Australia
a travel survival kit

Australia – a travel survival kit

Published by
Lonely Planet
PO Box
PO Box

Printed by
Colorcraft, Hong Kong

Photographs
NSW Government Tourist Bureau, Tony Wheeler, South Australian
Government Travel Centre, Tasmanian Government Tourist Bureau, Western Australia Department of
Tourism, Australian

From Lonely Planet: Australia Round Even &, Wide &
Laund from The Real

National Library of Australia
Cataloguing and Publication Data

Wheeler, Tony 1946–
Australia – a travel survival kit

Lonely Planet, 198
Includes index
1980, 0 908086

1. Australia – Description and travel –

919 404 2

© Tony Wheeler 198

Australia – a travel survival kit

Published by
Lonely Planet Publications
PO Box 88, South Yarra, Victoria 3141, Australia
PO Box 2001A, Berkely, CA 94702, USA

Printed by
Colorcraft, Hong Kong

Photographs
NSW Government Tourist Bureau, Northern Territory Government Tourist Bureau, South Australian Government Travel Centre, Tasmanian Government Tourist Bureau, Western Australia Department of Tourism, Australian Tourist Commission, Tony Wheeler

Cartoons & Illustrations
Tony Jenkins 15, 123, 167, 180, 325; Ernie Althoff (from *Australian Underground Comix*, Wild & Wooley, Sydney) 15; Elizabeth Honey 31; Michael Leunig (from *The Bedtime Leunig*, Angus & Robertson, Sydney) 53, 467; John Stanton 100; Richard Holt 10-11, 18-19; Todd Pierce 392

First published
February 1977

This edition
August 1986

National Library of Australia
Cataloguing in Publication Data

Wheeler, Tony, 1946 –
    Australia – a travel survival kit

    4th ed
    Previous ed.:South Yarra, Vic.:
    Lonely Planet, 1983
    Includes index.
    ISBN 0 908086 73 3.

    1.Australia – Description and travel – 1976 – Guide-books.I.Title.

919.4'0463

Tony Wheeler

Tony was born in England but spent his school years in Pakistan, the West Indies and the USA. He then did an engineering degree in the UK, worked for a short time as an automotive engineer, went back to university and did an MBA, then dropped out on the Asian overland trail with his wife Maureen. They've been travelling, writing and publishing guidebooks ever since, having set up Lonely Planet Publications in the mid-70s.

Mark Lightbody

Mark was born and grew up in Montreal. Educated there and in London, Ontario he holds a degree in journalism and has worked as a writer and editor. Mark has travelled in 45 countries on five continents and now lives in Toronto. He is the author of Lonely Planet's *Canada* guidebook and has also worked on our *Malaysia, Singapore & Brunei* guide and our *Papua New Guinea* guide.

Lindy Cameron

Born in the urban wilds of Gippsland, Lindy took on a career in jounalism as a writer and sub-editior on newspapers in Geelong and Melbourne. After travelling through Indonesia, India, Israel and Egypt she returned to Melbourne to join the LP team as an editor and tackled the island state for this edition.

Hugh Finlay

After three years travelling overseas, Hugh finally descended from the ozone and joined LP here in Melbourne. He was then sent off to unravel the deeper mysteries of Bendigo and Ballarat and emerged unscathed to put it all down on floppy disk for this new edition.

And the Next Edition

Things change – prices go up, good places go bad, bad places go bankrupt. So if you find things better, worse, cheaper (unlikely), more expensive, recently opened or long ago closed please don't blame us but please do write and tell us. We love letters from out on the road and good letters are rewarded with a free copy of the next edition (or any other LP title if you prefer).

This Edition

There's been one major change in Australia since the last edition of this guidebook – it's become a real travellers' centre. The proliferation of backpackers' hostels in Sydney, and the crowded poste restante counters are solid evidence. It's not surprising; travellers have always liked Australia but with the low dollar, it's become a real bargain.

Australia covers a huge area and updating this guidebook took a lot of effort from a number of people. Principle updater was Mark Lightbody who more-or-less retraced my steps from the previous edition (but counterclockwise instead of clockwise) using an Ansett Airpass (thank you Ansett). Mark did a round Australia circuit hitting all the main locations. Second string updaters were two keen travellers from the Lonely Planet office in Melbourne – Lindy Cameron covered Tasmania while Hugh Finlay covered the secondary centres in Victoria and did most of the leg-work on Melbourne. The whole office lent a hand and opinions on the Melbourne section.

Due to other projects I was not able to devote so much time to this updating but I did manage to cover a few new places in Victoria, South Australia and NSW, did an interesting outback trip from Melbourne to Adelaide via Broken Hill, Arkaroola and Wilpena Pound, caught the Adelaide Grand Prix and had another look at Adelaide, Sydney, the area around Sydney and, of course, Melbourne.

Not all the work on updating a guidebook takes place out 'on the road'. There's a great deal of desk work to be done, schedules and timetables to be checked, countless phone calls to be made. The bulk of this highly important side was done by Hugh Finlay. From him the text went to Richard Everist for final editing, to Anne Logan for typesetting, to Fiona Boyes for mapping, to Richard Holt for paste-up and finally to Sue Mitra for corrections. Thank you all of you.

Tony Wheeler

And More Thanks

Apart from the actual writers and Lonely Planet workers there are many people outside Lonely Planet to whom thanks must also go. First of all to Ansett Airlines who flew Mark Lightbody right round the country and also flew Lindy Cameron to Tasmania and back. Equally important thanks to all the travellers who wrote with suggestions, tips, updates, corrections and additions. Your letters played an important part in the many improvements to this addition. Thank you:

Mary Pat & Jeff Aardrup (USA), Michael Aaronsen (UK), Chuck Albertson (USA), Deb Andrews (Aus), Mary Ann Archambault (Aus), J F Aylard (UK), Philip Barker (UK), Dave Barkly (USA), Quentin Beasley (Aus), Andy Beer (UK), Walter Bissex (USA), Vibeke Bjerre (Nl), M Boyle (Aus), H Brooke (UK), Ginny Bruce (UK), Carl Butts (USA), Jacki Campbell, Brian Carson (UK), Luigi & Giordana Cerri (It), Dave Chapman (USA), Ken Cooper (Aus), Ken Cooper (Aus), Jenny Cram (Aus), Bill Dooly, Cathy Earl (Aus), Gai Evans (Aus), D J Fitzgerald (Aus), Four Swedish Girls (S), Jo Gardner (UK), Tom Gearen (USA), Lisa Girger, Norma Glanfield (Aus), Dorothy Goacher (Aus), J K Greye (UK), Richard Griffiths (UK), John Guest (Aus), John Hall (Aus), David Harcombs (Aus), Sean Hocking (UK), Jan Hoffer (C), Mads Jensen (Dk), Belinda Keane (UK), Kelly, Angus Kingon (Aus), Leanne Lamont (Aus), Stephen Langford (Aus), John A Lewis (UK), Steve Mark (Aus), Kathy Martinson, Mike Mathysson (Aus), Frances Miller (Aus), Ken Miller (NZ), Mrs Miller (Aus), Mary Morgan, Adrian Moss (NZ), Erica Murdoch (Aus), Kate Nash (Aus), Michael Nelles (Aus), Margaret Norris (Aus), Sandra Orr (Ire), Kevin Perrett (UK), Neil Pinkerton (Aus)T P Rebel (Nl), Cathryn Roesser, Helga Schmidbauer (G), B J Shepherd (Aus), Terry Siederer, Amanda Smith, Jack & Doreen Steer (Aus), R B K Stevenson (UK), Susan (USA), Ann Tipton (UK), Beryl Tucker (UK), Chris Tyler (UK), Lee Walkling (USA), Benjamin Westheimer (USA), Dieter Wettig (G), Yvonne Wignall (Aus), Dr Y A Wilks (Aus), J Woodell (UK), Chris Zinn (Aus) Aus – Australia, C – Canada, Dk – Denmark, G – Germany, Nl – Netherlands, Ire – Ireland, It – Italy, NZ – New Zealand, S – Sweden, UK – UK, USA – USA

Contents

Introduction

Where Australia is, south of South-East Asia, at the western end of the Pacific.

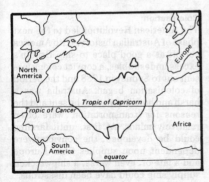

Where Australia isn't, but where it's antipodes (geographically opposite position) would be – in the Atlantic Ocean stretching from North Africa/Central America in the south to North America/Southern Europe in the north.

Australians have a well-earned reputation for being great travellers but I've met Australians on top of the Kyber Pass who haven't been on top of Ayer's Rock. It's kind of boring to say Australia is a big country but there are few places on earth with as much variety as Australia has to offer. And not just variety in things to see – in things to do, places to eat, entertainment, activities and just general good times.

What to see and do while tripping around our island continent is an open-ended question. There are cities big and small, some of them amazingly beautiful. If you fly in over its magnificent harbour, for example, Sydney is a city which can simply take your breath away. To really get to grips with the country, however, you have to get away from the cities. Australia is a country of cities, not the outback that provides the Australian myth, but it's in the outback where you really find Australia – the endless skies, the endless red dirt, the laconic Aussie characters. That still leaves you mountains and coast, superb bushwalks and big surf, the Great Barrier Reef and the Northern Territory's 'top end'.

Best of all Australia can be far from the rough and ready country its image might indicate. In the big cities you'll find some of the prettiest Victorian architecture going; Australian restaurants serve up an astounding variety of national cuisine with the freshest ingredients you could ask for (it's all grown here) and it's no problem at all to fall in love with Australian wines; plus Australia is one of those lucky countries where you can walk down almost any street at any time of day or night without worrying about your safety. It's not just exciting and invigorating, it's also very civilised. There's some fantastic travelling waiting for you around Australia, go for it.

Facts about the Country

HISTORY

Australia was the last great landmass to be discovered during the European period of exploration – if we accept the belief that a place simply doesn't exist until a European 'discovered' it. Although Captain Cook is the name commonly connected with Australia's discovery, it was probably a Portuguese who first sighted the country, and the credit for its early coastal exploration must go to Dutchmen.

Discovery & Exploration

Portuguese navigators had come within sight of the coast in the first half of the 16th century and in 1606 the Spaniard, Torres, sailed through the strait between Cape York and New Guinea which still bears his name. Dutch explorers then proceeded to chart much of the north and west coast right round to the Great Australian Bight, but what they found was a dry, harsh, unpleasant country and they rapidly scuttled back to the kinder climes of the Dutch East Indies. In 1642 Abel Tasman set out from Batavia, what is now Jakarta in Indonesia, to find out just what there was. He would have entirely bypassed the south coast had he not arrived in Tasmania which he gratefully named Van Diemen's Land after the Governor-General of the East Indies.

The prize for being Australia's original Pom goes back to the enterprising pirate William Dampier, who made the first investigations ashore nearly a hundred years before Cook. He would also have walked off with the award for being the first whinging Pom, as he came back with sensational, but accurate, reports of the wildlife, and the general conclusion that it was a lousy place with the 'miserablest people on earth' as its only inhabitants.

For a long period this dismal continent was forgotten until, in 1770, Captain Cook arrived at the east coast of Australia after making a scientific expedition to Tahiti to observe the planet Venus. The fertile east coast was a different story from the inhospitable land the earlier explorers had seen to the south and west. Cook sailed north all the way to Cape York, making the first temporary settlement on the way when his ship *Endeavour* was badly damaged on a reef off North Queensland. There was no support ship so it could well have been a permanent settlement had it not been possible to repair it.

If a country needs a founding figure, then Australians did very well with their's – Cook was resourceful, intelligent and humane. A self-made man, if ever there was one, his incisive reports of the new continent make fascinating reading, even today. By the time he met his untimely end in the Sandwich Islands (Hawaii now) in 1779, he had led two further expeditions to Australia and the whole continent was roughly mapped.

Colonisation

The American Revolution led to the next phase of Australian history. With America cut off as a good place to ship Britain's excess undesirables, a convict colony was sent out to Sydney in 1788 and the period of colonisation began. Australia was a harsh and horrible place to be sent and the reasons for 'transportation' were often relatively minor. At first, until farming could be developed, the convicts were dependent upon supplies from Europe and a late or, even worse, a shipwrecked supply ship could have been disastrous.

By 1792 the first difficult years had been survived but the cruel power of the military convict guards continued to make Australia a prison hell. Gradually, as free settlers started to supplement the original convicts, Australia became a more hospitable land and a new period of discovery started as the vast inland area was explored. The Blue Mountains at first proved an impenetrable barrier, fencing in Sydney to the sea, but in 1813 a path was finally forced through and the western plains were reached.

Australia never enjoyed the systematic push westward that characterised the European settlement of America. Here, colonial expansion often took place for one of two reasons: to find yet another place to keep convicts (particularly the real nasties), or to occupy another patch of land before anyone else (particularly the French) arrived – a false alarm as no other European power ever tried.

Thus, in 1803, the first settlement in Tasmania was founded close to the present site of Hobart, before the French could arrive. By the 1820s Hobart was actually a rival town to Sydney. Port Phillip Bay in Victoria was considered as a site for the second settlement in Australia at the same time, but was rejected, so it was not until 1835 that settlers from Tasmania, in search of more land, arrived at the present site of Melbourne. For similar, 'keep-anybody-else-out' reasons, Perth was first settled in 1829, but as it was isolated from the rest of the country, growth here was very slow.

The first settlement in the Brisbane area was made by a party of convicts sent north from NSW because the (by now) good citizens of Sydney were getting fed up with having all those crims about the place. By the time the Brisbane penal colony was abandoned in 1839, free settlers had arrived in force. Adelaide was initially set up in 1837 as an interesting experiment in free enterprise colonisation – it failed due to bad management and the British government had to take over from the bankrupt organisers.

Stability & Growth

Australia then progressed steadily for a period but it was the discovery of gold that next lit the development fuse. Gold was discovered in Victoria in 1851 and in little

more than a year the population had doubled. Similar discoveries in other states, in particular the WA gold rush of the 1890s, boosted populations and levels of economic activity. Although few people made fortunes, many settled in the country and became farmers and workers. At the same time the Industrial Revolution in England started to produce a strong demand for raw materials. With the agricultural and grazing potential of such a vast country Australia's economic base was secure.

The 19th century development of Australia also had a darker side. The Aboriginals were looked upon as little more than animals and were thoughtlessly pushed off their tribal lands. In some places, Tasmania in particular, they were hunted down and destroyed like vermin. Today, the Aboriginals are a dispossessed, lost people and belated efforts (generally unsuccessful) are being made to find them a place in modern society. Equally belatedly, the strength of much of their culture is being discovered, along with a realisation of the close harmony in which they lived with their rugged environment.

The gold rushes brought floods of diligent Chinese miners onto the Australian goldfields and violent white opposition led to a series of unpleasant race riots and a morbid fear of Asian immigration which persisted right into this century. The shipping of large numbers of convicts to Australia naturally provided it with a ready-made criminal class and escaped convict 'bushrangers' preyed upon unwary settlers. Later bushrangers, not always escapees, became the nearest thing Australia was to develop to cowboy-style folk heroes.

An Australian Identity?

Although Australia became increasingly self-sufficient and independent from the 'mother country' of England, it followed the British lead on most matters of foreign policy and duly marched off to the Boer War in South Africa and then to WW I.

continued on page 12

Boomerangs and Stone axe

Quartzite tools

Baskets

Pointing bones

Sand drawing

Legendary hero

Emu tracks

X-ray style kangaroo

Spirit figures

Painting on bark

Snake design

Australia, as a political entity, actually came into existence in 1901 when the separate states were federated and the decision to find a national capital was made.

Despite Australia's strong basis for self-sufficiency, it was far from economically independent of the rest of the western world and the depression of the '30s had an enormous effect on Australia. In WW II Australia once more marched off dutifully beside England but with the entry of Japan into the war, soon found fighting right on the doorstep. When Singapore abruptly collapsed and the Japanese swept down through Indonesia, Australia not only found itself being bombed from Japanese bases on the island of Timor, but also involved in a bitter hand-to-hand struggle along the terrible Kokoda Trail in Papua New Guinea. It was in Papua New Guinea, only a short flight from the north of Queensland, and in the Coral Sea off the Queensland coast, that the tide of the Pacific war turned against Japan.

The war had two immediately obvious effects on the country: a realisation of its dependence upon the US on the other side of the Pacific, and a clearer understanding that while Australia might be a European type of country, it is actually in Asia. With the prosperity and growth of the '50s and '60s, Australia appeared to once again slip into a period of sleepy inactivity. The conservative Liberal-Country Party coalition lethargically dominated the political arena; intellectuals and artists felt they had to escape to prove themselves and the whole place more or less went into mothballs. The only change was a retrograde one; England was replaced as the parent figure by America, and Australia slavishly marched off to Vietnam, just as it had followed Britain into various imperial wars.

Australia Today

The Vietnam fiasco did its bit to wake Australia up and the real upheaval came with the election of a Labor government in 1972. Unfortunately Gough Whitlam's government was long on great ideas but short on the practical experience of governing – and the oil crisis certainly didn't help them. In 1975 the Labor government was overturned by the Liberal-Country coalition in an underhanded manner that still rankles today. After seven years of conservative rule, Bob Hawke led the Labor Party back to power in 1983 and has been trying with limited success to improve relations between the militant unions and the business community ever since.

Australia's position today is still one of uncertainty as to what it is doing and where it is going. It is certainly no longer just a chunk of Europe, displaced in the Pacific. But just what is it? A farm and a mine for the Japanese industrial juggernaut? Should it co-operate with its rapidly growing Asian neighbours or should it try and shut itself off from them? Will it prosper by taking on the world at what it can do best or should it try and protect inefficient industries by shutting out potential competition with high import duties and fierce quota restrictions?

This confusion even extends to Australia's image of itself. It's certainly not the wide, empty land of the outback legend, for most of the population lives in large cities. It's certainly not the independent-spirited place some people would like to believe either, for much of the country's employment and many industries are propped up by grants, aids, bounties, protection and other forms of government support and intervention. Any answers?

Explorers

At the start of the last century, by which time 'unknowns' on maps were becoming pretty few and far between, most of Australia was still one big blank. It was even suspected that it might be two large, separate islands and, until the middle of the century, it was hoped that there might be a vast inland sea in the centre. Some of the early explorers, particularly the men who braved the hostile centre, suffered great hardships and, on more than one occasion, lost their lives. Some of those early explorers include:

Bass & Flinders George Bass charted the coast south of Sydney almost down to the present location of Melbourne in 1797-98. In 1798-99, in company with Matthew Flinders, he sailed right round Tasmania (Van Diemen's Land) thus establishing that it was an island and not joined to the rest of Australia. Flinders went on, in 1802-03, to sail right round Australia.

Eyre Edward John Eyre left Adelaide in 1840 to try to reach the centre of Australia. He gave up at Mt Hopeless and then decided to attempt a crossing to Albany in Western Australia. The formidable task nearly proved too much as both food and water were virtually unobtainable and his companion, Baxter, was killed by two of their Aboriginal guides. Eyre struggled on and by a stroke of luck came across a French whaling ship in Rossiter Bay. Reprovisioned, he managed to reach Albany. The road across the Nullarbor Plains from South Australia to Western Australia is named the Eyre Highway.

Leichardt A German scientist, Leichardt travelled up through North Queensland and skirted round the Gulf of Carpentaria to Port Essington, near modern Darwin, during 1844-45. He turned back during an 1846-47 attempt to cross Australia from east to west, but soon re-started and was never seen again.

Burke & Wills Leaving Melbourne in 1860, the Burke & Wills expedition's attempt to cross the continent from south to north was destined to be one of the most tragic. Leaving a depot at Coopers Creek in Queensland, they intended to make a dash north to the Gulf of Carpentaria with a small party of four. Their camels proved far slower than anticipated in the swampy land close to the gulf and, on their way back, one of the party died of exhaustion.

Burke, Wills and the third survivor, King, eventually struggled back to Coopers Creek, virtually at the end of their strength and nearly two months behind schedule, only to find the depot group had given up hope and left for Melbourne only hours earlier. Not realising that the group's departure had been so recent, they remained at Coopers Creek and Burke and Wills both died of starvation before a relief party arrived.

Stuart Departing from Adelaide in 1860, chasing a £2000 reward for the first south-north crossing, John Stuart reached the geographical centre of Australia, Central Mt Stuart, but shortly after was forced to turn back. A second attempt in 1861 got much closer to the top before he again had to return. Finally in 1862 he managed to reach the north coast near Darwin. The overland telegraph line, completed in 1872, and the modern Stuart Highway, follow a very similar route.

Kennedy In 1848 Edmund Kennedy set out to travel by land up Cape York Peninsula while a ship, *HMS Rattlesnake*, explored the coast and islands. Starting from Rockingham Bay, south of Cairns, the expedition almost immediately struck trouble when their heavy supply carts could not be dragged through the swampy ground around Tully. The rugged land, harsh climate, lack of supplies, hostile Aboriginals and missed supply drops, all took their toll and nine of the 13-man advance party died. Kennedy was speared to death in an attack by Aborigines when he was only 30 km from the end of his fearsome trek. His faithful Aboriginal servant, Jacky Jacky, was the only expedition member to finally reach the supply ship.

FACTS & FIGURES
Population

Australia's population is about 15½ million. The most populous states are the south-eastern states of New South Wales and Victoria, each with a capital city (Sydney and Melbourne) with a population of about three million. The population is principally concentrated along the south-eastern coastal strip from Adelaide to Cairns, and the similar but significantly smaller western coastal region of Western Australia. The centre of the country is very sparsely populated. There are about 150,000 Aboriginals.

Area

Australia's area is 7,686,884 square km, about the same as the 48 mainland states of the USA and half again as large as Europe, excluding the USSR. Australia is about 4000 km from east to west and 3200 km from north to south and has a coastline 36,735 km long.

Government

Australia has a parliamentary system of government based upon that of the UK, with a prime minister leading the party holding the greatest number of lower house seats. The lower house is the House of Representatives, the upper house is the Senate. Voting in Australian elections is compulsory and also somewhat complicated as a preferential voting system is used where each candidate has to be ranked in order of preference. This can result in Senate elections with 50 or more candidates to be ranked.

The federal parliament is based in Canberra, the capital of the nation. Like Washington DC in the USA, Canberra is in its own separate area of land, known as the ACT or Australian Capital Territory, not in one of the states. The ACT is, however, completely surrounded by NSW. Each state also has its own state government led by a state premier.

The two main political groups are the Australian Labor Party (ALP) and the coalition between the Liberal Party and the National Party. The latter was, until recently, known as the National Country Party since it mainly represents country seats.

Economy

Australia is an affluent, industrialised nation but much of the country's wealth comes from the land, either from agriculture or mining. The small population base means that most Australian manufacturing industries are comparatively weak and require protection from imports in order to survive. Nevertheless in 1984 and '85 the rate of growth of the Australian economy was one of the highest in the developed world.

GEOGRAPHY

Australia is an old, worn-down country – much of it uncompromisingly bleak and inhospitable. Much of the interest that Australia's 'red centre' holds is its sheer emptiness – come to the centre of Australia and see great expanses of nothing! Almost the entire population is crowded into a narrow strip along the east coast and an even smaller section around the south-west corner of the continent.

From the east coast a narrow, fertile strip merges into the almost continent-long 'Great Dividing Range'. The mountains are mere reminders of the mighty range that stood here millions of years ago and only in the Snowy Mountains section, straddling the NSW/Victoria border, and in Tasmania, do they have winter snow.

West of the range the country becomes increasingly flat and dry until virtually all habitation ceases and the endless flatness is broken only by salt lakes, occasional mysterious protuberances, like Ayers Rock and the Olgas, and some starkly beautiful mountains, like the MacDonnell Range near Alice Springs. In places the scant vegetation is sufficient to allow some grazing, so long as each animal has a seemingly enormous area of land, but much of the Australian outback is an eternally barren land with harsh, stone deserts and dry lakes with evocative names like Lake Disappointment.

In the far west there is a repeat of the mountain range and coastal strip which heralds the Indian Ocean, but this is only in the far south. In the north-central part of Western Australia, the dry country runs right to the sea. The extreme north of Australia, the 'top end', is a tropical area within the monsoon belt. Although the annual rainfall here looks very adequate on paper, it comes in more or less one short, sharp burst. This has prevented the top end from ever becoming seriously productive.

Wildlife

Australia's got a normal enough collection of zoos, but visitors from abroad will probably be more interested in the reserves and wildlife parks for Australia's own exotic collection of animals. Actually, these reserves are of equal interest to most Australians as many of these animals are quiet, reclusive creatures not readily seen in the wild. It's quite surprising how many Australians have never seen a kangaroo in the bush – but they're very common if you just look in the right place (and at the right time). Some favourites:

Kangaroos There are actually larger numbers of Australia's national animal now than when Europeans first arrived, due to the better availability of water and other necessities of kangaroo life. The danger to kangaroos is to certain species. There are many different types of roo: wallabies are part of the kangaroo family – they're smaller editions of the big bounders, and odd examples include the quokka, a cat-sized wallaby found only on two islands off the west coast, and the even-smaller rat kangaroos.

Possums Another species that has managed to get on well with man – far too well for many Australians, as they delight in getting into attics and creating havoc. Possums can become very tame; a whole family came down from the trees to demand their share of our meal in a campsite in the Barossa Valley. They'll live almost in the city centre – I've seen them right beside the Yarra River in the very heart of Melbourne. Like roos, they come in a variety of types from the tiny pygmy possum to the common brush-tailed possum.

Wombats With a name like that it'd be hard to dislike a wombat – imagine a cross between a very small bear and a very large guinea pig and

One in three in Australia works for the government. One in ten is unemployed. At times it is difficult to tell which is which. "Road works" is a bit of wishfull thinking that occupies a good few. Suntanned gladiators in an arena full of potholes. Never in the history of man have so many taken so long to do so little.

Alternate

Side track

Tea boy 'Boiling the billy'

Men Wo....

Paint

....four

Deviation

Diversion

Some of the varied ways of announcing 'Not finished yet mate maybe next year.'

Road 'work' crew, Queensland Australia

you've got one. Wombats are solid, powerfully built creatures, prodigious diggers and, like possums, can become quite tame.

Koalas They may look cuddly but the teddy bear-like koala actually has a rather short temper and a very uncooperative nature. They'd rather be flaked out in a handy eucalyptus tree.

Tasmanian Devil Unlike other marsupials (animals which carry their young in a pouch) the devil is carnivorous. It's an ugly, fierce-looking little monster, about the size of a small dog, and is found only in Tasmania. When Europeans arrived, Tasmania also had an awkward dog-like creature known as the Tasmanian Tiger, but it was gradually exterminated and, in 1936, the last known tiger died in Hobart Zoo. Despite frequent 'sightings', there has been no positive evidence of a Tasmanian Tiger since that time, although a sighting in 1982 has been accepted by the state's National Parks & Wildlife Service as 'irrefutable and conclusive'.

Platypus Undoubtedly Australia's weirdest animal, the platypus is a sort of stepping stone between reptiles and mammals. It has a duck-like bill, webbed feet, lays eggs but suckles its young, and the male has a poisonous spur on its hind feet! The platypus is amphibious and very graceful when cruising around underwater. The only other monotreme, or egg-laying mammal, is the echidna, or spiny ant-eater, which is also found in Australia.

Snakes We've got a few of these too, although fears of the poisonous types are largely exaggerated. They're generally shy creatures, only too ready to avoid trouble. The deadliest varieties are the taipan and the tiger snake, although death adders, copperheads, brown snakes and red-bellied black snakes are also worth keeping away from.

Emus The only larger bird than the emu is the similarly flightless African ostrich. They're a shaggy, scruffy looking bird and often rather curious – they're only too happy to wander over and have a look at you. The emu is unusual in that after the female lays eggs she plays no further part in their rearing – the male hatches them and raises the young. Cassowaries are slightly smaller and much more colourful. They're found in the rain forests of north Queensland.

Parrots & Cockatoos There are an amazing variety of these often colourful birds throughout Australia. The noisy galahs are amongst the most common – they certainly make their presence known. Rosellas have one of the most brilliant colour schemes and in some parks they're not at all backward about taking a free feed from the visitors. Budgerigars are mainly found towards the centre; they often fly in enormous flocks numbering 10,000 or more brightly coloured birds.

Crocodiles There are a number of types of crocodiles found in northern Australia, ranging from the potentially dangerous saltwater crocodiles, to smaller, more shy, harmless varieties.

Kookaburra A member of the kingfisher family, the kookaburra is heard as much as it is seen – you can't miss its loud, raucous guffaw. Kookaburras can become quite tame and pay regular visits to friendly households, but only if the food is excellent. You can't impress a kookaburra with anything less than top class steak.

Spiders Two to keep away from are the Redback, a relative of the American Black Widow, and the Sydney Funnel-web. The latter are found solely in Sydney, while the former are more widespread and have a legendary liking for toilet seats. Both are extremely poisonous and have been lethal. There is a well-tried antivenene for the Redback, but a Funnel-web bite is a nastier thing altogether.

Bower Birds The bower bird has a quite unique mating practice. The male builds a bower which he decorates with blue and green objects to attract females. In the wild, flowers or stones are used, but if man-made objects (clothes pegs, plastic pens, bottle tops, anything blue or green) are available, they'll certainly use them. The females are impressed by the males' neatly built bower and attractively displayed treasures, but once they've mated, all the hard work is left up to her. He goes back to refurbishing the bower and attracting another female, while she hops off to build a nest.

Other That's only a small selection of the creatures you may get a glance at. Others include penguins, particularly the delightful fairy penguins, which perform a nightly parade on Philip Island in Victoria; turtles, which

continued on page 20

THE BEAR FACTS

HAVE YOU EVER SEEN A KOALA ON THE GROUND? NOTICE HOW STUPIDLY HELPLESS HE IS; HOW HE SHUFFLES AND STUMBLES.

© WORDS + PICTURES - ERNIE ALTHOFF.
THEORY - PETER ANDREW.

EVEN IN THEIR EUCALYPTUS HABITAT, THEY ARE VERY INACTIVE AND DROWZY, STARING SLEEPILY DOWN AT YOU THROUGH THEIR **TINY** EYES AS THEY MUNCH THEIR LEAVES.

AT LAST THE FACTS CAN BE REVEALED. OUR TEAM OF SCIENTISTS HAS FOUND THAT A CHEMICAL EXISTS IN GUM LEAVES THAT AFFECTS KOALAS THE SAME WAY THAT THE KILLER WEED **MARIJUANA** AFFECTS HUMAN BEINGS.

THERE THEY SIT ALL DAY, PERMANENTLY EATING, PERMANENTLY STONED! HIGH IN THE TREES, HIGH IN THEIR MINDS; NEVER COMING DOWN AND PASSING THE HABIT FROM GENERATION TO GENERATION.

IMAGINE IF WE LIVED THE WAY THEY DO!

IT'S A GOOD THING THAT AUSTRALIA HAS A FINE HEALTHY UPSTANDINGLY NOBLE ANIMAL LIKE THE KANGAROO FOR ITS NATIONAL CREATURE, INSTEAD OF THIS GROTTY LITTLE DOPE FIEND.

Trap-door Spider

Platypus

Echidna

Tasmanian Devil

Fairy Penguin

Estuarine or Saltwater Crocodile

Wombat

Red Kangaroo

Kookaburra

Emu

Koala

Children's Python

frequent a number of beaches in Queensland; and seals of various types which can be seen in a number of places in the south. Until Australia's black swans were first seen, it was thought all swans were white. Frogs are common, particularly in Queensland. In the dry areas, you can see an amazing variety of lizards; some grow to a very hefty size. And I've not mentioned the undersea life you may come across, especially on the Barrier Reef.

OCCASIONS & HOLIDAYS

The Australian seasons are inverted compared to the northern hemisphere and the summer holiday season also coincides with Christmas. At that time of year things are likely to be rather crowded in the holiday areas, rather quiet in the cities. There are happenings and holidays in Australia year round – the following is just a brief overview. Some of the most enjoyable Australian festivals are the ones which are most typically Australian – like the surf lifesaving competitions on beaches around Australia during the summer months, or the outback race meets when tiny stations come alive and eccentric bush characters appear out of nowhere.

January

This is the busiest summer month with lots of beach events, pop festivals and the like. Australia Day is a national holiday, falling on the first Monday after 26 January.

February

In Hobart there's Regatta Day with boat races and other water activities. The Snowy Mountains Festival takes place in Cooma, NSW.

March

On even numbered years a Festival of the Arts takes place in Adelaide. It's Australia's biggest arts festival with music, drama and light entertainment. Wine enthusiasts flock to the Hunter Valley north of Sydney for the Hunter Valley Vintage Festival with wine tasting, grape picking and treading contests. Moomba, a week long festival, takes place in Melbourne, and sometimes-staid Melbourne actually shines a little.

March-April

The Festival of the Rocks takes place the week before Easter in Sydney. There's a street procession, a Rocks pub crawl and a mock court on the green. Over Easter Sydney also has the Royal Agricultural Show with livestock contests and exhibits, ring events and rodeos.

April

Anzac Day, the national war memorial day, is another public holiday on 25 April. On odd numbered years the Barossa Vintage Festival takes place in South Australia with all the usual wine-related activities and entertainment.

May

As the southern states drift into winter the emphasis moves north and particularly to the Northern Territory where there are all sorts of colourful events; like the Bangtail Muster in Alice Springs with a colourful float parade and other events. There is also a whole series of country race meets at remote Northern Territory stations over the coming months.

June

In Darwin the Beer Can Regatta features boat races for boats constructed entirely out of beer cans – there are plenty of those in the world's beer drinking capital. In Sydney there's a bathtub race across the Heads.

July

Scuba divers travel to Heron Island in Queensland for the Divers Rally.

August

In the Northern Territory there's something on almost every weekend in

Alice Springs. The Camel Cup features camel racing while the Apex Rodeo is one of the biggest rodeos in Australia – the town fills up with swaggering Territorian cowboys. The big event is the Henley on Todd Regatta on the last Saturday in the month, when boats race down the Todd River – even though the Todd River hardly ever has any water in it!

Meanwhile in Sydney, Australia's biggest race takes place with up to 25,000 competitors running the 14 km from Hyde Park to Bondi Beach in the City to Surf. I've survived it three times. At the Whitsundays in Queensland it's time for another aquatic festival with yacht races and a 'Miss Figurehead' contest while near Yeppoon, also in Queensland, it's time for the national 'cooeeing' contest.

September

Sporting attention turns to Melbourne with the Grand Final for Australian Rules Football and the MCG fills up beyond its 100,000 spectator capacity. It's the biggest sporting event in Australia. Also in Melbourne, there is the Sun Superrun, another big fun run with the competitors pounding across the huge Westgate Bridge. The Royal Melbourne Show attracts agricultural folk and lots of children and the Royal Perth Show also takes place in Perth. Up on the Sunshine Coast in Queensland it's time for the Sunshine Coast Spring Festival. Motor racing enthusiasts flock to Bathurst in NSW where the annual 1000 km touring car race on the superb Mt Panorama circuit is one of Australia's best known car races.

October

In late October or early November the Australian Formula 1 Grand Prix takes place on a round-the-streets circuit in Adelaide. There's more wine fun with the Bushing Festival in McLaren Vale, South Australia, while in Swan Hill, on the Murray River in Victoria, it's time for the Annual Pioneer Festival. Cairns, in the far north of Queensland, has Fun in the Sun.

November

The Melbourne Cup on the first Tuesday in November is Australia's premier horse race. It's a public holiday in Victoria but the whole country shuts down for the three minutes or so which the race takes. In beautiful Paddington, Sydney, the Queen St Festival features a street fair and arts activities.

December

The Sydney-Hobart Yacht Race starts on 26 December, a fantastic sight as the yachts stream out of the harbour and head south. In Hobart there's a Mardi Gras to celebrate the finish of the race.

ACTIVITIES

In each state section there is some information on a number of popular participant sports and activities. Around the country you'll also find plenty of opportunities for golf, squash, tennis, trail riding (horse and motorcycle), fishing and so on.

Surfing is almost a religion for many Australians who follow the waves around the country and there are a number of important surfing contests. Australia is also a great place for bushwalking. It's unfortunate that some of the superb walks are not better known as walking enthusiasts rate walks like Cradle Mountain-Lake St Clair the equal of any of the better known walks in New Zealand.

If you can't find what you want from the telephone yellow pages then contact the state tourist info office. If you want your sport as a spectator rather than as a participant there is also plenty of scope. You'll find football of assorted types including the unique Australian Rules

Football (related to Gaelic Football) which is played most avidly in Melbourne. Then there's motor racing and motorcycle racing, cricket, horse racing, yacht racing, cricket matches and lots more.

LANGUAGE

Any visitor from abroad who thinks Australian (that's 'strine') is simply a weird variant of English/American will soon have a few surprises. For a start half of Australia doesn't even speak Australian – they speak Italian, Lebanese, Turkish or Greek (Melbourne is said to be the third largest Greek city in the world). Then those who do speak the native tongue are liable to lose you in a strange collection of totally unique Australian words, words with completely different meanings to English speaking countries north of the equator and commonly used words which are shortened almost beyond recognition.

There is no real regional variation in the Australian accent and the city/country difference is mainly a matter of speed. Of course some of the most famed Aussie words are hardly heard at all – I don't think I've ever heard anyone called 'cobber', plenty of 'mates' though. If you want to pass for a native try speaking slightly nasally, shortening any word of more than two syllables and then adding a vowel to the end of it, making anything possible into a diminutive (even the Hell's Angels can become mere 'bikies') and peppering your speech with as many insults as possible. The brief list that follows may help:

abo – Aboriginal
amber fluid – beer
am I ever – not half
apples (she'll be) – it'll be all right
arvo – afternoon
ASIO – Aussie CIA
avagoyermug – traditional rallying call, especially at cricket matches
award – minimum pay rate

back of Bourke – back of beyond

bail up – hold up, rob
banana bender – Queenslander
barbie – barbecue
barrack – cheer on team at sporting event
battler – hard trier, struggler
beaut, beauty, bewdie – great, fantastic
beef road – outback road for transporting cattle
beg yours – I beg your pardon
bell (give someone a) – phone someone up
bible basher – religious fanatic
bikies – motorcyclists
billabong – water hole in dried up riverbed, more correctly an ox bow bend which has been cut off
billy – tin container used to boil up tea in the bush
bitumen – surfaced road
black stump – where the 'back of Bourke' begins
blowies – blow flies
bludger – lazy person, one who won't work
blue (to have a) – to have an argument or fight
bluey – swag
boomer – big, particularly large kangaroo
bonzer – great, ripper
bottle shop – liquor shop
Buckley's chance – no chance at all
bug (Moreton Bay Bug) – a small yabby
Bulamakanka – place even beyond the back of Bourke, way beyond the black stump
bull dust – fine dust on outback roads, also bull-shit
bunyip – Australia's yeti or Loch Ness monster
bush – country, anywhere away from the city
bush (go) – go back to the land
BYO – Bring Your Own (booze) to a restaurant
Chiko roll – a typical piece of vile Australian junk food
chook – chicken, as in 'chook 'n chips'
chunder – vomit
cobber – mate

cockie – small farmer
cooee – bush call, signal
come across – will she?
come good – turn out all right
compo – compensation, as unemployment compensation
cow cockie – small cattle-farmer
crook (to be) – to be ill
cut lunch – sandwiches

dag, daggy – dirty lump of wool at back end of a sheep, also term of abuse
daks – trousers
damper – bush loaf made from flour and water
deli – delicatessen, milkbar
didgeridoo – long, tube-like Aboriginal musical instrument
dill – idiot
dingo – native Australian wild dog
dinkum, fair dinkum – honest, genuine, really?
dinky-di – the real thing
donk – car engine
don't come the raw prawn – don't try and fool me
drongo – worthless person
duco – car paint
dunny – outhouse

fair go! – give us a break
fair crack of the whip! – fair go!
fall pregnant – become pregnant
financial (to be) – to be OK for $$
fire plug – fire hydrant
FJ – most revered Holden car
flake – shark meat, used in fish & chips
floater – meat pie floating in pea soup, yuk
fossicking – hunting for gems or semi-precious stones
fuckwit – stupid, incompetent person

galah – noisy parrots, thus noisy idiots
garbo – person who collects your garbage
gibber – stony desert
give it away – give up
g'day – good day, traditional Australian greeting
good on yer – well done

grazier – large-scale sheep or cattle farmer

hoon – idiot, hooligan
hump – to root, also to carry as in 'hump your bluey'
humpy – Aboriginal's shack

interstate – to be in another state

joey – baby kangaroo
journo – journalist

king hit – hit from behind, stab in the back
kiwi – New Zealander
knock – criticise, deride
knocker – one who knocks

lair – layabout, ruffian
lairising – acting like a lair
lamington – square cake covered in chocolate icing & coconut
larrikin – a bit like a lair
lay-by – put a deposit on an article so the shop will hold it for you
lollies – sweets, candy
lolly water – soft drinks
lurk – a scheme

Manchester – household linen, sheets
middy – medium beer glass
milkbar – corner shop
milko – milkman
mozzies – mosquitoes

never never – way out in the outback
new Australian – recent immigrant
no hoper – hopeless case, ne'er do well
northern summer – summer in the northern hemisphere
no worries – she'll be right

ocker – basic, down-to-earth Aussie
off-sider – assistant
OS – overseas, as 'he's gone OS'
outback – remote part of the bush, back of Bourke
OYO – own your own (flat or apartment)
Oz – Australia

pastoralist – large-scale grazier

pavlova – traditional Australian meringue & cream dessert

pineapple (rough end of) – stick (sharp end of)

piss turn – boozy party

pom – English person

poofter, poof – gay male

poser – one who poses, as driving in a flash car

postie – mailman

pot – large mug of beer

push – gang of larrikins

ratbag – friendly term of abuse

ratshit – lousy

rapt – delighted, enraptured in

reckon! – you bet!, absolutely!

rego – registration, as 'car rego'

ripper – good (also 'little ripper')

road train – semi-trailer-trailer-trailer

root – euphemism for sexual intercourse

rubbish (to) – deride, tease

salvo – member of the Sally Army

school – group of drinkers

schooner – large beer glass

scuse I – excuse me

sea wasp – very dangerous jelly fish

sealed (road) – surfaced road

semi-trailer – articulated truck

she'll be right – no worries

shoot through – leave in a hurry (particularly 'shoot through like a Bondi tram')

shout – buy round of drinks (as 'it's your shout')

sickie – day off work ill

sly grogger – after hours drinking place

smoke-o – tea break

spunky – sexy

squatter – pioneer farmer who didn't bother about buying or leasing his land from the government

squattocracy – Australian 'old money' folk, who made it by being first on the scene and grabbing the land

station – large farm

stickybeak – nosy person

strides – daks

strine – Australian language

sunbake (to) – to sunbathe (well the sun's hot in Australia)

surfies – members of the surfboard persuasion

tall poppies – achievers, what knockers like to cut down

tea – evening meal

technicolour yawn – vomit

thingo – thing, whatchamacallit

tinny – can of beer

too right! – absolutely!

true blue – dinkum

tucker – food

two pot screamer – person unable to hold their drink

two-up – traditional heads/tails gambling game

uni – where you go for an education

ute – utility, pickup truck

wag (to) – to skip school

walkabout – lengthy walk away from it all

wet (the) – rainy season in the north

wharfie – docker

whinge – complain, moan

whinging pom – the very worst sort of pom

wog – an illness

woolgrower – sheep farmer

wowser – spoilsport, puritan

yabby – small freshwater crayfish

yahoo – noisy, unruly person

yakka – work

yous – plural of you

If English isn't your first language and you've come to Australia to learn it colleges specialising in teaching English include:

Australian College of English, 20th floor, Bondi Junction Plaza Building, 500 Oxford St, Bondi Junction, NSW 2022 (tel (02) 389 8936

Milner International College of English, 195 Adelaide Terrace, Perth, WA 6000 (tel (09) 325 5708)

The English College, 291 Sussex St, Sydney, NSW 2000 (tel (02) 267 6042)
The English Teaching Laboratory, 113-115 Oxford St, Sydney, NSW 2010 (tel (02) 331 4589)

HERE IT IS A GIANT BLACK MARLIN I HOPE I WIN A BOOK FROM YOU FOLKS! I'VE USED THEM QUITE EXTENSIVELY ON MY TRAVELS AND IF I WIN I'D LIKE "AFRICA ON THE CHEAP".

Greetings from N.Q.
I hope this is your first 'MARLIN' CARD.

HELLO!
I'M ETTIE, COMING FROM DENMARK, I HOPE THIS WILL BE THE FIRST BIG MARLIN YOU GET.

Dear Lonely Planet,
You probably already have this one but just in case, here is a big Black Marlin.

Dear Lonely. P.
I take you up on your Page 224 offer. One Giant Fish.

Big Things

In the last edition of this guide we had a little competition for people to send us postcards of 'big things' – like the 'Big Pineapple' at Nambour. There's some sort of national mania in Australia for constructing 'big things' and some of them are superb examples of Australian kitsch. In all we got something like 250 postcards of about 60 different 'big things' – they decorated a whole wall of our office. Most frequently sent were the Big Marlin (27 cards), Big Pineapple (15), Big Trout (12), Big Banana (11), Big Shell (11), Big Lobster (10), Big Captain Cook (9), Big Rocking Horse (8), Big Apple (8), Big Darwin Stubby and Big Stubby (7 each), Big Orange (7), Big Buffalo (6), Big Sugar Cane (6), Big Cheese (5) and Big Mandarin (5).

Facts for the Visitor

VISAS & IMMIGRATION

Once upon a time, Australia was fairly free and easy about who was allowed to visit the country, particularly if you were from Britain or Canada. These days, only New Zealanders get any sort of preferential treatment; almost everybody else has to have a visa to visit Australia. Even New Zealanders have to have at least a passport these days. Visas are issued by Australian consular offices abroad; they are free and valid for a stay of up to six months. Applications for visa extensions can be made at Department of Immigration & Ethnic Affairs offices in Australia. Some offices, like Sydney, can be very thorough, requiring things like bank statements and interviews.

As well as the visa, visitors are also required to have an onward or return ticket and 'sufficient funds' – the latter is obviously open to interpretation. Like those from any country, Australian visas seem to have their hassles. We've heard from Japanese and other young Asian travellers from time to time about the difficulties of obtaining Australian visas. One young Japanese even recommended applying for an Australian visa in a country where there was no Australian embassy, since in that case, the application would be handled by the British Embassy and the 'British do not care who goes to Australia'! If you do hit visa problems, while trekking around Asia for example, the best advice is to try in the next city. Extending your six-month stay can also be difficult, mainly because the office is notoriously slow at renewing visas. We've actually heard of people still waiting for an extension after they'd been in Australia for a year! Apply for an extension and then don't worry about it, is probably the best advice; you shouldn't have to be responsible for the snail's pace of Australian bureaucracy.

Young visitors from certain countries – Britain, Ireland, Canada, Holland and Japan – may be eligible for a 'working holiday' visa. Young is fairly loosely interpreted as around 18-26 and working holiday means up to 12 months, but the emphasis is supposed to be on casual employment rather than a full-time job. This visa can only be applied for in your home country. Officially, working in Australia is completely verboten on a regular tourist visa, but in actual fact it's relatively simple to do. As long as you can find a job, that is. There are no social security cards, national insurance cards or the like in Australia yet, although it seems quite likely that the 'Australia Card' will be introduced in '86 and this may make things a bit more difficult. At the moment there are generally not too many questions asked. Travellers kicking around Australia often seem to pick up odd jobs as they go, although, like anywhere in the western world, times are tough and jobs are no longer there for the asking.

Although Australia doesn't have any borders with other countries, we still manage to get plenty of illegal immigrants. Twice since the early '70s the government has granted an amnesty for illegal immigrants; if they had been in the country for at least six months and were otherwise acceptable they could stay. On both occasions the number of illegal immigrants who stepped forward was highly surprising.

A few of the more useful Australian consular offices overseas include:

Canada
    Australian High Commission, The National Building, 130 Slater St, Ottawa K1P 5H6 (tel 613 236 0841)
    also in Toronto & Vancouver
Denmark
    Australian Embassy, Kristianagade 21, 2100 Copenhagen (tel 26 2244)

Germany, West
Australian Embassy, Godesberger Allee 107, 5300 Bonn 2 (tel 02221 376941-7)

Greece
Australian Embassy, 15 Messogeion St, Ambelokpi, Athens (tel 360 4166/15)

Hong Kong
Australian Commission, Connaught Centre, Connaught Rd, Hong Kong (tel 5 227171/8)

India
Australian High Commission, Australian Compound, No 1/50-G Shantipath, Chanakyapuri, New Delhi (tel 69 0336)

Indonesia
Australian Embassy, Jalan Thamrin 15, Jakarta (tel 323109)
also in Denpasar

Ireland
Australian Embassy, Fitzwilton House, Wilton Terrace, Dublin 2 (tel 76 1517/9)

Italy
Australian Embassy, Via Alessandria 215, Rome 00198 (tel 84 1241)
also in Milan & Messina

Japan
Australian Embassy, No 1-14 Mita 2 Chome, Minato-ku, Tokyo (tel 453 0251/9)
also in Osaka

Malaysia
Australian High Commission, 6 Jalan Yap Kwan Seng, Kuala Lumpur (tel 42 3122)

Netherlands
Australian Embassy, Koninginnegracht 23, 2514 AB The Hague (tel 070 63 0983)

New Zealand
Australian High Commission, 72-78 Hobson St, Thorndon, Wellington (tel 73 6411/2)
also in Auckland

Papua New Guinea
Australian High Commission, Waigani, Hohola (tel 25 9333)

Philippines
Australian Embassy China Bank Building, Paseo de Roxas, Makati (tel 87 4961)

Singapore
Australian High Commission, 25 Napier Rd, Singapore 10 (tel 737 9311)

Sweden
Australian Embassy, Sergels Torg 12, Stockholm C, S-101 86 Stockholm (tel 24-46-60)

Switzerland
Australian Embassy, 29 Alpenstrasse, Berne (tel 43 01 43)
also in Geneva

Thailand
Australian Embassy, 37 South Sathorn Rd, Bangkok 12 (tel 286 0411)

UK
Australian High Commission, Australia House, The Strand, London WC2B 4LA (tel 01 438 8000)
also in Edinburgh & Manchester

USA
Australian Embassy, 1601 Massachusetts Avenue NW, Washington DC, 20036 (tel 202 797 3000)
also in Los Angeles, Chicago, Honolulu, New York &San Francisco.

CONSULATES & EMBASSIES

The principal diplomatic representations to Australia are in Canberra and you'll find a list of the addresses of relevant offices in the Canberra section. There are also representatives in various other major cities, particularly from countries with major connections with Australia like the USA, UK or New Zealand; or in cities with important connections, like Darwin which has an Indonesian Consulate. Big cities like Sydney and Melbourne have nearly as many consular offices as Canberra. Look up addresses in the telephone yellow pages under 'Consulates & Legations'.

CUSTOMS

For visitors from abroad the usual sort of 200 cigarettes, bottle of whisky regulations apply to Australia, but there are two areas you should be very careful about. Number one is, of course, dope – Australian customs have a positive mania about the stuff and can be extremely efficient when it comes to finding it. Unless you want to make first-hand investigations of conditions in Australian jails (not very good), don't bring any with you. This particularly applies if you are arriving from Indonesia or South-East Asia. You will be the subject of suspicion!

Problem two is animal and plant quarantine; they are naturally keen to prevent weeds, pests or diseases getting into the country – with all the sheep in Australia, that scruffy Afghani sheepskin coat over your arm is not going to be popular. Fresh food is also unpopular, particularly meat, sausages, fruit, vegetables and flowers. There are also various restrictions on taking fruit or vegetables between states.

When it is time to split there are duty free stores at the international airports and their associated cities. Treat them with healthy suspicion, though. 'Duty Free' is one of the world's most overworked catch phrases and it is often just an excuse to sell things – at prices you can easily beat by a little shopping around. City duty free shops are generally better value than the airport ones.

MONEY

Australia's currency is good, old-fashioned dollars and cents. When they were changing over from pounds, shillings and pence some years back, there was consideration of calling the new unit the 'Royal'; that foolish idea soon got the chop. Over the past couple of years Australia's dollar has weakened against many other countries' currencies, most particularly against the US dollar. For Americans, in fact, Australia has become a real bargain. Note that travellers' cheques generally enjoy a better exchange rate than cash in Australia. Current exchange rates are:

There is a variety of ways to carry your money around Australia with you. If your stay is limited then travellers' cheques are the most straightforward, but if you're planning to stay longer than just a month or so, it's worth considering some other possibilities which give you more flexibility and are more economical. With travellers' cheques it is obviously easiest to travel with Australian dollar travellers' cheques as these can be exchanged immediately at the bank cashier's window without having to have them converted from a foreign currency. Changing travellers' cheques denominated in other currencies – yen, Deutschmarks, pounds, US dollars or whatever – is certainly no problem though. It's done quickly and efficiently and never involves the sort of headaches and grand production that changing foreign currency in the US always entails. American Express, Thomas Cook and other well-known international brands of travellers' cheques are all widely used in Australia.

If your stay in Australia is for longer than a month or so, and this applies equally to Australians setting off to travel around the country, then it's worth considering an alternative to travellers' cheques. One of the neatest solutions is to open a passbook savings account. All the banks operate these systems and with your passbook you can withdraw money from any branch of the bank in question in the country. There are limitations as to how much you can pull out in one hit but

A$1	=	US$0.69	US dollars	US$1	=	A$1.45
A$1	=	NZ$1.23	New Zealand dollars	NZ$1	=	A$0.74
A$1	=	UK£0.45	pounds sterling	UK£1	=	A$2.22
A$1	=	S$1.55	Singapore dollars	S$1	=	A$0.64
A$1	=	HK$5.40	Hong Kong dollars	HK$1	=	A$0.18
A$1	=	Y116	Japanese Yen	Y100	=	A$0.85
A$1	=	DM1.55	Deutsche marks	DM1	=	A$0.64
A$1	=	fl 1.87	Dutch guilders	fl 1	=	A$0.53
A$1	=	C$0.95	Canadian dollars	C$1	=	A$1.04

it's quite reasonable. This way, instead of paying to buy travellers' cheques, you actually get paid for having your money on deposit. Probably the best bank for the traveller to be with is the Commonwealth Savings Bank. This is a government-owned bank with branches all around the country, as well as in almost every post office. So finding a place to withdraw money is no problem at all and the hours are also longer than normal banking hours. If the branch has 'black light' signature identification facilities you can draw out up to $500 per day or $700 per week if you are interstate. Otherwise you can withdraw $200 with suitable identification. In London, you can simply walk into the Commonwealth Bank branch there and ask them to transfer whatever you require to Australia and open an account for you.

Credit cards are widely accepted in Australia and this is another alternative, for the better-heeled, to carrying large numbers of travellers' cheques. The most common credit card, however, is the purely Australian Bankcard system. Visa, Mastercard, Diners Club and American Express are widely accepted but mainly in the ritzier sort of places. If you're planning on renting cars while travelling around Australia, a credit card makes life much simpler; they're looked upon with much greater favour by rent-a-car agencies than nasty old cash.

Another cash possibility for those with an Australian account is a cash card, which you can use in the automatic banking machines now found all over Australia. You just put your card in the machine, key in your number and can then withdraw up to $200 a day from your account. Bankcard can also be used to draw out cash but in that case you are charged interest until you pay it back.

On departure day from Australia, you're allowed to take out what you brought in if you stayed for less than six months. Otherwise you're allowed A$250 in local currency, A$250 in foreign currency and the balance (whatever it might be) in travellers' cheques.

COSTS

In comparison to the USA, Canada and European countries, Australia is cheaper in some respects and more expensive in others. The international fall in the value of the Australian dollar, however, has made it remarkably good value for foreign visitors. Manufactured goods tend to be more expensive because they're either imported and have all the additional costs of transport and duties or, if they're locally manufactured, they suffer from the extra costs entailed in making things in comparatively small quantities. Thus you pay more for clothes, cars and other manufactured items. On the other hand, food is both high quality and low in cost.

Restaurants and hotels tend to have their prices jacked up by the high labour cost in Australian service industries. As soon as 5 pm rolls around, everyone goes on to overtime rates. On the plus side, what you see is what you get – there are no service charges, no add-on sales or value-added taxes, even tipping doesn't feature in the picture. If something costs $x (including a hotel room or a restaurant meal), then that's what it costs, not $x plus 10% plus 12% plus whatever else you can load on.

CLIMATE

Australian seasons are opposite to those in Europe and North America. Christmas falls in the middle of summer while August is mid-winter. Summer starts in December, autumn in March, winter in June and spring in September. The climatic extremes in Australia are relatively mild and even in Melbourne, the southernmost capital city on the mainland, it's a rare occasion when the mercury hits freezing point. Of course, the poor Tasmanians, further to the south, have a better idea of what cold is.

As you head north the seasonal variations become smaller and smaller until, in the far north – around Darwin – you are in the monsoon belt where there are just two seasons: hot and wet or hot and dry. When the wet hits Darwin around November or December, it really does get wet. In the Snowy Mountains in the south of NSW and the north of Victoria, there's a snow season with good skiing. The climate in the centre is desert-like, hot and dry during the daytime but often bitterly cold at night.

Australia is such a big country that there is a best 'season' for some place almost year round. Down in the south, for example, Victoria and Tasmania are probably at their best at the height of the summer, although spring and autumn are pretty good too. You might head south for the skiing but otherwise Melbourne can be rather cold, grey and miserable in the July-August winter months when it's best to avoid it! By contrast, in the far north the real season is mid-winter. Darwin in July-August is just right, whereas in mid-summer (December-January) it's often unbearably hot and humid, the sea is full of sea wasps, plus if there are cyclones about, this is when they'll appear. Similarly in Alice Springs the mid-summer temperatures can be far too high for comfort, while in mid-winter the nights may be chilly but the days are delightful.

Apart from climatic seasons, when travelling around Australia it's worth bearing the holiday seasons in mind too. Christmas is not only the regular holiday season associated with Christmas, it's also the middle of the long, summer, school vacations. This is the most likely time of year to find accommodation booked out and long queues everywhere. School holidays also take place in May and August and these too can be more difficult times to travel. The school holidays often vary by a week or two from state to state.

A synopsis of average maximum and minimum temperatures and rainfall follows. Note that these are average maximums – even Melbourne gets a fair number of

summer days topping 40°C (100°F). Temperatures in Australia are all expressed in degrees centigrade. As a rough rule of thumb 20°C is about room temperature or 70°F; 30°C is getting hot, say 85°F; while 40°C is a very hot day.

Adelaide – maximum temperatures are from 25 to 30°C from November to March; minimums drop below 10°C between June and September. Rainfall is heaviest, 50-70 mm per month, from May to September.

Alice Springs – there are daily maximums of 30°C and above from October to April; minimums drop to 10°C and below from May to September. Rainfall is low year round; December to February gets an average of 30 mm plus.

Brisbane – daily maximums are rarely below 20°C year round, peaking towards 30°C from November to February; rainfall is fairly heavy year round, with December to March getting over 130 mm per month.

Canberra – mid to high 20s°C in the summer and daily minimums often close to freezing between May and October; rainfall is usually 40-70 mm a month, year round.

Cairns – average maximums are around 25-33°C year round, with minimums rarely dropping below 20°C; rainfall is below 100 mm a month from May to October (lowest in July and August), but peaks from January to March with around 400-450 mm.

Darwin – even temperatures year round with average maximums round 30-34°C and minimums around 20-25°C; rainfall is minimal from May to September, but December to March gets 250-400 mm a month.

Hobart – only from December to March do averages top 20°C, but from April to November average minimums are below 10°C; rainfall is about 40-60 mm a month, year round.

Melbourne – Melbourne hits 20°C and above from October to April and drops below 10°C from May to October; rainfall is even year round at 50-60 mm almost every month.

Perth – average maximums reach 30°C from December through March, but minimums rarely drop below 10°C; rainfall is lightest from November to March (20 mm and below) and heaviest in May to August (120-200 mm).

Sydney – only in the middle of winter do average minimums drop below 10°C, with summer maximums around 25°C from November through March; rainfall is in the 75-130 mm range year round.

BOOKS & BOOKSHOPS

Australians have a fascination with Australia – and with Australians. In almost any bookshop you'll find a section devoted to Australiana. There are books on every Australian subject you care to mention. If you want a souvenir of Australia, something to take back home, one of the numerous coffee-table photographic books, like *A Day in the Life of Australia*, can't be beaten. There are numerous other Australian books to enjoy – look for children's books with very Australian illustrations, or cartoon books by some of Australia's excellent cartoonists.

We've also got a lot of bookshops and some of the better bookshops are mentioned in the various city sections.

A couple of good sources of wildlife posters, calendars and books are the Wilderness Shops in each capital city and the Government Printing Office in Sydney and Melbourne.

MEDIA

Australia has a wide range of media although a few big companies (Rupert Murdoch being the best-known internationally) tend to dominate. There's a national advertising-free television and radio network, the Australian equivalent of the BBC, which is known as the ABC. In Sydney and Melbourne there are also three commercial television stations and a government-sponsored multi-cultural station. Around the country the number of stations varies from place to place; in some remote areas the ABC may be all you can receive.

Radio usually has a couple of ABC stations, plus a whole host of commercial stations, both AM and FM, featuring the whole gamut of radio possibilities from pop to 'beautiful music'.

Each major city tends to have at least one important daily, often backed up by a tabloid paper and also by evening papers. The *Sydney Morning Herald* and the Melbourne *Age*, are two of the most important dailies. Plus, there's *The Australian*, a Murdoch owned nation-wide daily paper.

Weekly newspapers and magazines include the *National Times*, an Australian edition of *Time* and a combination edition of the Australian newsmagazine *The Bulletin* with *Newsweek*.

FILM & PHOTOGRAPHY

If you come to Australia via Hong Kong or Singapore it's worth buying film there but otherwise Australian film prices are no longer too far out of line with the rest of the western world. Including developing, 36-exposure Kodachrome 64 slide film retails at about $12 but with shopping around you can find it for $8 or less, particularly if you buy it in quantity.

There are plenty of camera shops in all the big cities and standards of camera service are high. Developing standards are also high, with many places now offering instant developing of print film. Australia is the main centre for developing Kodachrome slide film in the South-East Asian region, as well as for Australia.

Photography is no problem, but in the outback you have to allow for the exceptional intensity of the light. Best results in the outback regions are obtained

early in the morning and late in the afternoon. As the sun gets higher, colours get washed out. In the outback, especially in the summer, you must also allow for temperature extremes and do your best to keep film as cool as possible, particularly after exposure. Other film hazards are dust in the outback and humidity in the tropical regions of the far north.

HEALTH

So long as you have not visited an infected country in the past 14 days (aircraft refuelling stops do not count) no vaccinations are required for entry. Cholera vaccination is not required and yellow fever vaccination is only required if you come from an area where it is endemic. Naturally, if you're going to be travelling around in outlandish places apart from Australia, a good collection of immunisations is highly advisable.

Medical care in Australia is first-class and only moderately expensive. A typical doctor visit costs around $15 to $20. Health insurance cover is available in Australia, but there is usually a waiting period after you sign up before any claims can be made. A health and accident insurance policy is a wise investment.

POST

Australia's postal services are relatively efficient but not too cheap. The main postal rates are:

standard letter in Australia	33c
aerogram to anywhere in the world	45c
air-letter – up to 20 gm (postcard)	
New Zealand	50c (35c)
Singapore, Malaysia	60c (40c)
Hong Kong, India	65c (45c)
USA, Canada	80c (50c)
UK, Europe	90c (55c)

Post offices are open 9 am to 5 pm Monday to Friday, but you can often get stamps from local post offices operated from newsagencies or shops on Saturday mornings. All post offices will hold mail for visitors and some city GPOs will have very busy poste restantes. Cairns, for example, can get quite hectic. You can also have mail sent to you at the American Express offices in big cities if you have an Amex card or carry Amex travellers' cheques.

TELEPHONES

The Australian phone system (run by the government owned 'Telecom') is really remarkably efficient and, equally important, easy to use. Local phone calls all cost 20c for an unlimited amount of time. You can make local calls from red phones – often found in shops, hotels, bars, etc – and from STD phones.

If you want to make a long-distance (trunk) call from a public phone, look for a grey-green STD (Standard Trunk Dialling) phone which allows you to dial direct and only pay for the time actually used – there's no three-minute minimum as there is on operator-connected calls. Almost all public phones are STD these days. The trick is to have plenty of 20c and 50c coins and be prepared to feed them through at a fair old rate. You can insert a handful of coins at the beginning and they just drop down as they're used up. When you're about to be cut off, a red light flashes faster and faster and you can either hurriedly insert more coins or simply speak quicker! If you complete your call before the money is used up the change is returned.

STD calls are cheaper at night, in ascending order of cost:

economy	9 pm to 8 am
night*	6 to 9 pm
intermediate	12.30 to 1.30 pm
day	8 am to 12.30 pm & 1.30 to 6 pm
	*the night rate also applies from 8 am to 9 pm on Sunday

From some STD phones you can also

make ISD (International Subscriber Dialling) calls just like making STD calls. ISD phones are not yet very widespread but you will often find them at airports and at city GPOs or other central city Telecom centres. Dialling ISD you can get through overseas almost as quickly as you can locally and if your call is brief it needn't cost very much – 'Hi, I'll be on the flight to London next Tuesday' can cost half the price of a postcard. All you do is dial 0011 for overseas, the country code (44 for Britain, 1 for the USA or Canada, 64 for New Zealand), the city code (1 for London, 212 for New York, etc), and then your number. And have plenty of coins to hand. A call to the USA or Britain costs $2.10 a minute, New Zealand is $1.50 a minute.

FACTS

Emergencies

For police, fire or ambulance, dial 000.

Electricity

Voltage is 220-240 volts and the plugs are three-pin, but not the same as British three-pin plugs. Men who shave electrically should note that, apart from in fancy hotels, it's very difficult to find converters to take either American flat two-pin plugs or the European round two-pin plugs. You can easily bend the American plugs to a slight angle to make them fit, however.

Measurements

Australia went metric in the early '70s. We buy petrol and milk by the litre, apples and potatoes by the kilogram, measure distance by the metre or km, and our speed limits are in km per hour. But there's still a degree of confusion; it's hard to think of a six-foot guy as being 183 cm.

Opening Hours

Although Australians aren't great believers in long opening hours, they are a long way ahead of the Kiwis, thank you! Most shops close at 5 or 5.30 pm daily and noon on

Saturdays. They are closed all day on Sundays. There is usually a late shopping night, when the doors stay open until 9 or 9.30 pm – it's Thursday night in Sydney, Friday nights in Melbourne.

Banks are open from 9.30 am to 4 pm Monday to Thursday, and until 5 pm on Friday. Some large city branches are open 8 am to 6 pm, Monday to Friday. Some are also open to 9 pm on Fridays. Of course there are some exceptions to Australia's unremarkable opening hours and all sorts of places stay open till late hours and all weekend – particularly milk bars, delis and city bookshops.

Tipping

Australians have a world-wide reputation as lousy tippers because in Australia tipping isn't done much and it isn't a habit the way it is in the US or Europe. Perhaps it is part of the great Australian egalitarian 'I'm as good as you are, mate' feeling. So taxi drivers don't expect tips (of course, they don't hurl it back at you if you decide to leave the change). In contrast, just try getting out of a New York cab, or even a London one, without leaving your 10 to 15%. In fact Australian taxi drivers will often round fares down – if it comes to $8.10 you're quite likely to be told 'make it eight bucks, mate.'

Nor do any but the flashiest restaurants require tipping; there isn't even the service charge that gets added to the bottom of the bill as in many other countries. So, if you are going to tip, make sure it is for what tipping was supposed to be for in the first place – especially good service.

INFORMATION

There are a number of information sources for visitors to Australia and, in common with a number of other tourist-conscious western countries, you can easily drown yourself in brochures and booklets, maps and leaflets. Forests fall to inform you abut what Australia has to offer.

Australian Tourist Commission

The Australian Tourist Commission is the government body intended to inform potential visitors about the country. There's a very definite split between promotion outside Australia and inside it. The ATC is strictly an external operator; they do minimal promotion within the country and have no contact with visitors to Australia. Within the country, tourist promotion is handled by state or local tourist offices.

The ATC have a number of items of interest for potential visitors. First there's the booklet called the *Down Under Wonder*, which is a good introduction to the country, its geography, flora, fauna, states, transport, accommodation, food and so on. They also have a good map of the country and an excellent guide to the Great Barrier Reef. Note, however, that this literature is intended for distribution overseas only; if you want copies, get them before you come to Australia. Addresses of the ATC offices for literature requests are:

Australia
    324 St Kilda Rd, Melbourne 3004 (GPO Box 73B, Melbourne 3001)
Singapore
    Australian Travel Centre, 17th Floor, Goldhill Square, 101 Thomson Rd £17-03, Singapore 1130
Canada
    120 Eglington Avenue East, Suite 220, Toronto, Ontario ONT M4P 1E2
Europe
    Neue Mainzer Strasse 22, 6000 Frankfurt/ Main 1, West Germany
Japan
    Sankaido Building 7F, 9-13, Akasaka 1-Chome, Minato-ku, Tokyo 107
New Zealand
    15th Floor, Quay Tower, 29 Customs St West, Auckland 1
UK
    4th Floor, Heathcote House, 20 Saville Row, London, W1X 1AE
USA
    3550 Wilshire Boulevard, Suite 1470, Los Angeles, CA 90010

State & Local Offices

Within Australia, tourist information is handled by the various state and local offices. Each state and the ACT and Northern Territory have a tourist office of some form and you will find information about these centres in the various state sections. Apart from a main office in the capital cities, they often have regional offices in main tourist centres and also in other states. As well as supplying brochures, price lists, maps and other information, the state offices will often book transport, tours and accommodation for you. Unfortunately, very few of the state tourist offices maintain information desks at the airports and, furthermore, the opening hours of the city offices are very much of the 9-5, weekdays and Saturday morning only variety. Addresses of the state tourist offices are:

Australian Capital Territory
    ACT Government Tourist Bureau, London Circuit & West Row, Canberra City 2601
New South Wales
    NSW Government Travel Centre, Corner of Pitt & Spring Sts, Sydney 2000
Northern Territory
    Northern Territory Government Tourist Bureau, 31 Pitt St, Darwin 5700
Queensland
    Queensland Government Tourist Bureau, Adelaide & Edward Sts, Brisbane 4000
South Australia
    South Australian Government Tourist Bureau, 18 King William St, Adelaide 5000
Tasmania
    Tasmanian Government Tourist Bureau, 80 Elizabeth St, Hobart 7000
Victoria
    Victorian Government Travel Centre, 230 Collins St, Melbourne 3000
Western Australia
    Western Australian Government Travel Centre, 772 Hay St, Perth 6000

A step down from the state tourist offices are the local or regional tourist offices. Almost every town in Australia seems to maintain a tourist office or centre of some type or other and in many cases these are really excellent, with much local information not readily available from the larger, state offices. In Cairns, Queensland, for example, there's an office of the Queensland Government Tourist Bureau and also of the Far North Queensland Promotion Bureau. There are similar situations in a number of other places around the country, particularly where there is a strong local tourist trade.

Automobile Associations

Australia has a national automobile association, the Australian Automobile Association, but this exists mainly as an umbrella organisation for the various state associations and to maintain international links. The day-to-day operations are all handled by the state organisations who provide an emergency breakdown service, literature, excellent maps and detailed guides to accommodation and campsites.

The state organisations have reciprocal arrangements between the various states in Australia and to the equivalent organisations overseas. So, if you're a member of the NRMA in NSW, you can use RACV facilities in Victoria. Similarly, if you're a member of the AAA in the US or the RAC or AA in the UK, you can use any of the state organisations' facilities. But you need to bring proof of membership with you. More details about the state automobile organisations can be found in the relevant state sections. Some of the material they produce is of a very high standard, in particular there is a superb set of regional maps to Queensland produced by the RACQ. The state offices are:

New South Wales
    National Roads & Motorists Association (NRMA), 151 Clarence St, Sydney 2000
Northern Territory
    Automobile Association of the Northern Territory, 79-81 Smith St, Darwin 5790
Queensland
    Royal Automobile Club of Queensland (RACQ), 190 Edward St, Brisbane 4000

South Australia
 Royal Automobile Association of South Australia (RAA), 41 Hindmarsh Square, Adelaide 5000
Tasmania
 Royal Automobile Club of Tasmania (RACT), Patrick & Murray Sts, Hobart 7000
Victoria
 Royal Automobile Club of Victoria (RACV), 123 Queen St, Melbourne 3000
Western Australia
 Royal Automobile Club of Western Australia (RAC), 228 Adelaide Terrace, Perth 6000

National Park Organisations

Australia has an extensive collection of national parks, in fact, the Royal National Park just outside Sydney is the second oldest national park in the world. Only Yellowstone Park in the USA pre-dates it. The National Park organisations in each state are state-operated, however, not nationally. They tend to be a little hidden away in their capital city locations, although, if you search them out, they often have excellent literature on the state parks. They are much more up front in the actual parks where, in many cases, they have very good guides and leaflets to bushwalking, nature trails and other activities. The state offices are:

New South Wales
 National Parks & Wildlife Service, 189-193 Kent St, Sydney 2000
Northern Territory
 Conservation Commission of the Northern Territory, Gap Rd, Alice Springs 5750
Queensland
 National Parks & Wildlife Service, 239 George St, Brisbane 4000
South Australia
 National Parks & Wildlife Service, 129 Greenhill Rd, Unley 5061
Tasmania
 National Parks & Wildlife Service, 16 Magnet Court, Sandy Bay 7005
Victoria
 National Parks Service, 240 Victoria Parade, East Melbourne 3002
Western Australia
 National Parks Authority, Hackett Drive, Crawley 6009

National Trust

The National Trust is dedicated to preserving historic buildings in all parts of Australia. They actually own a number of buildings throughout the country which are open to the public and many other buildings are 'classified' by the National Trust to ensure their preservation.

The National Trust also produces some excellent literature, including a fine series of walking-tour guides to many cities around the country, large and small. These guides are often available from local tourist offices or from National Trust offices and are usually free whether you're a member of the National Trust or not. Membership of the trust is well worth considering, however, because it entitles you to free entry to any National Trust property for your year of membership. If you're going to be doing much travelling around Australia, this could soon pay for itself.

Annual membership costs $16 for individuals, $24 for families and includes the monthly or quarterly magazine put out by the state organisation which you join. Addresses of the various National Trust state offices are:

Australian Capital Territory
 42 Franklin St, Manuka 2603
New South Wales
 Observatory Hill, Sydney 2000
Northern Territory
 14 Knuckey St, Darwin 5790 (GPO Box 3520)
Queensland
 Old Government House, George St, Brisbane 4000 (GPO Box 1494)
South Australia
 Ayers House, 288 North Terrace, Adelaide 5000
Tasmania
 25 Kirksway Place, Hobart 7000
Victoria
 Tasma Terrace, Parliament Place, Melbourne 3002
Western Australia
 Old Perth Boys School, 139 St Georges Terrace, Perth 6000

TIME ZONES

Australia is divided into three time zones: Western Time is +8 hours from Greenwich Mean Time (WA), Central Time is +9½ hours (NT, SA), and Eastern Time is +10 (Tas, Vic, NSW, Qld). During the summer things get slightly screwed up as daylight saving time does not operate in Western Australia or Queensland (of course), so those two states are an hour behind.

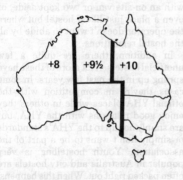

ACCOMMODATION

Finding a cheap place to stay can be a major stumbling block to seeing Australia at a reasonable price. It's not impossible, however, and these days Australia certainly offers as good value as you'll find in most western countries. We're actually very well-equipped with youth hostels and campsites, the cheapest shelter you can find. Furthermore, there are plenty of motels around the country and in holiday regions like the Queensland coast intense competition tends to keep the prices down.

Hostels

The number one accommodation choice for backpackers has to be the youth hostel chain. Australia has a very active youth hostel association and you'll find hostels all over the country with more popping up all the time. It's indicative of the growing popularity of hostelling not only that the official hostel association is opening more

hostels, but also that more and more 'unofficial' hostels are springing up.

Youth hostels provide basic accommodation, usually in small dormitories or bunkrooms. The nightly charges are rock bottom – usually just $5 to $7 a night – but in return there are a number of rules and regulations you have to observe. The most important one is that to stay at a youth hostel you must be a YHA (Youth Hostel Association) member. In Australia this costs $16 a year plus an $8 joining fee. Youth Hostels are an international organisation, so if you're already a member of the YHA in your own country, your membership entitles you to use the Australian hostels. Hostels are great places for meeting people, great travellers' centres and, in many busier hostels, the visitors will outnumber the Australians.

The rules and regulations for use of the hostels are all fairly simple and are outlined in the *Australian Youth Hostels Handbook*, which is available from any YHA office in Australia. This booklet also lists all the hostels around Australia with useful little maps showing how to find them, so it's quite invaluable. YHA members are eligible for various discounts at various places and these facilities are also listed in the handbook. The first rule is that you must have a sheet sleeping bag – a regular sleeping bag or sheets will not do. If you haven't got one they can be rented at many hostels (usually for $1), but it's cheaper, after a few nights' stay, to have your own. YHA offices and some larger hostels sell the official YHA sheet bag. Secondly, the hostels are generally not open during the day time. You've got to get up and out in the morning and generally can't get back in until 5 pm. Other rules are mainly of the no-alcohol, don't-disturb-people-at-night variety.

Most hostels have cooking facilities and some place where you can sit and talk. There is usually some sort of laundry facility and hostels often have excellent noticeboards. Many hostels have a maximum-stay period – because some hostels are permanently full it would hardly be fair for people to stay too long when others are being turned away. Hostels keep their costs down by getting you to do the work. Before departing each morning there will be some chore you must complete.

The YHA defines their hostels as the simpler 'shelter' style and the larger 'standard' hostels. They range from tiny little places to big modern buildings with everything from historic convict buildings to a disused railway station in between. Most hostels have a warden who checks you in when you arrive, keeps the peace and assigns the chores. Because you have so much more contact with a hostel warden than the person in charge of other styles of accommodation he or she can really make or break the place. Good wardens are often great characters and well worth getting to know. Accommodation can usually be booked ahead with the warden or, in some cases, with the state head office. The YHA handbook tells all.

The national head office of the Australian YHA is at 60 Mary St, Surry Hills, NSW 2010, (tel 212 1151). The state membership offices of the YHA are:

New South Wales
    355 Kent St, Sydney 2000 (tel 29 5068)
Northern Territory
    PO Box 39900, Winnellie 5789 or enquire at the Darwin youth hostel
Queensland
    462 Queen St, Brisbane 4000 (tel 831 2022)
South Australia
    Cnr King William & Sturt Sts, Adelaide 5000 (tel 51 5583)
Tasmania
    28 Criterion St, Hobart 7000 (tel 34 9617)
Victoria
    122 Flinders St, Melbourne 3000 (tel 654 5422)
Western Australia
    257 Adelaide Terrace, Perth 6000 (tel 325 5844)

Not all of the approximately 125 hostels listed in the handbook are actually owned by the YHA. Some are 'associate hostels' which provide all the usual hostel facilities and abide by all the hostel regulations but are owned by other organisations or individuals. Others are 'alternative accommodation' and do not totally fit the hostel blueprint. They might be a motel which keeps some hostel-style accommodation available for YHA members or a campsite with an on-site van or two kept aside, or even a place just like a hostel but where the operator doesn't want to abide by all the hostel regulations.

In addition, there are quite a few unofficial hostels. A lot more of these have sprung up in the past few years. In some cases they're in competition with the official YHA places while in others they enjoy good relations with the YHA, but are simply not up to the YHA's standards or simply don't want to be a part of the association. Youth hostelling is very popular in Australia and city hostels are often packed right out. When this happens, they're generally only too happy to recommend other hostel-style possibilities you can turn to.

The Ys

In a number of places in Australia accommodation is provided by the YMCA or YWCA. There are variations from place to place – some are mainly intended for permanent accommodation, some are run like normal commercial guest houses. They're generally excellent value and usually conveniently located. You don't have to be a YMCA or YWCA member to stay at them, although sometimes you get a discount if you are. Accommodation in the Ys is usually in fairly straightforward rooms, usually with shared bathroom facilities. Some Ys also have dormitory-style accommodation. Note, however, that not all YMCA or YWCA organisations around the country offer accommodation; it's mainly in the big cities.

Another organisation which sometimes

offers accommodation is the CWA (Country Women's Association), but this is mainly in the country and mainly for women only.

Colleges

Although it is students who get first bite at these, non-students can also stay at many university colleges during the uni vacations. These places can be relatively cheap and comfortable plus there is the opportunity to meet other people. Costs can be as low as $6 a day, or less, for room only (if you're a student), although around $12 is more normal. With meals it can go up to around $25. There's usually a student and a higher non-student rate.

A problem with this type of accommodation is that it is usually available only during the vacations (summer is November through February, the others are in May and August). Additionally, it must almost always be booked ahead; you can't just turn up. Many of Australia's new universities are way out in the suburbs (we call them 'bush unis') and are inconvenient to get to unless you have wheels.

The Australian Tourist Commission puts out a comprehensive booklet listing all the college accommodation possibilities – ask for *Campus Accommodation*.

Hotels

For the budget traveller, hotels in Australia are generally older places – new accommodation will usually be motels. To understand why Australia's hotels are the way they are, requires delving back into the history books a little. At the same time the powers that be decided Australia's drinking should only be at the most inconvenient hours, they also decided that drinking places should also be hotels. So every place which in Britain would be a 'pub' in Australia is a 'hotel', but often in name only.

The original idea of forcing them to provide accommodation for weary travellers has long faded into history; many of them have just a handful of rooms which are always 'occupied'. This ludicrous law is gradually being rolled back as 'tavern' licenses are issued which allow alcohol to be provided without the required sideline of having rooms. A 'private hotel', as opposed to a 'licensed hotel', really is a hotel and does not serve alcohol. A 'guest house' is much the same as a 'private hotel'.

New hotels being built today are mainly of the Hilton variety; smaller establishments will usually be motels. So, if you're staying in a hotel, it will normally mean an older place, usually with rooms without private facilities. Unfortunately many of them are definitely on the drab, grey and drear side. You get a strong feeling that because they've got the rooms they try to turn a dollar on them, but without much enthusiasm. Fortunately some are also colourful places with some real character. They're also often very centrally located. Although the word 'hotel' doesn't always mean they'll have rooms, the places that do have rooms usually make it pretty plain that they are available. If a hotel is listed in an accommodation directory you can be pretty sure it really will offer you a bed. If there's nothing that looks like a reception desk or counter, just ask in the bar.

You'll find hotels all around the town centres in smaller towns while in larger towns the hotels that offer accommodation are often to be found close to the railway stations. In some older towns, or in historic centres like the gold-mining towns, the old hotels can be really magnificent. The rooms themselves may be pretty old-fashioned and unexciting, but the hotel facade and entrance area will often be quite exotic. In the outback the old hotels are often places of real character. They are often the real 'town centre' and you'll meet all the local eccentrics there. While researching the last edition I stayed in one little outback town with a population of about 10, seven of whom were in the bar that night.

A bright word about hotels (guest houses and private hotels, too) is that the breakfasts are usually A1. A substantial breakfast is what this country was built on and if your hotel is still into serving a real breakfast you'll probably feel it could last you until breakfast comes around next morning. In these places, B&B stands for 'bed & breakfast'. Generally, hotels cost about $15 to $22 for a single, around $25 to $30 for a double. When comparing prices, remember to check if it includes breakfast or not.

The state auto clubs produce accommodation directories listing hotels and motels in almost every little town in the country. They're updated every year so the prices will generally be fairly current. They're available from the clubs for a nominal charge if you're a member or a member of an affiliated club enjoying reciprocal rights. Alternatively, the state tourist offices also put out frequently updated guides to local accommodation. In airports, bus and railway stations, there are often information boards with direct-dial phones to book accommodation. Sometimes these places offer a discount if you book through the direct phone. Some hotels around the bus and railway stations also offer discounts to bus-pass travellers. The staff at bus stations are good local sources of information on cheap and convenient accommodation.

Motels, Serviced Apartments & Holiday Flats

If you've got wheels and want a more modern place with your own bathroom and other facilities, then you're moving into the motel bracket. Motels cover the earth in Australia, just like in the US, but they're usually located away from the city centres. Prices vary and with motels, unlike hotels, singles are often not much cheaper than doubles. Sometimes there is no difference at all between a single and a double. The reason why is quite simple – in the old hotels many of the rooms really are singles, they're relics from the days of single men heading off somewhere to find work or whatever. In motels, the rooms are

almost always doubles. You'll sometimes find motel rooms as low as $22 and in most places will have no trouble finding something for $40 or less. You can take $28 to $35 as a reasonable average for an economically priced motel room.

Holiday flats and serviced apartments are much the same thing and bear some relationship to motels. Basically, holiday flats are found in holiday areas, serviced apartments in cities. A holiday flat is much like a motel room but usually has a kitchen or kitchen facilities so you can fix your own food. Usually holiday flats are not serviced like motels – you don't get your bed made up every morning and the cups washed out. In some holiday flats you actually have to provide your own sheets and bedding but others are operated just like motel rooms with a kitchen. Note that most motels in Australia will provide at least tea and coffee-making facilities but a holiday flat will also have cooking utensils, dishes, cutlery and so on. Basically a holiday flat is a bit like having your own small flat or apartment but on a short-term basis.

Holiday flats are often rented on a weekly basis but even in these cases it's worth asking if a daily rate is available. Remember also that paying for a week, even if you only stay for a few days, can still be cheaper than having those days at a higher daily rate. If there's more than just two of you, another advantage of holiday flats is that you can often find them with two or more bedrooms. A two-bedroom holiday flat is typically priced at about 1½ times the cost of a comparable single bedroom unit.

In holiday areas like the Queensland coast, motels and holiday flats will often be virtually interchangeable terms – there's nothing to really tell one from another. In big cities, on the other hand, the serviced apartments are often a little more obscure although they are often advertised in the newspaper small ads. As with hotels, you'll find motels and other similar accommodation listed in car-club accommodation directories, tourist office lists and at airports and other arrival points.

Camping & Caravanning

The camping story in Australia is partly excellent and partly rather annoying! The excellent side is that there are a great number of campsites and you'll almost always find space available. If you want to get around Australia on the cheap then camping is the cheapest way of all with nightly costs for two people around $5 to $8.

The drawbacks are first of all that campsites are often intended more for caravanners (house trailers for any Americans out there) than for campers and the tent campers get little thought in these places. The New Zealanders could certainly show Australian campsite operators how it's done. Over there campsites often have a kitchen and a dining area where you can eat. If it's raining you're not stuck with huddling in your car or, even worse, tent. The fact that most of the sites are called 'caravan parks' indicates who gets the most attention.

Equally bad, in the cities most sites are well away from the centre. This is not so inconvenient in smaller towns but, in general, if you're planning to camp around Australia you really need your own transport. In this respect European countries can show how it's done, with many cities having campsites right in the middle of town, like in Florence, for example, where the site is beautifully situated overlooking the river and town centre. Brisbane is the worst city in Australia in this respect because council regulations actually forbid tents within a 22 km radius of the centre. Although there are some sites in Brisbane within that radius, they're strictly for caravans, no campers allowed.

Still, it's not all gloom – in general Australian campsites are well kept, conveniently located and excellent value. Many sites also have 'on-site vans' which

you can rent for the night and give you the comforts of caravanning without the necessity of towing a caravan around with you. An on-site van typically costs around $15 to $20 a night. A variance of this is 'cabins' which have much the same facilities as a caravan but without the pretence that it might be towed away somewhere. As with hotels and motels, the state car clubs put out camping directories, and information sheets are also available from state and local tourist offices.

I've made trips around Australia using every sort of accommodation, going from youth hostels to motels, but one of the most successful was a trip Maureen and I made on a motorcycle. We had a little tent strapped across the handlebars and managed to camp almost everywhere we went, from Canberra to Cooktown, Airlie Beach to Ayers Rock. On the few occasions when sitting in a tent listening to the rain beat down (one of those times being in Alice Springs, believe it or not!)was too oppressive, we managed to find an on-site van to shelter in. In Alice Springs we were allowed to use a vacant on-site van free during the daytime.

Other Possibilities

That covers the usual conventional accommodation possibilities but there are lots of less conventional ones. You don't have to camp in campsites, for example. There are plenty of parks where you can camp for free, or roadside shelters where short-time camping is permitted. Australia has lots of bush where nobody is going to complain about you putting up a tent.

In the cities if you want to stay longer, the first place to look for a flat or a room is the classified ad section of the daily paper. Wednesdays and Saturdays are the usual days for these ads. Noticeboards in universities, youth hostel offices, certain popular bookshops and other contact centres are good places to look for flats to share or rooms for rent.

Australia is a land of farms (sorry,

stations) and one of the best ways to get to grips with Australian life is to spend a week on a farm. Many farms offer accommodation where you can just sit back and watch how it's done or have a go yourself. The state tourist offices can advise you on what's available; the costs are pretty reasonable. Or how about life on a houseboat (see South Australia)?

FOOD & DRINK

The culinary delights can be one of the real highlights of Australia. Time was, like 20 years ago or even less, when Australia's food (mighty steaks apart) had a reputation for being like England's, only worse. Well, perhaps not quite that bad, but getting on that way. Miracles happen and Australia's miracle was immigration. The Greeks, Yugoslavs, Italians, Lebanese and many others who flooded in to Australia in the '50s and '60s brought, thank God, their food with them.

So in Australia today you can have excellent Greek moussaka (and a good, cheap bottle of retsina to wash it down); delicious Italian saltimbocca and pastas; good, heavy German dumplings; you can perfume the air with garlic after stumbling out of a French bistro; try all sorts of Middle Eastern and Arab treats; and, of course, the Chinese have been sweet & souring since the goldrush days. In the last few years there has even been an amazing increase in the number of Indian restaurants so you can now find good tandoori food in most big cities as well.

Australian Food

Although there is no real Australian cuisine there is certainly some excellent Australian food to try. And I don't mean witchetty grubs, the giant-sized maggots that are an Aboriginal delicacy – you eat 'em live!

Any mention of Australian food has to include a couple of firm favourites, although they are not going to win any competitions. For a start there's the great Australian meat pie – every bit as sacred

an institution as the hot dog is to a New Yorker. It is just as frequently slandered as tasteless, unhealthy and not nearly as good as it used to be. The meat pie is an awful concoction of anonymous meat and dark gravy in a soggy pastry container. You'll have to try one though; the number consumed in Australia each year is phenomenal and they're a real part of Australian culture. See the Port Douglas (Queensland) section for the place to find a meat pie that really is worth eating.

Even more central to Australian eating habits is Vegemite. This strange, dark-coloured yeast spread is something only an Australian could love. You have to be born here to appreciate it. Australians spread Vegemite on bread and become so addicted to it that anywhere in the world you find an Aussie, the jar of Vegemite is bound to be close at hand. Australian embassies the world over have the location of the nearest Vegemite retailer as one of their most-asked-for pieces of information. Another Australian staple is beetroot, the purple vegetable which manages to show up in almost any salad. It's hard to imagine a real Aussie hamburger without the obligatory slice of beetroot.

The good news about Australian food is the fine ingredients. Leave the fancy cooking to the French; simple food and simple preparation is what works best in Australia. Nearly everything is grown right here in Australia so you're not eating food which has been shipped half way around the world. Everybody knows about good Australian steaks ('This is cattle country, so eat beef you bastards', announces the farmers' bumper stickers), but there are lots of other things to try. Australia has a superb range of seafood: fish like John Dory and the esteemed Barramundi, or superb lobsters and other crustaceans like the engagingly named Yabbies or Moreton Bay Bugs! Even vegetarians get a fair go in Australia; there are some excellent vegetarian restaurants and, once again, the vegetables are as fresh as you could ask for.

Where to Eat

If you want to feel right at home there are McDonalds, Kentucky Frieds, Pizza Huts and all the other familiar names looking no different than they do anywhere from New York to Amsterdam. There are also Chinese restaurants where the script is all in Chinese, little Lebanese places where you'd imagine the local PLO getting together for a meal and every other national restaurant type you could imagine.

For real value for money there are a couple of dinky-die Australian eating places you should certainly try, though. For a start Australian delis are terrific and they'll put together a superb sandwich. Hunt out the authentic looking ones in any big city and you'll get a sandwich any New York deli would have trouble matching, and I'm willing to bet it'll be half the price.

That covers your lunchtime appetite and in the evening the number one value is to be found in the pubs. Look for 'counter meals', so-called because they used to be eaten at the bar counter. Some places still are just like that, while others are fancier, almost restaurant-like. Good counter meals are hard to beat for value for money and although the food is usually of the simple steak-salad-french-fries variety, the quality is often excellent and prices are commendably low. The best counter meal places usually have serve-yourself salad tables where you can add as much salad, French bread and so on as you wish.

Counter meals are usually served as counter lunches or counter teas, the latter a hangover from the old northern English terminology where 'tea' meant the evening meal. One catch with counter meals is that they usually operate fairly strict hours. The evening meal time may be just 6 to 7.30 or 8 pm. At the appointed hour the gates are slammed shut! Pubs doing counter meals often have a blackboard menu outside but some of the best places are quite anonymous – you simply have to know that this is the pub that does great food and furthermore that it's in the bar hidden away at the back. Counter meals vary enormously in price but in general the better class places with good serve-yourself salad tables will be in the $5 to $7 range for all the traditional dishes: steak, veal, chicken, and so on.

For rock-bottom prices the real shoe-stringers can also check out university and college cafeterias, the big department store cafeterias (Woolworths and Coles, for example), or even try sneaking into public service, office cafeterias. Australians love their fish & chips just as much as the English and, just like in England, they can be enormously variable – all the way from stodgy and horrible to really superb. We've also got the full range of take-away foods, from Italian to Mexican, Chinese to Lebanese.

Drinks

In the non-alcoholic department Australians knock back Coke and flavoured milk like there's no tomorrow and also have some excellent mineral water brands. Coffee enthusiasts will be relieved to find good Italian cafés serving cappuccino and other coffees, often into the wee small hours and beyond. Beer and wine need their own explanations.

Beer

Australia's beer must be considered alongside the country's drinking habits. Way back in WW I the government of the day decided that all pubs should shut at 6 pm as a wartime austerity measure. Unfortunately when the war ended this wartime emergency move didn't. On one side the wowsers didn't want anybody to drink and if Australia couldn't have prohibition like America, stopping drinking at 6 pm was at least a step in the right direction in their view. The other supporters of this terrible arrangement were, believe it or not, the breweries and pub owners. They discovered that shutting the pubs at 6 pm didn't really cut sales at all and it certainly cut costs. You didn't have to pay staff until late in the evening and you certainly didn't have to worry about making your pub a pleasant place for a drink. People left work, rushed around to the pub and packed as much beer away as they could before 6 pm. They certainly didn't have time to admire the decor.

This unhappy story didn't even end after WW II. In fact it carried right on into the '50s before commonsense finally came into play and the 'six o'clock swill' was consigned to the bin where it belonged. Since that time the idea of the Australian pub as a bare and cheerless beer barn has gradually faded and there are now many pleasant pubs where an evening drink is a real pleasure. More recently, drinking hours have been further liberalised and in the last few years pubs have been able to open later in the evening and on Sundays.

Enough of the history, now for the beer – to most partakers, it's superb. Fosters is, of course, the best-known international brand with a firm following in England and even some supporters in the USA. Each Australian state has its own beer brand and there'll be someone to sing the praises of everything from Fourex (Queensland) to Swan (Western Australia) and even some fine local brands like Coopers (Adelaide). A word of warning to visitors – Australian beer has a higher alcohol content than British or American beers; Australian beer sold in the US has to be watered down to meet US regulations. And another warning, drinking drivers lose their licences; unfortunately, drunk driving is a real problem in Australia. Take care.

Beer Consumption

Australians are not the world's greatest consumers of beer – that achievement goes to the West Germans, who knock back nearly 150 litres per capita per year. But Darwin is reckoned to be the number one city for beer drinking. Its peak year was 230 litres per man, woman and child; with so much beer disappearing down Darwinians' throats, it's no surprise that they can run a boating regatta solely for boats made out of beer cans. When a party of

Darwinians sailed to Singapore in a beer-can boat, it was locally mooted that they inspired boatloads of Vietnamese refugees to take their chances in the opposite direction.

Australians are reckoned to be about the third biggest beer consumers in the world, about five to 10 litres behind the Germans, a litre or so less than the Belgians and neck and neck with the thirsty Czechs. The poms are about 25 litres back in 10th place. Americans don't even rate. Australia's per capita beer consumption has, however, been on a steady decline for the past decade or so.

Wine

If you're not a beer fancier, then turn to wines. Australia has a great climate for wine producing and some superb wine areas. Best known are the Hunter Valley of New South Wales and the Barossa Valley of South Australia, but there are a great number of other wine-producing areas, each with their own enthusiastic promoters.

The Australian wineries have often been compared with their Californian counterparts since the climate and soil are similar and the history of wine making in both areas has been alike. Recently, European wine experts have begun to realise just how good Australian wines can be. They can certainly mix it with the best. Australia's wines are cheap and readily available. We pay less for our wine than the Californians do and the price of a decent bottle in England, Common Market or not, is positively horrifying.

It takes a little while to become familiar with Australian wineries and their styles but it's an effort worth making! All over Australia, but particularly in Melbourne, you'll find restaurants advertising that they're BYO. The initials stand for 'bring your own' and it means that they're not licensed to serve alcohol but you are permitted to bring your own with you. This is a real boon to the wine-loving but budget-minded traveller because you can bring your own bottle of wine from the local bottle shop or from that winery you visited last week and not pay any fancy restaurant mark-ups. In fact, most restaurants make no charge at all for you bringing your own booze with you, even though it's conceivable that without it they might sell you a bottle of mineral water or something.

An even more economical way of drinking Australian wine is to do it free at the wineries. In all the wine-growing areas, most wineries have free tastings; you just zip straight in and say what you'd like to try.

THINGS TO BUY

Australia is not a great place for buying amazing things – there's nothing in particular which you simply 'have' to buy while you're here. There are, however, lots of things definitely not to buy – like plastic boomerangs, Aboriginal ashtrays and all the other terrible souvenirs with which tacky, tourist souvenir shops in the big cities are stuffed full. Most of them come from Taiwan anyway.

Top of the list for any real Australian purchase, however, would have to be Aboriginal art. It's an amazingly direct and down to earth art which has only recently begun to gain wide appreciation. If you're willing to put in a little effort you can see superb examples of the Aboriginals' art in its original form, carved or painted on rocks and caves in many remote parts of Australia. Now, and really just in time, skilled Aboriginal artists are also working on their art in a more portable form. There are Aboriginal art galleries in most big cities but the best displays are probably in the Northern Territory. Nobody captures the essence of outback Australia better than the Aboriginals so if you want a real souvenir of Australia this is what to buy.

Otherwise there are some alternative interesting possibilities. Like the sturdy farming gear worn by those bronzed Aussie he men on outback stations – boots, jeans and shirts, all made to last. Or there are all sorts of sheepskin products from car seat covers to Ugg boots. Surfing equipment is, of course, a major industry in Australia. You can find some terrific Australian books of the coffee table variety and Australian children's books can be equally attractive.

Recently some amusing Australiana shops have popped up selling delightfully silly examples of Australian kitsch – like lamingtons-in-perspex paperweights or a vegemite jar in an 'in case of emergency break glass' box.

Australia's national gemstone is the opal, found particularly in South Australia. They're very beautiful but buy wisely, as with all precious and semi-precious stones there are many tall tales and expert 'salesmen' around.

Aboriginal Art

A real appreciation of Aboriginal art, by westerners, is a comparatively recent development. Much of it was a temporary creation, like amazingly intricate sand paintings which were destroyed after ceremonial use. Or it was very permanent but also very remote, like the superb rock carvings and paintings still being discovered in places like the wild Kakadu National Park in the Northern Territory. Today, however, you can find excellent examples of all forms of their art in the Aboriginal craft shops in most state capitals, but particularly in Darwin and Alice Springs.

A useful introduction to these crafts can be found in the *Aboriginal Art* series of pamphlets. They include a general introduction and a number of separate brochures on rock art, baskets, carving, sculpture, painting and weapons. One of the best known crafts is the bark paintings from Arnhem land. These traditionally show Australian native animals in a style known as X-ray paintings because some of the internal organs are shown. From the central Australian deserts the sand paintings are a more recent addition. Sand paintings were traditionally made for ceremonial occasions and were often of great size. They used an intricate pattern of dots, whorls, circles and lines, brightly coloured to symbolise events and stories. Recently artists have started to reproduce these dramatic patterns with paint on hardboard. Interestingly they can still only be produced by certain initiated men and considerable planning is required before a painting can be produced.

Carvings are found in many regions but some of the best known are the large carvings by the Tiwi people from Bathurst and Melville Islands. Their ceremonial grave poles are particularly interesting. In the Kimberley region of Western Australia the large nuts of the boab tree are carved with intricate patterns. Boomerangs, woomeras (spear throwers) and didgeridoos (a long tube-like musical instrument) are other wooden objects. Baskets are woven from bark fibres or pandanus palm in a number of Aboriginal communities

Getting There

Basically getting to Australia means flying. Once upon a time the traditional transport between Europe and Australia was by ship but those days have ended. Infrequent and expensive cruise ships apart, the only regular shipping service to Australia runs between Singapore and Fremantle, the port for Perth on the west coast. Fares on this service vary with the cabin class and the cheaper cabins are often booked out some time ahead. There's no real saving on this ship compared to air travel.

The basic problem with getting to Australia is that it's a long way from anywhere. In recent years there have been lots of cheaper fares introduced and there is certainly a lot more competition than there used to be – Qantas no longer has it absolutely all its own way – but there's no way you can get around those great distances, and hence high costs.

Australia has a large number of international gateways. Sydney and Melbourne are the two busiest international airports with flights from Asia, the Pacific, Europe, New Zealand and North America. Perth also gets many flights from Asia and Europe and has direct flights to New Zealand. Other international airports include Hobart in Tasmania (New Zealand only), Adelaide, Port Hedland (Bali only), Darwin, Cairns, Townsville, and Brisbane. One place you can't arrive at, directly from overseas, is Canberra, the national capital.

FROM EUROPE

Official discount fares to Australia are Apex advance purchase fares and excursion fares. Stop-overs are not permitted on Apex fares and are limited on the excursion fares. A return Apex London-Sydney can run from £800 up to £1150 depending on when you go out and back. One-way Apex fares range from £400 to £600. There are also excursion fares which are somewhat more expensive than Apex fares ranging from around £1150 to £1300 again depending on the season. They do not require advance purchase and firm advance reservations but they do have restrictions on the minimum and maximum period of stay and there are restrictions on stopovers or extra charges. The one-way excursion fare, which permits one stopover, is £510 to £700. The regular economy one-way fare is £1007.

You can generally find tickets through London bucket shops at fares pleasantly lower than the Apex prices and with stopovers permitted. These do not involve any of the Apex cancellation penalties but you have to shop around and the prices tend to vary from week to week and airline to airline. Currently one-ways to Australia are available from London bucket shops from around £400.

For up to date information on what's available scan the travel ads in the giveaway papers *Australasian Express* and *LAM*, or get a copy of the weekly what's on guide *Time Out*. Although most bucket shops (the label is usually applied to discount travel agents) are pretty straight up and down there are always some sharp operators around. *Time Out* gives some useful advice on precautions to take. A couple of the major London operators who are usually OK are Trailfinders at 46 Earls Court Rd, London W8 and STA Travel 74 Old Brompton Rd, London W7.

On to New Zealand

There are no official cheap fares from London to New Zealand which include a stop-over in Australia. The cheapest way of doing it is either to get a discounted ticket to Australia and then get a cheap Australia-New Zealand fare, which requires advance purchase, or shop around for a cheap ticket from the bucket shops such as one using UTA through Australia or fares via the USA which include New Zealand as a stop-over en route to Australia. With a US and a New Zealand stop-over you can get to Australia for around £550.

FROM NORTH AMERICA

From North America you can fly to Australia with Qantas, Air New Zealand, Canadian Pacific, Pan Am, Continental and UTA. The USA is not a good place for unofficial cheap tickets although there are plenty of official cheap deals around. Pan Am is about to be replaced on the Pacific route by United Airlines and there are likely to be a number of special short term deals offered when they commence operations.

The regular economy fare is US$1198 Los Angeles-Sydney on a single carrier. Stop-overs are permitted but you must fly all sectors with the same airline. For US$1418 you can get essentially the same ticket but with the option of flying other trans-Pacific carriers along the way. Booked 14 days in advance, a one-way fare on a non-direct route is US$800.

Special economy return fares also permit stop-overs but the fares vary with the season, must be booked at least 14 days in advance and there is a cancellation penalty once you have booked and paid for your ticket. The fares are US$996 in the low season and US$1296 in the high season. Basically the low season for flights to Australia covers the April to August winter months, the high season covers the November to February summer months.

Of course if you shop around you can find better deals. Check the Sunday travel sections of papers like the *Los Angeles Times, San Francisco Examiner* or the *New York Times*. Deals available depend on the season and demand but you can get a one-way ticket for US$700 or less (down below US$500 in the off-season), and returns from as little as US$850. Recently even better deals have been available out of Canada. In the US good agents for

discounted tickets to Australia are the two student travel operators CIEE and STA, both of which have offices in various places around the country.

Via New Zealand

Many travellers from the US will want to visit both New Zealand and Australia. The cheapest way to do this is to buy an advance purchase Epic return fare USA-New Zealand and then a cheap return ticket New Zealand-Australia. The fare saving varies with the season. From the US West Coast, Epic returns range from around US$1000 to US$1500, one-way from around US$700. As with direct flights to Australia you'll probably find cheaper deals by shopping around.

Another possible way of combining New Zealand and Australia from the USA is with Circle Pacific fares. See the section on these fares below. Note that Auckland is the usual entry point from the USA but that there are flights between most Australian state capitals and the major New Zealand cities. For more information on New Zealand see Lonely Planet's *New Zealand – a travel survival kit.*

FROM NEW ZEALAND

Air New Zealand and Qantas operate a network of trans-Tasman flights linking Auckland, Wellington and Christchurch in New Zealand with Brisbane, Sydney and Melbourne on the east coast of Australia. More recently direct flights have started from Townsville, Adelaide and Perth to New Zealand. TAA also fly between Christchurch and Hobart in Tasmania. So basically you can fly between a lot of places in New Zealand and a lot of places in Australia.

Fares vary depending on which cities you fly between but the economy one-way range is from NZ$485 to NZ$529 while Apex returns, which also vary with season range between NZ$598 to NZ$806. The TAA Apex return between Christchurch and Hobart ranges from NZ$508 to NZ$608 depending on the season.

FROM ASIA

Ticket discounting is widespread in Asia, particularly in Singapore, Hong Kong (currently the discounting capital), Bangkok and Penang. There are a lot of fly by nights in the Asian ticketing scene so a little care is required. For much more information on South-East Asian travel and on to Australia see Lonely Planet's *South-East Asia on a Shoestring*.

Typical one-way fares out of Asia include Hong Kong from around HK$3500, Singapore from around S$800. Bangkok and Penang are other good ticket-centres. These fares are to the east coast capitals. Brisbane is sometimes a bit cheaper than Sydney or Melbourne. From Singapore it's cheaper to Perth or Darwin.

You can also pick up some interesting tickets in Asia to include Australia on the way across the Pacific. UTA were first in this market but Qantas and Air New Zealand are also offering discounted trans-Pacific tickets. On the UTA ticket you can stop-over in Jakarta, Sydney, Noumea, Auckland and Tahiti or Hawaii.

Stop Press: Timor-Darwin Flights

In early 1986 the Indonesian airline Merpati introduced flights between Darwin and Kupang, Timor (Indonesia). They leave Kupang at 2.30 pm on Fridays, and Darwin at 9 am on Saturdays and take just over two hours. Excursion fare is US$98 one-way but check with Merpati as there may be some conditions on this; the normal one-way fare is US$194, return is US$388.

This means that you can island-hop through Nusa Tenggara and exit direct to Australia rather than having to make your way back to Bali.

ROUND-THE-WORLD-TICKETS

Round the world tickets have become very popular in the last few years and many of these will take you through Australia. The official airline RTW (Round the World) tickets are much cheaper than the official fares and you can also put together interesting unofficial RTW packages in ticket discounting centres in Asia and Europe.

The official tickets are put together, usually by a combination of two airlines, and permit you to fly anywhere you want on their route systems so long as you do not backtrack. Other restrictions are that you (usually) must book the first sector in advance and cancellation penalties then apply. There may be restrictions on how many stops you are permitted and usually the tickets are valid for from 90 days up to a year. Typical RTW packages that include Australia are Continental-KLM, Continental-Air India, Qantas-TWA, Qantas-British Airways and Qantas-Air Canada. Canadian Pacific do a whole series of combinations which permit you to travel via Australia. Purchased in the UK RTW tickets through the South Pacific typically cost around £1150, in the US the tickets are priced from about US$2400.

US they're priced from around US$2400.

A do-it-yourself RTW package might be London-Singapore with a London bucket shop ticket, then Singapore-Los Angeles via Australia and New Zealand with one of the discounted trans-Pacific tickets like UTA's and then a stand-by ticket from LA back to London. London bucket shops offer RTW tickets through Australia for as little as £800.

CIRCLE PACIFIC TICKETS

Circle Pacific fares are a similar idea to RTW tickets. They permit you to use a combination of airlines to circle the Pacific – combining Australia, New Zealand, the USA and Asia. Examples would be Continental-Thai International, Qantas-Northwest Orient, Canadian Pacific-Cathay Pacific and so on. Typically fares range between US$1800 and US$1900. Using Continental with Thai you could, for example, fly Los Angeles-Hawaii-Auckland-Sydney-Bangkok and back to the USA.

ARRIVING & DEPARTING
Arriving in Australia

For information about how to get to the city from the airport when you first arrive in Australia check the Airport Transport section under the relevant city. At all of Australia's international airports there is an airport bus service, either private or government-run, and there are always taxis available.

Leaving Australia

Australia is much better than it used to be for cheap ticket deals but is still relatively 'straight'. At present some discounting is going on for tickets to Europe, nothing much at all to Asia. Apex tickets are available to all the usual destinations. The big catch about leaving Australia, however, is the terrible departure tax. It's A$20, one of the worst in the world, and it definitely discourages visitors to the country.

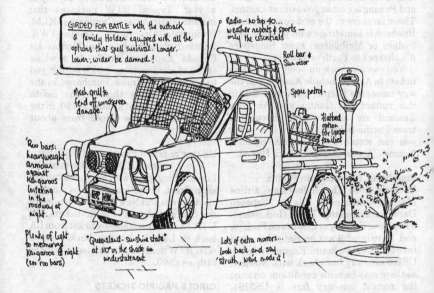

GIRDED FOR BATTLE with the outback a family Holden equipped with all the options that spell survival. 'Longer, lower, wider be damned!'

Mesh grill to fend off windscreen damage.

'Roo bars: heavyweight armour against kangaroos loitering in the roadway at night.

Plenty of light to mesmerise kangaroos at night (see 'roo bars)

"Queensland - sunshine state" at 110° in the shade is understatement.

Radio - no top 40... weather reports & sports - only the essentials

Roll bar & sun visor

Spare petrol

Flatbed option for larger families

Lots of extra mirrors... look back and say 'struth, we've made it'

Getting Around

FLYING

Australia is so vast (and at times so empty) that unless your time is unlimited, you're quite possibly going to have to take to the air sometime. It has been calculated that something like 80% of long distance trips by public transport are made by air. Unfortunately the two major domestic airlines are far from the cheapest per km in the world, although they are among the safest.

The two airlines are TAA (Trans Australia Airlines) which is government owned, and Ansett, which is privately owned with newspaper magnate Rupert Murdoch being one of the principal shareholders. The difference in ownership makes almost no difference to the traveller as both airlines are remarkably similar. In fact their sameness is one of the most interesting things about them. They offer a nearly identical service, absolutely identical prices and until recently, identical aircraft.

This follow-the-leader mentality was quite amazing just a few years ago. If Ansett wanted to buy two new Boeing 727 series 200s then TAA would also buy two new Boeing 727 series 200s. If one airline's planes arrived before the other's, they were held back until both airlines could introduce them on the same day. Then, as the ultimate absurdity, TAA and Ansett usually operated services at virtually exactly the same time. If TAA flew from A to B daily at 9 am and 3 pm, then Ansett would fly from A to B at 9.05 am and 3.05 pm (or perhaps 8.55 am and 2.55 pm). If they were going to have just one flight a week then they would probably go on the same day too!

Fortunately things have changed a bit. The respective aircraft fleets are now quite different (TAA has Airbuses, Ansett has 767s). Nor do they now operate quite such slavishly similar schedules, although there is still a certain degree of similarity on certain routes. Still, despite increased competition the fares are identical and, what is worse, they are a lot higher than they used to be. In the last few years airfares have risen with an almost clockwork regularity.

There are a number of reasons for the high cost of Australian air travel (although compared to prices in Europe the situation is not really all that bad). One is the government policy of loading the cost of air operations in Australia on to the domestic carriers – government policy is to recoup the entire cost of air traffic control, airport operation and so on from the airlines. In other countries it is often at least partially covered by general taxation.

Another reason is the poor utilisation of the aircraft, since very few flights are made at night. Except for flights between Perth and the east coast – only a couple a night for each airline – most of the fleet sits on the tarmac every night. Stringent regulations about night operations at Sydney and Brisbane airports (no arrivals after 10 pm) are a major reason for this.

Again it's government policy which accounts for another continuing absurdity of Australian air travel; namely the ruling that Qantas shall only fly abroad, Ansett and TAA only within Australia. There are some overseas sectors (Cairns-Port Moresby or Darwin-Bali for example) which would be much more suitable for the domestic carriers. Similarly Sydney-Perth and Melbourne-Perth are domestic sectors so Qantas 747s fly these long stretches, often only half full, and domestic passengers aren't allowed to use them. There's now a small crack in these regulations as TAA flies to New Zealand (but only from Tasmania) and Ansett has some Pacific connections on behalf of the Pacific island nations, but there's a long way to go.

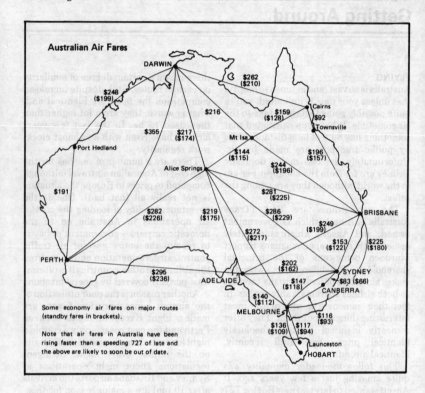

Australian Air Fares

DARWIN

$262 ($210)

$248 ($199)

$216

Cairns $159 ($128)

$92 Townsville

$355

$217 ($174)

Port Hedland

Mt Isa

$196 ($157)

$144 ($115)

$191

Alice Springs

$244 ($196)

$281 ($225)

BRISBANE

$282 ($226)

$219 ($175)

$286 ($229)

$249 ($199)

$272 ($217)

$153 ($122)

$225 ($180)

PERTH

$202 ($162)

SYDNEY

$295 ($236)

ADELAIDE

$147 ($118)

$83 ($66)

CANBERRA

$140 ($112)

MELBOURNE

$116 ($93)

Some economy air fares on major routes
(standby fares in brackets).

Note that air fares in Australia have been
rising faster than a speeding 727 of late and
the above are likely to soon be out of date.

$136 ($109)

$117 ($94)

Launceston

HOBART

Of course the biggest reason for the lack of competition is that the two domestic airlines simply don't have to. They've got a perfect little duopoly going and nobody else is allowed into the game. It's only when people simply stop flying or public complaints become overwhelming that something happens. In the last few years a combination of these factors has resulted in some cheaper fare possibilities – Apex round trip fares and standby fares for examples. Service has improved too – you actually get meals on longer sectors these days. Once upon a time they'd fly you from one end of Australia to the other with a cup of tea and a biscuit. There's also some internal competition too – East-West Airlines has been flying people on major routes at lower fares.

Cheap Fares – Standby For travellers the best story on the cheap fares side is the availability of standby fares on some main routes. The air fares chart shows the regular fares and the standby fares in brackets. Basically standby fares save you around 20% of the regular economy fare – Melbourne-Sydney, for example, is $148 economy, only $118 standby. You have no guarantee of a seat when travelling standby. You buy your ticket at the airport, register at the standby desk and then wait for the flight to board. If at that time there is sufficient room for the standby passengers, on you go. If there's room for 10 additional passengers and 20 are on standby then the first 10 to have registered get on. If you miss the flight you can standby for the next one (you'll be that much further up the line if some standby passengers have got on) or you can try the other airline.

A catch with standby fares is that they only work on a sector basis. If you want to fly Melbourne-Perth and the flight goes via Adelaide you have to standby on the Melbourne-Adelaide sector and then for the Adelaide-Perth sector. Furthermore the fares will be a combination of the two sectors, not a reduction from the direct Melbourne-Perth fare. Fortunately there are a lot more direct flights these days.

If you intend to standby the most likely flights will be, of course, the ones at the most inconvenient times. Very early in the morning, late at night or in the middle of the day are most likely. Many inter-capital flights in Australia are really commuter services – Mr Businessman zipping up from Sydney to Brisbane for a day's dealings – so the flights that fit in with the 9 to 5 life are the most crowded. 'Up for the weekend' flights – leaving Friday evening, coming back Sunday afternoon – also tend to be crowded. At other times you've got a pretty good chance of getting aboard. At various times I've flown standby to quite a few places around Australia and I've always managed to get there although once or twice it has not been on the first flight I tried. Incidentally Australia's parallel scheduling can create some scenes of real comedy in the standby game. If you don't get on the TAA flight you can still try the Ansett one, but that leaves just five minutes later and the Ansett desk is right at the other end of the terminal! Run!

Cheap Fares – Other Possibilities If you're planning a return trip and you have 30

days warning then you can save 35% by travelling Apex. You have to book and pay for your tickets 30 days in advance and once you're inside that 30 day period you cannot alter your booking in either direction. If you cancel you lose 50% of the fare.

Excursion fares, called *Excursion 45* by TAA and *Flexi-Fares* by Ansett, give a 45% reduction on a round-trip ticket, can only be booked between 14 and four days prior to travel and the maximum stay away is 21 days. The airline guarantees you a seat on the day you nominate, but as you only get notified which flight you are on the day before you travel, your arrangements need to be flexible to a certain degree.

University or other further education students under the age of 26 can get a 25% discount from the regular economy fare. A student photo identity card is required for Australian students. Overseas students can use their International Student Identity Card, a New Zealand student card or an overseas airline ticket issued at the 25% student reduction. The latter sounds a good bet!!

International visitors to Australia can get a 30% discount on internal flights to connect with their arriving or departing international flight – so if you're flying in to Sydney from Los Angeles but intend to go straight on to the Black Stump you get 30% off the Sydney-Black Stump flight.

There are also some worthwhile cheap deals with regional airlines such as East-West. By linking with Skywest in Western Australia and flying Sydney-Ayers Rock-Perth, East-West have a near national service. They have some useful flights like Sydney-Melbourne via Albury $9 less

than the big two regular fare but $28 less on standby. Keep your eyes open for special deals at certain times of the year. When the Melbourne Cup horse race is on and when the football grand final happens (also in Melbourne) lots of extra flights are put on. These flights would normally be going in the opposite direction nearly empty so special fares are often offered to people wanting to leave Melbourne when everybody else wants to go there.

Round Australia Fares Ansett and TAA

Fare A: $540
Maximum 6,000 km, 5 Stopovers

both have special round the country fares – TAA's is called *Airpass*, Ansett's is *Kangaroo Airpass*. Both have two tickets available – 6000 km for $540 and 10,000 km for $860 and they must be used within 45 days of the first day of use. Students under 26 with a student card are eligible for a 25% reduction. Some possible routes are illustrated below:

Stop Press

As of mid '86, the government airline TAA has been renamed Australian Airlines as part of a programme to modernise it's image.

Fare A: Total 5919 km
Melbourne-Canberra-Sydney-Alice Springs-Adelaide-Hobart-Melbourne

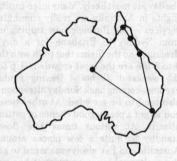

Fare A: Total 5515 km
Sydney-Proserpine-Townsville-Cairns-Alice Springs-Sydney

Fare A: Total 4952 km
Melbourne-Canberra-Sydney-Townsville-Proserpine-Gold Coast-Melbourne

Fare A: Total 5621 km
Perth-Alice Springs-Cairns-Mackay-Gold Coast-Sydney

Fare B: $860
Maximum 10,000 km, 8 Stopovers

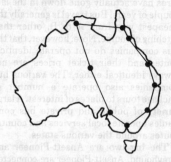

Fare B: Total 7848 km
Melbourne-Sydney-Gold Coast-Rockhampton-
Townsville-Cairns-Darwin-Alice Springs-
Adelaide-Melbourne

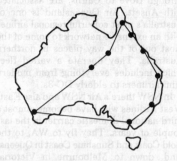

Fare B: Total 9013 km
Melbourne-Sydney-Brisbane-Mackay-Townsville-
Cairns-Mt Isa-Alice Springs-Perth-Melbourne

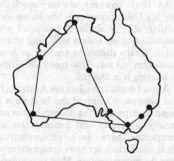

Fare B: Total 9582 km
Melbourne-Perth-Port Hedland-Darwin-
Alice Springs-Adelaide-Melbourne-Canberra-
Sydney

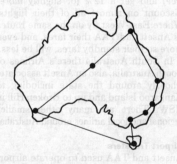

Fare B: Total 9929 km
Melbourne-Canberra-Sydney-Gold Coast-
Townsville-Alice Springs-Perth-Hobart-
Melbourne

If you want to see a lot of Australia but haven't got much time these fares are excellent value as they are much cheaper than the addition of all the separate fares. They're not even bad value compared to the bus pass tickets since on a bus pass quite a lot of your travel time is spent actually travelling. You don't have to finish in the city you start from and it's possible to backtrack. You can also miss out sectors if you wish and travel by land.

Other Airlines

There are a number of secondary airlines apart from the two major domestic carriers. In WA there's Ansett WA with an extensive network of flights to the mining towns of the north-west and to Darwin in the Northern Territory. Air NT, who operate from Darwin down to Alice Springs and Ayers Rock and across through Gove to Cairns, are associated with Ansett. Air Queensland is one of Australia's most colourful regional airlines with an extensive network to some of the most out of the way places in northern Australia. They operate a varied fleet which includes everything from modern mini-airliners to elderly DC-3s.

In NSW there's Air NSW and also East-West Airlines who have become almost a third national domestic carrier in the last couple of years. They fly to WA, to the Gold Coast and Sunshine Coast in Queensland, down to Melbourne in Victoria, across to Tasmania and also to Norfolk Island, apart from their extensive NSW connections. If you're between 15 and 25 you can join East-West's Club 25 (it's free) and get a 12% (or slightly more) discount on almost all of their flights. Where East-West fly on the same routes as Ansett and TAA their fares, and even more so their standby fares, will be less.

In South Australia there's Airlines of South Australia, also an Ansett associate, who fly around the state including to Kangaroo Island and up to Broken Hill in NSW. There are many other smaller regional and local airlines around Australia.

Airport Transfers

Ansett and TAA used to operate airport bus services all around the country but that stopped a couple of years ago. There are, however, private or public bus services at almost every major town in Australia. In one or two places you may have to depend on taxis but in general you can get between airport and city reasonably economically and conveniently by bus.

BUS

The nationwide bus system has gone through a major shake-up in the past few years. ' There are still the two major nationwide bus operators but there are now a number of secondary, national operators, quite apart from the string of more localised firms. A result of this new competition is that on many routes bus fares have actually gone down in the last couple of years! Bus travel is generally the cheapest way from A to B, other than hitching of course. Note, however, that the bus companies do not operate identical routes and their ticket prices are not always identical either. The various bus companies also operate a number of package tours to places of interest. A large variety of public and private bus companies operate local services and country routes around the various states.

The big two are Ansett-Pioneer and Greyhound. Ansett-Pioneer are connected with Ansett Airlines and in most cases operate from the Ansett city terminals. Greyhound, despite the similar logo, are not related to Greyhound Buses in the USA. Both, however, are very much like the big US companies – the buses look similar, they're similarly equipped with air-conditioning, toilets and quite often a video. As the distances are just as great, Australian bus travel has many similarities to bussing it in the US.

A great many travellers see Australia by bus because it's one of the best ways to come to grips with the country's size and variety of terrain and because the bus companies have such comprehensive route networks – far more comprehensive than the railway system. Most importantly, the big two have unlimited travel passes which can be excellent value. Here's a brief run down on the passes:

Greyhound Eaglepass The Eaglepass allows unlimited travel on Greyhound routes for either 30 days for $465 or 60 days for $690. Overseas, 21-day Eaglepasses are available for the equivalent of A$340. For overseas members of the Youth Hostels Association there's a 10% discount. The pass gives you 25% off local sightseeing tours.

Although both companies go to all the major centres, Greyhound does have a more extensive network and more import-

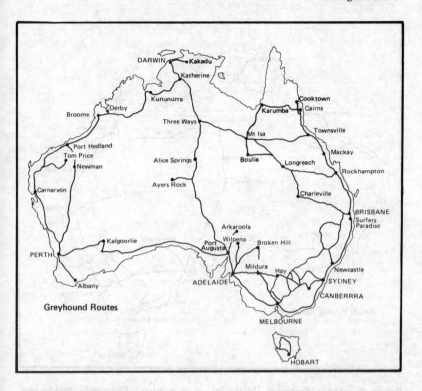

Greyhound Routes

antly, more frequent services. One place where services are infrequent – along the north-west coast of WA – the Greyhound and Ansett-Pioneer passes are interchangeable. Both companies now extend to Tasmania since their passes can be used on Tasmanian Redline Coaches' services. In Western Australia, the Eaglepass can be used on Westrail bus services from Perth to Albany. Your Eaglepass will also take you up into the Flinders Ranges of South Australia which is another advantage over Ansett-Pioneer.

Ansett Pioneer Aussiepass The Aussiepass is available in three variations – 15 days for $260, 30 days for $465 and 60 days for $690. A major plus for the Aussiepass is that it covers free sightseeing in Adelaide,

Canberra/Cooma, Melbourne, Perth and Sydney. In Alice Springs, Brisbane, Cairns, Darwin, Surfers Paradise and Townsville, you get a 50% discount on sightseeing tours. This can be useful where attractions are too far from the centre of a city to get to easily by yourself. or by public transport. The Phillip Island fairy penguins outside Melbourne are a good example. Note, however, that the Aussiepass included free sightseeing at one time, then dropped it, then offered it again at additional cost and now offers it again for free. They seem rather uncertain about offering it or not!

Another Ansett Pioneer advantage, according to some travellers is that their city terminals are often more conveniently located than the Greyhound ones.

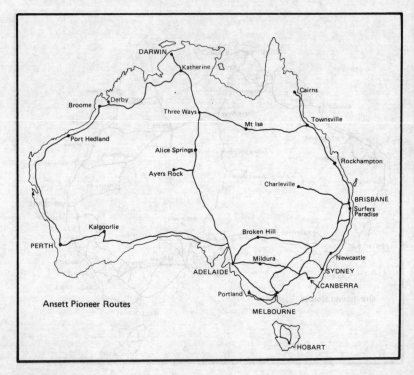

Ansett Pioneer Routes

Deluxe Coachlines Koalapass Deluxe is the third largest operator having extended it's network rapidly in the past few years. It now runs virtually identical routes to Ansett Pioneer and it also goes to Albany in the south-west of WA. The Koalapass costs much the same as the others – 32 days for $450, 62 days for $670 and 90 days for $900.

The maps show the comparable route networks for Ansett Pioneer and Greyhound. Big city terminals are generally well equipped – they usually have toilets, showers and other facilities. Greyhound also have a special 'super-saver' ticket which will take you from any place to any other place in their network for a maximum of $220. Any of these super-saver tickets also entitle you to 10% off accommodation

at a number of generally non-budget-traveller motel groups and 20% off sightseeing in most major centres and 25% off Budget Rent-a-Car anywhere in Australia.

Greyhound has introduced a new luxury, non-smoking, limited-stop service between the major centres, called the 'Silver Eagle'. This is generally a couple of hours faster and costs about 10% more.

In most cases you can make stop-overs along the route on your ticket, within certain time restrictions, with either company. If you want to know what bussing around Australia is like, look for a copy of *Bussing Around Australia*, available from bookshops or Greyhound offices for A$7.95. It relates an Eaglepass circuit of the country by two elderly (well they certainly sound elderly from the tone of the book!) and rather 'organised' travellers.

There are many other bus companies in Australia (such as VIP) although none, apart from Deluxe, have as comprehensive a route network as the big two. In Tasmania – where neither Ansett Pioneer or Greyhound operate – they include Tasmanian Redline, the major operator, plus a number of more localised operators. McCafferty's have a fairly comprehensive route system from Sydney up into Queensland as far as Mackay. Skennars also operate in Queensland and down to Sydney. In South Australia there is Briscoes, who run right up to Alice Springs in the Northern Territory, plus Stateliner who operate right around the state including the Flinders Ranges. In Western Australia there's Westrail, who

don't have many trains anymore so have turned to buses instead.

In many cases services are operated on behalf of Ansett Pioneer or Greyhound by these local operators. In some states there are restrictions on using interstate buses for intrastate travel – these rules particularly affect travel in NSW. It means you can't, for example, use a Sydney-Melbourne bus to get somewhere in NSW only.

RAIL

Australia's railway system has never really recovered from the colonial bungling which accompanied its early days over a century ago. Before Australia became an independent country it was governed as six separate colonies, all administered from London. When the colony of Victoria,

Principal Railways

for example, wanted to build a railway line it checked not with the adjoining colony of New South Wales but with the colonial office in London. When the colonies were federated in 1901 and Australia came into existence, by what must rate as a sheer masterpiece of planning, not one state had railway lines of the same gauge as a neighbouring state!

The immense misfortune of this inept planning has dogged the railway system ever since. The situation between Victoria and New South Wales is a typical example. When NSW started to lay a line from Sydney to Parramatta in 1850 their railway engineer was Irish and convinced the authorities it should be built to wide gauge – five foot three inches. Victoria also started to build to this gauge in order to tie in with the NSW system if, at some time in the future, a Melbourne-Sydney rail link was completed. Unfortunately NSW then switched railway engineers and their new man was not Irish and not enamoured of wide gauge. NSW railways accordingly switched to standard gauge – four foot eight inches – but Victoria decided their railway construction had gone too far to change now. Thus when the NSW and Victorian railway lines met in Albury in 1883 they, er, didn't meet. The Victorian railway lines were seven inches wider apart than the NSW ones. For the next 79 years a rail journey between Melbourne and Sydney involved getting up in the middle of the night at the border and changing trains!

In 1962 a standard gauge line was opened between Albury and Melbourne and standard gauge lines have also been built between the NSW-Queensland border and Brisbane. In 1970 the standard gauge rail link was completed between Sydney and Perth and the famous, and very popular, *Indian-Pacific* run was brought into operation. There are also, however, narrow gauge railways in Australia. They came about because they were believed to be cheaper. The old *Ghan* line between Adelaide and Alice Springs was only replaced by a new standard gauge line a couple of years ago.

Apart from different gauges there's also the problem of different operators. In the early '70s during the Whitlam era the Australian National Railways (ANR) was set up to try and bring the railways under one national umbrella, but due to non-Labor governed states not wanting to co-operate the ANR only operates railways in South Australia, the Melbourne-Adelaide service plus the two really well known services, the Adelaide-Alice Springs *Ghan* and the Sydney-Perth *Indian-Pacific*. Other services are operated by the state railways or a combination of them for interstate services.

Rail travel in Australia today is basically something you do because you really want to – not because it's cheaper (it isn't) and certainly not because it's fast. Rail travel is generally the slowest way to get from anywhere to anywhere in Australia. On the other hand the trains are comfortable and you certainly see Australia at ground level in a way no other means of travel permits.

Australia is also one of the few places in the world today where new lines are still being laid or are under consideration. The new line from Tarcoola to Alice Springs, to replace the rickety old *Ghan*, was an amazing piece of work and its success has inspired thoughts of finally building a railway line between Alice Springs and Darwin.

Although not all important services are operated by ANR there is co-operation under the Railways of Australia banner. You can write to them at 325 Collins St, Melbourne, Victoria 3000 for a copy of their handy and concise timetable of all the major Australian railway services. State booking office phone numbers are NSW (02) 217 8812, Queensland (07) 225 0211, South Australia (08) 217 4455, Tasmania (002) 34 6911, Victoria (03) 62 3115 and Western Australia (09) 326 2811.

Main Routes

Sydney-Melbourne
  day and overnight services every day of the week, 13 or 14 hours

Sydney-Murwillumbah
  daily overnight service for the Gold Coast, 17 hours

Sydney-Canberra
  seven days a week, five hours

Sydney-Brisbane
  daily overnight, 16 hours

Brisbane-Rockhampton
  six days a week, 10 hours

Brisbane-Cairns
  six days a week, 36 hours

Townsville-Mt Isa
  twice weekly, 20 hours

Melbourne-Adelaide
  daily overnight, 12 hours

Melbourne-Mildura
  six days a week, overnight, 10 hours

Sydney-Adelaide
  three days a week via Broken Hill, 28 hours

Sydney-Perth
  three days a week, 2½ days

Sydney-Alice Springs
  weekly, two days

Adelaide-Perth
  five days a week, 1½ days

Adelaide-Alice Springs
  once weekly (twice May to October), 23 hours

Perth-Kalgoorlie
  six days a week, eight hours

Austrail passes, allowing unlimited travel on all Australian rail systems, are available, but only for purchase overseas and only for foreign passport holders. Costs are the local currency equivalent of A$290 for 14 days, A$370 for 21 days, A$450 for one month, A$630 for two months and A$730 for three months. These passes are for economy class travel and do not cover meals and berth charges on trips where these are charged for as additional costs. The agent for Austrail passes in the UK is Thomas Cook and in the US it is Tour Pacific.

Students can get substantial discounts on the railways but need to have the concession card available from universities and colleges. Overseas students may have difficulty getting one but it's worth asking about as it allows travel in the sit-up cars of ANR trains. Perth-Adelaide would cost $79 and Adelaide-Alice Springs $58, which is cheaper than the bus.

DRIVING

Australia is a big, sprawling country with large cities where public transport is not always very comprehensive or convenient. Like America the car is the accepted means of getting from A to B and many visitors will consider getting wheels to explore the country – either by buying a car or renting one.

Driving in Australia holds few real surprises. We drive on the left hand side of the road just like in England, Japan and most countries in south and east Asia and the Pacific. There are a few local variations from the rules of the road as applied elsewhere in the west. The main one is the 'give way to the right' rule. This means that if you're driving along a main road and somebody appears on a minor road on your right, you must give way to them – unless they are facing a give-way or stop sign. This rule caused so much confusion over the years – with cars zooming out of tiny tracks onto main highways and expecting everything to screech to a stop for them – that most intersections are now signposted to indicate which is the priority road. It's wise to be careful because while almost every intersection will be signposted in southern capitals, when you get up to towns in the north of Queensland, stop signs will still be few and far between and the old give-way rules will apply.

The give-way ruling has a special and very confusing interpretation in Victoria where if two cars travelling in opposite directions both turn into the same street, the vehicle turning right has priority. This causes no end of headaches and confusion but fortunately, this rule only seems to apply in Victoria.

There's another special hazard in Melbourne – trams. You can only overtake trams on the inside and must stop behind them when they stop to pick up or drop off passengers. In central Melbourne there are also a number of intersections where a special technique, mastered only by native Melbournians, must be employed when making right hand turns. You must turn from the left hand side of the road. Be aware of trams – they weigh about as much as the *Queen Mary* and do not swerve to avoid foolish drivers.

The general speed limit in built-up areas in Australia is 60 kph (about 38 mph) and out on the open highway it's 100 to 110 (60 to 70 mph) depending on which state you're in. The police have radar speed traps and are very fond of using them in carefully hidden locations in order to raise easy revenue – don't exceed the speed limit in inviting areas where the gentlemen in blue may be waiting for you. On the other hand when you get far from the cities and traffic is light, you'll see a lot of vehicles moving a lot faster than 100 kph.

On the Road

Australia is not criss-crossed by multi-lane highways. There simply is not enough traffic and the distances are too great to justify them. You'll certainly find stretches of divided road, particularly on busy roads like the Sydney-Melbourne Hume Highway or close to the state capital cities – the last stretch into Adelaide from Melbourne, the Pacific Highway from Sydney to Newcastle, the Surfers Paradise-Brisbane road, for example. In general, however, Australian roads are of a good, surfaced standard (though a long way from the billiard table surfaces the poms are used to driving on) on all the main routes. Many roads are rather bumpy and patched, but the generally light traffic makes it hard to justify perfect roads. Make no mistake, away from the cities, traffic is generally light.

You don't have to get very far off the

beaten track, however, to find yourself on dirt roads and anybody who sets out to see the country in reasonable detail will have to expect to do some dirt-road travelling. If you really want to explore outlandish places, then you'd better plan on having four-wheel drive and a winch. If you're going to be doing any amount of driving on highways in the Northern Territory or WA, it's a good idea to carry a plastic emergency windscreen – they are available for a few dollars.

Driving standards in Australia aren't exactly the highest in the world but to a large extent the appalling accident rate is due to the habit that suitably boozed country drivers have of flying off the road into gum trees. Drive carefully, especially on the weekend evenings when the drinking-drivers are about. Note also that the police are doing their best to make

drinking and driving a foolish practice, even if you don't hit something. Random breath tests and goodbye licence if you exceed '.05' are the order of the day.

Australia was one of the first countries in the world to make the wearing of seatbelts compulsory. All new cars in Australia are required to have seat belts back and front and if your seat has a belt then you're required to wear it. You're liable to be fined if you don't. In some states small children are only allowed in the front seats if they're belted into an approved safety seat.

Petrol is available from stations sporting the well-known international brand names. Prices vary from place to place and from price war to price war but generally it's in the 55 to 60c a litre range (say around $2.45 to $2.70 an imperial gallon). In the outback the price can soar and some outback service stations are not above exploiting their monopoly position. Distances between fill-ups can be long in the outback and in some remote areas deliveries can be haphazard – it's not unknown to finally arrive at that 'nearest station x hundred km' only to find there's no fuel until next week's delivery!

Although overseas licences are acceptable in Australia for genuine overseas visitors, an International Driving Permit is even more acceptable. Between cities signposting on the main roads is generally quite OK but around cities it's usually abysmal. You can spend a lot of time trying to find street-name signs and as for indicating which way to go to leave the city – until recently you were half way to Sydney from Melbourne before you saw the first sign telling you that you were travelling in the right direction.

Buying a Car

If you want to explore Australia by car and haven't got one or can't borrow one, then you've either got to buy one or rent one. Australian cars are not cheap – it's a factor of the small population once again. Locally manufactured cars are made in small, uneconomic numbers and imported cars are heavily taxed so they won't undercut the local products. If you're buying a second-hand vehicle reliability is all important. Mechanical breakdowns way out in the outback can be very inconvenient – the nearest mechanic can be a hell of a long way down the road.

Shopping around for a used car involves much the same rules as anywhere in the western world but with a few local variations. First of all, used car dealers in Australia are just like used car dealers anywhere in the world from Los Angeles to London – they'd sell their mother into slavery if it turned a dollar. For any given car you'll probably get it cheaper by buying privately through newspaper small ads rather than through a car dealer. Buying through a dealer does give the the advantage of locally registered guarantees, but a guarantee is not much use if you're buying a car in Sydney and intend setting off for Perth next week. Used car guarantee requirements vary from state to state – check with the local automotive organisation.

There's much discussion amongst travellers about where is the best place to buy used cars. Popular theories exist that you can buy a car in Sydney or Melbourne, drive it to Darwin and sell it there for a profit. Or was it vice-versa? It's quite possible that car values do vary from place to place but don't count on turning it to your advantage. What is rather more certain is that the further you get from civilisation, the better it is to be in a Holden. New cars can be a whole different ball game of course, but if you're in an older vehicle, something that's likely to have the odd hiccup from time to time, then life is much simpler if it's a Holden. When your fancy Japanese car goes kaput somewhere back of Bourke it's likely to be a two week wait while the new bit arrives fresh from Fukuoka. On the other hand, when your rusty old Holden goes bang there's probably another old Holden sitting in the ditch with a perfectly good widget waiting to be removed. Every scrap yard in Australia is full of good ole Holdens.

Note that in Australia third party personal injury insurance is always included in the vehicle registration cost. This ensures that every vehicle (as long as it's currently registered) carries at least minimum insurance. You're wise to extend that minimum to at least third party property insurance as well – minor collisions with Rolls-Royces can be surprisingly expensive. When you come to buy or sell a car there are usually some local regulations to be complied with. In Victoria, for example, a car has to have a compulsory safety check (roadworthiness certificate – RWC) before it can be registered in the new owner's name – usually the seller will indicate if the car already has a RWC. In NSW, on the other hand, safety checks are compulsory every year when you come to renew the registration. Stamp duty has to be paid when you buy a car and as this is based on the purchase price, it's fairly common practice for buyer and seller to agree privately to understate the price! It's much easier to sell a car in the same state that it's registered in, otherwise it has to be re-registered in the new state.

Finally, make use of the automotive organisations – see the information section for more details about them. They can advise you on any local regulations you should be aware of, can advise you in general about buying a car and, most importantly, for a fee will check over a used car and report on it's condition before you agree to purchase it.

Renting a Car

If you've got the cash there are plenty of car rental companies ready and willing to put you behind the wheel. Competition in the Australian car rental business is pretty fierce so rates tend to be variable and lots of special deals pop up and disappear again. Whatever your mode of travel on the long stretches, it can be very useful to have a car for some local travel. Between a group it can even be reasonably economical. There are some places – like around Alice Springs – where if you haven't got your own wheels you really have to choose between a tour and a rented vehicle since there is no public transport and the distances are too great for walking or even bicycles.

The three major companies are Budget,

Hertz and Avis with offices in almost every town that has more than one pub and a general store. The second string companies which are also represented almost everywhere in the country are Thrifty and National. Then there are a vast number of local firms or firms with outlets in a limited number of locations. You can take it as read that the big operators will generally have higher rates than the local firms but it ain't necessarily so, so don't jump to conclusions.

The big firms have a number of big advantages, however. First of all they're the ones at the airports – Avis, Budget, Hertz and, quite often, Thrifty, are represented at most airports. If you want to pick up a car or leave a car at the airport then they're the best ones to deal with. In some but not all airports other companies can also arrange to pick up or leave their cars there. It tends to depend on how convenient the airport is.

The second advantage of the big companies is if you want to do a one-way rental – pick up a car in Adelaide, leave it in Sydney. There are however, a variety of restrictions on these. Usually it's a minimum hire period rather than repositioning charges but Thrifty also charge an additional $5 per day. Only certain cars may be eligible for one-ways. Check the small print on one-way charges before deciding on one company rather than another. One-way rentals are generally not available into or out of the Northern Territory or Darwin. Special rules may also apply to one-ways into or out of remote areas.

The major companies all offer unlimited km rates in the city but in country and 'remote' areas it's a flat charge plus so many cents per km. The big companies all go on about how economical they are and what great cars they've got. You can take most of it with the usual pinch of scepticism. During the course of researching the last edition I even rented a clunker from Hertz with over 100,000 km on the clock which would have been rejected by

Top: View of Sydney city centre with the Opera House and Harbour Bridge (ATC)
Left: In complete contrast, rolling fields near Byron Bay in the north of New South Wales (NSWGTB)
Right: Old meets new in the centre of Perth, Western Australia (TW)

Top: Gar's Mahal, the High Court building by Lake Burley Griffin in Canberra (TW)
Left: At the War Memorial in Canberra, the remains of a Japanese midget sub sunk in Sydney Harbour in WW II (TW)
Right: Looking from the the War Memorial across to the old Parliament House.

rent-a-wreck – admittedly it was in a 'remote' area. On straightforward off-the-card city rentals they're all pretty much the same price. It's on special deals, odd rentals, longer periods that you find the differences.

The chart below shows typical metropolitan rates for small and medium cars, per day.

	small	medium
Avis	$39	$45
Budget	$35	$45
Hertz	$42	$48
Thrifty	$38	$43

city rates
  unlimited km
country rates
  $5 is added to the city rates, 250 km is included, with an excess of 23c a km for Avis, 20c a km for the others. By the week unlimited km are included.
remote areas
  $10 is added to the city rates, 100 km is included, with an excess of 23c a km for Avis, 20c a km for the others.

Small cars are typically Ford Lasers or Toyoto Corollas – a Laser is the same as a Mazda 323, known in the US as a Mazda GLC.

Medium cars are typically Mitsubishi Sigmas, Nissan Bluebirds or Holden Camiras. Sigmas are the medium size Mitsubishi car, sold in some countries as a Colt. Nissan (Datsun) Bluebirds are also known as Datsun 200s or Nissan Maximas. Camiras are the same as a Vauxhall Cavalier, Opel Ascona or Chevrolet Cavalier.

There are a whole collection of other factors to bear in mind about this rent-a-car business. For a start if you're going to want it for a week, a month or longer then they all have lower rates. If you're in Tasmania, where competition is very fierce, there are often lower rates especially in the low-season. If you're in the really remote outback (some place like Darwin and Alice Springs are only vaguely remote) then the choice of cars is likely to be limited to the larger, more expensive

ones. Daily insurance is usually an extra $10. You usually must be at least 21 to hire an Avis, Hertz or Budget car and 23 for Thrifty.

Finally, with the big companies, look for special deals. In the big cities, where most cars are hired to businessmen from Monday to Friday, there are often special weekend rates. Budget even offers a 'standby' rate. Keep your eyes open and there may be special one-way hires available. While researching the last edition I even saw cars offered free in Townsville, so long as you got them to Cairns within 24 hours!

OK, that's the big hire companies, what about all the rest of them? Well some of them are still pretty big in terms of numbers of shiny new cars. In Tasmania, for example, the car hire business is really big since many people don't bring their cars with them. There's a plethora of hire companies and lots of competition. In many cases local companies are markedly cheaper than the big boys but in others what looks like a cheaper rate can end up quite the opposite if you're not careful. Quick, what's cheaper: $30 a day, or $12 a day plus 12c a km in excess of 100 km – if you do 200 km? And if you do 300?

A fairly recent upheaval in the local rental business is the proliferation of 'rent-a-wreck' companies. They specialise in renting older cars – at first they really were old and flat figure like $10 a day and forget the insurance was the usual story. Now many of them have a variety of rates. If you just want to travel around the city, or not too far out, they can be worth considering.

Mokes

In lots of popular holiday areas – like on the Gold Coast, around Cairns, on Magnetic Island, around Alice Springs, in Darwin – right at the bottom of the rent-a-car rates will be the ubiquitous Moke. To those not in the know a Moke is a totally open vehicle looking rather like a miniature Jeep. They're based on the Mini so

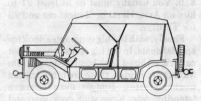
they're front-wheel drive not four-wheel drive and they are not suitable for getting way off the beaten track. For general good fun in places with a sunny climate, however, they simply can't be beaten. No vehicle has more air-conditioning than a Moke and as the stickers say 'Moking is not a wealth hazard' – they cover lots of km on a litre of petrol.

If you do hire a Moke there are a few points to watch. Don't have an accident in one, they offer little more protection than a motorcycle. There is absolutely no place to lock things up so don't leave your valuables inside, and the fuel tanks are equally accessible so if you're leaving it somewhere at night beware of petrol thieves – not that there are a great number in Australia, but it does happen.

Renting Other Vehicles
There are lots of other vehicles you can rent apart from cars. In remote outback areas you can often rent four-wheel drive vehicles. In many places you can rent campervans – they're particularly popular in Tasmania. Motorcycles are also available in a number of locations – they are popular on Magnetic Island for example.

Best of all, in many places you can rent bicycles. Many Australian cities now have special bike tracks and often a bicycle will be the ideal way of getting around. There

are no hasseles with parking, and in all, it's hassles with parking, and altogether, it's an ideal way of seeing a city – so long as the hills aren't too steep or the traffic too horrendous. In the course of researching the last edition I rented bicycles in half a dozen places as widely scattered as Surfers Paradise, Darwin and Broome.

BIKING
Motorcycles are a very popular way of getting around although the accident rate is also rather frightening – perhaps due to the practice of letting novice riders start learning on multi-cylinder super-bikes? The climate is just about ideal for biking most of the year and the long open roads are really made for large capacity highway cruisers. Maureen and I have ridden two-up from Melbourne all the way to Darwin (via Sydney-Brisbane-Cairns-Cooktown-Mt Isa-The Alice-Ayers Rock) on a 250 cc trail bike, so doing it on a small bike is not impossible, just more boring.

Doing it on a pushbike is closer to being impossible – or at least it is for any normal, reasonably sane human being! Yes, plenty of people have ridden pushbikes around Australia but you have to have a large helping of masochism and a fair share of nuttiness in your character to attempt it. There are certainly some places (apart from cities) where the old pushbike can be just the thing for getting around. Tasmania, for example, is certainly bikeable size for an enthusiast and there are a lot of other compact areas worth considering.

Many keen, but not crazy, bicycle riders see Australia by riding the interesting bits and then putting their bike aboard a train, bus or plane for the dull bits. It's generally not too expensive to transport your bicycle this way, often free in fact, and when you get to your destination you've got you're own wheels immediately to hand. Bike rental has also become a much more reasonable proposition in the last few years – you can now hire bikes by the hour, day, or longer periods in a great number of locations around the country.

HITCHING

Travel by thumb may be frowned upon by the boys in blue in some places but it can be a good way of getting around and it is certainly interesting. Sometimes it can even be fast, but it's usually foolish to try and set yourself deadlines when travelling this way – you are depending on luck. Successful hitching depends on several factors, all of them just plain good sense.

The most important is your numbers – two people are really the ideal, any more makes things very difficult. Ideally those two should comprise one male and one female – two guys hitching together can expect long waits. Women's lib or not I do not recommend women hitching unaccompanied and a woman should never hitch solo.

Factor two is position – look for a place where vehicles will be going slowly and where they can stop easily. A junction or freeway slip road are good places if there is stopping room. Position goes beyond just where you stand. The ideal location is on the outskirts of a town – hitching from way out in the country is a hopeless as from the centre of a city. Take a bus out to the edge of town.

Factor three is appearance – the ideal appearance for hitching is a sort of genteel poverty – threadbare but clean. Looking too good can be as much of a bummer as looking too bad! Don't carry too much gear – if it looks like it's going to take half an hour to pack your bags aboard you'll be left on the roadside.

Factor four is knowing when to say no. Saying no to a car load of drunks or your friendly rapist is pretty obvious but it can be time saving to say no to a short ride that might take you from a good hitching point to a lousy one. Wait for the right, long ride to come along. On a long haul, it's pointless to start walking as it's not likely to increase the likelihood of you getting a lift and it's often an awfully long way to the next town.

Trucks are usually the best lifts but they will only stop if they are going slowly and can get started easily again. Thus the ideal place is at the top of a hill where they have a downhill run. Truckies often say they are going to the next town and if they don't like you, will drop you anywhere. As they often pick up hitchers for company, the quickest way to create a bad impression is to jump in and fall asleep. It's also worth remembering that while you're in someone else's vehicle, you are their guest and should act accordingly – many drivers no longer pick up people because they have suffered from thoughtless hikers in the past.

Hitching in Australia is really very easy, we are supposed to be friendly remember, and if you take care with your rides it is reasonably safe. Of course people do get stuck in outlandish places but that is the name of the game. If you're visiting from abroad a nice prominent flag on your pack will help, and a sign announcing your destination can also be useful. Uni and youth hostel noticeboards are good places to look for hitching partners. The main law against hitching is 'thou shalt not stand in the road' – so when you see the law coming, step back.

SHIPPING

Not really. Once upon a time there was quite a busy coastal shipping service but now it only applies to freight and apart from specialised bulk carriers, even that is declining rapidly. The only regular shipping service is between Victoria and Tasmania and unless you are taking a vehicle with you the very cheapest ticket on that often-choppy route is not all that much cheaper than the air-fare. You can occasionally travel between Australian ports on a liner bound for somewhere but very few people do that.

TOURS

There are all sorts of tours around Australia including some interesting camping tours. Adventure tours include four-wheel drive safaris in the Northern

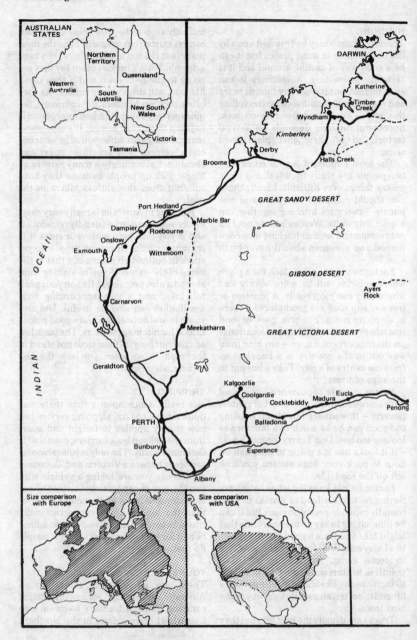

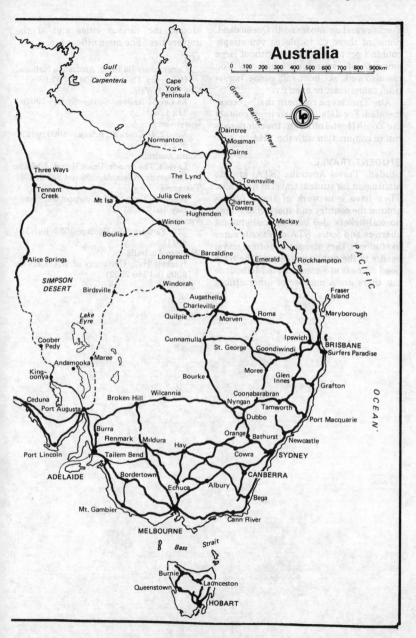

Australia

0 100 200 300 400 500 600 700 800 900km

Gulf of Carpenteria

Cape York Peninsula

Normanton

The Lynd

Great Barrier Reef

Daintree
Mossman
Cairns

Townsville

Charters Towers

Three Ways

Tennant Creek

Mt Isa

Julia Creek

Hughenden

Mackay

Winton

Barcaldine

Emerald

Rockhampton

Boulia

Longreach

PACIFIC

Alice Springs

SIMPSON DESERT

Birdsville

Windorah

Augathella
Charleville

Quilpie

Morven

Roma

Fraser Island

Maryborough

Lake Eyre

Coober Pedy

Andamooka

Maree

Cunnamulla

St. George

Goondiwindi

Ipswich

BRISBANE
Surfers Paradise

King-oonya

Ceduna
Port Augusta

Bourke

Moree

Glen Innes

Grafton

OCEAN

Port Lincoln

Burra

Broken Hill

Wilcannia

Renmark
Mildura

Coonabarabran
Nyngan

Tamworth

Port Macquarie

Dubbo

Orange
Bathurst

Newcastle

ADELAIDE

Tailem Bend

Hay

Cowra

SYDNEY

Bordertown

Echuca

Albury

CANBERRA

Mt. Gambier

Cann River

Bega

MELBOURNE

Bass Strait

Burnie

Queenstown

Launceston

HOBART

Territory and up into far north Queensland. Some of these go to places you simply couldn't get to on your own without large amounts of expensive equipment. You can also walk, ski, boat, raft, canoe, horse-ride, camel-ride, or even fly.

Aus-Trail is one company that's recommended. For details of their trips, contact the Youth Hostel offices as the company is run in conjunction with the YHA.

STUDENT TRAVEL

Student Travel Australia (STA) are the main agent for student travel in Australia. They have a network of travel offices around the country and apart from selling normal tickets also have special student charters and tours. STA don't only cater to students, they also act as normal travel agents to the public in general. The STA head office is at Faraday St in Melbourne but there are a number of other offices around the various cities and at the universities. The main offices are:

ACT
  Concessions Building, Australian National University, Canberra 2600 (tel 47 0800)
New South Wales
  1A Lee St, Railway Square, Sydney 200 (tel 212 1255)
Queensland
  Shop 2, 40 Creek St, Brisbane 4000 (tel 221 9629)
South Australia
  Level 4, The Arcade, Union House, Adelaide University, Adelaide 5000 (tel 223 6620)
Tasmania
  Webster Travel, 60 Liverpool St, Sandy Bay, (tel 795 8771)
Victoria
  220 Faraday St, Carlton 3053 (tel 347 6911)
Western Australia
  Hackett Hall, University of WA, Crawley 6009 (tel 380 2302)

Australian Capital Territory

Area　　　　2366 square km
Population　250,000

Don't miss the national capital, a beautiful, planned city with monuments, museums, a brand-new art gallery and Australia's parliament house.

Like many other world capitals, Canberra is a planned city. When the separate colonies of Australia were federated in 1901 and became states the decision to build a national capital was part of the constitution. The site was not selected until 1908, diplomatically situated between arch rivals, Sydney and Melbourne. An international competition to design the capital was won by the American architect, Walter Burley Griffin. In 1911 the Commonwealth government bought up the land of the Australian Capital Territory (ACT), and in 1913 decided to call the **capital Canberra, believed to be an Aboriginal term for 'meeting place'.**

Early development of the site was painfully slow due to WW I; not until 1927 did parliament first convene in the capital. In the interim, Melbourne acted as the national capital. The depression virtually halted development again and it was not until after WW II that things really got underway. In the 50s, 60s and 70s progress was incredible and for some time Canberra was Australia's fastest growing city. Satellite cities sprang up at Belconnen and Woden and, in 1960, the population topped 50,000, sprinted to 100,000 by 1967 and today is around the 250,000 mark.

Canberra is unlike other large Australian cities. It is amazingly ordered and neat, and it is an inland, not a coastal, city. It is still principally a place of government and public services and there are few local industries. It is no distance at all from good bushwalking and skiing country in NSW and the population is fairly young.

INFORMATION
The Canberra Tourist Bureau only has a couple of offices, unlike the other state tourist offices which seem to be widely scattered.

ACT
　　Canberra Tourist Bureau, Jolimont Centre, Northbourne Ave, Canberra City, ACT 2601 (tel 45 6464)
NSW
　　Canberra Tourist Bureau, 64 Castlereagh St, Sydney, NSW 2000 (tel 233 3666)
Victoria
　　Canberra Tourist Bureau, 247 Collins St, Melbourne, Vic 3000 (tel 654 5088)

ACTIVITIES
Bushwalking The Canberra Bushwalking Club's address is The Environment Centre, Kingsley St, Acton (tel 47 3064). A book called *25 Family Bushwalks In & Around Canberra* by Graeme Barrow can be found in most city bookshops for about $4. Several of the parks and reserves in the south of the ACT have good bushwalks. Tidbinbilla Fauna Reserve has marked trails. Other good areas include Mt Kelly-Gudgenby, around Cotter Reserve and Mt Franklin.

Boating Canoes, paddle boats and sailing boats can be rented by the hour, or for

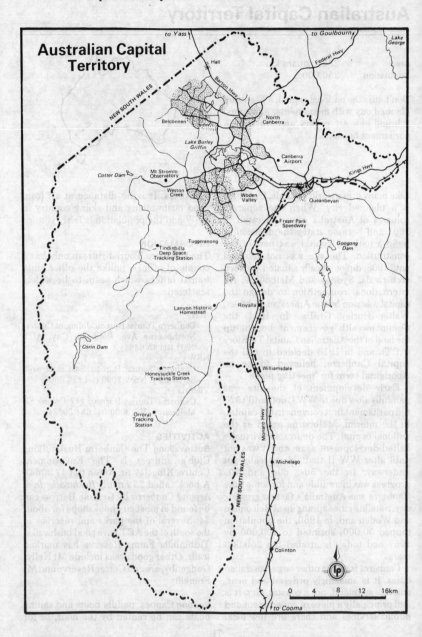

Australian Capital Territory

to Yass

to Goulbourn

Lake George

Hall

Federal Hwy

Barton Hwy

NEW SOUTH WALES

Belconnen

North Canberra

Lake Burley Griffin

Canberra Airport

Cotter Dam

Mt Stromlo Observatory

Kings Hwy

Weston Creek

Woden Valley

Queanbeyan

Fraser Park Speedway

Googong Dam

Tuggeranong

Tindinbilla Deep Space Tracking Station

Lanyon Historic Homestead

Royalla

Corin Dam

Williamsdale

Monaro Hwy

Honeysuckle Creek Tracking Station

Orroral Tracking Station

Michelago

NEW SOUTH WALES

Colinton

0   4   8   12   16km

to Cooma

longer periods, from Dobell's Boat Hire, Ferry Wharf, Acton; so you can get out on Lake Burley Griffin. They're only open on weekends, though, except during school holidays.

The Canberra Rowing Club (tel 48 9738) and the YMCA Canoe Club (tel 49 8733) both welcome visitors. The YMCA Sailing Club (tel 81 1396) will tell you about YMCA-organised races. A brochure on safety procedures and weather conditions on the lake is available – no power boats are permitted.

Bicycling Canberra has a series of bicycle tracks – they are probably the best and most extensive bike riding facilities in Australia.

A map of Canberra Cycle Ways is available, as is a brochure called *Canberra: On a Bike Tour*. You can rent bikes from the Youth Hostel or from Mr Spokes Bike Hire (tel 91 6779) near the Acton Ferry Terminal.

Skiing The NSW Snowy Mountain snowfields are within four hours' easy drive of Canberra so check the NSW section for info. The ACTTB can supply the latest news on conditions, as can the YMCA (tel 49 8733), who also have lodges at Guthega and Thredbo. A number of local garages, as well as the conventional ski shops, hire out equipment.

Swimming & Diving It's a 150 km drive to the nearest surf beaches at Batemans Bay in NSW – there's a daily bus service. There are a number of swimming pools around the city plus river or lake swimming at Kambah Pool (21 km), Pine Island (27 km) on the Murrumbidgee River and Casuarina Sands (19 km) near Cotter Dam. There's even a nude bathing stretch along the Murrumbidgee.

Swimming in Lake Burley Griffin is definitely not recommended. There are some skin-diving possibilities around Batemans Bay.

Canberra

The capital is amazingly orderly and planned-looking. There's no gradual disintegration into a jumble of used-car lots as you get further from the centre. In fact, it's so squeaky clean and artificial that the city has a very mixed reputation in Australia. Its popular image is of a soulless string of suburbs, a playground for politicians and public servants who, if they're far enough up the scale, jet away to somewhere more interesting come the weekend. There's probably still a fair bit of truth in that image but Canberra today is becoming more and more a real city, yet it's basically as attractive as ever.

Information

The Canberra Tourist Bureau (tel 45 6464) is in the Jolimont Centre on Northbourne Avenue. It's open every day, 8.30 am to 5 pm. They're helpful and friendly and have a good collection of maps, brochures and information leaflets. There's a free film on Canberra shown on the hour. Interstate information is also available (tel 45 6446). Also located at the Jolimont Centre is the Greyhound Bus Terminal, the airport bus departure point, other bus lines (but not Ansett Pioneer) and the post office. The Jolimont Centre is the block bounded by Northbourne Avenue, Alinga St, Moore St and Rudd St.

There's another information centre at Northbourne Avenue, Dickson, which you pass as you drive into the city. Lastly, there is an information booth on City Walk near the merry-go-round. The NRMA (tel 43 3777) has an office at 92 Northbourne Avenue where you can get a copy of their excellent map of Canberra.

The YHA has a useful walking-tour leaflet. There is a university information centre at Balmain Crescent, Acton, with an info noticeboard. The Petrie Plaza and Monaro Mall shopping complexes both have community noticeboards. Check the interesting noticeboard in Smith's Bookshop, too. As a capital city should be, Canberra is well stocked with overseas information centres and libraries – good places to keep up with foreign magazines, papers and films. For detailed information on Canberra, it may be worth purchasing *The Canberra Handbook*, published by the Australian National University (ANU) and retailing for $2.75. There are also books on cycling and bushwalking around Canberra. Canberra has a number of good bookshops; Dalton's, in Garema Place, is probably the best.

If you're getting mail sent to you in Canberra have it addressed to Poste Restante at the Canberra City Post Office rather than the GPO Canberra which is inconveniently situated behind the parliament building.

Orientation

Canberra is neatly divided into two parts by the natural looking, but artificial, Lake Burley Griffin. The north side of the lake can be thought of as the living part and the south side as the working part. Today, as Canberra expands in all directions, that's a haphazard description, but it will do, since, for the short-term visitor, most accommodation is to the north, while the major government attractions are principally to the south.

The huge circle north of the lake, Vernon Circle, is the centre point for the north side. Close to this circle you will find the tourist office, post office, airline and bus terminals, and the shops and restaurants of the Civic Centre, Canberra's oldest and most established shopping centre. This area is the main Canberra downtown centre and is known as 'Civic'. City Walk and Petrie Plaza pedestrian malls are found here; where they meet there is a fine old merry-go-round, marking the centre of things.

From Vernon Circle, Commonwealth Avenue runs arrow-straight across the lake to Capital Circle, the site of the new parliament building, which is currently under construction. Capital Circle is the apex of Walter Burley Griffin's parliamentary triangle – bordered by Commonwealth Avenue, Kings Avenue and the lake. Most of the government buildings are concentrated within this triangle including the National Library, the High Court, the National Gallery and the old parliament building. Kings Avenue also runs across the lake to the north side. Away from Civic spreading in all directions are numerous suburbs and neighburhoods, each with its own small, modern shopping centre. The biggest of these are Belconnen to the north-west and Woden to the south-west. Together with Canberra Central these two form the rough Y-shape the city planners first envisaged.

Lookouts

The hills that range around the city provide fine views of the lake as well as across the city itself. Try 825 metre Black Mountain, topped by the controversial 195 metre Telecom Telecommunications Tower. It's even got – wait for it – a revolving restaurant on the top. According to reports, the food is the revolving restaurant norm; expensive and far inferior to the views. The view alone costs $1 and is available from 9 am to 10 pm.

There are good bushwalks around the mountain. Apart from the 9 am Canberra Explorer bus there is no public transport up the hill. Between a group, a taxi to the top wouldn't be too expensive, or you can walk up there; quite a pleasant stroll apart from the mad traffic.

Other mountain viewpoints, all with roads running up to the top, are: 722 metre Red Hill, 840 metre Mt Ainslie and 665 metre Mt Pleasant. Mt Ainslie is close to the city on the north-east side and has particularly fine views across the city and out over the airport – you can see the Ansett and TAA aircraft lining up behind each other. From up top you'll also appreciate what a green and park-like city Canberra is. There are trails leading up Mt Ainslie from behind the War Memorial.

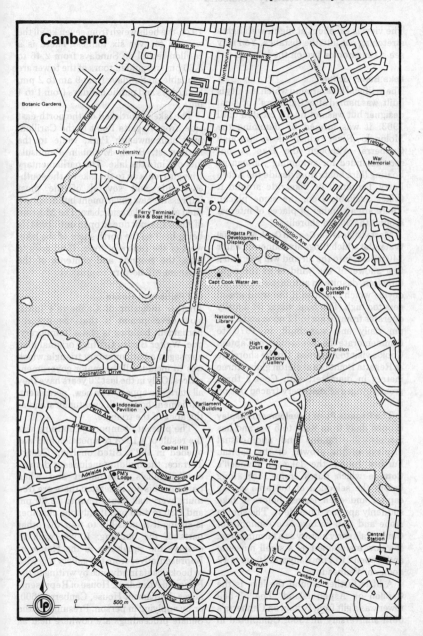

Canberra

Botanic Gardens

University

Masson St

Girrahween St

Northbourne Ave

Limestone Ave

Barry Drive

Cooyong St

Doonkuna St

GPO

London Circuit

City Centre Ave

Ainslie Ave

Vernon Circle

London Circuit

Treloar Cres

War Memorial

Edinburgh Ave

Marcus Clarke St

Anzac Pde

Ferry Terminal,
Bike & Boat Hire

Regatta Pt
Development
Display

Parkes Way

Constitution Ave

Capt Cook Water Jet

Blundell's
Cottage

National
Library

High
Court

National
Gallery

Carillon

Coronation Drive

King Edward Tce

King George Tce

Flynn Drive

Forster Cres

Fenner Cres

Perth Ave

Indonesian
Pavillion

Parkes Place

Parliament
Building

Kings Ave

Bowen Drive

Arkana St

Commonwealth Ave

Capital Hill

Brisbane Ave

Adelaide Ave

PM's
Lodge

Capital Circle

State Circle

Sydney Ave

Telopea Pk

Wentworth Ave

Dominion Circuit

National Circuit

Hobart Ave

Canberra Ave

Circle

Central
Station

Melbourne Ave

Empire Circuit

Mugga Way

Manuka

Canberra Ave

Turrana Circle

Arthur Circle

0   500 m

The view is excellent at night, with lights stretching out into the distance. You may see a kangaroo or two on the hike up.

Lake Burley Griffin

The artificial lake, around which the city is built, was named after Canberra's original designer but was not finally created until 1963. It was formed by damming the Molonglo River which flows through Canberra. Although the lake is not recommended for swimming you can go boating (hire boats from beside the Acton Ferry Terminal) or bike ride around it (bikes available from the same place). There are a number of places of interest around the 35 km shoreline.

Most visible is the **Captain Cook Memorial Water Jet** which flings six tonnes of water 140 metres into the air and will give you a free shower if the wind is in the right direction, despite an automatic switch-off device which operates if the wind speed gets too high. The huge water jet usually operates from 10 am to 12 noon and 2 to 4 pm daily and was built in 1970 to commemorate the bicentenary of Captain Cook's visit to Australia. On the shoreline at Regatta Point is a skeleton globe, three metres in diameter, with Cook's three great voyages of discovery traced out on it.

The **Regatta Point Development Display** is open daily from 9 am to 5 pm and has models, illustrations and audio-visual displays of the growth of the capital. Further round the lake is **Blundell's Cottage** which dates from 1858, long before the selection of the area as the capital and even longer before a lake suddenly appeared beside it. The simple stone and slab cottage is a reminder of Canberra's early history as a farming area. It's now maintained as a small museum and is open 2 to 4 pm daily and 10 am to 12 noon on Wednesdays.

A little further around the lake is the **Carillon** on Aspen Island. The 53-bell tower was a gift from Britain on Canberra's 50th anniversary in 1963. Completed in 1970, the bells weigh from seven kg all the way up to over six tonnes. There is a carillon recital on Sundays from 2.45 to 3.30 pm and guided tours of the tower are available on Sundays from 9 am to 2 pm, Saturdays and public holidays from 1 to 4 pm.

The lake is bordered on the north-east side, from Regatta Point to the Carillon, by Commonwealth Park, while to the north-west, Black Mountain Peninsula juts out into the lake. The parliamentary triangle fronts on to the lake on the south-east side and several of the most impressive new government buildings are sited along the lakeside here. The Museum of Australia, not due to open until 1991, is being built on the north shore of the lake, west of the centre of town. If all goes to plan, the grounds and contents of the museum will be very impressive.

Old Parliament House

Another indicator of Canberra's initial slow development is that the present parliament building is just a 'temporary' one. Walter Burley Griffin's original plan envisaged a parliamentary triangle which was to include all the major government offices. Only in the last 20 years have they all started to appear. The new, 'permanent' parliament house will eventually stand at the apex of the triangle.

The present, 'temporary' building was the result of a 1923 competition and was opened in 1927. Sited on King George Terrace, the building includes a display on Australia's government and when parliament is not in session there are free tours every half hour, 9 am to 12.30 pm and 1.30 to 4.30 pm. If only one chamber is sitting it is possible to tour the other parts of the building. If you wish to observe the squabbles in the House of Representatives from the gallery it is wise to book tickets in advance by writing to the Principal Attendant, House of Representatives, Parliament House, Canberra 2600, or by applying in person. Presumably the Senate proceedings are nowhere near as interesting since no advance ticketing is required.

Items of interest in the parliament building include an early issue of the Magna Carta and the speaker's chair which is a replica of the speaker's chair in the House of Commons in Westminster. Since that original chair was destroyed in WW II in an air-raid, the House of Commons' speaker's chair is now a replica of the Australian replica! The building is open almost every day of the year and generally from 9 am to 5 pm.

New Parliament House

The new, and 'permanent', parliament building was finally given the go-ahead in 1979. An international design competition was won by a New York architect; number 177 from a total entry of over 300. The design won because of its successful integration with Capital Hill and its relationship to the old Parliament House, which will be retained. Though far from complete the massive 10 year project is beginning to take shape and emerge from Capital Hill. There seems to be some controversy concerning the design and even as to whether it will be large enough but judgements should be withheld until 1988 when it is planned to open, in time for the country's bicentennial celebrations. Meanwhile, the Exhibition Centre, on South Circle, displays what is going on and what the end product will look like – open daily.

Australian War Memorial

Canberra's tourist attraction (and the second most popular in all of Australia, second to Sydney's Opera House) is the massive war memorial at the foot of Mt Ainslie, looking directly along Anzac Parade towards Parliament House on the other side of the lake. The war memorial was conceived in 1925 and finally opened in 1941, not long after WW II entered its Pacific theatre. The museum houses an amazing collection of pictures, dioramas, relics and exhibitions, including a fine

collection of old aircraft. The exhibition rooms are undergoing modernisation to make them more relevant to new generations. If the completed section on Gallipoli is any indication the concept is well worth while. As the work continues, various rooms will be temporarily closed.

Outside lie the twisted remains of one of the Japanese miniature submarines that raided Sydney Harbour during WW II. Or, rather, the remains of two, reconstructed to make most of one. One of the three submarines which took part in the raid is still in the harbour, having never been found. In 1985 the submarine was removed for restorations that were to take a year or so. A recent addition to the outdoor collection is a Russian tank.

It's easy to get the impression in Australia that there's an unhealthy obsession with war memorials – we seem to have a hell of a lot of them. Perhaps it has something to do with Australia coming together as a nation, not through any fight of its own, but through going off to fight other peoples' wars. The whole national fascination with war memorials reaches its highest level right here. Still, only the jaded can miss the feelings of futility and loss which are depicted here. In this way, perhaps ironically, the memorial offers a rather moving plea for peace.

For anyone with a toy-soldier interest, the miniature battle scene recreations are absorbing. Also note the many paintings; they succeed in bringing history to life. The memorial is open 9 am to 4.45 pm every day except Christmas Day and admission is free.

Royal Australian Mint

The mint in Deakin produces all Australia's coins – as much as 70 tonnes of coins a week. Through a series of plate-glass windows (to keep you at arm's length from the ready) you can see the whole process take place, from raw materials to finished coins. There's also a rare coin collection in the foyer. The mint is open 9 am to 4 pm from Monday to Friday.

National Library

On Parkes Place, beside Lake Burley Griffin, the National Library is probably the most elegant building in Canberra. The library has a number of displays, including rare books, paintings, early manuscripts and maps, plus a cannon from Cook's ship the *Endeavour* and a fine model of the ship itself. The foyer is dominated by three huge tapestries. The library's exhibition area is open 9 am to 10 pm Monday to Friday, 9 am to 4.15 pm Saturday, Sunday and public holidays. There are guided tours Monday to Friday at 11.15 am and 2.15 pm.

Embassies

With Canberra's slow development as the capital, it is hardly surprising that embassies were also slow to show up, preferring to stay in the established cities, particularly Sydney and Melbourne, until Canberra really existed. The British High Commission, in 1936, was the first diplomatic office to arrive in Canberra followed, in 1940, by the US Embassy. Today there are about 60 high commissions and embassies in Canberra (Commonwealth countries have high commissions instead of embassies).

Enthusiasts for embassy spotting can pick up the tourist office's *Embassies in Canberra* folder or buy *Canberra's Embassies* by Graeme Barrow (Australian National University Press) which is a useful little guidebook to the city's diplomatic offices. A few of them are worth looking at although many of Canberra's embassies operate from nondescript suburban houses. The US Embassy, however, is a splendid facsimile of a Williamsburg, Virginia mansion, a style of architecture which in turn owes much to the English Georgian style.

Although, as you might expect, the South African Embassy gets its fair share of protests, the building is an imposing structure on State Circle. The Thai Embassy, with its pointed, orange-tiled roof, is in a style similar to the typical Thai

temples of Bangkok. The Indonesian Embassy is no architectural jewel, but beside the dull embassy building there's a small display centre exhibiting Indonesia's colourful culture. It's open 10 am to 12 noon and 2 to 4 pm; if you're lucky you might catch an impromptu shadow-puppet play put on for a visiting school group. The steps up to the centre are flanked by stone, Balinese, temple guardian-statues.

Papua New Guinea's High Commission looks like a 'haus tambaran' cult-house from the Sepik River region of PNG. There's a display room with colour photos and artefacts, open weekdays from 10 am to 12 noon and from 2 to 4 pm. As for the British High Commission, the present building dates from 1953, but it's strictly dullsville.

Addresses of the embassies above plus some of the other embassies in Canberra which might be useful for a visitor, include:

Austria
    107 Endeavour St, Red Hill (tel 95 1533)
Canada
    Commonwealth Avenue, Yarralumla (tel 73 3844)
Germany (West)
    119 Empire Circuit, Yarralumla (tel 73 3179)
Indonesia
    8 Darwin Avenue, Yarralumla (tel 73 3222)
Ireland
    20 Arkana St, Yarralumla (tel 73 3022)
Japan
    112 Empire Circuit, Yarralumla (tel 73 3244)
Malaysia
    7 Perth Ave, Yarralumla (tel 82 2444)
Netherlands
    120 Empire Circuit, Yarralumla (tel 73 3111)
New Zealand
    Commonwealth Avenue, Yarralumla (tel 73 3611)
Norway
    Hunter St, cnr of Fitzgerald St, Yarralumla (tel 73 3444)
Papua New Guinea
    Forster Crescent, Yarralumla (tel 73 3322)

Singapore
    81 Mugga Way, Red Hill (tel 73 3944)
South Africa
    cnr State Circle & Rhodes Place, Yarralumla (tel 73 2424)
Sweden
    Turrana St, Yarralumla (tel 73 3033)
Switzerland
    7 Melbourne Avenue, Forrest (tel 73 3977)
Thailand
    111 Empire Circuit, Yarralumla (tel 73 1149)
UK
    Commonwealth Avenue, Yarralumla (tel 73 0422)
USA
    State Circle, Yarralumla (tel 73 3711)

High Court

The High Court building, on the lake-side, is open from 10 am to 4 pm daily. Opened in 1980, it's a structure of such grandiose magnificence that it has been dubbed 'Gar's Mahal', a reference to Sir Garfield Barwick, the Chief Justice of the Australian High Court, who was primarily responsible for much of the grandeur and overkill. To tell the truth, there is a touch of Indian Moghul palace about the ornamental watercourse, burbling alongside the entrance path.

Australian National Gallery

On Parkes Place, beside the High Court and Lake Burley Griffin, the art gallery opened in 1982 after many years of build-up. It started way back in the '70s when the gallery, which didn't even have an exhibition space at that time, paid a 'truly fabulous' sum for Jackson Pollock's 'Blue Poles'. More gee-whiz purchases from time to time since that first big buy have kept the gallery firmly in the public eye. It was worth it because the gallery is a fine building with a really superb collection of Australian art and collections from the rest of the world which are particularly strong post-1950 and form a good basis for further expansion prior to that time. Admission to the $50 million collection is $2. There's also a pretty good restaurant

with views over the lake, vegetarian and fish dishes, and sandwiches.

Institute of Anatomy

The Institute's collection, while still together, is in mothballs waiting for the new Museum of Australia to be built. The new tenant in the building is the National Film & Sound Archives, which presents public exhibitions. It is open daily from 10 am to 4 pm, near the university at McCoy Circuit in Acton.

Science Centre

The Australian National University is developing a participatory science museum; opening dates have not been set as yet.

Ginninderra Village

This 1880 village recreation is out on the Burton Highway, less than 20 km from town, and has period crafts and demonstrations and picnic grounds. It's open daily and is free.

Old Buildings

The Church of St John the Baptist was built between 1841 and 1845 and thus predates the city of Canberra. The stained-glass windows in the church show pioneering families of the region. There is an adjoining school-house with some early relics. The Royal Military College, Duntroon, was once an early homestead, parts of it dating from the 1830s. On Denman St, Yarralumla, the old Canberra Brickworks is the site of the brickworks used for Canberra's early construction. You can see the brick kilns plus some old cars and steam engines. It's open daily. On weekends a flea market offering a variety of bric-a-brac sets up here.

Other Buildings

You can do no more than drive by and peek in the gates of the Prime Minister's Lodge – Australia's 10 Downing St or White House. Ditto for Government House at Yarralumla, although there's a lookout beside Scrivener Dam at the end of the lake, which gives a good view of the building – the Governor-General's residence. It is worth driving by the building locally known as 'the Martian Embassy' – situated on McCoy Circuit in Acton – the National Film & Sound Archives does indeed look like a misplaced flying saucer.

On Parkes Way there is an Australian-American Memorial, a 79-metre-high shaft topped by an eagle; it's a memorial to US support for Australia during WW II. You can get a guide-yourself leaflet for the Australian National University from the Information Office opposite Union House. The university was founded in 1946. The Serbian Orthodox Church in Forrest has its walls and ceiling painted with a series of Biblical murals. Canberra also has a mosque, for the diplomatic staff from Islamic countries, on the corner of Hunter St and Empire Circuit.

Botanic Gardens

Yes, a botanic garden was part of Walter Burley Griffin's grand plan too – a botanic garden dedicated to Australian native flora. Like so much of Canberra it took a long time for his vision to become a reality and planting only started in 1950. The garden was, finally, officially opened in 1970. Situated on the lower slopes of Black Mountain the beautiful gardens have several arrowed, educational walks. One of the walks indicates plants used by Aboriginals and the uses made of them. A highlight of the garden is the rain-forest zone, achieved in Canberra's dry climate by a 'misting' system which creates a suitably damp environment, in a gully. The gardens are reached from Clunies Ross St and are open 9 am to 5 pm daily. There are guided tours at 10 am and 2 pm on Sunday. There is a small restaurant with a pleasant outdoor section as well as tables inside.

The Museum of Unusual Bicycles

This free exhibition of about 50 bikes of all kinds and ages is good for kids – there is a BMX track next door with bike rentals. It's in Dickson on Badham St near Dickson Place and is open daily.

Places to Stay

Hostels The *Canberra Youth Hostel* (tel 48 9759) is at Dryanda St, O'Connor, about six km from the city centre. Nightly charges are $7, $1.50 for bed and linen. There is a bus service to the city about every half hour (see Getting Around for details) or you can hire bicycles at the hostel. It's a nice hostel, but the warden takes effort.

The *YWCA* (tel 47 3033) is very central at 2 Mort St in the city. They take only females and have twin rooms at $13 per person or dorms at $10. Singles are generally full with permanents; no meals available but there are low long-term rates.

Ainslie Village, at the end of Quick St, Ainslie (tel 48 6931) is cheap but not really meant for travellers. If there's room they take you in, however. It's a government hostel and charges are $10 a night or $35 a week, plus $10 for linen if you need it. Meals are very cheap. Prices are less for the unemployed.

Guest Houses & Private Hotels Just as you enter Canberra from Sydney or Melbourne on Northbourne Avenue, there are three prominently sign-posted guest houses. There's not much between them in standards and prices. You can walk into town but it's a fair distance and buses do run along Northbourne. *Chelsea Lodge* (tel 48 0655) at 526 is $18 for bed and breakfast, doubles $26. It's cheaper by the week and, like the other two places, considerably less in the off season.

The *Blue & White Lodge* (tel 48 0498), with another place a few doors down, is at 524 and has a wide range of prices, all including cooked breakfast. Shared rooms with from two to four people are $12 per person. Singles are $18 bed & breakfast, weekly rates are cheaper. At 522, the *Platon Lodge* (tel 47 9139) has the same prices as its neighbours. All three are plain and straightforward but clean, quite comfortable and, in true Australian fashion, the breakfast is very filling.

Closer to the centre, but still a bit of a walk, is the *Tall Trees Lodge Motel* (tel 47 9200) on a quiet residential street at 21 Stephen St, Ainslie. It's a modern, one-storey place with central heating and a spacious lawn. Prices are single $22, twin $25 in the lodge and $38/41 in the motel with air-con.

Within easy walking distance of the city centre, *Gowrie Private Hotel* (tel 49 6033) is a large tower block at 210 Northbourne Ave, Braddon. It's an ex-government place with no less than 568 rooms. A single is $18 including breakfast and $30 for a double. The manager told me prices would soon be taking a hefty jump so it may be worth calling to ask. Three-course meals are available and reasonable at $5. There are other items in the $3 range in the cafeteria. You have to wander down the corridor to a bathroom, but the place is very well-equipped with cafeteria, recreation facilities, TV lounges and laundries.

Macquarie Private Hotel (tel 73 2325), across the lake at 18 National Circuit, Barton has 500 rooms and the same set-up and prices as the Gowrie: single $18, for the week $75; double $30, for the week $120. There are a number of other guest houses around Canberra, but they're mostly not as conveniently situated or their prices are a lot higher.

Hotels Not much in this category but there's the *Hotel Kingston* (tel 95 0481) about 4.5 km out, at the corner of Canberra Ave and Gile St in Manuka, with singles/doubles at $18/26.

Motels Most motels in Canberra are quite expensive. *Acacia Motor Lodge* (tel 49 6955) at 65 Ainslie Avenue is $40 for one, $50 for two, and it's only 500 metres from the Civic Centre. It has barbecue facilities in the courtyard. Cheaper but not so

central *Motel 7* (tel 95 1111) on Jerrabomberra Avenue, Narrabundah is about eight km out from the centre and is excellent value. It's got most mod-cons, a swimming pool, 63 units and costs just $30 for a single, $33 for a double, room only. The rooms are small but the prices are lower. You can get there on a 323 bus.

The *South Side Motor Park* (tel 80 6176) on Canberra Avenue, Symonston charges $25/30 for their rooms with private facilities, others also have cooking. There is also a caravan park. Next up the price range would be a couple more motels in Canberra South: *Regency Motel* (tel 95 0074) at McMillan Crescent, Griffith where singles/doubles are $25/30 and up. As with many of these motels, the Regency has cheaper rates on weekends.

The *Victor Lodge* (tel 95 7432), at 29 Dawes St, Kingston is a simple place without private facilities: single $25, double $44, includes breakfast. In Woden Valley there's *Gunther's Lodge* (tel 81 5499) at 106 Cotter Road, Curtin. It's small, but rooms are well equipped and there's a pool. Singles/doubles are $28/36, room only. Prices of other motels range upwards to the sky.

Colleges The Australian National University has quite a selection of residential places which may well have empty rooms during the May, August, or November to February uni vacations. Charges are $12 for students, $16 for non-students, for a room and food. In fact, they can't get enough people these days, so you may even get in during term if you stay for a week or so. The Canberra College of Advanced Education also has a hostel which takes students only, usually in groups of five or more. To find out what the story is check with:

Australian National University
  Ursula College (tel 48 9055)
  Bruce Hall (tel 49 2828)
  Burgmann College (tel 47 9811)

Toad Hall* (tel 49 4722)
Burton & Garran Halls* (tel 49 3137)

College of Advanced Education*
Accommodation Officer (tel 52 2121)

* students only

Camping There are a couple of camping sites close to Canberra catering for people with tents. The *Canberra Lakes Carotel* (tel 41 1377) is 6½ km north of the city on the Sydney road. Tent sites here cost $7.50 per tent. There are also on-site vans from $25 for four people and a variety of chalets, flats and cabins from as little as $8 per person. The *South Side Motor Park* (tel 80 6176) is eight km south of the city on the main road to Queanbeyan and charges from $7.50 for two people with a tent. There is also the *Crestview Tourist Park* (tel 97 2445) 81 Donald Rd, Queanbeyan (tel 97 2445). A site will cost $7 if you have a tent and there are also on-site vans and cabins from $20. More rural camping (and cheaper, too) can be found 22 km out at the Cotter Reserve.

Places to Eat
Canberra has a reasonable selection of places in Civic and then a few away from the centre as well.

At the back of *Smith's Bookshop* on Northbourne, near London Circuit is a small comfortable café serving very good lunches, and light snacks like croissants and milkshakes through the day and evening. It's a casual place, with a good artsy noticeboard, where you can linger. It is open from Monday to Thursday from 9.30 am to 5.30 pm, Friday from 9.30 am to 2.30 am and on Saturdays from 9 am to 1 pm and 7.30 pm to 2.30 am. During the day enter through the store; later on there's a separate door in the lane.

Another recommended choice is the small, colourful restaurant in the *TAU Community Arts Centre*, on Mort St between Cooyong and Elouera. Though they serve meals like pasta with broccoli and cottage cheese for $5.50, it's mainly

Middle Eastern fare. The bread and hummus ($2) with home-made soup is a good lunch as are the large falafels. Open Monday to Friday from 11 am to 3 pm and from Thursday to Saturday, 6 pm until late.

The *Yum Yum Tree* take-away counter has very good, very thick roast beef sandwiches for $2 and the other usual offerings. It's in the Bailey Arcade, off the City Walk mall, near the merry-go-round. The *Private Bin* at 50 Northbourne Avenue, described eloquently by a local as a 'basic, pig-out joint', is certainly good for those with big appetites. Buffets are from $5.50, the roast of the day is $3.95, chicken, schnitzel dishes are $5 to $6 – good helpings. Also on Northbourne Avenue the *Honeydew* at 55 is a 'gourmet wholemeal' place with main courses from $8.

There are two pizza places at Garema Place, in the centre. *The Pizzeria* and *Sorrento's* are both inexpensive and popular. The latter is busy at night with those coming for 'the best capuccino in Canberra'.

Nearby, over on Bunda St, through the Garema Arcade, is *Gus's* with some outdoor tables where you can get cheap European meals of goulash and spaghetti for around $4 and good cakes.

The *Lovely Lady Pancake Parlour* chain has a branch office here on Alinga St, just up from the bus exchange. Open 24 hours, meals are $4 to $6.

There are quite a few ethnic places as might be expected of a capital city. The *Canberra Vietnamese Restaurant* upstairs at 21 East Row, Civic, is recommended. Four people can really do their stomachs a favour for about $30. Try the squid with lemon grass and chili – excellent spicing. It's a very friendly place and on the weekends there's live music. There are other Vietnamese places; one a few doors down, one at 1 Sargood St out in O'Connor is said to be pretty good. *Dalat* in Yarralumla has had mixed reviews lately.

For Malaysian, the *Rasa Sayang*, 43

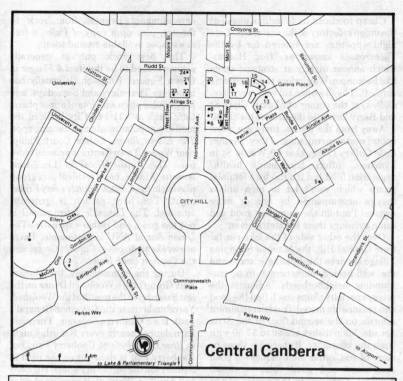

Central Canberra

1 National Film & Sound Archives
2 Acadamy of Science
3 Lakeside International Hotel
4 Canberra Theatre Centre
5 Bushgear
6 Malaysian Restaurant
7 Smith's Bookshop
8 Private Bin Bistro
9 Sinbad's Restaurant
10 Action Info Centre (local buses)
11 Merry-go-Round
12 Woodstock Restaurant

13 Dalton's Bookshop
14 Pizzeria
15 Gus's
16 Angus & Robertson
17 YWCA
18 Ansett Airlines
19 Canberra Vietnamese Restaurant
20 Ansett Pioneer
21 Tourist Office
22 TAA
23 Post Office
24 Greyhound & other buses

Wooley St. Dickson is quite good and has fair prices. In the centre of town the *Malaysian Restaurant* at 71 London Circuit has dishes in the $6 to $7 bracket.

The *Anarkali Pakistani Restaurant* in the Boulevard Centre has reasonable food but the small portions mean it's not great value. Curries and kebabs are about $8.

The *Acropolis* at 35 East Row, Civic is cheaper, you get a Greek feed for around $5 for a main course. In traditional manner, you choose from an appetising display of food. Greek wines are available for retsina fans. It's open to 9 pm, closed on Sundays. *Sinbad's* at 25 East Row is a cheap Lebanese take-away.

Cheap food can be found, as usual, at the union refectory in the university. Late night appetites are catered for by the *Tuckerbuses* known as 'Dog Houses' which appear nightly at strategic spots like Belconnen Way before the Macquarie turn-off. They're open till very, very late. *Dolly's*, at the corner of Marcus Clark St and Barry Drive, is the best of the them.

Away from the centre, there are a few spots worth mentioning. *Tilley Devines Cafe Gallery (Tilley's)* at 69 Wattle St in Lyneham, offers home-made health/ vegetarian food but it's run by a feminist group which won't let in men unless they're accompanied by one or more women! I'm told the soups are good and some evenings there is entertainment.

Over the other side of the lake not far from Capital Hill, the Manuka Shopping Village services the diplomatic corps and the well-heeled bureaucrats from surrounding neighborhoods. Amongst the pricey specialty shops you'll find the good and reasonably priced Turkish restaurant *Alanya*, on the second floor of the Style Arcade. Main dishes are $6 to $7.50 with lamb the speciality. If there are three or more of you, order the banquet – a good assortment and good value – closed Sundays. *Grandes*, in the centre of the village, is a small, popular Italian café with sweets, snacks and coffees.

West of Capital Hill, the inconspicuous *Gambit* is in the Deakin Shopping Centre. Their fresh, tasty lunch specials are so popular you have to book (tel 82 4362). They have sandwiches, salads, omelettes and crepes – like the generous camembert and crab ones for $5. It's open Monday to Friday to 5.30 pm and Saturdays, which aren't so busy, to 2.30 pm.

Entertainment

Canberra is not renowned for its night life – despite the liberal licensing laws which allow hotels unlimited opening hours, in contrast to the rest of Australia. Some say you really need to go to Queanbeyan if you want to go out – it's a normal city! For all entertainment listings, from rock to theatre, pick up a copy of *Pulse*, a free newspaper available around town.

The best rock pub is generally acknowledged to be the *Boot & Flogger* in Green Square, Kingston. It usually has bands on Thursdays and Saturdays, and is a popular place with lots of atmosphere. *Cafe Jax's* at 131-141 City Walk in the mall is a popular music and dancing spot. *The Elbow Room*, Cobee Court Philip, near Woden Town Centre is a casual blues bar. The *Ainslie Hotel* in Limestone Avenue, Ainslie, has a resident jazz group playing in the *Carlton Lounge* every Friday night. The beer garden is generally crowded. The *Lakeside International* is not too good, and rather expensive. The *Union Bar* at ANU is reasonable. There are weekend discos at *Captain Greggs* and the *Captain Cook Hotel*.

During the summer only, the Monaro Folk Group hold a Woolshed Dance on the last Saturday of the month at the Woolshed, Yarralumla (near the Governor-General's pad). It's a Canberra occasion. There are barn dances nearly every Saturday night in *Blue Belly Joe's* at Canberry Fair, but Canberry Fair is right out on the road to Sydney (on the corner of Federal Highway and Antill St, Watson). It consists of rides and amusements in a park-like setting, seven km north of the Civic Centre.

Not surprisingly, Canberra has quite a lot of film showings. Check with the various cultural centres, *Maison de France* and the *Goethe Centre*, and the ANU film group – to find out what's on. There are a number of cinemas around the Civic Square area. The *Boulevard Blue & Red Theatres* here both show repertory type films (tel 47 5060). The National Library runs free film series on Thursday evenings with good, varied programmes.

The *Canberra Theatre Centre* comprises a complex of stages where you can see anything and everything. There are lunchtime shows at *Brief's*, beside the Canberra Theatre. *J's Roller Rink* is at the National Exhibition Centre Showground; $2.50

includes the skates and it's open from 7.30 to 10 pm. Lastly, the various clubs have live entertainment and, of course, pokies. They also have very cheap meals.

Events

The Canberra Festival takes place over 10 days each March and celebrates the city's birthday. Music, food, displays and a big parade are some of the activities. Commonwealth Park holds many of the events and is the site of a carnival.

Getting There

Air Most flights to Canberra are from Sydney or Melbourne, although there are now some direct flights from Brisbane and Adelaide. Although Canberra is Australia's capital it is not an international airport. Air fares to Canberra are rumoured to be inflated as the airlines know that most flights are being paid for by the government!

During 1985 the airport was undergoing some much needed expansion. This work should be completed well before the bicentennial.

From Sydney it's just half an hour to Canberra; the fare is $83 or $66 standby. Melbourne is about an hour's flight for $116 or $93 standby. You can also standby on the direct flight to Adelaide for $180 or Brisbane for $178.

Road Ansett Pioneer and Greyhound operate between Sydney and Canberra but only Ansett Pioneer have traffic rights unless you're on an interstate ticket. Sydney-Canberra takes about five hours and costs $29 – rather more than the train.

Ansett Pioneer, Greyhound and Deluxe operate Melbourne-Canberra. The trip takes about 11 hours and costs $30. Deluxe are now only marginally cheaper than the big companies and their services are not nearly as frequent. Ansett Pioneer (tel 45 6624) is located at the Canberra Rex Hotel, a few blocks from the centre on Northbourne Avenue. Greyhound (tel 52 2659) is at the Jolimont Centre in Northbourne Avenue.

You can book for these buses and also for buses to Yass and other regional centres at the Tourist Bureau. Four times a week there's a Canberra-Orange bus which costs $30.30. A bus runs Canberra-Wollongong five times weekly for $18. A bus also runs to Batemans Bay on the coast and continues from there to Moruya.

Rail The Monaro Express runs daily, leaving Sydney at 7.30 am and arriving at Canberra at 12.11 pm. Canberra-Sydney departs at 5.30 pm and arrives at 10.15 pm. The fare for first class is $27, for regular, $19. There is no direct train between Melbourne and Canberra; you take a regular Sydney train as far as Yass ($31.70) and then a bus ($5) for the one-hour ride into Canberra. Although all the Melbourne-Sydney trains go through Yass, only the Intercapital Daylight connects directly with the bus. Otherwise you might have to kill five hours or so in Yass. Leaving Melbourne at 9 am, you arrive in Yass at 5.15 pm and Canberra at 6.16 pm. Going the other direction, you leave Canberra on the bus at 10.45 am and arrive at Melbourne at 8.20 pm. There is no service on Sunday. Phone 95 1555 for railways information in Canberra.

Getting Around

Airport Transport Canberra's airport is just seven km from the city centre and though it's only busy at regular rush hours, the expansion and renovations occurring are much needed. Note all the government cars lined up outside waiting to pick up returning 'pollies'. Hertz, Budget, Avis and Thrifty have airport desks. There's an airport bus which leaves from outside the tourist office in town but only twice a day, Monday to Friday at 9.05 am and 4.20 pm. It's about $2. Other than that it's a taxi ride as there are no city buses to the airport. The taxi fare isn't too hefty, however. TAA (tel 68 3333) is in the

Alinga Place Civic Centre; Ansett (tel 45 1111) is at 4 Mort St.

Bus Apart from cruises on Lake Burley Griffin, road is about the only way there is to get around the ACT. Canberra is a sprawling place, a perfect suburb in fact, and even crossing the street is a long walk at some of the wider boulevards.

Around Canberra there are quite frequent bus services on modern buses. The bus information kiosk is on the corner of Alinga St and East Row and is open Monday to Saturday 6 am to 11 pm and Sunday from 9 am to 6 pm. Phone 51 6566 for information, 7 am to 6 pm Monday to Friday, 7 am to 12.30 pm Saturday and 9 am to 7 pm Sunday. At other hours phone 46 2133. A free map of the whole bus system is available, as well as individual timetables for each route.

There's a flat fare of 70c per journey or 60c before 9 am and after 9 pm and all day Saturday. Sunday fares are just 10c. You can get an unlimited use Day Tripper for $2.60. Four of the city buses, or Action buses as they are called, are known as sightseeing specials and go to locations of interest to visitors. The information bureau has pamphlets on them. For example, route 904 goes to the Botanic Gardens and the tower atop Black Mountain.

You can also buy a Canberra Explorer ticket for $7 a day or $14 a week. The Explorer runs hourly every day around a 25 km route with 22 stops at points of interest to visitors. You get a printed guide and can get on and off the bus wherever you like. The $14 weekly ticket includes use of the ordinary Action local buses. The main advantage of the Explorer bus over the cheaper Action day pass is that it goes up Black Mountain, but only once a day at 9 am. Otherwise, the ordinary $2.60 Action day pass will get you everywhere except Black Mountain – if you don't mind an occasional walk and having to sort out the bus routes.

To get to the youth hostel on weekdays

and Saturday mornings, catch a 380 bus to the Scrivener St stop in Miller St. On Saturday afternoons and Sundays you have to take a 360. Route 380 is half-hourly, route 360 is hourly. For the embassies take the 230 or 231 from platform 9. There's a free inner-city bus service, but it just goes around London Circuit and only during the middle of the day.

Car Rental The cheapest car rental outfit is Discount Rent-a-Car (tel 49 6551) at 16 Mort St, where rates range from $12 to $25 a day including 100 km, excess at 12c per km depending on the size of car. Next cheapest is old faithful, Thrifty, (tel 47 7422) at 13 Lonsdale St. Budget, Thrifty and Hertz can be found at Canberra airport. Hertz has cheap weekend deals from $20 a day.

Bicycles Canberra is a cyclist's paradise with its network of cycleways making it possible to ride around the city hardly touching a road. Get a copy of the invaluable *Canberra Cycleways* map from the tourist office. You can hire bikes from Mr Spokes Bike Hire near the Acton Ferry Terminal from $2.50 an hour, $9 daily, $18 weekly. Bikes are also hired out by the youth hostel.

Tours The Canberra Tourist Bureau has all the latest info on ACT tours. They can tell you about half-day city tours or half-day or longer tours to the surrounding countryside and sheep stations. A variety of other day trips visit the Mt Kosciusko Alpine area, the Snowy Mountains hydro-electric scheme or caves, nature reserves, satellite tracking stations, horse studs and fossicking areas around the ACT. They can also tell you about boat cruises on Lake Burley Griffin. Lake cruises are $4.50, south coast trips $16, a visit to a sheep station including a barbecue $15. There are three main tour operators, the tourist office has info on each.

Around Canberra

NEW TOWNS

Canberra, once 'seven suburbs in search of a city', now has a collection of satellite towns dotted around it. These new towns of Woden, Belconnen and Tuggeranong are separate, self-sufficient communities.

PICNIC & BARBECUE SPOTS

There are a number of popular picnic and barbecue spots in and around Canberra. Many of them have coin-operated, gas barbecue facilities and at places along the Cotter and Murrumbidgee Rivers there are good swimming spots. Black Mountain, of course, is virtually in the city itself, but others include Casuarina Sands (19 km) on the Cotter, Kambah Pool (21 km) on the Murrumbidgee, Cotter Dam (23 km) on the Cotter, Uriarra Crossing (24 km) near the junction of the Murrumbidgee and Molonglo Rivers, Point Hut Crossing (26 km) on the Murrumbidgee, Pine Island (27 km) on the Murrumbidgee and Gibraltar Falls (48 km) on Gibraltar Creek.

The spectacular Lower Ginninderra Falls are in Parkwood, out along Parkwood Rd to the north-west of Canberra. They're open 10 am to 5 pm daily and reached by a fine nature trail to Ginninderra Gorge. There's an admission charge.

The Tidbinbilla Nature Reserve (40 km), near the space-tracking station, has a series of marked bushwalking tracks, some of them leading to interesting rock formations. There's also a nature reserve with kangaroos, koalas, emus and other animals. The reserve has an information centre and is open 9 am to 6 pm; the animal enclosures are open 11 am to 5 pm.

Canberra is well-equipped with wildlife reserves. There's one at Mugga Lane, Red Hill – the Canberra Wildlife Gardens, which are open 9 am to 4 pm weekdays, and to 5 pm on weekends. Rehwinkel's Animal Park is on Macks Reef Rd, off the Federal Highway, 20 km north of Canberra and actually across the ACT border. It's open daily from 10 am to 5 pm. Still farther away, about a 2½ hour drive, is an African Lion Safari at Warragamba Dam, NSW. It's open Wednesday to Sunday.

OBSERVATORIES & TRACKING STATIONS

The Australian National University, Department of Astronomy's Stromlo Observatory is 16 km west of Canberra and has a 188 cm telescope plus a photographic exhibition which is open from 9.30 am to 4 pm daily. There are a series of space-tracking stations 40 to 60 km out of the city at Honeysuckle Creek, Tidbinbilla and Orroral. The latter is apparently no longer operating and as NASA develops more sophisticated equipment Honeysuckle Creek will become obsolete.

Tidbinbilla Station, known as the Canberra Space Centre, is to remain open to the public and has an information centre with models of spacecraft and is open from 9 am to 5 pm daily. It's also a popular centre for bushwalks and barbecues.

OLD HOMESTEADS

Lanyon Homestead, 26 km south of the city on the Murrumbidgee River near Tharwa, is a beautifully restored old homestead. The early stone cottage on the site was built by convicts and the grand homestead was completed in 1859. During the pioneering era it had a reputation as one of the most gracious homes in the area. This National Trust homestead is open from 10 am to 4 pm from Tuesday to Sunday. A major attraction of the fine old building is the collection of 24 Sidney Nolan paintings on display. There are separate admission charges to the homestead and to the gallery which houses the Nolan paintings.

Cuppacumbalong, also near Tharwa, is another old homestead, although neither as grand nor of such importance as Lanyon. It now houses a craft studio and gallery and is open 11 am to 5 pm from

Wednesday to Sunday. Opposite Lanyon there's a small memorial graveyard to a pioneer of the Australian wheat industry.

North of Canberra on the Barton Highway, the **Old Canberra Inn** is an old inn, built in 1850 and now restored as a restaurant and bistro. The **Ginninderra Schoolhouse Museum** is also nearby, a restored slab-hut built as a school in 1833. On the corner of Gold Creek Rd and the Barton Highway behind the schoolhouse is **Cockington Green**, a miniature replica of an English village, open 10 am to 5 pm daily, to 6 pm in summer.

QUEANBEYAN (population 17,800)

Across the border in NSW, Queanbeyan is virtually a suburb of Canberra, although it actually predates the capital. Until 1838 it was known as 'Queen Bean'. There's a history museum in the town and good lookouts from Jerrabomberra Hill and Bungendore Hill, both six km out.

DAY TRIPS

A popular drive, especially on a Sunday, is out past Bungendore to Braidwood (one hour or so) with its many antique shops,

craft stores and restaurants. There's also an old hotel for a beer or pub lunch. On the way from Canberra, Lake George is to the north. It's actually in NSW and it's known for its mysterious, periodic, disappearing act! At Bungendore the Village Square has shops, crafts, foods and a historic re-creation that tells the story of local bushranger William Westwood from the mid 1800's.

The free Canberra tourist map, with tourist drives, shows another good route to follow. It takes in Tharwa (see old Homesteads) which is set in fine, hilly grazing lands. There is a coffee shop at the historic site and a grocery store with 'hot pies, cold beer'. From here the route goes on to Gibraltar Falls (good walking in the area) and Tidbinbilla Nature Reserve. The Reserve information centre is only open to 3 pm on weekdays. The Space Tracking Stations are on the way back into town along the slow, winding, scenic road. A bus tour of this route is $15.

Lastly, an enjoyable day can be spent slowly riding around Lake Burley Griffin on a bicycle. There's a bike trail all the way around and a lot of birdlife.

New South Wales

Area   802,000 square km
Population   5,000,000

Don't miss Sydney, Australia's oldest, largest and most dramatic city with its beautiful harbour and well known Opera House.

New South Wales is the site of Captain Cook's original landing in Australia, the place where the first permanent settlement was established and today it is both the most populous state and has the country's largest city – Sydney. Of course NSW is much more than Sydney with its glistening Opera House and equally well known (if far less attractive) harbour bridge – but Sydney is certainly a good place to start.

It was down at Sydney Cove, where the ferries run from today, that the first settlement was made in 1788 so it is not surprising that Sydney has an air of age and history about certain parts of it which is missing from most Australian cities. That doesn't stop Sydney from being a far brasher and outwardly more lively looking city than its younger rival Melbourne. With a setting like Port Jackson (the harbour) to build around it would be hard for Sydney to be unattractive and from almost any angle it is an incredible looking city.

Sydney has much more than just the central city going for it; Paddington is without question one of the most attractive inner-city residential areas in the world and the whole Pacific shoreline of the city is dotted with good beaches sporting famous names like Bondi or Manly. Furthermore there are two particularly pleasant national parks marking the southern and northern boundaries of the city – Royal National Park and Ku-ring-gai Chase. Inland it is only a short drive to the Blue Mountains with some of the most spectacular scenery in Australia.

Nevertheless there is more to NSW than Sydney. The Pacific Highway runs north and south from the capital and good beaches and surf are waiting for you all along the coast. A short trip north is the Hunter Valley, one of Australia's premier wine-producing areas with a popular annual wine festival. Newcastle is the second city of NSW, a major industrial centre. Further north is the high plateau of the New England region and the long, sweeping, often deserted beaches of the north coast up to the Queensland border.

South of Sydney are the Southern Highlands with beautiful scenery and good bushwalks. There is more great coastline on the way down to Victoria too, plus Wollongong, the third city of NSW, another major industrial centre. The Great Dividing Range rises in the south of the state into the highest mountains in Australia with summer bushwalking and excellent winter skiing.

Finally there are the vast inland plains, sweeping expanses of agricultural and grazing land which finally dwindle into the harsh NSW outback. Out there you can find the town of Broken Hill, almost a small, independent state, run by powerful unions.

INFORMATION

There are NSW Government Travel Centres in Sydney, Melbourne and Brisbane

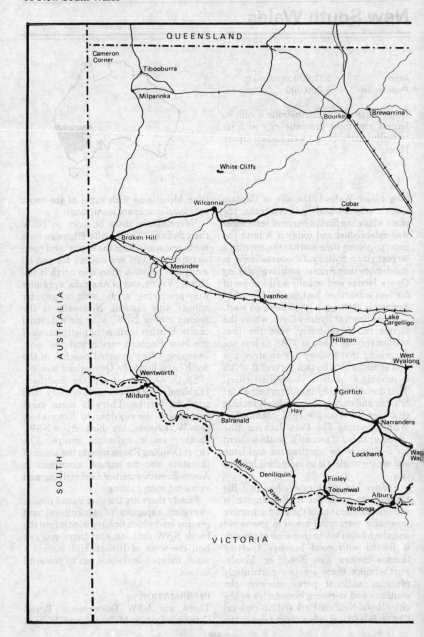

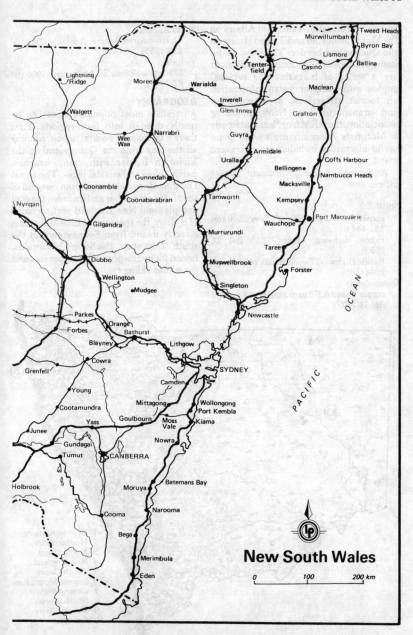

New South Wales

0   100   200 km

and also information centres at Albury on the Victorian border and Tweed Heads on the Queensland border. The most useful items produced by the tourist department are a series of magazine-size regional guides with comprehensive information on tourist attractions, accommodation and transport. The NSW motoring association, the NRMA or National Roads & Motorists Association also has some useful information including some excellent maps.

Addresses of the government tourist offices are:

NSW
corner Pitt & Spring Sts, Sydney 2000 (tel 231 4444)
Hume Highway, Albury 2640 (tel 21 2655)
Pacific Highway, Tweed Heads 2485 (tel 36 2634)

Queensland
corner Queen & Edward Sts, Brisbane 4000 (tel 31 1838)

South Australia
41 Hindmarsh Square, Adelaide 5000 (tel 223 4555)

Victoria
359 Little Collins St, Melbourne 3000 (tel 67-7461)

GEOGRAPHY

Australia's most populous state can be neatly divided into four regions. First there's the narrow coastal region, running all the way from the Queensland to the Victorian border with many beaches, parks, inlets and coastal lakes. The Great Dividing Range also runs from one end of the state to the other and includes the cool and pleasant New England section north of Sydney, the spectacular Blue Mountains directly inland from Sydney and, in the south of the state, the Snowy Mountains, famed for hydro-power developments and for winter skiing.

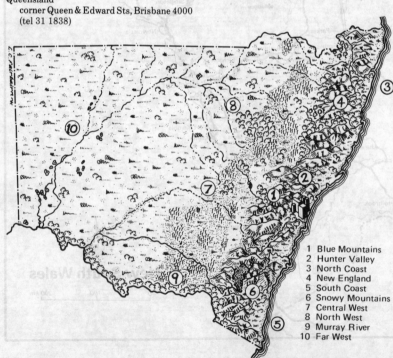

1 Blue Mountains
2 Hunter Valley
3 North Coast
4 New England
5 South Coast
6 Snowy Mountains
7 Central West
8 North West
9 Murray River
10 Far West

Behind the Great Dividing Range the fertile farming country of the western slopes gradually fades into the plains which cover two-thirds of the state. This far western region is NSW's stretch of the great Australian outback, often dry and barren, particularly towards the South Australian border, and with very little of the state's population. The south of the state has the Murray River as a natural border with Victoria.

GETTING AROUND

Air Sydney is connected to Canberra and to other state capitals by TAA and Ansett. Within the state Air New South Wales and East-West Airlines operate a comprehensive network. The chart below details some of the routes and the fare costs.

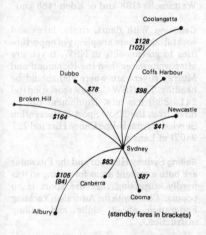

(standby fares in brackets)

Bus Ansett Pioneer, Greyhound, Deluxe and various other carriers operate services through NSW but in order to protect the railways they are extremely limited in the services they can operate. Interstate services cannot carry passengers on services within the state – thus there are lots of buses going up the Pacific coast from Sydney to Brisbane but you can't take those buses to Newcastle or other intermediate stops. Travellers on bus passes can, however, get on and off at will. Ansett Pioneer and Greyhound both have interstate services that cross the state in various directions.

There are at least six companies operating between the capital cities and competition is fierce, so it pays to shop around to see who has the best deal as some offer standby fares at various times. See the Sydney Getting There section for prices.

Rail The State Rail Authority of NSW has probably the most comprehensive rail service in Australia, see the bus section above for one of the reasons why. There are a variety of day tour fares and you can also get a 14-day Nurail Pass which gives you unlimited 1st class travel throughout the NSW rail system. Apart from trains of the usual Australian speed the NSW railways also boasts Australia's fastest train, the XPT (Express Passenger Train) service, which operates to most major NSW centres and to Canberra and can top (just) 160 kph (100 mph). XPT services are all 1st class, 40% more than economy, plus a $6 to $8 XPT zone fare. Some relevant economy fares and distances from Sydney include:

Albury	643 km	$34.50
Bourke	831	$39.10
Coffs Harbour	608	$34.50
Dubbo	462	$29.10
Goulburn	222	$13.40
Lightning Ridge	811	$39.20
Mudgee	308	$18.20
Murwillumbah	935	$41.60
Newcastle	168	$10.00
Nowra	153	$10.00
Orange	323	$19.40
Tamworth	455	$29.10
Wagga Wagga	518	$30.10
Yass Junction	315	$19.40

ACTIVITIES

Bushwalking The NSW Federation of Bushwalking Clubs or the National Parks & Wildlife Service are both good for information on bushwalking. A useful book on walks in the state is *100 Walks in NSW* by Tyrone Thomas which retails at around $6. There are a number of bushwalking shops in Sydney which have this and other titles on sale.

Closest to the city are walks like the fine clifftop paths in the Royal National Park or the walks in Ku-ring-gai Chase National Park where you can find some gigantic Aboriginal rock carvings. Inland, the Blue Mountains have a whole series of fine walks and some spectacular scenery. The Southern Highlands are also within easy reach of the city.

Further afield, the Kosciusko National Park in the south of the state has excellent longer walks, camping facilities and vivid wildflowers in late summer. It's best to let the snow have plenty of time to thaw and dry up after the winter. Barrington Tops National Park is north of Sydney, near the New England tableland and the Warrumbungle National Park is further west near Coonabarabran.

Running & Biking There are tracks and facilities at Narrabeen Lakes north of Sydney. Sydney joggers do their stuff at Centennial Park which is also popular with the pushbike people. In August, the City to Surf fun run is Australia's biggest foot race.

Swimming & Surfing This is the true-blue Sydney activity and all the beaches around Sydney – Palm Beach, Whale Beach, Avalon, Colaroy, Manly, Bronte, Maroubra, Cronulla, Bondi, Coogee (need I go on) have good swimming and/or surfing. The beaches in the Royal National Park are also popular.

Surf carnivals – lifesavers, surf rescue boats, all that stuff – start in December when there are competitions between lifesavers from the various beaches. Phone the Surf Life Saving Association to find out what's on where, or contact the NSW Travel Centre.

Officially, Sydney has 34 surf beaches and there are plenty more along the NSW

coast. The north coast is more popular during the winter months (warmer of course) at places like Seal Rocks (325 km), Crescent Head (497 km), Scott's Head (538 km), Angourie (744 km) and Lennox Heads (823 km). Byron Bay has been a surfing Mecca for almost as long as Australia has had surfies. South of Sydney there is Stanwell Park (56 km), Wollongong (82 km), Huskisson (187 km) and Mollymook (222 km).

Scuba Diving Excellent scuba diving and snorkelling can be found at a number of sites along the coast. North of Sydney popular spots include Terrigal (96 km), Port Stephens (235 km), Seal Rocks (325 km) or Byron Bay (850 km). Head south to Jervis Bay in the Royal National Park, to Wattamolia (198 km) or Eden (488 km).

Canoeing With dams, rivers, lakes and coastal lakes there are plenty of opportunities to go canoeing in NSW. If you are after whitewater then the Richmond and Murray Rivers are where you should be heading. The NSW Canoe Association (tel 241 3866) has info. Equipment can be hired from the NSW Sport & Recreation Service or from B-line Canoe Hire (tel 727 9402) at Lansvale.

Sailing Sydney Harbour and the Pittwater are both excellent areas for sailing so it is hardly surprising that the sport is so popular. Check with the Australian Yachting Federation about clubs and sailing instruction.

Skiing See the Snowy Mountains section for information about skiing in NSW.

Sydney
Population 3,400,000

As Australia's oldest and largest city it's not surprising that Sydney (Sinney to the locals) has plenty to offer. The harbour, around which the city is built, was noted by Captain Cook in 1770 and named Port Jackson by him. He actually anchored in Botany Bay, a few km to the south, and only passed by the narrow entrance to the harbour, not entering the magnificent stretch of water that lay within the heads. In 1788 when the convict 'First Fleet' arrived in Sydney it too went first to Botany Bay but after a few days moved north to Port Jackson. These first settlers established themselves at Sydney Cove, still the centre of harbour shipping to this day.

As Sydney grew it stretched back from that original landing spot but down near the waterfront in the area known as the Rocks you can still find some of the earliest buildings in Australia. Because Sydney grew in a somewhat piecemeal fashion, unlike other later Australian cities which were planned from the start, it's a tighter, more congested centre with narrower streets than the wide boulevards you find in other cities, Melbourne in particular. Despite that it's also a dazzlingly modern city, the place with the most energy and style in Australia. In Sydney the buildings soar higher, the colours are brighter, the consumption is more conspicuous! It all comes back to that stupendous harbour though. It's more than just the centrepiece for the city, everything in Sydney revolves around the harbour. Would the Opera House, for example, be anything like the place it is were it not perched right beside the harbour?

Information

Tourist Information The NSW Government Travel Centre (tel 231 4444) is at 16 Spring St on the corner with Pitt St. It's open Monday to Friday 9 am to 5 pm and has the usual range of brochures, leaflets and accommodation details. They have a display of all possible city and area tours and can make bookings. The Sydney Visitors Bureau (tel 235 2424) is in Martin Place, a mall area which runs between George and Elizabeth Sts. The office is nearer Elizabeth St, and is open the same hours as the NSW centre. The privately run Tourist Information Service (tel 669 5111) is a telephone info service operating seven days a week from 8 am to 6 pm.

The National Roads & Motorists Association (NRMA) is the NSW car club and it has its head office at 151 Clarence St (tel 260 9222) and a branch at 324 Pitt St (tel 260 9781). There's a YHA shop at the Sydney YHA office (tel 29 5068) at 355 Kent St. The national head office of the YHA is also in Sydney at 60 Mary St, Surry Hills. As usual the universities are good info sources and there are university newspapers at Sydney University and the University of NSW. The Wayside Chapel (tel 358 6570), up at 29 Hughes St, Kings Cross, is a crisis centre and good for all sorts of local information and problem solving.

Books *Sydney – the Harbour City Handbook* by Robyn Stone is a comprehensive handbook on sightseeing, accommodation, restaurants and entertainment in Sydney, including both low and high price places. It's published by George Allen & Unwin, 1981, and retails at $6.95. Another guide is *Out & About in Sydney* by Taffy Davies & Jill Wran. Although it also contains some info on cheaper places it is really more of a guide to the top end. Sydney has lots of good bookshops including a large Angus & Robertson and two Grahames on Pitt St, Dymocks and the Travel Bookshop on George St, and the anarchic Gould's Book Arcade, also on George St.

Things to Buy You can find Aboriginal art in several places in Sydney. The Dreamtime Aboriginal Art Centre is in the Argyle Art Centre in the Rocks. It mainly has bark paintings and, as usual, they are attractive but costly. The nearby Gallery of Aboriginal Art is closed but apparently re-opening at a new location. The Aboriginal Art Centre at the corner of Clarence and

Market Sts is both a gallery for contemporary work as well as a shop for traditional arts, again mostly painting. New Guinea Primitive Arts on the 6th floor at 428 George St with an absolutely amazing collection of artefacts from PNG, has just a few Aboriginal works – worth a visit. At 135 Bathurst St is the Bush Church Aid Shop, which sells artefacts made by Aboriginals from reserves all over Australia.

Duncan's Boomerang School has a very good shop at 202 William St, up by Kings Cross, and another one just down the hill a bit. They have an excellent array of boomerangs from $5 – a good souvenir or present. There is a video to watch to learn the basics and every Sunday from 10 am to noon there are free throwing lessons given in the park at the end of New Beach Rd, Rushcutter's Bay.

Back in the Rocks you can find a variety of original Australian designs at the Australian Design Centre at 70 George St, open daily, and lots of interesting goodies at the Environment Centre, 399 Pitt St. There's a shop in the Argyle Arts Centre in the Rocks which sells genuine Australian road signs – the kangaroo and koala warning variety. The Village Bazaar on Oxford St in Paddington has a superb arts, crafts and general odds and ends session on Saturdays. It's quite a scene.

Orientation

Sydney is much less simply laid out than most Australian cities – the streets are narrower, more winding and convoluted, and getting around is more difficult. It's a combination of history and geography that has led to this situation. Historically Sydney came into existence before the era of grand plans and wide boulevards that was to characterise most later Australian cities. Geographically Sydney's layout is complicated by the harbour with its numerous arms and inlets and by the general hilly nature of the city.

The harbour divides Sydney into two areas, north and south. Most of the places of interest in the city area tend to be south

of the harbour, including the city centre itself. The centre is connected to the north shore by the huge, but often jammed, harbour bridge. The central city area is relatively long and narrow although only a couple of roads, George and Pitt Sts, run all the way from the waterfront area known as the Rocks right to Central Station, which marks the southern boundary of the city. These are the two main streets of central Sydney and along them or near to them you'll find shops, shopping centres and arcades, airline offices and other central city businesses. The Rocks and the waterfront mark the northern boundary of the centre, an inlet marks the western boundary and a string of pleasant parks border it to the east.

Beyond this park strip are some of the oldest and most interesting inner suburbs of Sydney – Woolloomooloo, Kings Cross and Paddington. Further east again are some of the more exclusive suburbs south of the harbour and then the beachfront suburbs like Bondi. The airport is south of this area, beside Botany Bay, the second great harbour for Sydney.

The Rocks

Sydney's first settlement was made on the spur of land sticking out into the harbour from which the harbour bridge makes its leap across to the north shore. A pretty squalid place it was too. Later it became an area of warehouses and bond stores and then gradually declined as more modern shipping and storage facilities were opened.

The notorious 'rocks pushes' were gangs of larrikins (a great Australian word that) who used to haunt the Rocks. An outbreak of bubonic plague at the turn of the century led to whole streets of the Rocks being razed and the construction of the harbour bridge also resulted in much demolition.

Today a major redevelopment programme is making this into the most interesting area of Sydney and imaginative restorations are converting the decrepit old

Top: The City to Surf race to Bondi Beach race attracts up to 25,000 runners (NSWGTB)
Left: And what do you find at Bondi Beach? (NSWGTB)
Right: Australia isn't all sun and sand; a lone skier at Thredbo (NSWGTB)

Top: The El Alamein fountain in Kings Cross, Sydney (TW)
Left: Terrace rooftops zig-zag up the hill in the trendy inner-Sydney suburb of Paddington (NSWGTB)
Right: Painted doors in the 'hippy' centre of Nimbin, north New South Wales (NSWGTB)

warehouses into places like the trendy and very interesting Argyle Arts Centre or the amusing Old Spaghetti Factory. Despite the years of destruction there were still a great number of interesting and important buildings remaining when restoration commenced in 1970. Redevelopment has gone far enough for some people and local residents are fighting the government to prevent the loss of their old homes. You'll see banners to this affect across some buildings. It's a wonderful area to wander around, full of narrow cobbled streets, fine old colonial buildings and countless historical touches.

The arts centre was originally built as a bond store between 1826 and 1881. Today it has a collection of shops, boutiques, studios and eating places. Just beyond the arts centre is the Argyle Cut, a tunnel cut through the hill to the other side of the peninsula. It was begun in 1843 by convict labour but abandoned and not finished until many years later. This area is known as Millers Point and is a delightful district of early colonial homes, some around a real village green, almost in the heart of Sydney.

Get a walking tour map of the area from the Rocks Visitors' Centre, 104 George St, and explore on foot. The centre also shows a short film about the Rocks and four times daily there are one-hour walking tours from there. It's open weekdays 8.30 am to 4.30 pm, weekends 10 am to 5 pm. Also from here there's a free bus every 15 minutes to Pier 1, a complex of stores and restaurants at the bay in a renovated landmark. It's only a seven-minute walk, however.

Strolling around the Rocks you'll come across Cadman's Cottage (1816), the oldest house in Sydney. When it was built this was where the waterfront was and the arches to the south of the cottage once housed longboats. You can also find the site of the public gallows, a colonial museum, an old observatory in the pleasant park on Flagstaff Hill (open by arrangement only) and much more. The

Rocks also has several historic old pubs including the *Hero of Waterloo* and the *Lord Nelson*. There are also guided walking tours of the Rocks from the Argyle Arts Centre four times a day for $3.

Sydney Harbour Bridge
Down at the end of the Rocks the harbour bridge rises up on its path to the north shore. It's known affectionately as the 'old coathanger' and was a far from elegant, but very functional, symbol for the city until the Opera House came along. It was completed in 1932 at a cost of $20 million, quite a bargain today.

Crossing the bridge costs just 20c, southbound only, there is no toll in the other direction. Trivia fans may be interested to know the bridge has only been repainted a handful of times since it was completed but that repainting is a continuous process – painters start at one end, work to the other and by the time they get there it's time to start again. You can also walk across the bridge, there are stairs up to it from the Rocks. See the note in City Views. At rush hours the bridge gets very crowded and the possibility of a second harbour bridge or, more likely, a harbour tunnel is a subject for on-going discussion.

On the north shore, neatly framed beneath the bridge, is the grinning mouthpiece of another Sydney symbol – Luna Park. North Sydney has become a smaller replica of the Sydney centre in the past 20 years. Spiralling office rents and central congestion prompted the construction of this second city centre.

The Sydney Opera House
From the past symbol to the present one is a short walk around Circular Quay – to the controversial Sydney Opera House. After countless delays and technical difficulties and with cost escalations like a land-bound Concorde, the Opera House finally opened in 1973, 14 years after work began. And I was there! During a cheap Sunday afternoon concert or sitting in the

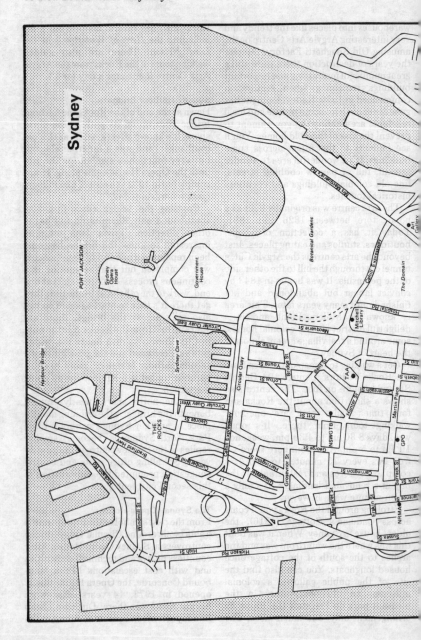

Sydney

PORT JACKSON

Harbour Bridge

Bradfield Hwy

THE ROCKS

Sydney Cove

Sydney Opera House

Government House

Botanical Gardens

The Domain

Art Gallery

Circular Quay West

Circular Quay East

Macquarie St

Phillip St

Bent St

Young St

Bligh St

Loftus St

Hunter St

Pitt St

O'Connell St

Castlereagh St

Elizabeth St

Martin Place

Mrs Macquarie Rd

Hospital Rd

Mitchell Library

TAA

GPO

NSWGTB

George St

Grosvenor St

Harrington St

Cumberland St

Gloucester St

Cahill Expressway

Circular Quay

Carrington St

Margaret St

Erskine St

Clarence St

York St

Barrack St

George St

Wynyard Park

NRMA

Kent St

Sussex St

High St

Hickson Rd

Windmill St

Hickson Rd

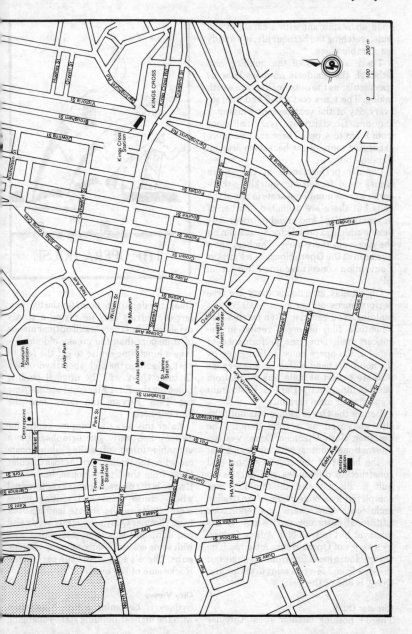

open air restaurant with a carafe of red wine, watching the harbour life, it's a truly memorable place.

There are tours of the building and although the inside is nowhere near as spectacular as the outside, they are worth taking. The tours cost $2.50 and operate every day of the year (except Christmas Day and Good Friday) every half hour from 9 am to 4 pm. There are also more expensive tours of the backstage area on Sundays only.

Popular performances at the Opera House tend to sell out quickly – there aren't a great number of seats in any of the halls but there are a limited number of 'restricted view' and standing-room-only tickets which go on sale for $5 at 9 am on the day – get there early. The best show I've seen at the Opera House? – a Fairport Convention concert recorded live for an LP.

On Sunday afternoons there are free performances on the outer walk of the building. You can also often catch a free lunchtime film or organ recital in the concert hall. One free performance to avoid at the opera house is that given by the notorious band of free-loading seagulls who are expert at collecting meals from outdoor diners at the Harbour Restaurant – guard your meal carefully.

Before the Opera House was built the site was used as a tram depot. The designer, Jorn Utzon, a Dane, won an international contest with his design but at the height of the cost over-runs and construction difficulties and hassles he quit in disgust and the building was completed by a consortium of Australian architects. How were the enormous additional costs covered? – not by the taxpayer but in true-blue Aussie fashion by a series of Opera House lotteries. The Opera House looks fine from any angle but the view from a ferry, coming in to Circular Quay, is one of the best.

Circular Quay
There's nothing circular about Circular

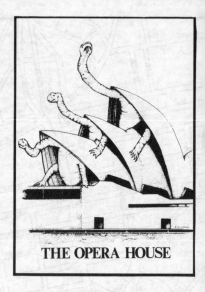

THE OPERA HOUSE

Quay, the departure point for the harbour ferries. Ferries may be plying a slowly dying trade but there is still no finer means of transport than the creaky old ships – take a lunchtime cruise to get the feel or zip to Manly on the high-speed hydrofoils. Circular Quay was the original landing point for the First Fleet and at that time the Tank Stream ran down into the harbour here.

Later this was the shipping centre for Sydney and early photographs show a veritable forest of sailing ship masts crowding the skyline here. Across Circular Quay from the Opera House, beside the Rocks, is the overseas passenger terminal where cruise ships and visiting liners moor. Some of the streets leading back from Circular Quay are slightly seedy and run down but this is an interesting area with some colourful early-morning-opening pubs. There's a pleasant little park on the Rocks side of the quay.

City Views
Sydney is becoming a mini-Manhattan with the highest-building stakes changing

from year to year. From up top you can see the convoluted streets that are a relic of the unplanned convict past. George St is the main shopping street, once known as High St, while Pitt St was famous for is brothels way back when. Bridge St was so-named because it was the site of the first bridge in Australia across the Tank Stream, which is now funnelled underground.

Highest, not only in Sydney but also Australia, is the Sydney Tower on top of the Centrepoint Complex. This is a tower built purely for the sake of being high – it's nothing more than a gigantic column with a circular viewing gallery and revolving restaurant on the summit. The construction of the tower was interesting. First the column was constructed, in 46 prefabricated sections stacked one on top of another, then the top 'drum' was assembled at the bottom of the column and slowly jacked up to its position at the top. It's 305 metres above street level. The tower is open 9.30 am to 9.30 pm daily except Sundays and public holidays when it's open 10.30 am to 6.30 pm. Admission is $3.50 for the observation deck. There is an exhibit on UFO's at the top for $4.50. A combination ticket is $6. Reservations for either of the restaurants is a good idea.

Sydney Harbour Bridge is a good vantage point and a good place for a picture of the Opera House and harbour. The south-eastern pylon on the pedestrian walkway is open on Saturday, Sunday and Monday, and school holidays 9.30 am to 5 pm, entry is 50c. At the top of the 200 stairs is a panoramic view of the city. There is a stone staircase up to the bridge from Argyle St in the Rocks.

Lastly, there is a good view from the rooftop of the Australian Museum and it's free!

City Parks

Sydney has plenty of parks including a string of them which border the city centre on its eastern side. Stretching back from the harbour front, beside the Opera House, is Sydney's Royal Botanic Garden with a magnificent collection of South Pacific plant life. The gardens were originally established in 1816 and in one corner of the gardens you can find a stone wall marking the site of the convict colony's first vegetable patch.

The harbour bridge freeway separates the botanic gardens from the Domain, behind Macquarie St. Here on Sunday afternoon after 2 pm impassioned soapbox speakers entertain their listeners. Continue down beyond the Domain and the art gallery and you'll find Mrs Macquarie's Chair cut into the rock of Mrs Macquarie's Point. Here the wife of that early governor is said to have sat to watch how hubby's construction projects were coming along, just across Farm Cove. It's a popular place to for taking photographs of the Opera House.

Third of this group of city parks is Hyde Park with its delightful fountains and the Anzac Memorial. This is a popular place for a city sandwich lunch on the grass since it's only a few steps from the centre. Sydney's biggest park with running, bicycling and horse tracks, duck ponds, barbecue sites and lots more is Centennial Park, just beyond Paddington. You can hire bikes from Centennial Park Cycles, 50 Clovelly Rd, Randwick – 9 am to 5 pm weekdays, 8.30 am to dusk on weekends.

Macquarie Place

Narrow lanes lead back from Circular Quay at the waterfront towards the real centre of the city. Find the pleasant little triangular open space of Macquarie Place where under the shady Moreton Bay figs you'll find a cannon and anchor from Phillip's First Fleet flagship HMS Sirius. There are a number of other pieces of colonial memorabilia in this interesting little square including gas lamps, a drinking fountain dating from 1857, a National Trust classified gentlemen's convenience and an obelisk indicating distances to various points in the colony of NSW.

Early Buildings

After the founding governor Phillip left in 1792 the colony was run by officials more intent on making a quick fortune through the rum monopoly than anything else and it was not until Macquarie took over in 1810 that order was restored. The narrow streets of parts of downtown Sydney are a reminder of that chaotic period. Some of the finest early buildings in Sydney were the work of convict architect Francis Greenway and there are examples of his buildings scattered around the city. St James Church and the Hyde Park Barracks are two of his early masterpieces on Queens Square at the northern end of Hyde Park.

Next to the barracks on Queen St is the Mint Building, originally built as a hospital in 1814 and known as the Rum Hospital because the builders constructed it in return for the lucrative monopoly on the rum trade. It became the mint in 1853 and the northern wing of the hospital is now the Parliament House. The Mint, with its collection of historic decorative arts, is open 10 am to 5 pm daily except Wednesday when it opens at 12 noon. In the same area the State Conservatorium of Music on Macquarie St was originally built, by Greenway again, as a stables and servants' quarters for government house.

City Centre

Sydney has some of the most attractive and imaginative shopping complexes in Australia including the delightful old Strand Arcade between Pitt and George Sts. The MLC Centre, Centrepoint and the Royal Arcade are just three of the many modern centres you will find off George and Pitt Sts in the centre. In the basement of the Hilton Hotel, under the Royal Arcade, you can find the Marble Bar, a Victorian extravaganza built by George Adams, the fellow with the prescience to foresee Australia's gambling lust and founded Tattersall's lotteries (best known for Tattslotto). When the old Adams Hotel (originally O'Brian's Pub)

was torn down to build the Hilton, the bar was carefully dismantled and reassembled like some archaeological wonder.

Sydney's real centre is Martin Place, a pedestrian mall extending from Elizabeth St down to George St beside the massive GPO. It's a popular lunchtime entertainment spot with buskers and more organised entertainment. The Cenotaph war memorial is here and also the Sydney Visitors Centre. In December a Christmas tree appears here in the summer heat.

Continuing along George St you'll come to the 1874 Town Hall and then the centre begins to fade, becoming rather grotty before you reach Central Station and the inner suburb of Glebe. Just off George St and before the station is the colourful Chinatown around Dixon St, packed with Chinese shops and restaurants.

Art Gallery of NSW

Situated in the Domain, only a short walk from the centre, the Art Gallery has an excellent permanent display and from time to time shows some really inspired temporary exhibits. The gallery also has a very good cafeteria, ideal for a genteel cup of tea. It's open 10 am to 5 pm Monday to Saturday, 12 noon to 5 pm Sunday. There's no charge to enter the gallery itself but entrance fees may apply at certain times for major exhibitions. Free guided tours of the gallery are available. Sydney is packed with other galleries, particularly in Paddo and Woollahra.

Museums

The Australian Museum at the corner of College and William Sts, right by Hyde Park, is a natural history museum with an excellent collection of Australian wildlife, a new Aboriginal gallery tracing Aboriginal history from the Dreamtime to the present and an intriguing 'arid Australia' section. See the latter before you head off into the centre. The Papua New Guinea Village display is also good. This is Australia's largest museum. It's open 10 am to 5 pm everyday except Monday when it's 12 noon to 5 pm. Admission is free and taped guided tours are available.

The Museum of Applied Art & Science on Harris St, Ultimo, has recently been refurbished and renamed the Power House Museum. It's also open daily and admission is free. Outside stands a life-size lunar-module model. There is also a Rail Transport Museum at Chullora and a Mining Museum at the top end of George St in the Rocks. Near Sutherland and the Royal National Park on the Princes Highway there's a Tramway Museum open on weekends – Sydney's last tram rumbled into the history books back in 1961. There's a 600-metre-long tram track.

At Birkenhead Point, just across the Iron Cove Bridge in Drummoyne, the Sydney Maritime Museum has ships and museum displays. It's open daily from 10 am to 5 pm except Mondays when it opens at 1 pm. There's an admission charge and you can get there on a 500 bus from Circular Quay or by ferry from number 2 wharf, Circular Quay. There's also a fishing museum here. Other Sydney museums include the Macleay Museum and Nicholson Museum at Sydney University, natural history at the former, Greek antiquities at the latter. At 157 Gloucester St in the Rocks there's the Hall of Champions Sports Museum. Kings Cross has a waxworks in the Village Centre.

The State Library of New South Wales has one of the best collections of early works on Australia in the country. It includes maps, documents, pictures and many other items which can be seen in the library galleries. The galleries are open 10 am to 5 pm Monday to Saturday, 2 to 6 pm on Sunday.

Other Displays

The Sydney Antique Centre is a con-glomeration of 60 antique shops located at 531 South Darling St, Surry Hills. Open everyday, there are items ranging from movie posters to silver, junk to jewellery.

Located on the top floor of the Argyle Centre, 33 Playfair St, the Energy Information Centre has educational and informative displays concerning energy use and conservation plus ideas to save money around the house.

From the Australian Wine Centre at 21 Circular Quay West on the water you can take a tour and get a free tasting.

Darling Harbour

To the west of the city centre this huge redevelopment of a run-down docks area is planned to be the third great Sydney 'attraction' – along with the Opera House and the Sydney Harbour Bridge. The first stages of Darling Harbour are planned to open for the bicentennial celebrations in 1988.

When eventually completed, Darling Harbour will be linked to the city centre by a monorail. The Sydney Entertainment Centre and the Power House Museum are already completed near the development which will eventually include a huge exhibition centre, various hotels and convention centres, a harbourside retail market (Festival Gardens) and a National Maritime Museum. The area will also include parks and gardens including a formal Chinese Garden linking Darling Harbour with Sydney's Dixon St Chinatown. This garden will be designed and built by experts from the Chinese province of Guangdong. Later on a National Aquarium will also be built here.

Paddington

The trendy inner suburb of Paddington has to be one of the most attractive inner city residential areas in the world. 'Paddo' is a tightly packed mass of terrace houses, built for aspiring artisans in the later years of the Victorian era. During the lemming-like rush to the dreary outer suburbs after WW II the area became a run-down slum. Then a renewed interest in Victorian architecture (of which Australia has some gems) combined with a sudden recollection of the pleasures of inner city life led to the quite incredible restoration of Paddo during the '60s.

Today it's a fascinating jumble of often beautifully restored terraces, tumbling up and down the steeply sloping streets. Surprisingly there was an older Paddington of fine gentlemen's residences, a few of which still stand although the once spacious gardens are now encroached upon by lesser buildings. Paddington is one of the finest examples of totally unplanned urban restoration in the world and is full of trendy shops and restaurants, some fine art galleries and interesting people. The best time to visit Paddo is Saturdays when you can catch the 'Paddo Fair' with all sorts of eccentric market stalls selling everything from Indian kaftans to pop art. I always manage to see something I just have to have.

While you're in Paddington visit the old Victoria Barracks where you can see the impressive changing of the guards at 10.30 am on Tuesdays except in December and January. The barracks were built between 1841 and 1848, at that time the area was sand dunes and swamps! Get a free copy of The Paddington Book (available from shops in the area) to help you find your way around.

You can get to Paddo on a 380 bus.

Kings Cross

'The Cross', Sydney's sin centre, is rather a pale shadow of similar places abroad but it's the only place in Oz that gives it a try. Apart from the seedy strip joints it has some good restaurants, lots of late night eateries, plenty of hookers, the pleasant Kings Cross Village Centre and lots of travellers. The Cross has a string of popular hostels and is an excellent place to stay. It has lots of activity and is very close to the city centre.

The attractive (when it's working) thistle-like El Alamein Fountain, down at the end of Darlinghurst Rd, is known locally as the 'elephant douche'! Victoria St, the site for a major tussle between conservationists and developers in the

early '70s is a pleasant tree-lined street with numerous restaurants and a number of the most popular travellers' centres in the Cross. From the city you can walk straight up Williams St to the Cross, grab one of a multitude of buses which run there or take the very quick Eastern Suburbs train service which takes you right to the centre of the Cross.

Between the city and the Cross is Woolloomooloo, the 'loo', one of Sydney's older areas with many narrow streets. This area, which was extremely run down in the early '70s, has gone through a complete restoration and is now very pleasant.

Beyond the Cross

At the harbour front near the Cross is Elizabeth Bay where you'll find Elizabeth Bay House at 7 Onslow St, a fine old home, built in 1832 and overlooking the harbour. It's open Tuesday to Friday from 10 am to 4 pm, Saturday from 10 am to 5 pm and Sunday from 12 noon to 5 pm, admission is $1.50, less for students.

Continuing through Kings Cross you come to Rushcutters Bay, trendy Darling Point and then even trendier Double Bay – swish shops and lots of badly parked Porsches and Benzes. Next up in this direction is Rose Bay then Vaucluse where Vaucluse House (admission $1.50) is an imposing example of 19th century Australiana. It was built in 1828 for William Wentworth and you can get there on a 325 bus.

Towards the end of the harbour is Watsons Bay with trendy Doyles restaurant, a couple of Sydney's most 'be seen there' harbour beaches and the magnificent view across the Heads. All along this side of the harbour there are superb views back down the harbour towards the city.

Other Suburbs

On the other side of the centre from Paddo and the Cross is Balmain, the arty centre of Sydney and in some ways a competitor for Paddo in Victorian-era trendiness.

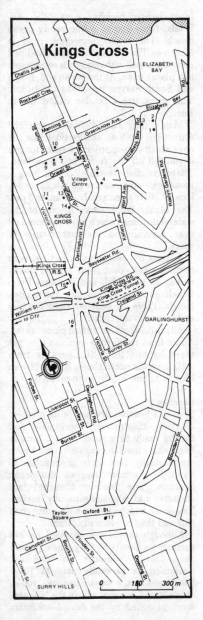

Kings Cross

1	Backpackers Accommodation
2	Young Travellers Hostel
3	Montpelier
4	El Alamein Fountain
5	Kings Cross Library
6	Clay's Bookshop
7	Wayside Chapel
8	Cross Country Travellers Hostel
9	Gala Private Hotel
10	Macquarie Hotel
11	Cactus Cafe
12	Atoa Guest House
13	Springfields Lodge
14	Benly Guest House
15	Canberra Oriental Hotel
16	McCafferty's Bus Depot
17	Balkan Restaurant

Glebe, closer to the centre, is another area which has been going up the social scale in recent years. While the eastern suburbs (the harbour to ocean area beyond the Cross) and the north shore (across the harbour) are the wealthy areas of Sydney the western suburbs are the real suburbs. Heading west you come first to Redfern. Parts of it are quite interesting but other parts are Australia's closest approach to a real slum. Further out it's the red-tile roofed, triple-front area of the slurbs, the dull Bankstowns of Sydney.

The Harbour

Sydney's harbour is best viewed from the ferries. It's extravagantly colourful and always interesting. People have often wondered out loud just which great city has the most magnificent harbour – Hong Kong, Rio, San Francisco or Sydney? I've still got to get to Rio but between the others I'd have to give Sydney first place. Out in the harbour Fort Denison, or Pinchgut as it was uncomfortably named, is an interesting reminder of convict days. It was fortified when Australians were having a bout of Russian-fears back in the Czar's days. There are tours there from Jetty 6, Circular Quay at 10.15 am, 12.45 and 2.15 pm from Tuesday to Saturday. The trip takes 1½ hours and costs $2.50 return. It's best to book, phone 2 0545 (ext 292), Monday to Friday only. There are tours that include other points of interest listed under 'Ferries' in Getting Around.

The Gap, the entrance to the harbour, is a popular spot for catching the sunrise and sunset. You can hire boats (rowboats, canoes, small sailboats and motorboats) from Walton's Hireboats, 2 The Esplanade, Balmoral. There are several other harbour boat-hire places. There's a fine four-km walking track along the harbourside at Ashton Park, below Taronga Park Zoo. Another harbourside walk takes you for three km around Cremorne Point.

A favourite harbour activity is following the 18-footer yacht races on Saturdays. Ferries, complete with on-board bookies so you can bet on the outcome, follow the exciting races. Eighteen-footers are a peculiarly Australian yachting class where virtually anything goes – the end result is boats carrying huge sails which result in them being fantastically fast and requiring great athletic ability to keep them upright. Unlike most yachting classes the boats carry advertising on their sails and are heavily sponsored. Ben Lexcen, designer of the America's Cup winning *Australia II*, first made his name as an 18-foot designer and skipper.

Taronga Park Zoo

A short ferry ride across the harbour will deposit you near Taronga Park Zoo which has one of the most attractive settings of any zoo in the world. Gradually the animal enclosures are being brought up to the same high standard. The ferry goes from Jetty 5, Circular Quay and the zoo is open daily 9.30 am to 5 pm, admission is $6, half price for kids.

Manly

It is an excellent, cheap, 30-minute ferry cruise to Manly at the ocean edge of the harbour. The frequent hydrofoils are a dollar or so more, bumpier, and do the trip in 15 minutes.

Manly is very pleasant, more like a small resort than a city suburb. A short walk from the ferry terminal, near the

inner harbour beaches, across the peninsula, takes you to a fine sandy ocean beach. The main connecting road is known as The Corso and is a palm-lined pedestrian mall with numerous restaurants and places to sit. At the ocean end, North and South Steyne run along the beach. This main street is also called Ocean Beach.

Manly also has a few commercial attractions such as sharks (just like the ones which are supposedly waiting for you if you fall off the ferry) at Marineland. There are daily feedings of the hungry monsters – admission is $5, students $3, kids $2.50. It's open daily, 10 am to 5 pm. The Manly Waterworks is one of the waterslide things which have appeared all over Australia in the last couple of years.

A string of oceanfront suburbs stretch north up the coast from Manly, finally ending in beautiful, and wealthy, Palm Beach and the spectacular Barrenjoey Heads. There are beaches along the way and buses do the route.

All in all, Manly isn't a bad place to stay. Apart from the ferries you can also get there by bus from St Leonards train station on the north shore. It might be an idea to go one way by each method.

Beaches

Sydney's beaches are one of its greatest assets – they're very accessible and they're really very good. In fact for city beaches it's hard to imagine better. There are basically two sorts of beaches in Sydney – harbour beaches and ocean beaches. The harbour beaches are sheltered and calm and generally smaller. The ocean beaches often have quite good surf and they're generally larger.

Although they'll get crowded on hot summer weekends Sydney's beaches are never really shoulder to shoulder. Swimming is generally safe at these beaches – at the ocean beaches you're only allowed to swim within the 'flagged' areas patrolled by the famed voluntary lifeguards. Efforts are made to keep the surfers separate from the swimmers. A high point of Sydney's beach-life is the surf-lifesaving competitions with races, rescues and surfboat competitions at various beaches throughout the summer months.

Shark patrols are operated through the summer months and the ocean beaches are generally netted – Sydney has only had one fatal shark attack since 1937. The shark-proof nets do not, incidentally, enclose the beaches – they're installed perpendicular to the beaches, not parallel to them. This dissuades sharks from patrolling along the beaches.

Many of Sydney's beaches are 'topless' but on some beaches it is not approved of so women should observe what other people are doing before forgetting their bikini tops. There are also a couple of nude beaches. A brief resume of some of the beaches:

Harbour Beaches On the south side one of the most popular harbour beaches is trendy Camp Cove, a small but pleasant sliver of sand popular with families and also topless. This was the place where Governor Philip first landed in Sydney. Back towards the city is Watson's Bay with the delightful, outdoor seafood restaurant Doyle's, where you can dine in the open and gaze back along the harbour towards the city.

In the opposite direction, just inside the heads (the harbour entrance), the tiny Lady Bay Beach achieved some notoriety in the process of becoming a nude beach. It's mainly a gay scene. There's another nude beach on the north shore of the harbour, Reef Beach, but it's quite a long walk to get to it. Two other popular harbour beaches are Balmoral, with it's little 'island', on the north side of the harbour and Nielson Park on the south side at Vaucluse.

South Ocean Beaches South of the heads there are a string of ocean beaches all the

way to the entry to Botany Bay. They include Bondi; with its crowds, surfies and even fibreglass mermaids in pathetic imitation of Copenhagen it's probably the best-known beach in Australia. Bondi's beachfront is backed by somewhat run down Victorian buildings which give it an air of a slightly seedy, antipodean Brighton but that makes Bondi sound a lot worse than it is. It's really quite an enjoyable place and Maureen and I often stay at Bondi when we're in Sydney. The south end of the beach is topless. Bondi is rather like Earls Court is (or was) for young Australians in London, only, in this case, Bondi is a favourite with New Zealanders and other young visitors to Sydney. It's a popular gathering place.

Tamarama, a little south of Bondi, is another beautiful sweep of sand with strong surf and it's also topless. Then there's Bronte, a wide beach popular with families, and Coogee, another wide, sweeping beach where you'll also find the popular Coogee Bay Hotel with its beer garden overlooking the beach. Other beaches towards Botany Bay, which is more for sailing than swimming due to the sharks, include Maroubra.

Surf Beaches Surfing is a popular pastime in Sydney, and with the large number of good beaches close at hand, it's easy to see why. Apart from Bondi and Tamarama, there's Clovelly and Maroubra south of the heads. North of the heads there's another dozen or so, the best being Narrabeen, North Avalon and Palm Beach, the north end of which is a nude beach.

Places to Stay
There's a wide variety of accommodation in Sydney including an excellent selection of rock-bottom priced hostels. Finding a place to stay in Sydney requires deciding which suburb you prefer first of all. The information that follows is subdivided by location as well as type. If you want to book a hotel or motel room the Public

Transport Commission performs this service and so does the Government Travel Centre. There are cheap places in the rooms to let ads in the Sydney Morning Herald every day, but particularly on Wednesday and Saturdays. Finding a room from the ads, even on a short term basis, is no problem.

When Maureen and I first set up Lonely Planet we lived in the basement of a Paddington terrace in Sydney and since then we've made lots of trips and visits to the harbour city and tried out all sorts of areas around the city either staying with friends or in a variety of cheap places, more than a few of which feature below.

The Cross, which is definitely the backpackers' centre, is great fun, a bit noisy and seedy, but if you like a little raucous squalor it's not at all a bad place to stay. Bondi is another very popular accommodation centre and also probably Sydney's best known beach. Like the Cross there's lots of activity and also lots of places to eat. If you'd like something quieter I can also recommend Manly. The distance is no big deal because you ride back and forth on the best transport Sydney has to offer – a harbour ferry.

Hostels Sydney has three official YHA hostels and an ever-increasing number of unofficial ones. The latter are all busy and cheap but vary a bit so you may have to jump around until you find one that best suits you.

The closest *Youth Hostel* (tel 692 0747) to the city centre is at 28 Ross St, just across the Parramatta Rd from Sydney Uni. This hostel, at Forest Lodge, has only 30 beds and is closed from 9.30 am to 5 pm. The other *Youth Hostel* (tel 569 0272) is at 407 Marrickville Rd, Dulwich Hill. It's seven km from town but only four km from the airport, and has 120 beds. Both these hostels charge $7 per night and you can arrange to get in after 10 pm if they have already booked you in. The third *Youth Hostel* (tel 692 8418), due to open in early '86 at 262 Glebe Point Rd, Glebe, will charge $8, have 96 beds and can be reached on buses 431 and 433 from

George St in the city. This hostel, like the one at Dulwich Hill is open all day until 10 pm.

The *YMCA* residence building burnt down and though there are plans to rebuild, there is no accommodation for the time being. Phone 264 1011 for the latest information. Ironically, the YWCA has recently opened so at least one Y remains. The *YWCA* (tel 264 2451) takes women or couples and is central at 5-11 Wentworth Avenue, at the corner of Liverpool St across from Hyde Park. Four-people dorms go for $12.50 per person, single rooms from $23, twins $35, more for a private bathroom, cheaper for stays beyond two months. There is a cheap cafeteria open to all.

The private hostels in Sydney are mainly around the Kings Cross area. Competition has kept prices the same for years and in some cases the cost of a bed has even dropped a dollar. They are generally open through the day but check-in is before 10 am and after 5 pm. Nearly all have noticeboards for rides, deals, messages etc. Most of the private hostels don't have a stay limit and some have a cheaper weekly rate. To get there, take a train to Kings Cross. When you don't have your gear you can walk it from the town centre.

The *Travellers Rest* (tel 358 4606) at 156 Victoria St is a well run place and has had a recent paint job. Dorm beds are $6 in small rooms with adjoining toilet areas. There are also singles/doubles at $14/18 ($18/22 with attached bathroom), and weekly rates are six times the daily rate. As in all hostels there are cooking facilities and, as in most, a TV lounge.

Up a few doors at 162 is the larger *King's Cross Backpackers Hostel* (tel 356 3232) in a nice old building with 78 beds and a kitchen. It's $6 for a dorm bed or $12 in a single, open all day, but you can't check in until after 4.30 pm. You can get a key so that you can come and go at night but after 11 pm they want the place quiet. There's a very good noticeboard here.

Next door at 160 is the *Atoa House* (tel 358 3693) with dorms, rooms and self-contained flats. It's also pretty big and busy but the toilet and laundry facilities could be better. Dorm beds are $6 nightly, or $42 per week. Singles/doubles are $16/23 or $91/140 by the week, flats are $30 a day.

Around the corner at 25 Hughes St is *The Young Cross Country Travellers Centre* (tel 358 1143). It sleeps two to four people in a room, linen is supplied but if you don't have your own sleeping bag you must pay a deposit on blankets and there's a a key deposit. It's also $6 a night, or $40 per week.

A few doors down is *The Annex* (tel 692 0897) at 19. It has a range of rooms from dorms, twin-bed shares to a few singles. The office is open from 9 to 11 am and from 5.30 to 7.30 pm. They have a nice garden out the back. There are quite a few 'permanents' here and last visit they even had a party room.

Also at Kings Cross is the *Young Travellers Hostel* (tel 357 3509) at 15 Rosyln Gardens. There's a kitchen and again no curfew. It's a fine old building and not in bad shape but many on the street are being completely renovated. For this hostel catch a 316 bus from Hunter St to the end of the run in Elizabeth Bay.

Not quite as central but still within walking distance of the city are a couple of places on South Dowling St, Surry Hills. At 635, across the street from the park, is *Kangaroo Bakpak* (tel 699 5915) in an old house. It's $5.50 a night, $35 a week in dorms. A little further along at 663 is *Beethoven Lodge* (tel 698 4203). It has the same nightly price but it's a few dollars less per week at $33. Both are open during the day and both are fairly basic.

Rather a long way out, but a pleasant trip on the ferry, is *Earl's Court* (tel 949 2133) at 95 West Esplanade, Manly which again costs $5 a night. It's very close to the Manly Ferry Wharf.

In Glebe, there is the *Hostel Glebe (Wattle House)* (tel 692-0879) at 44

Hereford St; a 30-bed hostel which charges $6 per night, $40 weekly. Catch bus 431 or 433 from the city.

In Coogee, the *Backpackers Hostel* (tel 665 8514) at 94 Beach St has been recommended. The charge is $6.50 per night in a dormitory and sheets and towels are available for hire. The hostel has excellent cooking facilities and there's a common room with TV and stereo.

If you don't mind staying out beyond the airport at Rockdale the *Sydney Airport Backpackers Accommodation* (tel 59 2850) at 46-48 Cameron St has accommodation at $6.50 per night.

Hotels, Private Hotels & Guest Houses

Unlike the hostels, hotels have recently become more costly and, in the city at least, rarer. Re-development has taken it's toll on the old places. The main areas to search are the city, Kings Cross or Bondi Beach but there are a few places scattered about the North Shore and Coogee as well. Check the hostel section also, as some offer single and double rooms as well as dormitories.

City The old standby *Peoples' Palace* remains at 400 Pitt St but has become the *Pacific Coast Budget Accommodation* (tel 211 5777), part of a small chain you'll see several times up the coast. It's old but well looked after with singles from $16 to $18, doubles and twins from $28 to $32. The more expensive have their own shower and toilet. For jittery women there is one floor for females only! Meals are available and there is a coin laundry. Be warned that a common Australian perversity, the 9 am check-out is in effect here.

Across the road from the People's Palace is another large private hotel, the *CB Private Hotel* (tel 211 5115). It's clean but very plain – in fact it's a lot like a South-East Asian hotel – open all night and cheap! There are 200 rooms and they keep them full by keeping the tariffs down – daily rates are $14/20 for singles/doubles or twins, $25 for three. Weekly rates are five times the daily rates. All these rates are room-only and no rooms have facilities, but there is a laundrette and public telephones. Both these hotels are near the Central Station.

Others in the area, including the *Cunningham* and the *Cozy*, don't take travellers. There is a pub worth mentioning in the city, however. *The Red Lion Inn* (tel 264 3120) at 344 Pitt St has basic rooms for $18 single, $30 twin (four of each) and although there is no breakfast available there's a coffee shop next door.

Down near the Central Station, at 356-358 Elizabeth St, is the *Central Private Hotel* (tel 212 1068) where all rooms have hot and cold water and a refrigerator. Singles are $20, doubles $25, twins $26 and extra people $8. Weekly rates are cheaper and breakfast, offered next door, is $2.50. The office is open 8 am to 7 pm. Also in this area is the *Aranui* (tel 212 1005) at 75 Wentworth St, near Campbell St, which is a bit of a dive for more or less permanent residents. It's now $12 a night and $50 a week.

A couple more in this 'no class' category are the *Haymarket Hotel*, 655 George St and *Gould's Private Hotel*, 700 George St. They're basic and not really for travellers.

Kings Cross This area is better for hotels or flats with lots of places, particularly on Victoria St. The *Bernly Private Hotel* (tel 358 3122) is pretty much in the centre of things at 15 Springfield Ave, off Darlinghurst Rd. It's a fairly modern place and though it appears small there are over 80 rooms. All have at least a sink and others have showers. TV's are extra. Singles are $16 to $18, twins/doubles $24 to $27 with weekly rates from $90 single, $135 double. *Springfield Lodge* (tel 358 3222) at 9 Springfield St is also good in the same simple, staightforward manner. Rooms with share bathrooms for $20 single, $26 double or with private facilities from $26. A stay longer than a week will net you a good discount. The rooms have a fridge and cooking facilities.

The Macquarie Private Hotel (tel 358 4415) is over on the corner of Hughes and Tusculum Sts. Prices for rooms without a toilet are $20 single, $26 double, or with toilet, $30 and $35. There's a 10% discount for non-smokers, a new twist I'd say. For a one week stay you pay for six days; for a second week just five days. Across the street at 23 Hughes St, the *Gala Private Hotel* has fallen into disrepair and 'doesn't want casuals, it's too much work'. Long term residents do keep it full though.

Alice's Tudor Private Hotel (tel 358 5977) at 64 Darlinghurst Rd offers good value with rooms that include air-con, showers, fridge, toaster and tea-making facilities. Singles are $25, which includes a small breakfast, and larger rooms are available.

Willowbridge Tourist Apartments (tel 331 3178) have three apartments for four or five people from $40 to $55. They're at 116-118 Darlinghurst Rd and the modern apartments have TV, washing machine, dryer and a fully equipped kitchen.

The *Plaza Hotel* (tel 358 6455) is right in the heart of noisy Kings Cross at 23 Darlinghurst Rd. The entrance is just off the main street, in the alley. The nightly cost is $12/16, per week it's $55/70 for singles/doubles. It's a very plain and basic place but it is quite OK.

There are some upper-class budget hotels around Kings Cross, the best known of which is probably the *Canberra Oriental* (tel 358 3155) (don't know how it came up with that odd name). It's at 223 Victoria St, right in the middle of the things, a strange location for a Temperance Union hotel in fact! There are a wide variety of rooms and all rates include a very good breakfast. Cheapest singles are $19.50 with a sink, and they go up through $23.50, $26.50, right up to $46 for the newest rooms with a bathroom and colour TV. Twins are $33.50 with a sink, and $38 up to $57 (no rock bottom twins). The restaurant also does lunch and dinner. There are many others, some on the main streets from $20 and up. Bayswater St has the *Barclay Hotel* and across the street the plain *Hotel Mansions* charges $18 and up for bed & breakfast.

East Sydney *The Park Hotel* (tel 357 5537) is at 20 Yurong St, East Sydney, right behind the museum and just across Hyde Park from the city. East Sydney is between the city and Kings Cross so it's very convenient. This is a very straight-forward place but it's clean and some of the recently done up rooms are quite pleasant. A catch is that you can check in only between 9 am and 7 pm on weekdays, 9 am and noon on Saturdays – any other time you're out of luck. The cost is $10 a night per person, but by the week it's only $45 for one, $80 for two.

Bondi Beach You can get to Bondi from the city by bus but it's far quicker to get the Eastern Suburbs train to Bondi Junction and change to a bus (buy a rail/bus ticket). There are quite a few places around Bondi, the most popular is probably at 11A Consett Avenue where the *Thelellen Lodge* (tel 30 1521) has room-only rates from $16 to $25 or share rooms at $12.50 per person, $2.50 for a light breakfast. The pleasant rooms have fridges and tea-making equipment. Next door is the *Bondi Beach Guest House* (tel 371 0202) at 11, which is also neat and clean. There's tea-making in all the rooms and a big kitchen.

A little worn and tattered but still serviceable, the *Hotel Biltmore* (tel 30 4660) is at 110 Campbell Parade, right across from the beach. The friendly woman who runs it has rooms at just $10 single, $15 double or by the week for $40/50 and up. There's a guest kitchen and a rather primitive TV lounge.

Further along at 2 Campbell Parade is the *Thelellen Beach Inn* (tel 30 5333), one of the big, old Bondi hotels with a variety of rooms from $23 a double and up. Each has a fridge, TV and tea-making. Also in this mould is the *Hotel Bondi* (30 3271) at

the corner of Campbell Parade and Curlewis St. A variety of rooms from $20 a standard single, $30 a double which include TV and tea-making facilities. There are more rooms at the front, with the view, for up to $42 with complete facilities.

The old *Hotel Astra*, a fine building with a prime location at 32 Campbell Parade, is now a rather posh retirement home; come back in a few years. The *Bondi Lodge* (tel 30 5863) is not officially an old folks home, but it may as well be. It mainly has guests by the week with rooms at $14/20 for singles/doubles.

Even cheaper is the guest house with no name at 124 Curlewis St (tel 30 9341). It too seems to be mainly semi-permanents, but younger ones. On my visit the place seemed a little on the rough side but it may be different in peak season. Its room charges start at $8 a night.

Over at 264 Bondi Rd is the *Sharon Private Hotel* (tel 130 1495), a very simple place (none of the rooms have washbasins) and it's a bit noisy. Rooms are inexpensive in the $15 to $18 range and there are cooking facilities.

The Bondi Beach Motel (tel 30 5344) at 68 Gould St, right in the centre of things, has been recommended. Rooms aren't cheap at $40 but have a fridge and tea-making facilities. Breakfast is available and there is a roof garden with a view of the beach area.

Coogee Coogee is down the coast a bit from Bondi. There are a couple of places worth mentioning here. The *Grand Pacific Private Hotel* (tel 665 6301) at the corner of Carr and Beach Sts costs from $10 to $18 single or $20 to $35 double. Weekly rates are $49 to $66 for singles, $80 to $120 for doubles. There's a shared kitchen and laundry and it's pleasantly close to the beach.

At the corner of Carr and Arden Sts, the *Oceanic Hotel* (tel 665 5221) charges $12 for singles, and $20 to $25 for doubles and twins in the more spartan rooms or from

$30 to $35 in the more luxurious ones. The cheaper rooms are usually full. This is a hotel with other attractions – popular bars and music on weekends.

North Shore There are a number of private hotels on the north shore but they tend to be up a notch in price. The *Elite Private Hotel* (tel 922 2060) is just across the bridge at 133 Carabella St, Kirribilli and has rooms from $22 for singles, $32 for doubles and $120/180 weekly. Tea and coffee are provided but a light breakfast is an extra $3.

At 3 Milson Rd, Cremorne Point, the *Waldorf Private Hotel* (tel 90 2621) is very handy to the ferry. Bed & breakfast is $22 single, $35 twin and $75/95 weekly, and like the Elite there's a guest kitchen.

If you don't mind being as far out as Manly (a nice trip to the city on the Manly ferry) then there are a few places to stay. Very close to the ferry is the *Manly Lodge* (tel 977 8514) at 22 Victoria Parade. It's a nice looking place with a Thai restaurant downstairs, and the beach is just up the street. Singles are $15, doubles $25 or $50/85 weekly. The *Sun Surf* (tel 977 3779) at 96 Ocean Beach Rd, North Steyne has the same prices.

Over at 61 Pittwater St is the *Pacific Coast Budget Hotel* (tel 977 6177), formerly a Peoples' Palace. It's old and simple but has a certain comfortable character which the temperance hotels in this small chain seem to exude. Charges are $14/24 for singles/doubles which includes a light breakfast.

Motels The most central motel with a reasonable tariff is *Cron-Lodge Motel* (tel 331 2433) at 289 Crown St, Surry Hills. Rooms cost $25 to $30, extra people are $5 and they have a fridge, tea and coffee making facilities, toaster, crockery and cutlery.

At Bondi the *Alice Motel* (tel 30 5231) at 30 Fletcher St is excellent value, particularly if you want weekly or longer rates. Rooms are the usual motel standard

(although the TVs are only black & white) and there's even a pool. Costs are $28 single, $32 to $40 for doubles and twins. In the off-season there are cheaper weekly rates.

Another fairly convenient low-priced place is the *Esron Motel* (tel 398 7022) at 96 St Pauls St, Randwick (between Coogee and the city) where fully equipped singles/doubles cost from $25/29 and again there's a swimming pool.

If you don't mind being out a bit the *Bombora Motel* (tel 977 5461) at 46 Malvern Avenue, Manly has all the usual facilities including a light breakfast included in its prices which are from $20 for singles, $30 for doubles. It's only one block from the beach.

Colleges The usual rules apply – vacations only, students for preference. Best bets are the two '*International Houses*'. The following colleges are at the University of NSW, Kensington. *New College* (tel 662 6066) costs $16 for students, $34 for non-students with full board, $10 and $24 for bed & breakfast and $22 for room-only for a non-student. They also have a cheaper weekly rates and bed & breakfast only rates. *Warrane College* (tel 662 6199) is a Catholic college which takes men only – $12 for students, $16 for non-students. *Kensington College* takes conference groups only. At *International House* (tel 663 0418) full board is $16 a day for students, $20 for non-students.

A lot of the colleges at the University of Sydney, Camperdown, tend to be booked out with conferences. Ones to try are *Wesley College* (tel 51 2024), *Women's College* (tel 51 1195), *St John's College* (tel 51 1240) which is closed December and January, *Sancta Sophia College* (tel 51 2467) which usually has conferences and otherwise prefers students, *St Andrew's College* (tel 51 1449) and *International House* (tel 660 5364). These all charge around $15 a night.

Camping Unfortunately Sydney's campsites tend to be rather a long way out of town and many of the closer places are for caravans only. The closest one to the city which does allow camping is the *Sundowner Caravan Park*, North Ryde, about 14 km out. The sites listed below are within a 30-km radius of the centre but if you're planning to camp phone and check first, some may only permit caravans.

Woronora Caravan Park (tel 521 2291), Menai Rd, Woronora, 30 km south, sites $8 to $10, on-site vans $20 to $25 per day.

Sheralee Tourist Caravan Park (tel 599 7161), 88 Bryant St, Rockdale, 13 km south, sites $10, on-site vans $18 to $38 per day.

Bass Hill Tourist Park (tel 72 9670), 713 Hume Highway, Bass Hill, 23 km south, sites $6, on-site vans $16 to $20 per day.

Sundowner Ryde (tel 88 1933), Lane Cove Rd, North Ryde, 14 km north, camping $8, on-site vans $29 to $33 per day.

Van Village Caravan Park (tel 88 3649), Plassey Rd, North Ryde, 14 km north, sites $8 to $9, on-site vans $24 to $26 per day.

Lakeside Caravan Park (tel 913 7845), Ocean Parade, Narrabeen, 26 km north, sites $5.

Ramsgate Beach Caravan Park (tel 529 7329), 289 The Grand Parade, Ramsgate, 18 km south, sites $12, on-site vans $25.

Places to Eat

Melbourne's food snobs like to look down their sensitive noses at Sydney eateries but actually there's probably little difference. If you're going to eat out in Sydney very often a good book is *Cheap Eats in Sydney* by Oliver Freeman and Robyn Fleming, $4.95. Sydney doesn't have the same distinct food areas the way Melbourne does – you'll find interesting restaurants all over Sydney: in the centre (particularly near Central Station and Circular Quay) but also in Paddo, Balmain, Glebe, Newtown, Redfern and most of the beach suburbs.

Greek There are plenty of Greek places around town. *The Minerva* at 285 Elizabeth St looks more expensive than it actually is. Most dishes are in the $5 to $7 range. The *Hellenic Club* (tel 264 5883) on the 5th Floor at 251 Elizabeth St, overlooking Hyde Park, is open Monday to Friday from 12 noon to 3 pm and for dinner Monday to Saturday from 5 to 9 pm. Main courses are in the $6 to $9 range. *The Illiad*, around the corner at 126 Liverpool St, is popular but more expensive than its neighbours.

Away from the centre, in the basement at 336 Pitt St, *Diethnes* is Greek in the more spartan tradition. Open Monday to Saturday, it has low prices and lots of good food.

If you're still in the souvlakia and moussaka mood, *Dilina* is at 158 Redfern St in 'beautiful' inner-city Redfern and does excellent-value set meals. They have Greek wines and are also closed on Sundays. Also good is the *Kakavia* at 458 Elizabeth St, Surry Hills. A three course lunch is $7.50; at dinner main courses are $6.50 to $8. There's lots of lamb, moussaka, etc and music on Friday and Saturday nights.

Italian The humble pizzeria is everywhere in Sydney. If a (very) late night pizza is needed then try *Pinnochio's Pizzeria* at 87 Darlinghurst St, Kings Cross – pizzas range from $4 to $8. They also have many other Italian dishes. *Angelo's* at 25 Oxford St, Paddington, is another popular pizza specialist.

If you follow the crowds, around 12.30pm, into a dull-looking little house in Chapel St, East Sydney (close to the Crown and Stanley Sts junction) you will find yourself in *No Names*. So called because it has no name, no sign, nothing but dirt cheap and very filling spaghetti and one or two other daily dishes. The starter is $3, main course $4. This is definitely a Sydney eating experience not to miss but it has become so 'in' of late that you may have to queue to get in (and no longer does a bottle of Fanta arrive with a plonk on your table at meal time, although Fanta is still about all there is on offer to drink). It's open until 9 pm every day.

Another popular Italian specialist is the

Italo-Australian Club upstairs at 727 George St, down towards the Central Railway Station. The restaurant is open to the public but is no longer very cheap and the food isn't always so special. Main courses are $6 to $8 and there are some non-Italian items as well.

Italian in name only, the *Old Spaghetti Factory* at 80 George St, The Rocks, is good cheap fun and the range of spaghettis (with recommendations on the wall to avoid spaghetti with chocolate sauce) are mass market but not at all bad. The factory is full of Victoriana and odd bits and pieces – everything from confessional booths in the bar to a Bondi tram shooting through the middle of the dining area. It's a Sydney showpiece not to be missed.

At Bondi Beach at 118 Campbell Parade is *Gelateria Italia*, a very popular place for inexpensive home-made pasta. This is also a good place for breakfast from Thursday to Tuesday.

Middle East In Surry Hills, where Cleveland and Elizabeth Sts meet, there are a host of Lebanese places most of which are good or even better than good. Try *Abdul's*, right on the corner, for an excellent-value square meal in unpretentious surroundings and good take-aways. Across the street is a small café-like spot that's very cheap and good – falafels, kebabs, and the vine leaves at 70c are tasty.

Emad's at 298 Cleveland St, just up from the corner, has good food in slightly posher surroundings. A couple of doors down at 302, *Salinda's* is also excellent value with an $8 fixed-price meal and a belly dancer on Friday and Saturday nights.

At 423 Cleveland St you can shift across to Turkey at *Erciyes* to try 'pide', a sort of Turkish pizza which is cheap and very good. There's also another one a few doors down. If you get out here and change your mind about what you want to eat, there's *L'Aubbergade*, a French place that's been here since the '50's. It's more expensive than the Lebanese, but good. A three

course meal can be had for $9.95 and it's open Monday to Thursday. Fish, lamb or rabbit might be on the blackboard.

The *Ya-Habibi* at 100 Campbell Parade, Bondi, is Middle East by the seashore – very good food at good prices. It used to be known as the Sheik's Tent.

Chinese Just a short walk up George St from the city is Sydney's Chinatown, based around Dixon St, Haymarket. Dixon St itself is a colourful pedestrian mall with trees, benches and lamps with hanging wind chimes. The area has a whole flock of restaurants but for a quick introduction try the food in the *Dixon Centre*, the modern building at the corner of Little Hay and Dixon Sts. Stalls offer food from Japan, Vietnam, Thailand, Malaysia, Singapore and other Asian countries. Meals are just $3 or so and the food is not only good it's also pretty authentic. You'll see many Orientals bent over bowls of noodle soups. Another food centre is in the newish semi-pagoda-style place at the corner of Dixon and Goulburn Sts.

The large *Old Tai Yuen* at 110 Hay St is more expensive but has been around a long time and has a good reputation. Across the street the *Mandarin Gardens* is also said to be good. Next door the Chinese pastry shop sells hot meat or vegetable pastries – the curried ones are not bad at all.

The *Eastern* at 52 and the *Lean Sun Low* at 54 Dixon St are two pretty standard places and they share the same kitchen. The *Shanghai Village* near Hay St has an extensive buffet for $7.50 in the evenings from 5.30 to 7.30 pm, a dollar less at lunch. Cheaper, more basic places are *Greenjade* and, a few doors down at 64, *Hong's Garden Seafood*, which is open to 2 am except Sundays when it closes at 10 pm.

Moving out a bit, the licensed *Malaya* at 787 George St is a long standing favourite with local uni students for its reasonably cheap Malay-Chinese food. The prices haven't been altered too much despite additions of more carpet and fancy decorations.

For a Chinese smorgasboard in the city, good value can be found at the *Lantern Restaurant* at 147 King St where the price is just $3.90, but it's closed on Sunday. The *Hing-Wah* in the Remington Centre, opposite Hyde Park on Liverpool St, offers a take-away lunch for only $2.90.

Out at Bondi Junction the *Yung Sang* is a good restaurant and take-away on the corner of Bronte Rd and Ebley St. Or obscurely located at 80 The Corso, Manly, you can get excellent value Singaporean-Chinese food at the *Manly Asian Kitchen*. It's on the mall but the door is around the back in the car park.

Other Ethnics For Indonesian, there's the *Java* at 435 Pitt St with most main dishes around $6. The *Bandung Indonesian* is a BYO at 142 Victoria Avenue in the Cross; from $4.50 for a nasi goreng. The *Bali* at 80 Oxford St, Darlinghurst near the Ansett terminal is simple, inexpensive, tasty and very popular. Most dishes are $6 to $7.50 although some are less; the lumpia at $1.20 is great.

Sydney also has lots of Vietnamese restaurants, many of them excellent value like *Tien* at 95-97 Glebe Point Rd, Glebe. It's open 5.30 to 10 pm everyday.

Glebe Point Rd, from Broadway up quite a few blocks towards the city, contains an interesting array of small shops, antique stores and numerous restaurants and cafés, many of them cheap. There's *BJ's*, a home-cooking place at number 99; a Lebanese place nearby, and at number 101, the *Rasputin*, a more expensive Russian restaurant.

A real Sydney favourite of mine is *Salama* at 37 Cameron St, Birchgrove (that's really Balmain). It's North African, the food is delicious and you can sit up or lounge back on cushions on the floor – it's remarkably low-priced and open Tuesday to Saturday.

Among Oxford St's many restaurants

the *Balkan* at 209 specialises in those two basic Yugoslavian dishes raznjici and cevapcici. Ask for a pola pola and you'll get half of each. It's basic and straight-forward food, filling, very cheap and definitely for real meat eaters only. The Balkan is closed on Tuesdays. There is a second location open for dinner only a few doors down at 215 Oxford St.

Down at 129 is the *Kaffe Mirabell* for Austrian and Swiss fare. A vegetarian dish is $4.80, others are $5 to $7 including a salad and there are home-made desserts. It's open 12 noon to 3 pm and 6 pm to late, daily except Sunday.

North of the harbour the *Curry Bazaar* at 334 Pacific Highway, Crows Nest, has good Indian food with main courses at $7.50 and $8. It's open Tuesday to Saturday.

Vegetarian The *Whole Meal* is a natural health food restaurant on the 1st floor of the Angel Arcade, 121 Pitt St, just down from Martin Place. Everything is really fresh and the prices are quite reasonable.

The *Hare Krishnas* put on a free meal at 112 Darlinghurst Rd, just south of Kings Cross, between 5 and 7 pm, which may include 'spiritual' food, of course. If you want to eat without participating in the service go around the block to the rear entrance.

Nearby at 187 Darlinghurst Rd is the very cheap *Eastern Noodle Shop* with things like noodles and vegetables at $2.50. *Badde Manors* is a popular café on Glebe Point Rd at the corner of Francis St. It's a nice casual place with vegetarian dishes, coffees and desserts, in an inter-esting part of town.

The *Pure & Natural Food Co* has salads, quiches, smoothies, and is a good place for breakfast. There are tables inside and out and it's in the city on Liverpool St at the corner of Castlereagh St.

In the city centre there are a couple of *Sanitarium* health food places. They're basically take-aways, very popular for lunchtime sandwiches. One is on King St between Pitt and George Sts, the other on Hunter St. For those with more time *Laurie's Vegetarian Diner* on Elizabeth St on the corner of Wentworth St does interesting vegetarian food.

In Bondi Junction, at 288 Oxford St is *Sennin*, a very nice place with an imaginative menu. Lunches are $4 to $5 from Wednesday to Friday only. Nearby and cheaper is *Jester's* at 87 Oxford St for sandwiches, jaffles and shakes.

At the corner of Hall and O'Brien Sts in Bondi Beach you'll find *Positive Vibrations*, open 5 pm to 1 am with a great variety of sweets and blender drinks. They also have an eclectic, off-beat menu of low priced meals and salads. It's worth a visit – where else can you get a Congo-Bongo, which includes smoked salmon and yoghurt?

Lentil As Anything, a health food restaurant at 38 Pittwater Drive, Manly, is good although more expensive. They have interesting pastas, curries, soups and it's BYO. It's open from 6.30 pm but closed Sundays and Mondays.

Odds, Ends, Basics & Others The *Penny Farthing Coffee Lounge*, 128 Liverpool St, is a good place for breakfast, sandwiches and cheap daily lunches. Also good for breakfast (eggs, toast and coffee for $2.55) is the 2nd floor cafeteria in *Woolworths* at the corner of Park and George Sts. They have cheap meals too.

For crepes, the *Crepe Connection* is reasonably priced if you stay away from the seafood. It's upstairs in the Pitt St Plaza, near the Hilton.

The *Elysee Coffee Lounge*, on the corner of Pitt and Bathurst Sts, is ordinary but is central, cheap and has a good selection of lunches and light meals.

Home-made Sweets & Snacks is a well named, small café at 181 Hay St. It also has croissants and soup.

Another place worth a mention is the cafeteria on the 5th floor of the Qantas building, where three-course meals can be had for $3. It seems this place is a corporate café where the public is welcome.

At 711 George St near the railway station, the *Mekong* is a cafeteria-style Cambodian place with all dishes under $5. The food is all on display and looks very good.

For a good hamburger there's the *Green Park Diner*, a stylish gay/trendy place at 219 Oxford St.

At Circular Quay the *Sorrento Cafe* is the place for fresh fish; a delicious John Dory lunch goes for $5. Also down at this end of the city *Phillip's Foote*, at 101 George St in the Rocks, has a good barbecue.

Up at Kings Cross the *Astoria* on Darlinghurst Rd, round the corner from the fountain, is famous for its good value, basic, home-cooked, Australian-style food. You can get a big meal for around $3.20. Still in the Cross, *New York* at 23 Bayswater Rd is another basic place offering straightforward food at very low prices. Another old-fashioned place offering great value is *Johnnie's Fish Cafe* at 57A Fitzroy St, Surry Hills, where there's take-away fish & chips and also eat-in facilities.

Back in the Cross the *Cactus Cafe* at 150 Victoria St is a small, more expensive place serving French-style food but with some exotic spicing from the Seychelles. It's open Wednesday to Sunday from 6 pm until late and has main courses from $10 to $13 plus desserts and coffee. At the top of William St by the Cross the *Music Cafe* is an easy going place with lasagna, quiches and other simple dishes from around $5.

Meals with a View If you're visiting the opera house and want to eat, consider the *Harbour Restaurant* – it's overpriced and the food is nothing to get excited about but the view is not to be missed. Just make sure it is a sunny day so you can sit outside. The expensive *Bennelong Restaurant* is to be avoided at all costs.

At Watsons Bay on Marine Parade, *Doyle's on the Beach* has good but very expensive seafood although the view and atmosphere are unsurpassed. It's very popular and doesn't take bookings so you've just got to get there early. Make sure the sun is shining – you go to Doyle's in order to eat outside.

The *Australian Restaurant*, on the 67th floor atop one of the country's tallest office buildings, offers great views and meals at a fair price. Salad with steak or fish, followed by a cheese-plate and coffee is $12. It's in the MLC Centre in Martin Place.

Another place to consider for the setting as much as the food is the *Sydney Tower* at Level 2 atop the Centrepoint Tower. There are actually two restaurants; the self-service carvery is much cheaper although still expensive. A complete revolution of the revolving dining room takes just over an hour.

The glossy *Pier One* centre in the Rocks also has meals with a view.

Chains & Pub Food The *McDonald* plague started its march around Australia in Sydney so there are plenty of them. There's one up on George St done up in art nouveau style – it's worth a hamburger just to look at it. There are also plenty of *Pizza Huts* and *Kentucky Frieds*.

There are two *Lovely Lady Pancake Parlours* in the city, at 10 Hickson St in the Rocks and at 485 George St, also one at Bondi. You'll see these restaurants in other towns; they never shut and offer a variety of pancake meals from $3.30 to $8.

The huge *Centrepoint Tavern*, under the central Centrepoint shopping complex, is popular for it's large assortment of quite reasonably priced meals and lower-priced children's dishes. The *London Tavern* at 119 Pitt St is similar and busy. There are also lots of regular counter meal style pubs – try the one across from the mining museum in the rocks.

Locations Since Sydney's restaurants are not found in specific quarters to anything like the same extent as Melbourne's a location guide follows:

City *Australian Restaurant* (international), *Centrepoint Tavern* (international), *Crepe Connection* (crepes), *Diethnes* (Greek), *Dixon Centre* (Chinese), *Eastern* (Chinese), *Greenjade* (Chinese), *Harbour Restaurant* (international), *The Hellenic Club* (Greek), *Hing-Wah* (Chinese), *Home-made Sweets & Snacks* (snacks), *Hong's Garden Seafood* (Chinese), *The Illiad* (Greek), *Italo-Australian Club* (Italian), *Java* (Indonesian), *Lantern Restaurant* (Chinese), *Laurie's Vegetarian Diner* (vegetarian), *Lean Sun Low* (Chinese), *London Tavern* (international), *Lovely Lady Pancakes* (pancakes), *Malaya* (Malaysian-Chinese), *Mandarin Gardens* (Chinese), *Mekong* (Cambodian), *The Minerva* (Greek), *Old Spaghetti Factory* (Italian), *Old Tai Yuen* (Chinese), *Penny Farthing Coffee Lounge* (sandwiches, breakfast), *Phillip's Foote* (barbecue), *Pier One* (international), *Pure & Natural Food Company* (sandwiches, breakfast), *Sanitarium* (sandwiches), *Shanghai Village* (Chinese), *Sorrento Cafe* (fish & chips), *Sydney Tower* (international), *Whole Meal* (vegetarian), *Woolworth's Cafeteria* (snacks, breakfast)

Inner City *Abdul's* (Lebanese, Surry Hills), *Angelo's* (pizza, Paddington), *Astoria* (home cooking, Kings Cross), *L'Aubbergade* (French, Surry Hills), *Badde Manors* (vegetarian, Glebe), *Bali* (Indonesian-Chinese, Darlinghurst), *Balkan* (Yugoslav, Darlinghurst), *Bandung Indonesian* (Kings Cross), *BJs* (home cooking, Glebe), *Cactus Cafe* (French-Seychelles, Kings Cross), *Curry Bazaar* (Indian, Crows Nest), *Dilina* (Greek, Redfern), *Eastern Noodle Shop* (Chinese & vegetarian, Kings Cross), *Elysee Coffee Lounge* (snacks), *Emad's* (Lebanese, Surry Hills), *Erciyes* (Turkish, Surry Hills), *Green Park Diner* (hamburgers, Darlinghurst), *Jesters* (sandwiches, Bondi Junction), *Johnnie's Fish Cafe* (fish & chips, Surry Hills), *Kaffe Mirabell* (Austrian, Darlinghurst), *Kakavia* (Greek, Surry Hills), *New York* (home cooking, Kings Cross), *No Names* (Italian, East Sydney), *Pinnochio's Pizzeria* (Italian, Kings Cross), *Rasputin* (Russian, Glebe), *Salama* (North African, Birchgrove), *Salinda's* (Lebanese, Surry Hills), *Sennin* (vegetarian, Bondi Junction), *Tien* (Vietnamese, Glebe), *Yung Sang* (Chinese, Bondi Junction)

Beaches *Doyle's on the Beach* (seafood, Watsons Bay), *Gelateria Italia* (Italian, Bondi), *Lentil as Anything* (vegetarian, Manly), *Lovely Lady Pancakes* (pancakes, Bondi), *Manly Asian Kitchen* (Singapore-Chinese, Manly), *Positive*

Vibrations (vegetarian, Bondi), *Ya-Habibi* (Lebanese, Bondi)

All Over *Kentucky Fried*, *McDonalds*, *Pizza Huts*

Entertainment

Listen to the What's On service at 6.30 pm on radio *2JJJ* for info or check for listings in the *Daily Telegraph* on Thursdays or the *Sydney Morning Herald's* Metro section on Fridays.

A lot of Sydney evening entertainment takes place in the Leagues Clubs or other 'private' clubs where the profits from the assembled ranks of one-armed bandits (you're in gambling country) finances big name acts at low, low prices. They may be 'members only' for the locals but as an interstate, or even better, international, visitor you're generally welcome to drop in. Simply ring ahead and ask, wave your interstate driving licence or your passport at the door. They're a Sydney institution so if you get a chance visit one. The most glittering and lavish of the lot is the *St Georges Leagues Club.*

There are several casino-type gambling clubs where visitors can lose money. *What's On* and other tourist guides advertise such places.

Music Sydney doesn't have the same pub music scene that you get in Melbourne although there are a fair few places where you can count on something going on most nights of the week. What Sydney does have is a whole stack of pleasant wine bars/bistros where for a low (even free) entry charge you can catch the music and also get a meal. Some wine bars, pubs, discos which are worth a look include:

The Basement (tel 27 9727), 29 Reiby Place, Circular Quay – Monday to Wednesday till 12.30 am, Thursday to Saturday till 3 am – free admission except after 10 pm on Friday and Saturday when it's $3 – excellent modern jazz.

Soup Plus Restaurant (tel 29 7728), 38 Pitt St, has straighter jazz in the basement daily except Sunday.

The Cock 'n Bull Tavern, corner Bronte & Ebley Sts, Bondi Junction – live music Tuesday, Wednesday, Sunday – disco Thursday to Saturday.

Salina's (in the Coogee Bay Hotel) (tel 665 0000), Coogee Bay Rd, Coogee Bay – Friday and Saturday – cover charge varies – rock.

Grand National (tel 32 3096), 161 Underwood St, Paddington – Friday and Saturday – live rock – free

Astra (tel 30 1201), Bondi Beach – Thursday to Sunday – sometimes a cover charge – rock – can get a bit rough.

The Royal Hotel, Bondi Rd at the beach – live rock – free.

Paradise Club, basement on Darlinghurst Rd, between the fountain and Kings Cross station, near McDonalds – every night except Sunday, 7 pm to 3 am – free – rock and pop – cheap food.

Benson's Wine Bar, 103 Oxford St, Bondi Junction – Tuesday to Sunday till 4 am – cover up to $3, Thursday to Saturday – rock – meals available.

Musicians Club, 94 Chalmers St, Surry Hills – Wednesday or Thursday to Saturday or Sunday – acoustic concert on Thursdays, bar section is closed.

There are many, many other places. For rock try the *Kings Cross Rex* next to the El Alamein Fountain in the Cross or the *Windsor Castle Hotel* in Paddo. For jazz you could try the *Booth St Dispensary* wine bar in Annandale, the *Sydney Brasserie*, in the city centre at 9a Barrack St or the *And Now for Something Completely Different Restaurant* in Chatswood.

Nightclubs Most nightclubs have stiff cover charges, but there are a few exceptions. The *Exchange Hotel* at the bottom of Oxford St is one. The dress restrictions are not too severe and although it's a predominantly gay place, there are many straights there and the atmosphere is good. It has three bars and two dance-floors and drink prices are the same as in a pub.

Stranded, in the Strand Arcade in the city costs $4 to get in, is well done and has a good young crowd. In Paddington there is *Paddos* in Elizabeth St.

Theatre Sydney has a selection of theatres and more adventurous new-theatre places. *The Nimrod* (tel 69 5003), 500 Elizabeth St, Surry Hills, has both a downstairs and upstairs stage and often simultaneous programmes. Or there's the *New Theatre* (tel 519 3403), 542 King St, Newtown, which isn't really so new at all since it's been going for years, and many others.

Film You'll find interesting films at the *New Mandarin*, 150 Elizabeth St, between Liverpool and Goulburn Sts – Chinese and repertory style films are regularly featured. The *Sydney University Union Theatre* can always be counted on for something good and at low prices. *The National Film Theatre of Australia* shows classic films at the Opera House and at the Paddington Town Hall Cinema.

Other non-commercial (or less-commercial?) cinemas worth trying are the *Double Bay Village Twin*, the *Rose Bay Wintergarden* and the *Academy Twin* in Paddington. Almost a sight in itself is the *State Movie Theatre* on Market St between Pitt and George Sts. Wow! They don't make them like this anymore.

If mainstream movies are what you want, Hoyts cinemas are half-priced on Tuesdays.

Odds & Ends In the summer there are free music and rock performances in parks on the weekends. There's music at lunchtime in Martin Place between Pitt and Castlereagh Sts. You can always sit and listen to the buskers around the Cross and a wander through the Cross at night is always an education! Try and see something at the Opera House – they have film shows, live theatre, classical music, opera and even rock concerts.

Getting There

Air Sydney's Kingsford Smith Airport, better known as Mascot because that's where it's situated, is Australia's busiest, both for domestic and for international flights. It's fairly central which makes

getting to or from it a breeze but it also means that flights have to stop at 10 pm due to noise regulations. The main runway stretches out into Botany Bay and these problems of space restrictions and noise hassles have prompted lots of discussion, but no action, on building a new airport.

You can fly into Sydney from all the usual international points and from all over Australia. Between Melbourne and Sydney, for example, there are flights every hour for $140 ($117 standby). Other flights include Adelaide $192 ($154), Alice Springs $309 ($273), Brisbane $146 ($117), Canberra $80 ($64), Perth $365 ($292).

Bus There are lots of bus services to and from Sydney with the big two operators and a host of others. Prices have actually gone down on some routes over the past couple of years. Ansett Pioneer and Greyhound both have services to or from Canberra ($25, 5½ hours), Melbourne ($35, 14½ hours), Adelaide ($69, 24 hours) and Brisbane ($35, 17 hours). Often there are alternate routes between the cities – you can, for example, travel Brisbane-Sydney via the coast or via New England, Melbourne-Sydney via the Hume and Canberra or via the coast.

Ansett Pioneer (tel 268 1881) operate from the Ansett terminal at Oxford Square, Oxford St, Darlinghurst. Greyhound (tel 268 1414) are at the Greyhound Terminal, also at Oxford Square. Two other companies operating regularly scheduled services to north NSW and Queensland are Skennars and McCaffertys.

There are quite a few independent bus operators with interstate services to and from Sydney. Across Australia Coachlines (tel 264 3691) is at Eden Travel, Shop 22, Wellesley Arcade, 210 Pitt St, and other agents. They operate air-conditioned, non-smoking coaches between Perth and Sydney twice a week. Fares to or from Sydney include Melbourne $30, Adelaide $60, Perth $130, no concessions.

VIP Express (tel 232 5166), with an

office in Imperial Arcade, Pitt St, goes to Brisbane or Melbourne for $25. Deluxe Coachlines (tel 212 4888) are at the Sydney Coach Terminal, corner of Castlereagh and Hay Sts.

In the introductory NSW travel section note the bus travel restrictions in NSW. On many routes you are not allowed to use the interstate bus services for intrastate stops, unless you're on a bus pass ticket. Thus, for example, you cannot take a Sydney-Brisbane bus to Newcastle or to other intermediate stops.

Rail All the interstate and principal regional services operate to and from the Central Railway Station. Between Melbourne and Sydney there are two overnight services daily (the Southern Aurora and the Spirit of Progress) plus the Intercapital Daylight Express from Monday to Saturday. The trip takes 12½ to 14 hours and the fares are $59 in economy, $83 in 1st. In 1st class, sleeping berths are an extra $33. There are no sleeping berths in economy. You can take a car on the Southern Aurora for $70. Monday to Saturday the Canberra-Monaro Express departs Sydney at 7.30 am and arrives Canberra at 12.19 pm. The fare is $16.

Travelling north there's a daily overnight service to Brisbane, the Brisbane Limited Express, which takes 16 hours and costs $59 economy, $83 in 1st class. You can also train to Murwillumbah, just south of the Queensland border, from where a connecting bus runs into the Gold Coast. This trip takes 16½ hours and the fare is $42 in economy, $58 in 1st. A sleeping berth is an extra $33 on top of the 1st class fare. This is a much cheaper way of getting to Queensland, especially if you want to start your Queensland travels on the Gold Coast. Cars can be taken on this train for $84.

Direct Sydney-Adelaide train connections are made four days a week by taking the Sydney-Perth Indian-Pacific between Sydney and Peterborough via Broken Hill and the connecting service

between Peterborough and Adelaide. The trip takes about 29 hours and the fares are $108 in economy or $180 in 1st class plus $33 for a 1st class sleeper. The Indian Pacific fare includes meals. You can also travel between the two cities via Melbourne and in that case the fares are a straight combination of the Melbourne-Sydney and Adelaide-Melbourne fares – this is cheaper than the direct route via Broken Hill. A third alternative is to take the 'Speedlink' train-bus connection. This takes you to Albury by the high speed XPT train where you connect with a V-Line coach. The fare is $68.50 in economy, $75 in 1st and the trip takes about 20 hours. It's faster and cheaper than other alternatives.

Sydney-Perth is on the four times weekly Indian-Pacific service, see the Perth section for more details on this train service. There's also a once-weekly direct service from Sydney via Broken Hill and Tarcoola to Alice Springs on the new Ghan line.

Services within the state include Sydney-Newcastle $10, Sydney-Albury $34, Sydney-Griffith $34.50, Sydney-Orange $19, Sydney-Wollongong $3.60. All these fares are economy. There's a 14-day Nurail Pass allowing unlimited use of railway services within the state. It's available in 1st class only and costs $120, no reduction for students. See the NSW introductory travel section for more details on rail travel.

Getting Around
For information on trains, buses and ferries, call 29 2622, 7 am to 10 pm every day.

Airport Transport The international and domestic terminals at Mascot Airport are some distance apart – a bus between the two costs $1.20. The private Kingsford Smith Airport Bus Service operates every hour between 6 am and 6 pm and costs $2.80. It runs every half hour, will take you to the door of your hotel or hostel but you must phone 677 3221 at least an hour beforehand to book.

The Yellow Airport Bus, part of the city bus system, runs every 20 minutes or so from the city and costs $2. Two stops are Circular Quay and Central Station. It's about a 30 minute trip to Circular Quay, 80c between the two airport terminals. Catch either of these from outside the terminal entrances.

The Watts Coach goes to/from Wollongong for $6 six times daily on weekdays but on weekends only if booked, phone 295 100.

If you're willing to walk half an hour from the Arncliff Station you can get into the city by train for just $1. There are some public bus services from the domestic terminals to the city (302 and 385 to Circular Quay) or Bondi Junction (064) but they operate mainly for airport workers and principally on weekdays.

A taxi between the airport and city will cost you about $10, depending on where you're going, possibly more if the traffic is heavy. Hertz, Budget and Avis have desks at the airport. Luggage lockers at the airport cost 50c.

In the city, TAA's main centre (tel 693 3333) is in the old Qantas building, corner of Phillip and Hunter Sts in Chifley Square, while Ansett's (tel 268 1111) is just beyond Hyde Park at Oxford Square on the corner of Oxford and Riley Sts.

Bus There are extensive bus services in Sydney but they are very slow in comparison to the rail services. Most are run

by the Urban Transit Authority, but some suburban services are run by private operators. Circular Quay, Wynyard Square and Central Railway Station are the main bus stops.

There's a 777 free city bus service which goes from York St down King St, along Pitt St, into Park St, around the Domain, down Market St and Clarence St and back to its starting point. The 666 free service operates from Hunter St near Wynyard Station on a loop out to the Art Gallery and back.

The Sydney Explorer is a tourist bus service which operates a continuous loop around the tourist sights of the city at roughly 15-minute intervals from 9.30 am to 5.30 pm daily. It costs $7 for the day, covers 18 km and 20 attractions, and you can hop on and off wherever you like. It would be much cheaper to get around these places by the ordinary bus (in fact it's possible to walk around the places visited by the bus), but the Explorer makes it easier as you don't have to work out the bus routes. It goes from Circular Quay via the Opera House, Mrs Macquarie's Chair, the Art Gallery, Kings Cross, Woolloomooloo, Central Station and back through the Rocks to Circular Quay. You also get concessions on the Manly and Taronga Park ferry for that day, and various other concessions.

Rail If you can get to your destination in Sydney by rail it's generally far quicker than by bus. Quite a lot of Sydney is covered by the suburban rail service, which has frequent trains. For state rail info call 20 942.

Ferries Sydney's ferries are one of the nicest ways of getting around in Australia. Apart from the harbour itself there are also services at the Royal National Park to the south and north on the Pittwater. Not only are there the fine old harbour ferries (Manly $1.10c, other places generally 90c) but also hydrofoils to Manly ($2). A pleasant intro to harbour ferries is the short 80c hop across to Taronga Park Zoo (you can also get a return ticket that includes admission to the zoo for $7).

All the harbour ferries depart from Circular Quay, close to where the original settlement in Sydney was made. The Urban Transit Authority has a free ferry and hydrofoil timetable for the Sydney Harbour services. Services on the Pittwater operate from Church Point and Palm Beach. There's also a service from Palm Beach to Patonga, which is also the first leg of a cruise up Cowan Waters. From Patonga it's possible to bus (changing once on the way) to Gosford.

There are a variety of more comprehensive harbour cruises as well as lunchtime and supper cruises. The Urban Transit Authority ones, if they are still running, are the best value. Many other companies offer harbour trips. Just walk around Circular Quay and you'll get leaflets detailing them. Cheapest is the 'Cat' from Jetty 2, running trips every half-hour, Monday to Friday, up to Watson's Bay for $5. The Sydney Harbour Explorer costs $9, permits re-boarding all day and operates a Circular Quay-Opera House-Watsons Bay-Taronga Park-The Rocks-Circular Quay circuit every 90 minutes. Captain Cook offers a range of tours of varying lengths and prices.

Special Deals The Public Transport Commission has several special deals. For $4.50 you can get a Dayrover which covers a day's travel on any suburban bus, train or ferry except the hydrofoils, after 9 am on weekdays or all day on weekends. You can even use them on the Harbour Cruises or Upriver Cruises. There is also a Weekly Rover available for $22.50 with the same conditions as the Dayrover. 'Mini Fares' are available during the same hours as the Dayrover tickets on return rail journeys over four km within the outer Sydney metropolitan and Sydney suburban areas – they give up to a third off normal fares. Return fares are less than two one-way tickets and cost less out of peak hours.

If you use the Eastern Suburbs rail line you can get a combination bus-rail ticket so you can change to a bus for a destination such as Bondi or Bondi Junction station. This works out cheaper than buying the tickets separately. Remember that even if you know you'll have to change trains, buy a ticket to your ultimate destination when you board the first train, it's cheaper. For more information, the Transport customer service phone number is 290 2988.

General Public Transport Gregory's produce *Sydney by Public Transport*, widely available from newsagents and bookshops for about $4. You can get info on all forms of public transport in Sydney from the Urban Transit Authority Travel & Tours Centre (tel 29 7614) at 11-31 York St, Sydney. There's a public transport map available for a small charge. It's not too helpful but does give you some idea of the services available and tells you where to enquire for further info on the particular services you require.

Car Rental There are a large number of rent-a-car operators in Sydney including all the big boys. You'll find Avis, Budget, Thrifty and Hertz all on William St up from the city towards Kings Cross, together with a number of local operators.

In the telephone yellow pages there's a long list of agencies under 'Motor Car Rentals (Drive Yourself)'. Most of the cheap outfits won't let you take their cars very far afield, so worth mentioning because they do is Bargain Car Rental (tel 648 4844) on the corner of Parramatta Rd and Alban St in Lidcombe. Their whole fleet is HQ Holdens, mostly automatics but some manuals, and you can use them anywhere in NSW (except the far west), in lower Queensland and in Victoria. Cost is $21.50 per day including insurance and 100 km. Their weekly rate is $129 including insurance and 600 km. Excess km cost 9c each. These rates aren't bad for around the city but if you're going to do any sort of distance it soon begins to compare badly with the big operators and their unlimited km rates.

Rent-a-Bug (tel 428 2098 or 747 3770) has a fleet of '70 to '74 VW beetles at $14 per day or $80 per week plus insurance and unlimited km but only for use in Sydney. They also have newer cars. Cheap Car Rentals (three locations north and south of the harbour) have VWs and Datsuns from $15 a day plus insurance with unlimited km. Rent-a-Wreck (tel 808 2888) have cars from $17 to $24 a day including insurance and unlimited km but again only for city use. Other cheaper outfits to try are: Rent-a-Bomb (tel 327 6499), Pam's Rent-a-Car (tel 358 6011) in Woolloomooloo, and Half Price in Kings Cross (tel 357 1191).

Bicycle Rental The bike hire places tend to be out in the suburbs. Centennial Park Hire (tel 398 5027) is at 50 Clovelly Rd, Randwick and charges $3 an hour, $18 a day. Others include: The Bike Shop (tel 958 1465) at 195 High St, Willoughby and Fit & Free (tel 547 1812) at 617 Princess Highway, Blakehurst but they are a very long way out.

Tours There is a vast array of city and area tours. See the tourist office on Pitt St for information, also the giveaway magazines from hotels, etc. Ansett-Pioneer, AAT and Clipper are three of the biggies. Half-day city tours are around $14 to $16, full-days $30 to $36. Longer day tours include Katoomba in the Blue Mountains (around $20), Hawkesbury River ($34), Old Sydney Town ($32), Jenolan Caves ($30), Canberra ($33), Hunter Valley Vineyards ($30).

For trips further afield, Rob King runs 14-day outback tours from the Dulwich Hill youth hostel for $18 per day.

Around Sydney

One of the major attractions of life in Sydney is the superb national parks to the north and south of the city. There is much more also within easy reach, however. In the early days of European settlement small towns were soon established around the major centre and although some of these, like Parramatta, have been engulfed by Sydney's urban sprawl, they're still of great interest today.

ROYAL NATIONAL PARK

Thirty km south of the city, this is the second oldest national park in the world, only Yellowstone National Park in the USA predates it. The park offers some superb bushwalks including spectacular walks along the cliff tops. There are also good surfing beaches, a number of pleasant, rocky swimming holes and the Hacking River runs right through the park. You can hire rowboats on the river at Audley and there are camping sites for longer stays. The park is carpeted with wildflowers in late winter and early spring. When I lived in Sydney this was a favourite getaway. Entry to the park costs $3 per car.

KU-RING-GAI CHASE NATIONAL PARK

As the Royal park is to the south so Ku-ring-gai is to the north. Just 24 km from

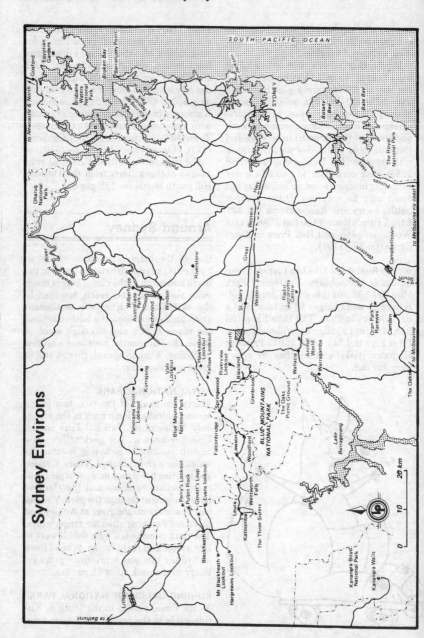

Sydney Environs

the centre you can get to the park by public transport. There are many bush-walks and the park also has some magnificent Aboriginal rock carvings which are quite easy to find. High points in the park offer magnificent views across the wide expanse of the Pittwater while from the northern tip of the park there's another fantastic view across to the hammerhead-like rock of Barrenjoey Point at the end of Palm Beach. Ku-ring-gai also has an excellent wildlife sanctuary and a camping area.

You can get to the park by public transport – take a bus from Wynyard to Church Point (1½ hours) then ferry, or take a bus from Wynyard to Palm Beach (nearly two hours) and ferry from there. There's a camping area at the Basin, where a ferry runs to Palm Beach. Entry to the park costs $3 per car.

On Namba Rd in Terrey Hills, close to the park, is the popular Waratah Park wildlife reserve. It's open Tuesdays to Sundays and on Mondays, as well, during school holidays.

BOTANY BAY

It's a common misconception amongst first time visitors to Sydney that the city is built around Botany Bay. Actually Sydney Harbour is Port Jackson and Botany Bay is several km to the south, although the city has expanded to encompass Botany Bay too. Botany Bay, named by Joseph Banks for the many botanical specimens he found here, was Cook's first landing point. The First Fleet also moored here at first, but quickly decided that Port Jackson was a better site for the first settlement. At Kurnell, on the south side of the bay, Captain Cook's landing place is marked with various monuments and a very interesting Captain Cook Museum with many exhibits and displays relating to the good captain's life and explorations. The centre is open 7 am to 7 pm daily. On the sea side of the landing point there's a stretch of spectacular rocky coast.

Across the bay entrance, beyond the oil tankers which bring crude oil to the Kurnell refinery, is La Perouse where the French explorer of that name turned up in 1788, just two days after the arrival of the first convict fleet. He gave the poms a scare as they weren't expecting the French to show in this part of their empire so soon. La Perouse sailed into the Pacific and totally disappeared. It was not until many years later that the wreck of his ship was discovered on a Pacific island revealing his unfortunate end. At La Perouse there's a fort on a small Bare Island. It was built in 1885 in order to repel or discourage a feared Russsian (yes Russian) invasion of Australia. The fort is open daily from 8 am to 5 pm and admission is free.

PARRAMATTA (population 128,000)

Sydney has sprawled out to encompass Parramatta, 24 km from the centre, but in the early days of European settlement this was the second settlement in Australia. Sydney soon proved to be a poor area for farming and in 1788 Parramatta was selected as the first farm settlement. Parramatta Park is the oldest area of the city. Elizabeth Farm House, built in 1793 by John Macarthur, is one of the oldest homes in the country. The Experiment Farm Cottage at 9 Ruse St was built for James Ruse in the early 1800s, open on Tuesday to Sunday from 10 am to 4.30 pm and admission is $1.50.

Roseneath is a fine example of 1830's colonial architecture. The Old Government House is another important early building in the Parramatta Park, where there is also a Tramway Museum. You can also find St Johns Cemetery in Parramatta, the oldest in Australia. The interesting pioneer headstones include one dating from 1791, again the oldest in Australia.

There's a Parramatta Information Bureau at Prince Alfred Park on Market St for information on the town. They have maps and brochures and a walking tour guide. Near Parramatta in Auburn is the Auburn Botanic Gardens which include an ornamental Japanese garden.

PENRITH (population 60,000)

Also on the edge of the capital's urban sprawl, Penrith is on the way to the Blue Mountains. From here you can visit the lion park at Warragamba Dam or Bullen's Animal World at Wallacia. At Doonside there's a large collection of native birds and other wildlife at the Featherdale Wildlife Park.

WINDSOR (population 4500)

One of Australia's earliest towns, Windsor has a number of important early buildings including the convict-built St Matthew's Church from 1817. It was designed, like the courthouse, by the convict architect Francis Greenway. George St and Thompson Square have a number of other historic buildings. On Thompson St the Tourist Information Centre and the Hawkesbury Museum are located in the old Daniel O'Connell Inn, dating from the 1840s.

The Australiana Village at Wilberforce is six km from Windsor – it has early buildings and a coal mine while on Sundays and public holidays sheep-shearing demonstrations, bushranger holdups and other pioneering activities take place. At nearby Ebenezer the Presbyterian church, built in 1809, is said to be the oldest in Australia still in regular use.

RICHMOND (population 2500)

Just eight km from Windsor, Richmond dates from 1810. Hobartville is an early mansion which is open Sunday to Thursday from 10.30 am to 5 pm. St Peter's Church dates from 1841 and a number of notable pioneers are buried in its cemetery.

CAMPBELLTOWN (population 37,000)

South of Sydney, this is another town which has been swallowed up by Sydney's outward expansion. Buildings in the town date right back to the 1820s including the 1824 St Peter's Church. Queen St in particular has some early houses. On the way south to Campbelltown is Liverpool (population 90,000), now completely swallowed up by Sydney but still with some fine examples of colonial architecture from the 1820s.

HAWKESBURY RIVER

North of Sydney the Hawkesbury River enters the sea at Broken Bay, between Ku-ring-gai Chase and the Bouddi and Brisbane Waters National Parks. This is one of the most attractive rivers in Australia and a very popular centre for boating of all types. At Bobbin Head you can hire boats from rowing dinghies to large houseboats and the river is dotted with coves, beaches, picnic spots and some fine riverside restaurants.

An excellent way to get a feel for the river is to take the river mailboat run which operates up the river every weekday, departing Brooklyn at 9.30 am and completing its run at 12.30 pm. Passengers can come along for $12, enquire at the NSW Government Travel Centre. On Wednesdays the Public Transport Commission in Sydney has a connecting train from Central Station in Sydney at 8.10 am and from Gosford at 8.53 am. The same boat also operates a variety of other cruises on the Hawkesbury and out to Broken Bay.

The tiny settlement of Wisemans Ferry is a popular spot up the river. There are still vehicular ferries operating across the river today and the Wisemans Ferry Inn is named after the original ferry operator. Across the river the Dharug National Park is noted for its many Aboriginal rock carvings which are thought to date back nearly 10,000 years. The Great Northern Road which continues north from Wisemans Ferry is a particularly interesting example of early convict road building because it has scarcely changed since its original construction.

Blue Mountains

The Blue Mountains were once an

impenetrable barrier to expansion inland from Sydney. Despite many attempts to find a route through the mountains, and a bizarre belief amongst many convicts that China, and freedom, was just on the other side, it was not until 1813 that a crossing was finally made and the western plains were opened up.

The Blue Mountains National Park has some fantastic scenery, excellent bushwalks and all the gorges, gum trees and cliffs you could ask for. The hills rise up just 65 km inland from Sydney and even a century ago this was already a popular getaway for affluent Sydney-siders who came to escape the summer heat on the coast. The mountains rise as high as 1100 metres and despite the intensive tourist development much of the area is so precipitous that it's still only open for bushwalkers. The blue haze, which gave the mountains their name, is a result of the fine mist of oil given off by eucalyptus trees. The droplets refract the light and intensify the blue.

Places to Stay

There are plenty of hotels, motels and campsites in the Blue Mountains and youth hostels in Katoomba and North Springwood.

Getting There

There are no bus services from Sydney to the Blue Mountains although buses do operate around the various towns of the Blue Mountains. Katoomba is now virtually an outer suburb of Sydney, 109 km from the centre, and trains operate regularly. The fare is just $5.60. To Lithgow the fare for the 155 km trip is $9.10.

SYDNEY TO KATOOMBA

At Glenbrook the 1833 Lennox Bridge is the oldest bridge still standing on the Australian mainland, there are older bridges in Tasmania. The famous artist Norman Lindsay lived in Springwood from 1912 until he died in 1969. His home at 128 Chapman Parade is now a gallery

and museum with exhibits of his paintings, cartoons, illustrations and, in the garden, his sculptures. It's open from 11 am to 5 pm on Fridays, Saturdays and Sundays.

KATOOMBA (population 14,000)

With its adjacent centres of Wentworth Falls and Leura this is the tourist centre of the Blue Mountains. The Scenic Skyway is a horizontal cable car crossing the gorge over Cooks Crossing with views of Katoomba Falls, Orphan Rock and the Jamieson Valley.

The Explorer's Tree, just west of Katoomba, was marked by the original explorers Blaxland, Lawson and Wentworth who crossed the mountains in 1813. Nearby there's a large aviary and there's also a deer park in Wentworth Falls. Two lookouts provide fine views of the Wentworth Falls which plummet 300 metres into the Jamison Valley. In Leura the National Trust has a garden at Everglades on Denison St with fine views over the mountains.

Information

There's a Tourist Information Centre at Echo Point. For more information on the Blue Mountains, particularly for walks, look for *How to See the Blue Mountains* by Jim Smith (Megalong Books). Be prepared for the great climatic differences between the Blue Mountains and the coast – you can swelter in Sydney but shiver in Katoomba.

Walks & Scenery

The Blue Mountains National Park is the second largest national park in NSW and has many superb bushwalks although there are also some equally good ones outside the park. There's a visitors' centre at Glenbrook on the eastern edge of the park. Immediately south of Katoomba is one of the park's landmarks, the magnificent Three Sisters rock formation. It's floodlit at night when it makes an awesome sight from Echo Point lookout.

Awesome is also the word to describe

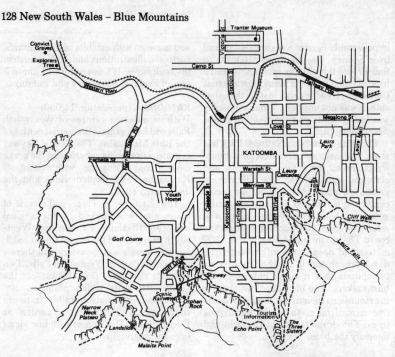

the bad taste of the 'three sisters' sculpture outside the restaurant by the funicular railway. The railway runs down to the base of the Jamieson Valley from near the restaurant and you can make a variety of easy, medium and even hard bushwalks to sites in the area. The railway was originally built in the 1880s for transporting miners to a coal mine and its 45° incline is one of the steepest in the world. The stroll to the aptly named ruined-castle rock formation is one of the best but watch out for the leeches if it has been raining.

Places to Stay

There's a great variety of accommodation at Katoomba including holiday homes, boarding houses, private hotels, regular hotels and motels, campsites and a youth hostel. Many places charge more at weekends than midweek. The places listed below are just a few recommendations to show the range available.

The *Youth Hostel* (tel (047) 82 1416) at 1 Wellington Rd in Katoomba has beds at $5.50. Other cheap accommodation includes the *Hotel Katoomba* (tel 82 1106) the corner of Park and Main Sts, near the railway station. Rooms are very plain – shared facilities, just a washbasin in the room – but with tea and coffee-making facilities. Singles/doubles are $16/25.

At Mt Victoria, 15 km west, the *Victoria & Albert Guesthouse* (tel 87 1241) charges $25 per person for bed and breakfast during the week, complete with open fires and billiard tables.

At the top of the hotel scale is the magnificent old *Carrington Hotel* (tel 82 1111) right in the middle of town on Katoomba St. The hotel dates from 1880 and doubles cost $62 to $78 on weekends. The *Hydro Majestic* (tel 88 1002) at Medlow Bath is a similarly superb relic of an earlier era.

Cheapest of the Katoomba motels are the *Blue Danube* (tel 82 1329) at the

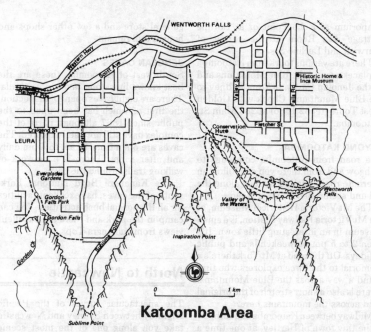

Katoomba Area

corner of Waratah and Lurline Sts (doubles from $32); the *Three Explorers* (tel 82 1733) at Lurline and Birdwood ($38 or $41 on weekends); and the *Echo Point Motor Inn* (tel 82 2088) at 18 Echo Point Rd ($38 and $42).

If you want to camp there's the *Katoomba Holiday Park* (tel 82 1483) at Scenic Drive (Cliff Drive) and Great Western Highway where tent sites cost $4 plus $1 per person or there are on-site vans for $18 (more on weekends). The *Katoomba Falls Caravan Park* (tel 82 1835) on Cliff Drive has tent sites from $3.60 and on-site vans from $21.60.

Places to Eat

Eat early in Katoomba, most places shut early in the evening. Many people eat at their guest houses where the tariff often includes meals. For cheap pub eats the *Hotel Katoomba* has meals from just $3 to $3.50. There are a string of snack bars, pizzerias and the like along Katoomba St –

like *Rene's Pizza Place* with small pizzas from $4, *Tom's Eats* with meals from $4.50 to $5.50 and small pizzas from $5, or *Blue's Cafe* with main courses from $6 to $9.

The splendid old *Carrington Hotel* has an equally splendiferous dining room with complete meals costing $15. The dining room has chandeliers, white tablecloths, the whole bit. Also take a look at the *Paragon Cafe* on Katoomba St for superb, unspoilt 1920s decor – ask to see the cocktail lounge at the back. Local residents say the food isn't that good.

Getting There & Around

Trains run regularly to Katoomba from Sydney; the two-hour trip costs $5.50.

You can hire bicycles from The Great Blue Mountains Bicycle Company. They have two-hour, four-hour and day rates and you can find them at the Ampol Service Station on the corner of Waratah and Katoomba Sts, the Kedumba

Emporium at Echo Point or at Lurline Cottage Tea Room at the corner of Warwick and Lurline Sts.

There are various tours from Katoomba to places around the Blue Mountains and to the Jenolan Caves, or from Sydney to the Blue Mountains. Check with Golden West Tours (tel 82 1866) at 283 Main St, Katoomba.

BEYOND KATOOMBA

The road from Katoomba continues to Lithgow and from there you can follow an alternate route back to Sydney along the old and scenic Bells Line of Road.

The Mt Victoria Historical Museum, at the Mt Victoria Railway Station, is a small museum in an interesting little town. It's open 2 to 5 pm on weekends and public holidays. Off the road at Mt York there's a memorial to the three explorers who first found a way across the Blue Mountains. There is also a short stretch of the original road across the mountains here.

Midway between Katoomba and Lithgow is the tiny town of Hartley, at one time a colonial travellers' stop there are still a number of original buildings from the 1830s and '40s. The convict built Court House is now a museum and is open from 10 am to 1 pm and 2 to 5 pm every day except Wednesday.

Near Bell, off Bells Line of Road, is the Zig Zag Railway, an amazing Victorian engineering feat which brought trains down from the Blue Mountains to the western plains. Construction of this complex line was completed in 1869 but with new technology the line was superseded in 1910. In the 1960s, however, railway enthusiasts restored the line and on weekends and public holidays steam trains operate.

Yerranderie, on the edge of the park about 100 km south-west of Sydney, is a ghost town now slowly being restored. Once a bustling gold and silver mining town of 2000 people, it basically disappeared after the boom period at the beginning of this century. The post office,

general store and a few other shops and houses still remain.

JENOLAN CAVES

South-west of Katoomba, these are the best known limestone caves in Australia. There are eight caves open for inspection, the first of which has been open to the public since 1867 although parts of the complex have still not been explored. The caves are open from 10 am to 4 pm daily and after 8 pm. There is a network of walking trails around the caves.

The Kanangra Boyd National Park, south of the caves, has excellent facilities for all the normal bush activities. You can camp in the park and there are excellent views from Kanangra Tops.

North to Newcastle

The spectacular curves of the Pacific Highway between Sydney and Newcastle take you along one of the most scenic routes in Australia. You cross the mouth of the Hawkesbury River and then run beside a couple of large coastal lakes before reaching Newcastle. There are also some interesting spots along the coast, off the highway.

GOSFORD (population 38,000)

Less than 100 km north of Sydney this is the centre for visiting the Brisbane Waters National Park. Old Sydney Town, see below, is a major Sydney-area attraction near here. Gosford also includes Eric Worrell's Reptile Park for snake enthusiasts, Henry Kendall's Cottage built in 1838 as an inn and lived in by the poet 1874-75, and the Somersby Falls near Old Sydney Town. Near Gosford, Woy Woy (population 12,200) is more or less a dormitory suburb.

Old Sydney Town

Only a few km from Gosford and about 70 km north of Sydney, Old Sydney Town is a major reconstruction of early Sydney with replicas of early ships including the brig *Lady Nelson* and trader *Perseverance*, houses and other buildings plus non-stop street theatre retelling events from the colony's early history. Children love the whippings, duels, hangings and floggings!

It's open 10 am to 5 pm Wednesday to Sunday and every day during NSW school holidays. Admission for adults is $8.50. There's a rail tour here from Sydney for $20 which takes all day. You can also get here on a $34 tour that includes a two-hour mail-boat ride along the coast, returning by bus.

Parks
Gosford is the jumping off point for the parks of the area. The Bouddi National Park is a coastal park, 17 km from Gosford with excellent bushwalking, camping and swimming. The beautiful Brisbane Waters National Park offers similar attractions at the mouth of the Hawkesbury.

GOSFORD TO NEWCASTLE
At Gosford you have the option of continuing straight up the Princes Highway or taking a coastal route around Tuggerah Lake. Wyong (population 3900) is on the Princes Highway while on the coastal route you can visit Terrigal (population 7500), a popular surfing centre. The Entrance (population 37,900) is a very popular resort at the ocean entrance to Tuggerah Lake.

Further north is another coastal lake, Lake Macquarie, although here the Pacific Highway runs on the ocean side of the lake. This is the largest seaboard lake in Australia and popular for sailing, water-skiing and fishing. Swansea, Belmont and Toronto (total population 17,000) are the main resorts on the lake. In Wangi Wangi, south of Toronto, you can visit the home of artist William Dobell. There are cruises on the lake on the *Wangi Queen* (tel 58 2311). There are train services to Toronto, bus services to Belmont and Speers Point.

Newcastle
Population 259,000

New South Wales' second largest city and one of the largest in Australia, Newcastle actually has a larger population than Canberra or Hobart. It's also Australia's second biggest port. Situated 167 km north of Sydney at the mouth of the Hunter River, it's a major industrial and commercial centre dominated by the massive BHP steelworks and other heavy industries although they're on the river and not seen from the town. It's also the export port for the Hunter Valley coalfields; coal exports are still Newcastle's lifeblood.

Originally named Coal River, the city was founded in 1804 as a place for the worst of Sydney's convicts and it soon gained the dubious distinction of being the 'hell of NSW'. The breakwater out to Nobbys Head with its lighthouse was built by convicts and Bogey Hole at King Edward Park was built as a bathing place for Major Morriset, a strict disciplinarian. It's a great place for a dip to this day.

Information & Orientation
There's a Visitor Information Centre (tel 26 2333) in the foyer of the City Administration Centre opposite Civic Park; Eric Dunkley, the man in charge, is a positive mine of information. It's open 8.30 am to 5 pm, Monday to Friday. Saturdays and Sundays you can get info from the art gallery from 2 to 5 pm. They have various brochures, a good map of Newcastle and an excellent city walks leaflet.

Just north of Newcastle there's another info centre at Hexham at the junction of the Pacific and New England Highways. The NRMA is at 8 Auckland St.

There are left-luggage lockers at Newcastle Railway Station – one-day use only and they cost 20c. The Scout Outdoor Centre opposite the Civic Hotel in Hunter St is a good place for outdoor gear.

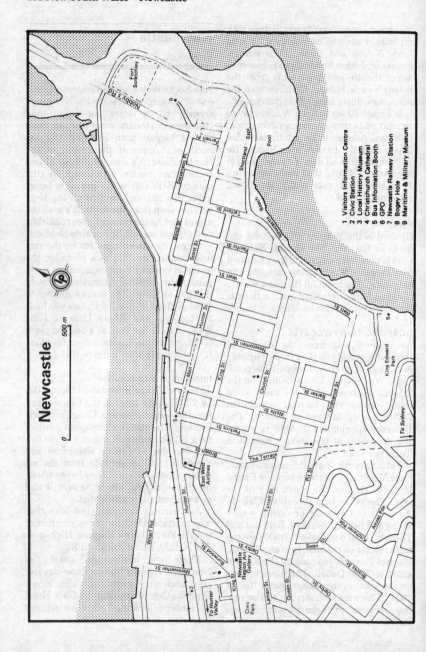

Newcastle

0 ____ 500 m

1 Visitors Information Centre
2 Civic Station
3 Local History Museum
4 Christchurch Cathedral
5 Bus Information Booth
6 GPO
7 Newcastle Railway Station
8 Bogey Hole
9 Maritime & Military Museum

The centre of Newcastle is a peninsula bordered by the ocean on one side and the Hunter River on the other. It tapers down to the long sandspit leading to Nobbys Head.

Around the City

Hunter Street is the three-km-long main street. There are bronze plaques at various historical points around the city. The Captain Cook Memorial Fountain is by the central Civic Park. The modern Newcastle Region Art Gallery was established in 1957 as a war memorial cultural centre but now only has a library from that original function. On the second floor there are changing displays of historic documents and photos. Cooks Hill, around the gallery area, has several well-established private galleries.

Newcastle also has several museums including the Maritime Museum and the Military Museum in Fort Scratchley (admission free) and the not terribly interesting Local History Museum on the Brown St extension (open Sundays only).

North of the city is the Stockton breakwater which is built over a sandbank known as Oyster Bar where many ships were once wrecked. The last to go aground here was a four-masted barque, the *Adolphe*, in 1904. The hull of the *Adolphe* and various other shipwrecks are now built into the breakwater; the *Adolphe* is the only one visible today. Fort Scratchley is at the north-east end of the city, on Nobbys Road. Originally built in the 1840s the present construction dates from 1882. The Bare Island fort in Botany Bay in Sydney is from the same period. The city was actually attacked by a Japanese submarine during WW II and the fort fired back. It's open from 12 noon to 4 pm except on Mondays and admission is free.

Beaches

Newcastle is exceptionally well-endowed with beaches, many of which have good surf. The main beach, Newcastle Beach, is only a couple of hundred metres from the centre of town and has an ocean pool which is open at night, and usually, good surf. Merewether Beach, further south, also has a pool which is open at night. Bar Beach is floodlit at night and the beach is protected by a rocky bar. Nobbys Beach is north of the centre and is more sheltered from the southerlies. It's often open when other beaches are closed. At the end of the beach is an old 1857 lighthouse.

BHP Steelworks

Situated at Port Waratah, six km west of the city, the steelworks were opened in 1915 and today employ about 6000 people. They have the capacity to produce nearly three million tonnes of steel a year although these days their output is far less.

Blackbutt Reserve

In the middle of Newcastle this 166 hectare bushland reserve has a variety of bushwalks as well as aviaries, wildlife enclosures (including koalas) and fern houses.

Places to Stay

Hostels Newcastle has quite a vacuum in the budget accommodation field but if you ask at the Visitor Information Centre backpackers may be able to stay at the Fort Scratchley State Emergency Centre for $3.

The *YWCA Hostel* (tel 24 031) at 82 Parkway is usually full with permanents. If you're lucky you may get in to sleep on a mattress on the common room floor or TV lounge floor. Ask for a key at night as the doors are locked at 10 pm.

Hotels The *Civic Casbah* (2 2904) at 465 Hunter St, has singles/doubles for $23/31. The *Grand* (tel 2 3489), on the corner of Bolton and Church Sts, is now a quiet place since the police station and courthouse are right across the road! Singles/doubles are $12/20.

At 95 Scott St opposite the railway

station the *George* (tel 2 1534) has a lot of permanents. Singles are $15 and they do counter lunches and teas here. You can get breakfast next door. Nearby the *Terminus Motel* (tel 26 3244) at 111 Scott St has motel-style rooms at $40/45.

The *Clarendon* (tel 2 4347) at 347 Hunter Street has 16 rooms and is said to be pretty good value – for $10 a single it should be. The *Cambridge*, a little further out at the corner of Hunter and Wood Sts is noisy but just $15.

If you don't mind the rock bands on some nights, the *Beach Hotel* (tel 63 1574) on Frederick St, Merewether, is just across from Merewether Beach, a short bus ride from town. It charges $15 for singles, $24 for doubles.

The same distance from the centre but away from the beach in Broadmeadow is the *Premier* (tel 61 3670) at 1 Brunker Rd, where bed & breakfast is from $18. There are frequent buses to Broadmeadow. There are other hotels scattered among the more distant suburbs.

Motels Newcastle tends to be expensive. Belmont, to the south, where there is a string of motels along the Pacific Highway, is probably the best bet. *Pelican Palms Motor Inn* (tel 45 4545) at 784 Pacific Highway is $24 to $30 and there's a pool.

Colleges Edwards Hall has accommodation in the uni holidays but it's expensive, the rooms are bare and there are no cooking facilities.

Camping *Walsh's Caravan Park* (tel 68 1394) at 293 Maitland Rd, Mayfield West, is the closest site to town but doesn't take tents. On-site vans on this very small site are $18 to $21.

Stockton is very handy for Newcastle by ferry, otherwise it's 19 km by road (there is a bus). *Stockton Beach Caravan and Tourist Park* (tel 28 1393) is right on the beach in Pitt St. Camping costs $5.50, on-site vans are $19 a night.

There are three sites at Belmont: *Belmont South Caravan Park* (tel 45 4750) is on the lake in Ethel St and has tent sites for $4.30 to $5, or less by the week. It's cheaper because it's a council camp. A bit further north there's no camping at *Gaytime Caravan Park* (tel 45 3405) at 687 Pacific Highway. On-site vans are $17 for two ($15 in the off-season) plus $1 for each extra person. They hold up to six people. *Belmont Bay North Caravan Park* (tel 45 3653) is on Gerald St and has camping ($5 for two) and on-site vans from $18 to $20. There's also a site in Redhead and several in Swansea.

Places to Eat
Newcastle offers some surprisingly good places to eat apart from the usual Kentucky Frieds, Pizza Huts, Big Al's and the like.

Counter Food At 471 Hunter St (through to King St) the *Casbah* is a glossy, new and very popular pub with food from $5 to $7, including a do-it-yourself steak barbecue plus a salad bar and 'Healthworks' for good sandwiches.

Rumours Tavern at 23 Watt St has main courses for $6 to $7. The *George* at 95 Scott St has counter lunches and teas. The *Crown & Anchor*, on the corner of Perkins and Hunter Sts has lunches for around $4 to $5, dinners for $8 to $9.

Others include the *Beach Hotel* in Frederick St, Merewether and the *Cricketer's Arms* on the corner of Bull and Bruce Sts, Cooks Hill.

Italian Newcastle has some real Italian institutions like the *Italian Club* at 46 Beaumont St in Hamilton. There are other Italian places in this area. Other favourites include *Don Beppino's* at 45 Railway St, Merewether, and *Arrivederci* on the corner of Glebe Rd and Watkins St at The Junction. *Arrivederci* is very busy and popular (probably due more to the opening hours than the pizzas) and is open to 2 or 3 am.

Restaurants *Taco Bill's* at 80 Darby St, for Mexican food, is open Wednesday to Sunday at 10 pm and is BYO. It's usually very popular and crowded. They don't take bookings so you often have to queue to get in.

The *Maharaja* is a licensed Indian restaurant at 653B Hunter Street, Newcastle West. It's open for lunch from Tuesday to Saturday and for dinner every night. The food is northern Indian (mainly meat dishes) but there are also vegetarian dishes. Slightly cheaper take-aways are also available.

At 131 Darby St *Café Gritz* is a pleasant little place with vegetarian and other food at $4 to $6. *Emilio's Pizzeria and Trattoria* is at 127 on the same street.

Specials *Alcron* at 116 Church St, overlooking the harbour, has a three-course 'sunset dinner' for $11.50. Sunset is 5.30 to 9.30 pm Monday to Thursday, 5.30 to 7.30 pm on other nights. Their a la carte prices are *not* cheap.

At 141 Scott St, just east of Newcomen St, the *Pancake Factory* is popular. It's open every day for lunch and dinner till fairly late in the evening, and serves various pancakes. There's a bar upstairs with music on some nights.

Frenchies at the Star complex at 569 Hunter St by the rock pool has a $5.50 lunchtime special for main course and dessert. The *Waratah-Mayfield RSL* has a Sunday lunchtime smorgasbord which is good value. *Clams* at 87 Frederick St, Merewether is famous for its seafood. It's next to the Beach Hotel and closed Sundays.

Entertainment
Newcastle entertainment tends to be limited to the weekends and Wednesdays. Phone the 2NX What's Happening line (11 6889), get Friday's *Newcastle Herald* or the *That's Entertainment* give-away on Wednesdays.

Pub Music *Delaney's* is a relaxed little pub

on the corner of Council and Darby Sts, Cook Hill, with music most nights of the week – usually good music, people and atmosphere. The *Cricketer's Arms* on the corner of Bull and Bruce Sts in Cooks Hill is also popular. The *Oriental*, opposite the Cricketer's Arms, has good jazz and a great atmosphere.

The *Bellevue Hotel*, on the corner of Hunter and Hannel Sts, has music every night except Monday. Further along again, at the corner of Hunter and Wood Sts, the *Cambridge* has live music every night and Sunday afternoons; different music on different nights.

In Merewether the *Beach Hotel* has good music (usually rock) on the usual nights. The *Prince of Wales*, also in Merewether, is very popular on Friday nights.

Other The *Newcastle Workers' Club* in Union St has regular visiting bands. There are lots of clubs in Newcastle although they tend to be fussy about dress and can be quite expensive. Newcastle also has some nightclubs like the *Palais Royale* (loud rock) and *Fannys*. Plays and concerts are held in the *Civic Theatre* behind the City Hall.

Getting There
Air You can fly between Sydney and Newcastle although the distance is so short you're unlikely to want to. The airfare from Sydney is around $44 depending on the airline. East-West fly directly between Newcastle and Brisbane or the Gold coast.

Bus Most Brisbane buses stop in Newcastle. Ansett Pioneer and Greyhound are both booked through Jayes Terminal at 204 King St; they cost $34 to Brisbane. Deluxe also run through Newcastle. You cannot take buses between Sydney and Newcastle (unless you are using a bus pass).

Rail Trains to and from Sydney operate

about 15 times daily, take about three hours and cost $10. Three of the services are fast 'flyers' but you must book a seat on these. Heading north, the trains are far from regular.

Getting Around

The Urban Transit Authority's buses cover all of Newcastle and the eastern side of Lake Macquarie. Their services are reasonably frequent but can be painfully slow. The Information Booth at the western end of the Mall has timetables but its actual opening hours don't bear much relation to the posted ones. Buses are rather expensive, but for a bit of sightseeing by local bus, try route 348 or 358 to Swansea or 366, 363 or 327 to Speers Point. Newcastle has the same special local transport deals as in Sydney.

Trains run to the western side of Lake Macquarie with connecting buses to the south-western shores. A private bus company operates to Stockton. A ferry operates across to Stockton from central Newcastle and costs 90c.

There's a bus to Nelson Bay and to Cessnock. To anywhere else in the Hunter region you have to go by train, although there's a bus up to Forster. Trains run to Maitland and the upper part of the Hunter Valley.

There doesn't currently seem to be anywhere in Newcastle hiring out bicycles. The regular rental car operators are here and Cheap Heap have cars at $12.50 a day.

The Hunter Valley

The Hunter valley has two curiously diverse products – coal and wine. In some places you can find both together. Steam trains still take coal to Hexham. Singleton, 77 km inland from Newcastle, and Muswellbrook, a further 47 km, are two wine producing/coal mining areas. The Pokolbin area is the centre of the Hunter Valley

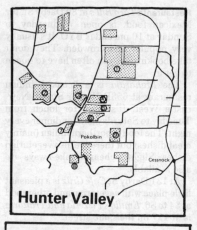

Hunter Valley

1 Rothbury Estate
2 Tyrell's
3 Hungerford Hill
4 Tamburlaine
5 Pokolbin Estate
6 Tulloch's
7 Linderman's Ben Ean
8 McWilliams Mt Pleasant
9 Saxonvale Happy Valley

vineyards and some of the wineries date back to the 1860s. You'll find many of Australia's best known wine names – such as Lindeman's, Drayton's McWilliams, Tyrells and Tullochs are represented here.

The first grapevines were actually planted in the Hunter in 1832 and the first winery was established in 1843 but depression in the 1930s and a subsequent loss of interest in wine reduced the wine industry to a shadow of its early 20th century peak. Then, in the mid-60s, the current wine boom started and today the Hunter Valley is one of Australia's premier wine producing areas.

The upper Hunter Valley, less well known than the lower valley, is wilder country but also has vineyards and a regular wine festival. The Hunter River runs for about 300 km in all.

Getting There

You cannot travel to the Hunter region with the main bus operators, unless you're on a bus pass or travelling from interstate, but there are a number of train services operating through the area. A variety of bus services operate around the Hunter Valley and between Sydney and Cessnock.

Wineries

There are about 20 vineyards in the valley where you can sample the wines or tour the winery. Generally the vineyards are open for tasting from 9 am to 5 pm (some a little earlier, some a little later) from Monday to Saturday. Some are also open on Sunday afternoons. Many of the wineries have picnic and barbecue facilities so you can enjoy your lunch while sipping on a bottle from their winery.

Starting from Cessnock a few of the more interesting wineries include Happy Valley (Saxonvale) with it's rather expensive restaurant. Lindeman's Ben Ean is not, surprisingly, the home of Ben Ean moselle which is blended from a number of grape-growing regions. Tulloch's, Pokolbin Estate and Tamburlaine are all side-by-side. Hungerford Hill bills itself as a 'wine village'. It has a restaurant, handicrafts shop, 'farmers' market' and wine tours as well as the usual tasting and wine sales facilities – commercial but interesting. Housed in a huge and splendid building the Rothbury Estate sells all its wines direct. Tyrell's is one of the longest established names in the Hunter. Finally Wyndham Estate, again with a restaurant, is several km north of the main vineyard concentration, a little north of the New England Highway.

CESSNOCK (population 17,000)

Cessnock is the main town and accommodation centre for the vineyards, only a few km from Pokolbin, right in the centre of the wineries. Wollombi is a tiny town south of Cessnock with some interesting old buildings and there are some good lookouts around the valley.

Places to Stay

Cessnock is the main town in the lower Hunter Valley and it has a variety of accommodation possibilities including several hotels and motels. The *Wentworth* (tel 90 1364) at 36 Vincent St is the cheapest hotel at $15 single, $30 double room. The *Cessnock Hotel* (tel 90 1002) on Wollombi Rd opposite the Post Office, has singles/doubles for $17/30. The *Cessnock Motel* (tel 90 2770), 13 Allandale Rd, has rooms from $26 to $34. For camping, try the *Southwood Park 'Caravillage'* on Carrs Rd – sites are $7.50 for two people. There's no youth hostel near to hand.

Places to Eat

For a good cheap meal in Cessnock try the Cessnock Workers' Club or the RSL (Chinese food). Both are straightforward with true-blue Aussie food! There are a few restaurants around the vineyards – all of them rather expensive, some of them rather indifferent. If you'd like to eat well while sampling Hunter wines they could make an interesting 'splash out' meal. It's wise to book ahead or, at the least, check if they're open since many of them open only on weekends or certain week nights.

MAITLAND (population 42,000)

Maitland, once a coal-mining centre, is only 30 km inland from Newcastle. It was settled by convicts in 1818 and at one time Sydney, Parramatta and Maitland were the three main centres in Australia. Early buildings include Brough House, now an art gallery, and Grossman House which is run by the National Trust. There are a number of old homesteads in the area including the 1820, convict– built Windermere Colonial Museum in nearby Lochinvar. Morpeth Town in particular has many reminders of it's early history.

Historical Homes & Buildings ($1.50) is a good guide to the old buildings in Maitland. The Maitland Lands Office has an excellent *East Maitland Heritage Walk* brochure.

A regular suburban train runs to Maitland from Newcastle so a visit to this interesting old town is a good excursion for people without their own transport.

AROUND NEWCASTLE

There are a number of other places of interest around Newcastle apart from the Hunter Valley. Raymond Terrace (population 7550), just 23 km north of Newcastle, has a number of early buildings from the 1830s and '40s including a courthouse which is still in use and Irrawang, an 1830 homestead.

North Coast

North of Newcastle a narrow band of country runs back from the coast and then rises into the Great Dividing Range area of New England. The coastal strip has some good resort towns and long, lonely beaches, some with notable surf. In places the Pacific Highway runs well inland from the coast and rougher roads will take you along quite deserted stretches of beach on the actual coastline.

Getting There

Airlines of NSW and East-West Airlines operate to various centres in the north coast region particularly Port Macquarie and Coffs Harbour. There are also services from Brisbane. By rail the train services between Sydney and Brisbane or Sydney and Murwillumbah (for the Gold Coast) both run up the coast. Ansett Pioneer, Greyhound, Skennars and various other bus operators have services along the coast between Sydney and Brisbane or regionally.

NEWCASTLE TO PORT MACQUARIE

It's about 250 km up the coast from Newcastle to the popular resort town of Port Macquarie. North of Newcastle is Port Stephen where Nelsons Bay (population 7900) is the main town. It's a popular fishing centre with many fine beaches and there are a variety of cruises from here.

Bulahdelah (population 1000) is the jumping-off point for the beautiful beaches and headlands of the coastal Myall Lakes National Park. You can drive from Bulahdelah to Bombah Point from where ferries cross to the park. The lakes and coastline with its sand dunes offer a variety of activities from swimming and boating to surfing and fishing, plus you can bushwalk or camp at Seal Rocks, a small fishing village south of Forster, Mungo Brush and Bombah Point. There are some excellent bushwalks from Bulahdelah.

Between Bulahdelah and Taree you can take a loop off the Pacific Highway through the twin towns of Forster-Tuncurry. This road takes you closer to the coast and beside the Myall Lakes park. Forster-Tuncurry (population 9300) are connected by a bridge at the sea entrance to Wallis Lake. Places of interest in the towns include the Arts & Crafts Centre in Forster, the Vintage Car Museum a couple of km south and Talabah Park (amusing for children) 20 km north. Green Cathedral is an open air 'cathedral' created by the Mormons on the shores of Lake Wallis, 13 km south.

Another alternative to the Pacific Highway is to travel further inland along Bucketts Way on the eastern slopes of the Great Dividing Range. Dungog (population 2100) is a main access point to the Barrington Tops National Park, noted for its wildlife and some unusual local flora. The park boundary is at Barrington Guest House although an all-weather road proceeds through the neighbouring state forest, giving access to the national park higher up. There are cabins in the neighbouring forestry area and camping on the Allyn River. Barrington Tops Forest Drive linking Gloucester and Scone (outside the main body of the national park) is a good drive if the weather is fine.

There are also some good walking trails along the Telegherry River in the Telegherry Forest Park. Chichester Dam on the Bandon Grove Road is a popular spot for barbecues. About the same distance north of Newcastle as Dungog is Stroud (population 500) with a surprisingly large number of early buildings, most of them dating back to the 1830s. Gloucester (population 2500) is at the foot of the hills known as the Bucketts. There are some good lookouts in the hills, particularly at Copeland Tops and Kia-Ora.

Taree (population 14,700) is the main town in the Manning River District. Just inland from Taree is Wingham (population 3950) where the Brush is a park close to the town, inhabited by countless flying foxes between September and May each year. Places of interest around Taree include the Bulga Plateau where you can see the 160-metre drop of the Ellenborough Falls 50 km north. The varied attractions of the Crowdy Bay National Park are 40 km to the east. There is good surfing on beaches only 16 km east of Taree.

Less than 50 km south of Port Macquarie and immediately north of the Crowdy Bay National Park are the fishing towns of Laurieton, North Haven and Dunbogan, collectively known as Camden Haven (population 2200). There's excellent fishing along the coast here and some fine bushwalks around the lakes close to the coast.

PORT MACQUARIE (population 19,600)
A major resort centre Port Macquarie makes a good stopping point on the trek up the coast from Sydney (430 km south) to Brisbane (602 km north). It was founded in 1821 making it one of the oldest towns in NSW and was a convict settlement until 1830. There is a wide range of accommodation and places to eat and the competition tends to keep prices down. It has also been blessed with a beautiful series of beaches starting right in the town – good for surfing, snorkelling or just collecting a suntan.

From the centre there's Town Beach (good swimming or surfing), Oxley Beach (an open sweep of sand), Rocky Beach (just that), Flynn's Beach (excellent surf), Nobby's Beach (interesting rock formations and a high headland at the north end), Shelly beach (good swimming, interesting, gem-like pebbles), Miner's Beach (secluded, good for sunbathing) and, finally, the endless stretch of Lighthouse (more good surfing).

Port Macquarie also has a selection of man-made attractions. On Wednesday and Saturday nights (Friday in the holiday season) you can observe the moon from the observatory near Town Beach for 45c. There's the Hastings Historical Museum on Clarence St (open daily, 50c). On Hay St you'll find the 1824-28 St Thomas Church which was built by convict labour and designed by the convict architect Francis Greenway (see Sydney). It's the third oldest church in Australia. Close by on Gordon St is a historically interesting cemetery.

There's a marine park and dolphin park called the King Neptune Park by Town Beach – open daily. On Pacific Drive, five km south of Port Macquarie, there's a 30-hectare flora and fauna reserve, Sea Acres Sanctuary, also open daily. For the kids there's Fantasy Glades on Parklands Avenue, five km south – also open daily. Finally, there are a number of river cruises from Port Macquarie. The tourist office can advise you where and when.

If you're heading north from Port Macquarie you can follow a dirt road (a bit rough) north to Crescent Head where you turn inland to meet the Pacific Highway near Kempsey. You take a vehicle ferry across the Hastings River just out of Port Macquarie. The beach at Crescent Head is virtually deserted with fine surf, good picnic spots, nice views.

There is an excellent information centre at the waterfront end of Horton St (the main street) and they can give you all the facts and figures on accommodation and things to do.

Places to Stay & Eat

There are lots of hotels, motels (something like 40 of them), holiday flats and campsites in Port Macquarie so you've plenty of choice. The competition keeps the prices down so you can find motels for around $20 a double.

In the town centre the *Macquarie Hotel* (by the tourist office) and the *Innes Tavern* both have counter meals – there's probably more choice at the Macquarie Hotel which also has grill-it-yourself steaks. You can get a cheap meal at the *RSL* (visitors welcome) otherwise there are plenty of take-aways, fast food joints and more expensive restaurants.

PORT MACQUARIE TO COFFS HARBOUR

Just inland from Port Macquarie is Wauchope (population 3650) with Timbertown, a working replica of a timber town of the 1880s. It's open 10 am to 5 pm daily. The Beranghi Folk Museum is in Kempsey (population 9000) but it's worth diverting off the Pacific Highway here to Trial Bay, 35 km north-east. Here the front section of the brig *The Trial* has been restored as a museum at the Trial Bay Gaol. The ship was stolen from Sydney by convicts in 1816 and wrecked here. The nearby Smoky Cape Lighthouse can be inspected on Tuesdays and Thursdays. South of Smoky Cape is the fine coastal region of the Hat Head National Park.

Macksville (population 2350) is on the Nambucca River and here you can visit the Mary Boulton Pioneer Cottage on River St or in nearby Bowraville there's yet another of Australia's many folk museums – the Joseph & Eliza Newman Folk Museum. Follow the road 27 km upriver to Taylors Arm and there you'll find the 1903 Cosmopolitan, the hotel immortalised in that sad song *Pub with No Beer*.

Down at the mouth of the Nambucca River the popular resort of Nambucca Heads (population 4050) has a couple of museums – the Nambucca Historical Museum on the headlands and the Orama

Mineral Museum. There are superb coastal views from the Yarrahappin Lookout here. A little inland is Bellingen (population 1600) a pleasant small town on the banks of the Bellingen River. Between here and Dorrigo (population 1200) is the rainforest of the Dorrigo National Park. The New England National Park, on the eastern side of the New England Plateau, is also in this region. The turn inland to Dorrigo is just beyond Urunga (population 2050), a popular fishing spot with a coastal lagoon.

COFFS HARBOUR (population 16,000)

With Port Macquarie, Coffs Harbour is the other major central north coast resort. It's got fine beaches and a Porpoise Pool on Orlando St (open daily) plus the Kumbaingeri Wildlife Sanctuary (14 km north, open daily) and the Bruxner Park Flora Reserve (nine km north-west in Korora) with fine views over the coast.

Coffs Harbour, capital of the NSW 'Banana Republic' is probably best known for its Big Banana – 10 metres long in reinforced concrete (you can walk through it) it's on the Pacific Highway three km north of town. The Big Banana, immortalised in thousands of visitors' photographs, is part of a banana complex! You can have a look around the banana plantation on the hill behind or sample banana cake, a banana split, a banana shake or even a chocolate covered banana. Open daily from 8.30 am to 5.30 pm, it's free. Just eight km south of Coffs Harbour, Sawtell (population 3700) is another popular, coastal resort town.

WOOLGOOLGA (population 2100)

Woolgoolga is a pleasant fishing port with a fine surf beach. The town has a sizable Indian Sikh population who have a gurdwara, the Guru Nanak Temple, on River St. There are fine beaches with good swimming and excellent bushwalks and camping at the Red Rock National Park, 10 km north. Adventure Village and Sam's Place, five km north where you can see pottery making demonstrations, are other local attractions.

GRAFTON (population 17,000)

Grafton is noted for its beautiful flame of the forest and jacaranda trees; there's a Jacaranda Festival in November each year. The turn of the century Schaeffer House is now a local historical museum but ice cream fans might find the ice-cream factory on Fry St (inspections at 2 pm weekdays) of more interest. There are walking tracks to the top of Glenugie Peak for fine views, south of the town. View-freaks can also try MacLean Lookout near the town.

Canoeing and bushwalking enthusiasts might care to sample the Guy Fawkes River National Park to the west of Grafton but it's a difficult area to get to and there are zero facilities. The Gwydir Highway, running west from Grafton to Glen Innes in the New England regions, runs through the Gibraltar Range National Park.

GRAFTON TO BALLINA

From Grafton the highway follows the Clarence River to Maclean (population 2600) close to the river mouth. This is one of the most important fishing ports in NSW. Attractions in the area include the Iluka rainforest, the Angourie surfing beach in the coastal Angourie National Park and the blue pool, a popular picnic spot at Angourie with a very deep pool only 50 metres back from the ocean. At the northern end of the park and right on the mouth of the Clarence River, Yamba (population 2500) is a prawning and fishing town and base for the park.

Further north is Evans Head (population 1800), again off the main highway and a busy prawning centre. You can make a loop off the highway through Evans Head and the Broadwater National Park just north of the town. There are good bushwalks here and Evans Head also has some superb surf beaches. You can see emus, koalas and wallabies in the Bund-julung Flora & Fauna Reserve, south of

the Evans River. Woodburn (population 650) is the place where you turn off the highway for Evans Head, or turn inland for Casino and Lismore. Those with an interest in Papua New Guinea's history may want to see the monument and remains of New Italy, a settlement formed from the tattered remnants of the Marquis de Rays' plan to colonise the New Guinea island of New Ireland.

BALLINA (population 11,000)

This busy town, where the Richmond River meets the sea, has an interesting little Maritime Museum. It's in the information centre on Norton St by the river on the north-east side of the town – open Monday to Friday, admission 50c. Here you'll find a balsa wood raft from the La Balsa expedition – a group of three rafts, manned by a 12-man international crew that drifted across the Pacific from Ecuador in South America to Ballina in 177 days in 1973. They proved whatever one does by crossing vast stretches of water in Heath Robinson creations!

Ballina also has the historic Shaws Bay Hotel, a shell museum, a busy little shipbuilding yard and 11 km west is the Tropical Fruit Research Station which you can visit on Thursdays at 2 pm. The Tourist Information Centre is beside the Maritime Museum.

LISMORE (population 24,000)

Inland from Ballina on the Bruxner Highway to Tenterfield in the New England district, Lismore is the centre of a productive rural district. There's a historical museum, an old Aboriginal ceremonial ground near the Tucki Koala Reserve and an open-air pioneer transport museum at Alstonville. Nightcap National Park has superb views and lots of wildlife, 25 km north of Lismore. Continuing inland from Lismore you reach Casino (population 9750) with many fine parks and a folk museum. On the road to Tenterfield, 20 km beyond Casino, there are some Aboriginal rock carvings.

Although Australia's 'back to the land movement' is past its heyday Nimbin, 30 km north of Lismore, is still a great alternative centre. In fact the back to the land folk, despite a few hassles from the cops, are almost establishment around these parts. Nimbin has a good *Youth Hostel* (tel (066) 89 1333), one km from the town centre and right by the river at Granny's Farm. A little west of Nimbin is Kyogle (population 3100), a good base for the mountains and forests in this area. Mt Warning is north-east, between Kyogle and Murwillumbah, while north on the Queensland border is Mt Lindesay with terrific views from its summit.

BALLINA TO BYRON BAY
From Ballina the Pacific Highway again runs a little inland but you'll hardly add a km to the journey if you follow the coast road from Ballina, eventually rejoining the Pacific Highway just beyond Byron Bay. It's an excellent road with fine views over the superb beaches at Lennox Head, Broken Head and Byron Bay (population 3200).

Byron Bay is a surfing Mecca due to the superb surf at Watego's Beach on Cape Byron. The cape is the most easterly point in Australia and the picturesque little lighthouse that tops the headland was built in 1901 and is said to be the most powerful in the southern hemisphere and the second most powerful in the world. There are fine views of the beaches from the cape.

The Everglades, five km south of Byron Bay, is a nature sanctuary with a notable collection of water lillies (open Tuesday to Sunday). King's Beach is a great free beach at King's Head, six km south of Byron Bay with a caravan park at nearby Broken Head.

Places to Stay
There's a 36-bed *Youth Hostel* (tel (066) 85 6445) at 78 Bangalow Rd, 1500 metres south of the railway station. The *Holiday Village* (tel 85 7660) in Jonson St is a fairly new place with a pool, spa and barbecue charging $6 a night single or double.

BYRON BAY TO TWEED HEADS
Soon after Byron Bay the coastal road rejoins the Pacific Highway. Mullumbimby (population 2500) is in beautiful sub-tropical countryside and from here you can visit the Nightcap National Park or Tuntable Falls. Cedar House is a fine old restored house with a vintage car collection in the town. Just after the Mullumbimby turn-off is Brunswick Heads (population 1900), a busy fishing centre.

The road continues through Burringbar (close to where one of Lonely Planet's busiest writers, Geoff Crowther, hides out on a banana plantation) to Murwillumbah (population 7800); this is a banana and sugar cane growing area. Murwillumbah has the very popular associate YHA *Riverside Hostel* (tel (066) 72 3763) on the Tweed River. They have canoes and bicycles available and also operate a variety of tours. There are many communes and 'back to the earth' centres in this area including a major Hare Krishna centre. The Kookendoon Wildlife Sanctuary is eight km north at Dungay.

Mt Warning, 1756 metres high, rises up behind Murwillumbah; a road leads to the top. The mountain was named by Captain Cook, as a warning not to run aground at Point Danger off Tweed Heads – as he nearly did. There are many good bush-walks around and on Mt Warning – allow about four hours to climb to the top and down again, although it has been done, in a competition, in 27 minutes! It's just 32 km along the bank of the Tweed River from Murwillumbah to Tweed Heads and the Gold Coast. Alternatively you can take smaller roads inland through the hills and down to the coast.

You can also take a coastal route by branching off the Pacific Highway between Mooball and Burringbar then following the delightful stretch of coast known as the Tweed Coast, much less commercial than the Gold Coast to the north.

TWEED HEADS (population 5100)
The last town on the coast in NSW, Tweed Heads marks the southern end of the Gold Coast strip (see Queensland) and is actually continuous with Coolangatta, the first town in Queensland. It's a quieter, less commercial place to stay than the resorts closer to Surfers. It's also a popular place for Queenslanders to hop across the state line and play the pokies (poker machines) or buy the magazines which are banned in Queensland.

At Point Danger there's the towering Captain Cook Memorial which straddles the NSW-Queensland border. The 18-metre-high monument was completed in 1970 (the bi-centenary of Cook's visit) and is topped by a laser beam lighthouse visible 35 km out to sea. The replica of the *Endeavour's* capstan is made from ballast dumped by Cook after the *Endeavour* ran aground on the Great Barrier Reef further north. It was recovered, along with the ship's cannons, in 1968. Point Danger was named by Cook after he nearly ran aground.

Tweed Heads also has Marineland on Coral St (open daily) with aquarium, dolphins and sharks. The Tweed Head Waterworks is another (yet another) of the waterslide centres. It costs $5 an hour but sometimes that hour can extend all day. Three km from Tweed Heads you can get a fine view over the Tweed Valley and the Gold Coast from the Razorback Lookout.

Information
Tweed Heads has a NSW Government Tourist Information Centre on the Pacific Highway, open 9 am to 5 pm every day of the week. Like Albury this is treated as a major entry point to NSW for interstate visitors.

Places to Stay
There's all sorts of accommodation in Tweed Heads, spilling over into Coolangatta and up the Gold Coast. See the Gold Coast section in Queensland for more details. Probably the cheapest motel is

the *Golden Wanderer* (36 1838) at 153 Pacific Highway with singles/doubles for $20/22. It's close to the busy main route through Tweed Heads so it can be noisy. Tweed Heads also has hotels and holiday flats like *Panorama* (tel 36 1620) at 16 Boundary St where flats by the week cost from $80 to $160.

Places to Eat
In the eats department there's excellent seafood downstairs at *Markwell's Seafood Restaurant*, 64 Griffith St, including an excellent fixed-price catch-of-the-day meal which includes salad and tea or coffee. They also have a superb seafood platter with everything from calamari and Moreton Bay bugs to prawns and oysters.

Fisherman's Cove on Coral St in Tweed Heads is another excellent and reasonably economical seafood specialist. There's very ordinary counter food at the *Coolangatta Hotel* (Marine Parade) across the border, or you could try the *Kirra Beach Hotel* which is cheap but bland.

New England

The New England region is the area along the Great Dividing Range stretching north from around Newcastle to the Queensland border. It's a vast plateau of valuable sheep and cattle country with many good bushwalking areas, good fishing, photogenic scenery and much to recommend it. The New England Highway is an alternative to the coastal Pacific Highway which it runs parallel to.

Getting There
East-West Airlines and other regional airlines operate a network of services to towns in the New England region. You can also travel to New England centres on the trains which operate from Sydney to the region. Although the NSW bus travel restrictions apply in New England there are many regional bus services and Ansett

Pioneer and Greyhound both operate through New England on their Melbourne-Brisbane or Sydney-Brisbane services.

NEWCASTLE TO TAMWORTH
Singleton (population 9600) is a coal mining town on the Hunter River and one of the oldest towns in NSW. In the 1841 jail at Burdekin Park there's a historic museum. Lake Liddell, north-west of the town, is a water sports centre. You're still in the coal-mining area at Muswellbrook (population 8600) and still on the Hunter River. Aberdeen (population 1100) overlooks the Liverpool Plains. Scone (population 3950) is located in beautiful country and has a Historical Society Museum. There's a coal seam at nearby Burning Mountain, Wingen, which has been burning for over a thousand years.

Murrurundi (population 900) is on the Pages River in lush, green countryside. Timor Limestone Caves are 43 km east and you can also reach Burning Mountain from here. Quirindi (population 2850) is high in the Liverpool Ranges, slightly off the New England Highway which continues north to Tamworth.

TAMWORTH (population 29,700)
Spend much time driving the country roads of Australia and listening to a radio and you'll soon realise that country music has a big following. Tamworth, believe it or not, is the country music centre of the nation; an Antipodean Nashville. Each Australia Day weekend the country music awards are handed out here and at CWA Park there's the Country Music Hands of Fame memorial with the hand imprints of many Australian country and western singers. It makes the inevitable Historic Museum seem almost mundane.

Tamworth also has Minamurra House, an old Victorian mansion, Old Mill Cottage which now houses an arts and crafts exhibit, the City Art Gallery and various other attractions. Nundle is a historic gold-mining town, 63 km south-east.

TAMWORTH TO ARMIDALE
Walcha (population 1700) is off the New England Highway on the eastern slope of the Great Dividing Range. There's a Tiger Moth, the first aircraft used in Australia for crop-dusting, on display at the Pioneer Cottage. East of the town is Apsley Gorge National Park with magnificent waterfalls. Back on the highway Uralla (population 2100) is where the noted bushranger Captain Thunderbolt met the bullet with his name on it in 1870, his grave is in Uralla's cemetery. In the 1850s this was a goldrush area and some fossicking is still carried on today near the Rocky River diggings.

ARMIDALE (population 18,900)
The main centre in the region and site of the New England University, Armidale is a popular halting point on the road to Brisbane. The 1000 metre altitude means Armidale is pleasantly cool in the summer. The university art collection is said to be the most important provincial collection in Australia. Armidale also has a Folk Museum, a number of other important early buildings and fine parks.

The Armidale area is noted for its magnificent waterfalls including the Wollomombi Falls, 39 km east, whose 457 metre drop makes them the highest falls in Australia. Other falls include the fine Chandler and Dangar Falls. You can also visit Hillgrove, a gold-mining ghost town.

ARMIDALE TO TENTERFIELD
Guyra (population 1850) is at an altitude of 1300 metres making it one of the highest towns in the state. There are fine views from Chandler's Peak and unusual 'balancing rocks' at Backwater. You're still at over 1000 metres at Glen Innes (population 6050) which was a good place to meet bushrangers a century ago. The town's old hospital now houses a huge folk museum with the unusual name 'Land of the Beardies'.

The road from Glen Innes to Grafton, near the coast, passes through the

Gibraltar Range National Park – lots of lush rainforest and wildlife. There are a range of visitor facilities at the park centre at Dandahra Creek. Glen Innes is still a centre for sapphire mining and you can fossick at Dunvegan Sapphire Reserve on Reddeston Creek.

Tenterfield (population 3400) is the last town of any size before the Queensland border. In the town you can visit Centenary Cottage, dating from 1871, Hillview Doll Museum with more than 1000 dolls on display, or Stannum, a fine old home built in 1888. Historians will find the Sir Henry Parkes Memorial School of Arts interesting.

Out of town, Thunderbolt's Hideout where bushranger Captain Thunderbolt did just that, is 11 km away. It's worth taking the rough road to the Boonoo Boonoo Falls, 32 km north. In Bald Rock National Park the rock which gives the park its name can be climbed and from the top you'll enjoy superb views over Queensland and NSW.

Wollongong

Population 208,000

Only 80 km south of Sydney this is NSW's third largest city, a heavily industrialised centre which includes the biggest steelworks in Australia at Port Kembla. Despite its industrial nature Wollongong is fronted by some superb surf beaches while the hills soar up behind it giving fine views over the city and along the coast.

Information & Orientation

The Leisure Coast Tourist Association has an information centre (tel 28 7068) at 90 Crown St which is open Monday to Friday, 9 am to 5 pm. As well as the usual tourist info they organise tours, book buses (but not trains) and have a free accommodation booking service. They're also a YHA agent.

The Wollongong GPO is at 296-8 Crown St near the railway station but you might find the Wollongong East post office, lower down Crown St opposite the tourist centre, more convenient. The NRMA (tel 29 8133) are on the corner of Burelli and Kembla Sts. Wollongong Saddlery & Bushcraft Equipment at 90 Burelli St have bushwalking gear and there are also surplus shops on Crown St.

Around Town

Enquire at the Port Kembla Visitors' Centre about tours of the steelworks. Wollongong has an interesting harbour, fishing fleet and fish market and an old 1872 lighthouse on the breakwater beside it. The lighthouse is open weekends and school holidays from 1 to 4 pm; don't confuse it with the larger lighthouse on the headland.

There's a Historical Museum in Market Square, open Wednesday 10 am to 1 pm, Saturday, Sunday and public holidays 1.30 to 4.30 pm, admission is $1. The museum has reminders of the town's early days – including a reconstruction of the 1902 Mt Kembla village mining disaster.

The modern Wollongong City Gallery on Kiera and Burelli Sts is open Tuesday to Sunday from 12 noon to 5 pm. The Sea Treasure Cave Museum in the tourist office has an interesting little collection of shells and sea animals.

Amongst the lookouts above the town is Bald Hill where pioneer aviator Lawrence Hargraves made his first attempts at flying early this century. Hang gliders hang out there today. If you want to have a go at hang gliding, courses are offered by Aerial Technics (tel 94 2545). Australian wildlife roams free at the Symbio Animal Gardens, Helensburgh. There's a huge Moreton Bay Fig at Figtree.

Out of Town

The hills rise suddenly and dramatically behind Wollongong and you get spectacular views over the town and coast from the Bulli Pass which runs high above

Wollongong

0 .5 1 km

To Sydney

Wollongong Harbour

1 Australian Iron & Steel Works Visitors Centre
2 Railway Station
3 Wollongong Post Office
4 Art Gallery
5 NRMA
6 Wollongong East Post Office
7 Ansett
8 TAA
9 Tourist Office
10 Historical Museum
11 Wollongong Beach
12 New Lighthouse
13 Old Lighthouse

Wollongong. The country is equally spectacular heading inland (and up) through the Macquarie Pass National Park to Moss Vale or through the Kangaroo Valley.

On the road to Moss Vale you can see a fine local example of Australian kitsch – a huge potato in the middle of town and a motel called the Spud Motel. Yes, this is a potato growing area.

South of Wollongong, Lake Illawarra is popular for watersports and there are also a number of reservoirs and dams in the vicinity. At Jamberoo there's grass skiing and a twin waterslide.

Places to Stay

The tourist office will make accommodation bookings free but there are no hostels or similar cheap accommodation in town.

Hotels *Tattersalls Hotel* (tel 29 1952) at 333 Crown St up by the railway station charges $14 per person room only, $5 more with breakfast. Reasonably priced snacks and meals are available at the bar. On Market St the *Hotel Illawarra* (tel 29 5421) charges $18/30 room only, $6 more with breakfast.

At the corner of Crown and Station Sts near the station the *Centre Plaza Motel* (tel

29 7444) has hotel-style rooms at $13/20 and motel rooms at $20/32.

Still within walking distance of the centre (but get off at North Wollongong Station if you're travelling by rail) is the *Hotel North Wollongong* (tel 29 4177) on the corner of Flinders St (the Princes Highway) and Bourke St. The room only price is $10 per person. Four km south at Figtree, the *Figtree Hotel* (tel 28 4088) offers a bit more with attached bathrooms and tea-making facilities for $19/27, plus $5 more per person for breakfast.

Guest Houses Many of Wollongong's guest houses won't take casual visitors but you could try *Breadalbane Guest House* (tel 29 1749) at 25 Kembla St or the *Excelsior Guest House* (tel 28 9320) at 5 Parkinson St. They're unlikely to offer daily rates but, by the week, singles cost around $60 or $70 per person for a shared room.

Motels Wollongong motels tend to be expensive, but note the *Centre Plaza Motel* under 'Hotels' above. The *Piccadilly* (tel 29 6544) at 349 Crown St (between the post office and the railway) costs $24 to $26 single, $34 to $40 double. All rooms are fully equipped.

South at Figtree, *Sunsets Figtree Village* (tel 71 1122) on the Princes Highway has similar facilities at $35/42. At Fairy Meadow, 3.5 km north of Wollongong, the *Cabbage Tree Hotel-Motel* (tel 84 4000) has units for $25/35 for singles/doubles.

Colleges *International House* on the Princes Highway in North Wollongong has accommodation during the vacations for about $12.

Camping As usual with Australian cities you have to go a little way out before you can camp. The Wollongong City Council have camping areas at Corrimal (at the beach), Bulli (in Farrell Rd, adjacent to the beach) and Windang (in Fern St with beach and lake frontage). Bulli is 11 km

north, Corrimal about half way there and Windang is 15 km south, between Lake Illawarra and the sea. All charge $5 for two people.

There's another camping ground in Windang – the *Oasis Holiday Park* (tel 95 1591) at 142 Windang Rd. It's more expensive to camp ($8 for two) but it does have on-site vans ranging from $22 to $27, plus holiday units at $28/31 and motel rooms at $39/45.

Places to Eat

Wollongong's pubs offer the best value for money although there are also lots of coffee lounges open during the day. The one in the Piccadilly Place, up Crown St near the railway station, is possibly a bit better than average. One non-pub eatery definitely worth mentioning is the *International Centre* at 28 Stewart St, between Kembla and Corrimal Sts, where you can enjoy moderately priced Italian food – $6 to $7.50 for main courses.

Reasonably priced snacks and meals at breakfast and lunchtime are available at *Tattersalls Hotel* at 333 Crown St by the railway. The *Grand Hotel* on the corner of Keira and Burelli Sts has a snack bar with reasonably priced lunches – $3 to $4, burgers for $1.20. The *Oval Room* in the Grand serves home cooked goodies with main courses around $6. *Hotel Wollongong* on Crown St has meals at $4 to $5, the *Hotel Illawarra* on Kiera St offers a $3 lunch with salad. The *North Wollongong Hotel* on the corner of Bourke St and the Princes Highway has a cook-your-own-steak set up.

There are a couple of good value Turkish places in Wollongong – the *Topkapi Kebab Restaurant* at 76 Crown St and the *Istanbul Kebab* next door to the Grand Hotel on Kiera St. There's also a Mexican restaurant in Wollongong – *Amigos* at 116 Kiera St is open for dinner from Tuesday to Sunday. Right by the fish market, which is right by the fishing boat harbour, you'll find *Rosemary's Fish & Chips* – the fish should be fresh!

Entertainment

Wollongong activity is mainly in the suburbs and not usually on a regular basis. The *Illawarra Mercury* has details of what's on. On the corner of Burelli and Keira Sts the *Grand Hotel* has jazz on Saturday evenings. The Leagues Clubs have occasional bands and non-members can usually get in, except at Corrimal. The Illawarra Leagues in Church St has something on every Wednesday night. The *North Wollongong Hotel* has music on Sunday afternoons, the *Charles Hotel* up at Fairy Meadow on Fridays and the *Cabbage Tree* (very popular) Wednesdays to Saturdays. Wollongong University Union often has something going on.

Paddy's Market in Burelli St isn't bad. The Wollongong Festival in the first week of the August-September school holidays offers all sorts of activities.

Getting There

Air The local airport at Albion Park, south of town, has some services but generally people fly to Sydney (Mascot) and travel by land. Watts Coaches (tel 29 5100) operate an Airporter Express bus between Wollongong and Mascot eight times daily. The trip takes about 1½ hours and costs $11 for adults. Departures are from 104 Crown St.

You can get to the airport much cheaper, but with a great deal more trouble, by taking a Sydney train to Hurstville, changing there to an Arncliffe train and then making a lengthy (half-hour) walk to the international terminal.

Bus There's a daily Greyhound service to Melbourne via the Princes Highway. The 17-hour trip costs $32.50. Deluxe Coachlines operates daily to Melbourne via Canberra and the Hume Highway for $47.50. This service takes 12 to 14 hours. Just to Canberra costs $20 and takes four hours. All buses operate from the tourist office.

Rail There's no bus to Wollongong from Sydney apart from the airport bus. Bus services are not allowed to compete with rail but the rail services are being considerably improved and the line electrified. The service is fairly frequent and costs $4.20. If you need to catch another train to get to the part of Sydney you're heading for you can buy one ticket for the complete journey which is cheaper than buying them separately. There's no passenger rail service south of Wollongong beyond Nowra nor is there a service to Canberra.

Getting Around

You can reach a lot of Wollongong from the railway line which has a reasonable service along it. Some of the beaches are accessible by rail and there's a service to Kiama. The tourist office has a map of the local bus routes and a timetable for each route. There are no special deals (like day passes) on Wollongong buses.

Pedal Power Cycles (tel 96 6875) at 286 Windang Rd, Windang hires bikes as does Lotap Cycle Hire (tel 84 2796) at Stuart Park. You can hire paddleboats, row boats, catamarans and power boats at Lake Illawarra and at Brighton Beach you can hire aqua-bikes. Half-day tours of Wollongong are available.

South Coast

The Princes Highway runs right along the south coast from Sydney through Wollongong and on to the Victorian border. Although this is a rather longer and slower route between Sydney and Melbourne than the quick Hume Highway it's infinitely more interesting. For much of the way the road runs right along the coast and there are lots of pleasant little towns, good surfing spots and other attractions. The northern part of this route is known as the Illawarra Coast and has fine views, good surf beaches and some busy prawning ports.

The southern part is known as the

Alpine Coast because it is only a short drive inland from the coast to the Snowy Mountains. There are many pleasant little fishing ports and beach resorts on this stretch of the coast from Bateman's Bay to the Victorian border.

WOLLONGONG TO NOWRA
South of Lake Illawarra, Shellharbour (population 1800) is a popular holiday resort from Wollongong. It's one of the oldest towns along the coast and back in 1830 was a thriving port but it declined after the construction of railway lines. There are good beaches on the Windang Peninsula near the town.

Kiama (population 7700) is famous for its blowhole; illuminated at night it can spout up to 60 metres high. On Blowhole Point, Marineland displays blue-ringed octupuses and other aquatic nasties. There is also a Historical Museum, good beaches and the scenic Cathedral Rock at Jones Beach.

Just south of Kiama is Gerringong (population 1700) with fine beaches and surf. Pioneer aviator Charles Kingsford Smith took off from Seven Mile Beach to fly to New Zealand in 1933. Take the time to have a look at the excellent Hilltop Gallery on Fern St.

Berry (population 1200) was an early settlement and has a number of National Trust classified buildings and the almost inevitable Historical Museum. Nearby Coolangatta has a group of buildings now converted for use as a motel – they were the first buildings in the area, constructed by convicts in 1822.

NOWRA & AROUND
On Shoalhaven River, Nowra (population 17,900) is popular for watersports. There are excellent views from Hanging Rock or you can visit the rainforests in Riverside Animal Park. Nearby is Kangaroo Valley with old buildings which include the Friendly Inn, a pioneer farm museum and a reconstruction of an 1880 diary farm.

On the coast from Nowra is Culburra-

Orient Port (population 2000), a quiet resort town with a busy prawning fleet. Jervis Bay has some beautiful holiday resorts around the bay. Ulladulla (population 6500) is an area of beautiful lakes, lagoons and beaches. There's good swimming and surfing at Bendalong or you can make the pleasant bushwalk to the top of Pigeon House Mountain in Moreton National Park.

BATEMANS BAY (population 5000)
This popular resort is at the mouth of the Clyde River – again there's good bushwalking and swimming. You can see penguins and other birds at Tollgate Island Wildlife Reserve. More birds are on view at Batehaven Birdland and there's a Shell Museum one km east.

Like other towns along the coast Moruya (population 2000) is a dairy centre but oyster farming is also carried on here. The old Coomerang House is of interest but south-west is the beautifully situated old gold town of Nerrigundah and the Eurobodalla Historic Museum.

About 80 km inland from Bateman's Bay on the route to Canberra is Braidwood (population 1000) with many old sandstone buildings classified by the National Trust and a historical museum.

NAROOMA & AROUND
Narooma (population 2700) is another oyster town. There are many inlets and lakes around Narooma while near Lake Corunna, Mystery Bay has coloured sand and rock formations. Tilba, just 15 km south of town, is a well preserved little town which has undergone remarkably little change this century. At the junction of the Princes and the Snowy Mountain Highways, Bermagui (population 800) is a fishing centre made famous 50 years ago by American cowboy-novelist Zane Grey.

Inland and on the Princes Highway is Cobargo, another remarkably unspoilt old town. Bega (population 4400) is a useful access point to the snow country. Mimosa Rocks National Park is immediately north of Bega while the town also has a couple of good lookout points and the Bega Historical Museum. Candelo, 39 km south-west, is a picturesque little village which, like Tilba, has had a Rip Van Winkle existence and seen few changes this century.

SOUTH TO THE VICTORIAN BORDER

Continuing south you reach Merimbula (population 2900) another swim-fish-surf centre. On the main street the Old School Museum is just that – once an old stone school building, now a museum. Steamships used to dock at the wharf.

At Eden (population 3100) the road bends away from the coast into Victoria. This old whaling town on Twofold bay has a Whaling Museum with a fine killer whale skeleton. To the north and south of Eden is the Ben Boyd National Park – good for walking, camping and swimming.

Boydtown, south of Eden, was founded by Benjamin Boyd – a flamboyant early settler. His grandiose plans aimed at making Boydtown the capital of Australia but his fortune foundered and so did the town – later he did too, disappearing without trace somewhere in the Pacific. Some of his buildings still stand including a partially finished lighthouse and a ruined church. The Sea Horse Inn, built by convict labour, is still in use today.

The Snowy Mountains

Australia's snowfields straddle the NSW/Victoria border but Mt Kosciusko is firmly in NSW and at 2238 metres its summit is the highest point in Australia. Much of the NSW Snowies are within the boundaries of the Kosciusko National Park, an area of year round activity with skiing in the winter and bushwalking in the summer. The Snowy Mountain Scheme is the best known hydro-electric power development in Australia and also irrigates extensive areas of the Murray region.

COOMA (population 8000)

Just 114 km south of Canberra, this is the gateway to the Snowies and was the construction centre for the Snowy Mountains Scheme. You can walk down Lambi St and see 21 National Trust classified buildings in this town.

A half km west of the town is the wreckage of the *Southern Cloud*, an aircraft which crashed in the Snowies in 1931 and was only discovered in 1958. The Travellers' Rest Pioneer Museum is six km west. It dates from 1861 when it was built as a hotel and staging post for Cobb & Co. Other attractions include the Avenue of Flags in Centennial Park with flags of the 27 nationalities involved in the Snowy Mountains Scheme. You can see wooden clogs made in Clogs Cabin while Raglan Gallery, dating from 1854, has painting, pottery and rugs. Fairy Tale Park, three km out of town, is intended for children.

The Cooma Visitors' Centre is on Sharp St, beside Centennial Park. Cooma is at the junction of the Monaro and the Snowy Mountains Highways. The Snowy Mountains Highway runs north-west to Tumut and then joins the Hume Highway a little south of Gundagai.

KOSCIUSKO NATIONAL PARK

The 6900 square km of New South Wales' largest national park includes caves, glacial lakes, forest and all of the state's ski resorts as well as the highest mountain in Australia. You can drive most of the way towards the top of the mountain past Perisher and Charlotte Valley. The last eight km is on foot although there is a trail right to the top. The explorer who first discovered the peak and climbed to the top named it after Count Kosciusko from his native Poland. The park is also the source of the Snowy, the Murray and the Murrumbidgee Rivers. Although it is snow that the park is most famous for it is also very popular in summer when there are excellent bushwalks and marvellous alpine wildflowers.

Only eight km along the Snowy Mountains Highway from Cooma you can turn to the snowfields area and Mt Kosciusko. The Alpine Way runs through Thredbo and can either be followed as a loop around the park, rejoining the Snowy Mountains Highway at Kiandra, or as a 'back roads' route into Victoria. Although part of the road is unsurfaced it's no problem unless there's deep snow.

Along the Snowy Mountains Highway, just before you enter the park, Adaminaby (population 400) is the jumping-off point for Lake Eucumbene. Cruise boats go across the lake to the animal sanctuary at Grace Lea Island. Kiandra is actually in the park. It was the site of an 1859 gold rush and the crude ski races organised by miners probably predate the popularity of skiing as a sport in Europe. From here you can turn south to Cabramurra, Australia's highest town, and continue south to Khancoban in Victoria, although this road is often closed by snow. From here you follow the Alpine Way back into NSW, past the Murray 1 lookout on the Snowy Scheme. The road makes a loop south around Mt Kosciusko and through Thredbo to Lake Jindabyne.

On the shores of the lake is Jindabyne (population 1600), a popular fishing centre. There's a National Park Information Centre at the entrance to the park, about midway between Jindabyne and Thredbo. A shuttle bus operates in winter from here to Smiggin Holes and Perisher Valley. In 1985 work was started on the 'Skitube', a tunnel railway which will eventually ferry passengers between Little Thredbo and the Perisher car park.

SKIING & SKI RESORTS

Snow skiing in Australia can be a marginal activity – the benefits of pushing the mountains up a 1000 metres higher or shoving the whole country 1000 km south (but only for the winter!) are frequently discussed topics on most ski slopes. The season is short (July, August, September is really all there is) and good snow is by no means a safe bet. Nor, despite claims that the Australian mountains offer more skiable snow than the Swiss Alps, are the mountains ideal – their gently rounded shapes means most long runs are relatively easy and the hard, fast runs tend to be short and sharp. For a final bummer the short seasons means the operators have to get their returns quickly and costs can be high.

Having told you the bad, here's the good – when the snow's there and the sun's shining the skiing can be just fine. So long as you're not some sort of Jean Claude Killy you will find all the fun (not to mention heart-in-the-mouth fear) you could ask for. Plus, the long open slopes of the Australian Alps are a ski-tourers paradise – nordic (cross-country or langlauf) skiing is becoming increasingly popular and many resorts now offer lessons and hire equipment.

For the budget-minded skier the cheapest (and by far the most fun) way to get out on the slopes is to gather a bunch of friends and rent a lodge for a week. You can all chip in for the food and booze and really enjoy yourselves. Costs vary enormously but if you can find a reasonably priced place it can be within the bounds of reason. Bring as much of your food and drink with you as you can as supplies in some resorts tend to be erratic and they're always expensive.

Other costs are tows, lessons, and equipment hire if you do not have your own. Tows vary depending on the resort but count on $20 to $30 a day or $125 to $175 a week. Lessons average about $8 to $10 a session. Boots, skis and stocks can be hired for $18 to $25 a weekend or $40 for a week including both weekends. It's a trade off whether to hire in the city and risk damage and adjustment problems or at the resort and possibly pay more. Last time I skied I managed to break a ski and stock on my first run of the week! There are usually hire centres in towns close to the resorts and many garages also hire ski equipment as well as chains. Snow chains must be carried in the mountains during winter even if there is no snow – there are heavy penalties if you haven't got them.

Australian ski resorts are short of the frenetic nightlife of many European resorts but compensate with lots of partying between the various lodges. Nor is there a great variety of alternative activities apart from toboggan runs. Australia also doesn't have the range of all-in skiing packages which are the cheapest way to get on the slopes in Europe. Weekends tend to get crowded because the resorts are so convenient, particularly from Canberra.

All the main resorts are connected by bus with Cooma which can be reached by road or air. Main resorts with distances in km from Sydney are:

Thredbo (482 km)
The best and most expensive skiing in Australia. Except in exceptional circumstances it is not possible to ski down to the village which is below the normal snow line. There's a youth hostel but it costs $19 a night in the ski season, $5.50 in summer. In the summer this is a popular bushwalking centre and the chairlift to the top of Mt Crackenback operates right through the year.

Perisher Valley (510 km)
Rated just one notch below Thredbo and on a par with the better Victorian resorts Perisher has a wide variety of runs including the highest lifted point (2030 metres) in Australia. Perisher has 40 km of trails.

Charlotte Pass (490 km)
At the base of Mt Kosciusko this is the most isolated resort in Australia. You often have to snowcat the last eight km from Perisher. It has good ski-touring country.

Smiggin Holes (514 km)
The name comes from a Scottish word for a hole scraped by cattle. It's just down the road from Perisher and run by the same management so you can get a combined ski-tow ticket for both resorts. A shuttle bus runs between the two resorts.

Guthega (480 km)
Is small and still relatively new.

TUMUT (population 6300)
On the other side of the park from Cooma this is an alternate entry point. Australia's largest commercial trout farm is at nearby Blowering Dam. The Tourist Information Centre here can tell you about visits to the various centres of the Snowy Hydro-Electric Scheme.

Talbingo Dam and the Yarrangobilly limestone caves (60 km east, about midway between Tumut and Kiandra) are other points to visit. The caves are only open for inspection on a part-time basis – check at the tourist office for exact times. There's also a thermal pool here at a constant temperature of 27°C and some beautiful country in the reserve around the caves.

Batlow (population 1400) is south of Tumut in a fruit-growing area. There's a 'Big Red Apple' centre if you're collecting notable Australian 'big' tourist attractions. Near Batlow is Hume and Hovell's lookout where the two explorers did indeed pause for the view in 1824. Paddy's River Dam was built by Chinese gold miners back in the 1850s. Continuing south from Batlow you reach Tumbarumba (population 2200) a site for the early exploits of bushranger Mad Dog Morgan. There's great mountain scenery and good bushwalks in the area and the Paddy's River Falls are only 16 km from the town.

Beyond Tumut on the Snowy Mountains Highway, before it reaches the Hume Highway, is Adelong (population 800), an old gold-mining centre with a National Trust classified main street. There's a pleasant picnic area two km from the town on the Gundagai Rd at the cascade falls.

Along the Hume Highway

The Hume Highway is the main road between Australia's two largest cities. It's the fastest and shortest road and although it's not necessarily the most interesting there are still a number of places of interest along that well worn route. You can also make some interesting diversions off the Hume. One of the simplest is right at the beginning – when you leave Sydney instead of taking the long, weary trek through the dull outer suburbs towards Camden and Campbelltown you can take the coastal Princes Highway past the Royal National Park to Wollongong. Then just after Wollongong you can cut inland on the Illawarra Highway through the picturesque Macquarie Pass and over beautiful rolling countryside to Moss Vale before rejoining the Hume. Further south you can make a diversion off the highway to visit Canberra or continue beyond Canberra to the Snowy Mountains, rejoining the Hume once again in Victoria.

A word of warning if you're driving along the Hume – this is the broken windscreen centre for Australia. You've not travelled in Australia until you've smashed a windscreen on the Hume so beware of loose stones on the roadside. I've broken one just outside Gundagai.

Getting There

There are flights to a number of the main towns along the Hume Highway. The Melbourne-Sydney bus services run on the Hume and the train services run close to it.

SYDNEY TO GOULBURN

Only 60 km out of Sydney, Camden (population 9000) is virtually an outer suburb of the capital city today. This was one of Australia's first European settlements – John Macarthur arrived here in 1805 and his sheep breeding experiments formed the basis for Australia's sheep farming industry. The town has many early buildings with National Trust classification. Places of interest include Gledswood Cellars, a winery built in an 1810 coaching house. Grape vines were first planted here in 1827 making Camden the first wine producing centre in Australia. Denbigh (1817-27), Camden Park (1834), Kirkham Stables (1816), the Church of St John (1840-49) and Hassall Cottage (1817) are other early buildings. At Camden Airport, south of Narellan, there's an aviation museum with 20 old RAF and RAN aircraft and others including a 1909 Bleriot. Green's Motorcade museum in Leppington has more than 50 veteran and vintage cars plus a motorcycle section.

Continuing along the Hume, Picton (population 1700) is another early settlement with a Tollkeepers Cottage, an old railway viaduct and the early St Mark's Church of England. The Rail Transport Museum at Thirlmere has about 40 locomotives and other pieces including an 1864 engine from railway pioneer Robert Stephenson. Wirrimbirra fauna and flora sanctuary is 13 km south.

Mittagong (population 4200) is a local agricultural centre and has a Doll Museum. West of Mittagong, Joadja is now a ghost town. It's on private property but visits can be made at certain times – check in Mittagong. Just south of Mittagong on the Hume is Berrima (population 700), a tiny town which was founded in 1829 and has changed remarkably little. There are numerous interesting old buildings in the town including the old Surveyor-General Inn and a historical museum.

Bowral (population 6800) is another agricultural centre and from here you can visit the Mt Gibraltar Wildlife Reserve. Four km south of Mittagong a winding 65 km road leads to the Wombeyan Caves where five limestone caverns are open for inspection between 10 am and 4 pm daily. The drive to the caves is through superb mountain scenery and the caves themselves are in a very attractive bush setting.

Moss Vale (population 4400) is a pleasant town off the Hume. Throsby Park House, built between 1834 and 1837, is a fine old home built by the area's first settler. Near Moss Vale is the Morton National Park with excellent bushwalks for the more experienced walker. Bundanoon (population 1000) is a pleasant little town near the entrance to the park.

GOULBURN (population 22,000)

Another Hume centre with a long history, Goulburn was proclaimed a town way back in 1833. Old buildings of interest include the 1840 Riversdale coaching house with its beautiful gardens (open daily except Tuesdays). St Clair History House (about 1843) is a fine old restored mansion.

You can visit the Pelican Sheep Station, 10 km south of the town and see sheep shearing and sheepdog demonstrations – contact Eric Sykes at the station. Goulburn also has a Steam Museum on Crookwell Rd which seems to keep rather irregular hours. Crookwell (population 2100) is north of Goulburn. This was once a gold-mining and bushranging region but today it's just quiet farming country.

GOULBURN TO ALBURY

At Yass (population 4300), 296 km south of Sydney, the Barton Highway branches off the Hume for Canberra. Yass is closely connected with the early explorer Hume, who gave the highway his name. He lived here for 40 years and on Comur St the Hamilton Hume Museum has some exhibits relating to him. Near Yass at Wee Jasper you can visit the limestone Cary's Cave on Sunday afternoons from 1 pm.

Gundagai (population 2300) is one of the most interesting small towns along the Hume. The highway now bypasses the town but it's worth the small extra distance to take the old road. It crosses a long wooden bridge over the flood plains of the Murrumbidgee River, a reminder that in 1852 Gundagai suffered Australia's worst ever flood disaster when 89 people

were drowned. Gold rushes and bushrangers were also part of the town's colourful early history and the notorious Captain Moonlight was tried in Gundagai's National Trust classified, 1859 court house. Other places of interest in town include the Gabriel Gallery on Sheridan St, the Historical Museum and the information centre, also on Sheridan St, with its 20,000 piece marble cathedral model.

Gundagai's most famous monument is eight km out of town. There, still sitting on his tuckerbox, is a sculpture of the dog who in a well known bush ballad, 'sat on the tuckerbox, five miles from Gundagai'. It's now a popular little tourist centre and roadside stop. Near here is the Five Mile Pub, an equally popular place to break your journey back in the pioneer days.

Holbrook (population 1300) was known as Germanton until WW I, when it was renamed after a local war hero. In Holbrook Park you can see a replica of the submarine in which he won a Victoria Cross. The local information centre is located in the interesting Woolpack Inn Museum, in an 1860 hotel.

ALBURY (population 41,000)

The NSW half of the Albury-Wodonga development centre is on the north side of the Murray River. It's a busy and expanding industrial centre and is also an access point from Victoria to the NSW Snowy Mountains. Places of interest in Albury include the Folk Museum in the old Turk's Head Hotel, the tree marked by William Hovell where he crossed the Murray on his expedition from Sydney to Port Phillip (Melbourne wasn't there then) in 1824, and the Botanic Gardens.

Outside the city there's the Ettamogah Wildlife Sanctuary, 11 km north, and the Jindera Pioneer Museum, 16 km north-west. The road across the state line between Albury and Wodonga runs across the Hume Weir dam, the lake behind the dam is very popular for water sports.

South-West & Murray River

A number of roads run through the south-west area of the state – alternative inland routes to Melbourne from Sydney like the road from Cowra to Wagga Wagga and Albury or to West Wyalong and Narrandera. Or there are routes to Adelaide like the road through Hay and Wentworth. The Murray River forms the boundary between NSW and Victoria and although most of the most interesting towns are on the Victorian side NSW also has several interesting centres.

WAGGA WAGGA (population 36,800)
Wagga is a major inland city on the Murrumbidgee River. It's a busy farming centre with a Botanic Gardens and zoo. Wallacetown Historical Arms Museum is 20 km south of Wagga. The name is pronounced 'wogga' not 'wagga' and is usually abbreviated to just the one word. Just north of Wagga is Junee (population 4000) with some historic buildings including the lovely old homestead Monte Cristo.

WEST WYALONG (population 3800)
An old gold-mining town at the point where the Mid Western and Newell Highways meet, West Wyalong's District Museum has a gold-mine model and also local fossils. When there's plenty of water available Lake Cowal, 48 km north-east, is the biggest lake in the state. When there isn't so much water, it isn't. Lake Cargelligo (population 1200) is north-west of West Wyalong and has lots of bird life.

NARRANDERA (population 5000)
Near the junction of the Newell and Sturt Highways, Narrandera is in the Murrumbidgee Irrigation Area, there's a 'MIA' information centre in the town. There's a koala centre near the town and a group of swimming pools at Lake Talbot. Only 30 km away is Leeton (population 6500) with Australia's biggest fruit cannery.

Between Narrandera and Deniliquin is Jerilderie (population 1000) immortalised by the bushranger Ned Kelly who held up the whole town for two days back in 1879, locking the local police force up in their own jail. Kelly relics can be seen in the Telegraph Office Museum on Powell St.

GRIFFITH (population 13,000)
This busy farming centre was planned by Canberra's architect, Walter Burley Griffin. Apart from fruit, grain and grapes Griffith has also gained something of a reputation for local marijuana production and for the unpleasant events that have befallen people who found out too much about the local marijuana growers' activities. There's a Pioneer Park Museum just north of the town and bushwalking in the Cocoparra National Park, 19 km north-east. There's a Tourist Information Centre on the corner of Banna Avenue and Jondaryan Avenue.

HAY (population 3000)
At the junction of three highways Hay is a major sheep raising centre. There are some fine beaches along the Murrumbidgee in this area. The town has some interesting old buildings like the Hay Gaol Museum, a fine old 1883 fountain and a plaque in Lachlan St marking Charles Sturt's journey on the Murrumbidgee and Murray Rivers in 1828-30. There's a mini-zoo in South Hay.

DENILIQUIN (population 7700)
A sheep raising centre where much irrigated farming is also carried out, the town has an Exhibition Centre with Aboriginal artefacts and other displays. A footbridge from Cressy St runs to the Island Wildlife Sanctuary. There's good swimming at Sandy McLeans Beach.

ALONG THE MURRAY
Although the Murray River forms the boundary between NSW and Victoria from the Snowy Mountains right to the South Australian border, most of the

important river towns are on the Victorian side. It's no problem to hop back and forth across the river as in many places roads run along both sides. Albury (see the Hume Highway section) is the main NSW town on the Murray and also the first big town on the river down from its source. The Murray was once an important means of communication with paddle steamers splashing up and down stream like on an antipodean Mississippi.

Corowa (population 3400) is a wine producing centre downstream from Albury. The Lindeman winery here has been operating since 1860. On the second Sunday of each month and on public holidays there are train rides on the miniature Bangerang Railway. Tocumwal (population 1100) is a quiet Murray town with a giant fibreglass codfish in the town square. The town has a sandy river beach and is a very popular gliding centre. The Rocks is a popular picnic spot 11 km from town.

WENTWORTH (population 1250)

Close to where the Darling and Murray Rivers meet Wentworth is overshadowed by nearby Mildura on the Victorian side of the Murray. The old paddle steamer *Ruby* is on display near the Darling River bridge in Fotherby Park. Wentworth has a Folk Museum & Arts Centre and the 1879-81 jail has a display of the sorts of things the authorities used when they wanted to be unpleasant to prisoners. Admission to the jail is $1.50.

North of Wentworth on Mungo Station is the Wall of China, a strange 30 km long natural wall. Tours operate there from Mildura in Victoria.

Central West

The central west region starts inland from the Blue Mountains and continues for about 400 km, gradually fading into the harsh environment of the far west of the

state. This region, directly inland from Australia's first European settlement in Sydney, has some of the earliest inland towns in the country. Bathurst is the natural gateway to the region and from here you can turn north-east through Orange and Dubbo or south-west through Cowra and West Wyalong. The Western Highway running from Bathurst through Cowra, Wagga Wagga to Albury is an alternative Sydney-Melbourne route. Like the coastal Princes Highway it's longer than the direct Hume route but provides very different scenery and makes an interesting alternative for anyone suffering from the well known complaint 'Hume-ennui'.

Getting There

Air Airlines of New South Wales fly from Sydney to a number of centres in the central west including Coonabarabran, Coonamble, Dubbo, Mudgee and Walgett. There are services from Dubbo to other locations in the central and far west of the state.

Bus The usual NSW bus travel complications apply to some extent in the central west region. Ansett Pioneer and Greyhound have services through the region on routes between Sydney and Broken Hill or Brisbane and Melbourne.

Rail Trains operate from Sydney to Mudgee and Dubbo and from there connecting buses operate to Bourke ($39.20), Brewarrina ($39.20), Cobar ($36.70), Coonamble ($34.50), Walgett ($36.70) and other centres.

LITHGOW (population 12,800)

On the western fringe of the Blue Mountains, Lithgow is noted for the famous Zig Zag railway along which trains descended from the Blue Mountains until 1910. The line was built in 1868 and was quite an engineering wonder in its day. Now restored, the line is operated for visitors on Saturdays from 11 am to 4.30

pm and on Sundays from 10 am to 4.30 pm. It's 10 km out of Lithgow.

In the city, Eskbank House on Bennet St is a gracious old home built in 1841. There are fine views from Hassan Wall's Lookout, five km south of town. The interesting little village of Hartley with its fine courthouse, built by convicts in 1837, is nine km away on the Katoomba side of Lithgow.

BATHURST (population 19,600)

Situated 208 km from Sydney, Bathurst is Australia's oldest inland city. It's a fine old town with many early buildings reflecting its long, by Australian standards, history. They include the 1835 Holy Trinity Church and the remains of the Old Government House of 1817 which stand behind the Folk Museum. Apart from the usual pioneering exhibits the museum also displays Aboriginal artefacts. Bathurst also has an Art Gallery and a Museum of Applied Arts & Sciences. Eight km out of town is Abercrombie House, a huge mansion of the 1870s.

Close to the town is the Mt Panorama motor racing circuit, a true road circuit and the finest racing track in Australia. One of Australia's best known car races, the Bathurst 1000 km for production cars, takes place here each October and it's the annual event for which Bathurst is best known. The track is only used twice each year, the other occasion being the Easter motorcycle events which always seem to be followed by an exciting bikie rampage. In fact mayhem during the races has become such a monotonous feature that you almost have the feeling that the newspapers have *Bikies Cops Clash* headlines all set up even before Easter rolls round. Part of the track is closed off and only open during the races but the rest of it is normal public road and you can drive round it any time. Apart from race time of course!

Mt Panorama also has a couple of more permanent attractions. The Sir Joseph Banks Nature Reserve at Mt Panorama has koalas, kangaroos and wallabies. The Bathurst Gold Diggings is a reconstruction of an early gold-mining town. Bathurst has a Tourist Bureau in the Civic Centre.

AROUND BATHURST

The Abercrombie Caves are 72 km south of the city – the spectacular Arch Cave is a major feature of these limestone caverns. Between Bathurst and Cowra is Blayney (population 2700) close to Carcoar, an interesting little place very much like an English village.

North of Bathurst the old mining town of Hill End was the scene for a gold rush in 1871-74 and has many fine old buildings from that era. It's a particularly interesting old town and well worth a visit. The Royal Hotel was opened at the height of the rush in 1872 and has been operating ever since. There's an information centre in the old Hill End Hospital. North-east of Bathurst is Rylstone (population 650) where there are some interesting Aboriginal rock paintings just outside the town (enquire at the shire council) while 16 km north there are fine tree ferns in Fern Tree Gully.

MUDGEE (population 6000)

Further north, 126 km from Bathurst, Mudgee is a pleasant town with many fine old buildings and a Colonial Museum. Mudgee is becoming well known for the many enthusiastic small wineries that have sprung up here. People who find the Hunter Valley altogether too commercial report that Mudgee wineries are a delight to visit. And they make some nice wine too.

Only 30 km north-west is Gulgong (population 1700) an old gold town which features on the Australian $10 note. Although there are many finely restored old buildings here none of the ones that appear on the $10 note still remain! This was also the boyhood home of poet Henry Lawson who also appears on the note. Tours run from here to the Nagundie Aboriginal waterhole on Wednesdays, weekends and public holidays.

Further east towards New England is Merriwa (population 900) at the western end of the Hunter with a number of historic buildings including an 1857 historical museum. Cassilis also has some historic old stone buildings and between there and Mudgee there are some Aboriginal cave paintings just off the road.

ORANGE (population 27,600)

This important fruit producing centre does not, curiously enough, grow oranges! It was considered as a site for the federal capital before Canberra was eventually selected. This was the pioneer poet Banjo Paterson's home town and there is a memorial to him in the city. There's an art exhibition in the modern Civic Centre in Byng St while the Historical Museum on Sale St has exhibits including an Aboriginal carved tree about 300 years old.

Australia's first real goldrush took place at Ophir, 27 km north of Orange. The area is now a wildlife reserve and it's still popular with fossickers. There are a number of other popular parks and centres around Orange. The Lake Canobolas Park is eight km south-west while a further six km brings you to the Mt Canobolas Park with a series of walking trails. You can hire bicycles to get around the Mini-Bike Tourist Park, 10 km north.

Molong (population 1400) is north-west on the road to Wellington and four km south-east of the town is the grave of Yaranigh, the Aboriginal guide of explorer Sir Thomas Mitchell.

COWRA (population 8400)

On the alternative inland route to Melbourne the pleasant town of Cowra was the site of a Japanese prisoner of war camp during WW II. In 1944 an amazing mass prison break was made by the Japanese, resulting in the death of nearly 250 prisoners, many of them by suicide. Four prison guards were also killed but all the escapees were soon rounded up. The strange tale of this impossible escape attempt was told in the book and film titled *Die Like the Carp*. There's a Japanese war cemetery five km south of the town and two km south-east of the cemetery a memorial marks the site of the escape attempt. A plaque tells the tale of the breakout.

The Wyangala dam and park is 40 km from Cowra and has good water sport facilities. North of Cowra is Canowindra (population 1700) notable for its fine, curving main street and for the time in 1863 when bushranger Ben Hall bailed up the whole town!

GRENFELL (population 2000)

This old gold-mining town is 56 km west from Cowra towards West Wyalong. It was the birthplace of Australia's famous poet and author, Henry Lawson. There are good walks in the Waddin Mountain National Park, 18 km south-east.

YOUNG (population 6900)

South-west of Cowra towards Wagga Wagga, Young is a fruit growing centre with an earlier gold-mining history. This was the site of the anti-Chinese riots at Lambing Flats in 1861 and you can find out more about this unpleasant incident in the Lambing Flats Historic Museum. Between Young and Wagga is Cootamundra (population 6500).

FORBES (population 8000)

Another old gold town Forbes has a Historical Museum and the notorious bushranger Ben Hall is buried in the town's cemetery. He was killed in a shoot out in 1865. A km south of the town is the Lachlan Vintage Village which is open daily but does not have working demonstrations on Mondays or Tuesdays. Between Orange and Forbes is Eugowra (population 700) where one of early NSW's most spectacular gold-escort robberies took place. The town has a small museum.

PARKES (population 9000)

On the Newell Highway Parkes has a Motor Museum, a Pioneer Park Museum and the pleasant Kelly Reserve on the north side of town. A huge radio telescope stands 23 km north of the town. It's open daily and there's a visitors' centre.

WELLINGTON (population 5300)

Only 50 km from Dubbo, Wellington is noted for its limestone caves including the Wellington Cave, nine km from town. In the town there's a historical museum housed in a former bank. Walking trails lead to the lookout at Binjang in the Mt Arthur Reserve. Wellington also has several wineries.

DUBBO (population 30,000)

North of Parkes and Orange and 420 km from Sydney, Dubbo is another agricultural, sheep and cattle-raising town with some old buildings and a pioneer museum on Macquarie St. The Old Dubbo Gaol, with the gallows on display, is another city attraction. There is a fair amount on the Governor family whose exploits are related in the *The Chant of Jimmy Blacksmith*.

Dubbo is a pleasant place, situated on the Macquarie River and Newell Highway, but its main point of interest is five km south-west of town. There the Western Plains Zoo is the largest open-range zoo in Australia with many animals in open enclosures. You can hire bicycles in the zoo and ride around the exhibits which are divided into their continent of origin.

North-West

From Dubbo roads radiate out to the north-west of the state. The Newell Highway runs north-east right across the state, an excellent road which provides the quickest route between Melbourne and Brisbane. The Castlereagh Highway runs more or less directly north into the

rugged opal country towards the Queensland border, the surfaced road ends just before Lightning Ridge. The Mitchell Highway heads off north-west to Bourke via Nyngan. At Nyngan the Barrier Highway forks off directly west to Broken Hill in New South Wales' far west.

ALONG THE NEWELL

Gilgandra (population 2700) has the Gilgandra Observatory & Display Centre with an audio-visual of the moon landing and NASA Gemini flights plus a historical display. Gilgandra is a junction town where the Newell and Castlereagh divide and a road also cuts across to the Mitchell.

At Coonabarabran (population 3000) you can visit Miniland, eight km west, where there are life-size prehistoric animal models and the almost inevitable historical museum. This is also the access point for the Warrumbungle National Park where there are excellent walks and rock climbing possibilities. You can get a walks map from the park headquarters at Canyon Camp. The final 10 km of the road into the park is fairly rough. The largest optical telescope in the southern hemisphere is at Siding Springs, 24 km west at the edge of the park.

Narrabri (population 7300) is a cotton growing centre with a solar observatory and also a cosmic ray research centre. The town also has agricultural research centres, one of them involved in research into cotton growing. The Mt Kaputar National Park is east of Narrabri while to the west is Wee Waa (population 1900) a wine and cotton growing centre.

The huge dish of an OTC overseas communications antenna marks Moree (population 10,400). The town is situated on the flood-prone Gwydir River. From Moree the road is fairly dull until you finally reach Boggabilla and cross the border to Goondiwindi in Queensland.

MOREE TO NEW ENGLAND

Between Moree and Glen Innes in the

New England area is Bingara (population 1250), a gemstone centre with an early gold mining history. The National Trust classified Historical Society Museum was probably the town's first hotel.

Inverell (population 9700) is further east and is a popular fossicking centre, particularly for sapphires. The town has a National Trust classified courthouse and a Pioneer Village with buildings collected together which date from the 1830s. Warialda (population 1300) is another gemstone centre in the vicinity. A little south of Inverell is Tingha (population 900) with the excellent Smith's museum of mining and natural history. Tingha is a tin-mining centre and a tin dredge still operates in Copes Creek.

South from here towards Tamworth is Barraba (population 1700) in fine mountain country. The views from the top of Mt Kaputar, which can also be reached from Narrabri, are particularly fine. The Nandewar Mountains and the Horton River Falls are other scenic attractions. South again is Manilla (population 2100), noted for its production of honey and mead.

ALONG THE CASTLEREAGH

The Castlereagh Highway divides from the Newell at Gilgandra and you can also reach the Warrumbungle park from Gulargambone. Coonamble (population 3100) is at the edge of the Western Plains and from here you can travel west to the extensive Macquarie Marshes with their prolific birdlife. The road continues north to Walgett in harsh, dry country near the Grawin and Glengarry opal fields. This is a popular area for opal fossickers.

Near the Queensland border, Lightning Ridge (population 1100) is a huge opal field claimed to be the only site in the world where black opals can be found. This remote centre is heavily into tourism with underground opal showrooms, an art gallery, a bottle museum and an opal mine which you can visit. The town centres around the Diggers Rest Hotel.

ALONG THE MITCHELL

From Dubbo the Mitchell Highway passes through the citrus growing centre of Narromine (population 3000). Warren, further north and off the Mitchell on the Macquarie Highway, is another jumping off point for the Macquarie marshes, as is Nyngan where the Mitchell and Barrier Highways divide. The huge marshes are breeding grounds for ducks, water hens, swans, pelicans, ibis, and herons. Nyngan (population 2500) was the scene for fierce conflicts between Aboriginals and early pioneers.

The country up in the north-west, the Western Plains which stretch away on the inland side of the Great Dividing Range, is a vast, tree-dotted plain eventually shelving off into the barren New South Wales outback – the 'back of Bourke'. From Nyngan the highway and the railway both run arrow-straight for 206 km to Bourke and further west really is the 'back of beyond'.

BOURKE (population 3300)

On the Darling River and the Mitchell Highway, nearly 800 km north-west of Sydney, Bourke is notable for nothing much apart from being the centre of a huge tract of outback. In fact 'back of Bourke' is synonymous with the outer-outback, the back of beyond. A glance at the map will show just how outback the area is – there's no town of any size for far around and the country is flat and featureless as far as the eye can see.

Look for the Cobb & Co signs on the old Carrier Arms Hotel in Bourke. Fort Bourke Stockade was just south of Bourke and there's a memorial to the tangle an early explorer had with hostile Aboriginals here.

Brewarrina (population 1200) is 100 km east of Bourke. The name is an Aboriginal word meaning 'good fishing' and there are Aboriginal stone fishing traps, known as the 'rocks' or the 'fisheries', just down from a weir they built in the Darling River.

The Far West

The far west of NSW is rough, rugged and sparsely populated but it also produces a fair proportion of the state's wealth – particularly from the mines of Broken Hill. The Barrier Highway is the main access route into the region but Broken Hill is actually closer to Adelaide than Sydney and it's really more closely aligned to the South Australian capital. Although Broken Hill is so far from everywhere there are a number of places of great interest in the west of the state.

MOOTWINGEE

In the Bynguano Range, 131 km north of Broken Hill, there is an aboriginal tribal ground with rock carvings and cave paintings – a national historic site which has, unfortunately, been badly defaced in the past by vandals. There is also much wildlife and birdlife in the area and it is a place of quite exceptional beauty. There is a very informative Visitors' Centre at the site and a ranger now protects the relics.

MENINDEE LAKES

This water storage development on the Darling River, 112 km south-east of Broken Hill, offers a variety of water sport facilities. Menindee (population 450) is the town for the area. Bourke and Wills stayed in the Maiden's Hotel on their unlucky trip north in 1860. The hotel was built in 1854 and has been with the same family for nearly 100 years. The Kinchega National Park is close to the town and the lakes, overflowing from the Darling River, are a haven for birdlife.

THE BARRIER HIGHWAY

The Barrier Highway heads west from Nyngan; it's 594 km from there to Broken Hill. This road is an alternative route between Sydney and Adelaide and is also the most direct route between Sydney and Western Australia.

Cobar (population 3600) has a modern and highly productive copper mine but it also has an earlier history as evidenced by its old buildings, like the fine Great Western Hotel with its endless stretch of iron-lacework ornamenting the verandah. Enquire at the Tourist Information Centre in the main street about mine tours.

Near Cobar you can see 'Towser's Huts', mud and stone huts rented out to miner in the 1890s. Weather balloons are released at 9 am and 3 pm daily from the met station near Cobar. The Mt Grenfell Aboriginal cave paintings are 40 km west of Cobar – you have to phone the homestead (Cobar 226) for permission to visit them.

Wilcannia (population 980) is on the Darling River and in the days of paddle steamers was an important river port. It's a much quieter place today but you can still see old buildings from that era – including the Athenaeum Chambers where the Tourist Information Centre is located.

About 100 km off the Barrier Highway is White Cliffs, an old opal mining settlement where you can fossick for opals. There's a walk-in opal mine here and the skeleton of a plesiosaur, found in a mine, is also on display. You can also see various early buildings including Clancy's Hut, an old miner's home. As in Coober Pedy in the outback of South Australia there are many underground homes.

BACK OF BOURKE

Back of Bourke really is just what the name says. There's no surfaced road anywhere west of here in NSW and if you cared to drive from Bourke to Broken Hill via Wanaaring and Milparinka it's unsurfaced for the whole 713 km apart from the final 10 km or so into Broken Hill. Milparinka, once a gold town, now consists of little more than a solitary hotel although some old sandstone buildings still remain.

In 1845 Charles Sturt's expedition from Adelaide, searching for a central Australian sea, were forced to camp near here for six months. The temperatures were high, the conditions terrible and their supplies inadequate. You can see the grave of James Poole, Sturt's second in command, about 14 km north-west of the settlement. Poole died of scurvy. There's a stone cairn built by the expedition members on Mt Pool, 20 km north-west.

Tibooburra (population 200) is right up in the north-west corner and has a number of local stone buildings from the 1880s and '90s, including two hotels. It used to be known as The Granite from the granite outcrops in the area. Tibooburra is an entry point for the Sturt National Park.

At Cameron's Corner, right on the north-west corner of the state, there's a post to mark the place where Queensland, South Australia and NSW meet. It's a favourite goal for visitors to this area and four-wheel drive is not necessary to get there. It is recommended that you inform the park ranger before venturing into the park, however.

This far-western corner of the state is a harsh, dry area of red plains, heat, dust and flies but also interesting physical features and prolific wildlife. The border between NSW and Queensland is marked by the dingo proof fence, patrolled every day by boundary riders who each look after a 40 km section. Always seek local advice before setting off to travel in this area, particularly on secondary roads.

Country Race Meets

Some of the country race meetings are real occasions – the one at Louth, about 100 km south-west of Bourke, is particularly revered. The town's population is about 50 and one year they recorded 29 planes 'flying in for the day'!

Broken Hill

Population 27,000

Far out in the far west, Broken Hill is a fascinating town, not only for its comfortable existence in an extremely unwelcoming environment but also for the fact that it

was once a one-company town which in turn brought about one equally strong union. The Barrier Industrial Council pretty well runs the place.

The Broken Hill Company, after which the town was named, was formed after a silver lode was discovered near the present town. Miners were already working on other finds in the area and a false goldrush in 1867 had failed to notice the real wealth of the area. Today they are still working the richest silver-lead deposit in the world. Broken Hill is 1170 km west of Sydney but only 509 km from Adelaide so in many ways it is more aligned to South Australia than NSW. Even the clocks are set on Adelaide (central Australian) rather than Sydney (eastern Australian) time. It's really a hell of a long way from anywhere though, an oasis in the wilderness.

Information

Broken Hill has a very imposing tourist information centre on the corner of Bromide and Blende Sts. It's open every day of the week. The building is also the main bus station, houses rent-a-car desks and has a snack bar. The RAA (tel 2414) has its office at 261 Argent St and provides reciprocal service to other autoclub members. Broken Hill has a daily newspaper, the *Barrier Daily Truth*. The city is laid out in a straightforward grid pattern, the central area is quite compact and easy to get around on foot.

Mining

Four companies now operate the Broken Hill mines and you can take tours of the surface works of the North Mine on weekday afternoons at 2 pm. The tour takes two hours and you must wear sturdy footwear. Delprat's mine has an underground tour where you don miners' gear and descend 130 metres underground for a tour lasting nearly two hours. The cost is $12 and on weekdays the tours leave at 10.30 am, on Saturdays at 2 pm; nobody under 12 years of age is allowed on the tours; phone 88 1604 for details. To get there go up Iodide St, across the railway tracks and follow the signs, about five minutes drive.

About 45 minutes drive south of Broken Hill is the Triple Chance Mine where you can fossick. The turn-off is 29 km south, then it's 14 km off the road. The mine is open Tuesday and Thursday from 9.30 am to 4.30 pm. The Gladstone Mining Museum in South Broken Hill has life size working exhibits in an old hotel. It's open 2 to 5 pm daily and admission is 80c.

Other

Walking tours of the city are organised Monday to Friday at 10.30 am, Sunday at 10.30 am and 2.30 pm. Enquire at the information centre.

Broken Hill has a Railway, Mineral & Train Museum housed in the old railway station. There are many old railway trains and other pieces of railway equipment. It's open daily from 9 am to 5 pm but closed for lunch for an hour from 12.30 pm. Admission is $1.

There's a relic of the Afghan camel trains of the last century in the Afghan Mosque, built in 1891. It's on the corner of William and Buck Sts in North Broken Hill, is open only on Sunday afternoons, and admission is 10c.

Artists

Broken Hill seems to inspire artists and there is quite a plethora of galleries in the town. They include the Civic Centre Gallery and the Pro Hart Gallery on Wyman St. Pro Hart, a former miner, is Broken Hill's best known artist and quite a local personality. His gallery, with an

1 Tourist Lodge
2 Tourist & Travel Centre
3 Black Lion Inn
4 Mario's Motel
5 Railway Museum
6 Mario's Palace Hotel
7 Civic Centre
8 Post Office
9 Grand Private Hotel
10 Royal Exchange Hotel
11 RSL Club
12 Silver Spade Motel
13 Pancake Kitchen
14 Papa Joe's Pizza

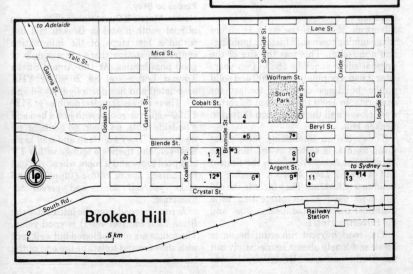

Broken Hill

amazing collection of paintings quite apart from his own work, charges admission ($2) but many others don't.

Some of the local artists are friendly local characters willing to spend the time to chat with visitors to their galleries. I particularly liked Hugh Schulz's gallery at 51 Morgan St – I liked his naive art style and he's an interesting man to talk with. The Ant Hill Gallery at 110 Wyman St features local and major Australian artists.

In the Civic Centre is the 'Silver Tree', a sculpture commissioned by the man who first discovered the town's fabulous mineral wealth back in 1883. It was only acquired by the city council and put on public display in 1975.

Around Town

Eight km from the town you can visit the Royal Flying Doctor Service at 4 pm each day. You must ring 2341 and book in advance. If you want to sit in on a School of the Air, which broadcasts lessons to kids in isolated homesteads, ring Broken Hill 3565 for the news. All visitors must be seated by 8.40 am for the 45 minute session.

Silverton

Silverton, 25 km to the west, is an old silver-mining town with historic buildings and a museum. This was the site of the original silver strike in 1883. Two years later it had a population of 3000 and solid public buildings designed to last for centuries. In 1889 the mines at Silverton were closed and the population shifted to Broken Hill.

Today it's an interesting little ghost town, used as a setting in the film *Mad Max II* (*The Road Warrior* in the States) and *A Town Like Alice*. A number of buildings still stand. They include the old jail, now used as an interesting little historical museum (admission 30c) and the Silverton Hotel.

The road beyond Silverton becomes bleak and lonely almost immediately but the Umberumberka Reservoir, 10 km

from Silverton, is a popular picnic spot and Penrose Park has animal and birdlife.

A variety of camel tours are operated from Silverton – contact Bill Canard (91 1682 or 91 1652) at Silverton. A day trek to the Mundi Mundi Plains costs $45. A day and a night costs $70. There are also short treks around Silverton for $10 or a two hour sunset trek for $20.

Further Out

Euriowie has interesting rock formations and Aboriginal artefacts. There are more again at Yanco Glen Hotel, just 30 km north of Broken Hill.

A really interesting way to see some of the country beyond Broken Hill is to go along on an outback mail run. Contact Barrier Air Taxi Service (tel 88 4307). Their Saturday mail run departs at 7 am and takes you round 25 outback stations before arriving back at Broken Hill at 5 pm. Cost is $90 including lunch. They also do various outback air tours – you can make a day trip to Cameron's Corner for $175 or to the Bourke and Wills 'dig' tree and Innaminka for $270.

Places to Stay

Hotels, Motels & Guest Houses There is no official youth hostel in Broken Hill but within a few steps of the information centre/bus station there are a couple of good possibilities. At 100 Argent St the Tourist Lodge (tel 88 2086) is YHA associated and has dorm beds at $6 and $7. There are also singles/doubles at $12/ 17.50 – spartan rooms with just a bed and a bedside table, no chair, no bedlight, no washbasin! They are clean and well kept, however, and there's a lounge with a TV and pool table and a room where you can fix yourself tea or coffee (supplied) and make yourself toast and cereal for breakfast.

Across the road from the info centre the *Black Lion Inn* (tel 4801) is good value. The rooms are old fashioned but well kept with showers and toilets at the end of the corridor.

Along Argent St there is a string of hotels, most of them very grand old places like *Mario's Palace Hotel* (tel 2385) at 227 with its reproduction of Botticelli's Venus on the ceiling over the stairs! Rooms are $25/38 with your own bathroom, cheaper with washbasin only. Further down at 320 Argent St, on the corner of Chloride St, the *Royal Exchange* (tel 2308) is an equally grand old place with comfortable rooms at $15/24 or $30/36 with your own facilities. The *Grand Hotel* (tel 5305) at 317 is $16 per person bed and breakfast. At 347, the *Theatre Royal Hotel* (tel 3318) is cheap at $14/22 for singles/doubles. There are lots more hotels around town.

Broken Hill also has plenty of motels, although most of them are expensive. *Mario's Hotel-Motel* (tel 5145) at 172 Beryl St is about the cheapest with singles/doubles for $25/38. The *Silver Spade* (tel 7021) at 151 Argent St is a friendly place and conveniently central with rooms at $29/38 and a swimming pool. Most of the motels in Broken Hill are in the $40 to $50 bracket.

Camping The *Broken Hill Caravan Park* (tel 3841) on Rakow St and the *Lake View Caravan Park* (tel 88 2250) at 1 Mann St both have camping sites ($4 to $7) and on-site vans ($15 for two).

Places to Eat
Broken Hill is door to door with clubs; this is a NSW club town if ever there was one. They generally welcome visitors and in most cases you can sign yourself in – they'll even leave the visitors book at the door with the membership secretary's signature already down beside 40 blank spaces for the night's visitors! Background music consists of the continuous rattle of one-armed bandits but for reasonably priced, reasonably good, very filling food then try, say, the *Broken Hill RSL*.

There are lots of pubs too (this is a mining town) like the *Royal Exchange Hotel* at the corner of Argent St and Chloride St. The *Pepinella Restaurant*

here has a long menu, mostly in the $8.50 to $11 bracket and an absolutely superb serve-yourself salad table. There are others, cheaper too, along Argent St. Otherwise there are snack bars including the popular cafe in the information centre, pizzerias like *Papa Joe's* on Argent St and some slightly up market places like the *Black Lion Inn*.

Getting There
Air Adelaide is the usual point to fly to Broken Hill from; it's $99 by Commodore Airlines (tel 88 1969). From Sydney it's $164 with Air NSW. You can also fly to Mildura, with connections to Melbourne or Adelaide, with Murray Valley Airlines.

Bus Stateliner-Greyhound and Ansett-Pioneer operate between Adelaide and Broken Hill. It's a seven-hour, $25 trip. Melbourne to Broken Hill by Greyhound is 12 hours and costs $51; from Mildura, $29.30. Ansett-Pioneer also go to Sydney – 17 hours and $59.70.

Rail Broken Hill is on the Sydney-Perth railway line so it can be reached on the four-times weekly Indian Pacific and there are also regular services between Adelaide and Broken Hill to connect with the Indian Pacific. The eight-hour trip to/from Adelaide is $30 and from Sydney it's $47.

Getting Around
There are plenty of taxis around Broken Hill. Tours operate around Broken Hill and out to surrounding attractions. Examples are various half day tours (including to Silverton) for $15, or day tours to the Menindee Lakes and Kinchega National Park for $37.50 or to the White Cliffs opal fields for $49.50.

Lord Howe Island

Only 11 km long and 2.5 km wide, Lord

Howe Island is a long way out in the Pacific, 600 km north-east of Sydney. The small and very beautiful island is heavily forested and has beautiful walks, a wide lagoon sheltered by a coral reef, some fine beaches and even a couple of mountains. It's small enough to get around on foot or by bicycle. The southern end of the island is dominated by towering Mt Lidgbird (808 metres) and Mt Gower (875 metres). You can climb Mt Gower in around six hours, round trip.

The lagoon has good snorkelling and you can also inspect the sealife from glass-bottom boats. On the other side of the island there's surf at Blinky Beach. The Lord Howe Island Historical Museum is usually open from 8 to 10 pm each evening. There's also a Shell Museum, open Monday to Friday from 10 am to 4 pm and movies are shown in the Public Hall on Saturdays and Tuesdays.

Information
For more information on Lord Howe Island check with the Lord Howe Island Tourist Centre, 20 Loftus St, Sydney. The phone number is 27 2867 or from elsewhere in the country (008) 22 1713.

Places to Stay
You can stay in full board lodges or in apartments, usually with facilities for preparing your own food. Food is more expensive than on the Australian mainland. Lord Howe is really off the budget track, apart from the expense of getting there you won't find much by the way of cheap accommodation. Most visitors to Lord Howe are on package tours.

Getting There & Around
You used to get to Lord Howe by romantic old four-engined flying boats from Sydney.

Today they've been retired and a small airport has been built on the island. Flights from Sydney with Lord Howe/Norfolk Island Airlines are $454 return. You can fly there from Port Macquarie with Oxley Airlines for $185 one-way.

Getting around the island you can hire bicycles from a number of locations for $2 a day. There are motorcycles and four rental cars on the island too but a bike is all you need. There is an overall 25 kph speed limit.

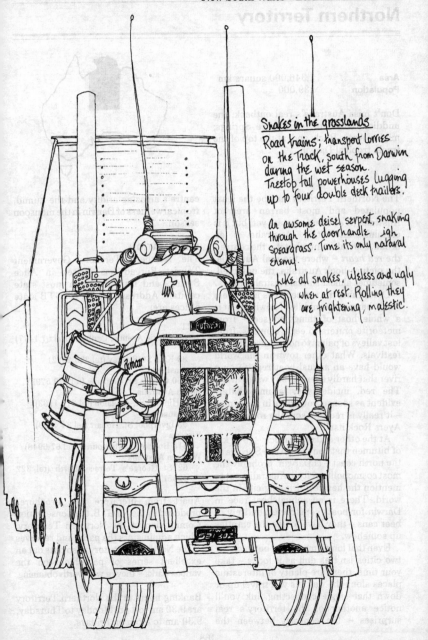

Snakes in the grasslands

Road trains; transport lorries on the Track, south from Darwin during the wet season. Treetop tall powerhouses lugging up to four double deck trailers.

An awsome deisel serpent, snaking through the doorhandle igh speargrass. Time its only natural enemy.

Like all snakes, Useless and ugly when at rest. Rolling they are frightening, majestic.

ROAD TRAIN

531 302

Northern Territory

Area	1,346,000 square km
Population	139,000

Don't miss Australia's real outback; the middle-of-nowhere town, Alice Springs; mighty Ayers Rock; and, at the top of the track, tropical Darwin.

The Northern Territory may be the least populated and most barren area of Australia (it's not even a state yet) but it is certainly interesting. Australia is an urban, coastal country but it is the centre – the *red heart* – where the real Australia, the picture-book Australia, the untamed, sometimes almost surreal Australia, exists.

Don't think the red centre is just Ayers Rock, bang in the middle of nowhere – it is a whole host of things to see – from meteorite craters to eerie canyons, from lost valleys of palms to noisy Alice Springs festivals. What other town in the world would have an annual boat regatta on a river that hardly ever has any water in it?? The red, incidentally, is immediately evident as soon as you arrive in the centre – it really is red, the soil, the rocks, even Ayers Rock itself.

At the other end of *the track* – 1500 km of bitumen that connects Alice Springs to the north coast – is Darwin, probably the most cosmopolitan city in Australia, not to mention the heaviest drinking city in the world. There is an annual boat race in Darwin for boats constructed entirely of beer cans – they have to use the empties up somehow.

Even that long, empty road between the two cities isn't as dull as it looks – take your time, there are plenty of interesting places along the way. As you travel up or down that single connecting link you'll notice another of the territory's real surprises – the contrast between the centre's amazing aridity and the humid, tropical wetness of Darwin in the monsoon season.

INFORMATION

The Northern Territory Government Tourist Bureau has offices in Alice Springs and Darwin and in most state capitals. Addresses of the NTGTB state offices are:

ACT
  35 Ainslie Avenue, Canberra (tel 57 1177)
NSW
  89 King St, Sydney (tel 235 2822)
Queensland
  260 George St, Brisbane (tel 229 5799)
South Australia
  9 Hindley St, Adelaide (tel 212 1133)
Tasmania
  93 Liverpool St, Hobart (tel 34 4199)
Victoria
  415 Bourke St, Melbourne (tel 67 6948)
Western Australia
  62 St George's Terrace, Perth (tel 322 4255)

Apart from literature and brochures produced by the NTGTB, the Conservation Commission of the Northern Territory, which administers the parks and reserves of the Northern Territory, also puts out an excellent series of pamphlets on the various parks – they're well worth obtaining.

Banking hours in the Northern Territory are 9.30 am to 4 pm Monday to Thursday, 9.30 am to 5 pm on Fridays.

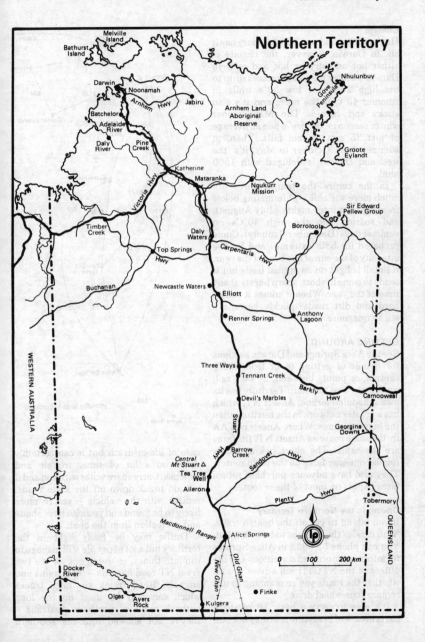

Northern Territory

Climate

Hot, cold, dry and wet – the territory has it all. In Darwin, however, the climate is either hot and dry or hot and wet. In Darwin's winter the temperatures drop to the high 20°Cs or low 30°s while in summer 40°C is the norm and it's also sticky and humid. The May-October winter season is 'the dry' when an average of just 25 mm of rain falls. Then, in summer, from October to May, it's 'the wet' and Darwin is deluged with 1500 mm!

In the centre the temperatures are much more variable – plummeting below freezing on winter nights (July-August), and soaring into the high 40°Cs on summer days (December-January). Come prepared for both extremes and for the intensity of the sun at any time of the year. Rainfall is light on an annual basis but it tends to come in short, sharp bursts at any time of the year. When it comes it comes hard and dirt roads quickly become a sticky quagmire.

GETTING AROUND

See the Alice Springs and Darwin sections for details of getting to or from those centres, or points between, by bus, rail, road or air. The Northern Territory has its own scheduled airline, Ansett NT, which has a greater network in the territory than the bigger airlines. Where Ansett or TAA fly the same route as Ansett NT, the fares are the same. The chart below details regular one-way fares on the main routes. They also have advance purchase return fares (Apex) on most of these routes.

Driving in the Northern Territory

If you intend to get off the beaten track, 'with care' is the thought to bear in mind. You can phone 52 3833 in Alice Springs for information on road conditions and the offices of the NTGTB will advise you on whether the roads you're planning to use require four-wheel drive.

It's wise to carry a basic kit of spare parts in case of breakdown. It may not be a

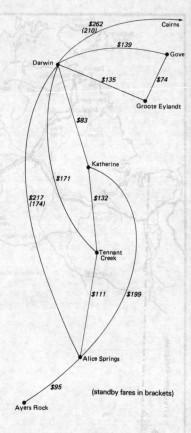

case of life-or-death but it can certainly save you a lot of time, trouble and expense. Carry spare water with you and if you do break down off the main roads, remain with the vehicle – you're more likely to be found and you also have shade and protection from the heat.

Traffic may be fairly light in the territory but a lot of people still manage to run into things, so watch out for the two great NT road hazards – road trains and animals. Road trains are huge trucks which can only be used on the long outback roads of northern Australia – they're not allowed into the southern cities. A road train is very long and very big. If you're trying to overtake one make sure you have plenty of room to complete the manoeuvre. If you're passing one travelling in the opposite direction it's wise to give it plenty of room – if a road train puts its wheels off the road to get by you, the shower of stones and rocks that result will not do you or your windscreen any good.

At night, especially, the territory's wildlife comes out to play. Hitting a kangaroo is all too easy and the damage to your vehicle, not to mention the kangaroo, can be severe. The Northern Territory also has buffaloes, wild horses and a number of other driving hazards which you are wise to avoid. There's really only one sensible way to deal with the road hazards after dark – don't drive!

ACTIVITIES
Bushwalking There are plenty of interesting bushwalking trails in the Northern Territory but care should be taken if you intend to venture off the beaten track. Around Alice Springs you can climb the surrounding ranges but wear stout shoes (the spinifex grass and burrs are quite amazingly sharp) and in summer you should wear a hat and carry water even for short walks. Walking in the top end is best in the dry although shorter walks are possible in the wet when the rain forests are at their best.

Rock Hounding There are plenty of worthwhile places in the territory for the avid fossicker. Check with the NTGTB about where to go and what permission is required. Places to look include the Harts Range (72 km north-east of Alice Springs) for beryls, garnets and quartz; Eastern MacDonnell Ranges (east of Alice Springs) for beryls and garnets; Anthony Lagoon (215 km east of the Stuart Highway, north of Tennant Creek) for ribbonstone; Brock's Creek (37 km south-west of Adelaide River, south of Darwin) for topaz, tourmaline, garnet and zircon.

Gliding The enormous thermals created by the dry heat of the centre are fantastic for gliding. There are gliding clubs in Darwin and Alice Springs. They operate from Batchelor, 88 km south of Darwin, and from Bond Springs, 25 km north of Alice Springs. Flying in to Alice Springs from Darwin once, I saw a glider far below, bright white against the red.

Swimming Because of the danger of sea wasps, stay out of the sea during the wet (October/November to April/May) – sea wasp stings are fatal. Darwin beaches are very popular, however, during the safe months. The sea is a long way from Alice Springs so the Speed St swimming pool is popular.

Darwin
Population 66,000

Cyclone Tracy may have done a pretty comprehensive job of flattening Darwin on Christmas Day 1974 but in true top end style it has bounced back. This time it has been built so the odd gust of wind won't stand it on its ear.

Darwin's hard drinking, frontier-town reputation hides the fact that it is one of the most cosmopolitan and easy-going places in Australia. There is a constant flow of travellers coming and going from Asia or simply making their way around Australia. It's one of those places where backpacks seem part of the everyday scene and people always seem to be heading off somewhere. Darwin is also a bit of an oasis – whether you're travelling south to the Alice, west to WA or east into Queensland – there are a lot of km to be covered before you get anywhere.

Darwin has had a stop-and-go history. It took a long time to decide on Darwin as the site for the region's main centre and even after the city became established its growth was slow and troubled.

There were various attempts to settle the top end, well before Darwin was founded, principally due to British fears of the French or Dutch getting a foothold on Australia. They were all remarkably unsuccessful. From 1824-29 Fort Dundas on Melville Island was tried then abandoned. From 1827-29 and 1838-49 further attempts at settlement were made at Fort Wellington and Victoria near Port Essington on the Cobourg Peninsula, well to the north-east of Darwin. These attempts also failed.

In 1845 Leichhardt reached Port Essington overland from Queensland and this aroused new interest in the top end. The Northern Territory was handed over to South Australia in 1863 and more ambitious plans were made for the area's development. Palmerston was established in 1864 at the mouth of the Adelaide River, not too far from Darwin's present location. In 1866 it was also abandoned when its location turned out to be a poor one. Finally Darwin was founded at its present site in 1869. The port had been named Darwin back in 1839 but at first the settlement was also known as Palmerston. It soon became unofficially known as Port Darwin and in 1911 the name was officially changed when the Commonwealth government took over the Northern Territory's administration.

Darwin's growth was accelerated by the discovery of gold at Pine Creek in 1871 but once the gold fever had run its course the city dropped back to slow and erratic development. The harsh and unpredictable climate combined with tenuous connections to the rest of the country held development back.

WW II really put Darwin permanently on the map. It became an important base for Allied action against the Japanese and the road south to the railhead at Alice Springs was surfaced, finally putting the city in close contact with the rest of the country. Darwin was attacked by Japanese forces 64 times during the war and 243 people lost their lives.

Today, Darwin is a modern city with an important role as the front door to Australia's northern region and as a centre for the mining activities of the Northern Territory. The population is rising quite rapidly and construction is visible all over town. Many southerners, and visitors too, come looking for work in and around Darwin. The port facilities are being improved and expanded and there is still hope that the standard gauge railway line from Alice Springs will be built.

Information

The Northern Territory Government Tourist Bureau (tel 81 6611) is at 31 Smith St Mall. It's open 8.45 am to 5 pm Monday to Friday, 9 am to 12 noon on Saturdays. They have a reasonable, though not astonishing, range of information and a good free map of Darwin's centre and outer area.

The Northern Territory Government Information Centre (tel 89 7972) is at 13 Smith St and is open Monday-Friday from 9 am to 4 pm. They also have maps and other information but it is more for non-tourist purposes.

There's a very popular public notice-board in the mall – a great place for buying and selling things or looking for rides. People often put notices up and then sit close by waiting for a result! Darwin has a daily newspaper, the *Darwin News*. The National Trust have their office on the corner of Knuckey St and the Esplanade – pick up a copy of their Darwin walking tour leaflet. The GPO with its busy poste restante is on the corner of Smith and Knuckey Sts.

Remember they're very fussy about 'dress rules' up here – if you don't meet their 'standards' you don't get in. Don't swim in Darwin waters from October to May. You only get one sting from a sea wasp each lifetime.

Events Aside from the Beer Can Regatta

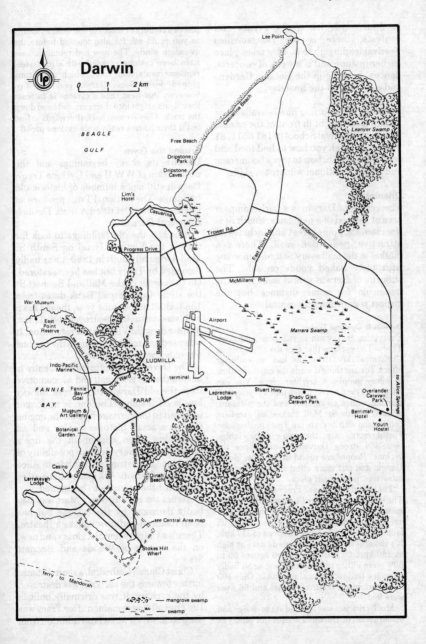

Darwin

0   1   2 km

BEAGLE GULF

Lee Point

Casuarina Beach

Leanyer Swamp

Free Beach

Dripstone Park

Dripstone Caves

Lim's Hotel

Casuarina

Trower Rd

Vanderlin Drive

East Point Rd

Progress Drive

McMillans Rd

War Museum

East Point Reserve

Airport

Marrara Swamp

Indo-Pacific Marine

Lee Point Rd

Dick Ward Drive

LUDMILLA

terminal

FANNIE BAY

Fannie Bay Gaol

Ross Smith Ave

PARAP

Leprechaun Lodge

Stuart Hwy

Shady Glen Caravan Park

Overlander Caravan Park

Museum & Art Gallery

Bagot Rd

Berrimah Hotel

Youth Hostel

to Alice Springs

Botanical Garden

Frances Bay Drive

Casino

Gilruth Ave

Larrakeyah Lodge

Stuart Hwy

Dinah Beach

see Central Area map

Stokes Hill Wharf

ferry to Mandorah

mangrove swamp

swamp

in June, with its sports events and contests, there is the Bougainvillea Festival leading up to it. This takes place earlier in June and is a week of concerts, dances, a picnic in the Botanic Gardens and a parade on the final day.

Activities Windsurfing hire is available at Mindil Beach right in front of the casino. The Bush Survival School (tel 81 6611, 81 9733) can teach you how to find food and water in the bush, how to toss a boomerang and other traditional wilderness skills.

Orientation

The centre of Darwin is a fairly compact area at the end of a peninsula. Smith St is the main shopping street and includes an attractive pedestrian mall. There's a market in the mall every Saturday morning with tasty baked goods on sale. The suburbs of Darwin sprawl away from the peninsula for some distance but the airport is conveniently central.

Darwin & Cyclone Tracy

Everything in Darwin is still pre– and post-Tracy. The cyclone that tore the city apart on Christmas Day 1974 has had an enduring effect. For one thing it made the city, according to many people, a brighter place. You can hardly ask for a better urban renewal plan than starting with a clean slate and the pleasant, relaxed Smith St Mall makes an excellent comparison with its drab, pre-Tracy predecessor. Furthermore, say the pro-cyclone lobby, there's a strong Darwinian spirit since the cyclone. People are proud of the new, glossy Darwin and put more effort into making it an attractive, permanent place.

The actual statistics of Tracy are frightening. The winds built up over Christmas Eve and by midnight began to reach their full fury. At 3.05 am the airport's anemometer cried 'enough', failing just after it recorded a speed of 217 kph. It's thought the peak wind speeds were as high as 280 kph. Of Darwin's 11,200 houses 50 to 60% were either totally destroyed or so badly damaged that repair was impossible. Only 400 houses survived relatively intact and 66 lives were lost.

Much criticism was levelled at the design and construction of Darwin's houses but plenty of places a century or more old and built as solidly as you could ask for also toppled before the awesome winds. The new and rebuilt houses have been cyclone proofed with strong steel reinforcements and roofs which are firmly pinned down. Some Darwin residents say, however, that next time a cyclone is forecast they'll jump right into their cars and head down the track. They'll come back afterwards to find out if their houses really were cyclone proof!

Around the Town

Despite its shaky beginnings and the destruction of WW II and Cyclone Tracy, Darwin still has a number of historic old buildings. The National Trust produce an interesting booklet titled *A Walk Through Historical Darwin*.

Amongst the old buildings to look for there's the Victoria Hotel on Smith St Mall. Originally built in 1890 it was badly damaged by Tracy but has been restored. On the corner of the Mall and Bennett St the stone Commercial Bank dates from 1883. Built in the same year, the old town hall was virtually destroyed by Tracy, despite its solid Victorian construction. It was used as a museum prior to the cyclone but only the walls remain.

The Government Information Centre is beside the old town hall and a locomotive from the old Darwin-Pine Creek railway line is on display. The line is no longer used but in the carriage behind the engine there's a small historic display and an interesting video clip about the line's history and the very definite possibility of a line being constructed north from Alice Springs to Darwin. Ask in the information centre for the carriage to be opened.

Across the road Brown's Mart was also badly damaged by the cyclone but has been restored and now houses a theatre. There's a Chinese temple, glossy and new, on the corner of Woods and Bennett Sts.

Christ Church Cathedral, a short distance further towards the harbour, was destroyed by the cyclone. It was originally built in 1902 but all that remained after Tracy was the porch, which was a later addition from

1944. A new cathedral has been built and the old porch retained.

Also badly damaged, the police station and old court house on the Esplanade have been restored and are used as government offices. Government House, built in stages from 1870, was known as The Residency until 1911 and has been damaged by just about every cyclone Darwin has been subject to. It is once again in fine condition, at the Esplanade corner.

Continuing round the Esplanade you reach a memorial marking where the telegraph cable once ran from Darwin into the sea on its crossing to Banyuwangi in Java (just across from Bali). This put Australia into instant communication with England for the first time.

Other buildings of interest along the Esplanade include the pleasantly tropical Hotel Darwin and Admiralty House, at the corner of Knuckey St, which is now used as a small local arts and crafts gallery. Underneath is a rather expensive cafe. Across the street is a museum in the old British & Australian Telegraph Company Residence (Lyons Cottage). It's free and open Tuesday-Friday 10 am to 5 pm, Saturday and Sunday 10 am to 4 pm. There are small, simple displays on Northern Territory history including pearling, sailing and exploration.

Further out from the centre the National Trust also operates the old Fannie Bay Gaol which was in use for nearly 100 years up to 1979. You can visit it from 2 to 3.30 pm, Monday to Friday, admission is $1.50.

Aquascene

This is one of those tourist attractions that's actually worth the cost of admission. At Doctor's Gully fish have grown accustomed to coming in for a free feed every day at high tide. It has taken 20 years to convince them that this is the place for a daily meal but now half the stale bread in Darwin gets dispensed to a positive horde of milkfish, mullet, catfish and batfish. Some of them are quite big – the milkfish grow to over a metre and will demolish a whole slice of bread in one go. It's a great scene and, of course, children positively love it – the fish will take bread right out of your hand. Feeding times depend on the high tides, admission is $1.50 for adults, the bread is free.

Botanic Gardens

The gardens' site was used to grow vegetables during the earliest days of Darwin. Tracy severely damaged the gardens, uprooting 75% of the plants. Fortunately vegetation grows fast in Darwin's climate and the Botanic Gardens, with their good collection of tropical flora, have been well restored. The gardens are now being extended down to Mindil Beach. It's an easy bicycle ride out to the gardens from the centre.

Museum of Arts & Sciences

Post-cyclone Darwin has acquired a really excellent museum. It's at Bullocky Point, Fannie Bay and houses a series of interesting exhibits within a fine new building. They include an Australian art collection, exhibits of Aboriginal art and archaeology, South-East Asian and Oceanic art exhibits, local historic items, natural science exhibits and temporary exhibitions. A museum highlight is 'Sweetheart', a huge five-metre long saltwater crocodile which became quite a local personality before meeting its unfortunate end. The museum is bright, spacious and not too big for museum over-kill to set in – its highly recommended. Admission is free and it's open Monday-Friday 9 am to 6 pm, Saturday and Sunday 10 am to 6 pm. You can get there on bus 4 or 6.

Indo-Pacific Marine

This small aquarium displays an interesting range of the sealife found around Darwin. Although it's small and the displays are nothing more than large, home-style aquarium tanks, it's a friendly place and you're able to ask questions and get a little expert fact and opinion. They have some nasty stonefish specimens and blue-ringed octopuses. In season there may be sea wasps. These unpleasant little creatures are hard to keep alive in tanks and at the end of the sea-wasp season they die off here just like they do in the sea. The aquarium is at 36 Philip St, Fannie Bay and it's open every day from 10 am to 4 pm except on Fridays when it doesn't open until 1 pm. Admission is $3.

Military Museum

At the East Point Reserve there are a series of wartime gun emplacements and a museum on Darwin's WW II activity. The city was the only place in Australia to suffer continuous attack during the war. In the dry season (May-October) the museum is open 9.30 am to 5 pm Monday-Friday. In the wet season (November-April) it's open 11 am to 4 pm. Year round it opens 9.30 am to 5 pm on weekends. Admission is $1.50. The East Point Reserve is about 10 km from the city, beyond Fannie Bay. In the early evening you can often see wallabies on the reserve and there are a number of walking tracks.

Beaches

Darwin has plenty of beaches but you're wise to keep out of the water during the October to May wet season because of the sea wasp danger. Popular beaches include Vestey's, Fannie Bay and Mandorah, across the bay from the town. The northern part of the seven-km long sweep of sand at Casuarina is an official free (nude) beach if you want to go in search of an overall sun tan. Like so many places in tropical Australia, Darwin has a waterslide – it's at Parap Pool on Ross Smith Avenue and is open daily.

Places to Stay

Darwin has hostels, guest houses, motels, camp sites – in fact a wide range of accommodation possibilities. Despite the plethora of accommodation it can still sometimes get very crowded at the height of the dry season. Darwin also has lots of guest houses for longer term stays. A wander around the central city area will soon turn up a few 'rooms vacant' signs. Darwin is a great meeting place and many travellers meet other travellers in Smith St Mall or in various coffee bars and find a place to stay that way.

Hostels & Guest Houses

Darwin has a youth hostel and a variety of guest-house-style places to stay. The city is well equipped in this bracket as there are plenty of reasonably priced rooms in an ex-government hostel and also in a former nurses' quarters – plus there's a YMCA and YWCA. Almost without exception the showers and toilets in these places are communal.

The *Darwin Youth Hostel* (tel 84 3107) has one major drawback in that it's 12 km out from the town centre. That problem is somewhat mitigated by Darwin's remarkably cheap bus service and hitching is fairly easy. The hostel is a former remand centre (they decided it wasn't good enough for criminals!) at Beaton Rd, off Hidden Valley Rd, Berrimah. That's just off the main Stuart Highway out of Darwin, a short distance beyond the airport. The nightly cost is $5 and the usual hostel rules apply although it's now open all day. There's a big common room, kitchen facilities, air-conditioning, a swimming pool and bicycles for hire. The warden also organises excellent day trips from Darwin – better value than the commercially operated ones. A bus 5 or 8 from the city will get you to the hostel (also from the airport). Get off at the Berrimah Hotel on the main highway. Coming in to Darwin, Ansett Pioneer and Greyhound buses will also drop you off there – they might even be persuaded to take you right to the hostel.

At 69 Mitchell, only a very short stroll from the centre of Darwin, the *Lameroo Lodge* (tel 81 9733) is a big ex-government hostel with 200-plus rooms. Despite the size, it is often full. It has a wide range of rooms and prices but the cheapest usually go first. If you have your own bedding, there are dorms for $6. Basic single rooms, sinks only, are $13, rooms with fridge and tea-making equipment are $15-17, with air-con $18-20. Doubles are $20, $25 and $30. The place has seen better days and maintenance and cleaning are a little on the slack side. Each block has what is called a kitchen but few people use them and there are no pots or pans. There is a cheap dining room for breakfasts and dinners and the Chinese cook whips up a very tasty evening meal for $4. There are lots of permanents and the place can be noisy but it's friendly and a lot of travellers stay too, so it can be good for meeting people. Also there is a pool and that's a definite plus. Weekly and longer rates are available and there's a luggage storage room, but don't leave valuables in it.

The lodge also operates the *Ross Smith Hostel* (tel 81 2162) near the corner of Parap Rd and Ross Smith Avenue. That's quite a way from the centre of town and it's really for permanents, not visitors.

Larrakeyah Lodge (tel 81 2933) has two locations – best known is the big, old building, formerly nurses' quarters, on Kahlin Avenue off Smith St about 1.5 km from the centre. There are two buildings here – Lambell House has singles/doubles at $13/18 without air-con. The more modern section has air-con and rooms are $22/25. There are good weekly rates at both buildings but they're likely to be demolished to make way for a new casino. Hence the new location of the *Larrakeyah Lodge* (tel 81 2933) is across from the Lameroo at 59 Mitchell St. This newly renovated place is the old Qantas staff building. It's modern with air-con singles/doubles with fridge for $22/28. There's also a TV lounge and laundry.

The YMCA and YWCA are both in-between the Lameroo Lodge and the old Larrakeyah Lodge, relatively close to the city. At Doctor's Gully, at the end of The Esplanade, the *YMCA* (tel 81 8377) has dorms at $7, singles at $10 ($11 with a fridge), doubles at $20 or $80 by the week. The rooms have fans. The Y is very popular and is often full. Office hours for checking in are 8.30 am to 9 pm weekdays, 9 to 10 am and 2 to 4 pm on weekends and females as well as males are accepted. There are no cooking facilities and no meals are available but there is a small swimming pool and garden.

The *YWCA* (tel 81 8644) also takes males or females. It's at 119 Mitchell St and all prices are bed & breakfast. Dormitory accommodation costs $9 (three-day limit), singles are $13 or $63 per week, twins are $11 per person or $17 per couple ($55 or $85 per week). Rooms are all fan-cooled (there's a handful with private facilities) and there's a laundry. There are some bedsitter rooms at $16 per person or $27 for couples. Use of the hostel's kitchen facilities costs $1.

Finally, there's a *Salvation Army Hostel* (tel 81 8188) at 49 Mitchell St, right in the centre. The emphasis here is rather more on permanent accommodation than at the other places – although all the others (the youth hostel apart) offer weekly or longer rates. The Sally Army rates are $11 single or $9 each in a shared room. By the week it costs $50 a single or $40 each, shared. For the unemployed the weekly rate is about $5 less.

Hotels & Motels There's not much in the way of hotels in Darwin, most of the older hotel-style places must have been swept away by the cyclone.

Right in the centre of town at 35 Cavenagh St the *Windsor Tourist Lodge* (tel 81 9214) has air-con rooms – all with shower and toilet, fridges and tea/coffee making facilities – at $25/30, room only. There are also triples at $35 but the rooms are a bit small and boxy. At 4 Harriet Place, just across Daly St from the centre, the *Crystal Motel* (tel 81 5694) is definitely misnamed – it's just a very basic guest house at $20 a night for a double, $80 a week.

Back on Cavenagh St, a little further

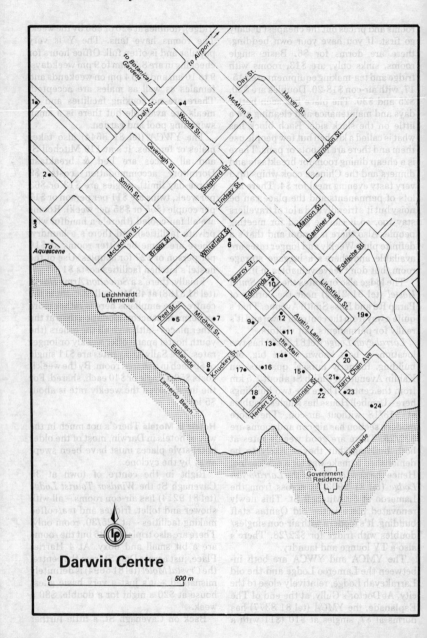

Darwin Centre

0   500 m

1 Larrakeyah Lodge (1)	13 Darwin Plaza
2 YWCA	14 Tourist Office
3 YMCA	15 Victoria Hotel
4 India Pakistan Curry House	16 Ansett
5 Lameroo Lodge	17 Salvation Army Hostel
6 Tiwi Lodge	18 Darwin Hotel
7 Larrakeyah Lodge (2)	19 Chinese Temple
8 National Trust	20 TAA & Garuda
9 GPO	21 Bus Terminal
10 Windsor Tourist Lodge	22 Government Information Centre
11 Aboriginal Heritage Gallery	23 Brown's Mart
12 Bookworld	24 Christchurch Cathedral

along from the Windsor Lodge at the corner with Whitefield St, the *Tiwi Lodge* (tel 81 6471) is a centrally located motel with rooms at $27.50/33. It's air-con and has the usual motel facilities. Also fairly central the *Aspa City Motel* (tel 81 6695) is at 38 Dashwood Crescent but it's rather more expensive at $36/40. Directly across from the airport on the Stuart Highway the *Leprechaun Lodge* (tel 84 3400) costs $40/46 for singles/twins. In Parap the *Shangri-La Motel* (tel 81 2163) at 52 Gregory St is another cheapie with rooms at $15/20 for singles/doubles or $24/30 with air-con. Darwin, as you can see, is not a great place for motel bargains.

In the motel/hotel category there are a couple of places rather further from the city centre. The *Berrimah Hotel* (tel 84 3999) is on the Stuart Highway out at Berrimah, close to the youth hostel. Rooms here are $30/34, they're modern motel-style. Across at Nightcliff you could try *Lim's Rapid Creek Hotel* (tel 85 3000) on Casuarina Drive where singles cost $20 to $25, doubles $27 to $30. The Chinese restaurant here is supposed to be pretty good.

Camping At first glance Darwin would appear to be very well equipped with camping sites but closer inspection reveals a different story. For a start many of them are quite a distance out from the centre – 20 to 30 km down the track. Secondly, a number of those that are more conveniently situated take caravans but not tent campers.

One of the best is the Pandanus Holiday Centre at Tracy Holiday Village at Tambling Terrace and Lee Point Rd, which is well located and has tent sites. Take the number 2 bus to get there. Shady Glen Caravan Park is on the Stuart Highway at Winnellie (across from the airport) and the Overlanders Caravan Park is at Berrimah (close to the youth hostel).

Some details of the sites include:

Coolalinga Caravan Park (tel 83 1026), 30 km south on Stuart Highway, camping sites $7 for two.

Pandanus Holiday Centre (tel 27 2897), 14 km north at Lee Point Rd, camping sites for $6, cabins $14 for two.

Howard Springs Caravan Park (tel 83 1169), 22 km south at 290 Whitewood Rd, Howard Springs, camping sites at $4, on-site vans $20 or $65 to $80 per week.

Overlander Caravan Park (tel 84 3025), 13 km south at the corner of McMillans Rd & Stuart Highway, Berrimah, camping sites at $4 for two, cabins at $12 per night, on-site vans from $10 to $20 per night or $50 to $97 per week, cabins at $12 per night or $65 per week.

Rural Caravan Park (tel 84 3891), 17 km south on Stuart Highway, camping sites at $5 for two.

Shady Glen Caravan Park (tel 84 3330), 9 km south at Stuart Highway, Winnellie, camping sites at $5.50 for two, on-site vans $14 to $20 per night or $80 to $100 per week.

Places to Eat

Fast Foods Darwin has always been a pretty cosmopolitan place to eat and the new, glossy Darwin carries on that pattern. It's also a place for fast foods and take-aways. For a quick snack or meal at lunchtime or early in the evening on the late shopping night try Darwin Plaza off Smith St Mall. There's a good collection of fast food counters here – the *Sheik's Tent* for Lebanese, the *Taco House* for Mexican, the *Thai Kitchen* for Thai/Chinese, *Energy Foods* for health foods and *Dairyland* for yoghurts and ice cream.

Also in the mall but on the other side is the *Central City Cafe*, a very popular little restaurant and take-away with a few outdoor tables. Sandwiches, fish & chips and omelettes are the regular fare. In *The Track*, another arcade/mall off Smith St, *Simply Foods* is a busy health food place. Here you'll find fruit juices, teas, fruit salads, exotic cakes, sandwiches and so on. It's a very popular meeting place and a good place to sit down and relax. Others in and around the mall are the *Little Lark Cafe* and *Crystal Cakes*.

The *Danish Connection* offers European open-face sandwiches. How about this one – prawn, asparagus and caviar – for $5? Stroganoffs, steaks and burgers are on offer too. It's in the arcade behind Thomas Cook Travel in the mall. The *Pancake Place* is a busy place with pancakes (crepes) sweet and savoury from $3.50 to $4.50. It's over on Cavenagh St near Knuckey St and it's BYO.

Finally there's *Kentucky Fried Chicken* on the corner of Mitchell St and Knuckey St, mentioned because it is open long hours every day. On Sundays and holidays it's about the only place open.

Counter Meals For counter meals there are a couple of good places right in the centre. The *Darwin Hotel* stretches from the Esplanade to Mitchell and the Bistro Room does meals in the $6 to $7 bracket – 12 to 2 and 6 to 8 pm. In the Smith St Mall the The Essington Carvery, upstairs in

the *Victoria Hotel*, has meals for $3.50 to $4.50 and similar opening times. Both of them offer that Darwin speciality, buffalo steaks!

The *Parap Hotel* does counter meals from $3.50 and more expensive meals in the Buff & Barr BBQ, an outdoor beer garden. You can also get counter lunches Monday to Friday and counter teas on Saturday from 6 to 9 pm at the *Berrimah Hotel's* Stuart Bistro. The Chinese restaurant at *Lim's Rapid Creek Hotel* is reputed to be fairly good.

Ethnic At Shop 12 in the Track, off the Smith St Mall, *Christo's* is a popular Greek restaurant, either eat in or take-away. At 37 Knuckey St, the *Capri Restaurant* has a restaurant section and a coffee lounge section, all the usual pizza and pasta dishes from around $4.50 plus main courses in the $6.50 to $10 bracket. There are good pizzas at *Enzrio's* on the corner of Cavenagh and Seeray Sts. Pizzas are also available at the *Pizza Kitchen* on Smith St, just beyond Daly St, near the Ys. They have a few outdoor tables here.

For very cheap curries there's the *India-Pakistan Curry House* at 90 Woods St. It's small and basic but chicken, lamb, vegetable or fish curry with rice is just $3.60. The *Maharaja Indian Restaurant* on Smith St near Searcy St is more expensive and extensive. For Chinese food, the *Jade Garden* in the Mall (upstairs) offers a nine course meal for $10.

Otherwise – well there are a string of French restaurants in Darwin, some said to be pretty good – plus steakhouses, seafood specialists, Greek and Italian restaurants and, of course, a number of Chinese.

Do-it-Yourself Darwin has plenty of supermarkets just like anywhere else in Australia. Food is, of course, rather more expensive than 'down south' but the difference is not as great as it used to be and the quality difference has also narrowed. You've got to expect higher costs when even the milk comes all the way from the Atherton Tableland near Cairns in Queensland. In summer Darwin is simply too hot for cows.

The Darwin Thirst

Darwin has a reputation as one of the hardest drinking towns in the world. In a dry year an average of 230 litres of the amber fluid disappear down each Darwinian throat. The Darwin thirst is summed up by the famed 'Darwin stubby' – a beer bottle that looks just like any other stubby, except that it contains two litres instead of 375 ml. The record for downing a Darwin stubby is one minute two seconds – but that was the pre-83 Darwin stubby which was a mite larger at 2.25 litres! That's half an imperial gallon, more than half a US gallon!

The Darwin beer thirst is celebrated at the annual beer can regatta in June. A series of boat races are held for boats constructed entirely of beer cans. Apart from the racing boats some unusual special entries generally turn up – like a beer can Viking longboat or a beer can submarine. Constructed by an Australian navy contingent the submarine actually submerged! The races also have their controversial elements – on one occasion a boat turned up made entirely of brand new cans, delivered straight from the brewery, sealed but empty. Unfair, cried other competitors, the beer must be drunk!

Entertainment

There are bands at the *Victoria Hotel* on Smith St Mall and at the *Berrimah Hotel*. *Lim's Hotel* has a disco and on Sunday has a band playing until 8 pm. Also on Sunday nights, the Darwin folk music club meets at 8 pm at the gun turret at East Point Reserve – bring along your guitar. There's also a folk dance club which meets on Tuesday nights at the water-ski club near the museum. There's free jazz from 4 to 8 pm Sundays in the *Don Hotel* and the same at the *Diamond Beach Casino Hotel*. For a quiet drink, the *Hotel Darwin* is pleasant in the evening. There's a patio-bar section by the pool.

The Darwin Film Society meets the first and third Tuesday of each month at 8 pm at the Darwin High School theatre –

temporary membership at the door. Films are also shown regularly at the various city libraries.

So long as you're 'properly dressed' it's quite good entertainment to watch people cast away large sums of money at the

Belly up to the bar in Katherine Northern Territories

Diamond Beach Casino Hotel. Callow youths at the door adjudicate whether the style of your shirt collar and the cut of your trousers is to their master's liking.

Two-Up

The Alice and Darwin casinos offer plenty of opportunity to watch the Australian gambling mania in full flight. You can also observe a true piece of Australia's cultural heritage, the all-Australian game of two-up.

The essential idea of two-up is to toss two coins and obtain two heads. The players stand around a circular playing area and bet on the coins showing either two heads or two tails when they fall. The 'spinner' uses a 'kip' to toss the coins and the house pays out and takes in as the coins fall – except that nothing happens on 'odd' tosses (one head, one tail) unless they're thrown five times in a row. In this case you lose unless you've also bet on this possibility. The spinner continues tossing until he or she either throws tails, throws five odds or throws three heads. If the spinner manages three heads then he or she also wins at 7½ to one on any bet placed on that possibility and he or she then starts tossing all over again. When the spinner finally loses the next player in the circle takes over as spinner.

Getting There

Air You can fly to Darwin from all the other states and Darwin is also an international arrival and departure point – principally for Indonesia and Singapore. The Darwin-Denpasar (Bali) flight, once an extremely popular arrival or departure point to Australia, can be as low as $226 one-way or $349 return if booked in advance and you return within 60 days, otherwise it's outrageously priced at $680 one-way for a normal economy fare. Garuda operates the flight twice weekly. Visas for Indonesia are available in Darwin for $3 and take about three days.

From other states the usual route is either via Mt Isa or Adelaide with TAA and Ansett. From WA there are TAA and Ansett flights from Perth via Port Hedland or Alice Springs while Ansett WA fly from Perth to Darwin with services through all the intermediate outback airports –

Karratha-Port Hedland-Broome-Derby-Kununurra. Ansett NT also fly via Gove to Cairns. Air North fly twice-weekly to Kununurra via Kakadu and Katherine.

See the Northern Territory introductory Getting There section for air fares within the Northern Territory. Fares to or from other states include Perth $354, Port Hedland $248, Cairns $262, Mt Isa $216, Brisbane $353 ($283 standby).

Buses You can reach Darwin by bus on three routes – the Western Australia route from Port Hedland, Broome, Derby and Kununurra; the Queensland route from Mt Isa to Three Ways and up the track, or straight up the track from Alice Springs.

In the Northern Territory Greyhound generally have more frequent services than Ansett Pioneer but Aussiepass and Eaglepass travellers can use either service on the Western Australia route. Ansett Pioneer (tel 80 3333) operate from the Ansett terminal on Mitchell St. Greyhound (tel 81 8055) have a terminal at the Lameroo Lodge, 69 Mitchell St.

Fares to or from Darwin include Alice Springs $107, 21 hours; Mt Isa $89, 26 hours; Townsville $124, 38 hours; Port Hedland $140, 36 hours and Perth $190, 2½ days.

Getting Around

Airport Transport Darwin airport is only about six km from the centre of town, conveniently central. The airport handles international flights as well as domestic ones, so it's quite busy. Hertz, Budget and Letz have rent-a-car desks at the airport. The taxi fare into the centre is about $8.

There is an airport bus shuttle which will pick up or drop off pretty well anywhere you like in the centre. Phone 81 1102 and book well before departure time, the cost is $2.50. You can also get out to the airport on a bus 5 or 8 for 30c. These same buses run right out to the youth hostel at Berrimah. In the city Ansett (tel 80 3333) is on Mitchell St, TAA (tel 82 3333) is at 16 Bennett St.

Bus Darwin has a fairly good bus service –
Monday to Friday. On Saturdays the
services are limited and on Sundays and
holidays they shut down completely. The
city services start from the small terminal
on Harry Chan Avenue, near the Government Information Centre where you can
get bus timetables. You can also phone 81
2150 or 27 9446 for information.

Except for services way down the track
(some of the route 8 buses) anywhere in
Darwin costs a standard 30c. Route 5 is
particularly useful, running from the city
via the airport to Berrimah (for the youth
hostel) and then up to Casuarina. On
weekdays there are 12 services a day from
6 am to 8.55 pm (ex-city) but only four on
Saturday mornings and none at all on
Saturday afternoons or Sundays. Route 8
also operates from the city via Berrimah to
21 km, 10 times a day but only twice on
Saturdays. Two or three times a day (once
on Saturdays) it runs right out to Howard
Springs and Humpty Doo.

Weekends are obviously a problem but
Mondays to Fridays you've got 20-plus
buses a day between the city and the
airport or the youth hostel and for just
30c.

Rental Cars Budget, Letz and Hertz are at
the airport. Thrifty and National are also
represented in the city. Darwin is classified
as a remote area and it is, therefore,
expensive if you plan to drive very far.
There are also a string of local car rental
organisations. Many of them rent Mokes
which are very popular in Darwin. Moke
Rentals (tel 81 8896) at 10 Hubert St is
typical at $18 plus $5 insurance per day,
plus 14c a km, although others can be
cheaper. Cheapa-Rent-A-Car (tel 81 8400),
149 Stuart Highway has cars and Mokes.
Mokes cost from $17, plus a km charge, or
$29 with 100 km free. Cars cost from $21 –
there are good weekly rates and they also
rent mopeds and minibuses.

Bicycles Darwin is surprisingly good for
bike riding and there is a fairly extensive
network of bike tracks. It's a pleasant ride
out from the city to the Botanic Gardens,
Fannie Bay, the East Point Reserve or
even, if you're feeling fit, all the way to
Nightcliff and Casuarina. The youth
hostel rents bikes for $5 a day. City Cycle
Rental (tel 81 9733) is at the Greyhound
Terminal, 69 Mitchell St – $5 a day and
weekly rates.

Tours There are all sorts of tours from
Darwin offered by numerous companies.
The tourist office has brochures on many
of them. Short afternoon city tours by Fun
Tours or Ansett Pioneer cost $15 to $20.
Coop & Co run horse & carriage city tours.
Tours further out to Yarrawonga Zoo and
Howard and Berry Springs, as well as the
city sights, cost $35. There are lots of
wildlife tours to see buffaloes and birdlife
($25 to $80 depending on the duration
and the distance covered) and tours down
the track as far as Adelaide River or on to
the Arnhem Highway ($40 to $80). As you
can see Darwin tours are not cheap.
Pandanas (tel 81 6611) offers canoe or
kayak trips on the Daly River. They're not
cheap either.

Further afield you can make day tours
by air to the Kakadu National Park or over
Arnhem Land. Several companies run bus
and/or camping trips to Kakadu. The two-
day ($135) camping trip run by Terra
Safari Tours is said to be good and is one
of the cheaper National Park trips. Other
companies do similar trips but many are
longer and quite expensive. Dial-a-Safari
offers trips to the Peppimenarti Aboriginal
area, an area just recently made accessible
and also to the Wangi area where a new
National Park, Stapleton, has been
proposed. Tours to the Aboriginal reserves
on Bathurst and Melville Islands cost
from $120 for a half-day tour. Trips to the
islands with Tiwi Tours have been recommended. Other tour destinations include
the Katherine Gorge or down the track.
Various boats can be hired around
Darwin. Crocodile enthusiasts can make
night, croc-spotting excursions for $20.

Things to Buy

Darwin has a number of souvenir shops and galleries but easily the best is The Aboriginal Heritage Gallery, 44 Smith St, in the mall. It's open every day but on Saturday only until 12 noon and on Sunday from 10 am to 2 pm. They've got a wide variety and fine examples of Aboriginal art. There are bark paintings from Arnhem Land, of course, but there are also interesting carvings by the Tiwi people of Bathurst and Melville Islands.

The Top End

There are a number of places of interest fairly close to Darwin. A group of people can hire a Moke and get out to them quite economically. There are also many tours operated out of Darwin to the sites along the track. The youth hostel warden also organises some interesting excursions for hostellers. The tourist office has a Parks & Reserves of the Top End pamphlet which gives basic information on them.

YARRAWONGA ZOO

Situated 20 km down the track, the zoo has a variety of top end wildlife including buffaloes, emus, brolgas, dingoes and crocodiles.

HOWARD SPRINGS

The springs are 30 km from the city. Turn off just beyond Yarrawonga. The forest-surrounded swimming hole is rather clogged by weeds and because the reserve is so convenient to the city it can get uncomfortably crowded. Nevertheless on a quiet day it's a pleasant spot for an excursion from the city and there's lots of birdlife.

ARNHEM HIGHWAY

Thirty-three km south of Darwin the Arnhem Highway branches off to the south-east. Only 10 km down the road you come to the *Humpty Doo Hotel*, a colourful

hotel with some real character. They do counter lunches and teas here all week, Sunday is particularly popular. The Fogg Dam, 60 km out, is a great place for bird watching. This was the site of the unsuccessful Humpty Doo rice project – the planners hadn't reckoned with the birds' appetites.

The *Bark Hut Inn* is a pleasant place to eat. It's near a billabong at Annaburroo Station, 85 km along the Arnhem Highway. The billabong is good for swimming and you can also camp there. The *South Alligator Motor Inn* is 180 km down the highway, just before the Kakadu National Park. From here you can make trips on the *Kakadu Princess* along the South Alligator River. Cruises usually cost $30 but on Fridays there are shorter two hour trips for $15.

DARWIN CROCODILE FARM

On the Stuart Highway, just a little south of the Arnhem Highway turn-off and 40 km from Darwin, the crocodile farm has a lake full of saltwater and freshwater crocodiles including some 'real biggies'. There's also a display of Northern Territory snakes. The farm is open 9 am to 5 pm daily. Feedings are on Wednesdays and Saturdays at 3 pm, Fridays at 10 am.

BERRY SPRINGS

The turn-off to Berry Springs is 46 km down the track and it's then 10 km further to the reserve. It's not as crowded as the Howard Springs reserve, principally because of its greater distance from the city, and there's a good walking track. The surfaced road ends soon after Berry Springs but it's possible to continue all the way to Mandorah on the Cox Peninsula. It's far easier to simply take the ferry across Darwin Harbour.

RUM JUNGLE

Seventy-seven km south of Darwin the road turns off to Batchelor and the abandoned uranium mine at Rum Jungle.

MANDORAH RESORT

It's only 10 km across the harbour by boat to this popular holiday resort on the tip of Cox Peninsula – you can also reach the resort by road but that's nearly 140 km, about half of it on unsurfaced roads. The ferry across to Mandorah costs about $9 return and the crossing takes about half an hour. It departs from Stokes Hill Wharf at 10 am and 12 noon on weekdays, also at 2 pm on weekends and public holidays. If you want to stay at the holiday resort you're looking at $40 or more a night for a double.

KAKADU NATIONAL PARK

Kakadu National Park, recently included on the UN World Heritage List, is one of the most spectacular in Australia. It consists of two distinct regions – the floodplains, billabongs and lagoons drained by the Alligator Rivers and the soaring, rocky Arnhem Land escarpment, cut by fantastic gorges, waterfalls and streams. Apart from the amazing scenery the park also has prolific wildlife and some superb examples of Aboriginal art. In fact the Aboriginal art is probably the best to be seen in any park in Australia.

The park is 220 km east of Darwin, between the South and East Alligator Rivers. The park headquarters are near Jabiru which is reached by the surfaced Arnhem Highway, from Darwin. There is also a uranium mining project at Jabiru and the close proximity of the uranium mines around the Kakadu park has caused much controversy. The park can also be reached by unsurfaced roads from Oenpelli and Pine Creek but these are often closed in the wet.

Highlights of the park include the Aboriginal art at Nourlangie Rock and Obiri Rock. The Jim Jim Falls (which drop 215 metres) and the Twin Falls in the south-east of the park are spectacular and there is much birdlife to be seen at the Yellow Water billabong. Cruises on the South Alligator River, on the park's western boundary, are also popular.

CONSERVATION COMMISSION

Although the roads in the park are unsurfaced they are generally quite accessible by conventional vehicles during the dry season. There are campsites at a number of locations in the park. Muirella Park on Nourlangie Creek is particularly pleasant.

Alternatively, there are a variety of tours into the park from Darwin. Probably the cheapest is a two-day tour which, with a YHA member discount, costs $95. Ask about it at the Darwin Youth Hostel. The others range from one-day, fly-drive tours for around $175, to two and three-day tours in the $135 to $350 bracket. You can also make four-wheel drive camping trips from the park headquarters for around $150 for two days. There are a number of operators into the park. It's quite easy to hitch around the park in the dry season. Uranium enthusiasts can tour the Ranger Uranium Mines at Jabiru for free. See Tours under Darwin for more details.

Crocodiles

The Northern Territory has a fair population of

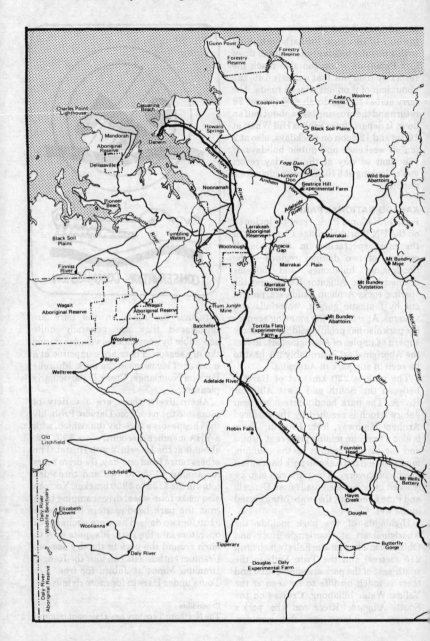

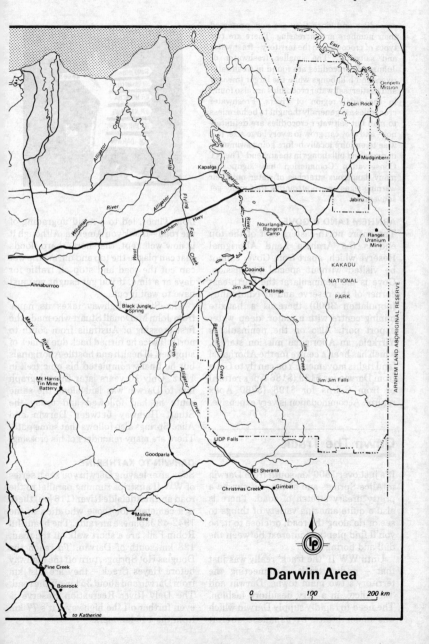

Darwin Area

0   100   200 km

crocodiles and since they are now protected their numbers are increasing. There are two types of crocodiles in the territory – freshwater and saltwater. The smaller freshwater or Johnston's crocodiles are found in freshwater rivers and billabongs while the larger (meaner and nastier) saltwater crocodiles are also found in the tidal region of rivers. Freshwater crocodiles are generally thought to be harmless to man but saltwater crocodiles are definitely not – and they can grow to a very large size. It is wise to enquire locally before going swimming in rivers and billabongs in the top end. The NT Conservation Commission has signposted many dangerous stretches of water but their warning signs are so attractive that many get souvenired.

ARNHEM LAND & GOVE

The entire north-eastern half of the top end is the Arnhem Land Aboriginal Reserve which, apart from Gove, cannot be visited without special permission. Gove is the peninsula at the north-east corner of the reserve and at Nhulunbuy (population 3600) there is a bauxite mining centre with a major, deep water export port. Also on the peninsula is Yirrkala, an Aboriginal mission station, which has been a centre for the Aboriginal land rights movement. You can fly to Gove from Darwin for $139 ($186 Apex return) or from Cairns for $198 ($260 Apex return). Accommodation is very expensive.

Down The Track

It's just over 1500 km south from Darwin to Alice Springs and at times it can be a pretty dreary stretch of road. There is also a quite amazing variety of things to see or do along the road, or close to it, so you'll find plenty of interest between the dull and boring bits.

Until WW II 'the track' really was just that – a dirt track – connecting the territory's two main towns, Darwin and 'the Alice', in a very desultory fashion. The need to rapidly supply Darwin which was under attack by Japanese aircraft

from Timor, led to a rapid upgrading of the road – thank you America. Although it is now well kept, the short, sharp floods that can plague the top end during the wet can cut the road and stop all traffic for days at a time. If you get caught you just have to wait it out.

The Stuart Highway takes its name from John McDouall Stuart who made the first crossing of Australia from south to north. Twice he turned back due to lack of supplies, ill health and hostile Aboriginals but he finally completed his epic trek in 1862. Only 10 years later the telegraph line to Darwin was laid along the same route he had followed and today the Stuart Highway between Darwin and Alice Springs also follows that same path. There are many reminders of his crossing.

DARWIN TO KATHERINE

Soon after leaving Darwin you see a series of WW II airstrips running parallel to the road and at Adelaide River (116 km) there is a cemetery for those who died in the 1942-43 Japanese air raids. The beautiful Robin Falls are a short walk off the road, 128 km south of Darwin. To reach the Douglas Hot Springs, turn off the highway before Hayes Creek – they are 214 km from Darwin and about 35 km off the road. The Daly River Recreation Reserve is even further off the highway – it's 77 km from the 146 km mark.

Pine Creek is reached after 248 km. It was a gold-mining centre around the turn of the century and some of the old buildings still survive. The railway station was built in 1889 and the hospital, located near the PO, is now owned by the National Trust. Some of the Aboriginal rock art galleries in the area are believed to be among the oldest art sites in the world. There's a pretty terrible youth hostel here which is in the process of being upgraded. You can borrow a gold-pan from the warden and try fossicking in the creek nearby.

At the 293 km mark you can turn off to Mt Todd and Edith Falls, 27 km off the road, where there is a camping reserve. Katherine is finally reached 340 km south of Darwin.

KATHERINE (population 4500)

Apart from Tennant Creek this is the only town of any size between Darwin and Alice Springs. It's a bustling little place where the road branches off to the Kimberleys and Western Australia. Katherine has long been an important stopping point since this is the first, permanent, running river if you're coming north from Alice Springs. The town includes some historic old buildings like the Sportsman's Arms, featured in *We of the Never Never*. The main interest here, however, is the spectacular Katherine Gorge, 32 km to the north-east. There is a daily bus from Katherine to the Gorge for $4. There are other parks and reserves in the area containing gorges and caves. Get the Conservation Commission pamphlet about them.

During the dry season the waters of the gorge are calm but in the wet from November to March the water can become a raging torrent. The difference in water levels between the wet and dry is simply staggering. During the wet the park's waterfalls are at their best but in general the dry season from April to October is the best time to visit. There's a park visitors' centre where you can obtain details of the

100 km of walking trails. Some of these trails require some preparation and the park ranger should be notified before you depart.

The most popular activity in the park is the boat trips up through the sheer-walled gorge. They operate regularly and are excellent value. The adventurous can continue further up the river on day-long expeditions. In the cooler months of June, July and August you may see an occasional croc sunning himself on the riverbank. They're Johnston's Crocodiles, a fresh-water variety, which are far too shy and kind-hearted to consider biting a human. If you want to say you've been for a dip in a crocodile-infested river this is your chance. Well, they're supposed to be harmless!

The Sixteen Mile Caves and Kintore Caves are also close to Katherine and the beautiful Edith Falls, which cascade down a hill in a series of pools, are also within the park boundaries. The gravel road to Edith Falls is closed during the wet season.

If you're heading for Western Australia, a stop at Victoria River Downs, 195 km west, is worthwhile. A local character called Max operates Red Valley Tours. The tours start from the the Victoria River Wayside Inn and for $15 you get shown freshwater crocodiles, fish and turtles being fed; have some real billy tea and get to have a go at playing the didgeridoo and trying to light a fire using firesticks. Max has a good knowledge of the flora and fauna and local history.

Places to Stay

There's a good youth hostel on the Victoria Highway, two km from the main street. Buses from the BP roadhouse go past it. Behind the hostel is a thermal spring – good for a late night dip under the stars.

The *Springvale Homestead* (tel 72 1044) is a tourist complex with budget rooms at $12.50 per person or you can camp for $3. If you don't have much gear, $6 will get you a tent and mattress, another $3, bedding. There is also a more expensive motel with rooms at $32/40. Boats can be rented at the site and local Aborigines perform a corroboree three nights a week during the dry season. The Homestead is eight km from town, past the Lower Level Reserve and the Katherine River.

There are more expensive motel-style places in town and a number of campsites. The *Gorge Caravan Park* (tel 72 1253) is actually at the gorge and costs $3 per person to camp. There are also a number of campsites at the town itself. The *Riverview Caravan Park* (tel 72 1011) is on the Victoria Highway, three km from the centre, and has a YHA 'tent hostel' at $4 a bed.

MATARANKA HOMESTEAD

Mataranka is 103 km south of Katherine and just north of the Roper Highway. About 10 km off the road, the delightful Mataranka Homestead is a terrific place to camp. There's a soothing thermal pool full of tiny fishes you can scoop up in your hands while basking in hot water – just a short walk from the campsite. The Waterhouse River is also only 200 metres from the homestead and you can walk along the river bank for three km to where it meets the Roper Creek. The wildlife to be seen in the area includes crocodiles, kangaroos, donkeys, wild horses, goannas and other reptiles and, of course, many colourful birds.

Places to Stay

The Mataranka Homestead has a campground which is $6 for two, rooms from $20 or with air-con from $33 and there's a *YHA Youth Hostel* costing $7. Transport is available from Mataranka to the Homestead – phone 75 4544 for details and accommodation bookings. Canoes are available for hire and there is a kiosk for groceries. There's also a motel and a hotel in Mataranka.

MATARANKA TO THREE WAYS

A little south of Mataranka and the Roper junction the Elsey Cemetery is right by the road, by the Warlock Ponds. You can see the graves of characters like 'the Fizzer', who came to life in the turn of the century classic of outback life – *We of the Never Never*. The foundations of the homestead can be seen across the road from the cemetery.

Continuing south you pass through Larrimah – at one time the railway line from Darwin terminated here but it was abandoned after Cyclone Tracy. Then there's Daly Waters, Newcastle Waters and Elliott and at all of them the land gets drier and drier. A large rock known as Lubra's Lookout overlooks Renner Springs and this is generally accepted as being the dividing line between the seasonal, wet land of the top end and the dry, dead heart of the centre. There's camping at Lake Woods, but no facilities.

About 50 km from Three Ways you pass Churchill's Head, a large rock said to look like Britain's wartime prime minister. Soon after there's a memorial to Stuart, at Attack Creek, where the explorer turned back on one of his attempts to cross Australia from south to north, after his party was attacked by a group of hostile Aboriginals. They were running low on supplies and this incident was the final straw.

THREE WAYS

Situated 537 km north of the Alice, 988 km south of Darwin and 643 km west of Mt Isa, Three Ways is basically a bloody long way from anywhere – apart from Tennant Creek, 26 km down the track. This is a classic 'get stuck' point for hitchhikers – fortunately there's a roadhouse at the junction but anybody who has hitched around Australia seems to have a tale about being stuck at Three Ways. The junction is marked by a memorial to John Flynn, the original flying doctor. A little south of Three Ways there's an old telegraph station from the days of the overland telegraph. But apart from that there isn't much else here.

TENNANT CREEK (population 2200)
Apart from Katherine, this is the only town of any size between Darwin and Alice Springs. It's just 26 km south of Three Ways, 511 km north of Alice Springs. There's an old tale that Tennant Creek was first settled when a wagonload of beer broke down here and the wagon drivers decided they might as well make themselves comfortable while they consumed the freight. Later, Tennant Creek had a small gold rush and you can see the old mines at Warrego and Nobles Nob, which is the largest open-cut gold mine in the country. The old telegraph station, just 10 km north of the town, by the highway, has a couple of unmarked graves.

About 100 km south of Tennant Creek are the Devil's Marbles, a haphazard pile of giant spherical boulders scattered on both sides of the road. The Rainbow Snake laid them, according to Aboriginal mythology. The Rainbow Snake obviously got around because there is a similar collection of boulders on a South Island beach in New Zealand and similar Devil's Pebbles 10 km north-west of Tennant Creek.

Places to Stay
There are several fairly expensive motels here and a *Youth Hostel* (tel 62 2719) on Leichardt St costing $4. The *Tennant Creek Hotel* (tel 62 2006) has rooms for

$28/40 including breakfast and a motel section that's just as expensive as all the others.

There are also two caravan/camping parks. The *Tennant Creek Caravan Park* (tel 62 2325) costs $6 for two to camp and has on-site vans for $20 to $22, cabins for $15 to $17. The *Outback Tennant Creek Caravan Park* (tel 62 2459) costs $8 for camping, $15 to $22 for on-site vans.

TENNANT CREEK TO ALICE SPRINGS
After the Devil's Marbles there are only a few places of interest to pause at on the trip south to the Alice. Near Barrow Creek the Stuart Memorial commemorates John Stuart who, after several attempts, made the first south-north crossing of the continent in 1862. Visible to the east of the highway is Central Mt Stuart, the geographical centre of Australia. At Barrow Creek itself there is an old post office telegraph repeater station. It was attacked by Aboriginals in 1874 and the station master and linesman were killed – their graves are by the road. A great number of innocent Aboriginals died in the inevitable reprisals.

The road continues through Tea Tree and finally Aileron, the last stop before the Alice. Although roadhouses and petrol are fairly plentiful (if expensive) along the track, it is wise to fill up regularly, particularly if you have a limited range – like on a motorcycle.

Alice Springs
Population 20,000

'The Alice', as it's usually known, was originally founded as a staging point for the overland telegraph line in the 1870s. A telegraph station was built near a permanent waterhole in the bed of the dry Todd River. The river was named after Charles Todd, Superintendent of Telegraphs back in Adelaide, and a spring near the waterhole was named after Alice, his wife.

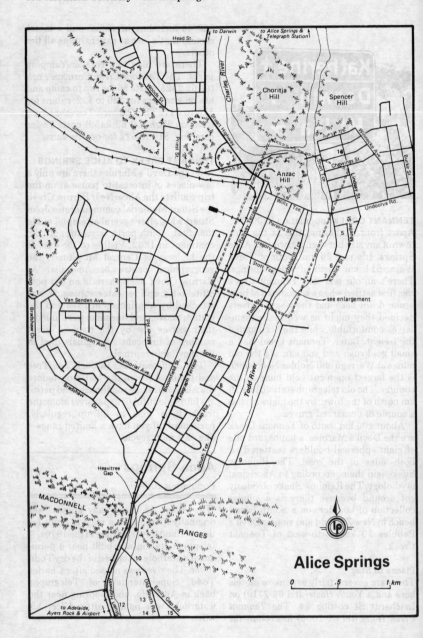

Alice Springs

0   .5   1 km

Top: The Henley-on-Todd Regatta in Alice Springs gets over the small problem that the Todd River
      rarely has any water by using bottomless boats (NTGTB)
Left: Close to the Alice Springs-Darwin road is the magnificent Katharine Gorge (NTGTB)
Right: In the 'top end' termite mounds are taller than a Land Rover (NTGTB)

Top: Not as well known as Ayers Rock, the nearby Olgas are equally spectacular (NTGTB)
Left: Ayers Rock is renowned for its size, isolation and its deep red colour (TW)
Right: Near Alice Springs, Palm Valley is a strange lost valley of primeval palm trees in the dry
    centre (NTGTB)

1 Diaorama	9 Casino
2 Aviation Museum	10 Heavitree Gap Caravan Park
3 Lasseter's & Namatjira's Graves	11 Pitchi Ritchi
4 Stuart Memorial Cemetery	12 Old Timer's Museum
5 Aruna Guest House	13 Auto Museum
6 Left Bank Guest House	14 El Mimi Date Farm
7 Desert Sands Motel & Campsite	15 Camel Farm
8 Toddy's Cabins	16 Arura Safari Lodge

A town, named Stuart, was first established in 1888, a few km south of the telegraph station, as a railhead for a proposed railway line. As the railway didn't materialise, the town developed very slowly. Not until 1933 did the town come to be known as Alice Springs.

The telegraph line through the centre was built to connect with the undersea line from Darwin to Java which, on its completion, put Australia in direct contact with Europe for the first time. It was a monumental task laying that line but it was achieved in a remarkably short time.

Today Alice Springs is a pleasant, modern town with good shops and restaurants. It acts mainly as a centre for the area and a jumping-off point for the many tourist attractions of central Australia. There is also a major US communications base, Pine Gap, near town and the American influence is very clear.

Alice Springs' growth to its present size has been recent and rapid. When the name was officially changed in 1933 the population had only just reached 200! Even in the 1950s Alice Springs was still a tiny town with a population in the hundreds. Until WW II there was no surfaced road leading to Alice Springs and only in the last 10 years has the road south to Adelaide started to be surfaced-there is still a lot of dirt road in that direction.

As part of the Northern Territory with its rosy-looking future, Alice, like Darwin, is experiencing a mini-boom. The population has increased by 7000 since 1982; there's a lot of construction and employment is relatively plentiful. There's even

hope that the rail link to Darwin might finally get underway. The city was has also deemed one of the best places on earth to see Halley's Comet on its 1986 world tour.

Information

The Northern Territory Government Tourist Bureau office (tel 52 1299) is at 51 Todd St in the Alice. It's open 8.45 am to 5 pm Monday to Friday and 9 am to 4 pm on Saturdays, Sundays and holidays. They're good and have maps and information on just about everything in and about town. *This Month in Alice* is a useful monthly information booklet produced on the Alice Springs area.

Alice Springs has a daily paper (*The Alice Springs Star*) and a weekly (*The Centralian Advocate*). Marron's Newsagency on Todd St claims to have the best selection of interstate newspapers of any country newsagent in Australia. The Connoisseur Book Shop in Todd Plaza (opposite the Flynn Church) and the Arunta Art Gallery at Todd St also have good selections of books.

Temperatures on summer days can climb extremely high (up to 45°C) and even winter days are pretty warm, however, I've been asked to re-emphasise just how cold winter nights can be. A lot of people do get caught off guard as temperatures do drop to below zero. In winter (basically June and July), about five minutes after the sun goes down you can literally feel the heat disappear. Despite Alice Springs' dry climate and low annual rainfall the occasional rains can be quite heavy.

Alice Events

Alice Springs has a string of colourful activities, particularly during the cool tourist months from May through August. The Bangtail Muster takes place in May – it celebrates the old practice of cutting horses' tails when they were rounded up and mustered before being shipped out. Today the Bangtail Muster is a colourful parade with floats satirising and making fun of local personalities and events.

Also in May there's the Camel Cup, a whole series of races for camels. You'll be surprised at just how many camels they can round up in the centre. All through the cooler months there are a string of country horse races at Alice Springs and surrounding out-stations like Finke, Barrow Creek, Aileron or the Harts Range. They're colourful events and for the out-stations it's the big turn-out of the year.

In August there's the Alice Springs rodeo when for one week the whole town seems to be full of cowboys, swaggering around in their stetson hats, Willie Nelson shirts, Levi jeans, and high-heeled boots – and all of them bow-legged.

Finally in late August there's the event which probably draws the biggest crowds of all – the Henley-on-Todd Regatta. Having a series of boat races in the Todd River is slightly complicated by the fact that there is hardly ever any water in the Todd River. It's as dry and sandy as a desert. Nevertheless a whole series of races are held for sailing boats, doubles, racing eights and every boat race class you could think of. The boats are all bottomless, the crew's legs stick out and they simply run down the course!

A Food & Wine Festival is held early in September, at the end of the Regatta. Various restaurants, ethnic groups and local wineries provide a range of food and drink through the day. The Top Half Folk Festival changes location annually but shows up in Alice every so often as it did in its 15th year, 1985.

Orientation

The centre of Alice Springs is a conveniently compact area just five streets wide, bounded by the dry Todd River on one side and the Stuart Highway on the other. Anzac Hill forms a northern boundary to the central area while Stuart Terrace is the southern end. Most of the places to stay and virtually all of the places to eat are in this central rectangle. Todd St is the main shopping street of the town. From Wills Terrace to Gregory Terrace there is a pedestrian mall.

Telegraph Station

Laying the telegraph line across the dry, harsh centre of Australia was no easy task, as the small museum at the old Telegraph Station, two km north of the town, shows. The original spring, which the town is named after, is also here. The spring made a good swimming hole in those days and it still does today.

It's easy to walk to the station from Alice – just follow the path on the western (left hand) side of the riverbed. Beside the barbecue place you reach after about 20 minutes, there's a path that branches off the vehicle track. Follow that for a more circuitous route to the station. If you can't find it on the way in then pick it up on the way back, following the path around the emu and kangaroo enclosures. You can also walk to the station from Burke St in the east side of town, or you can drive there. There's another pleasant circular walk from the station out by the old cemetery and Trig Hill.

In the May to September tourist season rangers give half-hour tours of the station at 11 am and 3 pm daily. The station, one of 12 built along the telegraph line in the 1870s, was constructed of local stone in 1871-72. The station continued in operation until 1932. The NT Conservation Commission has an interesting pamphlet on the station reserve.

Around Town

At the north end of Todd St you can make the short, sharp ascent to the top of Anzac Hill (or you can drive there). From the top you have a fine view over modern Alice Springs and down to the MacDonnell Range that forms a southern boundary to the town. There are a number of other hills in and around Alice Springs which you can climb but Anzac Hill is certainly the best known and most convenient. Right at the end of Todd St the picturesque signpost indicating how far Alice Springs is from almost anywhere makes a popular photographic subject.

The National Trust produces a useful walking-tour guide to the town's historic buildings and all of them are concentrated in the compact central area. Before you stroll down Todd St Mall note the footbridge over the Todd River from Wills Terrace. The road here crosses by causeway but until the bridge was built the Todd's infrequent flow could cut one side of the town off from the other.

Todd St is the main shopping street of the town and the one-way section has wide pavements to encourage relaxed strolling. Along the street you can see Adelaide House, built in the early 1920s. It's one of Alice Springs' earlier buildings. Originally it was the town's first hospital and now it is preserved as a museum. Across the road is Marron's Newsagency, one of the oldest shops in town – it's a fine verandahed building. Flynn, the founding flying doctor, is commemorated by the John Flynn Memorial Church on Todd St. At the back of the church there is a small museum of items relating to the setting up of the flying doctor service. A heritage walk is also outlined in the booklet *This Month in Alice*.

There are a number of interesting old buildings along Hartley St including the stone jail built in 1907-08. There's also a court house which was in use until 1980 and the Hartley St school. The Residency, on the corner of Parsons and Hartley Sts, now houses a museum. There's another museum, the Old Timers Museum, at the old folks' home, south on the Stuart Highway. It concentrates on the pioneering days of the centre and is open daily from 2 to 4 pm.

Flying Doctor & School of the Air

You can visit both these cornerstones of Australian outback life. The Royal Flying Doctor Base is close to the town centre on Stuart Terrace. It's open 9 to 11.30 am, 2 to 3.30 pm Monday to Friday and 9 to 11

am on Saturday. The half-hour tour costs $1.50. The School of the Air, which broadcasts school lessons to children on remote outback stations, is on Head St. It's open 1.30 to 3.30 pm Monday to Friday.

Aviation Museum

Alice Springs has an interesting little Aviation Museum housed in the former Connellan hangar on Memorial Avenue, where the town's airport used to be in the early days. The museum includes a couple of poignant exhibits which pinpoint the dangers of outback aviation.

In 1929 pioneer aviator Charles Kingsford-Smith went missing in the north-west in his aircraft 'Southern Cross'. Two other aviators, Anderson and Hitchcock, set off to search for Kingsford-Smith in their tiny aircraft 'Kookaburra'. North of Alice Springs they struck engine trouble and made an emergency landing. Despite their complete lack of tools they managed to fix the fault but repeated attempts to take off all failed due to the sandy, rocky soil. They had foolishly left Alice Springs not only without tools but also with minimal water and food. By the time an aerial search had been organised and their plane had been located both had died of thirst. Their bodies were recovered but the aircraft, intact and completely undamaged, was left. Kingsford-Smith turned up, completely unharmed, a few days later.

The aircraft was accidentally rediscovered, by a mining surveyor, in 1961 and in the '70s it was decided to collect the remains and exhibit them. They proved strangely elusive, however, and it took several years to find them again. They were finally located in 1978 by Sydney electronics whizz, Dick Smith. Fifty years of exposure and bushfires had reduced the aircraft to a crumbled wreck but it's an interesting display only a few steps from where the aircraft took off on its ill-fated mission. A short film tells the sad story of this misadventure.

Nor is this tragedy unique, for the museum also displays a Wackett which went missing in 1961 on a flight from Ceduna in South Australia. The pilot strayed no less than 42° off course and put down when he ran out of fuel. An enormous search failed to find him because he was so far from his expected route. The aircraft was discovered, again completely by accident, in 1965. The museum is not all tragedy – there are also exhibits of pioneer aviation in the territory and, of course, the famous flying doctor service. The museum is open Monday to Friday from 8.30 am to 4.30 pm, Saturday and Sunday 10 am to 4 pm. Admission is $1.75.

Other Attractions

Panorama Guth, at 65 Hartley St in the town centre, is a huge circular panorama which you view from an elevated, central observation point. It depicts almost all of the points of interest around the centre with uncanny reality. Painted by a Dutch artist, Henk Guth, it measures about 20-metres in diameter and admission is $1.50 – whether you think it's worth paying money to see a reproduction of what you may also see for real is a different question!

On the outskirts of town on Larapinta Drive the Diorama is a man-made tourist attraction. It's open from 10 am to 5 pm daily and admission to this rather hokey collection of three-dimensional illustrations of various Aboriginal legends is $1.50. Children love it. There is an excellent art collection in the foyer – the prize winners in the annual Alice Springs art contest. Eventually the collection will be housed in an Alice Springs art gallery.

Just beyond the Aviation Museum there's a cemetery with a number of interesting graves including those of Albert Namatjira, the renowned Aboriginal artist, and of Harold Lasseter who perished while searching for the fabled gold of 'Lasseter's Reef'. Alice Springs also has some pioneer graves in the small Stuart

Memorial Cemetery on George Crescent, just across the railway lines.

Pioneer Market Place is a small court-yard complex of shops dealing in crafts, bric-a-brac, souvenirs and food. It was here, in 1944, that the old Pioneer Theatre was set up; a walk-in rather than a drive-in movie cinema. At this open-air theatre patrons could sit under the stars of the Southern Cross and see the stars of Hollywood. Walk-ins were once common in rural Australia but many of them folded in the early 1980's, due partly to the advent of video. Some of the old deck-chairs still face the bare screen up on the wall and the equipment still sits in the projection room above Carmel's store. The Market Place is on Parson's St, at the corner of Leichardt Terrace, by the river. It's open daily, but weekends only till 2 pm.

The Olive Pink Flora Reserve – not far from the centre of town, over the Todd River off Barrett Drive – has a collection of shrubs and trees typical of the 200 km area around Alice Springs. It's open 10 am to 6 pm.

Pitchi Ritchi

Just south of the Heavitree Gap causeway is Pitchi Ritchi ('gap in the range'), a flower-and-bird sanctuary and mini folk-museum with a collection of sculptures by Victorian artist William Ricketts – you can see more of his interesting work in the William Ricketts' Sanctuary in the Dandenongs near Melbourne. The pleasant sanctuary is open 9 am to 5 pm daily and the admission cost is $1.50.

Date Garden & Camel Farm

On the Old South Rd, just beyond the Heavitree Gap, is Australia's only date garden. It's open daily from 9.30 am to 4.30 pm and there are tours on the hour.

The Camel Farm is on Emily Gap Rd and it is open 8 am to 5.30 pm daily. Here's your chance to ride a camel. It was these strange 'ships of the desert' and their Afghani masters who really opened

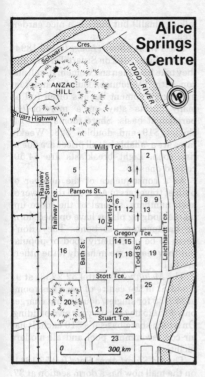

Alice Springs Centre

1 Signpost
2 Old Riverside Hotel
3 Papa Luigi's
4 Stuart Arms
5 Anglican Lodge
6 The Residency
7 Ansett
8 TAA & Greyhound
9 Pioneer Theatre (open air cinema)
10 Mia Pizza, Chopsticks & The Italian Restaurant
11 Post Office
12 Adelaide House
13 NTGTB
14 Telford Alice Motel
15 La Casalinga
16 Pines Homestead
17 Panorama Guth
18 Centre for Aboriginal Artists & Craftsmen
19 Library & Civic Centre
20 Billy Goat Hill
21 Salvation Army Hostel
22 YWCA
23 Royal Flying Doctor Base
24 Melanka Guest House
25 Youth Hostel

up central Australia. There's also a museum with displays about camels and early radio communications in the outback – admission is $2.25.

Stuart Auto Museum

Just south of Heavitree Gap the motor museum has a number of old cars and some interesting exhibits on pioneer motoring in the Northern Territory. They include the tale of the first car to cross the Northern Territory, way back in 1907. The museum is open 9 am to 5 pm daily and admission is $1.50.

Chateau Hornsby

Alice Springs actually has a winery. It's 15 km out of Alice Springs, five km off the road, before you get to the airport turn-

off. The wine they produce here (moselle, riesling-semillon and shiraz) is actually not at all bad although most of it gets sold to people intrigued at the novelty of a central Australian wine.

There's a pleasant restaurant here and it makes a nice lunchtime excursion from town – it's open for a lunchtime barbecue Thursday to Monday and for dinner on Friday and Saturday. You can pedal out to Chateau Hornsby by bicycle – after tasting a little free wine the distance back seems much shorter. Arura Safari Tours has a trip out here or to the Camel Farm for $5.

Places to Stay

Hostels & Guest Houses Alice Springs has a pretty good selection in this category. There's a youth hostel, a privately run ex-government hostel, a YWCA and several other similar places.

The *Alice Springs Youth Hostel* (tel 52 5016) is right in the centre of town at the corner of Todd St and Stott Terrace. It's a very busy place and though it has expanded to 60 beds, it still gets full. Facilities haven't kept up with the increased beds so you may have to get up early to get a warm shower. The kitchens and lounge are crowded but there are plans to solve at least some of these problems. It's not a good idea to leave clothes on the line overnight as things disappear. Nightly charges are about $5 and office hours are 7.15 to 10 am, 5.30 to 8 pm and 9.30 to 10 pm daily. There are mopeds and bicycles for rent. The warden is very friendly and will help with booking tours.

A very good alternative, and probably more relaxed, is the nearby *Sandrifter Safari Lodge* (tel 52 4859) at 6 Khalick St. It was formerly known as the Left Bank and sometimes still is. To get there, cross the Todd River on Stott Terrace and turn left past the caravan park. It's a simple, friendly place that's open all day and there's a kitchen (with a fridge that certainly keeps things cool – like solid!), laundry facilities and a couple of pet birds. Each room has just two beds and prices are $6 on a share basis, $10 to be alone. They sell a few basic groceries, rent bikes and organise tours to Ayers Rock.

Also good, and just a few minutes away, the *Alice Lodge* (tel 52 7805) is at 4 Mueller St, north-west of Khalick St. Located across from the park, the Lodge has room for 22 people in six double rooms and a dorm. Nightly rates are: dorm $6, single room $14, share rooms $10 per person. Weekly rates are also available. There's communal cooking and, in the pleasant garden, there is a pool and barbecue.

A similar place is the *Arura Safari Lodge* (tel 52 3843) on the corner of Lindsay Avenue and Warburton St in a residential area about 15-minutes walk from the centre of town, across the Todd River. Other than the stagnant looking pool, the place is immaculate with rooms with fridge and tea-making for $12.50 per person on a share basis or $17.50 a single. Dorms are $5 but there is a maximum stay of one week. The kitchen is small (we're talking small!) but there is a nice garden area.

The *YWCA's Stuart Lodge* (tel 52 1894) is centrally located on Stuart Terrace and they take both men and women. It's all air-con with TV lounge, laundry and tea-making equipment but it's often full as many guests stay on a more-or-less permanent basis. Share rooms are $14, singles $19 and doubles $28. Weekly rates are available but all prices are due to rise soon. Light breakfasts are $4.50, cooked ones $6.

As a consequence of the number of budget travellers in Alice and the power of such numbers, several of the more up-market lodging places have opened dorm or backpackers' sections. They don't seem to be particularly good or popular but they may come in handy if the others are full.

The *Melanka Lodge*(tel 52 2233) at 94 Todd St in the centre of town has rooms at $27/35 for singles/doubles but charges only $15/25 if you have your own bedding. On a twin share basis it's $10 each. It has air-con, swimming pool and all modern facilities.

The old *Stuart Arms Hotel* (tel 52 1811) on the mall now has a dorm section at $7. It's mainly known for the bars and was up for sale when this book was being researched so future policies are uncertain. Singles are $19, doubles $25.

The *Anglican Hostel, ('The Lodge')*, (tel 52 3108) is good value with singles for $19 ($72 per week), share or double for $15 per person ($50 per week) in rooms with their own facilities. Cheaper rooms are $10.50 daily or $40 per week and there are also self-contained flats. There is a communal kitchen and a pool. The whole place is spotless but it does have an institutional air about it.

The *Salvation Army Red Shield Hostel* (tel 52 1960) on Stuart Terrace on the corner of Hartley St is cheap but caters mainly to long term residents.

Out of Alice Springs, 75 km away on the western side of the MacDonnell Ranges, the *Hamilton Downs Youth Camp* has 60 beds at $10 for one night and $6 for subsequent nights. The Camp is an old homestead on the banks of Jay Creek. All food supplies and bedding need to be brought in with you. The owner provides free transport from Alice for groups of five or more people and can be contacted through the youth hostel.

Hotels & Motels Down Gap Rd, not too far south of the town centre, *Toddy's Holiday Accommodation* (tel 52 1322) is at number 41. They have a wide variety of rooms starting with dorms at $8 a night and $7 extra the first night if you need linen. Cabins with fridges and sinks are $25/35 for singles/doubles. Rooms with bathrooms are $30/40 and fully self-contained flats are $50/55. Family rates are available and the complex also has laundry facilities and a communal kitchen for those not in the self-contained units. There's a swimming pool, barbecue and small shop on the site. All in all, it's quite convenient and reasonably priced.

At 17 Gap Rd, not quite so far from the centre as Toddy's, are the *White Gum Holiday Units* (tel 52 5144). They're not for one-night stands since there's a minimum booking of three nights. The rooms are air-con, fully equipped, have kitchens with cooking facilities, utensils and a fridge, plus there's a swimming pool. The rooms will sleep four and cost $45/50 a night.

Generally, motels in Alice Springs aren't cheap. Amongst the cheaper ones the *Desert Inn* (tel 52 1411) at 15 Railway Terrace, near the centre, has rooms for $32/42 with every extra you could need. The *Outback Motor Lodge* (tel 52 3888) on South Terrace is a bit pricier at $36/42. The *Larapinta Lodge* (tel 52 7089) at 3 Larapinta Drive costs $35/45.

More expensive places include: the *Elkira Court Motel* (tel 52 1222) at 134 Bath St, in the town centre, with singles/doubles at $40/50 or $55/60 for the deluxe units; the *Oasis Motel* (tel 52 1444) at 10 Gap Rd is $45/50; the *Ford Resort Motel* (tel 52 6699) on Stott Terrace just over the Todd River, has good motel units at $40/50; the *Stuart Arms Hotel* (tel 52 1811) is on Todd St and has singles for $19 to $34 and doubles for $25 to $45.

Camping Alice Springs camping sites and their distance from the town centre are:

Carmichael Tourist Park (tel 52 1200), 3 km west on Larapinta Drive, camping costs $6 for two, cabins $20 to $30 (2-5 people), on-site vans $20.

Greenleaves Tourist Park (tel 52 4603), 2 km east on Burke St, camping $5 per person ($24 per week), on-site vans $20 single or double.

Stuart Caravan Park (tel 52 2547), 2 km west on Larapinta Drive, camping $6 for two people, on-site vans $23.

Wintersun Caravan Park (tel 52 4080), 2 km north on the Stuart Highway, camping $3 per person, on-site vans $23.

Ford Resort (52 6699), in the centre on Stott Terrace past the Youth Hostel, has a campground as well as motel units, pool and restaurant. Camping costs $4 per person.

Places to Eat

Snacks & Fast Food For a sandwich, jaffle or milkshake there's *Jule's Coffee Pot* in the town centre, off Todd St, opposite the John Flynn Memorial Church. Eat in or at the tables outside, open daily.

Neddy's Nosebag is a similar place, open Monday to Friday 8 am to noon, Saturday 9 am to 12 noon, for snacks and coffee. It's in the Stockade Arcade, running off Todd St, opposite the Stuart Arms.

You can get a burger, a hot dog or a quick $2 fried rice or chicken curry at *Grandad's* in the arcade across from the supermarket on Todd St – a popular spot for ice-cream too.

Cleo's Gourmet is a semi-healthfood place with salads, quiches and full meals. It's in the Ermond Mall, Hartley St, near Parson St, and has some outdoor tables.

On Lindsay St, near the corner of Undoolya St, across the river, there is a good and very cheap fish & chips shop but it's take-away only.

Kentucky Fried Chicken has appeared in Alice, across from the youth hostel. The Shell service station at the end of Todd St has quite a reasonable restaurant-snack bar.

Pub Meals On Todd St, the *Stuart Arms* does reasonably priced counter-style meals at lunchtime. Steaks and the like are in the $4 to $6 range.

Restaurants The *Eranova Cafeteria* at 70 Todd St is one of the busiest eating spots in town and is a comfortable place with a good selection of excellent food. Serve yourself pub-type meals – fish, vegetarian lasagna and desserts from $4 to $5.

Aussie Tucker is set up in the renovated Pioneer Market Place, on Parsons St, at the corner of Leichardt St. They specialise in central Australian beef which you can cook yourself or there's billy tea and damper – traditional outback tucker. They also have burgers, it's BYO and there are some outdoor tables.

There seems to be quite an Italian influence in Alice Springs. Down at the Anzac Hill end of Todd St is *Papa Luigi's Bistro* with a variety of meals – schnitzels, chickens, steaks and so on – all at $5, plus other meals like pastas and a fairly comprehensive selection of gelati ice-creams. This is a popular place to eat at lunchtime or in the evenings. Round behind it is *Il Sorrentino*, a rather more expensive Italian eatery.

La Casalinga at 105 Gregory Terrace, just off Todd St, is a three-part restaurant – first a take-away section, then a quite pleasant restaurant section where you can order from the take-away part at the same prices, and finally there's a tablecloths-and-candles section right at the back. In front, small pizzas cost $4 to $5 and it's up to $10 or so for large. They make a damn good pizza, too. Main courses are $6 to $8, pastas $3.50 to $5. The proper restaurant section is a bit pricier – a couple of dollars more for pizzas or main courses. There's also a bar but it's a bit expensive.

Over on Hartley St you'll find several places in the Ermund Arcade – like the *Mia Pizza Bar*, the 'pizza palace in the Alice'. Small pizzas cost from $4, spaghettis, lasagnas and other pastas are available and cost from $6 and up. Next door is the *Italian Restaurant* with starters at $5 to $6 and main courses at $8.50 to $9.50.

Alice Springs is better for Italian food than Chinese but the Ermund Arcade also has *Chopsticks* if you have to eat sweet & sour. Another Chinese place, perhaps more expensive, is the bright yellow *Golden Inn* on Undoolya St, just over the bridge from the centre. Aside from the usual items you can sample some Malaysian and Szechuan dishes.

The *Hacienda Overlander Mexican Steakhouse* at 72 Hartley St specialises in steaks, including buffalo, and Mexican food. Prices are in the $8 to $10 range for main courses. Other restaurants in this price bracket are *Bojangles* and the restaurant in the *Old Riverside Hotel*.

Entertainment

The *Stuart Arms Hotel* has rock bands most nights and on Saturday afternoon there's folk music. The *Old Riverside Hotel* has the popular Hitching Rail Bar and a disco. Another good place for a drink is the *Todd Tavern* with it's Maxim's Bar for beer and Bobby McGee's Disco for live rock and dancing – folk music on Sunday at 8 pm.

Alice Springs has a casino if you want to watch the Australian gambling enthusiasm in an unusual setting. The local film society puts on films at the Totem Theatre.

Getting There

Air You can fly to Alice Springs with TAA or Ansett from a variety of places. Ansett (tel 52 4455) and TAA (tel 50 5222) face each other across Todd St from corners at the Parson St intersection. Ansett NT are with Ansett.

See the Northern Territory introductory Getting Around section for details of air fares within the territory. To or from Alice Springs, Adelaide is the usual jumping off point and the fare is $219 (standby $175). Perth is $282 direct ($226 standby) but more expensive via Adelaide or Darwin. Mt Isa is $144 ($115) and Sydney $286 ($229). Since you can now fly direct to Ayers Rock from Adelaide, Perth and Sydney an interesting and more economical way into the Northern Territory from these state capitals would be to fly there first, rather than make Ayers Rock an out-and-back trip from Alice Springs.

Buses Ansett Pioneer and Greyhound both have bus services to Alice Springs on all three routes - Mt Isa to Three Ways and down the track, straight down from Darwin or straight up from Adelaide. Greyhound generally have the more frequent services in the Northern Territory.

In Alice Springs, Ansett Pioneer (tel 52 2422) operate from the Ansett office on Todd St. Greyhound (tel 52 7888) and Stateliner can be found at the CATA/TAA office also on Todd St. Fares (to or from) are: Adelaide, $99, 25 hours; Mt Isa, $58, 16 hours; Darwin, $76, 24 hours.

Deluxe Coachlines (tel 52 4444) is at 113 Todd St. They go to Darwin ($90), Townsville ($105) and Brisbane ($168). Briscos (tel 268 9444) at 8 Taminga St, Regency Park, Adelaide also have a bus service between Adelaide and Alice Springs. They operate three-times weekly and the fare is the same as Ansett Pioneer and Greyhound.

Driving & Hitching The basic thing to remember about getting to Alice Springs is that it's a very long way from anywhere. From Adelaide it's 1983 km and about 300 of those km are over an unsurfaced road which can easily be cut by rain. Fortunately the road is now surfaced from the South Australia-Northern Territory border to Alice Springs but it's still a long, long stretch of dirt to be covered before you get to that border. Coming in from Queensland it's 1180 km from Mt Isa to Alice Springs

or 537 km from Three Ways, where the Mt Isa road meets the Darwin-Alice Springs road, the track. Darwin-Alice Springs is 1525 km. The road from Mt Isa and from Darwin are both surfaced - they're just a very long way.

These are outback roads but you're not in the real outer-outback where a break-down can mean big trouble. Nevertheless it's wise to have your vehicle well prepared since getting someone to come out to fix it if it breaks down is likely to be very expensive. Similarly, you won't die of thirst waiting for a vehicle to come by if you do break down but it's still wise to carry water - waiting for help can get thirsty. Even the surfaced road can sometimes be cut by a short, sharp rainfall and in that case the only thing to do is to sit and wait for the water to recede. It usually won't take long on the surfaced road but waiting for the dirt roads to dry out can take rather longer.

Petrol is also readily available from stops along the road but the price tends to be high and variable. Some fuel stops are notorious for charging well over the odds so carrying an extra can of fuel with you can easily save you a few dollars by allowing you to bypass these places.

Hitching to Alice is not the easiest trip in Australia. Traffic is light and getting up the road from South Australia is likely to be very difficult. Coming the other way Three Ways is a notorious bottleneck for hitchers. You can spend a long time there. The noticeboard in the Alice Springs' youth hostel is a good place to look for lifts.

Rail 'The Ghan' between Adelaide and Alice Springs costs $118 in coach class (no sleeper and no meals) or $171 in economy, $236 in first, both including meals and a sleeper. It departs from Adelaide on Thursday morning at 11 am, arriving in Alice Springs the next morning at 10 am. From Alice Springs the departure is on Friday at 3.30 pm arriving in Adelaide the next afternoon at 2.15 pm. Cars can also be transported between Port Augusta in South Australia and Alice Springs: $210 for a car up to 5.5 metres long, $315 for larger cars. There is an additional service which only runs between May and October. It leaves Adelaide on Mondays and leaves Alice on Tuesdays.

'The Alice' is a direct Sydney-Alice Springs service. It leaves Sydney at 1.40 pm on Monday, arriving in Alice at 12.25 pm on Wednesday. It then leaves Alice at 5 pm on Wednesday, arriving in Sydney at 3.50 pm on Friday. This train runs at about 95% capacity so reservations are advised.

The Ghan

Australia's great railway adventure would have to be the 'Ghan'. The Ghan went through a major change in 1980 and although it's now a rather more modern and comfortable (dare I say 'safe') adventure, it's still a great trip.

The Ghan saga started in 1877 when it was decided to build a railway line from Adelaide to Darwin. It eventually took over 50 years to reach Alice Springs and they're still thinking about the final 1500 km to Darwin over a century later. The basic problem was that they made a big mistake right at the start, a mistake that wasn't finally sorted out until 1980. They built the line in the wrong place.

The grand error was a result of concluding that because all the creek beds north of Marree were bone dry, and because nobody had seen

rain, there wasn't going to be rain in the future. In fact they laid the initial stretch of line right across a flood plain and when the rain came, even though it soon dried up, the line was simple washed away. In the century or so that the original Ghan line survived it was a regular occurrence for the tracks to be washed away.

The wrong route was only part of the Ghan's problems. At first it was built wide gauge to Marree then extended narrow gauge to Oodnadatta in 1884. And what a jerry built line it was – the foundations were flimsy, the sleepers were too light, the grading was too steep and it meandered hopelessly. It was hardly surprising that right up to the end the top speed of the old Ghan was a flat out 30 km per hour! Early rail travellers went from Adelaide to Marree on the broad gauge line, changed there to narrow gauge as far as Oodnadatta and then had to make the final journey to Alice Springs by camel train. The Afghan-led camel trains had pioneered transport through the outback and it was from these Afghans that the Ghan took its name.

Finally in 1929 the line was extended from Oodnadatta to Alice Springs. Though the Ghan might have been a great adventure, it simply didn't work. At the best of times it was chronically slow and uncomfortable as it bounced and bucked its way down the badly laid line. Worse, it was unreliable and expensive to run. And worst of all, a heavy rainfall could strand it at either end or even in the middle. Parachute drops of supplies to stranded train travellers became part of outback lore and on one occasion the Ghan rolled in 10 days late!

By the early '70s the South Australian state railway system was taken over by the Commonwealth Government and a new line to Alice Springs was planned. The A$145 million line was to be standard gauge, laid from Tarcoola, west of Port Augusta on the trans-continental line, to Alice Springs – and it would be laid where rain would not wash it out. In 1980 the line was completed in circumstances that would be unusual for any major project today, let alone an Australian one – ahead of time and on budget. In late '80 the old Ghan made its last run and the old line has subsequently been torn up. Whereas the old train took 140 passengers and, under ideal conditions, made the trip in 50 hours, the new train takes twice as many passengers and does it in 24 hours. It's still the Ghan but it's not the trip it once was.

At present the extension of the line further north from Alice Springs to Darwin is still under

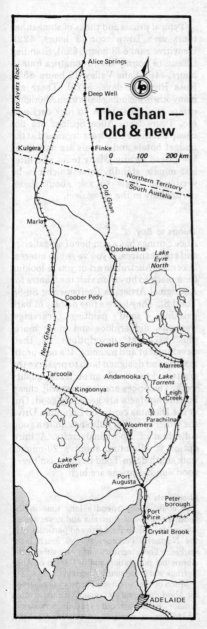

The Ghan —
old & new

to Ayers Rock

Alice Springs

Deep Well

Kulgera

Finke

0   100   200 km

Northern Territory
South Australia

Old Ghan

Marla

Oodnadatta

Lake
Eyre
North

Coober Pedy

New Ghan

Coward Springs

Tarcoola

Andamooka

Lake
Torrens

Kingoonya

Marree

Leigh
Creek

Woomera

Parachilna

Lake
Gairdner

Port
Augusta

Peter
borough

Port
Pirie

Crystal Brook

ADELAIDE

consideration. There's really no way the line would make economic sense but its value as a connection between the top end and the rest of the country plus the smooth construction of the Ghan line has kept the plan a firm possibility.

Getting Around

There is no public transport around Alice Springs apart from taxis. Fortunately the town centre is quite compact enough to get around on foot. If you want to go further afield you'll have to take a tour, rent a car or tackle the closer attractions by bicycle.

Airport Transport Alice Springs' airport is some distance south of the town, about $14 by taxi. There is an airport shuttle bus service (and they also go to and from the train station) that meets flights and takes passengers around to all city accommodation – $4 (or $5 return), less for the train station run. For bookings phone 52 3843. The airport is quite a busy one and the terminal is fairly small so when, as often happens, several aircraft arrive at once, it can get extremely crowded and chaotic.

Car Rental Hertz, Budget and Avis all have counters at Alice Springs' airport. Alice Springs is classified as a remote area so car hire can be a bit pricy. Winter rates can be somewhat lower and Thrifty are usually cheaper than the big three.

Moke rental, however, is not too bad. Moke Rentals (tel 52 1405) on Parsons St, opposite Ansett is typical and charges $18 a day, $5 for insurance plus 15c a km. The big rental firms also hire Mokes and their charges are usually inclusive of 100 or more km – get your calculators out and you may find they are equally good value. Check about distance restrictions because some companies specify that you cannot take their Mokes more than 50 km from town. This is OK for the closer places but there are plenty of attractions around Alice Springs which are more than 50 km out and are quite accessible for any reasonable vehicle. Hiring a Moke with a group of people is a fine way of exploring around the town.

Bicycles & Mopeds Alice Springs has a number of bicycle tracks and, particularly in winter, a bike is a great way of getting around town and out to the closer attractions. While researching the last edition I biked it as far out as Chateau Hornsby quite easily.

Thrifty Bike Hire at the Thrifty car rental office on Todd St hires good bikes for $6 a day ($10 a 24-hour day), they're open every day of the week and offer discounts for YHA members. Bikes are available for the same price from the Tip Top Jean Shop on Gregory Terrace by La Casalinga. They're open on weekdays and Saturday mornings, on the weekend you can hire their bikes from the Heavitree Gap Caravan Park. Bikes are also available at the Sandrifter Safari Lodge and the Arura for a reasonable price.

Thrifty also rents mopeds for $14 half day, $20 full day – discount for YHA members. Mopeds are also available at Action Moped (tel 52 8710) at the BP station in Todd St.

Tours The NTGTB can tell you about all sorts of organised tours from Alice Springs. There are the usual big name operators like Ansett-Pioneer and CATA but also a host of small local operators. There are bus tours, four-wheel-drive tours, even expensive balloon tours. Some specialise in animals, some people, others geography and scenery.

Rod Steinert's Dreamtime Tour is different to most and is evidently quite interesting. It's a half-day trip in which you meet some Aboriginals and learn a little of their traditional life. There are demonstrations on weapons and foods and samples of barbecued witchetty grubs and it costs $47. For around $110 you can go along on the Chartair outback mail runs and visit a string of outback stations to collect and deliver the mails. Phone 52 2544 or 52 6666 for details.

Typical prices and times of some other tours are: Town tour (3 hours, $22), Heavitree range (3 hours, $25), Standley Chasm (6 hours, $24), Namatjira tour (9 hours, $46), Palm Valley (12 hours, $55), Ross River (2 days, $125). There are many others including tours to an Aboriginal camp, to a ghost town, to rock carvings, etc. Tours from Alice Springs are not cheap but those which are organised at the budget hotels and hostels are usually as low priced as any. Many tours also offer last minute standby rates which can be very good deals so ask about these, particularly in the off-season.

Things to Buy

Alice Springs has a number of art galleries and craft centres. If you've got an interest in central Australian art or you're looking for a piece to buy then visit the Centre for Aboriginal Artists & Craftsmen at 86-88 Todd St. They have a fine display of bark paintings, sand paintings, carvings, weapons, didgeridoos and much more, plus excellent descriptions of their development and meaning. It's non-profit making and designed both to preserve the crafts and to provide an outlet for quality work. The prices aren't necessarily cheap but the artefacts are generally good. Out at the Diorama centre on Larapinta Drive the Outcrop Gallery also has quite a good collection of Aboriginal crafts. A third option is Mbantua, about a 20-minute walk south down Todd St but it isn't very good and the prices are high.

Aboriginals

You could easily spend a long time in the southern states of Australia and never see an Aboriginal. But in the north and particularly in the Northern Territory they're much more visible. The territory has a substantial Aboriginal population and in Darwin or Alice Springs you'll see many Aboriginals.

Much of the Northern Territory is reserved for Aboriginals and you cannot visit these often remote areas without special permission. There are a number of reasons for this exclusion; the unhappy result of the collision between our civilisation and theirs is certainly one of them. If you do intend to travel through Aboriginal lands then it's necessary to get in touch with the Northern Territory Lands Council in Alice Springs on 52 3800 for permission. Be aware of the fact that Aborigines, both on reserves and in town, do not appreciate their photos being taken, even at a distance.

The great tribes of the centre – the Arunta, the Pintjantjarra or the Gurindji – certainly still exist but the people camping in the sandy bed of the Todd River in the centre of Alice Springs are a sad reminder of former days when the tribes wandered an open land. Australia's modern record of dealing with the country's original inhabitants may not be perfect (although it's a thousand times better than that of the early colonialists) but a great deal of time, effort and money has been expended on trying to do the right thing – without a great deal of success. Integrating the Aboriginals into our still very alien way of life and finding a valid replacement for their old way of life, which we have almost totally destroyed, is going to be a serious and long-term problem.

It's possible to take Aboriginal language courses of 15 days or so, or maybe even single lessons, in town. You learn a sort of Pidgin-Aboriginal, some words, the basic pronunciation and how to hold your mouth to form some of the sounds.

Around Alice Springs

Outside of the town itself there are a great number of places within day-trip distance or with overnight stops thrown in if you have the time and inclination. Generally they're found by heading east or west along the MacDonnell Ranges which run east-west directly south of Alice Springs. Places to the south of town are usually visited on the way to Ayers Rock.

The scenery along the ranges is quite superb. There are many gorges that cut through the rocky cliffs and their sheer rock walls are extremely spectacular. In the shaded gorges there are often rocky waterholes and a great deal of wildlife which can be seen if you're quiet and

observant. They are often filled with wildflowers in the spring.

You can get out to these gorges on group tours or with your own wheels – some of the closer ones are even accessible by bicycle or on foot. A major advantage of having your own transport around the centre is the immense solitude and quietness you'll experience at many of these places. By yourself the centre's eerie emptiness and peacefulness can get through to you in a way that is completely impossible in a big group.

EASTBOUND
The Ross River road is only surfaced for the first 39 km but it stays in pretty good condition most of the way to Arltunga, about 100 km from Alice Springs. From here the road loops back west and rejoins the Stuart Highway 50 km north of Alice Springs, but this section is much rougher and may require four-wheel drive.

Emily & Jessie Gap
Heading south from Alice Springs you're only just through the Heavitree Gap when the sign points to the road east by the Heavitree Gap campsite. Emily Gap, 16 km out of town, is the next gap through the ranges – it's narrow and often has water running through it. Jessie Gap is only eight km further on and like the previous gap, it's a popular picnic and barbecue spot. On one visit to the Alice I was sitting there, having a lunchtime sandwich, when a huge flock of birds swished smoothly through the gap, tightening their formation as they passed by. I heard them coming long before they appeared in sight.

Corroboree Rock
Shortly after Jessie Gap the surfaced road ends at the Undoolya Gap, another pass through the range, but a good dirt road continues the 43 km to Corroboree Rock. There are many strangely-shaped outcrops of rocks in the range and this one is said to have been used by Aboriginals for their corroborees.

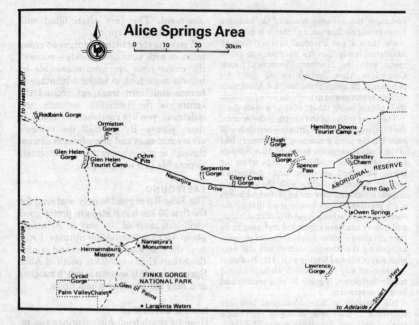

Alice Springs Area

0   10   20   30km

Trephina Gorge

About 75 km out, and a few km north of the road, is Trephina Gorge. It's wider and longer than the other gaps in the range – here you are pretty well north of the main MacDonnell Ranges and in a new ridge. A few km west of the gorge, reached by a track which can sometimes be unsuitable for conventional vehicles, are the delightful John Hayes Rockholes. A sheltered section of a deep gorge provides a series of waterholes which retain their water long after it has dried up in more exposed locations. You can clamber around the rockholes or follow the path to one side up to a lookout above the gorge – perhaps you'll see why it is also called the Valley of the Eagles.

Ross River & N'Dhala Gorge

Beyond Trephina Gorge it's another 15 km to the Ross River Homestead much favoured by coach tours. Rooms cost $38/48 for single/doubles. The N'Dhala Gorge is about 10 km south of the homestead and has some ancient Aboriginal rock carvings; you may also see rock wallabies. It's possible to drive through the gorge and return to Alice Springs by the Ringwood Homestead road but you may require four-wheel drive.

Arltunga

At the eastern end of the MacDonnell Ranges, 92 km north-east of Alice Springs, Arltunga is an old gold-mining ghost town. Gold was discovered here in 1887 and 10 years later reef gold was also discovered but by 1912 the mining activity had petered out. A few old buildings, a couple of cemeteries and the many deserted mine sites are all that remains here now. Alluvial (surface) gold has been completely worked out in the Arltunga reserve but there may still be gold further afield in the area.

The Ross River Highway from Alice Springs is formed gravel until just beyond

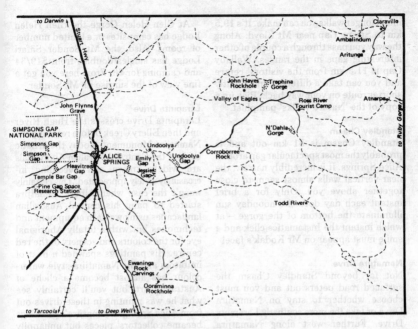

the Trephina Gorge turn-off but the rest of the way to Arltunga it is just a graded track and rain can make the road impassable. You can loop right round and join the Stuart Highway 50 km north of Alice Springs but this route is just a graded track all the way and can be rough going. With side trips off the road a complete loop from Alice Springs to Arltunga and back would be something over 300 km, a fair drive on outback roads.

WESTBOUND

Heading west, Larapinta Drive is surfaced for about 50 km out of town. The surfaced road ends where the road divides into Larapinta Drive heading slightly south-west and Namatjira Drive continuing more directly west. There are many spectacular gorges out in this direction and also some fine walks. A visit to Palm Valley, one of the prime attractions to the west of Alice Springs, requires four-wheel drive.

Simpson's Gap

Westbound on Larapinta Drive you start on the northern side of the MacDonnell Ranges. You soon come to Flynn's Grave; the flying doctor's final resting place is topped by one of the Devil's Marbles, brought down the track from near Tennant Creek. A little further on is Simpson's Gap, 22 km out, another picturesque cutting through the range. Like the other gaps it is a thought-provoking example of nature's power and patience – for a river to cut a path through solid rock may seem amazing, but for a river that rarely ever runs to cut such a path is positively mind-boggling. If you look very carefully across the gap to the jumble of rocks on the other side you'll see rock wallabies jumping nimbly from boulder to boulder.

The NT Conservation Commission recommends a couple of excellent walking trails from the parking area and visitors' centre. There's a short walk from the road up to Cassia Hill or there are a couple of much longer walks you can make. It's 19.5 km to Spring Gap near Mt Lloyd. Along the way you pass through a couple of other interesting gaps in the ranges. Wallaby Gap is 11.5 km from the visitors' centre and you can take a different and slightly shorter route on your way back. Pick up a copy of the 'Nature Walks' pamphlet.

Standley Chasm

Standley Chasm is 51 km out and is probably the most spectacular gap around Alice Springs. It is incredibly narrow, the near-vertical walls almost seem to close together above you. Only for a brief instant each day does the noonday sun illuminate the bottom of the gorge – at which instant the Instamatics click and a smile must appear on Mr Kodak's face!

Namatjira Drive

Not far beyond Standley Chasm the surfaced road peters out and you must choose whether to stay on Namatjira Drive or take the more southerly Larapinta Drive. Further west along Namatjira Drive another series of gorges and gaps in the range await you. Ellery Gorge is 93 km from Alice Springs and there's a big waterhole at the gorge. It's 13 km further to Serpentine Gorge, a narrow gorge with a pleasant waterhole at the entrance.

The large and rugged Ormiston Gorge also has a waterhole and it leads to the enclosed valley of the Pound National Park. Fish found in the waterholes of the pound bury into the sand and go into a sort of suspended animation when the water-holes dry up. When rains refill the holes they mysteriously reappear.

Only a couple of km further is the turn-off to the scenic Glen Helen Gorge where the Finke River cuts through the MacDonnells. The road standard is lower beyond this point but if you want to continue west you'll reach the red-walled Redbanks Gorge with its permanent water, 161 km from Alice Springs. Also out this way is Mt Sonder, at 1340 metres the highest point in the territory.

At Glen Helen Gorge the Glen Helen Lodge has campsites or a limited number of rooms. Also, the Mt Sonder Safari Lodge has singles/doubles from $19/34 and camping for $3. From here you get a fine view of the sunrise on Mt Sonder.

Larapinta Drive

Larapinta Drive crosses the Hugh River and then Ellery Creek before reaching the Namatjira Monument. Today the artistic skills of the Central-Australian Aboriginals are widely known and becoming increasingly widely appreciated. This certainly wasn't the case when Albert Namatjira started to paint his central Australian landscapes using western equipment and techniques but with a totally Aboriginal eye for the colours and scenery of the red centre. His paintings spawned a host of imitators and the Namatjira-style water-colour has almost become a cliche of Australian art, but you'll certainly see what he was painting in these drives out from Alice Springs. Namatjira's paintings became collectors' pieces but unhappily his new-found wealth prompted a clash with Alice Spring's staid European society of the time and he died an unhappy man. Only eight km further on you reach the Hermannsburg Mission, 125 km from Alice Springs. If you wish to continue further you'll need four-wheel drive.

Palm Valley

From Hermannsburg the trail follows the Finke River south to the Finke Gorge National Park, only 12 km further on. The track crosses the sandy bed of the river a number of times and four-wheel drive is required to get through. In the park, Palm Valley is a gorge filled with some geographically misplaced palm trees – a strangely tropical find in the dry, red centre.

South to Ayers Rock

You can make some interesting diversions

off the road south to Ayers Rock. The Henbury Meteorite Craters are only a few km off the road but you've got further to go to get to Ewaninga, Chambers Pillar, Finke or Kings Canyon.

EWANINGA & CHAMBERS PILLAR

Following the 'old south road' which runs close to the old Ghan railway line, it's only 35 km from Alice Springs to Ewaninga, with its prehistoric Aboriginal rock carvings. The carvings found here and at N'Dhala Gorge are thought to have been made by Aboriginal tribes who pre-date the current tribes of the centre.

Chambers Pillar, an eerie sandstone pillar, is carved with the names and visit dates of early explorers. It's 130 km from Alice Springs and four-wheel drive is required to get there. Finke is a tiny settlement, further down the line.

VIRGINIA CAMEL FARM

The camel farm, 90 km south of Alice, is run by Noel Fullerton, the 'camel king', who started the annual Camel Cup and has won it four times. In 1984 his 12-year-old daughter took first place. For a few dollars you can try your hand at camel riding and there are also one and two week safaris into Rainbow Valley and the outback. Interestingly, about 90% of the people who go on these long trips are women. It is also odd that the farm exports camels to places around the world including the Arabic nations of the Sahara, the original source of Australia's herd. It's been estimated that the central deserts are home to about 15,000 wild camels.

HENBURY METEORITE CRATERS

A few km off the road, 130 km south of Alice, are the Henbury Meteorite Craters, a cluster of 12 age-old craters which are amongst the largest in the world. The largest of the craters is 180 metres across and 15 metres deep. From the car park by the site there's a walking trail around the

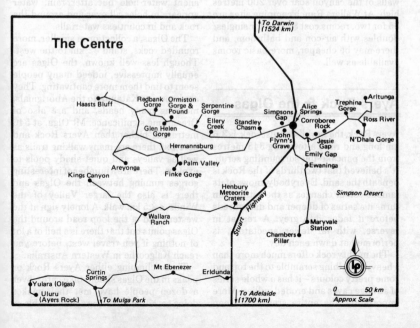

The Centre

To Darwin (1524 km)

Haasts Bluff
Redbank Gorge
Ormiston Gorge & Pound
Serpentine Gorge
Simpsons Gap
Alice Springs
Trephina Gorge
Arltunga

Glen Helen Gorge
Ellery Creek
Standley Chasm
Corroboree Rock
Ross River

Hermannsburg
John Flynn's Grave
Jessie Gap
N'Dhala Gorge

Areyonga
Palm Valley
Finke Gorge
Emily Gap

Kings Canyon
Ewaninga

Henbury Meteorite Craters

Simpson Desert

Wallara Ranch

Maryvale Station

Stuart Highway

Chambers Pillar

Curtin Springs
Mt Ebenezer
Erldunda

Yulara (Olgas)
Uluru (Ayers Rock)
To Mulga Park

To Adelaide (1700 km)

0   50 km
Approx Scale

craters with signposted features. There are no longer any fragments of the meteorites at the site but the Residency Museum in Alice Springs has a small chunk which weighs in at a surprisingly heavy 46.5 kg. The road in to the crater site is the start of the Kings Canyon Rd, a gravel road which can be rather slippery after rain.

KINGS CANYON

From the meteorite craters the road continues west to Wallara Ranch Tourist Chalet and Kings Canyon, 323 km from Alice Springs. This is an alternative, and rougher, route to Ayers Rock although you have to backtrack the 89 km between Wallara and the canyon. Dubbed 'Australia's Grand Canyon' it's a spectacular canyon with natural features like the 'Lost City' with its strange building-like outcrops and the lush palms of the 'Garden of Eden'. There are fine views over the canyon from its rim but it's a steep climb to the top. The walls of the canyon soar over 200 metres high. At Wallara Ranch camping sites are $5 for two, rooms cost $45/60 for singles/ doubles with air-con and bathroom, and there may be cheaper, more basic rooms available as well.

Ayers Rock & the Olgas

Ayers Rock, the world's largest rock, is 3.6 km long and rises a towering 348 metres from the pancake-flat surrounding scrub. It's believed that two thirds of the Rock is beneath the sand. Everybody knows of its famous colour changes as the setting sun turns it a series of deeper and darker reds before it fades into grey. A repeat in reverse, with far fewer spectators, is performed at dawn each day.

The mighty rock offers much more than a heavy-breathing scramble to the top and some pretty colours – it has a whole series of strange caves and eroded gullies. More importantly, the entire area is of deep cultural significance to the Aboriginals and there are many interesting theories about the paintings and carvings they have made. To them it is known as Uluru, the name given to the National Park which surrounds and encompasses the rock. There are several Aboriginal camps near Yulara and Ayers Rock.

The Aboriginal people now officially own the National Park, although it is leased permanently to the Commonwealth Government. Disputes continue over whether this compromise succeeds in protecting the rights of the traditional Aboriginal custodians at the expense of other Australians.

It is not difficult at all to spend several days here. There are walking trails around the rock and free, ranger-conducted walks delving into the plants, wildlife, geology and mythology of the area. It's a five-hour, nine-km walk around the base of Ayers Rock looking at caves and paintings. Maggie Springs, at the base, is a permanent water-hole but after rain, water appears in holes all over and around the rock and in countless waterfalls.

The Olgas, a collection of smaller, more rounded rocks, stand 32 km to the west. Though less well known, the Olgas are equally impressive, indeed many people seem to find them more captivating. They are known as Katajuta to the Aboriginals, meaning many heads, and are also of Dreamtime significance. Mt Olga, at 546 metres, is higher than Ayers Rock and here too, there are many walking trails as well as valleys and quiet shady pools to explore. There are a number of interesting gorges running between the Olgas and there is also the larger Valley of the Winds, a 2.5 km walk. A lonely sign at the western end of the loop road around the Olgas points out that there is a hell of a lot of nothing if you travel west, before you reach Kalgoorlie in Western Australia.

Those climbing either Ayers Rock or peaks in the Olgas should take care – over a dozen people have met their maker doing so, either by taking a fatal tumble or or

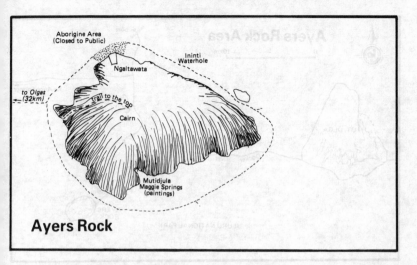

Ayers Rock

by having a heart attack. The entrance fee to the park is $1.50 and is collected at the Ayers Rock ranger office where maps and other info are available.

YULARA

Yulara Village has effectively turned one of the world's least hospitable regions into an easy and comfortable place for outsiders to visit. Lying just outside the National Park, 18 km from the rock and 37 km from the Olgas, the $165 million, joint government and private-industry tourist complex makes an excellent and surprisingly

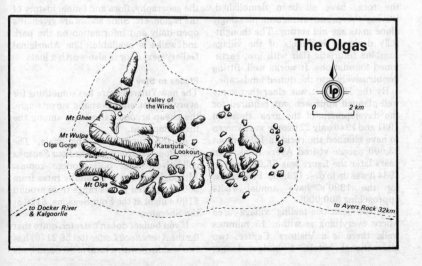

The Olgas

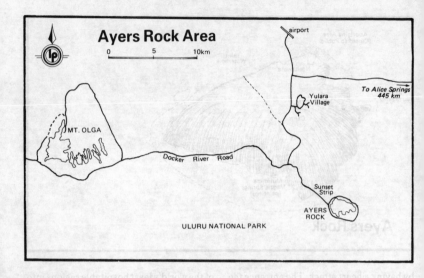

democratic base for exploring the area's renowned attractions. Opened in 1984, it supplies the only accommodation, food outlets and other services available in the area.

Motels, restaurants and other commercial businesses, once cluttered around the rock, have all been demolished, leaving the prime attraction pleasingly alone in its age-old setting. The thoughtfully designed buildings of the village combine futuristic flair with low, earth-toned foundations. It works well, fitting unobtrusively into the duned landscape.

By the 1970's it was clear that some well-planned approach was required for the development of the area. Between 1931 and 1946 only 22 people were known to have climbed the rock. In 1969 about 23,000 people visited Ayers Rock. Ten years later the figure was 65,000 and in 1984 it was up to over 120,000. Projections for the 1990's have annual visits approaching 300,000!

In the spacious-feeling village area where everything is within 15 minutes walk, there is a Visitors' Centre, two international hotels, a budget lodge, camping-ground, bank, post office, petrol station, newsagency, numerous restaurants, supermarket, craft gallery, a pub (of course), and even a police and fire station. An hour or so at the Visitors' Centre is recommended as it is actually a small museum and contains good displays on the geography, flora and fauna, history of the region, etc. Slide shows are given, it's open daily and information on the park and walks is available. The Aboriginal Gallery next door is also worth a look.

Places to Stay

The new Yulara centre has something for every budget and, perhaps surprisingly, the cheap accomodation was among the first completed.

At the top end of the scale, *The Sheraton Ayers Rock* and the *Four Seasons* collectively offer 330 modern rooms. Although you can get standby rates from $80 the quoted prices range from around $100 a night at the Four Seasons, $120 at the Sheraton.

If you budget doesn't stretch quite that far the *Ayers Rock Lodge* (tel 56 2170) has two buildings with a total of 80 dorm beds in rooms of 20. They go for $8 or $7 with a YHA card and you won't find a sturdier or quieter bunk. In winter you'll need extra bedding as the two blankets supplied are definitely not enough. There are also cabin-type rooms with either two bunk beds or a double bed and one bunk. These rooms are $32 each (less with kids) and bedding is $5 extra if you need it. All buildings are air-con in summer and heated in winter and the shared showers and toilets are spotless. Up behind the buildings there is a good lookout for early morning views of the rock.

A five or 10-minute walk away there is a campground with tent sites or unpowered van sites at $4 per person. On-site vans take up to six people and are $32.50 for two, each additional person is $4. There's a swimming pool and the reception kiosk sells basic food supplies.

The next stage of construction, due to begin in 1986 and costing another $50 million or so, will include more shops and lodging, this time in the mid-price range, say $40 to $50 per night and maybe a bed & breakfast arrangement.

Places to Eat

The Lodge has a take-away counter offering breakfasts at high prices, lunchtime sandwiches at $1.50 to $2.50 and cheaper dinners (stew), for $5. There are no kitchen facilities other than fridges and electric barbecues which you must feed with 20c coins. Barbecue packs with a steak and two sausages are $4.50, but the two-person version is better value. Altogether the food situation is not ideal and the 40c charge for a cup of hot water has already become infamous.

The campground kiosk sells canned goods, drinks, tea, coffee, breakfast cereals and the like. Over at the shopping square there is a fair-sized supermarket which sells frozen pizzas for $3.20. You can try to heat them up on the Lodge's barbecues. Also here, the tavern/bistro serves lunches of steak or fish for about $7 to $8, or dinners with more selection for

$7 to $11, it's not cheap but the portions are not bad. Beer is $1.75 a bottle and the place is certainly busy at night, when there is also music. Across the square, *The Old Oak Tree* is a coffee shop with burgers, sandwiches, and pizzas for $5.50 small, $8 medium. There are also more expensive restaurants in the hotels.

Getting There

Air A new airport about five km from Yulara was part of the development scheme, it's called Connellan Airport and takes Fokker F28s. This new airport has permitted longer range flights into Ayers Rock – you can now fly directly to Ayers Rock from Sydney (East-West, $284 one-way, $227 standby), Perth (East-West, $248 one-way, $199 standby), Adelaide (Airlines of South Australia, $242 one-way). Using one of these direct flights to Ayers Rock you could not only save some money over the equivalent fare to Alice Springs you could then continue to Alice Springs by land rather than have to do an Alice Springs-Ayers Rock roundtrip if you had flown to Alice Springs first of all.

You can fly between Alice Springs and Ayers Rock for $90. The flight takes one hour and there are two a day.

Bus & Tours A lot of people get to the rock and the village with one of the many tour operators in Alice Springs, and unless you're hitch-hiking, these are the cheapest, most convenient way to see some of the centre's attractions. Renting a car in Alice Springs with a few people works out the same as, or even more expensive than, most bus tours, which are generally quite good. The only drawback with the tours is that you usually don't get much time. It's a bit of a rush and you don't see everything you might like to but all the acknowledged highlights are squeezed in.

The road surfacing from Alice to Yulara was completed in 1984 and there are regular food and petrol stops along the way. The rock is 448 km from Alice, 246 km west of Erldunda on the Stuart

Highway, and the whole journey takes about six to seven hours. Mt Connor, which is seen on the left some way before Ayers Rock, is often mistaken for the rock itself. Along the way you may see kangaroos and dingoes or, at night, cows sleeping on the warm bitumen. Also note the old windmills which used to supply power and are now being replaced by solar energy.

The basic two-day bus tours generally include the trip there and back, guided walks of sections of Ayers Rock, a trip to the Olgas and a stop at the sunset viewing area known as Sunset Strip. Some include accommodation but on others it's extra. There are also three-day trips, some including Kings Canyon. You have to shop around a bit because different tours run on different days and you may not want to wait for a particular one. Other things to check for include the time it gets to the rock and the Olgas, if the return is done early or late in the day and how fast the bus is. Bear in mind the fact that prices can vary with the season and demand.

Greyhound, Ansett-Pioneer and CATA are the big three and all are very expensive; the two-day trip is in the $140 range. However, CATA has a standby deal where if you show up before departure time at around 7 am and there are seats available, you can get the trip for as low as $55. This is what half a dozen of us did and the whole tour was excellent. Accommodation was not included but $8 in the Lodge dorm wasn't a problem. CATA (tel 52 1700) is located in the TAA Building in Todd Mall.

Deluxe Coachlines' two-day tour is $60 but they also run a straight bus service which is $29 one-way or $50 return so you can see that for only an extra $10, the full tour is good value. If you're going to stay in the Lodge in Yulara you may want to book ahead, or at least check on the space situation. Aussiepass and Eaglepass travellers should note that the bus service to the rock is often booked up – if your schedule is tight it's best to plan ahead.

Landscanner Tourist Services (tel 52 4767), operating out of the Sandrifter Safari Lodge, has good value, popular trips. They leave from the hostel and include a night at Yulara's Lodge for $65. Arura Safari Tours (tel 52 7523) charge $65 which includes a sleeping bag and a night in the Yulara dorm, or $55 with no sleeping arrangements. For a three-day trip to the rock, the Olgas and Kings Canyon, Worana Tours (52 5710) are recommended and charge $100, also staying in the dorm, or you can just take the one-way trip from Ayers Rock to Kings Canyon and Alice for $35.

Note that you can sometimes go with a tour but stay an extra day or two and return with another tour by the same company. This usually costs an extra $30 or so plus your expenses at Yulara but is probably the cheapest way to stay a bit longer. Arura Safari offers these extensions. Both Arura Safari Tours and Landscanner offer more expensive tours to Ayers Rock which fly there and return by bus. They cost about $155, or $265 including a stop at Kings Canyon. Ansett NT run day-tours to the rock, but one day is too short a period to spend there.

Getting Around

There is a free bus service that tours around the village every hour on the hour, otherwise you put one foot in front of the other to get around. Going from place to place you can take walking trails over the dunes which lead to little lookouts overlooking the village and surrounding terrain. Bicycles for rent are planned but aren't available as yet. The petrol station has cars for rent but not cheaply.

Many people at Yulara come on tours from Alice which include trips to the rock, the Olgas and other sights, but for those without transport, there are bus shuttles from the village to the main sites and tours also operate from here. Though you can do everything on your own, at least one guided walk is probably a good idea as the commentary and information on Aboriginal beliefs and rituals is interesting. You would miss a lot just wandering around on your own, particularly at Ayers Rock. Ray Wilke, who's based out here, runs inexpensive guided tours and he knows the area well. His buses to the rock are $7 return, or $10 with the tour. Afternoon tours to the Olgas are $12 but he offers no simple bus-only trip. Another of his tours, for $20, focuses on Aboriginal life and traditions.

Ayers Rock Touring Company has buses going to the rock at 6.45 am, 11.30 am or you can catch the Ansett Trailways at 1.30 pm. Returns are at 9.45 am, 12.15 pm, 1 pm with Greyhound, or 5.15 pm and return tickets are $10. The last trip back includes a stop at the sunset viewing area, which I'd take advantage of. Village-

sunset trips are $5 return. Tours of the Olgas, also $10 return, depart at 10 am and return at 5 pm which gives you a nice long time; they aren't offered in summer due to the heat. The same company offers tours to both sites which include a walking tour; $10 for Ayers Rock, (the same price as the bus ticket alone), and $15 to the Olgas.

The small, old runway near the rock is now used for short scenic flights over the area. Call Chartair at 52 2066 in Yulara or go along to the sunset viewing point the night before as all the pilots are there and you can arrange times with them. The $25 spent on a half-hour early morning flight over the Rock and the Olgas is well worth it.

Queensland

Area	1,727,000 square km
Population	2,500,000

Don't miss the Great Barrier Reef and the delightful islands along the tropical coastline of Australia's holiday state.

Queensland is Australia's holiday state – you are certain to find something to suit whether you prefer glossy, neon-lit Surfers Paradise, long, deserted beaches with crashing surf, or the island resorts and excellent skin diving of the Great Barrier Reef.

In the far north the Cape York Peninsula is a disappearing stretch of wilderness against which people still test themselves. You can get an easy taste of this frontier in Cooktown, Australia's first (involuntary) British settlement and once a riotous goldrush town. Inland from Cairns there is the lush Atherton Tableland with countless beautiful waterfalls and scenic spots. Further inland is the outback mining town of Mt Isa, and in the south-west corner of the state you'll find Birdsville with its famous track.

Queensland started up as yet another 'ship them off out of the way' penal colony in 1824. As usual the free settlers soon followed and Queensland became independent of New South Wales in 1859, less than 10 years after Victoria.

In Queensland today agriculture and mining are the two major activities, the state has a substantial chunk of the nation's mineral wealth. Queensland also has Australia's most controversial state government – whether it is views on the environment, on Aboriginal land rights, on the censorship of films and magazines, or even on how the country should be run, you can count on the Queensland government to take an opposite stand to everybody else.

Unlike some other states, Queensland is not just a big city and a lot of fairly empty country; there are more reasonable sized towns in comparison to the overall population than any other state. Of course there is plenty of empty, outback country too. Also, for nearly 10 years it has had a higher annual growth rate than the other states. It's an interesting, quirky, curious kind of state.

INFORMATION

Queensland is probably the most tourist conscious state so there are plenty of offices of the Queensland Government Tourist Bureau (QGTB) both around the state and in other states. The interstate offices are:

ACT
> Garema Place, Canberra City, 2601 (tel 48 8411)

NSW
> 516 Hunter St, Newcastle, 2300 (tel 26 2800)
>
> 149 King St, Sydney, 2000 (tel 232 1788)

South Australia
> 10 Grenfell St, Adelaide, 5000 (tel 212 2399)

Victoria
> 257 Collins St, Melbourne, 3000 (tel 654 3866)

The RACQ has a series of excellent maps covering the whole state, region by region.

1 Gold Coast
2 Sunshine Coast
3 North Coast

4 Great Barrier Reef	7 The Gulf
5 Cape York Peninsula	8 Channel Country
6 Atherton Tablelands	9 Darling Downs

They're very detailed and packed with information on the reverse side. Available from RACQ offices.

GEOGRAPHY

Queensland has a series of distinct regions, generally running north-south parallel to the coast. First there's the coastal strip – the basis for Queensland's booming tourist trade. Along this strip you've got beaches, bays, islands and, of course, the Great Barrier Reef. Much of the coastal region is green and productive with lush rainforests, endless fields of sugar cane and stunning national parks.

Next comes the Great Dividing Range, the mountain range which continues right down through New South Wales and Victoria. In Queensland the mountains come closest to the coast and are most spectacular in the far north (where you'll

find Queensland's highest mountains, near Cairns) and in the far south (where they provide a superb backdrop to the Gold Coast).

Then there's the tablelands – flat agricultural land running to the west. This fertile area extends furthest west in the south where the Darling Downs have some of the most productive grain-growing land in Australia. Finally there's the vast inland area, the barren outback fading into the Northern Territory further west. Rain can temporarily make this desert bloom but basically it's an area of sparse population, of long empty roads and tiny settlements.

There are a couple of variations from these basic divisions. In the far north Gulf Country and the Cape York Peninsula there are huge empty regions cut by countless dry riverbeds which can become swollen torrents in the wet season. The whole region is a network of waterways so road transport sometimes comes to a complete halt.

GETTING AROUND

Air Ansett and TAA both fly to the major centres of Queensland, connecting them to the southern states and across to the Northern Territory. Within Queensland there is also a very comprehensive network of flights operated by Air Queensland; some of their flights go to tiny missions and outback stations. During the wet season their flights are often the only means of getting around the Gulf of Carpentaria.

Until 1982 Air Queensland was known as Bush Pilot Airways, BPA or 'Bushies' – certainly far more evocative names than the new one, so it's a shame they changed it. Bushies came into operation in the early '50s and gradually spread to cover the whole state.

Apart from regular and charter flights around the state the airline also operates a number of tours and day trips, both to the Queensland outback and to Barrier Reef resorts – although mainly to Lizard

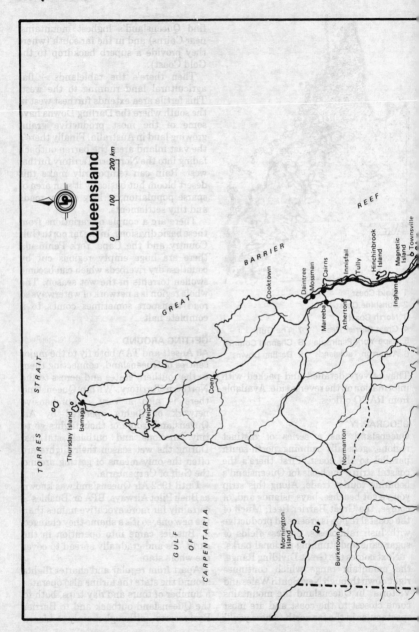

Queensland

0   100   200 km

TORRES STRAIT

GREAT BARRIER REEF

GULF OF CARPENTARIA

Thursday Island
Bamaga
Weipa
Coen
Cooktown
Daintree
Mossman
Mareeba
Cairns
Atherton
Innisfail
Tully
Hinchinbrook Island
Ingham
Magnetic Island
Townsville
Normanton
Burketown
Mornington Island

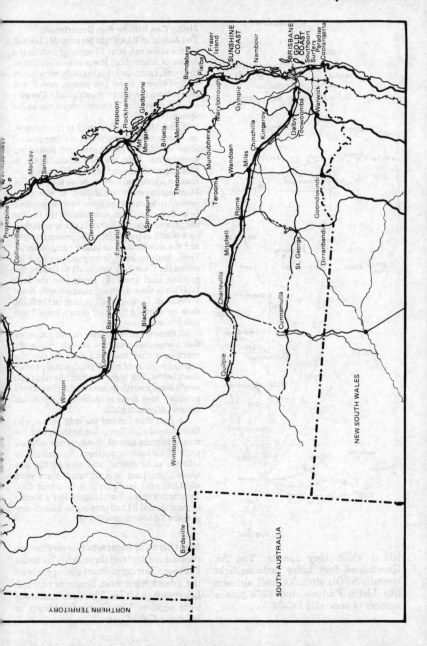

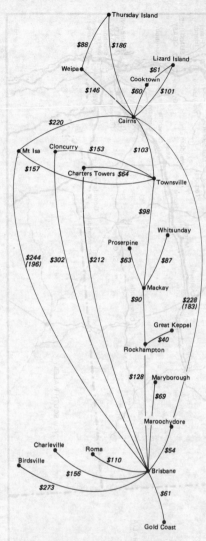

Thursday Island

$88 $186

Lizard Island

Weipa $61
                    Cooktown
$146 $60 $101

$220   Cairns

Mt Isa Cloncurry $153 $103

$157
    Charters Towers $64
                            Townsville

                    $98

                            Whitsunday

        Proserpine

$244
(196) $302 $212 $63 $87

                    Mackay

            $90 $228
                            (183)

                    Great Keppel

                        $40
            Rockhampton

            $128 Maryborough

                    $69

                    Maroochydore

Charleville Roma $54
                $110
Birdsville   Brisbane
    $156
$273
                    $61

                Gold Coast

Flying Can Still be Fun Department

The Ansett or TAA flight between Mt Isa and Cairns takes one hour 10 minutes but, in the course of researching the previous edition of this book, I managed to take nearly seven hours to fly between those two places, and it was hands down the most enjoyable flight I've ever taken in Australia. My magic carpet was an Air Queensland DC-3.

We left Mt Isa and flew north to Doomadgee, an Aboriginal reserve, where we dropped off some Aboriginal passengers and picked up some more. Then we flew north again to Mornington Island in the Gulf of Carpentaria, another Aboriginal reserve. As we took off from Mornington every inhabitant of the town seemed to be out in the street to wave goodbye as we flew over. Then it was across the Gulf to the prawning port of Kuranda where we picked up a bunch of people from the prawn trawlers and the crew from an oil tanker going on leave. From there we had the longest, two hour leg across the Cape York peninsula to Cairns, the parched land gradually rising into the lush tablelands then dropping dramatically down to the coast. I even got half an hour on the flight deck on that leg (no they didn't know I was going to write about it).

All three of our stops were on dirt strips, we flew low enough and slow enough to plot the route on a road map and we even saw the crashed remains of a WW II Liberator bomber down below. The flight was just like what you would hope a north Queensland airline would provide – beer came in stubbies in styrofoam coolers! A great flight.

I'm sure that I'm not the only person who likes this old-style flying and for those with the money to spare several operators now offer air tours of outback or northern Australia. You take the same aircraft and crew all the way around, stopping in a different place each night and next day flying on to your next stop. They're not cheap, but it sounds like a terrific experience and if I had the time and the money to spare I'd love to give it a try.

Bus There are numerous bus services up the coast and inland through Mt Isa to the Northern Territory. Buses also operate on the inland route from Brisbane through Longreach to Mt Isa. There are numerous local services like Cairns-Cooktown or Brisbane-Gold Coast.

Island which they operate. The Air Queensland fleet today includes light aircraft, STOL aircraft, small airliners like Metro Propjets and F27s plus a number of venerable DC-3s.

Rail There are three major rail routes in Queensland. The main one is the route from Brisbane up to Cairns with a local extension on the scenic route into the Atherton Tablelands. From Brisbane a service also runs inland to Charleville and Quilpie while from from Townsville there is a service inland to Mt Isa. The only interstate connection from Queensland is from Brisbane to Sydney. The 'Sunshine Rail Pass' provides unlimited travel on all services in Queensland. The fares in economy (and 1st class) are: 14 days for $161 ($245), 21 days for $195 ($301) and one month for $245 ($368).

Hitching Take care – Queensland is probably the worst state in Australia for hitching – on two counts. First, the police (who also have an Australia wide-reputation) don't like it and are likely to jump on hitch-hikers for little reason. Second, there are long lonely stretches of road where strange people are said to pick up unwary hitchers.

ACTIVITIES

Bushwalking A popular activity in Queensland year round, there are a number of bushwalking clubs in the state and several guidebooks about bushwalks. If you intend to camp in the national parks you must first obtain a permit although this can sometimes be arranged over the phone.

The Lamington National Park, 112 km south-west of Brisbane and inland from the Gold Coast, is popular, with rain forests, waterfalls and nearly 150 km of graded walking tracks. Fraser Island also offers good bushwalking possibilities and there are plenty of places in the north, around Cairns.

Fossicking There are lots of good fossicking areas in Queensland – get a copy of the QGTB's *Gem Field* brochure. It informs you of the types of gems available and the best places to find them. You'll need a 'miners right' before you set out.

Swimming & Surfing What else does one come to Queensland for? There are plenty of swimming beaches close to Brisbane on sheltered Moreton Bay. Popular board-surfing beaches are found south of the capital on the Gold Coast and north on the Sunshine Coast. North of Fraser Island the beaches are sheltered by the Great Barrier Reef so they're great for swimming but no good for surf fans. The clear, sheltered waters of the reef hardly need to be mentioned. There are also innumerable, good, freshwater swimming spots around the state.

Warning: from late November to March avoid swimming on unprotected northern beaches where deadly sea wasps (transparent jellyfish) may hang out. Observe warning signs and if in any doubt check with a local. If you're still in doubt, don't swim – you only get stung once in a lifetime.

Skin Diving There's plenty of opportunity for this activity in Queensland. The reef islands, Moreton Bay and the Sunshine Coast all have good diving spots. Evidence of qualifications must be shown when hiring equipment.

Other Watersports There are some popular canoeing places in Queensland, particularly on the Noosa River on the Sunshine Coast, on the Brisbane River, and in the far north. Townsville is another popular canoeing centre. Sailing enthusiasts will also find plenty of opportunities and many places which hire boats, both along the coast and inland.

The Great Barrier Reef

Facts & Figures
The Great Barrier Reef is 2000 km in length. It starts slightly south of the Tropic of Capricorn, somewhere out from Bundaberg or Gladstone, and it ends in the Torres Straits, just south of Papua

New Guinea. This huge length makes it not only the most extensive reef system in the world but also the biggest structure made by living organisms. At its southern end the reef is up to 300 km from the mainland, but at the northern end it runs much closer to the coast, has a much more continuous nature and can be up to 80 km across. In the 'lagoon' between the outer reef and the coast the waters are dotted with smaller reefs, cays and islands. Drilling on the reef has indicated that the coral can be over 500 metres thick.

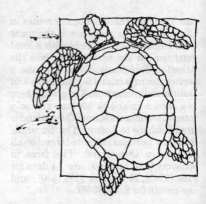

What is It?

Coral is formed by a primitive animal, a marine polyp, closely related to the sea anemones and jellyfish of the family *Coelenterata*. The vital difference is that these polyps form a hard exterior surface by excreting lime. When a polyp dies its hard 'skeleton' remains and these gradually build up the reef. New polyps grow on their dead predecessors and continually add to the reef.

Coral needs a number of preconditions for healthy growth. First the water temperature must not drop below 17.5°C – thus the Barrier Reef does not continue further south into cooler waters. The water must be clear to allow sunlight to penetrate and it must be salty. Coral will not grow below 30 metres depth because the sunlight does not penetrate sufficiently and it will not grow around river mouths. The Barrier Reef ends around Papua New Guinea because the Fly River's enormous water flow is both fresh and muddy – two antagonistic factors for coral growth.

Reef Types

Basically, reefs are either fringing or barrier. You will find fringing reefs around many of the Great Barrier Reef's islands. Barrier reefs are further out to sea and usually enclose a 'lagoon' of deep water. The Great Barrier Reef is out at the edge of the Australian continental shelf and the channel between the reef and the coast can be 60 metres deep. At places the

reef rises straight up from that depth. This raises the question of how the reef built up from that depth when coral cannot survive below 30 metres? One theory is that the reef gradually grew as the seabed subsided, and that the reef was able to keep pace with the rate of sinkage. The alternative is that the sea level gradually rose, and again the coral growth was able to keep pace.

Reef Inhabitants

The Barrier Reef would just be a very big breakwater if it wasn't for the colourful and highly varied reef life starting, of course, with the coral itself. Coral is highly varied in its types but almost all the polyp skeletons are white – it's the living polyps which give coral its colourful appearance. Equally colourful are the many clams which appear to be embedded in the coral. Each seems to have a different colour fleshy area. Other reef inhabitants include starfish, sea urchins, sea cucumbers and fish.

Crown-of-Thorn Starfish

One reef inhabitant which has enjoyed enormous publicity is the notorious crown-of-thorns starfish that tried to eat the Great Barrier Reef! For a time in the '70s it seemed like these starfish might do just that but the problem now appears to have slightly receded. At one time vast efforts were made by divers to clear stretches of the reef of these starfish. It is thought that crown-of-thorns starfish develop their taste for coral when the reef ecology is upset – as, for example, when the bivalves (oysters, clams) which comprise their normal diet are over-collected.

Nasties Hungry sharks are the usual idea of an aquatic nasty but the Barrier Reef's most unpleasant creatures are generally less dramatic. For a start there are scorpion fish with highly venomous spines. The butterfly cod is a very beautiful scorpion fish and it relies on its colourful, slow-moving appearance to warn off possible enemies. In contrast, the stonefish lies hidden on the bottom, looking just like a stone, and is very dangerous to step on. Although they're rather rare it's a good idea to wear shoes when walking on the reef. Stinging jellyfish are a danger only in coastal waters and only in certain seasons. The deadly sea wasp is in fact a box jellyfish. As for sharks, there has been no recorded case of a visitor to the reef islands meeting a hungry one.

Viewing the Reef

The cheapest way to get a good look at the reef is to do a day trip from somewhere like Cairns, where the reef is relatively close to the coast. Other options are to go to one of the islands on a package deal which include boat and snorkelling trips; or take a one or two day island trip and make reef trips from there independently.

Islands

There are two types of islands along the Barrier Reef. The larger islands, like those of the Whitsunday group, are the tops of flooded mountains. At one time these would have been a range running along the coast, but rising sea levels submerged it. They have vegetation like the adjacent mainland. Other islands may actually be on the reef, or may be isolated coral cays, like Green Island near

Cairns or Heron Island near Rockhampton. These are formed when the growth of coral is such that the reef is above the sea level even at low tide. Dead coral is ground down by water action to form sand and eventually hardier vegetation takes root. Coral cays are low-lying, unlike the often hilly islands closer to the coast.

Queensland has a great selection of islands and they're extremely variable in what they are and what they have to offer. Don't let the catchword 'reef island' suck you in. Only a few of the islands along the coast are real coral cays on the reef. Most of the popular resort islands are actually continental islands and some are well south of the Great Barrier Reef. It's not necessarily important since many of them will still have fringing reefs and in any case a bigger continental island will have other attractions that a tiny, dot-on-the-map coral cay is simply too small for – like hills to climb, bushwalks, and secluded beaches where you can get away from your fellow island-lovers.

The islands vary considerably in their accessibility – Heron is an $85 launch ride, others are just a few dollars by ferry. If you want to stay on an island rather than just day trip from the mainland that too can vary widely in costs. Accommodation is generally in the form of expensive resorts where most visitors will be staying on all-inclusive package deals. There are a few exceptions to this rule, however, plus on many of the uninhabited islands and also on a few of the resort ones, it's possible to camp. A few islands have proper sites with toilets and fresh water on tap while, at the other extreme, on some islands you'll even have to bring drinking water with you. From south to north a brief run down on the islands follows, see the relevant sections for more details:

South Stradbroke – sand island, mainly a day-trip from the Gold Coast.
North Stradbroke – sand island, usually a day or weekend trip from Brisbane but also has a

variety of fairly reasonably priced accommodation, cheap to get out to.

Moreton Island – sand island, 1927 square km, day-trip by plane from Brisbane at fairly reasonable cost or take the longer launch service, one small resort, fairly expensive.

Bribie Island – sand island, another day-trip island, also with accommodation, connected to the mainland by a bridge.

Fraser Island – sand island, 598 square km, very big, very much a get-away-from-it-all island, either difficult (four-wheel drive) or expensive (fly) to get to, also day and longer trips, wide variety of accommodation from camping through holiday flats to one resort.

Heron Island – coral cay, 0.4 square km, very tiny, first island on the reef and also first real reef island, expensive to get to and expensive accommodation, mainly for scuba diving enthusiasts.

Great Keppel – continental island, 14 square km, lots of variety, walks, beach, entertainment, a resort, cheaper accommodation, and camping – with the right to use some of the resort facilities.

Brampton Island – continental island, nine square km, reasonably expensive resort but excellent beaches.

Whitsunday Islands – more than 70 continental islands, from tiny dots up to 100 square km, resorts on Lindeman, Daydream, South Molle, Long Island and Hayman, the resorts are all fairly expensive although there is a cheaper resort on Long Island, lots of nice beaches, secluded spots, can camp on any of 20 uninhabited islands, possible to day trip to many islands, particularly the resort ones.

Magnetic Island – continental island, 52 square km, fairly big, very accessible and lots of day-trippers, wide variety of accommodation, possible to stay cheaply, not a reef island at all but you can get away from the crowds quite easily.

Orpheus Island – continental island, 15 square km, resort island, reasonably expensive.

Hinchinbrook Island – continental island, 374 square km, very big, one fairly simple resort, cheaper for larger groups, couple of camping places but not many facilities, not too expensive to get to.

Dunk Island – continental island (actually volcanic), 16 square km, very pretty, very expensive resort but cheap island to day-trip to.

Bedarra Island – continental island, very small, close to Dunk, resort island and very expensive.

Fitzroy Island – continental island with recently opened resort, popular for day-trips.

Green Island – coral cay, extremely small, reasonably cheap to visit but really a day-trip only, resort is expensive and lots of day-trip crowds.

Low Islands – coral cay, no more than a dot, very pretty but strictly a day-trip.

Lizard Island – continental island but right on the reef, 10 square km, very expensive to get to and very expensive to stay, camping possible but facilities very spartan, mainly for game-fishing enthusiasts.

Brisbane

Population: 1,100,000

When Sydney and the colony of New South Wales needed a better place to store its more recalcitrant 'cons' the tropical country further north seemed a good place to drop them. Accordingly, in 1824, a penal settlement was established at Redcliffe on Moreton Bay, but was soon abandoned due to lack of water and hostile Aboriginals. The settlement was moved to Brisbane and as Queensland's huge agricultural potential, and more recently the state's mineral riches were developed, Brisbane grew to be a town, then a city with a population that today is over a million – the third largest in Australia.

The skyscraper fever that has gripped Melbourne and Sydney is also taking over Brisbane, but to some it's still the 'large country town' which detractors have always been keen to label it. Brisbane is one of those places where you can always find something to see and do but basically there's nothing you absolutely cannot afford to miss. It's really just a gateway to Queensland's other attractions. In 1988 Brisbane is hosting Expo 88, a world fair

Top: Surfers Paradise – a beautiful beach backed by a real estate agent's dream (TW)
Left: Brisbane Town Hall is a grandiose structure by day; floodlit by night it's positively exotic (TW)
Right: When it comes to 'big' objects, Queensland has some of the best – this is the 'Big Pineapple' at Nambour (TW)

Top: The Millstream Falls in the Atherton Tableland are the widest in Australia (TW)
Left: During the dry the rivers running into the Gulf of Carpentaria make intricate patterns (TW)
Right: The Great Barrier Reef off the Whitsunday Islands (TW)

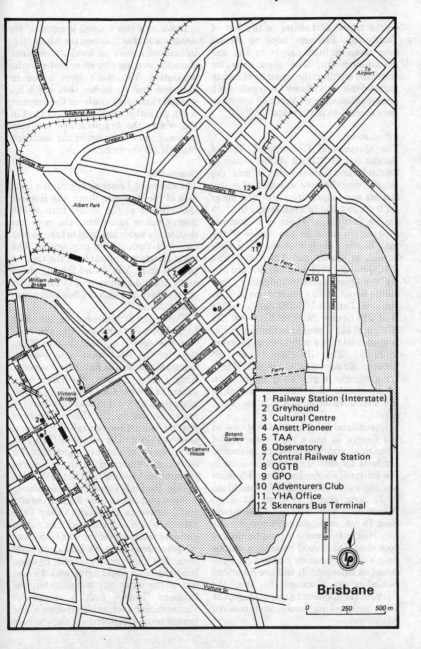

1 Railway Station (Interstate)
2 Greyhound
3 Cultural Centre
4 Ansett Pioneer
5 TAA
6 Observatory
7 Central Railway Station
8 QGTB
9 GPO
10 Adventurers Club
11 YHA Office
12 Skennars Bus Terminal

Brisbane

0   250   500 m

on the theme of Leisure in the Age of Technology. Planners hope to attract over seven million people to the six-month-long fair. The plan calls for emphasis on fun rather than facts and to that end the Walt Disney Corporation is a principal consultant. About 30 countries are expected to participate.

Information

The Queensland Government Tourist Bureau (tel 31 2211) is on the corner of Adelaide and Edward Sts. It has the usual comprehensive selection of maps, leaflets and helpful info. Opening hours are 9 am to 4.45 pm weekdays, 9 to 11.15 am on Saturdays. There is a Brisbane information kiosk in the centre of the mall beside *Jimmy's on the Mall* restaurant, at Queen and Albert Sts. The RACQ (tel 253 2444) is at 190 Edward St – see the Queensland introductory comments about their excellent maps. The National Parks & Wildlife Service office is at 239 George St. The YHA (tel 831 2022) is at 462 Queen St in the centre and is open from 8.30 am to 4.30 pm Monday to Friday. The GPO is on Queen St between Edward and Creek Sts. There are a number of give-away information guides circulated in Brisbane including the useful entertainment guide *Time Off*.

Queensland Aboriginal Creations at 135 George St has a good collection of Aboriginal and Torres Strait islanders' artefacts for sale. The Artifact Shop in the university's Anthropology Museum also has a good collection. It's open 10 am to 12 noon and 1 to 4 pm Monday, Wednesday and Friday. Queensland Book Depot, on Adelaide St opposite the City Hall, is Brisbane's biggest traditional book-shop. Other good bookshops include Angus & Robertson on Edward St, Folio Books on Elizabeth St and the American Bookstore on Elizabeth St. Jim the Backpacker in Queens Arcade, Queens St sells backpacking books and outdoor equipment.

Brisbane's city council is unusual for Australia in that it covers the whole city, instead of a host of local government councils covering city areas and suburbs separately. You don't have to be in Brisbane long to realise that it's a lot warmer than down south – in the summer it can get rather sticky and humid but in the winter the temperatures are very pleasant, especially when the southern capitals are shivering.

Orientation

The centre of Brisbane is situated on a loop of the Brisbane River; the Botanic Gardens are at the actual turn of the river. Once or twice when the river has flooded the water has tried to take a short cut right through the city centre. The main streets run uphill from the river or parallel to it. You'll find the big shops along Adelaide, Queen and Elizabeth Sts or on Albert and Edward Sts which run across them.

The Queen St Mall occupies the block from Albert St to Edward St. The Mall was hurriedly completed in late '82 in time for the Brisbane Commonwealth Games but proved an immediate success. King George Square, the large open square in front of City Hall, is a popular place to sit and watch the world pass by. Anzac Square by the Central Railway Station is another central city square. Queens Park at the corner of Elizabeth and George is another good spot for sitting. It's encircled by three fine old government buildings and on the William St side, the State Library of Queensland.

If you continue up Ann St from the city you'll arrive in Fortitude Valley ('the valley') which is Brisbane's restaurant and entertainment centre. The University of Queensland is at St Lucia, up-river from the city centre. Like Sydney, Brisbane has a Paddington and it's also one of the older city suburbs, but the Brisbane 'Paddo' isn't a centre for Victorian architecture like Sydney's. The terrace-house architecture of the southern capitals only pops up in odd, isolated pockets in Brisbane, but you'll find the tropical Queensland stilt-houses with their wide verandahs all over the place. Brisbane's airport at Eagle Farm is conveniently central. The city is surrounded by hills, many of them with fine lookouts.

City Hall

Brisbane's City Hall has gradually been surrounded by modern skyscrapers but the observation platform atop the tower still provides one of the best views across the city. It's open 9 am to 4 pm and the lift to the top is 40c. The City Hall also houses a museum and art gallery on the ground floor, which are only open on weekdays. A large open square fronts the City Hall and makes the building look even more grandiose and impressive – by night the backlighting and palm trees make it look positively exotic. Built in 1930 the building is one of the biggest city halls in Australia. It's at the corner of Adelaide and Albert Sts.

The Old Windmill

The Old Observatory and Windmill is one of Brisbane's earliest buildings, dating from 1829. It was intended to grind grain for the early convict colony but due to a fundamental design error it did not work properly – but no worries, cheap convict labour was freely available and it was quickly converted from windmill to treadmill. In 1837 it was made to work as it was originally intended but the building was then converted to a signal post and later a meteorological observatory. In 1864 a disastrous fire swept Brisbane and the windmill was one of the few early buildings to survive. It stands on Wickham Terrace, overlooking the city.

Other City Buildings

The National Trust's *Historic Walks* brochure will guide you round the most interesting early city buildings. The National Trust have their headquarters in the Old Government House building, built in 1862, at the end of George St. The State Parliament House is in George St overlooking the Botanic Gardens, it dates from 1868 but there is also a new Legislative Assembly annex.

The original parliament building is in French Renaissance style and has a roof of Mt Isa copper. St John's Cathedral at 417 Ann St is still under construction, work started in 1901. You can take a guided tour at 11 am on Wednesday. Queensland's first Government House, built in 1853, is now the Deanery for the Cathedral. The declaration of Queensland's separation from the colony of New South Wales was read here.

Queensland Museum

The museum, at the corner of Gregory Terrace and Bowen Bridge Rd in the valley, is old fashioned but has a number of intriguing exhibits. There is an absolutely enormous WW I German tank displayed outside – it carried a crew of 18 and this is the only known example to survive. Also outside are life size models of a Tyrannosaurus and Triceratops. Inside there is a good display of Australian animals and the taped bird calls are interesting – and amusing. It's a great old building surrounded by palm trees. I was told that it was constructed in just seven weeks. In 1988 the museum will be moving to a modern building of twice the size on the south side of the river at the new Cultural Centre. Many of the displays have already been removed from the old place but it's future has not been decided; let's hope it doesn't get an invitation to the Wrecker's Ball. The museum is open from 10 am to 4.45 pm Monday to Saturday, 2 to 4.55 pm Sunday and public holidays. Get there on a Chermside 172, Stafford 144 or Grange 126 bus from the red stops on Adelaide St, 50c.

Queensland Cultural Centre

Directly across the river from the city centre, in South Brisbane, this superb new complex houses the Queensland Art Gallery's excellent collection. Other features will be added to the centre as time goes on but there's already a 500-seat auditorium and a restaurant looking out on the city.

Other Museums

On Stanley St in South Brisbane the Queensland Maritime Museum displays include an 1881 dry-dock, working models and the frigate *HMAS Diamantina*. It's open Wednesday, Saturday, Sunday and public holidays 10 am to 4.30 pm. Doll enthusiasts might like to visit Panaroo's Playthings at 401 Lutwyche Rd, Windsor – open rather odd hours. Or postal enthusiasts could try the GPO Museum at 261-285 Queen St. It's open Tuesday and Thursday from 10 am to 3.30 pm. Brisbane's trams no longer operate but you can see some early examples at the Tramway Museum at 2 McGinn Rd, Ferny Grove, 11 km from the centre, guided tours at 3.30 pm Sunday.

Parks & Gardens

Brisbane has a number of parks and gardens including the Botanic Garden, on a loop of the Brisbane River, almost in the centre of the city. The park occupies 18 hectares and it's a good spot for bike riding. The riverbanks here are a popular mooring spot for visiting yachts.

Newstead Park is a pleasant riverside park where you'll also find one of the oldest houses in Brisbane, see Newstead House below. Further down-river at New Farm, the New Farm Park is noted for its rose displays and Devonshire teas. Other parks include the small city Roma St Park, Wickham Park, Bowen Park and Albert Park. Bulimba Creek is a popular recreation area with a variety of walking tracks and barbecue areas.

Lone Pine Sanctuary

The koala sanctuary at Fig Tree Pocket is one of Australia's best known and most popular animal sanctuaries because of its 'cuddle a koala' offer! The sanctuary also has wombats, emus, Tasmanian devils, platypuses and a variety of other Australian animals. It's open 9.30 am to 5 pm daily and admission is $4.50. The platypuses are only on view from 11.30 am to 12 noon and 3 to 4 pm. You can get to the sanctuary on a boat cruise for $9 or on a Lone Pine 84 bus from Adelaide St. It's 11 km from the centre.

Other Brisbane sanctuaries include the Alma Park Zoo at Kallangur which has a large collection of palms and Australian and overseas wildlife. It's 28 km from the city centre. Or there's Bunya Park on Bunya Park Drive, Eatons Hill, turn-off just past Albany Creek. Oasis Gardens is another possibility.

Mt Coot-tha Forest Park

This large park with lookouts is just eight km south-west of the city centre. The top is distinguished by a confusion of TV transmitter towers but the views are superb. On a clear day you can see the distant line of Moreton and Stradbroke Island, the Glass House Mountains to the north, the mountains behind the Gold Coast to the south and Brisbane, with the river winding through, at your feet. The view is particularly superb at night.

The new Botanic Gardens are in the foothills of the park. The gardens include an enclosed tropical display dome and an arid zone collection. There are some good walks around the park, like the walk to the J C Slaughter Falls. You'll also find the Sir Thomas Brisbane Planetarium (tel 377 5896) here; it's the largest in Australia. Admission is $3.50 and there are shows at 3.30 and 7.30 pm Wednesday to Friday, 1.30, 3.30 and 7.30 pm Saturday, 1.30 and 3.30 pm Sunday. You can get to the Mt Coot-tha lookout on a 10C bus or to the Botanic Gardens and planetarium on a Toowong 39 bus.

Eagle Farm Airport

Brisbane's airport, which handles domestic and international flights, is fairly central. A glass-walled building houses one of Australia's most famous aircraft – the tri-motor Fokker, 'Southern Cross' which made the first Pacific crossing with Brisbane's own Sir Charles Kingsford Smith at the controls.

Newstead House

On Breakfast Creek Rd, Newstead this is the headquarters for the Royal Historical Society of Queensland – it's the oldest home in Brisbane, built in 1846, and delightfully situated overlooking the river. It's open 11 am to 3 pm Monday to Thursday, 2 to 5 pm on Sundays and public holidays. Admission is $1. You can get there on an Airport 160 bus, or a Toombul 170, 171 or 190 bus. Newstead Park, where the house is situated, has a memorial to US WW II servicemen who passed through Brisbane and also, believe it or not, a memorial to Lyndon Johnson.

Other Old Houses

There are a number of interesting old houses and period re-creations around Brisbane. Early Street Historical Village is on McIlwraith Avenue, off Bennetts St in Norman Park, six km from the centre. It's a re-creation of early Queensland colonial life and it's open daily from 11 am to 4.30 pm. Get there on a Seven Hills 8A, 8B bus or a Carina 8C, 8D, 8E bus.

At 31 Jordan Terrace, Bowen Hills the Miegunyah Folk Museum is housed in an 1884 building, a fine example of early Brisbane architecture. It has been restored as a memorial to the pioneer women of Queensland and is open 10.30 am to 3 pm Tuesday and Wednesday, to 4 pm on weekends. Get there on an Airport 160 or Toombul 170, 171 or 190 bus.

Wolston House at Grindle Rd, Wacol was the first National Trust acquisition in Queensland. Built in 1852 of local materials it's open 10 am to 4.30 pm from Wednesday to Sunday and on public holidays. The 1884 Joss House on Higgs St, Breakfast Creek is the only Chinese temple in Brisbane.

Other Attractions

Yes, Brisbane has a water slide amusement centre – it's Mirage at 2098 Ipswich Rd, Oxley. There is also a go-kart track and other amusements.

Places to Stay

Brisbane is not Australia's best city for accommodation by a long shot (although it's a popular place) even the solitary hostel is a long way out from the centre. Plus, a curious city council regulation decrees that you can't camp within a 22 km radius of the city centre, so the more convenient caravan parks do not permit tent campers. There are, however, a number of guest houses and hotels with fairly reasonable prices both in the centre and close to it.

Hostel The *Brisbane Youth Hostel* (tel 57 1245) is at 15 Mitchell St, Kedron, eight km from the city centre. Get there on a 172 Chermside bus, getting off at stop 27A or 28A near Silvio's Pizza Restaurant then walk down Broughton Rd to Mitchell St. Bookings should be made to the city YHA office at 462 Queen St. Although it's some distance from the centre it's open all day and it's modern, popular and pleasant. There's room for 80 people and nightly costs are $5.50.

Hotels & Guest Houses Probably the best known cheap place is the *Budget Yale Inn* (tel 832 1665), 413 Upper Edward St, and it's pretty good. It's a 10-minute uphill walk from the city centre along Edward St and rates are singles $18, doubles $24, twins $26. They include a breakfast of cereal, toast and juice, and there are laundry facilities available.

If it's full, the *Dorchester Holiday Flats* (tel 831 2967) are a little further up at 484. Prices are singles $24 and doubles $30, a few dollars less by the week. There are cooking facilities and utensils so you can save money by eating in, and private bathrooms.

Back down toward town, on the corner

of Ann and Edward Sts, the *Hotel Canberra* (tel 32 0231) is an old standby. It's a well run temperance hotel with a varied selection of rooms. It was going up for sale during this update so its future is uncertain. Basic singles/doubles are $23/32. Rooms are $42/47 with tea-making and TV, extra with air-con. The dining room serves breakfast and dinners. You can also make use of the free luggage room. The beautiful, balconied *Palace Guest House* across the street is now boarded up and is not likely to re-open.

At 513 Queen St (at the junction with Adelaide) the *Atcherly* (tel 31 2591) is old and worn but still busy with singles at $20 and doubles at $40. Across the street the recently spruced up *National Hotel* (tel 832 2281) has rooms and self contained flats at reasonable prices.

Again up the hill from the centre, the *Astor* (tel 831 9522) is at 193 Wickham Terrace, with shared-facility rooms; singles $20, doubles $26 or first class rooms at $39/45. A little further along at 391 Wickham Terrace is the *Marrs Town House* (tel 831 5388) overlooking the city but within walking distance of the centre.

Prices for these modern rooms are a bit higher: singles $25, doubles $36 with TV and fridge; $35 and $45 with private facilities; breakfast is available at $4-7. There are good views, especially in the more costly rooms.

Out of the centre some way on Gregory Terrace the *Tourist Private Hotel Motel* (tel 52 4171) has rooms at $17.50 per person with breakfast, sharing a twin or double. Singles are $21. At 89-95 Gregory

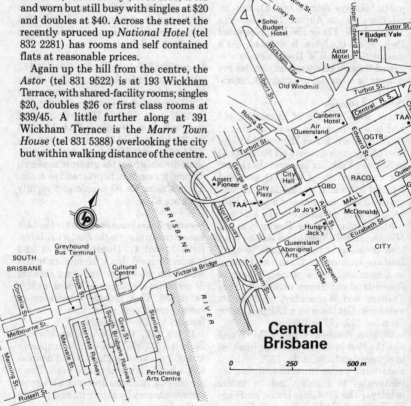

Central Brisbane

0   250   500 m

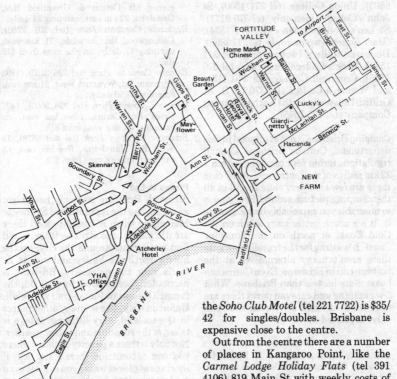

Terrace, the *Queensland Country Women's Association* has reasonable singles at $27.50 but the doubles are a whopping $48.

In Fortitude Valley the cheapest alternative is the *Fitzgibbons Osburne Hotel*, at the corner of Constance and Ann Sts, with singles/doubles $22/$28, and a pub downstairs.

Motels Some Brisbane guest houses fit better into the motel category and these generally offer the best value – places like the *Tourist* or the *Astor* on Wickham Terrace. Also on Wickham Terrace at 333

the *Soho Club Motel* (tel 221 7722) is $35/42 for singles/doubles. Brisbane is expensive close to the centre.

Out from the centre there are a number of places in Kangaroo Point, like the *Carmel Lodge Holiday Flats* (tel 391 4106) 819 Main St with weekly costs of $185/205 for singles/doubles. Hamilton is also not too far from the centre and the *Riverview Motel* (tel 268 4666) at 20 Riverview Terrace is $32/38. There are similar prices at the *South Pacific* (tel 358 2366) at the corner of Bowen Terrace and Langshaw St, New Farm; singles/doubles are $32/38. There are a couple of places in Aspley like the *Aspley Motor Inn* (tel 263 5400), 1159 Gympie Rd; singles for $30 and doubles for $35. Prices out in Moreton Bay are a little lower for both hotels and motels.

Colleges If you want to try your luck, the following colleges at the University of Queensland offer individual accommodation: International House (tel 370

9593), Union College (tel 371 1300), St John's College (men only, tel 370 8171), St Leo's College (men only, 371 1534), Grace College (women only, tel 371 3898), Duchesne College (women only, tel 371 1534), King's College (men only, tel 370 1125), Cromwell College (tel 370 1151) and Women's College (tel 370 1177). At Griffith University try the Nathan Housing Company (tel 275 7575).

Camping Brisbane is not at all good in this department. Curious Brisbane Council regulations forbid tent camping within a 22 km radius of the centre, and in any case there are few sites very close in. All in all the camping picture around Brisbane is so miserable you're probably best forgetting it. It's a much better story south on the Gold Coast or north on the Sunshine Coast. It's a drag for the traveller because there aren't many alternatives at the bottom-end in Brisbane. Even Cairns can boast more hostels than Brisbane. What few camping and caravan parks there are (and most of them are for on-site vans only) are listed below:

San Mateo Caravan Park (tel 341 5423), 2481 Logan Rd, Eight Mile Plain, 16 km south, no camping, on-site vans from $15 daily.

Sheldon Caravan Park (tel 341 6601), 27 Holmead Rd, Eight Mile Plains, 16 km south, no camping, on-site vans from $18 daily.

Amaroo Gardens (tel 397 1774), 771 Logan Rd, Holland Park, eight km south, no camping, on-site vans from $12.50 daily.

Alpha Caravan Park (tel 263 4442), 1434 Gympie Rd, Aspley, 13 km north, no camping, on-site vans from $20 daily.

Oxley Caravan Park (tel 375 4465), Kimberley St, Oxley, 13 km west, no camping, on-site vans from $20 daily.

Newmarket Gardens Caravan Park – forget it!

Wellington Point Caravan Park (tel 207 2722), Birkdale-Wellington Point Rd, Wellington Point, 29 km east, camping $6.50 daily, on-site vans $12 daily.

Greenacres Caravan Park (tel 206 4444), corner Mt Cotton & Greenfield Rds, Capalaba, 23 km east, camping $4 daily.

Redlands Caravan Park (tel 207 2752), Collingwood Rd, Birkdale, 21 km east, camping $7 daily, on-site vans from $15 daily.

Belcaro Caravan Park (tel 396 3163), 1893 Wynnum Rd, Wynnum West, 21 km east, camping $5.50 daily.

Carina Caravan Park (tel 398 9550), 1497 Creek Rd, Carina, nine km east, no camping, on-site vans from $15.

Brisbane Caravan Park (tel 399 4878), 18 Scott Rd, Hawthorne, five km east, no camping, on-site vans from $12.

Places to Eat

Although Brisbane certainly hasn't got anything like the reputation of Sydney or Melbourne when it comes to food there are still plenty of good places to try. You'll find restaurants around the city, up the hill in Fortitude Valley and out at St Lucia near the university. Brisbane is particularly well known for seafood, the famed Queensland mud-crab above all. Unfortunately, like so many other places in Queensland, very little advantage is taken of the sunshine and balmy weather. Not only is there a paucity of places where you can eat outside there's also a real shortage of places where you can eat even moderately late in the evening. Apart from the places featured below Brisbane also has the usual selection of Colonel McPizza Huts.

City You'll find a bit of everything around the central city area from good lunchtime sandwiches to flashy, night-time, splurge places. In the former category you could definitely do much worse than trying the cheap and excellent *The Source*, a long-running favourite in the vegetarian and health food department. It's in the Elizabeth Arcade at 99 Elizabeth St and has everything from tasty hot dishes to a tempting selection of exotic cakes. It's open lunchtimes and until 9 pm on Fridays.

Jo Jo's, a large place upstairs at the

corner of Queen and Albert Sts, is very popular. In the Perth section of this book you can read about my enthusiasm for Singapore-style 'food-centres', well this is a rather different interpretation of the same excellent idea. Jo Jo's offers a collection of fast food centres mainly Greek/Mediterranean but also Chinese, European, Middle Eastern, steaks, beer, wine, coffee, tea, desserts and so on. Tables are scattered about and prices are $6 to $9. The food is fresh, the portions good and the place is busy.

There are all sorts of other places to try around the city. In the Queen St Mall *Jimmy's on the Mall* is an excellent open-air cafe. *Parrots* at 993 Elizabeth is a big place with loud rock music, specialising in gourmet hamburgers, shakes, desserts etc. It's licensed and open every day. Another place which also makes real meat burgers, and some cheap Mexican items, is the *Manhatten Coffee Lounge* on the corner of Albert and Elizabeth Sts. The *Little Boys Gourmet Food Bar* at 229 Albert St is hard to beat for good, cheap take-aways.

At the City Plaza, corner of George and Albert Sts, there are a few restaurants, some with outside tables down by the fountain. *Tracks*, with the old train car outside, offers an all-you-can-eat lunch smorgasboard for $5.95. *Gino's East of Chicago*, downstairs in the Brisbane Arcade off the mall, is a very popular spot for pastas and pizza but it didn't seem to me to be great value.

The *Munich Steakhouse*, on the corner of Albert and Edward Sts, is a close relation to the Bavarian Steakhouse in Surfers. It's straightforward in the extreme – steaks, schnitzel and no messing about; lunch from $3.60, dinners $8 to $9. The *Arcade Bistro* is in the Brisbane Arcade in the centre and does equally straight-forward food with the accent on good value; steaks, a serve-yourself salad bar, pay as you enter, around $20 for two.

Another representative of the national pancake-house chain, the *Pancake Manor*,

is at 18 Charlotte St. As usual things are just 'lovely' and, also as usual, one of its major virtues is that it's open to midnight every night and 24 hours on Friday and Saturday nights.

Right in the centre at 254 Edward St the *Shingle Inn* is a genteel tea house for a genteel morning coffee. For a good cup of coffee, try *Aromas* in the Hoyt's movie theatre building in the Queen St Mall. It's beside McDonalds; walk in the theatre lobby.

Also, there are several Chinese places in the centre, especially around the corner of Elizabeth and Edward Sts. The *Oriental* is cheap with dishes in the $3.50 to $4 range. Another basic is the *New Eastern Cafe*, 110 Elizabeth St.

Lastly, the Main Roads Department cafeteria on the corner of Fortescue and Boundary Sts welcomes the public and serves a hot lunch with vegetables for $2.75. It's open from 12 noon to 1.30 pm weekdays.

Fortitude Valley Up the hill from the centre of town lies Fortitude Valley, another group of restaurants and shops, centred along and around Brunswick St, near Ann and Wickham Sts. There's a small but active Chinatown bordered by Wickham, Brunswick, Ann and Pips Sts. On Duncan St, within this rectangle, there are several Chinese restaurants. *Huong Cafe* on the corner of Duncan and Wickham Sts serves Vietnamese as well as Chinese food.

At 257 Wickham St the *Home Made Chinese Meal Kitchen* is a minute Chinese place about 100 metres across Brunswick St from the real restaurant block. The size has no relationship to the restaurant's reputation which is definitely on the large size! The excellent food and low prices (say $15 for two) can't be beaten.

The popular *Giardinetto's* at 366 Brunswick St is a small, pleasant, little Italian place with main courses in the $5.50 to $7.50 bracket and pizzas from around $4.50 for small ones. Round the corner at 683 Ann St the atmosphere is equally pleasant in *Lucky's Trattoria*, a fine Italian restaurant where two can eat for around $20. It's similarly priced to its near neighbour but is open only in the evenings.

Other Places Continue up beyond Fortitude Valley to Breakfast Creek to find the Breakfast Creek Wharf right beside the creek. It's at 190 Breakfast Creek Rd, Newstead, but as it's too far to walk, catch the 160 bus. In the wharf building there is a selection of excellent fish and seafood eateries. The fish and chips take-away place here is superb. There's an incredible selection, prices are low, and sometimes you get the whole fish! There's a pleasant park across the street to eat in.

Also in the building right beside the water, there's a well priced seafood place. Main courses $8 to $10; casual dress and it's open on Sunday. In between the two is the *Coral Trout*, an expensive, more formal place with a good reputation.

Gino's at 470 Kingsford Smith Drive, Hamilton is out towards the airport and does high quality pasta dishes and other Italian food along with the pizzas for around $25 for two.

At Redland Bay, on the coast southeast of the city, the *Redland Hotel* does great meals on Sundays for $5 where you can sit outside with views over Moreton Bay and its islands.

Counter Meals Brisbane has a good selection of the traditional steak and salad places, one of the best known being the famous *Breakfast Creek Hotel* at 2 Kingsford Smith Drive, Breakfast Creek. It's a great Victorian place dating from 1889; you can't miss it. This is a real Brisbane institution with a public bar where beer is still drawn from real wooden kegs. It's a rambling old place right by the creek and it has long been a Labor Party and trade union hang-out.

The *Spanish Garden Steak House* here is renowned for its superb steaks which are in the $7 to $9 bracket. They also do fine sandwiches from $1.25 and up, plus there's a good beer garden to eat and drink in. Get out here on a 160 bus from Adelaide St.

You'll see the tell-tale blackboards at lots of places around the city – like the *Carlton Hotel* at 103 Queen St which does cheap counter food. There's very cheap counter food, $2 to $8 in *la Cantina* in the *Hacienda Hotel* on Brunswick St, Fortitude Valley. It's open 5.30 to 7.30 pm Monday to Saturday. At 100 Leichardt St, the *Federal Hotel* does plain and simple pub food at rock bottom prices. Just follow up Upper Edward St to get to it. The *Springhill Hotel* up from the Yale Budget Inn, on the corner of Upper Edward and Leichardt Sts is another, and so is the nearby *Sportsmans* which isn't so cheap.

Entertainment
Brisbane has a number of pubs featuring live music; you'll find the full run down on what's on and where in the weekend papers or in the give-away entertainment paper *Time Off*. On a Friday night the mall is a real zoo, everybody's out strutting and buskers of all types ply their trades.

Rock specialists include the *Mansfield Tavern* in Mt Gravatt and the *Sunnybank Hotel* in Sunnybank. The *Blue Moon Cafe*, 540 Queen St in the city has live jazz till 3 am Thursday to Saturday nights. The *Adventurer's Club* at Kangaroo Point, across the river, has a variety of entertainment – jazz some nights, disco, and folk on others. The *Soulbin* in the Treasury Hotel, corner of Elizabeth and George Sts, plays soul and funk. *Swizzlers* at 78 Elizabeth St is a flashy, disco-style place with live rock.

Getting There
Air There are numerous Ansett and TAA flights daily to Brisbane from the southern

capitals and north to the Queensland regional centres. All flights to Sydney are direct, of course, while to Melbourne and Adelaide some flights go direct, some through Sydney. One-way fares include Sydney $153 ($122 standby), Melbourne $225 ($180 standby), Adelaide $249 direct, (more expensive via Sydney or Melbourne) ($180 standby). East-West fly to Sydney and Melbourne for about $10 less. See the relevant sections for details of the flights up the coast to regional Queensland centres. There are no flights between Brisbane and Coolangatta, the airport for Surfers and the Gold Coast. Travellers on round-Australia tickets can fly in to one port and out from the other however, travelling between the two by surface transport.

Brisbane is also a busy international arrival and departure point with frequent flights to Asia, Europe, the Pacific Islands, North America, New Zealand and Papua New Guinea.

Bus There are a lot of buses through Brisbane – particularly to Sydney. Ansett Pioneer (tel 226 1184) are at 16 Ann St and Greyhound (tel 240 9333) are at 79 Melbourne St, south of the river from the centre. Both operate regular Sydney-Brisbane services; Ansett Pioneer go daily while Greyhound have two daily services via the coastal Pacific Highway and one daily service via the New England Highway. The Sydney-Brisbane fare is $37 and the trip takes about 17 hours.

Both companies also operate daily up the coast to Rockhampton, Mackay, Townsville and Cairns – see the relevant sections for details. See the Gold Coast section for details on buses between Brisbane and Surfers Paradise. Greyhound have a daily direct Brisbane-Melbourne service via the New England and Newell Highways – 23 hours, $74. They also operate direct between Brisbane and Adelaide three times weekly – 36 hours, $96. Ansett Pioneer have direct

Melbourne-Brisbane services via Toowoomba or Surfers, three times weekly on each route. There are also direct services between Brisbane and Mt Isa with either company – see Mt Isa for details.

Ansett Pioneer and Greyhound are far from the only bus companies operating to and from Brisbane. There are a number of cut price operators like VIP Tours (tel 229 0550) and Deluxe offering Sydney-Brisbane for $25. Or there's McCafferty's (tel 211 3855) at 124 Adelaide St or at the South Brisbane Railway Station, Grey St, South Brisbane. They have services between Sydney and Brisbane either via the Pacific Highway or the New England Highway. Brisbane is linked to Toowoomba and hence to St George (further inland) or to Rockhampton and Mackay up the coast. You can also reach Rockhampton from Brisbane via the coastal Bruce Highway with McCafferty's.

Skennars (tel 831 8610) are at 22-34 Barry Parade, just off Wickham St about half-way up the hill from the city centre to Fortitude Valley. They have a comprehensive service around Queensland including buses to the Gold Coast, the Sunshine Coast, to various places in the New South Wales, New England area, to Port Macquarie on the coast, to the far south-west of Queensland (Charleville, Roma, etc) and to the north-west (Longreach, Mt Isa, etc). Connections also operate from Port Macquarie to Sydney and Tamworth. Including overnight accommodation in Port Macquarie, Skennars will transport you between Brisbane and Sydney for $76. Deluxe Coach Lines, 114 Elizabeth St, (tel 229 7655) serve Sydney $30, Adelaide $96 and Perth $160.

Rail You can reach Brisbane by rail from Sydney and continue north to Cairns or inland to Roma and Charleville. The daily Brisbane Limited Express (I guess that means that as an express it's very limited, it certainly isn't fast) takes 16

hours between Sydney and Brisbane. The fares are $83 in 1st, $59 in economy.

You can also travel north from Sydney on the Gold Coast Motorail Express to Murwillumbah, just south of the Queensland border. It's popular for people bringing their cars up to Queensland, and not wanting to drive all the way. The trip takes 16½ hours and costs $58 in 1st ($33 more for a sleeper), $42 in economy. That's quite a saving on the fare to Brisbane, particularly if you want to start your Queensland travels on the Gold Coast. There's a connecting bus service to the Gold Coast and Brisbane. It costs $84 for your car to come along for the ride from Sydney to Murwillumbah.

The Sunlander runs between Brisbane and Cairns, 1681 km and 37 hours to the north, six days a week. Inland to Roma, Charleville and Cunnamulla the Westlander runs twice a week. See the relevant sections for details. For information on trains in Queensland phone Queensland Railways (tel 225 0211) at 305 Edward St. The train station for out of town trips is in South Brisbane.

Getting Around
Airport Transport You can get to or from the airport on a 160 public bus for just 80c. By taxi it costs about $6 from the airport to the city, $5 to Fortitude Valley. Avis, Budget and Hertz have desks at the airport. In the city Ansett (tel 226 1111) are at the corner of Creek and Elizabeth Sts. TAA (tel 223 3333) are on the corner of Adelaide and Creek Sts. The international terminal at the airport is only open when there is a flight arriving or departing, otherwise it's deserted leaving nowhere to store luggage until your flight.

Buses Brisbane has a comprehensive bus network and a number of special fares. For a start you can buy a $3 Day Rover Ticket which allows unlimited use of the city bus services for the whole day. You can buy them from nominated newsagents

or, for 20c more, on board the bus. There's also a Concession Rover ticket for $1 which does not permit use on certain express buses. You can also get Fare Saver Cards which give you 10 tickets for $4 (single zone), $7.20 (two zones) or $9 (three zones). Regular bus tickets cost 50c for one zone, 80c for two, 90c for three. On Friday evenings to 9 pm a free bus runs along Adelaide and Queen Sts between Brunswick and North Quay.

For information on city buses it's worth visiting the information centre in the City Plaza behind the town hall or phone 225 4444. They can answer any queries you might have, or supply timetables. There is also a Public Transport Information Office in the Central Railway Station on Edward St and Anne St. Open 7.15 am to 5 pm, they have information on trains, buses and ferries.

Some useful buses include: the 172 Chermside bus for the youth hostel; the 162 also runs by the hostel and so does the 202 Chermside Express but this does not stop at the 27A youth hostel stop; for Mt Coot-tha take a 10C bus from Adelaide St; for the airport take a 160 airport bus for 60 cents.

Rail Brisbane has a suburban rail network too. There have recently been some extensive purchases of new equipment but some of the old railway carriages are still of such amazing antiquity that you'd think this was where Indian railays retired their rolling stock! The main suburban station is the big, new Central Station on Edward St. There is a line from here to the old interstate station, 60c.

River Brisbane doesn't make as much use as it might of its river but there are a number of popular day trips out and about on the river. Ferries run from Eagle St to East Brisbane and Hawthorne every half hour and across the river from Alice St by the Botanic Gardens. Fares across the river are just 40c.

Probably the most popular cruise is the trip to the Lone Pine Koala Sanctuary. It departs from the Hayles Wharf on Queens Wharf Rd every afternoon at 1.15 pm, returning at 5.30, and on Sunday mornings, costing $9, plus the sanctuary admission.

There's a one-hour scenic river cruise from the Creek St Ferry Terminal for just $1. It operates up to 20 times daily on weekdays, plus four times on Saturday mornings. Sundays and public holidays a cruise runs down the river to the mouth at Moreton Bay. Departures are from the Botanic Gardens at 2 pm and it returns at 5, the cost is $6. From the same dock, river cruises from 10 am until noon are $5. Both trips are available on the same ticket for $10. Other cruises include a visit to the Moreton Bay islands for $24 or a day-trip to Stradbroke Island for $35. A day-trip to the Tangalooma resort, including lunch, costs $23 and departs daily, except Monday and Tuesday, from the Hamilton Game Fishing Wharf. From the same dock, river cruises from 10 am to 12 noon are $5.

Car Rental All the big car rental operators have offices in Brisbane plus a number of more economical local operators like Shoestring Rent-a-Car (tel 52 3327) at 43 Ross St, Newstead with rates starting from $22, with 250 km free, for a Renault 12 or Datsun 120Y. The weekly rate is $135 and includes 1400 km free.

Bicycle Rental At 214 Margaret St, near the Botanic Gardens, Brisbane Bicycle Hire (tel 229 2592) is open 9 am to 5 pm daily to hire bicycles. Rates are $3.50 for an hour, $5.50 for two, $6.50 for three or all day for $12. A week costs $25.

Tours There are plenty of bus tours around Brisbane. They typically cost $8 or 9 for a half-day tour, $20 and up for a day tour. Around-Brisbane tours visit all the city sites, the Mt Coot-tha lookout and other attractions. Tours out of the city, costing $17 to $22, include the Tamborine Mountains, the Gold and Sunshine Coasts. Or you can cross the Great Dividing Range and visit the Darling Downs, also for $22. Boomerang Tours have the widest range of Brisbane bus tours. See the river transport section for details of river trips.

Around Brisbane

There are many places of interest around Brisbane, in fact several of Queensland's major tourist attractions are within day-trip distance of the city. The Gold Coast and the Sunshine Coast, for example, are an easy drive from the city and you can also visit the islands of Moreton Bay or head inland towards the Darling Downs.

NORTH OF THE CITY
Heading north towards Bribie Island and the Sunshine Coast you can visit Sandgate, a popular, old resort area just 19 km from the city, or the eccentric Shell Bungalow at Deception Bay, 32 km out, decorated with more than a million shells. Bribie Island is only 58 km north of Brisbane.

EAST OF THE CITY
Brisbane is about 30 km up the winding Brisbane River from Moreton Bay where you can visit Moreton Island with the Tangalooma resort, North Stradbroke Island or the old penal colony of St Helena. See the Moreton Bay section for more details. The Redlands area to the south-east is popular for market gardening.

SOUTH OF THE CITY
On the road south to the Gold Coast, Beenleigh (population 7800) is about the mid-point. The famous, old Beenleigh rum distillery has been operating since 1884 and is open for inspection at 11.30 am, 12.30 and 2.30 pm daily. An 1897 molasses tank makes a unique housing for

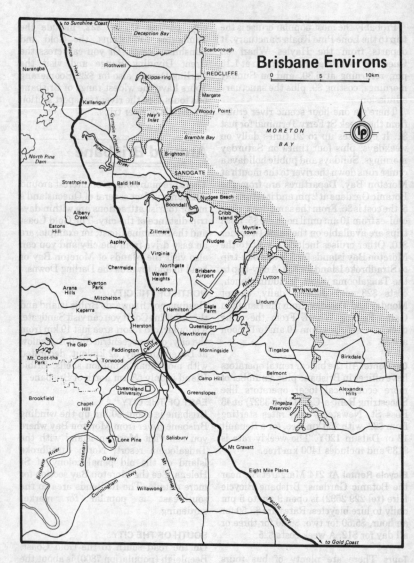

Brisbane Environs

0   5   10km

MORETON BAY

the Charthouse Museum collection. The town also has Bullen's African Lion Park & Zoo. It's open 9 am to 5 pm daily and the animals are fed at 2.30 pm daily, on Sundays and public holidays at 11.30 am

too. You can turn off the Pacific Highway for Mt Tamborine or take the Mt Lindesay Highway to the Woollahra Dairy Farm, a farm open to visitors and you can continue this way to Beaudesert.

WEST OF THE CITY

Heading inland from Brisbane towards the Darling Downs there are a number of places of interest along the Cunningham Highway to Ipswich and beyond and on the Brisbane Valley Highway to Toowoomba.

The Gold Coast

The Gold Coast is a 35 km strip of beaches starting at the NSW-Queensland border and running north. It's the most commercialised resort in Australia, virtually one continuous development culminating in the high rise splendour of Surfers Paradise – 'if you like Surfers you'll love Miami' commented one not quite entranced visitor. 'The Blackpool of the southern hemisphere' was a less kind description. Fortunately for the budget minded traveller all that nasty, hustling competition can make things surprisingly economical, despite the neon glitter, particularly if you avoid coming at the worst (school holiday) times.

Information & Orientation

The Queensland Government Tourist Bureau (tel 38 5988) is at 3177 Gold Coast Highway right in the middle of Surfers. It's open 9 am to 4.45 pm Monday to Friday and 9 to 11.15 am on Saturday. They have all the usual information and can offer suggestions for accommodation on the coast. Get a copy of the excellent free map guide produced by the shire councils of the Gold Coast and adjoining areas. It covers up to Stradbroke Island and down into northern NSW. There is also a Visitor's Information Kiosk on Cavill St down toward the sea. The airport in Coolangatta has a small information desk, too.

Surfers is, of course, the best known of the Gold Coast towns but the strip also includes Burleigh Heads, Palm Beach, Coolangatta, and Tweed Heads which is across the border in NSW. The Gold Coast airport is at Coolangatta, right at the southern end of the strip. To make it even more interesting inland, the MacPherson Ranges include some of the most spectacular mountain scenery in Australia. The beaches along the Gold Coast are really excellent but the various tourist attractions are basically artificial creations and your life will not be frantically the worse for it if you skip them.

Surfers Paradise

The centre of the Gold Coast is a real high rise jungle yet there is still construction every way you turn. In fact there is such a skyscraper conglomeration that in the afternoon much of the beach is cast into shadow! Still, people pack in for the lights, activities, shopping, attractions and that strip of ocean sand.

Where else would you see a waterslide right on the main street? The town has been promoting itself heavily in Japan and things are gearing up for a hoped for invasion. Five international class hotel are being built; one includes a casino which was opened in late '85. A number of illegal casinos have been operating in Surfers and the new, legal one is meant to nip this phenomenon in the bud.

Surfers has come a long way since 1936 when there was just the brand new Surfers Paradise Hotel here, a little hideaway nine km south of Southport. The hotel, on the corner of the Gold Coast Highway and Cavill Avenue, is now unrecognisable, but the beer garden carries on. Despite the changes and growth you don't have to go far north or south to find some relatively open, quiet, sunny beach.

The Gold Coast Highway is the main road right through Surfers, only a couple of blocks back from the beach. Traffic along the highway is non-stop and crossing the road can be quite a feat. Cavill Avenue has a pedestrian mall down towards the beach. Surfers has a

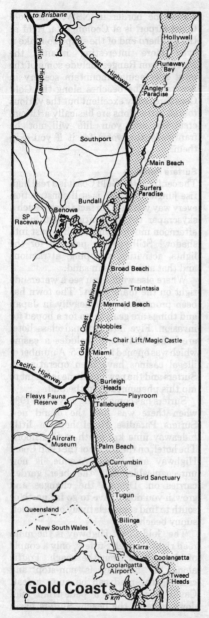

number of 'attractions' like a waxworks and the huge Grundy's amusement arcade.

If you want a place that somehow sums all that the Gold Coast is, you need look no further than 'Grundy's', off the Cavill Mall in Surfers. Only a few steps from the sea, the sand, the open air and the sun you're in a big, enclosed cavern where the neon lights have to burn all day long. Inside you've got all the space-invaders-style amusements necessary to keep your mind away from reality. You don't even feed the machines with coins – they consume 'Grundy tokens'. Finally, around the side, there are shoulder to shoulder junk food purveyors – maybe it's the neon lights but the food looks drier and more tasteless, the ice creams more garish and artificial than usual. In fact everything is artificial here, even the money. Just like Surfers?

Southport & North

Southport is sheltered from the ocean by the long, sand spit running up from Main Beach. This was the original town on the Gold Coast and although it pretty much goes about its own business, it's now modern and rather nondescript. It's certainly more like a real town than Surfers. Nerang and Scarborough are its main streets. At 3563 Main Beach Parade there's an Australiana Display, open daily.

There are a number of attractions between the Gold Coast and Brisbane including the big new Dreamworld, a Disneyland-style creation at Coomera with a $14 admission price! It's open every day and you can get there by bus. At Beenleigh, Bullen's African Lion Safari is a drive-through lion park open daily.

Main Beach

The northern end of the Gold Coast is a long, sand spit, pointing towards South Stradbroke Island. At present the north end of the spit is not developed at all and it's popular for secluded sunbathing. The road up the spit ends at Sea World, a huge aquatic amusement centre, one of the most popular attractions at Surfers. Sea

World has dolphin shows, sea lion shows, water ski shows, a miniature railway, rollercoasters and so on. Admission is $14. Fisherman's Wharf here is a complex of restaurants, shops and entertainment.

Nearby Bird Life Park has a huge walk-through aviary with Australian wildlife feathered and otherwise. There's also a Laserama with a 50-minute laser planet-arium show, and a 'Shark Expo' on Seaworld Drive. Popular Macintosh Park is at Narrowneck, by the Gold Coast Highway.

Down the Coast

South of Surfers, Cascades Gardens at Broadbeach is a good barbecue spot and the Pacific Fair shopping centre is the biggest shopping centre on the Gold Coast. At Mermaid Beach, Traintasia has a huge model train collection with 200 metres of track. It's at 2480 Gold Coast Highway and is open Monday to Saturday from 9 am to 5 pm. Continue to Nobbies Beach where there's a chairlift to a fairytale castle on a cliff top over the ocean.

At Burleigh Heads the small Burleigh Heads National Park has picnic tables, walking tracks and koalas and wallabies. West Burleigh is just inland from the heads and here Fleay's Fauna Reserve has an interesting collection of native wildlife. The platypus display is particularly interesting; this was the first place where this peculiar marsupial was bred in captivity. The reserve is open daily.

Morning and afternoon, flocks of technicoloured lorikeets and other birds flutter in for a free feed at the Currumbin Bird Sanctuary. You can flutter in for $7. The sanctuary is just 500 metres south of Currumbin Creek and is open daily from 8 am to 5 pm. Other creations here are the Land of Legend, Santaland and the Sea Shell Museum on Millers Drive. At Kirra, south of the airport, Yesteryear World features a large vintage and veteran car collection. There's also a zoo here at Natureland on Appel St.

Finally Coolangatta marks the southern end of the Gold Coast and the border to NSW. Coolangatta actually merges right in to Tweed Heads in NSW and you have to see the border marker to know you've gone from one state to the other. Wind-surfers are for rent at several places.

Inland

There are plenty of other attractions just inland from the coast. At Nerang, just in from Surfers, horse enthusiasts might like The Palms where miniature horses are bred. Near Mudgeeraba on Springbrook Rd you can brush up on your boomerang technique at Hawes Boomerang Farm & Factory. Also near here war and carnage enthusiasts can try out the Gold Coast War Museum & Battle Playground. There are lots of military vehicles and it's open 9 am to 5 pm daily. The Air Museum at Chewing Gum Field on Guineas Creek Rd, Tally Valley, six km in from Currumbin Bridge, has an interesting collection of old and very old aircraft; everything from Tiger Moths to jet fighters of the '50s. Wednesday to Sunday the Tally Valley market is held near here.

Places to Stay

The Gold Coast strip is virtually a continuous line of motels, broken only by junk food vendors. The QGTB has accommodation leaflets which list a vast number of places strung out along the highway. They'll also book places for you. Similarly the NSW tourist office in Tweed Heads, at the other end of the strip, has accommodation information but neither these nor the motoring club booklets are totally comprehensive. There are simply too many places to hope to list them all.

One of the easiest ways to find a place to stay is simply to cruise along the Gold Coast Highway and try a few places that look right and have the 'vacancy' signs hanging out. They're really all much of a muchness – more money simply gets you a newer TV, better location or bigger swimming pool. Prices are extremely variable according to the season. They'll rise during the Christmas, May and August school holidays and over Easter. Some motels push prices higher over Christmas than at other holiday peaks while if there's a cold snap in May or August prices may not rise at all. As a rule of thumb, a little searching should find a place at around $25 a double almost anytime of year.

A better bargain than motels, particularly if you're staying for longer, are the flats (apartments) which can also be found all along the coast. Again the lists from the tourist offices are not comprehensive. Basically a flat will have a kitchen, fridge, cooker, etc so you can fix your own food – but it won't have bed-sheets, towels, soap or be regularly serviced. Particularly during the peak seasons flats will be rented on a weekly rather than overnight basis but don't let that frighten you off. Even if they won't negotiate a daily rate, a $150 a week two-bedroom flat is still cheaper than two $30 a night motel rooms, even for just three days.

Finally there are other accommodation possibilities – hotels, guest houses and even hostels. There are so many places along the Gold Coast (an estimated 3000 different places to stay) that what follows is just a tiny sampler. You'll find lots of places just by wandering around.

Hostels The Youth Hostel (tel 31 5155) is found at the *El Dorado Motel*, 2811 Gold Coast Highway, about a 20 minute walk south from the centre of Surfers. Price is $5.50, there are kitchen facilities and you can use the pool or restaurant. Office hours are 8 to 10 am and 4 to 6 pm.

There is another hostel (tel 32 1777) but it's in Southport at 103 Nerang Rd at the *Bellevue Youth Centre*. They have 60 beds at $5. It's meant to close when a new one opens in Coolangatta, which will be '86 at the earliest – so ask about it.

Hotels & Motels All the older hotels are gone so budget places, for the most part, are now modern but small and plain motels. At the sea end of Caville Avenue the *Ocean Court Motel* (tel 39 0644) has singles/doubles at $25/32 and $80 by the week. It's an older motel and looks a little threadbare but the rooms are OK, you've got a balcony looking right out over the beach and it certainly couldn't be any more central. Also on Cavill Avenue *The Hub Motel* (tel 31 5559) at 21 has rooms at $15/30 and up, and the *Hawaiian Village Motel* (tel 31 7126) at 11 is $20/25, a couple of dollars more in the high season. Frankly, all prices in Surfers seem to be dependent on demand, the current temperature and what the mood of the day is.

Also very central, the *Hanlan Court Motel* (tel 31 5031) at 48 Hanlan St, a block over from Cavill Avenue, has singles or doubles at $25. A block over from the Gold Coast Highway at 32 Ferny Avenue, the *River Inn Motel* (tel 31 6176), is another somewhat flashier motel with rooms at $24 and up.

There are countless motels along the Gold Coast Highway, north and south of Surfers. Some are conveniently close to the centre. At 3205 Gold Coast Highway, just on the Southport side of the Surfer's centre, the *Winter Sun Motel* (tel 39 0833) is another straightforward motel, with a swimming pool. Nightly costs are just $20/25 and after night one it drops by a dollar a night. Close by is another cheapie, the *Paradise Springs Motel* (tel 31 5004) at 3204, with singles/doubles for $16/20.

Some other lower priced motels around the centre of Surfers include the *Siesta Motel* (tel 39 0355) at 2827 Gold Coast Highway with rooms at $20/25 or $100 a week. At 2923 the *Kyora Motor Inn* (tel 31 7745) is a little more luxurious and costs $25/30. At 2985 there's the *Silver Sands Motel* (tel 38 6041) at $18/22, with cooking facilities.

Down the Coast A few randomly selected places to consider, moving down the coast from Surfers: in Broadbeach, the *Whitehall Motor Inn* (tel 39 9003) on the corner of Elizabeth St and the Gold Coast Highway has rooms at $20/30. The *Motel Casa Blanca* (tel 39 9076) at 2649 Gold Coast Highway is $22/26.

At Palm Beach there's a string of reasonably priced places. *The Moana Motel* (tel 35 1131), at 1461 Gold Coast Highway, is on the beach, has rooms with fridges and colour TVs and is just $20/22. At 1500, the *Tally-Ho Motel* (tel 35 2955) with a barbecue area and self contained flats is even cheaper at $17/20. On the corner of 10th Avenue the *Tenth Avenue Motel* (tel 35 6133) has rooms at $20/24. The very simple *Tiki Flats* (tel 35 5001) at 1244 Gold Coast Highway has rooms from just $19. The *Palm Beach Motel* right on the beach is $19 and up for doubles.

There's a string of low priced motels along the Gold Coast Highway at Bilinga, near the airport, all with doubles around the $20 mark. You could try the Surfside at 351, the *Sundowner* at 329, the *New Bilinga Beach Motel* at 281, and the *Costa Rica* at 263.

In Coolangatta there is another cluster of accommodation and it's not a bad area to stay. Though sedate compared to Surfers it is a pleasant little town. There's a good beach and lots of surfing. There's an information desk at the airport and one on Griffith St.

The centrally located *Backpackers Inn Hostel* at 45 McLean St (tel 36 2422) has been highly recommended by several travellers. It costs $6.75 a night, has a friendly manager, a licensed restaurant and bar, TV and video room, mainly twin and double rooms and it's just two minutes walk from the beach. The old *Port O'Call Hotel* (tel 36 3066) at the corner of Griffiths and McLean has rooms for $10 and counter meals for $3. There's a big balcony round two sides where you can sit out and keep an eye on things.

Pacific Village Hotel (tel 36 2733) at 88

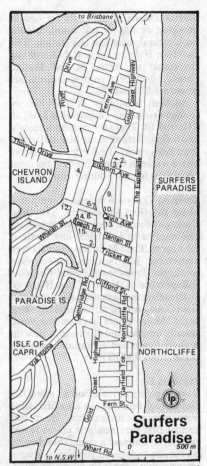

1	To Sea World
2	Bike Hire (three places)
3	Wintersun Motel
4	River Inn Motel
5	Bike Hire
6	East West Airlines
7	Bavarian Steak House
8	TAA
9	QGTB
10	Post Office
11	Ocean Court Motel
12	Ansett
13	Surfer's Paradise Hotel
14	Greyhound
15	Skennars

Marine Parade charges $22 for bed & breakfast or $29 for full board; heated pool, central, near the bus station. The *Bombora Holiday Lodge* (tel 36 1888) at the corner of Dutton St and Marine Parade, offers the same arrangements but prices are $31 and $36.

Another possibility is the *Kelvyn Golden Friendship Lodge* (tel 36 1318) at 6 Garrick St. There are numerous motels and holiday flats all along Marine Parade from $95 a week. The *Kirra Beach Hotel* on the water on the north side of the town has singles from $15 during slow periods.

Camping There are dozens of campsites along the Gold Coast strip. The Gold Coast city council operates six sites from Coolangatta to Labrador, just north of Southport. Their Main Beach site is very convenient, just north of Surfers. Just south, the *Broadbeach Island Caravan Village* is beside the Gold Coast Highway at Broadbeach. Camping sites along the Gold Coast are typically around $6 to $9 a night. Many places have on-site vans, usually from around $15 a night. Pick up a Gold Coast and hinterland camping leaflet from the QGTB.

Places to Eat

There's plenty of junk food all along the Gold Coast but you can also find some very pleasant restaurants. What you cannot find very easily is places to eat outside. It's almost a crime that despite all the sun and sea-air you almost always sit inside and listen to the air conditioning. Caville Mall is one of the few places where dining alfresco is possible – you could even take your *McDonalds* outside into the mall here.

In Surfers there's *Charlie's* in the mall with its busy outdoor tables under umbrellas, serving breakfasts, sandwiches, some Italian dishes and steaks. It's inexpensive and open 24 hours. There are others around the giant chess set, like the *Tamari Bistro* and *Georgio's* for pizza. *Caville Avenue Seafood* at 5 Cavill

Avenue has fish & chips and salad for $3.20. There's more expensive seafood next door. The *Springfield* at 44 is a moderate $6-a-dish Chinese place.

Emad's over at 10 Elkhorn St may not be noticed but it's a good, small BYO Lebanese place with shish kebabs at $3 and other dishes $3 to $7.50.

Orchid Avenue leading off Cavill Avenue has several eating-spots including the indoor/outdoor *Creperie* with crepes and Italian food for about $6, it's open daily. In the Mark Arcade on Orchid you'll find the *Curry Pot*, a BYO Indian place open from 6.30 pm, with meat dishes about $8, less for vegetarian. The Mark centre also has a *Pancake Kitchen* on the ground floor which has a great breakfast for $2.30.

The *Mexican Kitchen*, 150 Bundall Rd is one of the older restaurants and is reasonable. Up at the corner of Gold Coast Highway and Cavill Avenue the *Bavarian Steak House* has straightforward steak and chips style food for about $8 to $10.

In Southport, the *Malaysian Hut* at 52 Nerang St offers something different; lunch at $4.85 includes dahl, vegetables and curry. It's closed on Tuesdays. The *Health Habit* on Davenport St has only a few tables. Around the corner *Dimi's Place* also has good lunch bargains, inside or out. *Al's Restaurant* at the south end of Narang St has very cheap take-aways.

You'll need a car to get to *Gunter's Farmhaus* on West Burleigh Rd in West Burleigh. It serves plain, solid, down-to-earth German food and at very reasonable prices for a real restaurant meal.

On Sunday night the *Coconut Grove* in Mermaid Beach has an all-the-ribs-you-can-eat deal for $8.95 with soup, salad and bread.

In Coolangatta, a walk along Griffith St, the main street, will turn up plenty of places for a meal. The fish & chips joint at 43 is very cheap. *Mackwells'* at 64 is more expensive and offers barramundi among its wide selection. The *Gourmet Kitchen* in the central part of town is a nice place offering Australian and Chinese food. The *Queensland Hotel* has pub meals. There are more hotels and restaurants in Tweed Heads.

Lastly, a warning – in the off-season, in particular, restaurants close early – eat early or starve.

Entertainment

In Surfers *Bombay Rock* and *Industry* are rock bars. The *Swinging Vine*, downstairs on Cavill Avenue opposite TAA, is a place for jazz. The *Surfers Paradise Hotel* has a beer garden on the 2nd floor. *Jupiters Hotel* at Gold Coast City has a casino.

Down the Gold Coast Highway at Tallebudgera Bridge the *Play Room* is the live rock venue where you can catch the top Australian rock bands. In Coolangatta the large *Jet Club* has live bands and rock music for $2 to $8. It also has videos and is open until 3 am. The *Queensland Hotel* has music on weekends. In Tweed Heads, the *Twin Towns Services Club* makes lots of money from those nasty poker machines and some of the profits go to putting on big name shows.

Getting There

Air The Gold Coast is only an hour to two hours (depending on the traffic) from the centre of Brisbane but it also has its own busy airport with direct flights by Ansett and TAA from Sydney ($144, $102 standby), Melbourne ($220, $176 standby) and Adelaide ($247, $198 standby). You can also fly between Brisbane and Coolangatta for $61 – rather a lot of money compared to the bus fare! East-West Airlines fly daily to Sydney for $128 (standby $102).

Bus Greyhound operate a Brisbane-Surfers Paradise-Coolangatta service running down to Tweed Heads with up to 17 departures daily. The trip takes about 1½ to two hours to Surfers and costs $8.10. Note that arriving or departing Brisbane the bus does a city loop and will

drop you off or pick you up at stops around the city. The Greyhound terminal is across the river in South Brisbane. There are half a dozen services a day between Coolangatta and Murwillumbah including buses connecting with the Motorail train service from Sydney. There are also connecting Greyhound services through to Toowoomba. In Coolangatta the Greyhound terminal is on Warner St, (tel 38 8344). In Surfers it's on Beach Rd in the Cavill Park Building (tel 36 2366). Skennars and McCaffertys are also on Beach Rd. The fare from the Gold Coast to Sydney is approximately $30.

Skennars have an equally frequent Brisbane-Gold Coast service and they continue down the coast to Port Macquarie and Sydney. Their Coolangatta office is on Griffith St (tel 36 2574) while in Surfers they're in the Islander Motor Inn (tel 38 9944). McCaffertys operate between the Gold Coast and Toowoomba. In Tweed Heads they're on Boundary St (tel 36 1700).

Rail You can book rail tickets at the Greyhound office in Surfers. There's a daily train service between Sydney and Murwillumbah ($42) and a connecting bus between there and the Gold Coast.

Getting Around

Airport Transport Coolangatta Airport is the seventh busiest in Australia, right behind the state capitals. The airport bus, 'Kenney's', goes into town and Tweed Heads for $2. Hertz, Budget and Avis have desks at the airport but otherwise the plethora of rent-a-car agencies in Surfers are almost all unhappy about pick-ups or drop-offs from the airport.

TAA's office (tel 38 1188) is at 40 Cavill Avenue in Surfers. East-West (tel 50 3800) are at East-West World Travel, 3102 Gold Coast Highway in Surfers. Ansett (tel 38 3699) are also on the corner of Cavill Avenue and the Gold Coast Highway in the Cosmopolitan Building.

Bus There's a regular bus service running right up and down the Gold Coast between Southport at the north end and Tweed Heads at the south. It takes about an hour and 20 minutes from end to end and there are around 40 services a day from 7 am to past midnight. Surfers to Tweed Heads is $1.70, Coolangatta to Palm Beach is $1.35.

Car Rental There are stacks of rent-a-car firms along the Gold Coast, particularly in Surfers. There are so many that making any specific recommendations or even trying to list them is pointless – just pick up any of the give-away Gold Coast guides or scan the yellow pages. All the big companies are represented, plus a host of local operators in the Moke and small-car field and in the rent-a-wreck category. Budget give you a wad of free and reduced entry tickets with every car you rent. Rent-a-Bomb is one of the cheapest. Surfers Moped Hire rents them for $7 a day during the week. Moped World is on Cavill Avenue.

Bike Rental At 25 Elkhorn Avenue in Surfers, at the Repossessed Office Equipment place, there are bikes to rent. Silly Sycle on Islander Road is another bicycle rental place. At the other end of the strip at 159 Griffith St in Coolangatta, very close to the Queensland border, there is another bicycle and moped rental shop.

Tours There are all sorts of tours in and around Surfers, whether it's visiting the various tourist attractions or cruising the canals along which the Surfers rich live. River or canal cruises may include lunch, or in the evening, music, dancing and dinner. Bus trips up into the mountains behind the coast cost around $22 or for $25 you can make a boat trip to Stradbroke Island. There are joy flights over the coast including flights in old biplane Tiger Moths.

Back from the Coast

The Gold Coast is more than just the coastal strip – in fact the mountains of the MacPherson Ranges are probably the nicest thing about the coast.

TAMBORINE MOUNTAINS

Just 45 km north-west of the Gold Coast there are spectacular waterfalls, like the Witches Falls or Cedar Creek Falls, and seven national parks. The turn off to the mountains is from Oxenden, north of Southport on the road to Brisbane. Places of interest in the mountains include: Jasper Farm, a commercial fossicking site at Upper Coomera; Thunderbird eggs; Butterfly Farm where beautiful colourful butterflies are bred in captivity (it's open daily during the summer months); numerous short bushwalks, some with great views; wallabies in the Pine Grove Park; and enormous trees in the forest at Macdonald Park.

NERANG & SOUTH

Only nine km in from Southport this pleasant town in the Gold Coast hinterland has almost become a suburb of the coastal strip. Beyond, there is the Advancetown Lake, and Hinze dam – named after Russ Hinze, the grossly corpulent, right-wing Queensland politician who is the one man that could make almost anybody love Joh Bjelke Petersen.

In the Advancetown Hotel grounds, Pioneer House, a slab-wall pioneering home, is restored as a small museum. South of the lake is Springbrook where there's the Canyon, the 'Alpine Panorama' at the end of the road and the 'English Garden' with lots of 'old country' flavour. Natural Bridge is close to the Nerang-Murwillumbah road, an intriguing natural feature reached by a one-km-long walking track.

THE LAMINGTON PLATEAU

This was one of Queensland's first national parks with forests, beautiful gorges and a great many waterfalls. It's only about 30 km in from the coast and has lots of walking tracks, many leading to superb views. There's also a walking track for the blind which is equally interesting to sighted people who'd like to give their other senses a chance at communing with nature.

Much of the plateau is incorporated in the Lamington National Park which runs along the NSW border. O'Reilly's Green Mountain tops the western summits of the park. There's a tourist centre at Binna Burra Lodge, overlooking the Numinbah Valley. You can camp in the park with a permit from the ranger at Binna Burra or there's the *Binna Burra Mountain Lodge*, a great place to stay with excellent scenery, guides and good food. Information on the many walks in the park is available at Canungra.

Moreton Bay Islands

In all there are said to be 365 islands in Moreton Bay, an island for every day of the year. Actually most of them are little more than sandbanks barely rising out of the water, but there are a few larger islands of interest. Moreton Bay is at the mouth of the Brisbane River and the bay islands shelter this stretch of the coast. The south end of South Stradbroke is only just north of Southport, at the end of the Gold Coast, while the north end of Bribie Island is only just south of Caloundra, at the beginning of the Sunshine Coast.

NORTH & SOUTH STRADBROKE ISLAND

Until 1896 the two Stradbroke Islands were one but in that year a storm cut through the sand spit joining the two at Jumpinpin. Today South Stradbroke is virtually uninhabited but it's a popular

Moreton Bay

day-trip from the Gold Coast with a number of operators making cruises there.

North Stradbroke (Straddie to its friends) is a larger island with permanent population and it's a popular weekend escape from Brisbane, despite which it is still relatively unspoilt. In 1828 Dunwich was established on the island as a quarantine station for immigrants but in 1850 an arriving ship brought cholera and the cemetery tells the sad story of the 28 victims of the outbreak that followed.

Dunwich, Amity Point and Point Lookout are the three main centres on the island. The island has plenty of beaches, good surfing, some bays and inlets around Point Lookout, 18 Mile Swamp with lots of wildlife, Brown Lake, and Blue Lake in a national park.

All three centres on the island have camp sites but the only hotel is at Point Lookout. Ferries cross to North Stradbroke from Brisbane, Cleveland and Redland Bay. The vehicular ferry service from Redland Bay to Dunwich operates four to six times daily and takes about an hour to make the crossing.

MORETON ISLAND

Further out in the bay Moreton Island is still virtually a wilderness and is little visited. Apart from a few rocky headlands the island is all sand dunes with Mt Tempest, towering to 280 metres, probably the highest sand-hill in the world. The island has prolific birdlife and at its northern tip there's a lighthouse which was built in 1857. With all that sand it's hardly surprising that the sand miners have been looking at its potential and there is some controversy about whether sand mining will be permitted. Sand mining has taken place on North Stradbroke for some time.

Tangalooma, on the western side of the island, is a popular tourist resort sited at an old whaling station. There are a number of bushwalking tracks around the resort area apart from the usual resort attractions. Daily accommodation costs at the resort range from $60 to $85 per person.

If you catch the ferry to Reeders Point, you can pitch a tent under the trees by the beach. There's a shop in Korringal but it's expensive so bring what you can from the mainland. There's plenty of firewood around by the beach. For a bit of shark spotting, go to the Tangalooma Resort about 5 pm when they dump all the garbage off the end of the jetty.

Access to Moreton Island is by air (15

minutes, $30 one-way) or sea (2½ hours, $10) from Brisbane. Stradbroke Ferries operate from Cleveland to the south end of the island on Saturdays (returning Sunday) and from Bulimba to Korringal on Tuesdays and Fridays, from Manly on Saturdays and Sundays. There are day trips run to the island resort from Brisbane for $20 including lunch – see the Brisbane section.

BRIBIE ISLAND (population 4500)

At the north of Moreton Bay, Bribie Island is 31 km long but little developed. There's a bridge across Pumicestone Passage to the island at Bellara at the southern end but little else of the island has been touched. There's good surfing on the ocean side and a calm channel towards the mainland. Bongaree is the main town and buses run there from Caboolture and Brisbane three times daily.

THE BAYSIDE – north

Redcliffe (population 34,500), to the north of Brisbane, was the first settlement in Queensland as the original penal colony was established here in 1824. It was moved to Brisbane a year later, driven away by local Aboriginal opposition. The Aboriginals called the place Humpybong or 'dead houses' and the name is still applied to the peninsula. Redcliffe is now an outer suburb of Brisbane. South of Redcliffe, Sandgate is another long-running seaside resort which is now more of an outer suburb. At Beaufort Place on Deception Bay, north of Redcliffe, the Shell Bungalow is a curious house decorated with more than a million shells.

THE BAYSIDE – south

South of Brisbane is the Redland Bay area, a fertile market garden area for Brisbane. The (oh dear) Big Strawberry is at Boundary Rd, Thornlands. There's an old 1864 lighthouse at Cleveland Point and the 1853 Cleveland Court House is now a restaurant. The Redlands Museum is on Long St, Cleveland but is not open regular hours.

Ormiston House is a very fine home built in 1862 and now open for inspection Sunday afternoons between March and November. The first commercially grown sugarcane in Queensland came from this site. At Wellington Point, Whepstead there is another early home. Built in 1874 it is open on the first Sunday of the month from May to September.

There are many smaller islands in the bay including St Helena Island, once Moreton Bay's 'Alcatraz' although today only ruins of the prison buildings remain. There's a tour launch to the island on weekends but on weekdays it only runs if there's a group booking. The $10 cost includes a guided tour of the island. Phone 393-3726 or 396-5113 for details.

The Sunshine Coast

The stretch of coast from Bribie Island to Tin Can Bay near Gympie is known as the Sunshine Coast. It's competition for the Gold Coast but it's considerably less neon-lit and commercial. The Bruce Highway does not run through the coast resort area, to get there you have to leave the highway for Caloundra and then turn away from the coast again at Noosa. North of Noosa it's possible to drive up the long beach to Double Island Point and Rainbow Beach, the jumping-off point for Fraser Island. The coast is renowned for fine surfing and secluded beaches while inland there are extensive tropical fruit plantations and the scenic hills of the Blackall Range.

Information

There's a QGTB (tel 43 2411) office on Alexandra Parade, Alexandra Headland. It's open weekdays and Saturday mornings. In Noosaville there's the Noosa Information Centre on the Noosa-Tewantin Rd.

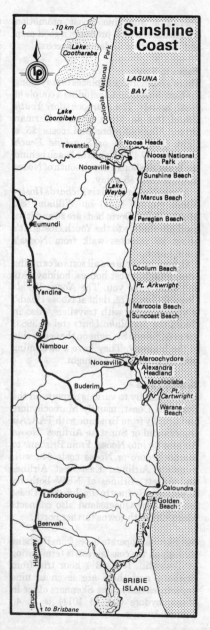

Sunshine Coast

There's a Sunshine Coast promotion organisation which produces a good map and information folder on the coast.

Places to Stay

There's no shortage of places to stay along the Sunshine Coast, including a couple of youth hostels. The *Maroochydore Youth Hostel* (tel 43 3151) is on Schirrman Drive, Maroochydore and costs $5 a night. The Noosa or *Sunshine Beach Hostel* (tel 47 4739) is on the beach behind the Duke St shops a beach south of Noosa itself. It costs $5 a day.

Also in Noosa Heads is *Richards Hostel Noosa* (tel 49 8151) on Williams St, Munna Point. Dorm beds are $6 and it's a good alternative to the Youth Hostel. It's about 20 minutes walk from Noosa's main beach.

Otherwise there are all sorts of camping sites, motels, guest houses, holiday flats and what have you. The *Noosa Woods Council Campsite*, right at Noosa Heads, is very popular with travellers. Also in Noosa the *Melaluka Units* (tel 47 3663) are at 64 Selene St, right on the ocean side of the highway. They have a swimming pool and charge $6 per night.

Getting There

Air You can fly to various airports on the Sunshine Coast, usually Maroochydore and usually from Brisbane with TAA, Air Queensland or Sunstate Airlines. Noosa Air also fly into Noosa. From Brisbane to Maroochydore or Noosa costs $40 with Sunstate Airlines. East-West Airlines and Ansett Airlines of NSW both fly direct from Sydney to the Sunshine Coast for $155. Air Queensland also connects Maroochy with towns further north.

Bus Skennars operate buses from Brisbane through all the coastal resorts terminating at Tewantin. It's a 3½ hour trip from Brisbane and there are seven to nine departures daily. The Skennars office in Maroochydore (tel 43 1011) is at 40 Second Avenue.

Getting Around

There's a ferry across the Noosa River from Noosaville for people heading up the beach to Double Island Point. Noosa is a popular jumping-off point for trips up the beach to Fraser Island. Lots of places along the coast hire cars, Mokes and four-wheel drives, particularly at Noosa Heads. Fun Wheels in Mooloolaba hire mopeds and bicycles too.

GLASSHOUSE MOUNTAINS

Shortly after Caboolture (population 6400), a prosperous dairy centre in a region which once had a large Aboriginal population, the Glasshouse Mountains are a dramatic visual starting point for the Sunshine Coast. They're only 72 km north of Brisbane and the 10 strangely shaped volcanic outcrops were named by Captain Cook. Depending on whose story you believe, he either noted the reflections of the glass-smooth rock sides of the mountains, or he thought they looked like glass-furnaces in his native Yorkshire. They are popular with rock-climbers.

CALOUNDRA (population 16,700)

At the southern end of the beach strip, Caloundra's quite a fair-sized town with a number of good beaches. Points of interest include the two-thirds scale model replica of the *Endeavour*, on display from 9 am to 5 pm daily at 3 Landsborough Parade, Seafarer's Wharf. A replica of the Bass and Flinders boat *Tom Thumb* is also on display. Caloundra also has a Military Museum on Caloundra Rd and the World of Matchcraft with amazing models made out of hundreds of thousands of matches.

AROUND MAROOCHYDORE

Around Maroochydore, the three centres of Mooloolaba, Alexandra Headland and Maroochydore (total population 17,500) are the main growth centres for the Sunshine Coast. Mooloolaba was the landfall for the Pacific 'La Balsa' expedition. On the corner of River

Esplanade and Brisbane St there's a Shell & Marine Display and a House of Dolls is at 31 First Avenue. Alexandra Headland has a long sandy beach, good for sunbathing.

At Maroochydore there's more good surfing and swimming, the Gallery of Sand Paintings at 209 Bradman Avenue, and lots of pelicans on the Maroochy River. Cotton Tree is a popular camping and picnic area on the river while at Bli Bli, 10 km north, there's a 'replica' of a Norman castle. Aptly dubbed Fairyland Castle (well it does have dungeons and a torture chamber) it's open daily. A couple of km further north is the Suncoast Pioneer Village; open daily, it has vintage cars and Australiana.

There are a long string of beaches north from Maroochydore to Noosa Heads –like Coolum, Peregian, Marcus Beach and Sunshine Beach. There are enough quiet little spots in between civilisation to usually allow you to find your own private beach.

NOOSA HEADS (population 17,000)
Like Maroochydore, Noosa is actually a combination of three separate centres. Here it's Noosa Heads actually on the headland, then Noosaville a short distance up the Noosa River, and finally Tewantin. The spectacular headland at Noose Heads marks the northern end of the Sunshine Coast beach strip. Noosa, the centre at the heads, is a trendy resort and deservedly so. It has great locations, lots of atmosphere, fine views and great beaches. Noosaville is mainly an accommodation centre while Tewantin is a quieter town further back from the coast, although it also has a number of attractions in its own right.

The headland at Noosa is a national park with fine walks, good surfing spots and pleasant sandy beaches between the rocky headlands from the Heads to Sunshine Beach. Granite Bay, at the northern tip of the park, is a popular though unofficial nude-bathing beach.

From Tingirana Lookout (also known as Laguna Lookout) at the top of the park headland there are superb views along the seemingly endless beach towards Double Island Point.

The park tracks include the walk to the Tanglewood wildlife sanctuary. Noosa Heads is a very popular centre with many travellers passing through. The *Noosa Youth Hostel* in Douglas St is a popular base for exploring this scenic area. Read the guest book to see just how good a time people have here!

Turning inland along the Noosa River you quickly reach Noosaville, access point to the Teewah Coloured Sands. At 82 Gympie Terrace in Noosaville, Tall Ships has a large and varied collection of ship models, it's open daily.

Tewantin has the House of Bottles on Myles St which amongst its exhibits of bottles includes (you guessed it) the 'Big Bottle', constructed out of 17,000 beer bottles. 'Big' things are popular on the Sunshine Coast and Tewantin also has the Big Shell on Gympie St. Both Tewantin 'bigs' are open daily. The coast road rejoins the Bruce Highway at Cooroy.

North of the Noosa River you can travel up the Noosa Lakes for up to 50 km into the national park. There are many boat trips on the lakes. Boreen Point on Lake Cootharaba is a particularly popular spot on the lakes. Eliza Fraser, who gave her name to Fraser Island following her shipwreck there, was held captive at the lake by Aboriginals.

BUDERIM (population 4000)
Off the Bruce Highway, Buderim is a fruit growing centre with a ginger factory open 8.15 am to 4.15 pm daily. Other attractions include Hans Wetzel's Movie Museum on Burnett St and Pioneer Cottage on Ballenger Crescent. At the Buderim turn-off from the Bruce Highway the Buderim Zoo & Koala Park is open Sunday to Friday – this is your chance to hold a koala. Also at the turn-off, Tanawah

World has a number of sights including a huge fibreglass dinosaur. There are good walks near Buderim in the Footes Sanctuary.

NAMBOUR (population 8000)

You often see sugar-cane trains crossing the main street of this sugar growing town. Pineapples and other tropical fruit are also grown in the area and the 'Big Pineapple' is one of Nambour's two, superbly kitsch, 'big' creations. Looming by the roadside you can climb up inside the 15 metre fibreglass wonder to see the full story of pineapple cultivation. There's a whole tourist centre behind it including souvenir shops, restaurant, snack bar, toy train rides around the plantation and an adjoining macadamia nut factory. As if that wasn't enough six km north is the (oh my God) 'Big Cow'. Yes you can climb inside it! Wappa Dam, near Nambour, is a good picnic spot. Near Yandina, just north of Nambour, you can fossick for thunder eggs.

COOLOOLA COAST

North of Noose Heads, and separated from the Sunshine Coast strip by the Noosa River, is the long beach backed by the Cooloola National Park and running north to Double Island Point. Four-wheel drive vehicles can drive the entire length of the coast along the 50 km beach and round to Wide Bay from where you cross to Fraser Island. The beach is noted for the Teewah Coloured Sands with 200 metre high cliffs of different coloured sands.

Just south of Double Island Point is the *Cherry Venture*, a 3000-ton freighter which was swept onto the beach during a cyclone in 1973. It was totally undamaged but proved completely impossible to refloat despite many attempts. There's more to the Cooloola park than just the coastline and beach and the inland part can be reached without the aid of four-wheel drive. There's a string of lakes connected by the Noosa River which can

be explored by boat. You can also reach Lake Coothuraba, the largest lake, by road and you can hire boats at Boreen Point. Boats cross the lake from here and it's then a two km walk to the Teewah Coloured Sands.

INLAND FROM THE COAST

The mountains rise up fairly close behind the coast and you can take the scenic Mapleton-Maleny road right along the ridgeline of the Blackhall Range. Parks in the range include the Mapleton Falls National Park and the Kondalilla National Park with the 75-metre-high Kondalilla Falls. There's lots of birdlife up here.

The small town of Flaxton, five km south of Mapleton, has a model English village and the Flaxton Inn in Tudor-style. A little south, Montville has a whole series of tourist attractions including an art gallery, a comprehensive model train collection in The Dome on Main St (daily except Wednesday) and a variety of local museums. On the road from Maleny to Kenilworth, Little Yabba Creek is a great picnic spot. Continue north to Imbil which has an unusual little museum and the Borumba irrigation dam nearby.

There's an alternative accommodation place, *Dealbata Host Farm* (tel (071) 46 0936) on Boolouaba Creek Rd, 40 km from Landsborough. It costs $4 a night or $15 for a self-contained flat for three people. Call for transportation assistance.

Further inland the South Burnett region includes Australia's most important peanut growing area, Kingaroy (population 5100) almost means 'peanuts' in Australia, not least because Joh-Bjelke Petersen, Queensland's Premier, big peanut himself, hails from here. Near Kingaroy, Nanango (population 1800), is another peanut town but with an earlier history of gold mining. North of Kingaroy, Murgon (population 2300) is the main town of the region.

Hervey Bay Area

North of the Sunshine Coast is the Hervey Bay area and Fraser Island. Extending from Maryborough to Bundaberg, Hervey Bay is the wide, sheltered bay in the lee of Fraser Island. There are several fair-sized towns along the Bruce Highway plus the locally popular beach ports on the bay. Inland from the coast is the Burnett region, one of the earliest farming areas in the state although gold was also found here. Grains, fruit and peanuts are all grown here.

GYMPIE (population 10,800)

Gympie came into existence with an 1867 gold rush and gold continued to be mined here right up to 1920. There's a 'heroic' statue to those early gold miners in the town and for a week each October there's a big Gold Rush Festival in Gympie. There's a Gold Mining & Historical Museum in the town (open 1 to 4 pm daily, 9 am to 5 pm on public holidays) and nearby is the cottage home of an early Australian Prime Minister, Andrew Fisher.

From Gympie a road leads through extensive pine plantations to Tin Can Bay (population 900) and Rainbow Beach, the gateway to Fraser Island. On the Bruce Highway through Gympie there's also (ho hum) another big pineapple where you can get tourist information; also available at 204 Mary St.

MARYBOROUGH (population 20,100)

Although to most people Maryborough is simply a pause on the route north, or a jumping-off point for Fraser Island, it's actually an interesting town in its own right and well worth looking around.

Today timber and sugar are Maryborough's major industries but its earlier importance as an industrial centre and seaport led to a series of imposing Victorian civic buildings, many of which survive in fine condition today. The National Trust has a free booklet detailing a walking tour around the centre and a longer driving tour. Even if you're just driving through, the walking tour is an interesting and educational hour's diversion.

The town has two fine parks: Queen's Park with an unusual domed fernery, a waterfall and the National Trust classified band rotunda; and Elizabeth Park which is noted for its roses. The imposing post office is just one of the buildings which reflect Maryborough's early prosperity – it was built in 1869. Some of the old hotels (a number have good counter meals in the evenings) are also fine examples of Victoriana. You'll find other reminders of Maryborough's early history as a port, by the river.

Maryborough's tourist information centre is located just after you cross the Mary River from Brisbane; they have copies of the walking tours booklet. The town has an alternate youth hostel in the *Criterion Hotel*.

HERVEY BAY (population 13,600)

Hervey Bay also refers to the string of small towns along the bay. There's no surf here so swimming is safe for small children and the area is packed with camping and caravan parks.

The coastal towns include Urangan from where barges cross to Fraser Island. There's also an aquarium at Dayman Point. On Tavistock St in Torquay there's the Urimbirra Park, a wildlife sanctuary and museum of Aboriginal, and other, artefacts. Pialba and Scarness both have historical museums while at Gatakers Bay there's the Parraweena Bird Sanctuary where flocks of lorikeets fly in for daily feeds at 7.30 am and 4 pm. Tourist information is available at the Hervey Bay Town Council Chambers, Torquay, from 8.30 am to 4.45 pm, Monday to Friday.

BUNDABERG (population 32,500)

At the north end of Hervey Bay, a 50 km

detour off the Bruce Highway, Bundaberg is a major sugar producing centre although tobacco, fruit and peanuts are also grown in the area. Some of the sugar ends up in the famous Bundaberg Rum. You can tour the rum distillery as well as several of Bundaberg's sugar mills. Bundaberg's Historical Museum is in the School of Arts Building on Bourbong St. Boyd's Antiquatorium is open 2 to 4 pm daily and amongst the exhibits is a replica of Stephenson's original steam locomotive 'The Rocket'. Bundaberg also has an art gallery and a doll museum.

Pioneer aviator Bert Hinkler was born in Bundaberg and made his first flight at the age of 19 in a home-made glider on Mon Repos beach in 1912. In 1928 he made the first solo flight between England

There are a number of Hinkler memorials around the town including a cairn on top of the Hummock, which is a 100-metre-high extinct volcano about 10 km out of Bundaberg, and is the solitary hill in the area.

Bundaberg also has an art gallery and an interesting doll museum.

Bundaberg's Alexandra Park Zoo has a tortoise which, records indicate, was brought to Australia from Madagascar back in 1847.

Just a couple of km out of town at 12 Ryan St, North Bundaberg, Tropical Wines produces a variety of tropical fruit wines.

Around Bundaberg there's the Dream Time Reptile Park four km out. There's good surf at Bargara (13 km) and Moore Park (23 km) while turtles nest at Mon Repos Beach (14 km). Three types of turtles lay their eggs at this beach; it's unusual since turtles generally prefer sandy islands off the coast.

The turtle season is from October to March and you're most likely to see the turtles laying their eggs around the time of the high tide at night. The turtles and their eggs are totally protected. There's a bus service operating from the city out to the various beaches.

Fraser Island

The world's largest sand island is off Tin Can Bay – it measures 120 km long by about 15 km wide. The island takes its name from Eliza Fraser, the wife of the captain of a ship which was wrecked off Rockhampton in 1836. Making their way south to look for help a group from the ship, including the captain and his wife, were captured by Aboriginals on Fraser Island (at that time known as Great Sandy Island). Only Eliza Fraser was to survive their captivity. Much more recently the island has been the subject of a controversial dispute between conservationists and sand-miners. The decision went to the conservationists after a bitter struggle.

The island is a delight for fishing, bushwalking, four-wheel drive and trail bike exponents and for lovers of nature in general. There are superb beaches, towering sand dunes and clean, clear fresh-water lakes and streams. The northern part of the island is a national park. The island is sparsely populated although there were once two to three thousand Aboriginals living here. Except for 20 km of surfaced road in the extreme south the island tracks are not suitable for conventional vehicles – it's four-wheel drive or motorcycles only. It's possible to drive right along the ocean beach, with occasional detours for creeks, but vehicles must be suitable equipped for travelling over soft sand.

Don't let this talk of sand, sand, sand, fool you, however. The island is carpeted in a lush rainforest and there are major pine plantations. The island also has a considerable number of lakes, creeks and streams varying from clear water lakes, some of them very deep, to marshy heathland. The island is chiefly popular for fishing; swimming can be dangerous due to severe undertows. Wildlife on the island includes dingoes (native dogs) and brumbies (wild horses).

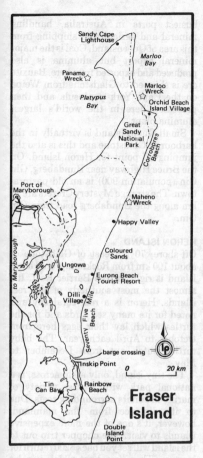

Fraser Island

number of other wrecks around the island. More than 99.9% of the island is pure sand, the few outcrops of rock are all at the most easterly point – Waddy Rock, Middle Rock and Indian Head; great views from the top of the latter.

Places to Stay

Most people staying on Fraser Island camp. Whatever your plans are you should come well equipped since supplies on the island are limited and only available in a couple of places. Starting from the south there's a *National Fitness Council* camp at Dilli Village (book in Brisbane, tel (07) 221 4905) with rooms from $10 per person, bed & breakfast.

Eurong has supplies, petrol, and motel-style accommodation at the *Eurong Beach Resort* with weekly rates of $135 for two people. Happy Valley, where again you can get petrol, is the main accommodation area on the island with half a dozen holiday flats all with rates around $30 a day for a unit.

Right up at the north, just beyond Waddy Rock, the *Orchid Beach Island Village* is a rather more expensive holiday resort – nightly costs with meals are around $55 per person. There's a campsite in the national park where camping is free with a permit from the park ranger.

Getting There & Around

If you're planning on travelling around the island solo and haven't got suitable transport you can rent four-wheel drive vehicles in Brisbane and Maryborough or at Eurong on the island. If you're going to drive through the state forest (not along the beach) you'll need a permit but this can be obtained over the phone by ringing Maryborough (071) 21 2408 or Gympie (071) 82 2244. The alternative is to take a day or longer tour.

The usual crossing point to the island is the 10-minute barge crossing from Inskip Point, reached by driving along the beach for 12 km from Rainbow Beach. To Rainbow Beach you can either take the

Starting from the south at Hook Point, you cross Fourth, then Third, Second and First Creeks, all of which drain the southern heathland. Dilli Village, the former sand-mining HQ, is between Third and Second. The beach here is aptly titled 75 mile beach. You then reach The Cathedrals, 25 km of coloured sand cliffs. Eli Creek is the largest creek on the east coast and just north of here lies the wreck of the *Maheno*, a 5000 ton liner that was blown on shore while being towed to a scrapyard in Japan, in 1935. There are a road from Gympie or drive up the beach after crossing the Noosa River at Tewantin. You can also ferry across from Urangan on Hervey Bay – usually to Ungowa. Bus tours of the island run from here and there are a variety of cruise-bus trips available. Ring (071) 28 9370, 28 9120 or 28 9217 for details from the various operators. There are joy-flights for $20 each for 30 minutes or $60 per plane load (five people) for 60 minutes.

Buses and trains run to Urangan from Maryborough, Monday to Friday and the trip takes 1½ to two hours. There are regular buses from Gympie to Rainbow Beach, 1¼ hours. From there you can get a bus-ferry service to the island via Inskip Point. Maryborough-Gympie buses take 1½ hours and run Monday to Friday. There's a regular charter flight on Wednesdays, Saturdays and Sundays from Maryborough and Brisbane. Return fares are $178 from Brisbane and $65 from Maryborough.

North to Rockhampton

AGNES WATERS & 1770

Turning east off the Bruce Highway at Miriamvale, there's a rough dirt road running 60 km out to Agnes Waters and 1770, which used to be known as Round Hill but was renamed in 1970 to commemorate Captain Cook's landing. Agnes Waters has a motel and caravan park and there's a camping ground at 1770, six km from Agnes Waters, with terrific scenery, on a large secluded bay. It's an area that's hardly developed and due to a gap in the reef, has one of the most northerly surf beaches on the east coast. Unfortunately it appears that this area may become a lot more developed in the future so see it while you can.

GLADSTONE (population 22,000)

Gladstone has only recently attained importance as a port. It's now one of the busiest ports in Australia, handling mineral and agricultural shipping from this area of Queensland. Coal is the major mineral export but alumina is also produced and exported from here. Bauxite ore is shipped to Gladstone from Weipa on the Cape York peninsula and then processed here in the world's largest alumina plant.

Small Quoin Island is virtually in the harbour at Gladstone and this is also the jumping-off point for Heron Island. On the Bruce Highway near Bundaberg, Gin Gin (population 900) is an old pastoral town. The strange Mystery Craters are 17 km along the Bundaberg road from Gin Gin.

HERON ISLAND

Off-shore, 70 km east of Gladstone or about 100 km from Rockhampton, Heron Island is right on the Barrier Reef. It's almost the most southerly of the reef islands. Heron is a real coral cay and noted for its many sea birds and for the turtles which lay their eggs here from October to April each year. The baby turtles hatch out from December to May.

The tiny island, only a km across, is a national park with a vast variety of marine life on its surrounding reefs. Due to its distance from the mainland, however, it's one of the more expensive islands to visit. The chopper trip out to the island will set you back $200 return for starters. There is a boat which is a lot cheaper at $85. When you get there you're up for a minimum of $75 a day per person for accommodation and meals which are better described as 'adequate' rather than 'luxurious'. But it's not creature comforts or easy accessibility which brings people here. Heron Island is famed for its superb skindiving and each November the Barrier Reef Divers Festival takes place here over four weeks.

BURNETT HIGHWAY ROUTE

As an alternative to the Bruce Highway

route you can travel north on the Burnett Highway, further inland. If you turn inland from Gympie you soon reach Gayndah (population 1700), one of the oldest towns in the state and the citrus-growing centre of Queensland. The District Historical Museum is open on weekends and public holidays.

On the way to Gayndah you pass by, or can divert to, Kilkivan, a popular fossicking area, the Kinbombi Falls with a series of swimming pools and the Ban Ban Springs. You can also reach Gayndah from Gympie or Maryborough via Biggenden, passing the volcanic crater lakes of the Coulston Lakes National Park on the way. Biggenden was once a gold mining centre. On the way to Biggenden from Maryborough you can visit the Woocoo Historical Society Museum in Brooweena, open Sunday afternoons or borrow the keys from the post office.

North of Gayndah is Mundubbera (population 1100), another citrus-growing centre and from here you can also reach the Auburn River National Park. Eidsvold (population 600) was a prosperous gold town for 12 years from 1888. Monto (population 1400) is in the heart of Rockhampton's cattle country. The spectacular Cania Gorge is 25 km north of the town. Just 142 km from Rockhampton is Biloela (population 4600) a busy irrigated agricultural centre. Mt Scoria, 14 km from the town, is a solidified volcano core. From here you continue through Mt Morgan to Rockhampton.

Rockhampton
Population 50,100

Australia's 'beef capital' sits astride the Tropic of Capricorn, there's a marker beside the road as you enter Rocky from the south. Rockhampton had a relatively small, early gold rush but cattle soon became the big industry in this area. A statue of a Braford bull marks the southern approach to the city and a Brahman bull the northern.

Information & Orientation
The QGTB (tel 27 8611) is at 119 East St and is open Monday to Friday from 9 am to 4.45 pm. There's also the Capricorn Information Centre at the junction of the Bruce, Burnett and Capricorn Highways in Curtis Park near the Tropic of Capricorn spire. The RACQ (tel 27 2255) is at 134 William St.

Rockhampton straddles the Fitzroy River with the city centre along the river to the south. The long Fitzroy Bridge connects the old central part of Rockhampton with the newer suburbs to the north. The town centre is actually quite small but the incredibly wide streets make walking a few blocks seem a fair distance.

Around Town
There are many fine early buildings in the town to remind you of pioneer days – particularly on Quay St where you'll find one of the best Victorian street frontages in Australia. More than 20 old buildings along the street bear National Trust classification and a National Trust walking tour brochure is available. There's an art gallery in the Pilbeam Theatre complex on Victoria Parade. Rockhampton also has one of those water-slide complexes (just like almost every other fair sized town on the Queensland coast), it's in North Rockhampton.

Near the airport St Aubin's Herb Farm is in an old 1870 homestead. There's an excellent tropical collection in the Botanic Gardens on Spencer St on the edge of the Athelstane Range. It overlooks Murray Lagoon, just three km from the city centre, to the south, near the airport. Established in 1869 it's said to be the finest tropical garden in Australia and has a walk-through aviary and a small zoo.

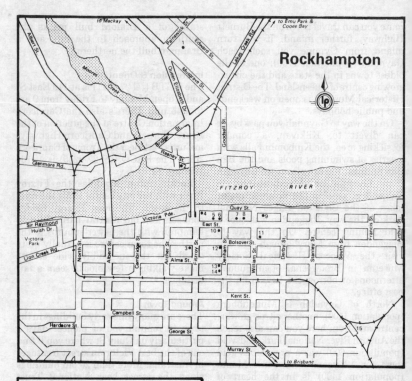

Rockhampton

1 Youth Hostel
2 Municipal Caravan Park
3 Criterion Hotel
4 TAA
5 Oxford Hotel
6 QGTB
7 Ansett
8 Heritage Tavern
9 Post Office
10 Crown Hotel
11 Leichardt Hotel
12 Winsall's Hotel
13 Texacana
14 Railway Station

Places to Stay

Hostel The *Rockhampton Youth Hostel* (tel 27 5288) at 60 Macfarlane St costs $5.50. People with cars can sleep in them and use the hostel facilities for $3. It's a new building across the river to the north

of town – about a 20-minute walk from the centre. Cross the bridge, turn right then left and keep walking along Musgrave St (parallel to the main highway) until you hit Macfarlane St. Except on Sundays you can also get there on a High St bus. Note that travelling south, Ansett Pioneer and Greyhound buses arrive in Rocky at terrible hours of the night. You can also book the Great Keppel hostel through the Rocky Hostel. The island hostel tends to be heavily booked so you have to plan ahead. The bus for the harbour and ferry leaves the hostel at 8 am and the combined bus/ferry return ticket is $15.

Hotels & Motels There are plenty of old fashioned hotels around the centre but nothing of great value in the motel line. On Quay St by the bridge the *Criterion*

Hotel (or rather Bonaparte's Criterion Hotel) (tel 2 1225) is a magnificent old building, one of the finest of the Quay St frontages. Hotel rooms here are $15/20 but there is also a new motel section at $25/30, about the best motel value in Rocky.

On the corner of East and Denham Sts the *Oxford Hotel* (tel 21 2837) is a straightforward central hotel with rooms at $13 per person, breakfast $4. At 49 William St at the corner of Bolsover, the *Crown Hotel* (tel 2 1684) is cheaper but not recommended. Across the street the *Queensland* isn't really any better; drinking's the game.

The *Grand Hotel* isn't special either but it's sort of funky with its old pioneer look, and it's quiet and the clientele seem to know when to quit. It's over at the corner of Archer and Bolsover, $12. The *Oriental*, corner of Alma and Williams Sts, is air-conditioned and has bed and breakfast for $20.

You'll find lots of motels and camp sites on the Bruce Highway into Rockhampton from the north and south. On the south side the *Lodge Motel* (tel 27 3130) is at 100 Gladstone Rd and has singles/doubles at $26/30. The *Traveller's Inn*, 110-114 George is $30/34 for singles/doubles. On the north side there's the *Kalka Hotel/Motel* (tel 28 5666) at the corner of Lakes Creek Rd and Water St, the 'back road' to Yeppon. Rooms here are $26/30. The *Capricorn* is one of many on Yaamba Rd and charges $22/26. As a rule north-side motels are cheaper.

Camping There are half a dozen campsites in Rocky including the attractively sited *Municipal Riverside Caravan Park* (tel 2 3779), just across the river from the centre and right beside the bridge. Camping here costs $5 for two people. Most of the other sites also have on-site vans as well as camping facilities although camping is generally a bit more expensive and none of them are so conveniently situated. There are a clump of them on the Bruce

Highway north of town towards the Yeppoon turn-off. *Ramblers Caravan Park* (tel 28 2084) has camping at $7.50 and on-site vans at $18.

Places to Eat

There are two things to note: Rocky is an early closer so head out early; and steak is a specialty, this is cattle country after all. The *Heritage Tavern* at the corner of Quay and Denham Sts is a flashier, more expensive version of a counter meal, in the $6 to $8 range, lots of meat. In the public bar much the same food is a few dollars less.

Also on the Quay, by the bridge, the beautiful *Criterion Hotel* has the usual counter menu with prices from $4 to $8 and is open until 9 pm.

Every other hotel in town has pub meals that are generally cheaper but they're not serving such quality steaks either. *Winsall's* on Alma call their counter section the Spanish Restaurant but it's fairly standard. It's open to 8 pm. The *Union Tavern*, corner of East and William Sts, has probably the cheapest feeding in town, fried rice and prawns is $2.

A fine alternative to all this is the *Copacabana*, which is pleasantly eclectic in food and decor. It's open early for breakfast; muesli and all the usual. Lunches offer sandwiches, hot meals, tacos. A good lasagna and a milkshake cost me $2.70; it's very popular but it closes at 4.30 or 5 pm.

The *Texacana*, up on Denham St near Alma St, is a saviour as it's the only place open after early evening. It's not bad and does burgers, shakes and other basics. The *Tropical Fruit & Juice Bar*, across from the Post Office on East St, has fantastic fruit salads for just $1.10, smoothies and vegetable salads.

At 61 William St, *My Old Dutch* offers pancakes and crepes. It's BYO but it's closed Sunday and Monday. Lastly, if you've got to have Chinese, there is the *Eastern* on Denham St near the corner of

Dension St. They serve lots of seafood dishes and most are in the $4 to $7 bracket.

On Sundays, from 4 to 8 pm, there's live jazz in the bar of the *Oriental Hotel*.

Getting There

Air You can fly to Rocky from all the usual places along the coast. Fares include Brisbane $123 ($99 standby), Mackay $89, Townsville $134 and Cairns $278. In Rockhampton, TAA (tel 31 0555) are at 75 East St. Ansett (tel 31 0755) are at 137 East St.

Bus Greyhound and Ansett Pioneer both travel up the Queensland coast between Brisbane and Cairns, and vise versa, on a daily basis. Brisbane-Rocky takes about 11 hours for $40. Coming south from Cairns it's 16 hours for $39, from Townsville about 10 hours, from Mackay about 3½ hours. Note that the southbound buses arrive at an ungodly hour in the middle of the night, with either operator.

Greyhound also operate inland from Rockhampton to Longreach – three times weekly, nine hours, $44. McCafferty's also operate buses on the coast between Brisbane and Rocky, twice daily. Their service between Rocky and Mackay operates inland through Emerald and Moranbah, rather than the direct route closer to the coast.

Greyhound's desk is in Duthies Real Estate (tel 27 7107), on the corner of Denham and Bolsover Sts. McCafferty's are on Denison St between Denham and Fitzroy Sts.

Rail The Sunlander runs from Brisbane through Rockhampton to Cairns six times a week. Brisbane-Rockhampton takes 9½ hours, it's another 24 hours north to Cairns. Twice weekly the Midlander runs between Rockhampton, Longreach and Winton. It's five hours to Emerald ($23 in economy), 16 hours to Longreach ($46) and 20 hours to Winton

($57). Phone 31 0211 for railway information.

Getting Around Rocky's airport is fairly conveniently situated about five km from the centre, $4 by taxi. Avis, Budget and Hertz all have desks at the airport. Rocky has a fairly modern railway station with luggage lockers but it's a fair walk from the city centre. From the centre take a High St bus for the youth hostel, north of the river. Rockhampton has a reasonably comprehensive local bus network – timetables from the town hall are 20c.

Buses operated by Youngs Bus Service run to Yeppoon via Emu Park and Cooee Bay. There's up to five services daily on weekdays, only two or three on weekends and the fare is $3.50. They also operate a bus to Mt Morgan (see Mt Morgan). There's a schedule in the tourist office window and one in the window of the Casket Newsagent on Denham St, corner of Bolsover St where the Young Buses stop. The 10 am and weekend afternoon trips leave from the Post Office.

Rotherys Coaches (tel 28 2847) offer tours of the city including historic sites and gardens for three hours for $8; Monday, Wednesday and Friday at 10 am from the Post Office.

Around Rockhampton

NORTH OF THE CITY

The rough and rugged Berserker Range starts 26 km north of Rocky, here you'll find several limestone caves. There are regular tours around Olsen's (or the Capricorn) Cave and Cammoo Cave, both just a few km off the Bruce Highway. Nearby you can also visit the Gangalook Museum with everyday items from the pioneering period. Gemland is just past the Yeppoon turn-off and has a rock and gemstone collection and gem cutting and polishing displays. The Queensland gem fields are inland from Rockhampton.

MT MORGAN (population 4000)

The Mt Morgan mines are 38 km south-west of Rockhampton. The gold and copper mine is open cut and is one of the biggest holes in the ground in Australia. The mine has been worked off and on for a century and is now nearly 300 metres deep. The town's population was much larger earlier this century.

Inspections of the mine take place at 9.30 am and 1.30 pm daily. There's a museum on East St (10 am to 1 pm weekdays, 10 am to 12 noon Saturdays and 2 to 4 pm Sundays) and a Tourist Information Centre in the School of Arts on Morgan St.

Young's Bus Service operates a regular bus from Rockhampton four times daily on weekdays, twice on Saturdays. The fare is $3.50, get a schedule at the tourist office.

Capricorn Coast

The 47 km stretch of coast east of Rockhampton is known as the Capricorn Coast. The main town is Yeppoon (population 6500) which has a small Shell Museum. The gigantic Iwasaki Resort, Japanese planned and owned, with hotels, sporting facilities, museum and park is just north of Yeppoon. The first stage of the 20-year (and much delayed) project is still not open.

There's a flora and fauna sanctuary at Cooberrie Park, 15 km north of Yeppoon (open daily). At Cooee Bay, a couple of km south of Yeppoon, the annual Australian 'cooee' (and husband calling) championships are held each August – the judges row out to sea to determine who can 'cooee' the furthest. Rossyln Bay Harbour is the jumping off point for Great Keppel island. At Double Head there's a blowhole, and there are good views from Wreck Point and Bluff Point while at Emu Park, 14 km from Yeppoon, there's the 'Singing Ship' – a series of drilled tubes and pipes

which emit a low, moaning sound when there's a breeze blowing. There are beaches all along the coast.

Places to Stay

If you're planning to just day trip to Great Keppel you may decide that it's better to stay in Yeppoon, 40 km from Rockhampton. It's a quiet seaside resort with cheaper accommodation, and in summer much cooler weather, than Rockhampton.

There are half a dozen caravan parks along the coast from Yeppoon to Emu Park. The *Island View Park* (tel 39 6284) at Kinka Beach, *Cool Waters* (tel 39 6102) at the Esplanade and the *Lakeside* (tel 39 2356) at Causeway all have on-site vans or cabins. The *Poinciana Tourist Park* (tel 39 1601) at Cooee Bay has camping sites for $6.50.

Yeppoon doesn't have Rocky's range of old hotels but it's much better equipped for motels. Try the *Sail-Inn Motel* (tel 39 1130) on James St with rooms at $26/30. The pleasant *Tidewater Motel* (tel 39 1632) is on Normanby St right down by the seafront. Singles/doubles are $22/28 and rooms have cooking facilities; some units for four or more are also available. There are also lots of holiday flats and units all along the Capricorn Coast – the best routine is just to cruise along the coast and look for them.

Places to Eat

There are quite a few places to eat around Yeppoon including the *Reef 'n Beef* on Normanby St. It's just a take-away place with a few tables but does good quality, well prepared food. The *Railway Hotel*, further up James St has an extensive menu but the food can be rather erratic.

Great Keppel Island

Owned by TAA, Great Keppel has been heavily promoted as the young peoples' resort – 'get wrecked on Great Keppel',

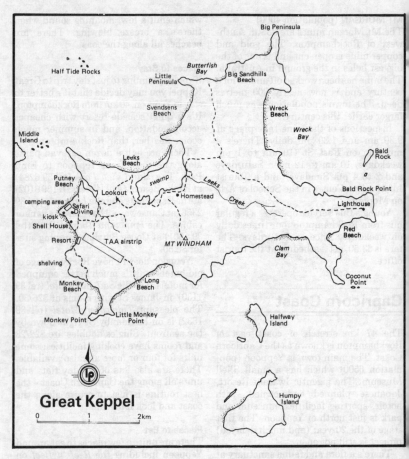

Great Keppel

0   1   2km

'after a holiday on Great Keppel you'll really need a holiday' etc, but you'll see all types and ages; singles and families, budgeters and those on the complete package. TAA has a variety of package tours to Great Keppel, depending where you start from seven days there will cost you around $900 to $1000 twin-share including airfare; in the high season it's about $150 more. The price includes accommodation, food and all the facilities. Great Keppel is heavy on entertainment – a resident rock band, lots of planned

activities, guaranteed exhaustion! People who go there usually reckon it's a lot of fun, although some recent reports suggest that TAA is trying to drive the low-budget crowd off the island with tricks such as imposing a cover charge in the bar for campers and hostellers.

Great Keppel is, however, one of the easiest and cheapest islands to visit if you are not on a package deal and Keppel – and this is a big plus – does have low budget places to stay. Although it's not actually on the reef, it is the equal of most islands up the coast. The island is 13 km offshore and it's one of my favourites – big enough that you won't see all of it in an afternoon but small enough to explore over a few days. In all it covers 14 square km and boasts 18 km of very fine beach.

It only takes a short stroll from the main resort area to find your own deserted stretch of white-sand beach. The water's clear, warm and beautiful. There is good coral at many points around the island, especially between Great Keppel and Humpy Island to the south. There are a number of fine bushwalking tracks plus, of course, the resort's famous entertainment value. There are maps available from the warden which are quite useful for orientation. Snorkelling equipment can also be hired from the warden for $5 and there's good coral diving at Monkey Beach.

The other islands in the Keppel group are all virtually undeveloped. Part of the reason for this is lack of water – only Great Keppel has a permanent water supply from wells. North Keppel island, nearly as big as Great Keppel, is dry. There is a fine underwater observatory by Middle Island, close to Great Keppel. A confiscated Taiwanese fishing junk was sunk next to the observatory to provide a haven for fish. A visit to the observatory costs $5, which includes the boat trip from the Great Keppel resort.

Things to Do

The resort hires out all its water sports equipment. Non-residents can rent snorkel gear at $4 for half a day and $8 for a full day. Scuba lessons and trips are offered. Behind the Shell House is a lookout. Beaches are found all over the island and in the centre you can visit an old restored homestead. Around the island you may spot wild goats. They were introduced in the early days so shipwrecked sailors would have something to eat. There's no indication however, as to how a tired, hungry, half-drowned man was supposed to catch a wild goat.

Places to Stay & Eat

You're looking at $70 or more per person per day at the resort but 90% of the people staying there will be on package tours. Great Keppel has a couple of terrific alternatives for the budget traveller. First of all there's the *Great Keppel Youth Hostel* which has room for 46 people and costs $6 a night. It's somewhat seedy but is still very popular and is often booked out for weeks ahead. You book the island hostel through the Rockhampton YH, but if you want to be certain of a berth it's wise to book through YH headquarters in Brisbane. The hostel is near the campground. Three times a week there's a $4 barbecue which is good value.

The other alternative is the *Wapparaburra Haven Tourist Park* (tel 39 1907) where you can camp for $5 for per person or, if you have a hostel card, $4 per person. They also have cabins which cost $45 single or double and $10 for each additional person; full kitchen facilities, laundry and linen. By mainland standards it's not cheap but for the islands it's a bargain.

At Wapparaburra there is a small kiosk open 8 am to 9 pm daily which sells fruit, vegetables, some meat, canned goods and basics. It's still a good idea to bring food with you as prices and selection on the mainland are better. In the evenings, in the small dining area, meals are available from $7.50 to $12.

Over at the resort there is also a takeaway counter with burgers at $1.80, meat pies etc. There's a daily lunch smorgasboard that's $10 for non guests, but I must say it looked good.

Half-way between the two, along the path, the *Shell House* with just a few shells actually, sells teas, coffee and homemade scones and cakes but they are not cheap. The bar and most entertainment at the resort is open to visitors and campers but a cover charge may apply. Get wrecked on the cheap.

Other possibilities include private camping at spots around the island but only at designated sites. South of Great

Keppel, there is camping on the very nice Humpy Island and it has well-water. The larger North Keppel has camping and a few cabins too, but again you must bring all your own food and do everything yourself. Though there is some well water here, it is limited and storage tanks are used. For either island (or any other) you need a permit from the parks people but it's free. Water taxis will supply transportation.

Getting There
There are a couple of companies operating boats across to Great Keppel and they can be booked in Rockhampton, Yeppoon or at Rossyln Harbour where the boats actually depart from. Rossyln Harbour is a little south of Yeppon on the Capricorn Coast.

Costs vary a bit between companies, the old *Seafari* at $14 return is the backpackers' special. The newer, faster ferries are $16. The tours vary from day to day and by the season but the basic trip is straight out to the island followed by an optional two-hour cruise around the island and/or visit to the underwater observatory. During the cruise you've got a chance to try boom-netting (getting soaked alongside!), coral viewing or snorkelling. One of the boat companies operates a hydrofoil as well as their regular launch. The *Keppel Kat* departs early and returns late, allowing for a reasonable day trip to Keppel.

You can get to Rossyln Harbour by car, by bus to Yeppoon from Rockhampton for $3 and then by taxi, or by a connecting bus to the boat service, which adds about $4 to the tour cost. There's a daily 80c car parking charge at Rossyln Harbour; alternatively you can leave your car at the Kempsea Car Park at Scenic Highway, Yeppoon for $1 per week.

From Rockhampton a day-trip package, including all transportation, costs $19. Tickets are available from the tourist office. For $22 you can take the *Romantique*, a catamaran, and have lunch on board.

Water taxis will drop off and pick-up at many of the islands for $30. Flying to Great Keppel costs $40 from Rockhampton one-way. There are also flying day-trips from about $40.

Capricornia

The country stretching inland from Rockhampton takes its name from its position, straddling the Tropic of Capricorn. There's a road that runs inland, virtually along the tropic, as far as Longreach (562 km inland) before turning north-west to meet the Townsville-Mt Isa road at Cloncurry. Although the area was first opened up by miners chasing gold and copper around Emerald, and sapphires around Anakie, it is cattle that provides the area's living today. To add to this, enormous coal deposits are starting to be exploited. The region straddles the central highlands and there are some interesting Aboriginal rock paintings to be found south in the Carnarvon Ranges.

EMERALD (population 4600)
Directly inland from Rockhampton, Emerald is known as the hub of the central Queensland highlands. It's an attractive town with streets lined with Moreton Bay Figs and a 1901 railway station classified by the National Trust. The country west of Emerald is noted for sapphires and other gems. They're found around Anakie and other nearby towns.

There's an arts and crafts centre in Rubyvale and the Desperado Mine can also be visited. On the way to Emerald from Rocky you pass through the coal mining centre of Blackwater (population 5400). North of Emerald is Clermont (population 1700) with the huge Blair Athol open-cut coal mine. There are a number of other coal mines in the Capricornia area or near to Mackay. South of Emerald is Springsure which is near the Old Rainworth Fort at Burnside.

CARNARVON NATIONAL PARK

Reached from Rolleston, south of Emerald, or from Injune, north of Roma, the rugged Carnarvon National Park is noted for its many Aboriginal rock paintings and carvings, some of which are very large. The park is in the middle of the Great Dividing Range and has some of the most spectacular scenery in Australia. The Carnarvon Gorge is particularly impressive.

AROUND BARCALDINE

Barcaldine (population 1400) is between Emerald and Longreach, another cattle centre the town also has a historical museum. North of here is Aramac (population 400), another small pastoral centre, while south is Blackall (population 1600). Near Blackall is Black's Palace, an Aboriginal site with burial caves and rock paintings.

LONGREACH (population 3000)

A modern and prosperous country town, Longreach's human population is considerably outnumbered by the neighbouring sheep population which is close to a million; there are a fair few cattle too. Although the Queensland & Northern Territory Air Services, perhaps better known as Qantas today, commenced operations in Winton, it was in Longreach that it got into its stride. The original Qantas hangar still stands at the airport. This hanger was also the first aircraft 'factory' in Australia – six DH-50 biplanes were assembled here in 1926.

Longreach was the starting point for one of Queensland's most colourful early crimes when in 1870 a bushranger sporting the title 'Captain Starlight' rounded up 1000 head of cattle (not his own, needless to say) and trotted them a mere 2400 km south through impossibly inhospitable country to South Australia where he sold them. He then made his way back to Queensland, was arrested and, unbelievably, acquitted – perhaps for sheer nerve.

The Australian Stockman's Hall of Fame & Outback Heritage Centre, opposite the airport, is being developed as a national tribute to the people who pioneered, developed, and recorded the history, of inland Australia. Stage 1, the Pioneer Cottage, is complete and is operating as an information centre and gift shop; open daily 9 am to 3 pm.

There is a *Youth Hostel* (tel 58 1529) in Longreach. It has 12 beds and charges $4.50 per night.

WINTON (population 1300)

On the road from Rockhampton via Emerald and Longreach to Mt Isa, Winton is a major sheep raising centre and also the railhead from which cattle are transported after being brought here from the channel country by road train. The small town has two claims to fame. Back in 1895 Australia's most famous poet-songwriter Banjo Patterson was on a station near here when he wrote Australia's best known ditty – *Waltzing Matilda*. Later Qantas started its operations here. These two diverse influences are united in the Qantilda pioneer museum! The countryside around Winton is rough and rugged with much wildlife, particularly brolgas, and sites with Aboriginal paintings.

Rockhampton to Mackay

The 343 km from Rockhampton to Mackay is one of the most boring stretches of the entire east coast Highway 1. For over 200 km from Marlborough north there is virtually nothing apart from a handful of roadhouses and a camp site at Lotus Creek. Not far north of Rocky, off the Bruce Highway, are Olsen's Capricorn Caverns, a series of limestone caves and passages. The large Cathedral Cavern is used for weddings and church services. Tours lead visitors though different parts of the underground

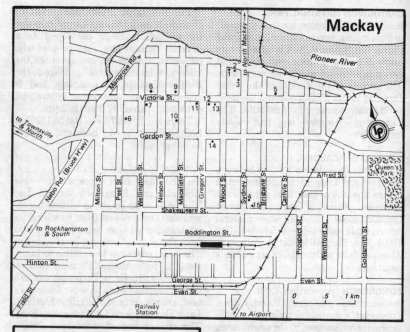

Mackay

Pioneer River

to North Mackay

Mangrove Rd

to Townsville
& North

Nebo Rd (Bruce H'wy)

Victoria St.

Gordon St.

Milton St.

Peel St.

Wellington St.

Nelson St.

Macalister St.

Gregory St.

Wood St.

Sydney St.

Brisbane St.

Carlyle St.

Alfred St.

Shakespeare St.

Boddington St.

Hinton St.

Prospect St.

Wentford St.

Goldsmith St.

George St.

Evan St.

Field St.

Railway Station

to Rockhampton
& South

to Airport

Queen's Park

0   .5   1 km

1 Post Office
2 QGTB
3 Ambassador Hotel
4 The Supper House
5 Pizza Napoli
6 Paradise Lodge Motel
7 Hotel Mackay
8 RACQ
9 Hotel Whitsunday
10 International Lodge
11 Ian Wood Travel (buses)
12 TAA
13 Ansett
14 CWA Hostel
15 Al Pappas

system daily except Saturday. You may see some of the hundreds of bats inhabiting the caves, or living tree roots, some of which are hundreds of metres long. Nearby, the Cammoo Caves, 22 km off the Bruce, feature stalactites, stalagmites and other unusual limestone formations.

Finally the road drops down over the range to the much more lush country around Sarina. This is the start of the sugar producing area around Mackay and there are also some fine beaches near the town.

Sarina (population 2800)

On the Bruce Highway, just 37 km south of Mackay, Sarina is noted for its excellent beaches and for the sugar-growing carried out extensively in the district. The Hay Point bulk loading terminal for coal is between here and Mackay. The coal produced from the gigantic coal fields inland from Mackay is railed down to the coast and exported from here.

Mackay
Population 35,400

Australia's 'sugar capital', Mackay is surrounded by sugar cane and processes a third of the total Australian sugar crop. The sugar is then loaded at the world's largest bulk sugar loading terminal. Sugar has been grown here since 1865. It's also a major coal port where a large part of Australia's coal production is shipped out, principally to Japan. The attractive town centre has many trees introduced from Sri Lanka.

Information

Mackay's tourist information centre is a Mackay attraction all by itself. Located on the Bruce Highway on the south side of town, it's housed in a Taiwanese fishing junk which was seized in 1976 when it was caught poaching clams within Australian territorial waters. The centre is open seven days a week from 9 am to 5 pm. The QGTB (tel 57 2292) is on River St, just down from the Forgan Bridge. It's open weekdays and Saturday mornings. More info at the Information Centre at 165 Shakespeare St. The RACQ (tel 57 2198) is at 214 Victoria St.

Orientation

Mackay is situated on the Pioneer River, the main streets of the town are laid out in a simple grid on the south side of the river, with wide streets and very long city blocks. The main intersecting streets are Wood and Victoria. The railway station is only a few blocks back from the centre and the airport is also fairly close to the city. The newer suburbs of Mackay are north of the river. Mackay's popular beaches are further north of the city.

Around Town

Good views over the harbour can be found at Mt Basset or at Rotary Lookout on Mt Oscar in North Mackay. The Rotary Lookout on Mt Oscar also gives good views. There are Botanic Gardens on Goldsmith St while Bayersville Zoo, by Harbour Rd, allows visitors to help feed the animals at 3.30 pm daily.

On weekdays at 3 pm you can make a 1½ hour tour of the Pleystowe Sugar Mill,

19 km from Mackay, during the mid-June to December cane crushing season. At 10.15 am and 3 pm you can also visit the Mackay Harbour sugar bulk terminals. Mackay is a jumping-off point for Barrier Reef cruises – particularly to Brampton Island. Mackay has good beaches at Blacks, Bucasia, Illawong, Lamberts and Shoal Point.

Places to Stay

Hostel *Backpackers Mackay* (tel 51 3728) is the youth hostel now that the one at Fairleigh is closed. It's at 32 Peel St, near Gordon St, four blocks from the bus station at the highway end of the city. There are 18 beds and a swimming pool and the nightly charge is $6. The *Tropical Caravan Park* (tel 52 1211), about a km beyond the Junk info centre on the south side of the city, has a couple of on-site vans held for hostellers until 9 pm. A bed costs $7 on a share-van basis.

For women only there's a *CWA Hostel* centrally located at 43 Gordon St near the corner of Wood St. Nightly costs are $8 in a share twin or $35 per week. The place is often full, however.

Hotels There's the usual selection of older hotels around the centre. The *Ambassador Hotel* (tel 57 2368) is at 2 Sydney St and has singles/doubles with breakfast for $15/20. It's quite pleasant and has a balcony and roof-top bar. The rooms are clean and have a sink. *McGuire's* (tel 57 2419) is on Wood St between Victoria and River Sts and costs $22/32. On the corner of Victoria and Peel Sts the *Austral Hotel* (tel 57 2639) is more basic with singles/doubles at $14/21. There are several others around the centre of town, two to try are the *Australian*, corner of Wood and Victoria Sts with a popular bar, or the *Cairns Hotel* at the same corner.

Motels The *Paradise Lodge Motel* (tel 51 1348) is conveniently central at 19 Peel St and pleasantly economical at $24/30 for singles/doubles. The rooms are straightforward but they're all air-con and have a TV and tea/coffee making facilities. A couple of blocks over at 40 MacAlister St the *International Lodge* (tel 51 1022) is even more central, similarly equipped and priced at $22/30. A few dollars more, the *Mackay Townhouse* (tel 57 6985) is at 73 Victoria St.

There's a whole string of motels along Nebo Rd, the main highway out of Mackay which runs past the junk and on to Rockhampton. Some cheaper motels along here include *Cool Palms* (tel 57 5477) at 4 Nebo Rd, fairly close to the centre; nightly costs are $30/32 with breakfast. The *City Gates Motel* is on Broadsound Rd and is budget priced at $24/25.

Opposite the junk on Nebo Rd the *Boomerang Hotel* (tel 52 1755) has motel units at $22/28.

Camping The *Central Caravan Park* (tel 57 6141) is at 15 Malcomson St, just across the river in North Mackay. Camping costs $6 and there are also on-site vans and cabins. At 152 Nebo Rd on the way out of town the *Premier Holiday Village* (tel 57 6976) is well equipped with camp sites at $7, on-site vans at $15, cabins at $20 and holiday units at $29. There are quite a few other sites in and around Mackay, at the beach suburbs and along the Hibiscus Coast.

Places to Eat

Counter Meals The *Hotel Mackay*, on the corner of Wellington and Victoria Sts, does cheap counter meals ($3.50 to $4) at lunch time Monday to Sunday and evenings too, Wednesday to Sunday.

The *Ambassador Hotel* overlooks the river from the corner of River and Sydney Sts. There's a terrace upstairs which is a popular place for a drink and the hotel does counter-style food every night of the week in the $6.50 to $9 range; lots of fish. Downstairs there are cheap counter lunches.

The big *Hotel Whitsunday*, on the corner of Victoria and Macalister Sts, does pretty basic counter meals for $3 to $4 in the public bar, or fancier food with a serve yourself salad table in the *Bistro Room*. Other pubs with counter food in the $4.50 to $6.50 range include *McGuire's* on Wood St and the *Australian Hotel* on the corner of Wood and Victoria.

If you're staying in one of the motels or campsites along Nebo Rd there are a couple of places which do counter meals. The *Boomerang Hotel*, opposite the junk, has meals which are around $5 to $6.

Snack Bars & Take-Aways Pretty slim pickings in this department. The *Tourist Chicken Bar* at 94 Wood St is a big place open to 8 pm. Curried chicken with rice for $3 plus all the usual stuff like fish & chips. Or try the *Capitol Cafe* at 36 Sydney St for sandwiches, fruit salad and the like. *Penny's Pantry* at 7 Wood St is a basic sandwich bar.

Restaurants The *Supper House* is a small, rather quaint place in an inconspicuous white bungalow at 109A Sydney St near Shakespeare St. Most meals are $5 to $7 including a salad and drink; it has crepes, Mexican and vegetarian. It's BYO and is open from 7 pm until late, nightly. Backgammon and chess boards are available.

Al Pappas on the corner of Alfred and Sydney Sts, a couple of blocks back from the central area, is a pleasant little place with pizzas and other Italian food to eat-in or take-away. The pizzas are really very good; small in the $3.50 to $4 bracket, large in the $4 to $5 range plus there are pasta dishes from $4.50 and up. Similar take-away food can be found at *Pizza Napoli* at 43 Victoria St for around $6.50 a main course.

For Chinese you've got several choices. The best bargain is probably the *Lychee Gardens* at the corner of Victoria and Wellington Sts with a lunch smorgasbord from Tuesday to Friday for $6 and a Sunday night special for $7. Others are the *Aspara* at 68 Victoria St and the more expensive *Mandarin* at 51 Wood St.

Entertainment

The *Ambassador Hotel* with its pleasant roof-top terrace is a popular place for a drink. There's free entertainment at the *Hotel Mackay*. The *Pacific Hotel* out at the beach at Eimeo also has entertainment and there's live music at the *Hotel Whitsunday*.

Getting There

Air Mackay is on the regular Brisbane-Cairns coastal route. Fares include Cairns $138, Townsville $97, Rockhampton $89 and Brisbane $159 (standby $128). In Mackay, Ansett (tel 57 1555) are at 97 Victoria St, TAA (tel 57 1444) at 105-109 Victoria St.

Bus Ansett Pioneer and Greyhound both operate through Mackay on their daily services along the coast. From Brisbane it takes 17 hours for $52, from Cairns it's 12 hours for $33, from Townsville five hours for $25. McCafferty's also operate Brisbane-Mackay but their service operates by the inland route from Rockhampton, through Emerald and Moranbah. Ian Wood Travel (tel 57 2858) on the corner of Victoria and Gregory Sts handles all three companies in Mackay.

Rail The six times weekly Sunlander between Brisbane and Cairns goes through Mackay, either at 4 am or 12 noon northbound, or about 10.30 pm or 7.30 am south-bound, depending on what day it is. The fare from Brisbane is $92 in 1st class, $61 in economy and the trip takes 20 hours. Southbound it takes 16 hours from Cairns and costs $74 in 1st and $49 in economy. The station is on Boddington St, tel 57 2551.

Getting Around

Airport Transport Mackay's airport is conveniently close to the centre; count on about $4 for a taxi to the city. Rental cars here are neither cheap or plentiful. You need to call ahead and reserve one at least a day in advance if possible. It will cost you about $50 to go to Airlie Beach in a small car – and that doesn't include the petrol! Avis, Budget and Hertz have counters at the airport.

Tours There are lots of half-day and day-tours in and around Mackay to the sugar mills, the national parks around Mackay and other local attractions. Ask at any travel agent for details.

Air tours include scenic flights out to the reef, flights landing on Bushy Atoll and on alternate Mondays you can go along on regular station runs to remote stations and coalfields inland from Mackay.

You can also book island cruises from Mackay – Brampton Island $18, Hayman Island $25 or the Barrier Reef $50.

Mackay to Proserpine

There are a number of places of interest along the road from Mackay to Townsville but the main attraction is the beautiful Whitsunday Island group. To reach the Whitsundays you turn off the Bruce Highway at Proserpine and drive down to Shute Harbour, the departure point for Whitsunday cruises. See the Whitsunday section for more details. You can also, if you've got the dollars to spare, fly from Mackay to the Whitsundays or to Brampton Island which is about mid-way between Mackay and the Whitsundays.

COAL MINES

The massive open-cut Queensland coal mines are about 200 km inland from Mackay at Blackwater, Goonyella and Peak Downs. Much of the coal is exported from the Hay Point coal terminal, 40 km south of Mackay. Free tours of the mines are available but it is usually necessary to phone ahead and book. The Blackwater tour bus departs from the main office on Wednesday at 10 am (tel 82 5166). The Goonyella tour bus departs from the Moranbah Town Square at 10 am Tuesday, the Peak Downs bus from the same location at 10 am Thursday. Ring 50 7122 for Goonyella, 50 7233 for Peak Downs.

NEAR MACKAY

The Eungella National Park is the largest national park in Queensland, it's 85 km directly inland from Mackay straddling the Clarke Range. There are fine lookouts in the park. The Eungella road runs through the Finch Hatton Gorge.

Cape Hillsborough National Park is 55 km up the coast and has walking tracks through the rainforest plus good beaches and camping areas. One of the most popular walking tracks is the Hidden Valley trail. To get to the park, turn off just before Seaforth from where it is 10 km on a gravel road to the park entrance.

BRAMPTON ISLAND

Mountainous Brampton Island covers eight square km – the island is a national park and wildlife sanctuary with lush forests surrounded by coral reefs. It is part of the Cumberland Group and is connected to nearby Carlisle Island by a reef which you can walk across at low tide. Accommodation on Brampton costs $50 to $95 per person. The island is reached by air or launch ($12) from Mackay. There are day trips from Mackay to the island.

NEWRY ISLAND

There are day trips three days a week from Victor Creek to pleasant Newry Island – a little known tropical island with good swimming, bushwalks and plenty of koalas. Departures are at 11 am on Wednesday, Saturday and Sunday and accommodation is available for $35 to $70 including meals.

Sugar Growing

Sugar is easily the most visible crop from Mackay north, past Cairns, up the Queensland coast. Sugar was a success almost from the day it was introduced in the region back in 1865 but the early days of the Queensland sugar industry have a distinctly unsavoury air as the plantations were initially worked by Pacific islanders who were virtually forced to work on the canefields. 'Blackbirding', as this slave trading was known, took a long time to be stamped out.

Today cane growing is a highly mechanised business and visitors are welcome to inspect the crushing plants during the harvesting season from August. The most spectacular part of the operation is the firing of the canefields in which rubbish is burnt off by spectacular night time fires – which also have the advantage of chasing off snakes and other unwelcome inhabitants of the fields.

Mechanical harvesters cut and gather the cane which is then transported to the sugar mills, often on narrow gauge railway lines laid through the canefields. These lines are a familiar sight throughout the cane country. The cane is then shredded and passed through a series of crushers. The extracted juice is heated and cleaned of impurities and then evaporated to form a syrup. The next process reduces the syrup to molasses and low grade sugar. Further refining stages end with the sugar loaded into bulk containers for export.

Sugar production is a remarkably efficient process. The crushed fibres, known as bagasse, are burnt as fuel; impurities separated off from the juice are used as fertilisers; and the molasses are used either to produce ethanol or as stock feed.

Proserpine
Population: 3000

A sugar-growing centre on the Bruce Highway, 125 km north of Mackay, this is the jumping-off point for Airlie Beach and the Whitsunday Islands. That's really Proserpine's function in life – to mark the place where you turn off the main road. From 9 am to 5 pm on weekdays during the sugar season (June to November) you can take a guide-yourself tour of the Proserpine Sugar Mills. There's also a Folk Museum in

Marathon St open 9.30 am to 12 noon, 2 to 5 pm from Friday to Wednesday.

Places to Stay & Eat

The *Plaza Lodge* (tel 45 1396) at 9 Hinschen St was once a sort of unofficial hostel but I recommend that you stay away. First you get verbal abuse, then the door slammed in your face. Who needs it?

The *Whitsunday Youth Hostel* (tel 45 1200) at 32 Herbert St keeps some beds for YHA members until 7 pm. The nightly cost is $7 if you share a room (an extra dollar if haven't got a sheet sleeping bag), $10 for a single. There is a kitchen, laundry facilities, and snacks are available in the restaurant.

The *Palace Hotel* on Main St has a few rooms and the cheaper motels include the *A&A Motel* (tel 45 1888) and the *Solaris Motel* (tel 45 1288) both on the Bruce Highway and both at around $28/34. There are also campsites available.

You can get a pizza at *Angels Restaurant* on Chapman St just off Main St. The *Midtown Café* has standard café meals and take-aways.

Getting There

Air Proserpine has an airport but it is not on either the TAA or Ansett itineraries. This is important for travellers on round Australia tickets since they cannot fly through Proserpine without extra charges for the Air Queensland flights. Air Queensland fly Townsville-Proserpine ($84) and Mackay-Proserpine ($64). There is only one flight per week, departing on Saturdays. Air Whitsunday uses the small airstrip near Shute Harbour.

Bus Ansett Pioneer and Greyhound both run through Proserpine on their daily Brisbane-Cairns service. The fare from Brisbane is $60, from Cairns $33, from Townsville $21. Mackay-Proserpine takes 1½ hours and there are several buses a day. The one-way fare is $10.50.

There is also a regular bus service between Proserpine, Airlie Beach and Shute Harbour. There are five trips a day in each direction. It's quite feasible to stay in Proserpine and make day trips from Shute Harbour as there are bus departures from Proserpine scheduled to connect with boat departures from Shute Harbour. Proserpine-Airlie Beach one way is $5 ($7.70 return), Airlie Beach-Shute Harbour is $1.25 ($2.25 return). Departures are from opposite the Hotel Proserpine on Mill St.

Rail Proserpine is on the six times weekly Brisbane-Cairns Sunlander service. The fare from Brisbane is $97 in 1st, $65 in economy. It takes 2½ hours between Mackay and Proserpine and costs $11.30.

Airlie Beach & Shute Harbour

Airlie Beach is the main accommodation centre on the mainland opposite the Whitsundays. If you plan to stay on the mainland and see the islands by day-tripping out to them you can stay here, in adjoining Cannonvale (back towards Proserpine) or along towards Shute Harbour. It's 25 km from the Bruce Highway turn-off at Proserpine to Airlie Beach and another eight km from here to Shute Harbour. There is a wide variety of accommodation and loads of ticket agents selling all the tours and trips out to the reef. There's a National Park campsite between Airlie Beach and Shute Harbour. Airlie Beach has grown phenomenally over the past 10 years.

There's a wildlife sanctuary and an adjoining aquarium up from Airlie Beach. The sanctuary has a collection of Australian wildlife and birds; lorikeets fly in to be fed at 3 pm daily. Mandalay Coral Gardens have fish and coral on display in tanks. Other attractions in and around the town

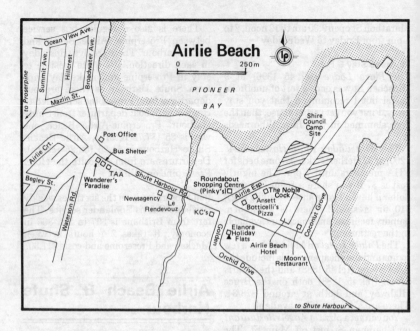

include the beautiful Cedar Creek Falls, off the road eight km along from Proserpine. The pools above the falls are popular for skinny-dipping.

The Conway National Park is densely forested and relatively unspoilt. There are some limited walking trails and some fine views across the Whitsunday Passage. The highest point is 563 metres. The park separates the passage from Repulse Bay, named by Captain Cook who strayed into the bay thinking it was the main passage.

There are some good beaches in the vicinity – Conway Beach to the south, Earlando and Dingo Beach to the north. Surprisingly, there is no real beach at Airlie Beach – something the local government would like to remedy. They are even talking about creating one!

Airlie Beach is the centre of activities during the annual Whitsunday Village Fun Race (for cruising yachts) each August or September. The festivities include a Miss Figurehead competition where the contestants traditionally compete topless. A more regular event is Tuesday and Thursday night toad races at the Airlie Beach Hotel. Rent-a-toad will hire you a steed if you haven't got your own. Beware of stingers in the water at Airlie Beach from October to April.

The noticeboard outside the newsagent on the main street lists rides, rooms to rent and so on. Many people come to Airlie Beach looking for casual work in hotels, restaurants or on the boats. Usually there are not enough jobs to go around. There is a sort of tourist office beside Le Rendezvous Restaurant with a pile of pamphlets on reef trips, etc.

Places to Stay

Hostels *Backpackers Hostel* (tel 46 7267) is on the corner of Lewis and Lamond Sts overlooking Airlie, two streets up from the shopping centre and it has a swimming pool and barbecue area. It has a view of

Airlie Beach and is open 24 hours a day. Nightly charge is $7 and there are 30 beds.

At the *Reef Oceanic Village* (tel 46 6137), a large new hotel complex, there is a budget section with dorm beds at $7. The village is just off the main road in Cannonvale, on the left side heading towards Airlie Beach, you can't miss the sign. There has been some talk of a large new hostel for Airlie Beach.

Hotels, Motels & Holiday Flats Airlie Beach's rapid expansion has put a bit of a squeeze on accommodation. Finding reasonably priced places to stay can sometimes be a bit difficult. Apart from the regular advertised places there are also quite a few holiday flats which start at $35, maybe $5 less in the off-season.

At Harper St, Airlie Beach, just a few steps back from the main road, *Elanora Holiday Units* (tel 46 6482) are simple and straightforward but well equipped with cooking facilities and other mod cons. Prices vary according to season but range from $32 for two people, $37 for three and $42 for four. The larger rooms can be less, especially when things are slow. The units are good value and central. The *Airlie Beach Hotel-Motel* (tel 46 6233) offers the usual motel facilities at $28/37.

Back in Cannonvale you could try *Cannonvale Villas* (tel 46 6177), probably the cheapest in the area with singles/doubles $20/25. There are a lot of other motels around Airlie Beach but you'll be pushed to find anything cheap. Most places are in the upper $30s and low $40s while some go to $50 and above. See camping below for more possibilities in cabins and on-site vans.

Camping Fortunately camping is much more straightforward. There are quite a few campsites in Cannonvale and Airlie Beach and more strung along the road to Shute Harbour. Come early though, they're often packed out. The National Park camp, almost down at Shute Harbour, is probably the best bargain although its range of facilities is not very wide. In Jubilee Pocket on the Shute Harbour Rd the *Island Gateway Village* (tel 46 6228) costs $5 to camp and there are on-site vans at $18. *Island Trader Cabins* are $22/24; good value.

There's a municipal campsite right in Airlie Beach where camping costs $4. The town council has been talking of getting rid of this very central campground in the next couple of years and transforming it into a park. Amongst the other popular sites is the convenient *Pioneer Park* (tel 46 5266) in Cannonvale.

Three km from the post office on the Shute Harbour Road the *Reef Oceana Village* has camping for $3, on-site tents for $4 and four-bed rooms at $7 per person. It has a swimming pool, laundry and licensed restaurant. The manager is friendly if a bit ineffectual at keeping the place clean.

Places to Eat

Food generally tends to be rather expensive, so it's more economical to buy supplies from the supermarkets and fix your own. *Airlie Beach Pizza Parlour* on Shute Harbour Rd, in front of Ansett, is surprisingly good although a bit expensive; pizzas from $5 to $8.50.

Noble Cock on Airlie Esplanade has take-aways of chicken and beef in rolls or as full meals. The portions are large and there are a few tables across the street to eat at.

The *Coffee Lounge* behind the Post Office offers inexpensive breakfasts and light meals, with a view. *Pinky's*, at the corner of Shute Harbour and Airlie Esplanade, is a moderately priced, trendy sort of spot with typical salads, quiches and crepes.

Moon's Seafood Restaurant on the corner of the Coconut Grove and Shute Harbour is a long standing, reputable dining room with dinners from $12 without wine. *Le Rendezvous, La Perouse* are also expensive. *La Perouse* has a French cook and a $15 dinner special. *KC's Chargrill* (no relation to KC's in Kathmandu!) has steaks for $10.50.

Dolphins, in the Palm Plaza, with a nice outdoor courtyard, is cheaper. Dinners are about $8 with a choice including Mexican, fish, satays; cheap lunches. In Cannonvale *Voyeurs* does Mexican, Spanish and Indian food.

Entertainment

There are night cruises and visits to the resort islands, music and toad races (this is Queensland) at the Airlie Beach Hotel or the Whitsunday Village. The cheap and popular Airlie Beach Hotel is the place for rock and pop music.

Getting There

See the Proserpine section for details on getting to Airlie Beach – basically you get there via Proserpine although there are direct flights from Mackay to the Whitsunday airstrip at Shute Harbour. Although they do not fly here TAA and Ansett both have offices in Airlie Beach because of their big holiday operations. TAA (tel 46 6273) are in the Wanderers Resort on Shute Harbour Rd; Ansett (tel 46 6255) is now in the Airlie Beach Travel Agency on the Esplanade. Almost all the island tours leave from Shute Harbour, see the Whitsunday Islands section following. For Greyhound tickets go to Whitsunday Travel Centre on Shute Harbour. Buses leave on the other side of the street from the bus shelter at the edge of town.

Getting Around There are a number of land-based tours around the peninsula although it's out on the water that has the real interest. You can rent bikes from Toys & Books on the corner of Shute Harbour Rd and the Esplanade in Airlie Beach – they're open Monday to Saturday and Sunday mornings. The usual rent-a-car agencies operate in Shute Harbour. Avis rents Mokes at $24 a day, insurance

included but there is a distance charge on top. Smaller outfits are a bit cheaper. Half-day bus tours to some man-made attractions are about $15. The coral gardens and bird sanctuary can be included.

Whitsunday Islands

The 70-odd islands of the Whitsunday group are probably the best known and most developed of the Barrier Reef islands. The group was named by Captain Cook who sailed through here on 3 July, 1770. They're scattered on both sides of the Whitsunday Passage. All the islands in the group are within 50 km of Shute Harbour, the jumping-off point for the many cruises through the group. The actual barrier reef is at least 60 km out from Shute Harbour; Hook Reef is the nearest part of the reef. Many of the Whitsundays are National Parks. The large block of mainland national park opposite them, stretching from Airlie Beach south to Conway, is known as the Conway Range National Park.

Curiously, the Whitsundays are misnamed – Captain Cook didn't really sail through them on Whitsunday. When he got back to England his meticulously kept log was a day out because he had not allowed for crossing the international date line! As he sailed through the Whitsundays and on further north Cook was also unaware of the existence of the Barrier Reef, although he realised there was something to the east of his ship making the water unusually calm. It wasn't until he ran aground on the Endeavour reef, near Cooktown, that he finally found out about the Great Barrier Reef.

Camping on the Islands

Although accommodation on the resort islands is expensive there is one cheaper location – Palm Bay on Long Island. In addition you can camp on any of the uninhabited islands, except those with a

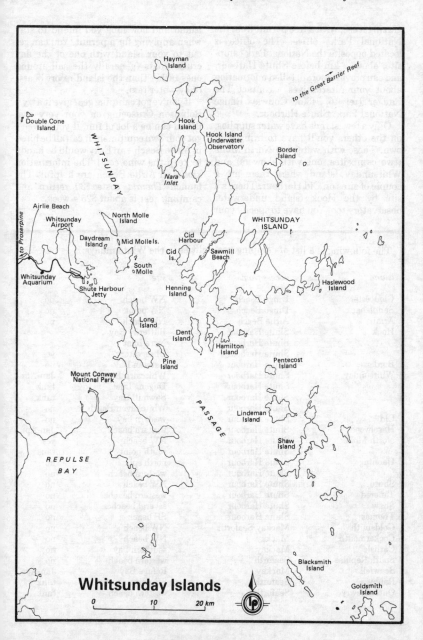

Hayman Island

to the Great Barrier Reef

Double Cone Island

WHITSUNDAY

Hook Island

Hook Island Underwater Observatory

Border Island

Nara Inlet

Airlie Beach

Whitsunday Airport

North Molle Island

Daydream Island

Mid Molle Is.

WHITSUNDAY ISLAND

Cid Harbour

Cid Is.

Sawmill Beach

South Molle

to Proserpine

Whitsunday Aquarium

Shute Harbour Jetty

Henning Island

Haslewood Island

Long Island

Dent Island

Hamilton Island

Pentecost Island

Pine Island

Mount Conway National Park

PASSAGE

Lindeman Island

Shaw Island

REPULSE BAY

Blacksmith Island

Whitsunday Islands

0   10   20 km

Goldsmith Island

grazing lease, with a free permit from the National Parks office. The office is located opposite the National Park campsite, about a km before Shute Harbour, and can provide more detailed information about your alternatives – contact The Ranger (tel 46 9430), Conway Range National Park, Shute Harbour.

Only a few islands have water supplies, on the others you'll have to bring your own. Those with water are North Molle (two campsites, one with showers) and Whitsunday Island where there are a couple of sites on Cid Harbour. There's a site by the Hook Island underwater observatory too. You have to specify your

island and how long you intend to stay when applying for a permit. You can get out to your island with one of the day cruise boats (generally the sail-around ones rather than the island resort boats) or by water taxi.

If you've got camping gear give it a try – Robinson Crusoeing on your very own island can be a lot of fun. If you haven't got your own equipment it can all be hired in Airlie Beach – an Esky would be handy to keep the wine cool! The information kiosks in Airlie Beach are helpful. The launch *Themla* costs $30 return and camping gear is about $25 a week.

The following is a list of camping possibilities in the Whitsundays:

island	access from	site	water
Gloucester	Dingo Beach	NW beach	no
Saddleback	Dingo Beach	NW point	no
Armit	Airlie Beach	NW beach	no
Hook	Shute Harbour	Butterfly Bay	
	Shute Harbour	Nara Inlet	
	Shute Harbour	Observatory	yes
Border	Shute Harbour	Cateran Bay	no
Whitsunday	Shute Harbour	Whitcairn Beach	Jan-Apr
	Shute Harbour	Dugong Inlet	tank
	Shute Harbour	Sawmill Bay	tank
	Shute Harbour	Whitehaven Beach	no
Cid	Shute Harbour	western bay	no
Haselwood	Shute Harbour	western beach	Jan-Apr
North Molle	Shute Harbour	NW beach	yes
	Shute Harbour	south point	tank
Henning	Shute Harbour	north spit	no
	Shute Harbour	western beach	no
Shute	Shute Harbour	NW beach	no
Tancred	Shute Harbour	western beaches	no
Shaw	Shute Harbour	several beaches	no
Thomas	Shute Harbour	SE beach	no
Goldsmith	Mackay/Seaforth	NW beach	no
Cockermouth	Mackay	NW beach	no
Carlisle	Mackay	southern bay	no
South Repulse	Seaforth	western beach	no
Scawfell	Mackay	Refuge Bay	Jan-Apr
Rabbit	Seaforth	SE point	tank
Outer Newry	Seaforth	western beach	tank

HAYMAN ISLAND

Hayman Island is one of the oldest Barrier Reef resort islands as it was first established in the early '50s. The most northerly of the Whitsunday group it has an area of four square km and rises to 250 metres above sea level. The resort is fronted by a wide, shallow reef which emerges from the water at low tide.

There are a number of small, uninhabited islands very close to Hayman. You can walk out to Arkhurst Island at low tide or from Langford Island, which has some fine coral around it, walk across to Bird Island. Black Island (they like to call it Bali Ha'i) is between Hayman and Hook Island.

There are a number of bushwalks around the island including an eight km circuit, two km across to Blue Pearl Bay or 3.5 km to Dolphin Point at the northern tip of the island. It's less than a km from the resort up to the Whitsunday Passage lookout overlooking Arkhurst Island.

Because the shallow reef is so extensive a toy train takes visitors in from the long jetty to the resort. Ansett has recently taken over the resort and has major plans to upgrade it. If you want to stay you can count on $70 to $110 per person per day depending on the room and the season ($60 standby).

Apart from the cruise boats you can also go out to Hayman by helicopter for $40 return – including transfer to Proserpine airport and lunch on the island – basically for those who really like helicopter rides.

SOUTH MOLLE

Largest of the Molle group of islands (four square km) South Molle is virtually virtually joined to Mid Molle and North Molle Islands. It has long stretches of sandy or coral beach and is criss-crossed by a network of walking tracks. Highest point is 198 metre Mt Jeffrey but the climb up Spion Kop is also worthwhile. Accommodation at the resort costs from $55 in the basic *Sealife Lodge* but it's

generally $70 to $90 per person in the other rooms. Standby rates can lower this considerably, at times to $60 double, but food costs are often not included in the daily rate so make sure to check.

DAYDREAM ISLAND

Also known as West Molle this small island is only a couple of hundred metres across at its widest point. It's about two km long. The island suffers from severe water shortages and at one time was abandoned as a resort. It now has the most delightful swimming pool on any of the resort islands – a long convoluted affair with a bar-island in the middle. Accommodation costs, per person, are $70 to $90 per day (standby $50).

LONG ISLAND

One of the closer in and least commercial of the resort islands, Long Island is about 11 km long but no more than 1½ km wide. It was named by Matthew Flinders. There are actually three centres on the island. *Happy Bay* is the main resort with a long expanse of a proper tropical-island sort of beach. This is where the cruise boats come to but it's not a flashy international sort of resort, more a quiet family type of place and the prices are also somewhat lower. At Happy Bay daily costs per person are $60 to $80 including all meals.

There are 13 km of walking tracks around the island and if you head south you'll soon come to another centre, *Palm Bay*. This is the cheapest island resort on the Whitsundays with fairly simple, separate, little units with cooking facilities. You can get some supplies here or bring them over from the mainland. At Palm Bay (tel 46 9400) a unit for four people costs from $70 to $75 a day, it's wise to book well ahead. Guests at Palm Bay are able to use facilities at the Happy Bay resort.

A third choice is *Whitsunday 100*, a new Ansett resort geared toward the youth market. It's relatively small and offers all manner of activity and lots of entertainment. Mini yachts are available to guests. Accommodation is $70 to $100 per person. Ansett takes advantage of the new airstrip at nearby Hamilton Island to service Whitsunday 100. The Mackay-Whitsunday 100 flight is $130 return. The launch fare from Shute Harbour is $20 return.

LINDEMAN ISLAND

This is the oldest of the Barrier Reef resorts, it was first established back in 1929 and covers eight square km. This is another family-style resort with lots of entertainment for kids. The island has 20 km of walking trails and its highest point is 210 metre Mt Oldfield.

There are a lot of small islands dotted around Lindeman and it's easy to get across to some of them. With plenty of little beaches and secluded bays it's no hassle at all to find one all to yourself. Costs per person, including all meals, are $65 to $85 per day depending on the room and the season. Regular flights to Lindeman with Lindeman Aerial Services (tel 079 57-3326) are $90 return from Mackay and $80 from Proserpine. The launch fare from Shute Harbour is $20 return.

HAMILTON ISLAND

One of the newest and most ambitious resort developments in the Whitsundays, Hamilton Island boasts the largest fresh-water swimming pool in Australia, a 400-boat marina and an extensive (and expensive) range of entertainment possibilities: helicopter joy rides, game fishing, parasailing, scuba diving, etc. Hamilton is fairly hilly, more than five square km in area, and rises to 200 metres at Passage Peak. The resort includes a fauna reserve, restaurants, shopping facilities, squash courts, sauna and hotel.

Prices vary from $140 for two people in a Polynesian-style *bure*, to $300 for six people in a three-bedroom apartment with all mod-cons and full cooking facilities (both prices daily, room only). Flights from Proserpine are $45, from Mackay $75 and the launch from Shute Harbour is $25 return.

HOOK ISLAND

Second largest of the Whitsunday Group, Hook Island has an area of 53 square km and rises to 450 metres at Hook Peak and 376 metres at Mt Sydney. There are a number of beaches dotted around the island but no resort development. It does, however, have the Hook Island Under-water Observatory, one of the most popular attractions in the Whitsundays. You descend to a viewing area in the reef, 10 metres below the surface. It's the next best thing to diving since you're right in there with the fish – not just looking down from above, as with glass-bottom boats.

Hook Island also has a camping area near the observatory. If you want to stay out on the islands without the resort costs and without doing the Robinson Crusoe, away from the world bit, then this is a good place to go. Once the day trip crowds have gone back to Shute Harbour it's very peaceful and pleasant. The beautiful, fjord-like Nara Inlet on Hook Island is a very popular deep-water anchorage for visiting yachties.

WHITSUNDAY ISLAND

The largest of the Whitsunday islands, Whitsunday covers 109 square km and rises to 438 metres at Whitsunday Peak. There is no resort development on the island but Whitehaven Beach on the north-east coast is probably the longest and finest in the group and at Sawmill Beach on the south-east side there is a national park camping area which has freshwater available.

CID ISLAND

East of Whitsunday island the Cid Harbour, wedged between Hook and Whitsunday Islands, was the deep-water anchorage used by part of the US Navy fleet before the Battle of the Coral Sea, turning point in the Pacific theatre of WW II. Today, visiting ocean cruise liners anchor here.

OTHER ISLANDS

There's a kerosene-lit lighthouse on Dent Island, guiding ships through the passage. Near Lindeman Island, Pentecost Island was named by Captain Cook and has a 208-metre-high cliff face shaped remarkably like an Indian head.

GETTING AROUND

Sea There are all types of boat trips out to the islands of the Whitsundays and beyond them to the Barrier Reef. The trips all depart from Shute Harbour, the end of the road from Airlie Beach. You can bus there from Airlie Beach or leave your car in the car park for $1.

You can divide the trips into several categories. First of all there are the straightforward go-see-the-islands cruises. You go to resort island A have an hour or two there to sample the beach, pool and bar then carry on to do the same at island B. Somewhere along the line you usually get a barbecue lunch thrown in. An excursion to the underwater observatory at Hook Island is usually also part of the picture. Typical prices for these cruises are $30. They're great if you want to make an on-the-spot assessment of the resort swimming pools.

A variation on these resort island trips is one that just takes you out to one island and leaves you there for the day. A day on Hayman Island, for example, is $20 including lunch, Lindeman is $30. There are similar day trips to Whitsunday and Daydream. Two-day all-inclusive tours start from $135.

Category two is the nowhere-in-particular trips, usually in smaller boats, you stay away from the resort islands, perhaps try a beach here, a bit of snorkelling there, maybe some fishing somewhere else. Many of the boats operating these trips are yachts. A day on the former America's cup contender

Gretel is yours for $25 for example. Other boats can be cheaper.

There are also outer reef trips where you power out to the outer reef for a spot of walking on the reef itself and perhaps a bit of snorkelling too. For these trips you need a fast boat to get you out to the reef in the minimum time possible and departure times are dependent on the tides. They're generally more expensive (you're looking at $65) but getting out to the reef is really an other-worldly experience that, if you can afford it, should not be missed. There are also week long sailing/camping trips with all food and gear provided but these are not cheap.

Finally there are all sorts of do-your-own-thing odds and ends. You could get yourself dropped off at an uninhabited island from one of the nowhere in particular boats or by the Water Taxi (tel 46 9202) from the Shute Harbour Jetty, or go out for a fishing trip. Or charter a boat and sail yourself. You can get small fishing dinghies with outboard motors from $18 a day, 22-foot yachts for $80 a day, catamarans at Airlie Beach for $10 an hour, big cruising yachts for a small fortune!

Air Scenic flights over the Whitsundays can run from $20, in a Tiger Moth $30, all the way up to $60 for a flight right out over the Barrier Reef – check with Coconut Airways or Air Whitsunday. For $100 Air Whitsunday will fly you out to Hardy Lagoon on the reef in their amphibious aircraft, there they have a glass bottom boat anchored and you get 1½ hours of coral viewing, reef walking and snorkelling before flying back.

Whitsundays to Townsville

BOWEN (population 7500)
The first settlement in north Queensland,

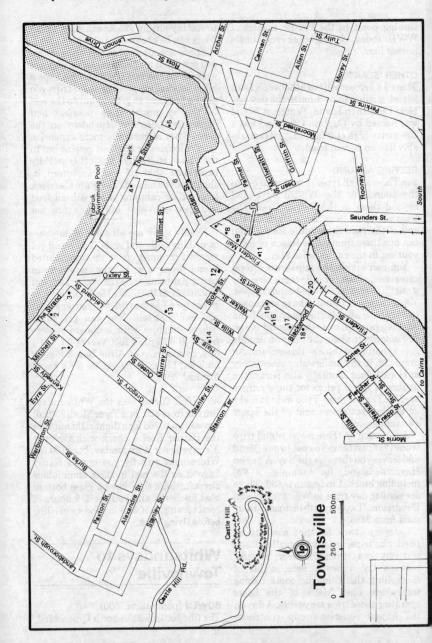

Townsville

Castle Hill

Castle Hill Rd.

0   250   500m

1	Allen Hotel
2	Seaview Hotel
3	Strand Motel
4	Waterfall
5	Greyhound Terminal
6	Magnetic Island Ferry
7	GPO
8	QGTB
9	Townsville International Hotel
10	Historic Swing Bridge (not used)
11	Ansett & Ansett Pioneer
12	Townsville Tourist Office
13	Wills Street Hostel
14	Coral House
15	Ansett & Ansett Pioneer (again)
16	Civic House
17	People's Palace
18	Sunseeker Guest House
19	Railway Station
20	Great Northern Hotel

dating from 1861, Bowen has a good historical museum at 22 Gordon St with exhibits relating to the town's early history. It's open from 10.30 am to 4 pm on weekdays, 3 to 5 pm on Saturdays. Beaches around Bowen are Queens Beaches, Greys Bay, Murray Bay, Horseshoe Bay, Rose Bay and Kings Beach – there are lots of beaches around Bowen and some of them are really excellent, beautiful beaches and often as secluded as you could ask for.

AYR (population 8800)
On the Burdekin delta Ayr is, once again, a sugar town. Rice is also grown in the area. On Wilmington St the House of Australian Nature has displays of orchids, shells, butterflies and beetles. It's open 8 am to 5 pm daily.

Across the Burdekin River is Home Hill (population 3200) with a historical museum. Between Ayr and Townsville you pass the Australian Institute of Marine Science on Cape Ferguson – phone 78 9211 to arrange to visit it.

Mt Elliot National Park, only 25 km south of Townsville, has good swimming holes in the Alligator Creek Gorge. There are also walking tracks, camping areas and an information kiosk here. Alligator

Creek Antique Museum is open Sunday to Thursday from 9 am to 5 pm.

Townsville
Population: 86,000

The third largest city in Queensland and the main centre in the north of the state, Townsville is the port city for the agricultural and mining production of the vast inland region of northern Queensland. The town was founded in 1864 by Robert Towns, a sea captain who foresaw the need for a port for the growing cattle stations inland. Today Townsville is the site of the James Cook University.

The city is dominated by Castle Hill with a lookout perched on top, 290 metres above the city on the Ross Creek. From the lookout you get a fine view of the centre and across to Magnetic Island.

The town has recently been heavily promoting itself and encouraging major development. In 1988 Townsville is to host the South Pacific Festival of the Arts. Sheraton International is building a hotel-casino and a massive 'Barrier Reef Wonderland' complex including an aquarium, museum and a super-wide screen film theatre is on the books for a bicentennial project. Furthermore there are plans for Australia's first floating hotel – offshore at the reef.

Information
The Townsville Tourist Organisation has a large information centre (tel 71 2724) at the corner of Sturt St and Stokes St. It's open 9 am to 5 pm Monday to Friday. Amongst the material there is a National Trust walking tour brochure, leading you around the cities fine Victorian buildings. The Queensland Tourist Bureau's office is in Flinder's Mall. The RACQ is at 711-717 Flinders St (tel 71 2168). The GPO is at the end of the mall, on the corner of Denham St, and the library is next door.

Mary Who at 143 Flinders St is an excellent bookshop. Aboriginal artefacts can be found in the Aboriginal Gallery at 137 Flinders St, also in the same Magnetic House complex, a group of early Townsville buildings. The visitors bureau runs a programme to introduce foreign visitors to Australians in their homes to share a drink or meal and conversation.

Orientation

The town is situated astride Ross Creek, which is rather larger than its name might suggest. The city centre is immediately to the north of the creek and Flinders Mall, the main shopping street of Townsville, is pedestrian only. You can easily get around the centre on foot – it's no distance to the railway station from the centre or along the river to the wharf for Magnetic Island. Opposite the wharf area are many of the town's attractive older buildings. Still further along new casino located on the water's edge. Most of the accommodation is also conveniently central.

Around Town

Townsville has one of the best city malls in Australia. It's bright, breezy, full of interest and a great place to wander or simply sit and watch the passing scenery. Giant games of chess, backgammon and snakes & ladders are part of the mall activities. The Strand is a long beachfront drive with parks and gardens, lots of bougainvillea, the Tobruk swimming pool and an impressive artificial waterfall.

Beside the Strand the old Queens Hotel on the corner of Wickham Terrace is now a TV and broadcasting station that used to have glassfronted studios so passersby could look in and see what was happening. The palm-fringed balcony of the Travelodge Hotel on The Strand affords good views. There's a coral display at Coral Gardens (9.30 am to 5 pm daily) on Tomlin St, just across from the town centre. Admission is $2.50 but it's not really worth it.

Townsville's main landmark is Castle Hill, towering over the town and river. There's a road up to the top and you can also walk there although it is quite a climb. There's a Townsville organisation dedicated to making Castle Hill into a mountain by adding the few metres of dirt necessary for its reclassification. Several years work has only resulted in a few cm of additional height.

Queen's Gardens on Gregory St, North Ward, is the original botanic gardens in Townsville. They're clearly visible below Castle Hill. Ho hum, Townsville has a water slide like every other big Queensland town; Crystal Cylinders is on Kings Rd.

Old Buildings

There are many fine old buildings in the town centre but Buchanan's Hotel, at 12 Sturt St with its superb ironlacework verandahs, burnt down. This was Townsville's finest building and one of the finest in far north Queensland. While discussion was going on about whether it could be rebuilt or the facade could be saved and a new building built behind, the demolition squad moved in and in true Queensland fashion down it went.

At the bottom of Stokes St, Victoria Bridge is one of the few remaining swing bridges in Australia. It's not in use but there are plans to restore it.

Galleries

There are quite a few galleries around town including the Perc Tucker Regional Gallery at the corner of Denham and Flinders Sts – 'one of the best regional art galleries in Australia'. It's closed on Sunday and Monday. There's also the Martin Gallery at 475 Flinders St and the Magnetic House Art Gallery also on Flinders St, down towards the Magnetic Island wharf. The latter has an eclectic collection of paintings, antiques, books and some really beautiful carpets.

The Australian Collection, on Flinders St East, near the ferry terminal is a gallery selling Aboriginal art and crafts.

It's run by Aboriginals, is quite good and is cheaper than the shops in the southern states.

Further Out

Four km out of the city the Jezzine Military Museum is on Mitchell St, North Ward and is open Wednesday to Sunday, 12 noon to 4 pm. The new botanic garden, the Anderson Park & Kokoda Pool, is six km out on Hugh St, Mundingburra. The Tropicforest Garden Estate is seven km out at 56 Bowen Rd, Rosslea and apart from rainforest walks it also has Australia's largest freshwater aquarium.

On the Town Common, only eight km from the centre, you can see a wide variety of wildlife, particularly early in the morning. During the winter there are sometimes thousands of the stately brolgas here as well as many other waterbirds. On the second Sunday of the month there are ranger-guided tours on the common.

At Stuart, about 11 km out of the city, there are free tours of the large copper refinery at 10.30 am and 1.30 pm on weekdays. A couple of km south of Stuart a road climbs to the top of Mt Stuart.

The new Billabong Sanctuary, 15 km south on the Bruce Highway, is now open although not complete. Animals include emus, kangaroos, dingoes and abundant birds which naturally frequent the billabong. There are good natural swimming holes at Mt Elliott National Park.

Further out from Townsville is the Mt Spec-Crystal Creek National Park, a pleasant day-trip from the city. There are panoramic views, swimming holes, bushwalks and camping areas. The turn-off to the park is 69 km north. The Jourama Falls National Park is nine km off the road, 89 km north of Townsville, it's also a popular outing from Ingham. There are more good swimming holes here - very pleasant in the summer heat. A 30-40 minute drive north will take you to Balgal

Beach near Rollingstone. There's camping and a food stall.

Mt Elliot is a larger park just 33 km from Townsville off the Bruce Highway. There's camping and swimming in Alligator Creek (don't let the name deter you) and good bushwalks where you can see wallabies. Camping in all National Parks is free but you do need a permit.

There are a lot of rodeos in Queensland, a number of them in the small towns inland from Townsville. The season is May to October and the tourist office should have details.

Places to Stay

Hostels The *Wills St Hostel* (tel 72 2820) is no longer an official YHA hostel but remains so popular that it's often full. It's at 23 Wills St, opposite the law courts – conveniently central but a hell of a long climb up the steps from the street. Your efforts are rewarded with a superb view over the town. The cost for the night is $6.50, there's a video, noticeboard, kitchen facilities and it's friendly

The fine, big, late 1800s building at 205 Flinders St, near the Magnetic Island Terminal, was being renovated to become a new hostel during the research for this edition. If all goes well it should be good; it's certainly a perfect location. It will probably be called *Backpackers Budget Accommodation* and the managers plan to offer trips around the area.

A third possibility is the *International Backpackers Hostel* (tel 72 5319) at 8 Morehead St in South Townsville. It's in a residential area and a bit of a walk from the centre although not that far from the ferry terminal. It recently changed ownership and future plans are as yet unknown.

Hotels & Guest Houses Many of the places in this category also have dorm or share rooms with kitchens and low prices, so they are really part hostel.

The People's Palace, now called *Pacific Coast Budget Accommodation* (tel 71

6874) is at the corner of Stuart and Blackwood Sts. The four-storey building has 72 rooms at $16/30 including a light breakfast or $4 more with private facilities. In an older section there are shared rooms at $8.50 per person. Cheaper weekly rates are available. Watch your belongings in the ground floor annex rooms as thieves have entered through windows. The hotel is central, friendly and dinner is available cheaply. The mainly elderly guests make it feel like an old folks home, however.

Across the road at 10 Blackwood St the *Sunseeker Private Hotel* (tel 71 3409) has share rooms at $5 each, singles at $14 and twins at $20. There's a pool and if you sign up for a scuba course you get the bed free. The owner also runs the *Carmen Guest House* (tel 71 2647) at 4 Wickham St across from the Tattersall Hotel. It's smaller and more basic but does have kitchen and laundry facilities; singles/doubles are $12/15.

A good and busy place is *Civic House* (tel 71 5381) back a block from the centre at 262 Walker St. Share rooms with three beds are $7 per person, two-bed shares are $10 per person, singles $15 and doubles $20. If you stay a week you pay only five nights. It's clean and has all the usual facilities including a TV room.

Back yet one more street, *Coral House* (tel 71 5512) at 32 Hale St has share for $8, singles for $14, doubles for $20. Weekly rates are $55/80. There's another place next door at number 34. You probably won't find anyone around in the middle of the day so go early or around dinner time. Both are fairly small and simple.

Somewhat away from the town centre, below Castle Hill, is *Courtly House* (tel 71 6222) at 3 Stagpole St in West End. They have a free bus service out there. It's an attractive old place surrounded by a large garden. Shares are $5 but you need your own bedding; singles/doubles are $12/16 and weekly rates are also available.

Finally there are a number of the traditional old hotels like the *Great Northern* (tel 71 6191) at 500 Flinders St

down by the railway station. Nightly cost is $16 per person, another $4 for breakfast. Some rooms have attached bathrooms for an extra $3. The *Seaview Hotel* (tel 71 5005) on the Strand has singles at $10 a night, $14 including breakfast. Another low cost hotel is the *Newmarket* at the corner of Blackwood and Flinders.

Motels The *Coachman's Inn* (tel 72 3140) is on top of the Greyhound Terminal at the corner of Flinders and King Sts, by the river. Singles/doubles in this modern motel are $32/37.

Other cheaper motels include *Motel 16* (tel 72 4166), at the corner of Queens Rd and Railway Avenue on Route 16, with rooms at $26/32. Or there's the *Strand Motel* (tel 72 1977) at 51 The Strand with rooms at $30/35 and the very central *Rex City Motel* (tel 71 6048) at 143 Willis St with rooms at $32/36.

Further out but still reasonably close to town is *Motel Rowes Bay* (tel 71 3494). It's at 74 Esplanade in Rowes Bay and has furnished flats at just $16 per night, motel units at $10/20. Family units good for four people are only $20.

Camping Townsville has a number of camping sites on the roads into the town, particularly on the Bruce Highway.

Places to Eat

Counter Meals For traditional pub fare there are numerous choices. The classic *Great Northern Hotel* by the railway station has typical meals at about $4.50. The *Newmarket* at the corner of Blackwood and Flinders Sts is similar but cheaper.

The *Exchange Hotel* on Flinders St opposite the Hayles Wharf has *Peppe's Restaurant* in the nice garden out the back with pastas from $5. It's closed Monday nights.

Also on Flinders, not far back toward town is the *James Cook Tavern*. Counter meals are in the $3.50 to $4.50 range and there are free sing-alongs in the evening

Over The Strand, the Seaview has *CoCo's Kitchen* with steaks and seafood in the pleasant outdoor beer garden. In the evening there's live music to help you digest. It's very busy on weekend nights.

Other There are numerous take-aways and fast food joints in the mall plus coffee shops for breakfasts and snacks. Many have tables under umbrellas on the mall. One of the most popular is *Toto's* which serves pizzas and is open long hours. The *Yoghurt Inn*, just a small counter in Shaws Arcade, serves all kinds of yoghurt concoctions, smoothies and fruit juices – very good at $2 or less.

Charlies, at the corner of the mall and Stanley St, is a good value restaurant – and open till 10 pm every night. Sandwiches, burgers or lasagna are in the $2 to $3.50 range and you can get a beer or a glass of wine for a dollar. They also have home-made pies and this is one of the few places open on Sundays.

On Flinders St, near the train station and not far from the corner of Blackwood St, *Zorba's* has Greek food in the $5 to $6 range and a filling dinner special for $4. It's open fairly late.

Fanny's Pancake Parlour at 145 Flinders is a BYO with all manner of stuffed pancakes for about $6 or burgers with salad and chips for $4. *Toppo's Spaghetti House* at 215 Flinders looks fairly plush but the Italian meals are not overly expensive at $5.50 to $8.

There's a mini restaurant-ghetto at the corner of Gregory St and The Strand down by the water. The *Rasa Penang* offers cheap Malaysian, *El Charro* is a very busy Mexican spot, the *American Spare Rib Joint* has take-away snack packs for $3.80 and *Tony's* bakes pizzas. There are a couple of others near the Allen Hotel including a fish & chip place. Around the corner the *Hotel Sea View* has a beer garden to wash things down.

For snacks and lunches you could try the *Fruit & Nut Shop* in the Cat & Fiddle Arcade or, at 438 Flinders St, the *Mango Tree* which has vegetarian and health food at lunchtime. There's more health food at *Mr Natural's Garden Cafe*, way down Flinders St past the railway station at 829. *Pizza Sorrento* is also up this end of town at 815.

At the post office end of the Mall *The Aussie Possie* is open from 8 am daily except Sunday for breakfast, lunch and dinner. They serve straight-forward, nononsense food and have tables out in the mall. On the Strand the *Ozone Cafe* is a popular take-away spot.

For a night out you could do worse than try *The Balcony* at 287 Flinders Mall. It's a pleasant open-air balcony looking out over the mall with main courses in the $4 to $6 range. Desserts are very reasonably priced and it's a nice, relaxing place to eat.

Entertainment

Quite a few pubs around Townsville feature music. There's rock music at the *Sea View Hotel*, the *Warehouse*, the *Manfield Hotel* on Flinders St and at the *Crown Hotel* where there's a $2 entry charge. The *James Cook Tavern* has free sing-alongs Thursday to Saturday nights. *The Tatts'*, as the *Tattersall Hotel* is known, is a bit on the rough side.

The *Bank*, at the wharf end of Flinders St, is a flashy, busy nightclub opening at 11 pm and costing $5. *Opus* at 450 Flinders St is a new wavy place with a DJ and videos. There are lots of bars in *Lowth's*, music in the basement. Every Wednesday night from 8 pm at the *South Side Pickers & Pluckers* in the *Shamrock Hotel* there's acoustic and country music. It's at Palmer St, South Townsville near the GPO.

Soon you'll be able to while away the time dropping money into the pokies at the new casino.

Getting There

Air Yes you can fly to Townsville from anywhere you care to mention. It's on the regular east coast run up from Brisbane to

Cairns and also connected to Mt Isa and through to Darwin and Alice Springs. Some typical one way fares are Brisbane $196 (standby $157), Rockhampton $133, Mackay $97, Cairns $92 and Mt Isa $157. Ansett (tel 81 6666) is at 350 Flinders St; TAA (tel 81 6222) is at the corner of Flinders and Stoke Sts.

Bus Ansett Pioneer and Greyhound both operate through Townsville on their services between Brisbane and Cairns and also from Townsville inland to Mt Isa and from there to Alice Springs or Darwin. It's 24 hours from Brisbane to Townsville ($65), six hours to or from Cairns ($22), 12 hours to or from Mt Isa ($64).

In Townsville, Ansett Pioneer (tel 81 6611) is at 44 Stanley St; Greyhound (tel 71 2134) is on the corner of Flinders and King Sts, down beyond the Hayles wharf; Deluxe Coach Lines (tel 72 6544) are at 194 Flinders St near the pier.

Rail The Brisbane-Cairns Sunlander rail service operates through Townsville. The service operates six times weekly and takes about 30 hours from Brisbane to Townsville at a fare of $109 in 1st, $73 in economy. A sleeping berth is $20 per night in 1st, $10 in economy. It's 7½ hours between Cairns and Townsville by rail and the fare is $38 in 1st and $26 economy.

The Inlander operates twice weekly from Townsville to Mt Isa. Travel times and fares are Charters Towers, three hours, $18.30 in 1st or $12.20 in economy; Cloncurry, 17 hours, $78 in 1st or $52 in economy; Mt Isa, 21 hours, $92 in 1st or $61 in economy. Sleepers cost an extra $18 in 1st, $9 in economy per night. Note the amazing trees in the Townsville railway station car park.

Getting Around
Airport Transport Townsville airport is fairly convenient for the city, about $4.50 by taxi. TAA (tel 81 6222) is at 344

Flinders St, Ansett (tel 81 6666) is at 350 Flinders St although they also have an office on the mall. Avis, Hertz and Budget have desks at the airport.

Bus The Townsville Explorer bus runs hourly from 9 am to 3 pm, Monday to Friday on a 32 km loop with stops near nine Townsville attractions. A $6 ticket is good all day.

Rental Vehicles There are a variety of local bus services around Townsville. The regular rent-a-car operators are all represented here including Natcar plus smaller firms like Brolga Moke Hire or Sun City Rent-a-Moke. You can rent bikes from Townsville Bike Hire at Graham Bourke, the chemist at 342 Flinders Mall.

Tours There are various town tours and also reef and island tours. Ansett Pioneer do city and area trips to places like Balgan Beach, Mt Spec, Ravenswood ghost town and the historic gold town of Charters Towers.

The Reef Link is a day trip to the Barrier Reef using a high speed boat which takes 90 minutes to get out to a waiting 'yellow sub', a semi-submersible with glass sides. Lunch is included and you get five hours at the reef with snorkelling.

Mike Bells Watersports has deals on equipment and activities. The Reef Travel Centre at 181 Flinders St East is a contact for many of the reef trips, boat tours, diving excursions etc. Prices range from about $25 to $30.

Magnetic Island
Population: 2,500

Magnetic is one of the most popular reef islands for travellers because it's so cheap and convenient to get to and has such a great selection of cheap places to stay. In

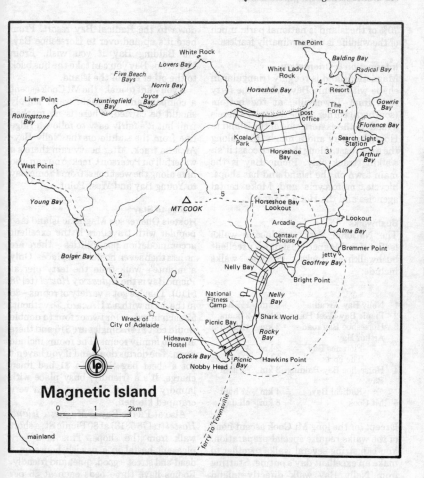

Magnetic Island

0   1   2km

White Rock

Lovers Bay

Five Beach Bays

Norris Bay

Joyce Bay

Liver Point

Huntingfield Bay

Rollingstone Bay

West Point

Young Bay

Bolger Bay

Wreck of City of Adelaide

Hideaway Hostel

Cockle Bay

Nobby Head

mainland

The Point

Balding Bay

White Lady Rock

Radical Bay

Horseshoe Bay

Resort

4

Gowrie Bay

post office

The Forts

Florence Bay

Koala Park

Search Light Station

Horseshoe Bay

3

Arthur Bay

MT COOK

5

1

Horseshoe Bay Lookout

Lookout

Arcadia

Alma Bay

Centaur House

Bremmer Point

jetty

Nelly Bay

Geoffrey Bay

Bright Point

National Fitness Camp

Nelly Bay

Shark World

Picnic Bay

Rocky Bay

Picnic Bay

Hawkins Point

ferry to Townsville

peak times, the number of people on the island can balloon up to 7000. It's also big enough and varied enough to offer plenty of things to do and see, including some really fine bushwalks.

Only 13 km offshore from Townsville (a 35-minute ferry trip), Magnetic Island is almost a suburb of Townsville and a popular day trip from that city. The island was given its name by Captain Cook, who thought his ship's compass went funny when he sailed by in 1770.

Nobody else has thought so since! The island has some fine beaches, lots of bird life, bushwalking tracks, a koala sanctuary and an aquarium. It's dominated by 500 metre Mt Cook.

There are several small resort towns along the coast and a variety of accommodation possibilities. Since the island is a real year round place it has quite a different atmosphere to the purely resort islands along the reef. This is one of the larger islands (52 square km) and about

70% of the island is national park; much of the wildlife is extraordinarily fearless.

Information & Orientation
Magnetic Island is roughly triangular in shape with Picnic Bay, where the ferry runs from Townsville, at the bottom (southern) corner of the triangle. There's a road up the eastern side of the island to Horseshoe Bay and a rough track along the west coast. Along the north coast it's a walking track only. Picnic Bay is the main town on the island and has shops, bicycle, motorcycle and Moke rental agencies and the Hotel Magnetic.

Bushwalks
The National Parks produce a walks leaflet for Magnetic Islands' excellent bushwalking tracks. Possible walks include:

1	Nelly Bay-Arcadia	5 km	1½ hours
2	Picnic Bay-West Point	8 km	2 hours
3	Horseshoe Bay road-Arthur Bay	2 km	½ hour
	-Florence Bay	2 km	½ hour
	-The Forts	2 km	1½ hours
4	Horseshoe Bay-Balding Bay	3 km	¾ hour
	-Radical Bay	4 km	¾ hour
5	Mt Cook	8 km	all day

Except for the long Mt Cook ascent none of the walks require special preparation. You can string several walks together to make an excellent day's outing. Starting from Nelly Bay walk directly inland along Mandalay Avenue and follow the signpost to Horseshoe Bay lookout from where the trail drops down and around to Arcadia. This is about a five km walk taking an hour and a bit.

Towards the end of the track there's a choice of routes. Take the longer track via the Sphinx Lookout which brings you on to the Horseshoe Bay road beyond Arcadia. You've then only got a short walk to the Radical Bay junction from where you can walk to the Forts and on

down to the Radical Bay resort. From here it's up and over to Horseshoe Bay, via Balding Bay if you wish. From Horseshoe Bay you can take the bus back to the other end of the island.

If you want to make the Mt Cook ascent a compass and adequate water supply should be carried. There is no marked trail but it's fairly easy to follow a ridge line from the saddle on the Nelly Bay-Arcadia track. After heavy rain there's a waterfall on Peterson Creek. You can also hike along the west coast from Picnic Bay to Young Bay and West Point.

Places to Stay
Hostels One reason Magnetic Island is so popular with travellers is the excellent accommodation possibilities – there are no less then seven hostel-like places. Only a minute's walk from the ferry pier at Picnic Bay is the *Hideaway Hostel* (tel 78 5110). They've got a variety of rooms – $5 in the dorm with a YHA card, $6 without, $7 each in rooms for two or four (a double would cost $14). Singles are $16 and there are also family rooms. The rooms include linen. The dorms don't and if you haven't got a sheet bag there's a $1 bed linen charge. It's a friendly, busy place with laundry facilities, TV room and a very cramped kitchen.

Also at Picnic Bay is *Magnetic Island Hostel* (tel 78 5313) at 80 Picnic St, a short walk from the shops. This is a very pleasant hostel in a newish house on a dead-end street – good, quiet and friendly. Rooms have three beds each at $6 per person and there is more than one big, spacious kitchen.

A little further out from the centre, about a 15-minute walk from the pier, is the *Magnetic Island Recreation Camp* (tel 78 5280) with space, including the overflow room, for 32 people. The price for YHA members is $4.50. For non-members it's $7.50 on the first night and $4.50 on subsequent nights. There's a kitchen and the hostel is open all day but the office is closed from 10 am to 5 pm. To get there walk along the Esplanade away from town to Granite St, then straight up to the top and turn right. The warden will collect you from the pier if you ring. There's a tennis court for hire at $2.50 an hour with free racquets for hostellers.

Moving north, a fourth possibility is *Camp Magnetic* (tel 78 5151), the Uniting Church Camp at Nelly Bay . They can take 36 in dorms and charge $5, or 50 cents more for non YHA members. There are cooking facilities and a pool. It's on Mango Parkway, a few blocks from the coastal road. Nearby is a similar sort of place, the *JOF Youth & Conference Centre* (tel 78 5106) on Clarke St, with the same prices. Beware of neighbourhood dogs if you ride a bicycle out here.

Up at Arcadia is the good and very popular *Centaur House* (tel 78 5668) at 27 Marine Parade. This was originally set up for nurses on holiday and even now nurses will get $1 off the nightly fee. Yes, you need an ID card. Regular cost is $5. It's not far from the beach and is central – about half way up the island.

Lastly, further along at Horseshoe Bay is *Geoff's Place* (tel 78 5577). He has a variety of accommodation spread over the treed grounds. You can camp for $3 per person or $5 in one of his tents, $8 for two people. There are also new A-frame wooden cabins each with a fridge for $15 a double, or rooms with shared facilities for $8/20 or with attached bathrooms for $18/25. Also at the site is a small take-away counter and evening meals are offered in a dining area. There's a TV lounge and bikes are for rent at $5 a day. At the moment there are no cooking facilities other than a barbecue but there's a lot of work and changes going on here. If you ask the bus driver he'll drop you off at the door. The beach is quite close by.

Hotels & Holiday Flats There are hotels and several resorts and motels on the island plus more than a dozen holiday flats. At certain times of year they can be rather packed so it's wise to phone ahead

and book if necessary. Right by the pier in Picnic Bay the *Magnetic Hotel Motor Inn* (tel 78 5166) has singles/doubles at $20/30. The *Arcadia Hotel* (tel 78 5177) is in Arcadia and has rooms at $39.

Then there are all sorts of holiday flats, most of which quote weekly rates although it's always worth asking if you want to stay for a shorter period. Prices vary with the season and with demand – even in the season you may find bargains if there just happens to be a room vacant. Single bedroom flats are typically in the $150 to $250 per week bracket, two-bedroom flats are in the $230 to $300 range. Check with the QGTB for a full list of flats.

One of the cheapest around is *Ti Tree Lodge Flats* at 20 Barbara St in Picnic Bay. One bedrooms flats are $120, two bedrooms $175. Another moderately priced one is *Foresthaven* (tel 78 5153) on Cook Rd, Arcadia. Rates are $130 and up for two bedroom flats. There are a couple of flats for rent up at Horseshoe Bay, too.

Places to Eat

In Picnic Bay, the *Magnetic Hotel* has *Jonah's Bistro* with tables outside, the more expensive *Trader Jacks* dining rooms and a cheap take-away. The *Tropical Inn* on the Esplanade in Picnic Bay is a good place for a meal, either take-aways or eat there. Food is reasonably expensive but the fish & chips are really excellent and just $1.60 if you eat there. You're entertained by the possums who appear on a shelf by the ceiling and drive the dogs crazy! *Crusoe's*, next door, is more expensive with main courses for $8 to $9.

The *Bosun's Grill* in the Arcadia Resort has daily lunches and dinners, sometimes a barbecue for $6 to $12. There is also a cheap take-away counter called *Pandora's Hut.* Toward Nelly Bay near the post office is the *Tea Gallery* which is open 8.30 am to 7.30 pm daily except Tuesdays when it closes at 5 pm. Meals cost $4.50 to $8 and range from spaghetti to prawn curry to fish. There's also a take-away place and a grocery store here.

At Horseshoe Bay on the waterfront you'll find *Dooley's Reef* with fish & chips and burgers for $2 or less and a few tables outside. Next door is a proper licenced restaurant with seafood meals at about $10, maybe a cheaper lunch special.

There's also a snack bar by the Arcadia Hotel, another place doing take-aways and light meals just around the headland at Alma Bay and the *Bee Ran Cafe* in Horseshoe Bay. The seafood place next door to the Bee Ran is, once again, reasonably expensive.

There is good bread and other bakery products at the *South Pacific Bakery* at Arcadia which also does pizzas. The *Tea Garden Gallery* in Arcadia is pleasant with tables out the front and in the back garden. Main courses are about $5.

Getting There
Ferries across Cleveland Bay to the island leave from the Hayles Magnetic Island wharf (tel 71 6927) at 168 Flinders St. They go to Picnic Bay and sometimes to Arcadia as well. There are about eight to 10 departures a day on weekdays and Saturdays, a dozen on Sundays and public holidays. A round-trip ticket costs $5.80.

Tickets are also available which include a day's bus travel on the island and entry to Shark World, but they're no saving on paying as you go along. You can take cars across on a vehicle ferry to Arcadia which operates twice daily on weekdays, once on Saturdays. It costs $10 return for a motorcycle, $36 for a car – fairly expensive so unless you're staying for long you'll probably find it cheaper to hire a Moke there, use the bus service or hitch.

Getting Around
Bus The Magnetic Island Bus Service operates up and down the island between Picnic Bay and Horseshoe Bay six to 10 times a day. You just have to watch the schedule if you need to meet a ferry

departure. Some bus trips include Radical Bay, others the koala park. You can either get tickets from place to place or a full day pass for $4. An all-inclusive ticket of boat, bus and lunch is available for $11.90 and another includes entry to Marine Gardens Shark World.

Bicycle Hire Alternatively you can hire bicycles, motorcycles or Mokes. Magnetic Island would be an ideal size for biking around if only the bikes available were a bit better. You can rent bikes in Picnic Bay on the Esplanade near the pier for $4.50 a day. Tandems are $7 for a half-day or $14 a full day. You can also try Brandy's Bike Hire (tel 78 5407) or the Arcadia Holiday Resort where they cost $6 for 24 hours. They all have hourly rates, too. Clevo's (tel 78 5407), a sportswear and fishing gear shop, rents bikes for $5 per day and tandems for $10 with a $2 deposit on all bikes. Next door you can also hire bikes or book tours.

Motorcycle Hire The motorcycles are much better – Magnetic Motor Cycle Hire on the Esplanade in Picnic Bay charges $18 a day for an 80 cc, $15 for a 50 cc. Petrol is included and there's no mileage charge. You need a motorcycle licence for the 80s, just a driving licence will do for the 50s. You certainly don't need anything bigger than that to explore Magnetic Island. There's another motorcycle hire place at the Tropical Inn on the Esplanade. The rates include insurance, unlimited km and petrol plus a crash helmet. You must have a motorcycle licence. If you're a YHA member you get a $2 discount.

Moke Rental Finally you can hire Mokes – in fact you soon get the impression that 90% of the vehicles on the island are Mokes, there seems to be nothing else. There are several Moke hire places in Picnic Bay, the other towns or from the various accommodation centres. Typical rates are $16.50 per day and 10 cents per km plus $5 per day for insurance. The Ahm outfit in Picnic Bay or Arcadia is cheaper. You must be over 21 years old to rent. Cheaper rates are available for longer periods, varying if they include a weekend or not. The hassle with Mokes is that there is no safe place to leave things but this is no problem at all on Magnetic Island, where you can't go far enough from home base to need very much!

Hitching Another cheap and easy altern-ative is to hitch around. Plenty of people do it – just start walking, and if you don't get a lift you end up in the next town before long.

Tours Next door to Clevo's you can book $15 half-day trips around the island. At Ahm Moke rentals you can book for the $60 Reef Link yellow submarine reef trip.

PICNIC BAY TO NELLY BAY

Many travellers stay in Picnic Bay because it's convenient for the ferry, has a good selection of shops and places to eat and has one of the most popular places to stay. There's a lookout above the town and just to the west of Picnic Bay is Cockle Bay with the wreck of the *City of Adelaide*. Heading around the coast from Picnic Bay you soon come to Rocky Bay where it's a short, steep walk down to a beautiful and secluded beach.

Next round the coast is Nelly Bay with the Marine Observatory, also billed as 'Shark World'. It's really a bit dismal, just a bunch of fairly small sharks swimming around in an oval swimming pool. The labelling and explanation on the adjoining aquarium tanks is minimal. All in all it could do with a good clean up and some major improvements. If you must it's open 8.30 am to 5 pm daily and admission is $3.50. The sharks get their daily feed at 2 pm. Nelly Bay has a good beach with shade, barbecue areas and a reef at low tide. At the far end of Nelly Bay there are some pioneer graves.

ARCADIA

Round the headland you come to Geoffrey Bay with shops and a walking track, then there's Arcadia with the Arcadia Hotel and, just round the headland, the very pleasant Alma Bay beach. Arcadia also has the Mountain View Fernery & Orchid Display on Rheuben Terrace. Admission to the fernery is $2 and includes a half-hour guided tour.

RADICAL BAY & THE FORTS

The road runs back from the coast until you reach the junction to the Radical Bay road. There's a choice of routes here. You can take the road which runs down to the Radical Bay resort with tracks leading off to Arthur Bay and Florence Bay or you can take the track via the forts. On the Radical Bay road there's also a track leading off to the old searchlight station on a headland between Arthur and Florence Bays. There are fine views from up here and the bays are also pleasant and secluded.

Alternatively you can take the track to the forts, starting from right at the Horseshoe Bay-Radical Bay junction. You can drive most of the way down to the forts but it's also a pleasant stroll and the views from the WW II forts are very fine. The forts comprise a command post and signal station, gun sites and an ammunition store. As an alternative to backtracking to the road junction you can continue downhill from the forts and rejoin the Radical Bay road just before the resort. From here you can walk across the headland to Balding Bay and Horseshoe Bay.

HORSESHOE BAY

Whether you continue along the road from the junction or walk across from Radical Bay you eventually end up at Horseshoe Bay, the end of the road and the other end of the island from Picnic Bay. Here there are more shops and accommodation possibilities, a long stretch of beach, a lagoon bird sanctuary and a koala park, a long drive off the main road, where admission is $3. Most people say it's not worth that much, although it is good for kids.

At the fine beach there are rentals for boats, surfboards and those big plastic water tricycles. You can also walk from here to Maud Bay, round to the west, or down the beach and across the headland to Radical Bay. Along the Radical Bay track another trail branches off down to pretty little Balding Bay, a popular place for skinny-dipping.

Townsville to Cairns

It's 374 km from Townsville to Cairns and there's plenty of interest along the way – lush rainforests, several towns, a number of islands offshore and from Innisfail an alternative route on to the Atherton Tablelands.

INGHAM (population 5600)
There's a lot of Spanish and Italian influence in this important sugar-producing town. The Ingham cemetery has some impressive Italian mausoleums. Lucinda, 24 km from Ingham, is the port from which the sugar is shipped and it has a jetty nearly six km long!

There are a number of places to visit around Ingham including the Wallaman Falls, 48 km inland, where the water falls 278 metres, the longest single drop in Australia. Only seven km off the highway is the Victoria Mill, the largest sugar mill in the southern hemisphere. You can see a large display of Queensland gemstones at the Jack Fraser Gemstone Gallery in Trebonne, eight km from Ingham. Forrest Beach and Taylors Beach, both 17 km out, have good swimming.

ORPHEUS ISLAND
North of Townsville and a little south of Hinchinbrook, Orpheus is a small 14 square km volcanic island surrounded by

a coral reef. It's about 20 km off-shore from Lucinda Point near Ingham and only 15 km from the Great Barrier Reef. The island, which is a national park, is heavily forested and there is lots of birdlife. Turtles also nest on the island and it's a quiet, secluded, small resort with outrageous prices. You can get there from Tully by helicopter or by launch.

CARDWELL (population 1200)
The road south of Cardwell climbs high up above the coast with tremendous views down across the winding waterways known as the Everglades which separate Hinchinbrook from the coast. There are good views across Rockingham Bay too. From Cardwell there are boat trips to Hinchinbrook, the Everglades and other islands. All the way from Brisbane to Cairns this is the only town on the Bruce Highway which is actually on the coast. At 235 Victoria St the Wishbone Tree is a local gallery and museum which even does Devonshire teas! Near Cardwell are the Murray Falls with fine rock pools for swimming and the Edmund Kennedy National Park.

From Cardwell the *Hinchiker II* can take you cruising for a day, on a snorkelling trip or just out to one of several small islands were camping was possible. Other trips go to Hinchinbrook Island resort for the day for $20. Camping trips are about this price too, for drop-off and pick-up. If you haven't got camping gear they'll rent that to you too. You can decide which island to be marooned on and for how long. Popular islands are Hudson, Bowden, Coomb and Wheeler of the Family Group. Goold Island is also good and there are various places on Hinchinbrook Island. Contact Hinchinbrook Charters (tel (070) 66 8734) in Cardwell.

HINCHINBROOK ISLAND
Halfway between Townsville and Cairns and usually reached from Cardwell, the entire large 374 square km island of Hinchinbrook is a protected reserve. The

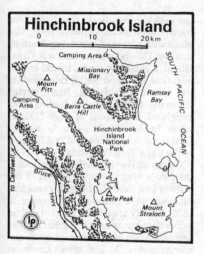

Hinchinbrook Island

0   10   20 km

Camping Area

Missionary Bay

SOUTH PACIFIC OCEAN

Mount Pitt

Ramsay Bay

Camping Area

Barra Castle Hill

Hinchinbrook Island National Park

to Cardwell

Bruce HWY

Leefe Peak

Mount Straloch

island is only separated from the mainland by a narrow channel. There's one resort on the island, on the northern peninsula, Cape Richards, but there are also a couple of campsites. The terrain of the island is varied – lush tropical forest on the mainland side, towering mountains in the middle and long sandy beaches and secluded bays on the eastern side. The island covers 635 square km and the highest peak, Mt Bowen, is 1050 metres. There are a number of walks around the resort and much wildlife, especially pretty-faced wallabies. Zoe Bay, with its beautiful waterfall, is one of the most scenic spots on the island.

The Cape Richards Resort operates a launch service across to Cape Richards from Cardwell for $20 return. It operates daily except Monday. The resort is a fairly simple and straightforward place and guests can prepare their own meals – the units have kitchens – although there's also a dining room with meals available. If you want to fix your own food there's a small shop at the resort. Daily cost is $85 per person for full board in the units which take up to four people.

The island campsites, for which permits

must be obtained from the park rangers at Cardwell, Cairns or Townsville, are at Haven (water available from Pages Creek) and Machushla (bring drinking water with you).

TULLY (population 2800)

The wettest place in Australia gets a drenching average of 440 cm a year, about 14 feet. There are some fine beaches around Tully, generally backed by lush (would you believe) rainforest. They include Mission Beach, an eight km long stretch of sand with a memorial to the ill-fated Edmund Kennedy Cape York expedition at Tam O'Shanter Point at the southern end of the beach. Day-trips operate from Mission Beach to Dunk Island and there are a number of campsites and caravan parks along the beach. Other places of interest around Tully include Clump Point, Bignil Bay, Kareeya Gorge and the Murray Falls.

MISSION BEACH

On the coast 30 km from Tully, Mission Beach was named after an Aboriginal mission which was here in 1914. The eight km beach is fringed with coconut palms and edged by rainforest. Perry Harvey, a local tour operator, is running a 'man versus starfish' battle and to help in this he is prepared to take up to four people out to the reef, free of charge, to gather starfish. The normal cost of a trip out in his boat is $30. You can find him at Clump Point on Mission Beach. There's also an associate *Youth Hostel* (tel (077) 43 5557) on Bingil Bay Rd, 200 metres east of Garners Beach. It's a 24-bed, pole-framed treehouse with views of the Pacific Ocean and it costs $3 per night.

DUNK ISLAND

One of the flashier Barrier Reef resorts is off Tully at Brammo Bay on Dunk Island. From 1897 to 1923 E J Banfield lived here and wrote his book *The Confessions of a Beachcomber*; the island is remarkably little changed from his early description.

The five square km island has more than 19 km of walking tracks through the rainforest and is noted for its prolific bird-life (nearly 150 species are seen here) and many butterflies. There are superb views over the entrances to the Hinchinbrook Channel from the top of 271 metre Mt Koo-tal-oo.

Launches run daily to Dunk Island, only five km off the coast, from Clump Point for $12 return or you can travel by air from Townsville or Cairns. Nightly costs at the Dunk Island Resort range from $92 per person. At tiny Bedarra Island there's a very small resort. It's a heavily wooded island only six km from Dunk. Including meals, nightly costs at Bedarra are $135 per person!

INNISFAIL (population 8000)

A sugar city for over a century Innisfail has a large Italian population although on Owen St you can also find a joss house. It's a busy town which produces a large proportion of the state's sugar.

From here you can visit Australia's only tea plantation at Nerada, 35 km to the west (open Tuesday to Sunday) or climb Mt Bartle Frere, the highest mountain in Queensland. There's a good road from here up to the Atherton Tableland.

Mourilyan, seven km south of Innisfail, has a tourist office and also a sugar museum. Just north of Innisfail is Babinda (population 1500), close to the Bellenden Ker National Park. Popular swimming and picnic spots around here are the Boulders, just 10 km inland, and Josephine Falls in the national park.

Further north Gordonvale (population 2400) is almost at Cairns. The winding Gillies Highway leads from here up on to the tableland.

Cairns

Population: 48,000

The 'capital' of the far north and probably the best known city up the Queensland coast, Cairns is a colourful and easy-going place with plenty of interest and variety to offer. Off-shore from Cairns is Green Island, a coral-cay resort. Inland are the beautiful, cool and fertile rainforests of the Atherton Tableland. North stretch the string of superb beaches leading to the delightful little town of Port Douglas while further north again is historic Cooktown and then the wild 'last frontier' of the Cape York Peninsula.

Cairns marks the northern terminus of the Bruce Highway and the end of the railway line from Brisbane. It came into existence in a half-hearted manner in 1876, initially as a port for the gold and tin mines developing inland. Earlier the bay had been used as a shelter for beche-de-mer gatherers. At first it was known as Trinity Bay and engaged in a fierce rivalry with Port Douglas. Later, sugar growing became the major activity of the region and it remains so today. Cairns is at its best from May to October, it gets rather sticky in the summer. The annual 'Fun in the Sun' festival takes place in October.

Cairns today is quite a travellers' centre, there is a great deal to see and do around the town and it is an arrival or departure point for the US west coast and for Papua New Guinea.

Information

The Visitors' Information Centre (tel 51 7366) is on the corner of Sheridan and Aplin Sts and is open from 9 am to 5 pm daily. The Queensland Government Tourist Bureau is at 12 Shields St. The RACQ have their Cairns office at 112 Sheridan St, see them if you want information about the road to Cooktown or if you're contemplating a Cape York expedition. The National Parks & Wildlife Service is in Moffat St, off Sheridan St, near the airport. The Civic Centre (Cairns' arts and cultural centre) is on the corner of Florence and Sheridan Sts. The GPO with its very busy poste restante counter is on the corner of Spencer and Abbots Sts. 'Cairns' is pronounced in a manner that sounds suspiciously like 'Cannes' to non-Australians.

There are a number of give-away information sources in Cairns with maps and listings of accommodation, restaurants, rent-a-car agencies and so on. Walker's Bookshop at 96 Cairns is the best bookshop in town. Absell's Newsagency, on Lake St opposite Ansett, has charts and survey maps of the far north. The Cairns Bushwalkers organise regular bushwalks and can probably arrange transport if you want to go along. Contact them in Cairns (tel 55 1865) or in Mareeba (tel 92 1491). Kouda Traders at 52 Shields St have a fine collection of Aboriginal art and artefacts for sale.

Orientation

The centre of Cairns is a relatively compact area running back from the waterfront. The railway station is within walking distance from the centre of town and the airport is only a few km to the north. Cairns is surrounded to the south and north by mangrove swamps and the sea right in front of the town is shallow and at low tide becomes a long sweep of mud – lots of interesting waterbirds though. Along the waterfront is The Esplanade and a pleasant strip of parkland, nice for a stroll.

The main intersection is Lake and Shields St. At this junction a small mall has been created, more like an inner city park, with a bandshell, benches and tree and flower planters. Around dinner time you won't believe the absolute racket made by the gathering birds.

Around the City

The earliest part of the port of Cairns is down around the junction of Wharf St and The Esplanade. Part of this colourful area was known as the 'Barbary Coast'. Here you'll find many fine old buildings with typically tropical wide verandahs. There's an interesting National Trust walking tour brochure to guide you around the old part of Cairns. Walk along the pleasant Esplanade and look for the colourful posters illustrating all the birds you might spot here. Further along is the rather sad Cataline memorial to the aircrew who operated from Cairns during WW II.

Cairns Reef World is on The Esplanade and is open 9 am to 5 pm daily, it displays a wide variety of fish and coral. Feeding time is 2 pm daily, admission is $3. Down at the Green Island wharf departure area is Windows on the Reef, a $4 audio-visual show about the reef and coral, simulating a dive.

Orchid growing is a big business in Cairns, as you can see at Limberlost Nursery (113 Old Smithfield Rd, Freshwater) or Roraina Orchids (342 Sheridan St, Cairns North). In Edge Hill the Royal Flying Doctor Service, 1 Junction St is open to visitors 10 to 11.30 am and 1.30 to 3.30 pm on weekdays.

At Laroc Miniature Coral Jewellery Factory you can watch the work and view a film depicting the production processes from the reef to ring. It's at 82 Aumuller St, three km from the centre. Cairns has one of those water slide operations which seems to have proliferated up and down the Queensland coast – $2.50 entry then $3 a half hour for the slides. It's at the end of Lake St. You can tour the Carlton & United Brewery at 113 Spence St on Tuesday and Thursday afternoons and see NQ Lager and Cairns Draught in production. Tickets are available from the tourist office at 44 McLeod St.

On the corner of Lake and Shield Sts the Cairns Museum is housed in the old School of Arts building of 1907, a fine example of early north Queensland architecture. The museum, only opened in 1980, has exhibits of Aboriginal artefacts, a display on the construction of the Cairns-Kuranda railway, the contents of a now demolished Chinese joss house, exhibits on gold mining in the area and natural history displays. It's open Monday

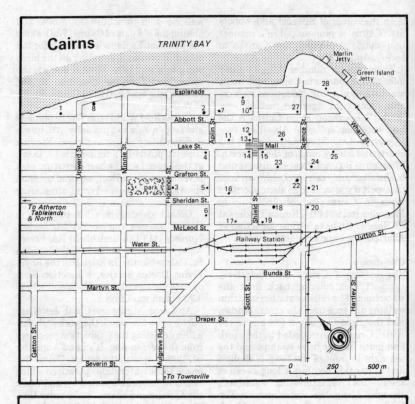

Cairns
TRINITY BAY

Esplanade

Abbott St.

Lake St.

Grafton St.

Sheridan St.

McLeod St.

Water St.

Martyn St.

Draper St.

Severin St.

Upward St.

Minnie St.

Florence St.

park

To Atherton
Tablelands
& North

Gatton St.

Mulgrave Rd.

↓ To Townsville

Marlin Jetty

Green Island
Jetty

Aplin St.

Mall

Spence St.

Wharf St.

Railway Station

Bunda St.

Scott St.

Hartley St.

Dutton St.

Shield St.

0   250   500 m

1 Catalina Memorial	15 Hides Hotel
2 Central House	16 Budget Accommodation
3 Civic Centre	17 Cairns Tourist Office
4 Cycle Works	18 Breakfast Place
5 RACQ	19 Grand Hotel
6 Trinity Fish & Chips	20 Healthy, Wealthy & Wise
7 Air Queensland	21 Mexican Pete's
8 Caravell's Hostel	22 Rusty's Bazaar
9 Youth Hostel	23 Greyhound Terminal
10 Air Niugini	24 The Inn Corner
11 Walker's Bookshop	25 Cairns Waterworks
12 QGTB	26 Ansett
13 TAA	27 GPO
14 Cairns Museum	28 Reef World

to Friday from 10 am to 3 pm and admission is \$1.

The Freshwater Connection, Kamerunga Rd, Freshwater, is a railway station complex from where you can catch the train to Kuranda, it leaves from Cairns station also. The complex has restaurants, a bar and a museum – this includes a rebuilt house from 1910. It's 10 km from the centre of Cairns.

You may want to take a look at House of 10,000 Shells at 34 Abbot St. There are lots of souvenirs, junk and kitsch, some nice jewellery and a good, extensive collection of shells. One section is articles for sale, another is more like a museum which includes a large, garish shell house.

The Saturday morning market is also worth a visit.

Further Out

There are arrowed walks around the Flecker Park Botanic Gardens off Collins Avenue, Edge Hill. The walk up to Mt Whitfield provides fine views over Cairns. It's open daily. Centenary Lakes in North Cairns is another, more recently opened, garden with a variety of birdlife on the park lakes.

At Smith Creek you can tour the Bulk Sugar Terminal at 3.30 pm on weekdays from late-July to early-December. There are short cruises around the mangrove swamps off Smith Creek, daily from the Marlin Jetty. Marlin are caught off Cairns from September to December and major catches are weighed at the game-fishing wharf on The Esplanade. Perhaps in another century big-game fishing will be looked upon with the same distaste as African big-game hunting is now.

Places to Stay

Cairns has hostels, motels, hotels (not too many surprisingly enough), quite a few pleasantly old-fashioned guest houses, lots of holiday flats and a wide selection of campsites. The seafront Esplanade is one of the best places to look for accommodation in Cairns – you'll find an example of almost every accommodation possibility going, including hostels.

There are also quite a few places along the beaches north of Cairns, particularly holiday flats. Note that the accommodation scene in Cairns is extremely competitive. In a slack season there's likely to be a lot of price cutting and you can often find some real bargains. Off-season seems to vary with who you talk to but any slow period for any reason will mean a drop in prices.

Hostels There are five hostels in Cairns. all popular, busy and at times full. The biggest of the lot is the huge *Caravalla's* (tel 51 2159) at 77-81 The Esplanade, down by the water. It has spread into the motel next door and has a total of about 160 beds in rooms running off passageways going every which way. There's a pool and kitchen facilities, the office is at number 77 and prices range from $5 to $7. The motel rooms at $7 each have two or three beds and include a fridge, TV and shower. There's always lots of activity here.

Further along, Mrs Caravalla's son runs a second *Caravalla's* (tel 51 2431) at 149 The Esplanade. With beds for 70 it's a little more low key and a homier feel is fostered by the Friday night wine and cheese parties free for guests. There are twins, rooms of four beds, some bigger ones and one larger mixed-sex dorm – beds cost $5.50 or $6 in the twin rooms. There's a big kitchen, a small TV lounge and a friendly warden. The only small problem with the Caravallas is that there are some semi-permanents and they as usual, can really take over a room more than a traveller might like.

A third choice, also very central, is the *Parkview* (tel 51 3573) at 176-180 Grafton St. It's busy, there are always people sitting out around the pool in front of this big, yellow place – its also been swallowing up the neighbours. The office is open from 7.30 am to 12 noon and 5 until 8.30 pm.

The *Cairns Backpackers Inn* (tel 51 9166) at 255 Lake St near the corner of Grove St is a bit of a walk from the centre but not enough to be a real chore. It's very good, probably quieter than the others, and the wardens are pleasant. It's open during the day with office hours from 7 to 10 am and 4 to 9 pm. There's a pool, large lounge area and tours and trips to the reef are organised. Like the others, prices are about $6.

Lastly, at 67 The Esplanade is the YHA *Youth Hostel* (tel 51 2225) called the *International Hotel*. It has 100 beds and charges $6 per night. A travel agency in the hostel arranges reef trips with good discounts for YH members. A courtesy bus operates between the airport, railway and bus stations and the hostel.

Guest Houses, Private Hotels & Holiday Flats There's a wide selection here, too, and again The Esplanade has several to try.

The *Old Lido*, beside Caravalla's at 147 The Esplanade, is not recommended and isn't really for travellers. At 153 is the *Silver Palm* (tel 51 2059) where rooms cost $15 to $20 including use of a kitchen, laundry and TV room – very clean and good value. A few doors down is the *Bell Air*. It's a very neat, nice looking place but unfortunately it's not friendly at all.

Much further along The Esplanade (it's confusing because at the turn it's a different name for a block or so and then goes back to being called The Esplanade) there are several others. At 223 *Linga Longa* (tel 51 3013) is excellent value with large, clean, self-contained flats at just $20 a day, $119 a week. The owner is gregarious, too. At 237 the *Costa Blanca* is more expensive and has a pool.

Moving back from The Esplanade there are many others. The *Central Hotel* (tel 51 1033) is a huge, castle-like place with turrets at the corner of Lake and Spence Sts. Air-con singles are $18 to $25, doubles are from $25.

The *Wintersun Motel Holiday Apartments* (tel 51 2932) at 84 Abbot St have a varying array of rooms starting with budget twin shares at only $8 per person, or singles at $15 with share-kitchens and bathroom and facilities. Better doubles with air-con, colour TV, tea and coffee making equipment, fridge and toaster cost from $25 to $28. The self-contained apartments can be reasonable value with four people. Prices here can rise during peak times in the better equipped rooms.

At 86 Abbot St is a pleasant place *Central House* (tel 51 2869) which costs $10/20 and has a pool, communal kitchen and laundry, large reading room and fans in the rooms. It's cheaper by the week at $60/90.

Back on Grafton St at 151 the *Grafton Lodge Guest House* (tel 51 6638) has a pool and kitchen and also costs $10/20 for fan-cooled rooms. Conveniently around the corner from the train station is *Pacific Coast Budget Accommodation* (tel 51 1264) at 100 Sheridan St. Rooms are $15/24 including a continental breakfast and there are also kitchen facilities. There are similar hotels down the coast and in Sydney.

The *Railway Hotel*, opposite the station, is an old pub-style hotel which rents rooms at reasonable prices. There are other small, simple guest houses on McLeod St, one opposite the station towards Spencer St, one at number 50 and another at 54. These are generally for long-term residents but they are cheap and may come in handy if things are tight.

Motels The *Cairns Motel* (tel 51 2771) at 48 Spence St is about as central as you could ask for. Rooms are fan-cooled, singles/doubles cost $28/36.

Like everything else there are quite a selection of motels along The Esplanade. At number 81 the *Esplanade Motel* (tel 51 2326) is a small, two-storey place with fan-cooled rooms, tea/coffee making facilities, fridge and TV for $30/35.

Motel Pengana (tel 51 2131) at the corner of The Esplanade and Alpin is a bit more expensive and rooms have all the features. The *Blue Water* at 131 is cheaper and has set rates.

Acacia Court (tel 51 5011) at 230-238 Lake St is really holiday flats but there's a pool and laundry facilities. Rooms are fully-equipped and nightly costs are $29/36.

The *Reef Motel* (tel 51 3540) at 215 Abott St is a new motel with singles/

doubles at \$25/30 including a 'tropical breakfast'.

Hollywood Inn (tel 51 3458) at 239 Sheridan St has rooms at \$25/33 and cheaper rates by the week – they have one and two-bedroom holiday flats and smaller 'flatlets' but there's a three-night minimum.

There are quite a few motels along the Bruce Highway, which runs right through the city. Cheaper places include the *Glenlee* (tel 54 1009) at 560 Bruce Highway with singles/doubles at \$28/30, or at 43-45 the *Sun Scene* (tel 55 4357) with rooms for \$24/28.

Camping There are about a dozen camp-sites in and close to Cairns and others up the coast. Almost without exception they take campers as well as caravans. Some of the more central sites include:

Cairns Golden Key Caravan Park (tel 54 1222), 532 Mulgrave Rd, camping \$7.25, on-site vans \$20.50.

City Caravan Park (tel 51 1467), corner of Little and James Sts, camping \$6, on-site vans \$18.

Coles Caravan Park (tel 53 1163), 28 Pease St, camping \$5.25, on-site vans \$18.50, cabins \$25.

Four Seasons Caravan Park (tel 54 1479), 495 Mulgrave St, camping \$7.25, on-site vans \$20.50.

Places to Eat

For a town of its size Cairns has quite an amazing number (and even more import-ant, a variety) of restaurants. Unfortun-ately they suffer from the same problem you'll find south in Surfers – a tendency to close early and virtually no attempt to take advantage of the climate by providing open-air dining. A great waste!

Snacks & Fast Food Lots of places around town do good sandwiches, fast foods and take-aways including a number of health food places. *Rusty's Bazaar* at 61-69 Grafton St is a small market-like complex which has several good, cheap lunch and

snack places. *Goodings* has excellent salads, shakes, sandwiches and they're open early if you fancy croissants for breakfast. There's also a place here offering inexpensive seafood salads and sandwiches. *Life in the Raw* has good and very cheap vegetarian food but is only open Thursday to Saturday.

The restaurant with no name on the south side of Sheridan between Shield and Spence Sts is the best breakfast place in Cairns. Open daily from 6 am it has a wide selection and dirt cheap prices. Another economical breakfast spot is the *Orange Tree Coffee Lounge* in the arcade off Shield St at Lake St, near TAA.

The *Burger Inn* at 85 Grafton St offers real hamburgers, not plastic patties, with about 20 different dressings, some spicy. *Fish & Chips* at 49 Aplin St serve excellent batches of what their name suggests.

Nibbles, a take-away in the Andrejic Arcade from 55 Lake St through to Grafton St, is a good place for sandwiches. They do odd fruit and vegetable juices.

Sly Cones do yoghurt, ice cream, fruit and nuts combinations – very tasty. It's near the International Hotel on The Esplanade.

Counter Meals Most of Cairns' counter meal places tend to be very straight-forward but also very cheap. You can get a meal for \$3 to \$4 in quite a few of Cairns old hotels – some to try include *Fitzgerald's Pub* on the corner of Grafton and Shields Sts, the *Great Northern Hotel* at 69 Abbott St or the *Railway Hotel* on McLeod St, opposite the railway station.

Also opposite the railway station is the *Grand Hotel*, where there's a fancier counter meal section (it's also open to 8.30 pm, later than the Cairns norm). Meals are in the \$5 to \$7 bracket and there's a serve-yourself salad bar.

Right in the city centre *Hides Hotel* has the *Tropical Lounge Bistro* with some of the best counter food in Cairns. It's open 6 to 9 pm, main courses are in the \$5.50 to

$8 range (mostly around $6 to $6.50) and also has a serve-yourself salad table.

Restaurants Easily the best deal in town is the Sunday night meal at *Healthy, Wealthy & Wise*, a Hare Krishna vegetarian restaurant at 69 Spence St near Sheridan St. It's free and open to all, but they also do all-you-can-eat lunches at $4 and dinners for $6 during the rest of the week.

Nonna's is a small, simple but cosy spot offering cheap home-made pastas. It's down near Carravalla's at 79 The Esplanade. For a splurge there are several seafood places along The Esplanade too. Shop for a dinner special or the nightly fixed-price full meal.

The *Swagman's Restaurant* is open everyday to 9 pm, Fridays and Saturdays to 10 pm and that's a big plus in itself. There's plenty of seafood, most $5 to $6 and the marinated kebabs on rice are good and sizeable. It's in the mall and you can sit outside, so it's quite pleasant.

Over at the corner of Grafton and Spence Sts is the *Inn Corner*, a popular place with good pizzas, or Indian and Malaysian meals at $8 to $9. It's only open Thursday to Saturday. Down the road at 42 Spence St is *Toko Baru*, a good but slightly expensive Indonesian restaurant. Next door is the modest *Borobudur*. It also has Indonesian food, but dishes are under $5 – not a bad choice.

Across the street *Mexican Pete's* has terrific decor and good food from $5 to $8.50. On some nights there is live music. Another Mexican restaurant is *Little Gringos* at 93 Grafton St with meals for around $8. The *Pancake House* is near Mexican Pete's and is also popular, with main courses for about $6.

At 47 Aplin St is the *Casa Gomez Spanish Restaurant* with a mix of seafood and Spanish dishes. It's a more expensive place. Nearby is *Thuggee Bills* at 42B Aplin St. If your Indian history isn't good enough the Thugs were a gang of ritual murderers who plagued parts of

India during the days of the Raj – until they were finally wiped out by a British officer, Thuggee Bill. Good curries but rather more expensive at $7 to $9 for main courses.

Entertainment

Radio 4CA have the run down on who is playing where around the Cairns pubs. Facing each other across Lake St down by Spence St the *Great Northern* and the *Central Hotel* both have live music in the evenings. *Hides Hotel* also often has live entertainment. Cairns Folk Music Club meets on Sunday evenings at 7.30 pm in the Crown Hotel and the Folk & Jazz Club meets in the *Crown Hotel* on Shields St from 7.30 to 10 pm on Sundays; cover charge is $1.50. People at the hostels will know where to go for a rage.

Getting There

Air Ansett and TAA both fly to Cairns from all the regular places. In particular there are as many as eight to 10 flights daily coming up the east coast from Brisbane and the southern capitals. Some typical fares include Melbourne $348, Sydney $298 ($227 standby), Brisbane $229 ($183), Townsville $92, Mt Isa $160, Darwin $263 ($210), Alice Springs $236 ($188). In Cairns TAA (tel 50 3777) are on the corner of Shield and Lake Sts. Ansett (tel 51 3366) are at 84 Lake St.

Air Queensland (tel 50 4222) live at 62 Abbott St; Cairns is their HQ and they have a comprehensive network around north Queensland – see the introductory Getting Around section. Cairns is also an international airport with regular flights to and from North America and Papua New Guinea. Air Niugini (tel 51 4177) is at 4 Shields St and the Port Moresby flight costs $205 and goes four times a week. Qantas (tel 50 4222) fly to Vancouver, San Francisco and Los Angeles via Honolulu.

Bus Greyhound and Ansett Pioneer both operate daily on the coast route from

Brisbane. Fares vary slightly between the two carriers. From Brisbane it's 28 hours ($75), Rockhampton 16 hours ($36), Mackay 13 hours ($33), Townsville five hours ($21.50). Ansett Pioneer (tel 51 2411) are at 58 Shields St and Greyhound (tel 51 3388) are at 78 Grafton St. Deluxe Coachlines (tel 51 8177) are at 105 Lake St.

Rail The Sunlander from Brisbane to Cairns operates six days a week. The train takes about 40 hours to make the 1681 km trip. The fare from Brisbane is $120 in 1st, $80 in economy. Sleeping berths cost $20 per night in 1st, $10 in economy. You can break your journey anywhere along the way, within certain guidelines. By rail it's about 7½ hours to Townsville, 16½ to Mackay, 24 to Rockhampton. Between Cairns and Kuranda, trains run twice a day and a one-way tickets costs $4.30.

Getting Around

Airport Transport Cairns' airport at Aeroglen is fairly convenient for the city, about $6 to $7 by taxi. A shuttle bus runs from the new airport terminal into town and will take you to your hotel for $3. It leaves the airport after each flight. To get out there phone 53 4722 for pick-up times. Avis, Budget and Hertz have desks at the airport.

Bus There are a number of bus services in and around Cairns. Local bus schedules are posted on the wall at the Queensland Tourist Office on Shield St. Northern Beach Lines (tel 55 3079) operate from Cairns as far as Ellis Beach about five times a day on weekdays, twice only on Saturdays and Sundays. The fare to Ellis Beach is $2. On weekdays there are a couple of other trips which don't run all the way north to Ellis Beach.

The Port Douglas Rocket leaves daily at 12.10 pm for Port Douglas and Mossman. Coral Coaches go to Cape Tribulation daily from the Ansett-Pioneer Terminal for $13.50, (cheaper if you book

through hostels). They also go to Port Douglas including Hartley's Creek, twice a day, Monday to Friday.

Other bus services include Mossman twice a week, up through the Atherton Tableland to Herberton and also to Cooktown twice a week. Plus, of course, there's the famous Kuranda train trip. See the relevant sections for more details.

Car Rental Cairns is another place where it's worth considering renting a car if you don't already have your own transport. There are places of interest in the town itself and most visitors manage to get out to at least one of the islands off the coast, but there is also plenty to see and do around Cairns whether it's making the beach crawl up to Port Douglas or exploring the Atherton Tablelands. As in other areas of tropical Australia Mokes are about the cheapest cars to rent and they're also ideal for the sunny climate and for relaxed, open-air sightseeing. Almost all the rental firms in Cairns have Mokes.

All the major firms are represented in Cairns; you'll find most of them along Lake St, where Hertz, Budget and Avis all live within a stone's throw of each other. Other local firms include Mini Car Rental at 142 Sheridan St with Mokes at $13 a day plus 13c a km, or Hondas at $14 plus 14c. Unlimited mileage rates are $26 for Mokes and $30 for Hondas. Weekly rates are also available. Insurance is $7 a day.

Sheridan Rent-A-Car at 196A Sheridan St is one of the cheaper dealers with Mokes and cars. Cairns Rent-A-Car at 147C Lake St is another to try and if you want to go bush bashing they hire out four-wheel drive Suzukis. Lo-Cost Rent-A-Car is on Sheridan.

Note that most Cairns rental firms specifically prohibit you from taking most of their cars up the Cape Tribulation road, on the road to Cooktown, or on the Chillagoe Caves road. A sign in the car will announce this prohibition and the contract will threaten dire unhappiness if you do so. Of course lots of people ignore these prohibitions but if you get stuck in the mud half way up to Cape Tribulation it could be a little embarrassing.

Bicycle & Motorcycle Rental Cycle Works on the corner of Aplin and Lake Sts have 10-speed bikes at $8 a day, $20 deposit. There's also bicycle rental at 61 Sheridan St, the Bicycle Barn, with the same rates. At Bill Lee Long's Sports Store, 72 Lake St you can get a tandem for $10 a day. Mini Car Rentals, 142 Sheridan, has mopeds for $12 a day, $4 an hour. Cairns Motorcycle Hire, 36 Sheridan, rents bikes with unlimited mileage and includes a helmet.

Tours There are a vast number of tours in and around Cairns. Day tours include the city sights, up to the Atherton Tableland or to Kuranda, or up the coast to Port Douglas. Others visit tea or sugar plantations or Dunk Island. There are a number of tour companies and their trips and prices vary slightly so it's worth checking around.

There are bus trips up to Cape Tribulation or three day tours to Cooktown (about $125). Austrek at 103 The Esplanade runs outback and reef trips. For trips to Cape Tribulation check the hostels, they run them frequently and offer the best rates. They also have trips to other out of town attractions.

If you want to get out to the outer reef again the hostels are the best bet. Caravalla's, for example, offer a $25 snorkelling trip to the reef and an island. Hayles runs more established commercial trips to the outer reef. They're located on Wharf St. Of course there are also trips out to Green and Fitzroy Islands off Cairns or Low Island off Port Douglas.

Scuba-diving trips, reef cruises, fishing trips and Cairns' famous game fishing are other possibilities. Pro-Dive (tel 51 9915) at Marlin Jetty offer a range of reasonably priced scuba-diving trips and courses. These include a five-day learner's course with three days of lectures and pool training, and an overnight cruise to the outer reef with meals and equipment included, for $200.

There are also cruises around the Cairns 'everglades' (mangrove creeks) leaving from the Marlin Jetty. One uses a paddle-wheeler. Raging Thunder offers whitewater rafting on the Barron River; the three-hour trip is $25. Details and bookings at the tourist office. A competitor is R'n'R at 26 Abbot St.

Aerial trips are another possibility. The North Queensland Air Club run a variety from brief scenic flights to quite extensive area tours. Aussie Air Safaris has a scenic reef flight for $48, a day trip to Cooktown for $95, and a three-day trip for $590. Air Queensland also have a number of standard tours out of Cairns.

Green & Fitzroy Islands

There are two popular islands off from Cairns, both of which attract lots of day-trippers (too many some think) and some overnighters too. Just up the coast off Port Douglas there's another reef island, popular for day-tripping although nowhere near as commercialised as Green Island. North of Green Island, Michaelmas Cay is a popular rendezvous for trips out to the Barrier Reef. Further still, although also reached from Cairns, is Lizard Island – an expensive and exclusive hideaway and certainly not over-run by tourist hordes at all.

Getting There
There are a wide variety of day-trips to the two islands either to one, the other or both. Check departure/return times and the travelling time when choosing your boat. Typical trips are the regular Green Island cruise for $20 return, 90 minutes travel each way. The faster catamaran

makes the trip in just 45 minutes and costs $32 return. The Green Island Express, 40 minutes, is $21 return or the Hayles Budget Launch, 90 minutes, is only $12 return. On the budget trip with lunch and a glass-bottom trip, the total fare is $24.

A different trip is to Green Island and the Barrier Reef. It includes three hours at Hastings Reef and two hours at the island for $60 – this includes lunch and snorkelling. Another possibility is the same trip, but to Michaelmas Cay instead of the reef, for $50. The cruises leave from the Marlin Jetty or Green Island Jetty. Others go to Fitzroy for the day, $17 boat only, or to both islands for $27.

GREEN ISLAND

Offshore from Cairns, 27 km to the north-east, Green Island is a true coral cay and the island and its surrounding reef is all national park. Green Island is a popular day trip from Cairns although it also has overnight accommodation. It's a really beautiful island although marred by casual, shonky development. Nevertheless, if you take a 10-minute stroll down to the other end of the island you can forget the tourist development is even there. The beach, right around the island, is beautiful, the water fine, the fish still reasonably prolific although the coral is not as extensive as it used to be.

The man-made attractions start at the end of the pier with the underwater observatory ($3) with lots of fish to be seen around the windows five metres below sea-level. On the island there's the Barrier Reef Theatre with a Barrier Reef film and (yawn) Marineland Melanesia ($3) with a wide variety of fish and corals in aquarium tanks plus larger creatures (sharks, turtles, stingrays, crocodiles) in pools or enclosures and a display of PNG art.

Places to Stay

At the Coral Cay Resort (tel (070) 51 4644)

the nightly cost including dinner, bed and breakfast is $39 to $55 per person in the off-season, $45 to $65 in the tourist-season.

FITZROY ISLAND

Six km off the coast and 26 km south-east of Cairns, Fitzroy Island has only been developed as a resort island since 1981. It's a larger continental island with beaches which are covered in coral so they are not ideal for swimming and sunbaking. There's good coral only 50 metres off the beach in the resort area. Day-trips to the island operate from Cairns and you can also make day-trips which combine Fitzroy and Green Islands.

Places to Stay

The nightly tariff including meals at the island resort is $75 per person.

Atherton Tableland

Inland from the coast between Innisfail and Cairns is the lush, rolling countryside of the Atherton Tableland and the Evelyn Tableland. From the coast the land rises up sharply then rolls gently back towards the Great Dividing Range. The altitude tempers the tropical heat and abundant rainfall and rich volcanic soil combine to make this one of the greenest places in Queensland. It's an easy-going area yet little more than a century ago this peaceful, pastoral region was still a wild jungle.

The first explorers came here in 1874 to '76, looking for a repeat of the Palmer River goldrush, further to the north, a few years before. The Aboriginal population was violently opposed to this intrusion but they were soon over-run. Some gold was found and rather more tin but though mining spurred the development of roads and railways through the rugged, difficult land of the plateau it was farming that soon became the principal activity.

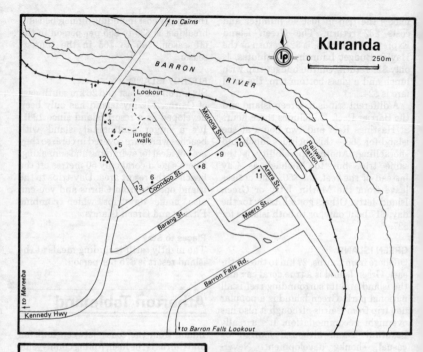

Kuranda

0 ————— 250m

BARRON RIVER

to Cairns

Lookout

Morong St.

jungle walk

Coondoo St.

Barang St.

Arara St.

Meero St.

Railway Station

to Mareeba

Kennedy Hwy

to Barron Falls Lookout

Barron Falls Rd.

1 Pioneer Cemetery
2 Garden Cafe
3 Kuranda Inn
4 Kuranda Market
5 Honey House
6 Frog's Restaurant
7 Post Office
8 Top Pub (Fitzpatrick's)
9 Aboriginal Museum
10 Bottom Pub (Kuranda Hotel)
11 Mrs Miller's Youth Hostel
12 Heritage Homestead

Today the tableland is a pleasant escape from the coastal heat and it also offers beautiful scenery and some of Australia's most appealing waterfalls. In the south of the Evelyn Tableland are Queensland's two highest mountains – Mt Bartle Frere (1656 metres) and Mt Bellenden-Ker (1591 metres). Getting there is half the fun and the railway ride to Kuranda is one of the tableland's major attractions.

Getting There

The most popular route up to the tablelands is the incredibly scenic railway line that winds up from Cairns to Kuranda, with its famous station. The train rises 300 metres in 21 km. With a stop at the Barron Falls, the trip takes 1½ hours each way. There are two departure points, the Cairns Railway Station or the Freshwater Connection, 10 km from the centre. One car on the train includes a commentary. The one-way fare is $4.30, return is $8.60. Through a hostel the return may be $8 or so. There are one or two a day leaving in the early morning and returning early afternoon.

There are also non-tourist trains to Kuranda which follow the same route but don't stop at the waterfalls. They run twice a day and the fare is $1.80. Phone 51 1111, extension 15 for details.

in the same area while the Honey House Motel, in front of the market site, has a variety of honeys on sale plus glass-fronted beehives so you can see the busy little workers doing their stuff. On the main street there's a small Aboriginal museum and crafts centre – admission 50c.

At the edge of town, at the corner of Coondoo St and the Cairns road is the Kuranda Village Centre, mainly a small shopping complex. Downstairs a gallery/theatre screens an audio-visual presentation called Cape York Experience. It costs $2.50 ($2 with Youth Hostel card) and gives a 17 minute impressionistic rather than informative glimpse of the northern cape. There are also books and photos for sale.

Across the road is the new Heritage Homestead with an old war plane sitting crashed at the gate. Inside is a fairly well laid out, but small history museum with an emphasis on the entertaining side. The entrance fee is $3.

The *Kuranda Queen*, down below the train station, does short river cruises departing each hour, $5.

Horse-drawn carriage tours are given through 'Jum Dum' Creek environmental park. Just off the highway on Black Mountain Rd, there's a jungle walk at the Tropical Sanctuary & Wildlife Garden. Close to Kuranda, the Rainforest World Tourist Park has rainforest tours in WW II army amphibious vehicles for $3.

Down on the plains, where the Kennedy Highway branches off for Kuranda, there's a monument to the trail blazers who cut the difficult roads into the tableland.

Places to Stay

Kuranda has one of Australia's most popular *Youth Hostels* (tel 93 7355) at 6 Arara St. It's in a fine old building, run by Mrs Miller, and it accommodates no less than 120 people. The nightly cost is $6 and the men's quarters are better than the women's – say the women! It also has a

You can reach Kuranda by bus or car as well – it's a half hour trip. White Car Coaches operate buses from the Ansett-Pioneer Terminal up into the Tablelands everyday. Fares are Kuranda $3.50, Mareeba $10.50, Atherton $15.50, Herberton $19.70.

KURANDA (population 500)

The railway line from Cairns climbs through superb scenery to Kuranda, at the top of the Macalister Range, 34 km away. The line was completed, at great expense, in 1888 and goes through 15 tunnels during its steep ascent. The final stretch is through the spectacular Barron Falls gorge – it's even more spectacular after heavy rain although hydro-power generation has detracted from its magnificence. Kuranda's picture-postcard railway station, decked out in tropical flowers and ferns, is justly famous.

Other attractions include the colourful Sunday morning market with produce and local arts and crafts on display – there's quite a large alternative establishment up here. The Sunday market has become so busy and popular that another, although somewhat smaller, has been added on Wednesday mornings. Non-market days remain very quiet.

There are a couple of short jungle walks

swimming pool, mini-golf, table tennis and videos. There's a big house next door with rooms for couples.

Alternatively the *Honey House Motel* (tel 93 7261) is small, right in the centre and costs $21/30 for singles/doubles. The *Bottom Pub* also has accommodation. *Cassowary House* on Black Mountain Rd has rooms for $25. There's a caravan park just beyond the town. Note that there is no bank in Kuranda.

Places to Eat

There are plenty of places to eat in Kuranda including counter meals at the hotels – the top pub and the bottom pub. The *Tea Gardens & Restaurant*, in the Youth Hostel, has sandwiches, steakburgers and the like for $2 to $4, lunch specials at $4.75. Down the street, the *Trading Post* offers local tea and damper (bush bread) – $3.50 for two people. Next door is *Frogs*, a more expensive but very pleasant restaurant.

The *Garden Cafe* around the corner is nice and breezy – you can eat outside and there's a take-away section. Rolls and burgers are $2, main courses are $5 to $8.50. They have fruit juices and smoothies too.

Right above is *Snatchmo's Restaurant*, a BYO where you can eat on the verandah. It's open from 6.30 pm Thursday-Saturday and all day Sunday and has Asian food. On weekends there's music.

The *Honey House* is excellent for scones, cream and honey and has honey-tasting sessions. During the week when things are slow, and businesses are closed, you can always get a sandwich (more expensive than usual), at *Mandomoni Café* in the Kuranda Village Centre. There is also a bakery downstairs.

MAREEBA (population 5900)

From Kuranda the Kennedy Highway runs west over the tableland to Mareeba, the centre of a tobacco and rice growing area. Between here and Dimbulah, further west, is Australia's major tobacco-growing area. From Mareeba the Kennedy Highway turns south to Atherton in the centre of the tableland.

CHILLAGOE

From Mareeba you can continue 140 km west to the Chillagoe Caves – the road is dirt but it's a very interesting trip. There are tours, usually twice daily, at 9 am and 1 pm, of the extensive limestone caves. There are other caves you can explore yourself but you'll need a torch. Chillagoe itself also has a museum with reminders of its heyday as a mining town. From Mareeba the Kennedy Highway turns south to Atherton in the centre of the tableland.

ATHERTON (population 4200)

Although it's a pleasant, prosperous town, Atherton, like Mareeba, has little of interest in its own right although there are a number of places worth exploring in the vicinity. From Atherton or nearby Tolga it's a short drive to Lake Tinaroo, the large lake created for the Barron River hydro-power scheme. Atherton is named after John Atherton, a pioneer in the region who also foresaw the agricultural potential of the tablelands.

South of the Gillies Highway are two picturesque crater lakes – there was once much volcanic activity in this area. The highway gradually descends from the tableland beyond Yungaburra (population 450) and eventually joins the Bruce Highway at Gordonvale, south of Cairns.

Lake Eacham is the smaller lake with a 6.5 km round-the-lake walk. The lake is popular for swimming and has turtles who will take bread scraps from visitors. Walkers may well glimpse other wildlife around the lakes. There is also a walking track around the larger lake, Lake Barrina. The massive 'Twin Kauri' pines are a feature of the walk. Most of the year there are also twice daily cruises on the lake. Both lakes have picnic and barbecue facilities as does Lake Tinaroo.

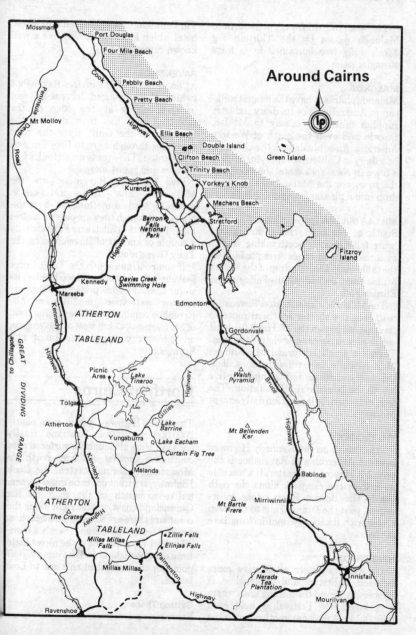

Around Cairns

Mossman
Port Douglas
Four Mile Beach
Pebbly Beach
Pretty Beach
Ellis Beach
Double Island
Green Island
Clifton Beach
Trinity Beach
Yorkey's Knob
Machans Beach
Stratford
Fitzroy Island
Cairns

Cook Highway

Peninsula Developmental Road

Mt Molloy

Kuranda

Barron Falls National Park

Kennedy Highway

Kennedy
Davies Creek Swimming Hole

Mareeba

ATHERTON

TABLELAND

GREAT DIVIDING RANGE

to Chillagoe

Picnic Area

Lake Tinaroo

Tolga

Atherton
Yungaburra
Lake Barrine
Lake Eacham
Curtain Fig Tree
Malanda

Herberton

ATHERTON

TABLELAND

The Crater

Kennedy Highway

Millaa Millaa Falls

Ravenshoe

Millaa Millaa

Palmerston Highway

Zillie Falls
Elinjaa Falls

Nerada Tea Plantation

Edmonton

Gordonvale

Walsh Pyramid

Gillies Highway

Mt Bellenden Ker

Bruce Highway

Babinda

Mirriwinni

Mt Bartle Frere

Innisfail

Mourilyan

The western road from Yungaburra to Malanda passes by the 'Curtain Fig Tree', a fig tree curtained by a huge strangler palm.

MALANDA
Malanda claims to have the longest milk-run in Australia since its dairy industry supplies milk all the way to Mt Isa, Darwin and even the north of Western Australia. An equivalent in the US could be a dairy in California supplying milk to a town in New York state! Just north of the town are the Malanda Falls which drop into a pleasant swimming hole.

MILLAA MILLAA (population 350)
South of Malanda the 15-km gravel 'waterfall circuit' is worth taking. It goes by some of the most picturesque falls on the tableland – the long drop of the Millaa Millaa Falls, the wider Zillie Falls and the Elinjaa Falls.

The Millaa Millaa-Atherton/Ravenshoe road (not the shorter southern route to Ravenshoe) passes the McHugh Lookout with a superb panoramic view of the area. There's a small Historical Museum on Main St while down towards Innisfail on the coast you can turn off the highway five km to the Nerada Tea Plantation. The factory is open for inspection daily except Mondays.

THE CRATER
Further north on the Kennedy Highway between Atherton and Ravenshoe is the eerie Mt Hypipamee crater. It's a scenic walk from the car park along the path beside the Barron River, close to its source, past the Dinner Falls to the deep crater with its spooky, evil-looking lake far below.

HERBERTON
On a slightly longer alternative route between Atherton and Ravenshoe is Herberton, an old tin-mining town where a colourful Tin Festival is held each September. A major attraction here is the Tin Pannikin – a local museum in an old hotel which has been rebuilt like a well known cartoon pub.

RAVENSHOE
At an altitude of 915 metres Ravenshoe (which is pronounced 'ravens-ho' not 'raven-shoe') is at the edge of the tableland and has been dubbed the 'gateway to the Gulf' since the road continues through here to Croydon and Normanton. The area is noted for its fine timbers and gemstones.

Five km past Ravenshoe are the Millstream Falls – the widest falls in Australia and something of a mini-Niagara although they are only 13 metres high. The Little Millstream Falls are only a couple of km out of Ravenshoe on the Tully Gorge road.

If you continue south the Tully Gorge lookout is 25 km out but it too has lost its water flow to hydro projects. There are various watersport facilities at the Koombooloomba Dam. The mining town of Mt Garnet is 47 km west of Ravenshoe, on the way you pass the Innot Hot Springs.

North of Cairns

The Bruce Highway, which runs nearly 2000 km north from Brisbane, finally ends in Cairns although the surfaced road continues another 80 km north to Mossman. This final stretch, the Cook Highway, is a treat not to be missed since, unlike so much of the road up the Queensland coast, it runs right along the coast and there are some superb beaches. Shortly before Mossman, there's a turn-off to Port Douglas, one of the nicest little towns in Queensland and the jumping-off point for the delightful trip out to Low Island.

Getting There
Buses run several times daily up the coast

to Ellis Beach ($2). There are daily buses to Mossman (for about $7). See the Cairns 'Getting Around' section for details or ask at the tourist office there.

ALONG THE COAST

It's beach after beach all the way along the Cook Highway. They start almost immediately north of Cairns with turn-offs to Machans Beach, Holloway Beach, Yorkey's Knob, Trinity Beach (catamarans for hire), Clifton Beach and Palm Cove where there is Wild World incorporating the former Australian Bird Park and Crocodile Park. Apart from those animals there are reptiles, snakes and the obligatory kangaroos. Shows are in the afternoon. Admission for adults is $8, kids $4, and it's open daily from 9 am. Across the road there's an opal showroom. Catamarans can also be hired.

Round the headland from Buchan Point the road runs along the coast and hugs it the rest of the way to Port Douglas. Ellis Beach is an unofficial nude-bathing beach at its southern end while at the central part of the beach there's a campsite and place to eat. Further north there's Pretty Beach and Pebbly Beach before the superb sweep of Four Mile Beach which stretches south from the headland at Port Douglas.

Soon after Ellis Beach you reach Hartley Creek Jungle Reserve with a collection of native Australian wildlife of the far north. Frankly, as a reserve it's no great shakes, most of the enclosures are a bit shoddy and dull but the sheer showmanship of the proprietor makes it one of the most interesting reserves in Australia. When he feeds Charlie the crocodile you know for certain why it's not wise to get bitten by one! And you've never seen anything eat apples until you've seen a cassowary knock back a dozen of them. The park is open daily (at least during the winter season) but you want to go there at crocodile feeding time so check the times in Cairns. Entry is $3.50, an extra dollar at showtimes.

PORT DOUGLAS (population 675)

In the early days of the far north's development Port Douglas was actually a rival for Cairns, or Trinity Bay as Cairns was then known, but Cairns got the upper hand and Port Douglas became a sleepy little backwater. It was just a quiet little fishing town until people began to realise what a delightful, laid-back little place it was. Now it's quite a busy tourist centre but still a great place to visit with a string of interesting little shops and restaurants to wander around when the magnificent beach, the boats and the lookout get dull. If you've spent a long time travelling up the coast this is a great place to sit back and recharge your batteries before heading on somewhere else.

The two old hotels on the main street have to be the best part of Port Douglas. It's hard to imagine a nicer country pub than the Central Hotel, and the Court House Hotel on the corner is just about as pleasant.

On the old wharf the Ben Cropp Wreck Museum has a collection of bits and pieces salvaged from various wrecks plus a continuous film show. It's open 9 am to 5 pm daily and admission is $2. Barrier Reef Shells on Macrossan St have a good display of shells while up the hill the Nautilus Boutique produces rather beautiful shell jewellery. There's a fine view over the coastline and out to sea from the Flagstaff Hill lookout.

Information

The only banks here are the ANZ and National Australia. There are movie screenings twice a week in the town hall.

Places to Stay

The Traveller's Hostel (tel 98 5200) is a new and welcome addition to the accommodation front and is really a superb place to stay. It's at 111 Davidson St, beside the caravan park on the way into town from Cairns. There are 60 beds at $6 (with more coming) in 10 rooms and a

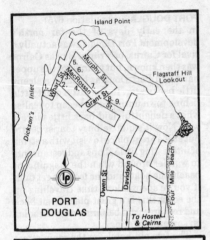

1 Ben Cropp Museum
2 Catalina Restaurant
3 Court House Hotel
4 Central Hotel
5 Post Office
6 Bike Hire
7 Mockas Pies
8 Roberts Patisserie
9 Barrier Reef Shells

kitchen, pleasant TV/lounge area, swimming pool and undercover parking. During the winter, you'd be well advised to book ahead as this place has become very popular. At the caravan park, tent sites are $3.50 per person per night. On-site vans are fully equipped (except for linen) and cost $20.25.

There are a number of other campsites along Four Mile Beach into Port Douglas, some of them within easy walking distance of the centre.

Cheapest of the motels is the *Port Douglas Motel* (tel 98 5248) on Davidson St at $27/32. On the corner of Macrossan and Garrick Sts the *Balboa Holiday Flats* (tel 98 5354) are just $22 for a double but there are only three of them. There are also holiday flats at *Whispering Palms* (tel 98 5128) on Langley Rd from $27 for two. *Island Point Motel* is $30 to $35 as is

the *Central Hotel*, which is right in town. Check the noticeboard by the post office if you're looking for longer term accommodation.

Places to Eat

There are plenty of places to eat in Port Douglas including the famous *Mocka's Pies* on the main road. Pie connoisseurs have claimed their $1 (and up) pies are absolutely the best in Australia. You'll have to judge for yourself but I've got to admit I'm on the connoisseurs' side!

Another spot to check out is *Robert's Patisserie* at 31 Macrossan St. Robert is a pastry cook from Germany who you may see in his old country leather shorts. The pleasant café is filled with all kinds of German curios and kitsch – even a working cuckoo-clock. The various pastries, cakes and sandwiches are very good, ranging from 75c to a couple of dollars.

Also on the main street *Arty's Place* has pizzas. On Grant St there is a bakery for breads, buns and pastries.

You can get counter lunches and teas in both of the delightful pubs on the main street – the *Central Hotel* and the *Court House Hotel*. In the latter there's a pleasant outdoor eating place and prices are generally around $5. Port Douglas also has other more expensive eating places, including the nice outdoors *Catalina Seafood Restaurant*. But to eat a pie from Mocka's while sitting in the park by the waterfront, is hard to beat. The *Central Hotel* has live music on Sunday afternoons.

Getting There

The Port Douglas Rocket leaves Cairns daily at 12.10 pm. Coral Coaches also have a twice daily bus to Port Douglas on weekdays.

Getting Around

Bicycle Rental You can hire bikes for $6 a day, or $3 a half day from a shop on Macrossan, the main street, down towards the waterfront.

Tours The *MV Reefer* (great name!) does snorkelling trips, including equipment, from $55 with a maximum of seven people, BYO grog. The *MV Quicksilver* is said to have good trips to the outer Barrier Reef, a 90-minute ride. There's a 'learn to dive' shop at the pier. Kunard Kompany on Macrossan St offers various regional adventure trips. Trailblazer Tours go to Cape Tribulation and the Daintree. Tropical Walkabouts offer guided day walking tours in the area's rainforest and other interesting locations. Details at the hostel.

LOW ISLAND
Off-shore from Port Douglas is a fine little coral cay topped by an incredibly well kept old lighthouse. This is a very different sort of reef island from the hyped-up Green Island off Cairns and worth making the trip out to see.

The *MV Martin Cash* goes out every day at 10.30 am and the cost is $30. There are also trips available including transport from Cairns for $35. The price includes glass-bottom boat, snorkelling gear and lunch.

MOSSMAN & DAINTREE
The far north sugar town of Mossman (population 1600) is almost the end of the road north but visit the beautiful river and waterfalls at Mossman Gorge, five km out of the town. The road continues north-west to the real end of the surfaced road at Daintree but before there you can turn off the surfaced road to the ferry crossing on the Daintree River and continue up the dirt road to Cape Tribulation. Between Mossman and the ferry turn-off is the fine beach at Wonga. From the Daintree ferry you can take the *Crocodile Express* on daily trips up the river to Daintree for $10.

The Daintree rainforest area has become the focus of attention in 1985 due to the insensitive Queensland Government's insistence in pushing a road through the forest along the coast from Cape Tribulation to Bloomfield, despite widespread condemnation. The roadworks have caused massive amounts of soil to wash-out onto the reef, raising fears about the long-term affects on both the reef and the fragile balance that now exists in the forest.

CAPE TRIBULATION
After Port Douglas the road turns away from the coast to Mossman and then Daintree but shortly before Daintree you can branch off the road, onto a small dirt road that runs down to the Daintree River. There, beside the 'Beware of Crocodiles' sign, a cable ferry crosses the river to the start of the Cape Tribulation road. It's 41 km to Cape Tribulation on a dirt road all the way; there are a number of creek crossings to be made but except after periods of heavy rain, it's no problem in conventional two-wheel drive cars.

In the '70s this was a hippie outpost with a number of settlements, particularly at the infamous Cedar Bay, further north towards Cooktown. There the Queensland police mounted a raid on the unfortunate inhabitants in search of the dreaded weed, burnt down their homes and charged them with, would you believe it, vagrancy! Today, with improvements to the road, Cape Tribulation is becoming more popular for visitors. It's not surprising as this stretch of coast is incredibly beautiful. It's one of the few places in Australia where the rainforest runs right down to the water.

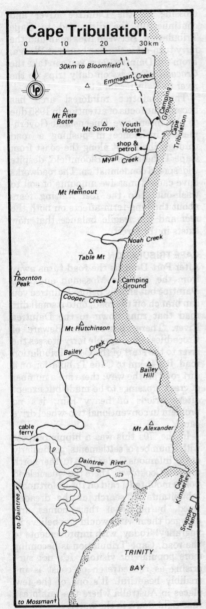

Cape Tribulation

0   10   20   30km

30km to Bloomfield

Emmagen Creek

Mt Pieta Botte

Mt Sorrow

Youth Hostel

shop & petrol

Myall Creek

Camping Ground

Cape Tribulation

Mt Hemnout

Noah Creek

Table Mt

Thornton Peak

Camping Ground

Cooper Creek

Mt Hutchinson

Bailey Creek

Bailey Hill

cable ferry

Mt Alexander

Daintree River

to Daintree

Cape Kimberley

Snapper Island

TRINITY BAY

to Mossman

The cape itself was named by Captain Cook, since it was a little north of here that his troubles and tribulations really started when he ran his ship on to the Endeavour Reef. The mountain rising up behind the cape was also named by him – Mt Sorrow! On the road up to the cape, stop at the lookout point high above the mouth of the Daintree River, and further on, pause on the bouncing rocks – a beach where the smooth stones bounce very high if thrown down.

Cape to Cape Safaris run four-wheel-drive-truck safaris from Cape Tribulation up to Thursday Island. It's $500 for 14 days. They have an office in Cairns but the trips leave from Cape Tribulation.

Places to Stay

There's a campsite by Cooper Creek, about half way up to the cape. *Palm Beach Camp* is right up by the cape; you can camp there for $2.50 and there are cabins for $21.

Just before the cape and right underneath Mt Sorrow is a new *Youth Hostel*. Nightly costs in this very pleasant place are $6 with a limit of five nights. There's a modern kitchen and solar-heated water. There's also the *Drysdale Arms*, a new addition to the lodge incorporating a bar, restaurant, swimming pool and common room for chess, backgammon and cards. Bushwalks are often arranged from the hostel or from the store just back down the road. They cost $3 or $7, depending on how many go and they are reckoned to be well worth it. To book in advance, write to PMB 3, Cape Tribulation, QLD 4873 or phone the YHA in Brisbane.

Getting There

Coral Coaches depart from the Ansett Pioneer terminal in Shield St, Cairns daily except Saturday at 9 am and the fare is $13.50 including the ferry charge. The bus leaves the cape at 1 pm for the return journey. Holders of Ansett Pioneer Aussiepasses can use them on this trip. For bookings phone (070) 51 2411.

It's quite easy to hitch since when you've crossed the Daintree ferry there's nowhere else to go but up the road. Note that most of Cairns' hire-car companies specifically prohibit the use of their vehicles on the Cape Tribulation road, which does not stop lots of people from doing just that! The ferry costs $3 for car and driver plus $1.20 per passenger; the return trip is free.

COOKTOWN (population 900)

North of Cairns you have to turn inland and follow a pretty terrible stretch of dirt road to Cooktown, 341 km north. Further north of Cooktown it soon becomes four-wheel drive only. Cooktown can lay claim to being Australia's first, albeit involuntary, British settlement. In 1770, Captain Cook careened his barque *Endeavour* here after making an equally involuntary close inspection of the Great Barrier Reef. To float the ship off the reef before putting into Cooktown for repairs, cannon and shot were hurled overboard. Divers have recently brought them up. The spot on the banks of the Endeavour River where the ship was repaired is marked and at Grassy Hill Lookout you can imagine yourself standing, like Cook, searching for a way out through the maze of reefs.

Cooktown later became an unruly goldrush centre for the Palmer River rush. At its peak the population was over 30,000 and there were no less than 94 hotels! In 1874 Cooktown was second only to Brisbane in size in Queensland. Today the population is less than a thousand and the Chinese Graveyard and the joss house relics in Cooktown's fascinating museum are the only reminders of the 2500 Chinese miners whose industrious presence led to some wild race riots. The biggest activity in Cooktown today is the flight of fruitbats that head out from the swamps every night.

Quiet though it is (only three pubs remain open today), Cooktown is a quite delightful place and if you can get there

NATIONAL TRUST OF QUEENSLAND
JAMES COOK HISTORICAL MUSEUM
COOKTOWN, N.Q.

Souvenir Ticket

it's a place not to be missed. Apart from just taking in the atmosphere you can visit the James Cook Museum in the Sir Joseph Banks Gardens, inspect the fine old Bank of NSW building or perhaps hitch a ride on a yacht heading north for Thursday Island and the South Pacific. While in Cooktown, Banks collected 186 plant species and the first kangaroo seen by the expedition was spotted here. Cooktown has a memorial to Cook, of course, but there's also a cairn to the unlucky explorer Edmund Kennedy and to the equally tragic Mary Watson (see Lizard Island) who is buried in the Cooktown Cemetery. Ask someone about the local 'burning rocks'. On the way to Cooktown you pass the black granite boulders known as Black Mountain or to Aboriginals as Kalcajagga – the mountain of death. Helenvale, just south of here and off the road, has the colourful old Lion's Den Hotel, an old mining pub.

Places to Stay

There are a few motels, hotels and holiday flats in Cooktown. The cheapest is the *Alamanda Inn* (tel 203) on Hope St which charges $15/22 for room-only singles/doubles. The *Seaview Motel* (tel

77) on Charlotte St costs $28/40 for singles/doubles including a light breakfast. There are also several campsites in Cooktown. The *Peninsula Caravan Park* (tel (070) 95 3730) has sites for $5 for two and on-site vans for $14.

Good counter meals are available at several of Cooktown's hotels.

Getting There

McGrath's Bus Service (tel 51 1064) operates Cooktown-Cairns on Wednesdays, Fridays and Sundays and from Cairns on Mondays, Wednesdays and Fridays. The trip takes a little over eight hours, the road is sealed to a little beyond Mt Carbine (about one-quarter of the way there) and the fare is $30. The RACQ in Cairns can advise you on road conditions. Air Queensland fly to Cooktown five times a week; the fare is $48.20.

There are a variety of tours available from Cooktown both locally and further afield into Cape York. Daily river cruises for $5 also operate along the Endeavour River from Cooktown.

Cape York Peninsula

The north of Queensland ends in a huge triangle pointing like a finger towards Papua New Guinea. The tip of Cape York is the most northerly point on the mainland of Australia and from here a scatter of islands dot Torres Strait. This is one of the wildest and least-populated parts of Australia, away from the great deserts of the centre.

As you head north a few cattle stations, small work parties along the overland telegraph line to Bamaga and a number of Aboriginal communities and reserves are all you will find. Getting up to the north along the rough and rugged Peninsula Development Road is still one of Australia's great road adventures – it's a trip for the tough and experienced since, even at the height of the dry, the main river to be

forded barely drops below a metre in depth.

Driving to the Top

Every year a handful of hardy travellers, equipped with four-wheel drive vehicles or trail motorcycles, make the long haul up to the top of Cape York. Apart from being able to say you've been as far north as you can get in Australia, you also test yourself against some pretty hard going and see some wild and wonderful country into the bargain. It's no easy trip – for a start, from December to March, during the wet season, nothing moves by road at all. Even if you could move in the mud, the rivers would be totally impassable at this time of year. From May to November, conventional vehicles can usually travel north of Laura as far as Coen and, with care and skill, even across to Weipa on the Gulf of Carpentaria. If you want to continue north from the Weipa turn-off to the top of the cape, however, then you're going to need four-wheel drive, a winch and plenty of strong, steel wire.

August to October is usually the only time you can get to the very top. The major problem is the many river crossings; even as late as June or July they will still be swift-flowing and frequently alter their course. The rivers often have very steep banks on entry and exit and the Jardine River only drops below a metre in depth at the very height of the dry season. The Great Dividing Range runs right up the spine of Cape York and rivers run to the Coral Sea on the east side and to the Gulf of Carpentaria on the west. Although the rivers in the south of the peninsula only flow in the wet season, those further north flow year round.

The ideal set-up for a Cape York expedition is to have two four-wheel drive vehicles travelling together – one can then haul the other out where necessary. Motorcycles also make it up to the top, floating the machines across the wider rivers. There are usually large truck inner-tubes left at the river crossings for

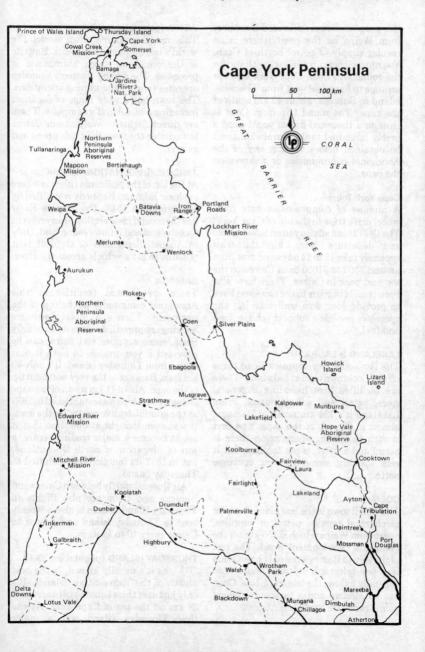

Cape York Peninsula

0   50   100 km

GREAT

BARRIER

REEF

CORAL

SEA

Prince of Wales Island
Thursday Island
Cowal Creek Mission
Cape York
Somerset
Bamaga
Jardine River Nat. Park
Northern Peninsula Aboriginal Reserves
Tullanaringa
Bertiehaugh
Batavia Downs
Iron Range
Portland Roads
Mapoon Mission
Weipa
Lockhart River Mission
Merluna
Wenlock
Aurukun
Rokeby
Northern Peninsula Aboriginal Reserves
Coen
Silver Plains
Howick Island
Lizard Island
Ebagoola
Strathmay
Musgrave
Kalpowar
Munburra
Lakefield
Edward River Mission
Hope Vale Aboriginal Reserve
Koolburra
Mitchell River Mission
Fairview
Laura
Cooktown
Koolatah
Drumduff
Fairlight
Lakeland
Ayton
Cape Tribulation
Dunbar
Palmerville
Daintree
Inkerman
Highbury
Mossman
Galbraith
Port Douglas
Walsh
Wrotham Park
Delta Downs
Lotus Vale
Blackdown
Mungana
Chillagoe
Mareeba
Dimbulah
Atherton

this purpose. Beware of crocodiles. Apart from Weipa on the coast, there is no regular supply of petrol north of Coen. You must either carry enough with you for the round trip Coen-Cape York-Coen or arrange to have fuel sent from Thursday Island to Bamaga, about 40 km south of the cape. The round trip from Coen is close to a thousand km so you'd need a pretty large fuel tank! Permission must be obtained before visiting any of the Aboriginal communities or reserves on the cape.

Cape York Tours

A number of companies operate four-wheel drive trips to the top of Cape York. The QGTB can advise you on latest prices and departure dates, but the trips typically take 12 to 14 days and cost from around $500 to $1000 from Cairns to the top and back to Cairns. There have also been trail-bike tours to the top – you have to provide your own trail bike but the operators provide a support vehicle, food and fuel.

LAKELAND & LAURA

The Peninsula Development Road turns off the Cooktown road at Lakeland. There are facilities here including a general store, petrol and a hotel-motel. From Lakeland it's 734 km north to Bamaga, almost at the top of the cape. The first stretch to Laura, where again there is petrol and a hotel, is not too bad, but it gets steadily worse as you continue north.

COEN

This small town is the last place north for mechanical repairs, petrol or supplies, apart from Weipa which is 153 km off the Peninsula Development Road. The rest of the way to Bamaga the only habitation is a few telegraph stations – the road generally follows the telegraph line. Coen has an airstrip and a racecourse where picnic races are held each August.

WEIPA (population 2400)

This modern mining town works the world's largest bauxite deposits. Bauxite is the ore from which aluminium is processed. The mining company Comalco operates tours of the mining operations. The town has a wide range of facilities including a motel and a campsite. There are direct flights to Weipa from Cairns but outside the town the roads are as bad as ever.

JARDINE RIVER NATIONAL PARK

At the top of the peninsula this was where explorer Edmund Kennedy was killed by Aboriginals in 1848. The Jardine River has the second greatest flow of any river in Queensland and it flows year round. Only in August, September or October is it possible to get a vehicle across the river.

BAMAGA

There are limited facilities at this Aboriginal community at the top of the peninsula. There's a motel (advance bookings required), a campsite in nearby Seisa, some supplies and petrol can be provided if you arrange to have it sent across from Thursday Island. It's only 40 km from Bamaga to the very northern tip of the cape. About 11 km south of the cape is Somerset which was established in 1863 as the administrative centre for the area. It was even thought at one time that it might become a major trading centre, a sort of Singapore of north Queensland, but in 1877 its functions were shifted to Thursday Island.

Air Queensland fly between Cairns and Bamaga and there are also flights to Thursday Island. There is also a weekly boat to Thursday Island and a boat to Cairns every 10 to 12 days.

THURSDAY ISLAND (population 2300)

'T.I.', as it's usually known, is the best known of the Torres Strait Islands. It's only just over three square km in area and 39 km off the top of Cape York. At one time Thursday Island was a major pearling centre and pearlers' cemeteries tell the hard tale of what a dangerous occupation this was. Some pearls are still produced here, from seeded 'culture farms'. Although Thursday Island has lost its former importance as a stopping point for vessels, it's still a popular pause for passing yachties. It's an attractive and easy-going little place and has a small Quetta Memorial Museum attached to the Quetta Memorial Cathedral. The *Quetta* was a ship wrecked near Thursday Island in 1890 with the loss of 133 lives.

Although Thursday Island's name is of uncertain origin there are other islands nearby also named after days of the week, possibly by Captain Bligh. Possession Island, close to Cape York, was where Captain Cook 'claimed' all of the east coast of Australia for England in 1770. There are regular flights to Thursday Island from Cairns with Air Queensland, the fare being $190. Keen travellers continuing on to Papua-New Guinea can easily find fishing boats crossing the Torres Straits to Daru, from where you can fly or ship to Port Moresby.

There's a hostel called *Jumulu* at Aboone which charges $9.13 per night with meals. Torres Strait Island camping is now council approved but phone in advance at Cairns 69 1304. For information on sea transport from Cairns, contact Going Places Travel (tel 51 4055) at 26 Abbott St, Cairns.

LIZARD ISLAND

The furthest north of the Barrier Reef resort islands, Lizard Island was named by Joseph Banks after Captain Cook spent a day here, trying to find a way out through the Barrier Reef to open sea. A Queensland tragedy took place here in 1881 when a settler's wife (the husband was away on a fishing trip) fled the island with her son and a Chinese servant after Aboriginals killed her other servant. The three eventually died on a barren island to the north. Their tragic story, as recounted in her diary, is told at the

LIZARD ISLAND

Cooktown Museum. Today the beautiful island is a pricey resort, reached by a 50-minute Air Queensland flight from Cairns. Lizard Island is about 100 km north of Cooktown. The island has superb beaches, swimming and snorkelling.

There are tour trips from Cairns to the island for the day, or you can fly there from Cairns for $96 or from Cooktown for $58. On the island accommodation including all meals and use of all the facilities costs $150 per person per day.

The Gulf

North of Mt Isa and Cloncurry is the Gulf country, a sparsely populated region cut by a great number of rivers. During the November to April 'big wet', the dirt roads turn to mud and even the surfaced roads can be flooded so June to September is the safest time to visit this area. Burke and Wills were the first Europeans to pass through the Gulf country but the coast of the Gulf of Carpentaria had been chartered by Dutch explorers even before Cook's visit to Australia. The actual coastline of the Gulf is mainly mangrove swamps which is why there is little habitation right on the coast – Burke and Wills did not actually manage to reach the sea, but knew they were close to it because of the tidal movement on the rivers.

The main roads into the Gulf region are from Cloncurry to Normanton (surfaced all the way) with a turn-off to Burketown at the point where the road from Julia Creek (also all surfaced) meets it. Between Cloncurry and Normanton the flat plain is interrupted by a single, solitary hill beside the road. It's colourfully named Bang Bang Jump-up. The Gulf Development Road also runs to Normanton from the Atherton Tableland area. The last stretch into Normanton on this route can be made on the famous (though a little pointless!) Gulflander rail service which runs once weekly in each direction between Croydon and Normanton. The 151-km trip, which is done in a very vintage-looking rail motor, is made from Croydon on Thursday and from Normanton on Wednesday.

BURKETOWN

This tiny town is probably best known for its isolation – when the rains come it can be cut off for weeks at a time. In the centre of a cattle-raising area, Burketown is 65 km south of the Gulf and can be reached by road from Cloncurry, Julia Creek or Camooweal. The 332 km trip to Camooweal from Burketown only passes one supply stop the whole way, tiny Gregory Downs.

Small, remote, isolated and forgotten though Burketown is, the Shire of Burke has made considerable efforts to ensure that it's not forgotten. Amongst their efforts they will issue a Burketown passport which grants you 'citizenship' of the shire and, more important, three free beers at the Albert Hotel, the Gregory Hotel and the Escott Barramundi Fishing Lodge, 12 km out of town, plus a free meal from the Saltpan Store.

Happy
The Hungry Shire of Burke

NORMANTON (population 900)

The main town in the Gulf region had a population of 3000 at the peak of its goldrush days in 1891. Karumba, 69 km from Normanton and actually on the gulf, is the prawn-fishing centre for the Gulf region. Croydon, connected to Normanton by that curious rail-car service, is an old goldmining town and has many historic and interesting old buildings.

Townsville to Mt Isa

It's 887 km from Townsville inland to Mt Isa and they're generally pretty boring km although there are several points of interest along the way.

Getting There

The Inlander railway service and the Ansett Pioneer and Greyhound bus services both operate through Charters Towers and the other towns on the route to Mt Isa. You can also fly – Townsville to Charters Towers is $65, Charters Towers to Mt Isa $113. By train it's $11.50 in economy, $17.30 in 1st from Townsville to Charters Towers. The Inlander takes a bit over three hours and operates twice a week but there is also a slightly faster Rail-Motor Service which operates from Townsville only as far inland as Charters Towers every weekday. By bus it's less than two hours to Charters Towers for $12.20. By planning your trip it is possible to day-trip to Charters Towers from Townsville on some days of the week.

CHARTERS TOWERS (population 6800)

Only 130 km inland from Townsville, this interesting old town's principal activities today are fruit growing and cattle raising, but from 1872 to 1916 this was a fabulously rich goldmining town with a peak population of 30,000. The beautiful old buildings with their classic verandahs and lacework are a living reminder of those days.

There's a war museum at 61 Gill St and on Mosman St there's the restored 1887 Stock Exchange Arcade. In the same building is the Assay Room Mining Museum while Mosman St also has a Folk Museum and the Zara Clark Museum with a number of historic vehicles. The old Venus Battery is about four km from town off Milchester Rd. Ore was first crushed here in 1872 and it continued operating right into the 1970s. Charters Towers also has the Rotary Lookout on Buckland's Hill and a small wildlife sanctuary in Lissner Park.

There's a tourist information centre at 61 Gill St.

On the way to Charters Towers from Townsville you can turn south at Mingela, 95 km out, to Ravenswood. This was a classic boom-and-bust goldrush town where gold was first discovered in 1868. Fossickers still find gold in the creek beds near this intriguing almost-a-ghost town.

CHARTERS TOWERS TO MT ISA

It's about 750 km on from Charters Towers to Mt Isa, a fairly unexciting trip although, fortunately, the last stretches of unsurfaced road were finally surfaced in 1976. Towns you pass through along the way are:

HUGHENDEN (population 1600)

An early explorer camped here in 1862 while in search of the ill-fated Burke and Wills expedition. Hughenden is on the main road and rail route to Mt Isa and the Porcupine Gorge National Park, a sort of Grand Canyon in miniature with walls rising sheer over 120 metres, is about 50 km north.

RICHMOND & JULIA CREEK

Richmond (population 800) and Julia Creek (population 600) are two more small towns. From Julia Creek a surfaced road turns off north to Normanton on the Gulf.

CLONCURRY (population 2000)

The centre for a copper boom in the last century, Cloncurry was the largest copper producer in Australia in 1916, but the mines and smelters declined soon after. Today it's a pastoral centre and a major base for the Flying Doctor Service. Points of interest in the town include the old Chinese and Afghan cemeteries, the courthouse, the indoor museum on Scarr St (with Burke and Wills relics) and the outdoor museum on Ramsay St. It's a rough trip about 100 km south of Cloncurry to the ghost town of Kurilda.

MARY KATHLEEN At Corella River, just before you reach Mary Kathleen, there's a memorial cairn to the Burke and Wills Expedition. Only 55 km from Mt Isa, Mary Kathleen is a small town, once controversial due to its uranium mine, which is now closed.

Mt Isa
Population: 23,700

Mt Isa is a one-activity town – an immensely rich copper, silver, lead and zinc mine. The town is a comparative oasis in the wilderness – travelling east or west you'll feel a considerable relief when 'the Isa' finally hoves into sight, and this is despite the fact that what you're likely to see first is the billowing smoke stack. It's a kind of rough-and-ready town, the image of an outback mining place despite its shiny new buildings. The deposits here were discovered in 1923 and today this is the major town of north-west Queensland. Virtually the whole town is run by Mt Isa Mines and ore produced is railed 900 km to Townsville on the coast. The underground mine is now closed to visitors, however the one above is still open and no reservations are needed.

Information & Orientation

There's a tourist office on Camooweal St, open Monday to Friday from 9 am to 5 pm. The Crusade Bookshop at 11 Simpson St is the best bookshop between Townsville and Darwin. The town centre is a fairly compact area, immediately south of the Leichardt River which separates it from the mining area.

Around Town

There's a major new Civic Centre in the city and the August Rotary Rodeo is quite an occasion, but the mines are the major attraction. Daily surface working tours take place from the Visitors Centre, Kings Cross, at 8.30 am and 1.30 pm, Monday to Friday.

Above Marian and Hilary Sts there's a lookout with a signpost giving directions all over the world. A more recent addition is the Frank Aston Museum, an underground complex cut into a hill close to the town centre. It's open 10 am to 3 pm daily with a display of mining equipment and other exhibits from the pioneering days.

Lake Moondarra, 20 km north of Mt Isa, is an artificial lake popular for water sports activities, but the main water supply for the town comes from Julius Dam, 105 km out.

Australia's newest National Park, Lawan Hill Gauge, lies 350 km northwest of Isa. The park is an oasis of gorges, ponds, rivers and canyons that the Aborigines have enjoyed for maybe 30,000 years. Their paintings, artefacts and old campsites abound. Also in the park are extensive and virtually unexplored

limestone formations. Getting there is the problem – it's a beautiful, pristine place that's miles from anywhere or anybody.

Places to Stay

Hostel Mt Isa has a 28-bed *Youth Hostel* (tel 43 5557) at Wellington Park Rd, opposite the velodrome. It's open all day and charges $5.50 per night.

Hotels, Motels & Lodges The *Tourist Inn* (tel 43 3024) on the corner of Marian and Camooweal Sts, has singles/doubles for $12/20.

Otherwise head along Marian St where there are a variety of places within a km or so of the centre. At 97 Marian St, the *Copper Gate Motel* (tel 43 3233) is $24/30. The rooms are a little old-fashioned but they're self-contained, air-con, have a TV, fridge and cooking facilities so they're pretty good value.

In and around the centre there are a number of very basic accommodation places, several of them single-sex. The *Queensland CWA Hostel* (tel 43 2216) at 5 Isa St, takes women and children only at $8 a night or $40 a week. There's a kitchen and laundry facilities.

Low-priced but not single-sex, the *Boomerang Lodge* (tel 43 2019) is rather a long way out from the centre at 11 Boyd Parade. Rooms are $24/30 and they're air-con, have shower and toilet, plus there's a communal kitchen and TV lounge and a swimming pool. Finally there's *The Welcome Inn* (tel 43 2241) at 118 Camooweal St with rooms at $16/24. The rooms don't have private facilities but they are air-con and have tea/coffee-making equipment and fridges.

Camping Mt Isa also has a string of campsites, a number of them conveniently close to the city centre. At 112 Marian St the *Mt Isa Caravan Park* (tel 43 3252) has tent sites at $3 per person and on-site vans for $18. The *Riverside Caravan Park* (tel 43 3904) at 195 West St has

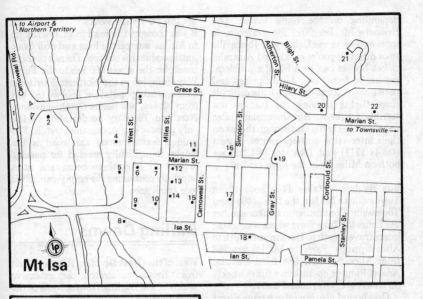

Mt Isa

1 Railway Station
2 School of the Air & Flying Doctor
3 Bonanza Restaurant
4 Civic Centre
5 City Cafe
6 Mt Isa Hotel
7 Queensland CWA Hostel
8 Argent Hotel
9 TAA
10 Verona Motel & Tourist Inn
11 Post Office
12 Greyhound
13 Ansett
14 Tourist Information Centre
15 Kentucky Fried
16 Crusade Bookshop
17 Tavern
18 Frank Aston Museum
19 Lookout
20 Boomerang Lodge

similar prices. There are a number of other sites around town.

Places to Eat

Excellent counter meals at lunchtime or in the evenings at the *Tavern* and also at the *Argent Hotel* – both on Isa St. At either place there is a variety of main courses in the $6 to $7 bracket, a serve-yourself salad table plus cheaper dishes and entrees.

Or you could try the *Bonanza Family Restaurant* on the corner of West and Grace Sts. It's a very glossy, American-style place (part of a Queensland chain) serving meals in cafeteria fashion. Next door is the rather more expensive *Phoenix Centre* and, of course, there are a number of pizzerias, cafés and so on including the *City Cafe* on West St, which offers no less than 19 varieties of burgers! *Frankies*, on the corner of Marian and Miles Sts, has burgers, sandwiches and 20 flavours of ice-cream. The tables outside are a good place to while away a few hours while waiting for a bus.

Getting There

Air Ansett and TAA both fly through Mt Isa with non-stop flights to and from Alice Springs $144 ($115 standby), Brisbane $244 ($196), Cairns $160 ($128) and Darwin $216. There are also many flights to other main centres but that fares vary depending on the route taken. The Brisbane-Mt Isa fare, for example, is more expensive via Cairns and Townsville than direct. If you're on a round-Australia ticket Mt Isa can be a bit of a problem, getting in from, say, Alice Springs and then out to Cairns can be a little difficult since flights through the Isa are not terribly frequent. Air Queensland also has a number of flights through the Isa on their interesting outback routes. Ansett (tel 44 1711) and TAA (tel 44 1222) are both on Miles St in the town centre.

Bus By bus it takes 11½ hours from Townsville to Mt Isa, the fare is $64 from Townsville. Continuing on it takes another 7½ hours to Three Ways where connecting buses travel north to Darwin and south to Alice Springs. Fares to Mt Isa are $58 from Alice Springs, $84 from Darwin. Ansett Pioneer operate five times weekly on this route; Greyhound daily.

Greyhound also operates a more direct route between Brisbane and Mt Isa via Charleville. This takes about 27 or 28 hours and costs $115 five times weekly. Ansett Pioneer (tel 44 1767) are at the Ansett terminal in Miles St. Greyhound (tel 43 6655) also have a terminal on Miles St.

Rail The Inlander operates Townsville-Hughenden-Cloncurry-Mt Isa. Departures from Townsville are on Tuesday and Friday at 4.45 pm, arriving in the Isa 21 hours later – a stunning 42 kph pace! From Mt Isa departures are on Thursday at 2.20 pm and Saturday at 10.20 am. Townsville-Mt Isa costs $86.90 in 1st, $57.90 in economy. Sleeping berths cost an extra $18 in 1st, $9 in economy.

Getting Around
There is little public transport around Mt Isa. A taxi to the airport costs around $7.50. Hertz, Budget and Avis have airport desks. Campbell's Coaches do a day-tour around Mt Isa for $20 including lunch.

MT ISA TO THREE WAYS
If you thought the road from Townsville to Mt Isa was pretty long and dull, wait until you hit this stretch. There's nothing much for the whole 650 km to the Three Ways junction in the Northern Territory. Camooweal (population 250) is 188 km from Mt Isa, just before the Queensland-Northern Territory border and it's the only place of any size on this stretch. The unique feature along this road is the 'goals' thoughtfully erected for passing drivers to hurl their beer cans at – hopefully containing the empty-can debris to a small area.

Darling Downs

West of the Great Dividing Range, inland from Brisbane, stretch the extensive plains of the Darling Downs, some of the most fertile and productive agricultural land in Australia. In the state's early history the Darling Downs were something of a back door into the region. Nobody was allowed within a 50-mile radius of the penal colony of Brisbane but settlers gradually pushed their way north from NSW through this area.

Places to Stay
There are youth hostels and hostel-style accommodation in the Darling Downs region at Jondaryan, Roma and Warwick.

Getting There
Rail The Westlander runs from Brisbane to Roma and Charleville twice a week. From Charleville it turns south to Cunnamulla or you can change trains and continue west to Quilpie. It's 777 km from Brisbane to Charleville and the trip takes 17 hours. Fares from Brisbane are: Roma $58 1st class, $34 economy; Charleville $74 1st class, $49 economy; Cunnamulla and Quilpie $87 1st class, $58 economy. Sleeping berths cost an additional $18 in 1st class, $9 in economy.

IPSWICH (population 61,500)
Virtually an outer suburb of Brisbane this was a convict settlement as early as 1827 and is now a gateway to the Darling Downs, either to Warwick or Toowoomba. The Redbank Railway Museum is 10 km back towards Brisbane, while at Wacol the Wolston House historic homestead can be visited from Wednesday to Sunday.

TOOWOOMBA (population 64,000)
On the edge of the Great Dividing Range and the Darling Downs, 138 km inland from Brisbane, this is the largest city in the region. It's a pleasant, gracious city with parks, tree-lined streets and many early buildings which include the National Trust classified Bull's Head Inn on Drayton Rd and the Early Settler's Museum on Parker St. There's also a Cobb & Co Museum on the corner of James and Water Sts, a Teddy Bear Museum in Bell St and various art galleries.

Near Toowoomba is Oakey (population 2900) where the Brookvale Park is a picnic and barbecue spot with visiting wildlife. Shearing demonstrations can be seen at the 1859 Jondaryan Woolshed where there is also a youth hostel. Pittsworth (population 1800) is another typical Darling Downs town with a folk museum.

WARWICK (population 8850)
South-west of Brisbane, 162 km inland and near the NSW border, this is the oldest town in Queensland after Brisbane itself. It's a busy Darling Downs farming centre noted for the roses that grow in its parks and for its annual rodeo in October. There are various parks and lookouts in the area and Pringle Cottage in the town, dating from 1863, has been preserved as a local museum. There is a Tourist Information Centre in the Warwick Town Hall.

Between Warwick and Goondiwindi is Inglewood (population 1000) while east of Warwick near the NSW border is Killarney

(population 750), a pretty little town in an area of fine mountain scenery with a number of scenic waterfalls. Texas (population 800) is another small border town with a historical museum in the old police station.

South of Warwick is Stanthorpe (population 4000) near the NSW border. At an altitude of 915 metres it's the coolest town in the state and a popular area for fruit production and winemaking. There are good bushwalks and rock-climbing opportunities in the Girraween National Park and on Mt Lindsay.

GOONDIWINDI & FURTHER WEST
Continuing west from Warwick you reach Goondiwindi (population 3600) right on the NSW border and Macintyre River. It's a popular stop on the Newell Highway route between Melbourne and Brisbane. There's a small museum in the old customs house and a wildlife sanctuary at the Boobera Lagoon.

If you continue inland from Goondiwindi you reach St George (population 2200), where cotton is grown on irrigated land. Much further west is Cunnamulla (population 1600), 254 km north of Bourke in NSW and very definitely out in the outback. This is another sheep raising centre and is noted for its wildflowers after rain. The Yowah opal fields are about 150 km further west.

OTHER TOWNS
Near Toowoomba other agricultural towns include Gatton (population 4200) and Dalby, a crossroads town in what is probably the richest grain-growing area in Australia. About 20 km south-east of Gatton is the pioneer village at Laidley, open on Sunday afternoons.

South of Toowoomba towards Warwick, Allora (population 700) also has a historical museum, which is open on Sunday afternoons. Cunningham's Gap National Park is 50 km east of Allora and has extensive bushwalking tracks. Boonah (population 1900) is just off the Brisbane-

Warwick road, near the Fassifern Valley National Park, and Clifton (population 700) is another town in the same area.

North of Toowoomba is Crows Nest (population 1000) which took its name from a local Aboriginal, Jim Crow, who lived in a hollow tree near the town site. Follow the Valley of Diamonds signs to the Crows Nest Falls National Park where there are good walking trails to the gorge and falls.

ROMA (population 5700)

An early Queensland settlement and now a sheep and cattle raising centre Roma also has some curious small industries. There's enough oil around Roma to support a small local refinery, producing just enough petroleum for local use. Gas deposits here are rather larger; Roma supplies Brisbane through a 450 km pipeline. There's also a small local winery, the Romavilla Winery which is open daily. Roma is a crossroads town for travellers heading north, south, east or west.

On the way to Roma from Toowoomba and Dalby you pass through Chinchilla (population 3100). In the western part of the Darling Downs, 355 km from Brisbane, Chinchilla is yet another busy agricultural town and has an interesting folk museum. Just beyond Chinchilla is Miles (population 1300) with a historical museum and brilliant wildflowers in the spring.

West of Roma towards Charleville is Mitchell (population 1200) from where an interesting but rugged unsurfaced road leads north into the Carnarvon Range National Park in the Great Dividing Range.

CHARLEVILLE (population 3500)

Way inland from Brisbane, about 800 km from the coast, Charleville is the terminus of the Westlander railway service and the centre for a huge cattle and sheep raising region. This was an important crossroads for early explorers and something of an oasis in the outback. It was a real frontier town around the turn of the century. There are various reminders around the town of the early explorers and a historical museum in the 1880 Queensland National Bank building on Albert St.

The Channel Country

The remote and sparsely populated south-west corner of Queensland, bordering the Northern Territory, South Australia and NSW, takes its name from the myriad channels which criss-cross the area. In this inhospitable region it hardly ever rains but the water from the northern monsoon pours into the channel country along the Georgina, Hamilton and Diamantina Rivers and Coopers Creek. Flooding towards the great depression of Lake Eyre this mass of water arrives on this huge, virtually flat plain and meanders aimlessly, eventually drying up in waterholes or salt pans or simply sinking back into the ground.

Only on rare occasions (the early '70s during this century) does the vast amount of water that pours west actually manage to reach Lake Eyre and fill it. For a period after each wet season, however, the channel country does achieve a short fertile period and cattle are grazed here. Soon the land returns to its barren, dusty dryness.

During the October to May wet season, even surfaced roads are often cut and the dirt roads become quagmires. In addition, the summer heat at that time is unbearable so a visit to this region is best made in the cool, dry winter period from May to September. Visiting this area requires a sturdy vehicle, four-wheel drive if you want to get off the beaten track, and some experience of outback driving. West of Cunnamulla and Quilpie you should carry plenty of petrol and water and should notify police so that if you don't turn up in the next town, the necessary steps can be taken.

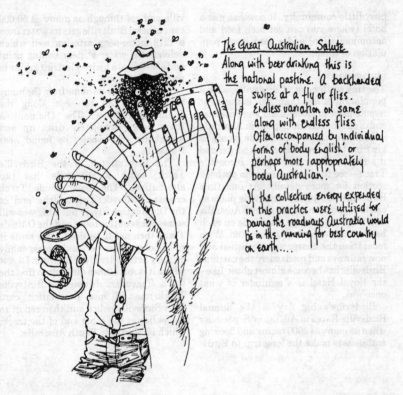

The Great Australian Salute

Along with beer drinking this is the national pastime. A backhanded swipe at a fly or flies. Endless variation on same along with endless flies Often accompanied by individual forms of 'body English' or perhaps more appropriately 'body Australian'.

If the collective energy expended in this practice were utilized for paving the roadways Australia would be in the running for best country on earth....

MT ISA TO CHARLEVILLE

The main road through the channel country is the Diamantina Development Road that runs south from Mt Isa through Dajarra and Boulia to Bedourie and then turns east through Windorah and Quilpie to Charleville. In all it's a long and lonely 1340 km although, fortunately, about half of the road is surfaced.

Boulia (population 300) is the 'capital' of the channel country and near here the mysterious 'Min Min' light, a sort of earthbound UFO, is sometimes seen. Bourke and Wills passed through here on their long trek. Windorah is either very dry or very wet but it's a welcome stop in the middle of nowhere. Quilpie is the railhead from which cattle, grazed here during the fertile wet season, are railed to the coast. Charleville is a comparatively large town.

OTHER ROUTES

The Kennedy Development Road runs from Wilton to Boulia and is partly surfaced with a couple of stops on the way. From Quilpie to Birdsville you follow the Diamantina road through Windorah but then branch off south to Betoota. It's 394 dull, dull, dull km from Windorah to Birdsville. Betoota, with one store and one pub, is absolutely all there is along the way.

South of Quilpie is Thargomindah from where camel trains used to cross to Bourke in NSW. Nocundra was once a busy little community. It now has just a hotel (where you can get fuel, food and accommodation) and a permanent population of three!

BIRDSVILLE

The tiny settlement of Birdsville, with a population of less than 200, is the most remote place in Queensland and possesses one of the most famous pubs in Australia – the *Birdsville Pub*. Birdsville is only 12 km from the South Australian border and it's the northern end of the Birdsville Track – see the South Australia outback section for more details. At one time Birdsville was quite a busy little place as cattle were driven south to South Australia and a customs charge was made on each head of cattle leaving Queensland. With federation the charge was abolished and now railways and roads carry the cattle so Birdsville has become almost ghost-like – the Royal Hotel is a reminder of what once was.

Birdsville's big day is the annual Birdsville Races in August or September when as many as 3000 racing and boozing enthusiasts make the long trip to Birdsville and get through as many as 50,000 cans of beer! Birdsville gets its water from a 1219-metre-deep artesian well which delivers the water at near boiling point and also drives a hydro-electric turbine to provide electricity.

The town takes its name from the many birds which can be seen along the Diamantina River. The Diamantina River never completely dries up and waterholes can usually be found near Birdsville.

The first stretch of the Birdsville Track, south of Birdsville, has two alternatives. The usual Inside Track crosses the Goyder Lagoon (the 'end' of the Diamantina River) but a big wet will sometimes cut this route and the Outside Track then has to be used. This route is much longer, however, and crosses sandy country at the edge of the Simpson Desert where it is sometimes difficult to find the track. Travellers driving the Birdsville Track must fill in a 'destination' card with Birdsville police and then report to the police at the other end of the track, which is Marree in South Australia.

South Australia

Area	984,000 square km
Population	1,350,000

Don't miss beautiful Adelaide, the wine country to north and south, the mighty Murray River and the terrific Flinders Ranges.

South Australia is the most urbanised and also the driest of the states. Even Western Australia doesn't have such a large proportion of desert. Adelaide, the capital, once had a reputation as the 'wowser's' capital and was contemptuously referred to as 'the city of churches'. The churches may still be there but otherwise times have changed.

Today the city's cultural spirit is epitomised in the biennial Adelaide Arts Festival. The death of wowserism is nowhere better seen than in the Barossa Valley Wine Festival which takes place on alternate years. South Australia's relatively liberal attitude is demonstrated in Australia's first legal nudist beach just a short drive south of the city. Since 1985 Adelaide has also been the site for the Australian Formula One Grand Prix.

Outside Adelaide the state is best known for its vineyards and wineries. The famous Barossa Valley, north of the city, is probably the best known wine-producing area in the country, even though the amount of 'Barossa wine' produced annually far exceeds the grape-growing capacity of the valley! South Australia also has the fine Clare and Coonawarra Valleys and the southern vineyards are only a very short drive from the city. Wine festivals in South Australia are frequent and fun.

Further north the rough and rugged Flinders Ranges make an ideal area for all sorts of outdoor activities; this is another of my favourite Australian places. The far north and west of the state has some of the most barren and inhospitable land in Australia although several years of unexpectedly heavy rain turned some of the inland salt lakes at least temporarily into the real, water-filled thing in the mid '70s.

The drive across the Nullarbor used to be one of the more accessible of Australia's outback driving adventures but the new road, opened in '76 (it was already surfaced westward from the South Australia-Western Australia border), has civilised even that long drive. The road actually runs close to the cliff tops along the Great Australian Bight. That still leaves you the Murray River, the interesting coast towards the Victorian border, fascinating Kangaroo Island, plus the Eyre, Yorke and Fleurieu Peninsulas to explore.

GEOGRAPHY

South Australia is Australia's most urbanised state; apart from Adelaide, the state is sparsely settled. Adelaide, the Fleurieu Peninsula to the south and the country to the north, with the well-known wine-producing Barossa and Clare Valleys, are green and fertile but most of the rest of the state is definitely not. As you travel further north it becomes progressively drier and more inhospitable and most of the north is a vast area of desert and dry salt-lakes with only scattered, tiny settlements.

One area of this dry land is not to be missed, however, and that's the magnificent Flinders Ranges, a desert

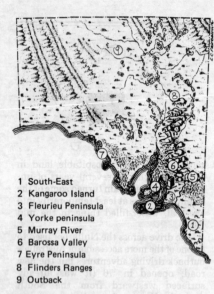

1 South-East
2 Kangaroo Island
3 Fleurieu Peninsula
4 Yorke peninsula
5 Murray River
6 Barossa Valley
7 Eyre Peninsula
8 Flinders Ranges
9 Outback

NSW
31 King St, Sydney 2000 (tel 232 8388)
South Australia
18 King William St, Adelaide 5000 (tel 212 1644)
Victoria
25 Elizabeth St, Melbourne 3000 (tel 61 2431)
Western Australia
111 St Georges Terrace, Perth 6000 (tel 321 0141)

There is a bed & breakfast pub programme operating throughout South Australia. The tourist office has a booklet listing participating hotels, which are good value and are mostly old, well-looked-after pubs.

GETTING AROUND
Air Ansett-owned Airlines of South Australia is the main regional operator in South Australia. They operate F27s on routes which principally fan out from Adelaide to places like Mt Gambier, Kangaroo Island, Port Lincoln, Streaky Bay and Ceduna. They also fly over the NSW border to Broken Hill. There are a number of other local operators in South Australia including a whole collection who fly to Kangaroo Island.

There are also flights to Oodnadatta, Innamincka, Birdsville, Hawker and Broken Hill. The chart shows the main South Australian air fares.

ACTIVITIES
Bushwalking Close to Adelaide there are many good walks in the Mt Lofty Ranges including the Belair Park, Cleland Park, Morialta Park, Deep Creek Park, Bridgewater-Aldgate, Barossa Reservoir and Parra Wirra Park.

In the Flinders Ranges, 400 km from Adelaide, there are excellent walks in the Wilpena Pound area as well as further south in the Mt Remarkable National Park or further north in the Arkaroola-Mt Painter Sanctuary area. Some of the walks in this area are for the more experienced walker since conditions can

mountain range of exceptional beauty and great interest. South Australia is also noted for its peninsulas and coastline. Starting from the Victorian border there's the south-east region with Mt Gambier, the wine-producing Coonawarra area and the long, coastal lake of the Coorong. Then there's the Fleurieu Peninsula with nearby Kangaroo Island, the Yorke Peninsula, the remote Eyre Peninsula fading into the Great Australian Bight, and finally the Nullarbor Plain which leads to Western Australia.

INFORMATION
The South Australian Government Travel Centre has offices in Melbourne and Sydney as well as in Adelaide. They have a series of regional brochures which are amongst the most useful literature produced by state tourist offices in Australia. These brochures have maps, sightseeing and accommodation details, even restaurants. The travel centres can also supply more basic leaflets on travel details, accommodation costs and so on.

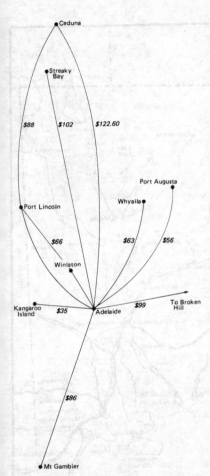

longer weekend walks in the Flinders Ranges. Hiking information can also be obtained from bushgear shops such as Thor Adventure Equipment, 40 Weymouth St, Adelaide.

Swimming & Surfing There is no surf at popular city beaches like Glenelg but as you travel further south there are plenty of good beaches and good surf. Seacliff, Brighton (sailing too), Somerton, Glenelg, West Beach, Henley Beach, Grange, West Lake, Semaphore, Glanville and Largs Bay are all popular beaches. Skinny-dipping is permitted at Maslins Beach, 40 km south of the city. You have to get over to Pondalowie on the Yorke Peninsula for SA's best board riding.

Other good surf areas can be found along the Eyre Peninsula; also close to Adelaide at Boomer and Chiton; between Victor Harbor and Port Elliott; and also near Goolwa.

Scuba Diving There are lots of diving possibilities around Adelaide and with proof of diving experience you can hire equipment in the city. Several of the shipwrecks off Kangaroo Island are easily accessible to scuba divers. Port Noarlunga reef marine reserve (18 km south) and Aldinga (43 km south) are good centres for boat diving. The reefs around Schnapper Point are suitable for snorkelling. At Rapid Bay (88 km south) you can dive from the jetty and there is abundant marine life.

Wallaroo on the Yorke Peninsula, Port Lincoln on the Eyre Peninsula and Second Valley (65 km south of Adelaide) are some other good areas.

Sailing & Canoeing There is good sailing all along the Adelaide shoreline of Gulf St Vincent and there are lots of sailing clubs. The Murray River and the Coorong are popular for canoeing trips and visitors can hire equipment and join in canoe trips organised by canoeing associations in South Australia.

be extreme. Get a copy of *Flinders Ranges Walks*, produced by the Conservation Council of South Australia.

The Heysen Trail is a walking trail from Encounter Bay at the bottom of the Fleurieu Peninsula up to the Barossa Valley. It's hoped to link this up with a series of walking trails right up into the Flinders. There are several bushwalking clubs in the Adelaide area which organise weekend walks in the Mt Lofty Ranges or

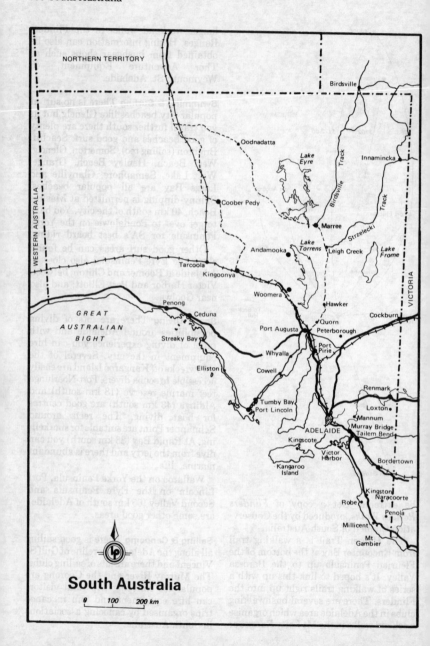

NORTHERN TERRITORY

WESTERN AUSTRALIA

VICTORIA

Birdsville

Innamincka

Oodnadatta

Lake Eyre

Birdsville Track

Coober Pedy

Marree

Strzelecki Track

Andamooka

Lake Torrens

Leigh Creek

Lake Frome

Tarcoola

Kingoonya

Woomera

Hawker

Cockburn

GREAT AUSTRALIAN BIGHT

Penong

Ceduna

Port Augusta

Quorn

Peterborough

Streaky Bay

Whyalla

Port Pirie

Elliston

Cowell

Renmark

Loxton

Tumby Bay

Port Lincoln

Mannum

Murray Bridge

Tailem Bend

ADELAIDE

Kingscote

Victor Harbor

Bordertown

Kangaroo Island

Kingston

Naracoorte

Robe

Penola

Millicent

Mt Gambier

South Australia

0   100   200 km

Adelaide

Population: 980,000

Adelaide is a solid, dare I even say, gracious city. It even looks solid; when the early colonists built they generally built in solid stone. It goes further than architecture however, for despite all the liberalism of the Dunstan years, Adelaide is still an inherently conservative city; an 'old money' place. In part that's due to Adelaide's role in Australia. It can't compete with Sydney or Melbourne in the big city stakes nor with Perth or Brisbane as a go-ahead centre for the resources boom, so it goes its own way; for the visitor that's one of the nicest parts about it. Adelaide is civilised and calm in a way no other Australian city can match. What's more, it has a superb setting – the city centre is surrounded by green parkland and further out the whole metropolitan area is rimmed by a fine range of hills, the Mt Lofty Ranges, which crowd the city against the sea.

Information

The South Australian Government Travel Centre (tel 212 1644) is at 18 King William St right in the centre of Adelaide. It's open 8.15 am to 5.30 pm on weekdays, 9 am to 2 pm on Saturdays, Sundays and public holidays. On Wednesday evenings at 8 pm they show films about South Australia.

The Royal Automobile Association of SA (tel 223 4555) is also very central at 41 Hindmarsh Square – they have a good bookshop section.

The Adelaide YHA office (tel 51 5583) is on the first floor of the Recreation and Sports Centre at the corner of King William and Sturt Sts. It's only open Monday, Wednesday, Thursday and Friday from 11 am to 3 pm and on Tuesday evening from 6.30 to 8.30 pm.

City Books at 108 Gawler Place is an excellent bookshop on two levels; or try Standard Books, a big bookshop of the old-fashioned school with a wide range at 136 Rundle Mall. Try the excellent Europa Bookshop at 58 Pulteney St by Hindmarsh Square for an excellent selection of foreign-language books. For Aboriginal arts and crafts visit the New Gallery of Aboriginal Art at 28 Currie St.

Orientation

Adelaide is laid out on a very straightforward grid pattern, interspersed with several squares. The main street through the centre of town is King William St with Victoria Square forming the dead centre of the central city area. The GPO is on King William St by Victoria Square. Continue north up King William St and the tourist bureau is on the other side of the road.

Running across King William the streets change name from one side to the other. The main shopping and restaurant street is Hindley on the west side changing to Rundle St on the east. Rundle St is a mall from King William through to Pulteney Sts. The next block up is North Terrace with the railway station just to the west and a string of major public buildings including the university and the museum to the east. Continuing north you're in the North Parklands with the Festival Centre; then it's across the Torrens River and into North Adelaide, also laid out in a straightforward grid pattern.

Around the City

Adelaide's most interesting streets are Rundle Mall and Hindley St. Rundle Mall was one of Australia's first city malls and is certainly one of the most successful. It's colourful, always full of activity and you'll find most of the big city shops along it. Street buskers add to the fun. Across King William St (the main drag of Adelaide), Rundle Mall becomes Hindley St. This is the Adelaide left-bank/sin centre if such a solid place as Adelaide can be imagined to have such a centre.

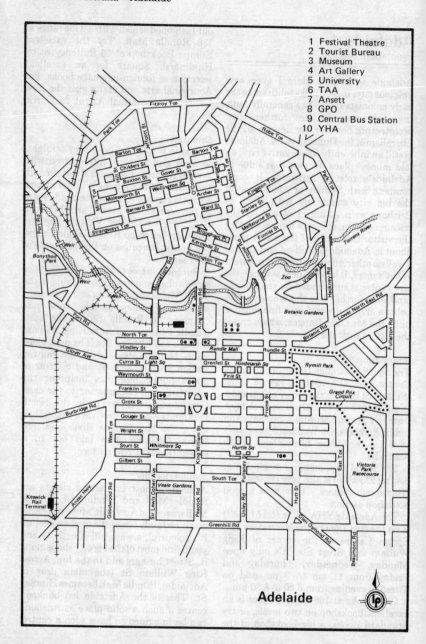

1 Festival Theatre
2 Tourist Bureau
3 Museum
4 Art Gallery
5 University
6 TAA
7 Ansett
8 GPO
9 Central Bus Station
10 YHA

Adelaide

Well, you'll find the odd strip club and 'adult book shop' along here, together with plenty of reasonably priced restaurants and snack bars.

Running parallel to both these streets is North Terrace, a fine old boulevard with city buildings on one side and the university, state library, art gallery, museum, and Government House on the other.

South Australian Museum

On North Terrace the fine museum is an Adelaide landmark with huge whale skeletons exhibited in the front window. In front of the building there's a three-thousand-year-old Egyptian column thought to have been erected by Rameses II. The museum has a huge Aboriginal collection and excellent collections from New Guinea and Melanesia. It's a fine museum, not to be missed and has been undergoing improvements inside and out. Opening hours are 10 am to 5 pm every day, except Wednesday when it's 1 to 5 pm and Sunday, 2 to 5 pm. On Sundays and public holidays, free tours are given at 2.30 pm.

Other Museums

On North Terrace by the railway station, the Constitutional Museum is the only political history museum in Australia. It features a 100-minute audio-visual on the state's history. To see the full show, which includes a tour, is $3. An abbreviated half-hour show and tour is $1. The museum is housed in the old Legislative Council building and is open Monday to Friday 10 am to 5 pm, weekends 1.30 to 5 pm. Admission is $2.50.

Behind the Art Gallery of SA on North Terrace, the South Australian Historical Museum was erected in 1867 and is open Monday to Saturday from 10 am to 5 pm (Wednesday to 9 pm) and on Sundays from 1.30 to 5 pm.

There's a Railway Museum on Railway Terrace off West Beach Rd at Mile End South. It tells the history of railways in

the state and displays early railway engines. Admission is 60c and it's open on the first and third Sunday of the month from 2 to 5 pm. At Electra House, 131 King William St, there's a Telecommunications Museum open weekdays from 10.30 am to 3.30 pm.

St Kilda, 30 km from the centre, has an Australian Electrical Transport Museum with historic transport vehicles, open Sundays 1 to 5 pm. There's a Shipping Museum (open by appointment) on the corner of Causeway and Semaphore Rds in Glanville.

Other museums are: the Historical Museum at Hindmarsh Place, Hindmarsh, which is open on Sunday afternoons; the National Motor Museum at the Birdwood Mill, Birdwood, open daily; and the Pioneer Village Museum on South Rd in Morphett Vale, also open on Sundays.

Art Galleries

On North Terrace the Art Gallery of South Australia has a good contemporary section both of Australian and overseas artists. The South-East Asian ceramic collection is also of particular note. The gallery has a pleasant little coffee shop with outside tables.

Other galleries include the Festival Centre gallery near the playhouse; Quality Five, a group of five craft galleries located in the City Cross Arcade; and a number of other private galleries around town.

Ayers House & Edmund Wright House

On North Terrace close to the city centre, this fine old mansion was originally constructed in 1846 but was added to and extended over the next 30 years. Now completely restored, it houses two restaurants but is open for visitors on weekends between 2 and 4 pm. There are also tours on the hour between 10 am and 4 pm Tuesday to Friday; admission is $2. The elegant bluestone building serves as the headquarters of the SA National Trust.

At 59 King William St, Edmund

Wright House was originally built in 1876 for the Bishop of South Australia in an elaborate Renaissance style with intricate decorations. It is now used as government offices and for official functions.

Other City Buildings

The imposing town hall, built in 1863-66 in 16th century Renaissance style, looks out on King William St. Faces of Queen Victoria and Prince Albert are carved into the facade. The post office across the road is almost as imposing. On North Terrace, Government House was built between 1838 and 1840 with a later addition in the centre in 1855. The earliest section is one of the oldest in Adelaide. Parliament House on North Terrace is fronted by 10 Corinthian marble columns. It was commenced in 1883 but not completed until 1939.

Holy Trinity Church, also on North Terrace, was commenced in 1838 and was the first Anglican church in South Australia. Other early churches are St Francis Xavier Cathedral on Wakefield St (commenced between 1856 and 1858) and St Peter's Cathedral in Pennington Terrace, North Adelaide (built between 1869 and 1876). St Francis Xavier Cathedral is beside Victoria Square, where you will also find a number of other important early buildings: the 1847-50 Magistrate's Court House (originally used as the Supreme Court); the 1869 Supreme Court; and the Treasury Building. Adelaide's Central Market (open on Tuesdays, Fridays and Saturdays) has all sorts of food and bargains.

Festival Centre

The Adelaide Festival Centre is close to the Torrens River, looking uncannily like a squared-off version of the vastly more expensive Sydney Opera House. It performs a very similar function with its variety of auditoriums and theatres. The complex was completed in 1977 and there are tours hourly on Monday to Friday

from 10 am to 4 pm and on Saturdays at 10.30 am, 11.30 am, 2 and 3 pm. They can be changed without notice so it's wise to phone 213 4600 and check. The tours cost $2.

One of the most pleasant aspects of the Festival Theatre is its riverside setting; people picnic on the grass in front of the theatre and there are several places to eat. You can also hire pedal paddle-boats from right in front of the centre. There are often free concerts and exhibitions here. In the Piano Room, on weekends from 2 to 4 pm, you can catch a free jazz or blues band or maybe a comedy revue.

Adelaide Arts Festival

South Australia enjoys two of Australia's major festivals: the Barossa Valley Vintage Festival on odd numbered years; and the Adelaide Arts Festival on the even years. The three-week festival of the arts attracts culture-vultures from all over Australia to dance, drama, music and other live performances; plus a writers' week, art exhibitions, poetry readings and other activities with guest speakers and performers from all over the world. Today the festival boasts 300 or more separate performances and next takes place in 1988 and 1990 in February-March.

Adelaide Grand Prix

The Australian Formula One Grand Prix takes place in Adelaide in late October or early November each year. The first event was in 1985 and was a huge success. The track is laid out on city streets immediately to the east of the city centre. The cars reach 300 kph down Dequetteville Terrace.

Although this must be one of the easiest Grand Prix in the world for spectator parking, on the first running getting into the circuit proved very difficult and the general admission area desperately needs proper viewing embankments if spectators (other than those right in the front) are going to get a good view. It's expensive

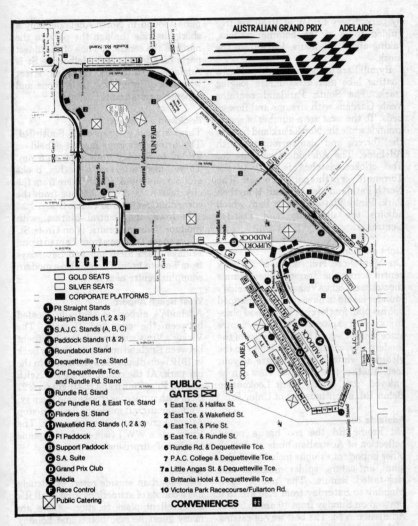

AUSTRALIAN GRAND PRIX   ADELAIDE

FUN FAIR

General Admission

PADDOCK

SUPPORT PADDOCK

GOLD AREA

FLAG

PADDOCK

S.A.J.C. Stands

LEGEND

☐ GOLD SEATS
☐ SILVER SEATS
■ CORPORATE PLATFORMS

1 Pit Straight Stands
2 Hairpin Stands (1, 2 & 3)
3 S.A.J.C. Stands (A, B, C)
4 Paddock Stands (1 & 2)
5 Roundabout Stand
6 Dequetteville Tce. Stand
7 Cnr Dequetteville Tce. and Rundle Rd. Stand
8 Rundle Rd. Stand
9 Cnr Rundle Rd. & East Tce. Stand
10 Flinders St. Stand
11 Wakefield Rd. Stands (1, 2 & 3)
A F1 Paddock
B Support Paddock
C S.A. Suite
D Grand Prix Club
E Media
F Race Control
☒ Public Catering

PUBLIC GATES ☒

1 East Tce. & Halifax St.
2 East Tce. & Wakefield St.
4 East Tce. & Pirie St.
5 East Tce. & Rundle St.
6 Rundle Rd. & Dequetteville Tce.
7 P.A.C. College & Dequetteville Tce.
7a Little Angas St. & Dequetteville Tce.
8 Brittania Hotel & Dequetteville Tce.
10 Victoria Park Racecourse/Fullarton Rd.

CONVENIENCES ♿

but quite a spectacle; just make sure you come early enough to get a view. With practice sessions and supporting races the event goes on for five days and all Adelaide gets into it.

Botanic Gardens & Other Parks

On North Terrace the botanic gardens have pleasant artificial lakes and are only a short stroll from the city centre. The glass Palm House was made in Germany in 1871. The central area of Adelaide is completely surrounded by green parkland, and the Torrens River, itself bordered by park, separates Adelaide from North Adelaide which in turn is also surrounded by park. Every Friday at 10.30 am free guided tours of the botanic gardens, taking about 1½ hours, leave from the kiosk.

Rymill Park in the East Parkland has a boating lake and a 600-metre jogging track. The South Parkland contains Veale Gardens with streams and flower-beds. To the west are a number of sports grounds while the North Parkland borders the Torrens and also surrounds North Adelaide. The Adelaide Oval, site for Test cricket matches, is north of the Torrens River in this part of the park. The North Parkland also contains Bonython Park, Pinky Flat and Elder Park which adjoins the university and Festival Centre.

Light's Vision
On Montefiore Hill, north of the city centre across the Torrens River, stands the statue of Light's Vision. Here Adelaide's founder is said to have stood and mapped out his plan for the city. It is a good place to start your exploration of the city centre since you get a good bird's eye view of the modern city, with green parkland and the gleaming white Festival Centre at your feet. Another fine Adelaide view can be enjoyed from Windy Point Lookout in Belair Rd, a continuation of Unley Rd.

Adelaide Zoo
On Frome Rd the zoo has a noted collection of Australian birds as well as other important exhibits including sloths, giant ant-eaters, spider monkeys and ring-tailed lemurs. The zoo is open Monday to Saturday from 9.30 am to 5 pm and on Sunday from 10 am to 5 pm. Admission is $4. The best way of getting to the zoo is to take a cruise down-river on board the *Popeye*. The trip costs just $1 and departs from Elder Park in front of the Festival Centre. The return trip is $1.80.

North Adelaide
Interesting old bluestone buildings and pubs abound in North Adelaide, only a short bus ride through the park to the north of the centre. It's one of the oldest parts of Adelaide and Melbourne St is Adelaide's swankiest shopping street with lots of interesting little shops and expensive restaurants.

Brickworks Markets
Three km out of town at 36 South Rd, Thebarton, this large market is held on Friday to Sunday from 9 am to 5 pm. There's food, arts, crafts, clothes, books and plain old junk. To get there from the city take a 29, 301 or 302 bus from the corner of Grenfell and Currie Sts.

In town, the Central Market, with produce, fish and crafts, is on Grote St. It's open on Tuesdays from 7 am to 6 pm, Fridays 7 am to 10 pm and Saturdays from 7 am to 1 pm. There's also a modern shopping centre next to it.

West Beach Airport
Adelaide's airport is centrally located between the city and Glenelg. The Vicker's Vimy which made the first flight between England and Australia way back in 1919 is on display in a showroom in the car park. At the controls were Sir Keith and Sir Ross Smith and the flight took 27 days with numerous stops along the way. A similar aircraft made the first non-stop Atlantic crossing in the same year. The Vimy was a WW I twin-engined biplane bomber of surprisingly large size.

Glenelg
The suburban seaside resort of Glenelg has a couple of attractions: first of all it's an excellent place to stay – there are many guest houses, hotels and holiday flats here if you can't find something suitable in the city; secondly it's one of the oldest parts of Adelaide – the first South Australian colonists actually landed here, so there are a number of places of historic interest. As a bonus Glenelg is exceptionally easy to get to. Adelaide's only tram runs from Victoria Square in

the centre right to Glenelg Beach. It costs $1 (70c between 9 am and 3 pm) and is commendably fast as its route keeps it separate from the road traffic.

At the jetty in front of the Town Hall and by the beach is Bay World; you can't miss the camel out the front. Pick up a map or walking or cycling-tour brochure from the helpful information desk here. Aside from the souvenirs sold here there is a museum-aquarium with sea-life in tanks and apparently a shrunken human head amongst the curios. Admission is $2. You can also rent bicycles here before you set off to explore. Glenelg is one of the most popular of the Adelaide beaches which stretch in a long chain south of the city. On Macfarlane St the Old Gum Tree marks the place where the proclamation of South Australia was read in 1836. Governor Hindmarsh and the first colonists landed on the beach near here. Apart from Glenelg's fine early buildings it also has a popular amusement park behind the beach including one of those all-the-rage waterslides.

The boat harbour shelters a large number of yachts and Glenelg's premier attraction: a reproduction of *HMS Buffalo*, the original settlers' conveyance. Used as a rather expensive restaurant, it's also open to visitors for $2 from 10 am to 5 pm daily (closed 12 noon to 2.30 pm on Wednesdays). The original *Buffalo* was built in 1813 in India.

Jetty Rd, the main street, is lined with shops and restaurants and the tram line goes right down the centre. Shell Land, at the corner of Mary and Melbourne Sts, has a large collection of sea shells.

Marineland Park

Just north of Glenelg and adjoining Adelaide airport is the dolphins-through-the-hoops marine park on Military Rd, West Beach. The seals and dolphins go through their paces at 11 am, 12.30 pm and 3 pm daily. The park also has an aquarium with sharks and rays and a 360° audio-visual show. Admission is $5.50.

Other Suburbs

In Jetty St, Grange you can see Sturt's Cottage, the home of the famous early Australian explorer. Preserved as a museum, it's open Wednesday to Sunday and public holidays from 1 to 5 pm. In Semaphore there's Fort Glanville, built in 1878 when Australia was having its phase of Russia-phobia as a result of the Crimean War. It's open during the summer. In Port Adelaide you can make boat trips from North Parade Wharf except during July.

Places to Stay

Adelaide is not the best city in Australia for cheap and central accommodation, although things have improved marginally in the past few years and there are now a few bargains in the centre. The city also has standard old hotels and moderately-priced guest-houses. Other than that you have to move out of the centre, particularly to the beach suburb of Glenelg which has several campsites as well.

Hostels Adelaide's *Youth Hostel* (tel 223 6007) is fairly central at 290 Gilles St, about a 20-minute walk from the mall. It's recently been renovated and expanded from the old, always-full, 16-bed hostel that it used to be. It's all very neat and new-looking and the warden seems to run a tight ship. There's a book outside the door listing alternative places if the hostel is full when you arrive. The office hours are 8 to 9.30 am and 5.30 to 10 pm and the doors are locked the rest of the time.

Nearby is the very pleasant, low-key *Adelaide Backpackers Hostel* (tel 223 5680) at 263 Gilles St. Catch a 191 or 192 bus from Pulteney St in the centre or take any bus going to the South Terrace area although it's not really that far to walk. It's a small hostel with three dorm-rooms with a total capacity of about 50 people, a small lounge and a kitchen. It's a friendly, casual place which charges $6 with a $1 charge for linen if you need it.

The office is open from 8 to 10 am and from 5 to 10 pm.

The *YMCA* (tel 223 1611) at 76 Flinders St is very central, takes guests of either sex and is not a bad place at all. Dorms are $6, share-twin rooms are $8 and singles $10. Weekly rates are six times the daily rates. The Y also has a very economical cafeteria serving breakfasts and dinners. There's also a TV lounge, laundrette and sporting facilities including squash and a sauna. Office hours are 9 am to 9.30 pm Monday to Thursday, 9 am to 9 pm on Friday, and 9 am to 12 noon and 4 to 8 pm on weekends and holidays. Even if there is room, you won't get in outside these hours.

Lastly, women might try the Salvation Army's *Sutherland Lodge* (tel 223 3423) and for men there's the *Mens' Hostel* (tel 51 2554) on Whitmore Square.

City Hotels The *Metropolitan Hotel* (tel 51 5471) at 46 Grote St is central and cheap at $12 for room-only and they give a discount to bus-pass travellers.

Around the corner and down the block from the youth hostel, the *Afton Private Hotel* (tel 223 3416) at 260 South Terrace costs $12 but with a YHA card you get a discount rate of $8, going down to $6 on subsequent nights. By the week it's $51 for non-YHA members. There are kitchen facilities and if you arrive after 8 pm phone ahead before turning up. It's a big place with 100 rooms but is apparently always full in winter.

Other central hotels include the *Plaza Private Hotel* (tel 55 6371) at 85 Hindley St. Rooms with wash-basins cost from $20/29. The Plaza is an old but well-kept place built around a very pleasant palm-filled central courtyard. Alternatively there's the *Angas Hotel* (tel 223 5649) at 78 Angas St where the rate is $15/25 including a light breakfast. At 205 Rundle St the *Austral Hotel* (tel 223 4660) gives a 10% discount to Aussiepass and Eaglepass travellers. Room-only costs $16/28 for singles/doubles.

The *Criterion Hotel* (tel 51 4301) at 137 King William St is conveniently close to the Central Bus Station and costs $15 per person for room-only. At 437 Pulteney St the *Hotel Hanson* (tel 223 2442) costs $20/35 for singles/doubles including breakfast. This is a flashier place with air-con, colour TV and tea and coffee-making facilities but there are only seven rooms.

Finally the *Centralia* (tel 51 4536) at 65 North Terrace costs $15/26 and the *Somerset Hotel* (tel 223 2768) at the corner of Pulteney and Flinders Sts is $14 per person; both room-only. The *King's Head* is at 357 King William St and charges $16/30 including a full breakfast.

City Motels & Guest-Houses Right in the city centre is the *Clarice City Motel* (tel 223 3560) at 220 Hutt St, also just around the corner from the youth hostel. There are some cheap rooms here in the old part of the building but the motel units are $29/34. At 262 Hindley St is the *Princes Arcade Motel* (tel 51 9524) with bed & breakfast rates of $29/36.

Other Motels Although you'll find motels all over Adelaide – some are also covered under Glenelg – there's a 'motel alley' along Glen Osmond Rd, which is the road that leads in to the city centre from the south-east. This is quite a busy road so places can be a bit noisy.

Powell's Court (tel 271 7995) is only two km from the centre at 2 Glen Osmond Rd, Parkside. Rooms are $30/32 which doesn't sound like great value but they all have kitchens and there are also rooms big enough for three or four for not much more than the price of a double. All the usual mod-cons (TV, air-con) are there as well as fridges and cooking facilities.

The *Sunny South Motel* (tel 79 1621) is four km out at 190 Glen Osmond Rd, Fullarton and offers the usual sort of motel standards for $30/33 and up. Across the road is *Princes Highway* (tel 79 3080) at 199 Glen Osmond Rd, Frewville which costs $27/30 and up.

Alternatively there's the *Sands* (tel 79 6861) at 198 Glen Osmond Rd, Fullarton which costs $28/32; or the *Motel 277* (tel 79 9911) at 277 Glen Osmond Rd, Glenunga, four km from the centre. It's excellent value at $28 for a standard double (there are also twin-rooms with kitchens) but prices go up at holidays and long weekends. Weekly rates are five times the daily rate.

Glenelg Accommodation Glenelg is the main city beach suburb, just 10 km from the city centre on the other side of the airport. It's easily reached by Adelaide's one remaining tram line, a popular 15-minute excursion. There's a lot of accommodation here: a couple of old hotels, a number of good guest houses, a handful of reasonably priced motels and a lot of holiday flats. The main road down to the sea in Glenelg is Jetty Rd, along which the tram runs. The road along the seafront is South Esplanade, which becomes North Esplanade on the other side of the boat harbour entrance.

Down at the waterfront at 2 Jetty Rd is the spacious old *Glenelg Pier Hotel* (tel 295 4116). This is a seaside hotel of the old school and rooms are $14/25, or $26/34 with private facilities. The tariff includes a light breakfast. At 16 South Esplanade the old-fashioned *Oriental Private Hotel* (tel 295 2390) costs $15/30 including a substantial breakfast. The *St Vincent Hotel* (tel 294 4377) at 28 Jetty Rd has rooms ranging from $20/36 for singles/ doubles with breakfast.

Colley House (tel 295 7535), at 22 Colley Terrace opposite the reserve, offers serviced apartments all the way from $28 to $65. There are a lot of flats and apartments in Glenelg; most quote weekly rather than daily rates.

At 7 North Esplanade the *Alkoomi Holiday Motel* (tel 294 6624) has double rooms from $29 to $38 all with private facilities, fridges and tea/coffee-making equipment. The adjoining *Wambini Lodge* (tel 295 4689) is similarly priced.

The *Norfolk Motel* (tel 295 6354) is at 69-71 Broadway, a few blocks south of Jetty Rd. It's a fairly small motel with 20 units for $32/36 including breakfast. The *Bay Hotel Motel* (tel 294 4244) is $25/30 with air-con, colour TV and tea/coffee-making facilities. It's at 58 Broadway, about half a km from the beach. The hotel section does counter lunches. There are lots of restaurants and take-away places down Jetty Rd; Glenelg is noted for its Greek food.

The tourist office has a list of holiday flats here and in other beach suburbs. They average $28 to $40 depending on the time of year.

Other Beach Suburbs Glenelg isn't the only beach suburb with accommodation possibilities; you can also find plenty of places to stay at West Beach and Henley Beach, a little further north. West Beach in particular has a variety of holiday flats while at Henley Beach there are holiday flats and the reasonably priced *Delmonte Private Hotel* (tel 353 5155) on the Esplanade with rooms at $20/30.

University Colleges The usual vacation-only, students-preferred rules apply but the Adelaide universities are no longer such good places to try for a room. Phone the University Welfare officer at 223 4333, extension 2915, Monday to Friday from 9 am to 5 pm if you want to give it a try. You can also try the Flinders University Halls of Residence.

Camping There are quite a few camping sites around Adelaide although some of the more convenient ones do not take tents, only caravans. The tourist bureau has a useful brochure on camping and caravan parks around the city. The following are within a 15 km radius; all camping charges are per site.

Recreation Caravan Park (tel 278 3540), National Park, Belair, 13 km south, camping sites $5, on-site vans $17.

Sturt River Caravan Park (tel 296 7302), Brookside Rd, Darlington, 13 km south , camping $6.50 per day.

Adelaide Caravan Park (tel 42 1563), Bruton St, Hackney, two km north-east and by the Torrens River, camping $8 per day but limited number of tent sites, on-site vans from $18 per day.

Glenbrook Caravan Park (tel 42 2965), Portrush Rd and River St, Marden, five km north-east, camping $6 per day, on-site vans from $17 per day.

Marion Caravan Park (tel 276 6695), 323 Sturt Rd, Bedford Park, 12 km south, camping $5 per day, on-site vans $17 per day and they take five or six people.

Brownhill Creek Caravan Park (tel 271 4814), is situated in the foothills of the Mount Lofty Ranges at Mitcham, eight km south, camping is $7 per day, air-con on-site vans are $17.

Norwood Caravan Park (tel 31 5289), 290 Portrush Rd, Kensington, three km east, no camping, cabins from $22 per day for two and powered caravan sites $8.

Levi Park Caravan Park (tel 44 2209) is well located at Lansdowne Terrace, Walkerville, five km north-east, camping costs are $6.50 per day for four, on-site vans are $19 per day.

West Beach Caravan Park (tel 356 7654) Military Rd, West Beach, eight km west, camping $6.30 to $7.20 per day depending on season.

Marineland Caravan Village (tel 353 2655), Military Rd, West Beach, eight km west, no camping, on-site vans $25 to $35 per day depending on the season.

Windsor Gardens Caravan Park (tel 261 1091) is situated at 78 Windsor Gardens, six km north-east, camping costs here are $6 per person per day.

Places to Eat

Although Adelaide does not have the variety or quality range that Melbourne or Sydney can offer it certainly has quite enough to ensure survival with style! Furthermore, Adelaide is well equipped with places where you can eat outside. Licensing laws are more liberal in South Australia than in Sydney or Melbourne so a higher proportion of restaurants are licenced. Those which claim to be BYO are often just licensed restaurants which allow you to bring your own alcohol if you wish.

Open Air & Lunch Adelaide is one of the best cities in Australia for *al fresco* dining; the climate is dry so you're unlikely to get rained on, it's sunny so being outside is nice, and it's not so super-hot that for much of the year you're risking sunstroke.

Hindmarsh Square is a good place to start looking if you're after a lunch in the sun. There's a collection of snack bars and restaurants around the square and tables with umbrellas to complete the picture. On the north Pultenay St corner *Carrots* is a long-running health-food place although it has had the odd name change over the years. It's a nice, airy place to sit and look out over the square while you're munching on a slice of hunza pie or carrot cake or sipping a fruit juice. It's open only from Monday to Friday from 10 am to 4 pm and they have magazines and books to flip through. Nearby is the *Park Tavern*, an attractive-looking pub.

On the west side of the square, with the tables and umbrellas, you can try *Crank's Salad Bowl* for fried brown rice, vegetable pies, soya bean pizzas and the like – mainly in the $1 to $2 range. Next door is the *Governor on the Park Restaurant*, a rather pompous name for an inexpensive Lebanese café. It's a small and comfortable BYO place with felafel for $2.50 and shish kebab for $3.50. Next door to that is the *Jasmin Indian Restaurant* with main courses generally about $6.50. There are actually two locations – the other is just a few doors down. They're closed on Sundays but are licenced and serve very good food. At the corner is the *Moonraker Snack Bar* with the usual take-aways and very cheap meat pies.

Another place to try is the *Festival Bistro* in the Festival Centre which overlooks the Torrens River. It has sandwiches and snacks and is open late into the evenings but is closed on

Sundays. The gardens around the Festival Centre are a good place for a picnic.

Snacks, Fast Foods & Late at Night If you're after late-night eats then the *Pie Carts* which appear every night from 6 pm till the early hours are an Adelaide institution. If a pie floater (the great Australian meat pie floating on a thick pea soup) is your thing then look for their vans at the corner by the GPO and on North Terrace near the railway station. If a floater does not sound like your thing (and I sincerely hope it isn't for your stomach's sake!) then they also have other, more straightforward pies.

The *Pancake Kitchen* (see below) and *Bertie's Pancake Factory* at Imperial Place (close to the Grenfell and King William Sts intersection) are open late.

Adelaide has *McDonalds* and other front runners in the fast food stakes but *Hungry Jacks*, a similar chain, has a branch right in the centre on the corner of Pultenay and Rundle Sts. The railway station has a cafeteria and the YMCA's restaurant is very economical. Adelaide University's union building is also conveniently close to the city centre – try the Tavern there.

On Frome St, between North Terrace and Rundle St, *Govinda's* is a Hare Krishna vegetarian place offering an all-you-can-eat vegetarian lunch plus fruit juice or lassi for $4.50; it's not open on the weekends. The modern Southern Cross Arcade runs through to St James place from King William St, just down from Rundle Mall. There are lots of fast food and take-away places here, good for a quick lunch. Downstairs, close to King William St, is the *Health Haven* with a good choice of cheap vegetarian dishes. Upstairs at the other end of the arcade, *Hav-a-Chat* is the best lunch bar here offering lots of salads, seafood sandwiches and rolls that are quite generous; or quiches with a choice of two salads for $2.40.

The Gallerie Shopping Centre runs from North Terrace through to Gawler Place. Here you'll find *The Food Affair* with booths offering Chinese, Greek, pizza, health-foods, crepes and fish & chips. It's not a bad place to eat and it's very busy at lunchtime. A plate of food is $4 to $5; a slice of pizza or various specials are about $3. It's open only to 6 pm except on Fridays when it's 9 pm. It's on the basement level beside the John Martins Department Store.

Just a cup of tea or coffee? Head for *Kappy's* in Stephen Place, just off Rundle Mall in the city. It's a delightfully old-fashioned and very genteel tea house where you can get a nice cup of tea and slice of raisin toast! The *First Left* at 165 Pultenay St, just down from Hindmarsh Square, is a comfortable, airy café. It's open long hours and is one of the few that is open on Sunday. It's pleasant for just a cake and coffee but if you want a full meal, one of the staff will drag the blackboard menu over to your table. Spinach pie and salad is $4.

The *Left Bank* is on Charles St (more like an alley) running south off North Terrace near King William St. Despite it's enormous size, it still feels like a café and has snacks, light meals and fairly inexpensive breakfasts. As with most things in Adelaide, it's closed on Sundays. The *Al Fresco Gelateria* at 260 Rundle St has tables out on the footpath; a good place for a gelati, cappuccino or a variety of sweets.

Counter Meals Adelaide is very well-represented in this category, particularly at lunchtime. Just look for those tell-tale blackboards standing outside. They don't come any cheaper than at the *Old Queen's Arms*, a few blocks from the centre at 88 Wright St. It's straightforward food at prices that are hard to beat; meals go for around $3.

The *Talbot Hotel* at 104 Gouger St has a nice deal with the Gouger Cafe next door. You get their excellent seafood at $5 to $8 for main courses in the hotel's pleasant beer garden. This is a more up-market pub where some money has been spent on decor. Another block along brings you to Franklin St where you'll find the Central Bus Station and a couple of hotels including the *Hotel Franklin* at 92 Franklin St which also does $3 breakfasts.

Hindley and Rundle Sts have a number of pubs with good food. On the corner of Rundle St and East Terrace *The Stag* is a ordinary-looking pub with a high reputation for its food; main courses are generally $5 to $7, counter lunches are as low as $2.50. On the corner of Grenfell St and Hindmarsh Square the *Park Tavern* is a ritzily done-up pub with a bistro where you'll pay $7 to $10 but there's also a cheaper counter meal section where you can get an excellent dinner for $2.50 to $3.50. The *Somerset*, centrally located at the corner of Pultenay and Flinders Sts, has steaks and grills for about $5.

Across in North Adelaide, *The British* at 58 Finniss St has a 'touch of the British' about it, plus a pleasant beer garden where you can grill the food yourself at the barbecue. Main courses are $5 to $6. Out at Glenelg on the beach end of Jetty Rd, the *Glenelg Pier Hotel* does low-price and filling meals at lunchtime.

Hindley Street If Adelaide has a food centre it has to be Hindley St. Down here you'll find a whole series of Italian, Greek, Lebanese, Chinese and Eastern European restaurants, interspersed with Adelaide's small and seedy collection of strip clubs, not to mention the 24-hour Third World Bookshop. The cheaper ones offer meals at $5 to $6; the more expensive ones are $7 to $8.

At 33 Hindley St you'll find *Chinatown* down in the basement. It's an unpretentious-looking place with most dishes in the $5 to $7 bracket and the food really is good. Lunches are cheaper at around $3.50 to $5. Across the road at 68 Hindley St the *Feed Bag* is strictly American fast-food-style but it's cheap,

clean, open reasonably late and is not bad at all, plastic though it may be. The daily specials are good value.

Central Pizza at 73 Hindley St offers Italian fare even on Sundays when much of the street is closed. It's open from midday to midnight and most dishes are around $3.50 to $5.

One of the nicest places on the street is the cheap and friendly *Abdul & Jamil's Quiet Waters*. Downstairs in this pleasant Lebanese coffee lounge they serve really good food; vegetarian dishes for around $2.50 to $4.25 and meat dishes, mainly lamb, about $5. It's tastefully decorated and has live music on Wednesday and Saturday. Another Lebanese place is *Beirut at Night* at 104 which has a catchy sign but is very plain inside. It has cheap take-aways and meals are $4.50 to $7.

Pagana's at 101 Hindley St does pastas from $4 to $6 or main courses from $6 to $10. It's good authentic Italian food and there's wine at 65c a glass. Then there is a string of steak/charcoal-grill places. *Noah's Arc* at 116 has felafels for $2. Another Middle Eastern place is the *Jerusalem Shish Kebab House*, found at number 133.

You can get Australian food with an authentic touch at the *Water Hole Down Under* at 142 Hindley St. Good Aussie tucker; even witchetty-grub soup, which is apparently tasty even though the heads are a bit crunchy. As much coffee as you like for $1.20 and the tea comes in a billy complete with gum leaf. The *Royal Admiral Hotel* at 125 has fresh fish with salad and chips for $5.50 and also the usual counter meals. For Malaysian there's *Shah's* next door where main courses are $6 to $7.

There are also numerous Greek places. The *Athens* is a typically narrow place at 121. Flashier is *Hindley's Olympic Restaurant* at 139 with souvlaki and spiced lamb.

The *Hikory Hollow* at 141 specialises in ribs for about $7. Further along at 179 is the *Deep South Restaurant* offering

American soul food and a few Mexican items as well. It's open from 6 pm till late every day and has live soul or blues music on Thursday to Saturday nights. Across the street and up a bit is the *BBQ Inn*, a steak and charcoal-grill place which is a little on the expensive side. A similar place but Greek orientated is the *Ludo's Barbecue* at 142.

Just off Hindley St on Club House Lane, the *King Luc* is a low-price Chinese place with lunches from $3.20.

Around the City Lots more places can be found around the city. The other end of Rundle St, for example, has quite an Italian flavour. Just go down Hindley St, through Rundle Mall, and at 201 Rundle St is *Don Giovanni's*, still a very popular Italian eatery with reasonable prices; a $5 lasagna is *big* and the calzone rustica is superb. Pizzas range from $2.40 for small to $6.50 for large. *Mezes* is a small, casual Greek place at 285 Rundle St with an open-view kitchen. Main courses are $5 to $6.50 and it's open till late.

Right in the centre you can stick with seafood at the rather plastic and fast-food flavour *Chief Charley's* at 12 Grenfell St which does a $5.80 all-you-can-eat fish special – good value. At 69 Grote St *Ellinis* is a Greek restaurant specialising in seafood; excellent food and reasonably priced with main courses about $10. A meal without wine would cost about $15 but would be good; a good place for a splurge.

Gilbert Place, a small lane across the corner of King William and Hindley Sts in the centre, has several places worth a look. The *Pancake Kitchen* is notable for being open 24 hours a day, seven days a week and it's also pretty good value. Where else but Australia would you find 'steak & pancakes'? Next door is *Phillips Coffee Cup*, specialising in about 10 kinds of omelettes at about $5 each. Round the corner is *Lino's City Spaghetti House* – a pleasant Italian place with dishes (schnitzels, parmigianas, etc) in the $6 to

$7 range and pastas a bit cheaper. The long-running but more expensive *Arkaba Steak Cellar* is also in this compact little group.

To feel the sea-breeze, head across to Gouger St which is the fish and seafood centre of Adelaide. Some of the places here have been running for many years and recently a lot of new places have joined them. There's *Paul's* at 79 and the *Gouger Cafe* at 98. Main courses in the latter are $6.50 to $7.50. It also handles the counter meals next door in the *Talbot Hotel*, or there's *George's* at 111 and *Stanley's* at 76.

Also on this street is *Ranis* at 83A which serves South Indian food very cheap. A couple of vindaloos, beef Madras and other curries are under $5, vegetarian dishes for $4; all served mild, medium or hot. It's a no-frills place so you're not paying for the decor. At 55 Gouger St is the *Mamma Getta Restaurant* and if you haven't guessed, it's Italian. Most dishes are under $6 and the pastas are just $4.30. At the corner of Morphett St is the *Tequila Sunrise* which has moderately priced Mexican food.

Lastly, there are a few places in North Adelaide if you're in the area. *Rabuka* at 33 O'Connell St is unusual with it's African angle. Meat and vegetarian dishes using coconut, couscous and dates are about $5 to $7.50. There are quite a few eating places along here including a fish & chips take-away, a Lebanese place and a couple of Italian ones; most of them are on the pricey side. Apart from Rabuka, *Scrumptious* at the corner of Ward and O'Connell Sts is about the best bet for a light meal. It's a small but good snack bar with milkshakes, filled croissants and espresso coffee.

Down in Glenelg there are numerous places along Jetty Rd offering something for everyone. On Durham St, near the jetty off Jetty Rd, is *Kalina's*, a vegetarian place with a very eclectic menu with a lean toward Polish cuisine. At lunch time, moussaka and cabbage rolls are $4;

dinners are $6.50 but include a large salad. They have lots of vegetable pies and a wide selection of herbal teas. All in all it's a pleasant little place. The *Pier Hotel* also serves counter meals.

Lastly, maybe worth a visit is the *Halifax Lounge* at 65 Flinders St. It's run by one of the local churches and offers a place to go from 10 am to 4 pm. There's tea and coffee and you can hang around reading and writing if you like.

Entertainment

There are lots of pubs with entertainment in Adelaide and a host of 'what's on' information, including a regular newssheet put out by the SAGTB; also check Thursday's *News* newspaper.

The usual rock pub circuit operates around Adelaide. It includes places like the *Arkaba* at 150 Glen Osmond Rd or the *Highway Inn* on the Anzac Highway in Plympton. The *Findon Hotel* on Grange Rd, Findon also has rock bands.

Popular city pubs with regular rock music include the *Angas Hotel* on Angas St, the *Producers Hotel* at 235 Grenfell St, and the *Tivoli* at 261 Pirie St. On trendy Melbourne St, North Adelaide, the *Old Lion Hotel* is a trendy hotel with everything from bars and dining room (expensive) to a disco and more rock music. Adelaide University often has big-name rock bands on at the union. The *Rockhouse Cabaret* at 173 Hindley St is another live-music bar. The *Reggae Club* is on Cornish St, Stepney.

Adelaide also has a string of places with folk and jazz, particularly on Friday and Saturday nights. You'll find them in the 'what's on' guides too. On the third Sunday of each month there's the Hills Folk Club Concert at the *Bridgewater Inn* in Bridgewater starting at 6.30 pm and costing $2.50. At the *Saloon* in O'Connell St, North Adelaide there's a jam-session starting at midnight on Fridays. There's always something on at the Adelaide Festival Centre; the SAGTB's 'what's on' guide tells all. In the amphitheatre at the Festival Centre there are usually free concerts with good local bands on Sundays from 2 to 4 pm. Also check the Piano Bar here for free shows.

There is a good selection of interesting film centres in Adelaide. The university film club often shows good films in the union or check out the Chelsea at 275 Kensington Rd, Kensington Park – good films and student discounts. There are free lunchtime films at the State Film and Video Library. The Downtown Leisure Centre at 65 Hindley St has heaps of pinballs and rollerskating. The various hostels often have 'things to do' notices posted on the noticeboards.

Getting There

Air Ansett and TAA fly to Adelaide from all the other state capitals and Adelaide is also the major departure point for Alice Springs and Darwin. All flights from Melbourne and most flights from Sydney for the Northern Territory go via Adelaide. Fares to or from Adelaide include Brisbane $249 ($199 standby), Sydney $202 ($162), Melbourne $140 ($112), Perth $294 ($236), Alice Springs $218 ($175), Darwin $335 ($268).

Bus Ansett Pioneer, Greyhound and Deluxe all operate to Adelaide from Sydney, Melbourne, Perth, Alice Springs and other main centres. From Melbourne it's 11 hours and $30, Sydney is 22 hours and $59, Perth 35 hours and $85, and Alice Springs 27 hours and $95 ($74 standby). There is also a whole collection of other buses, particularly on the Perth route.

Ansett Pioneer (tel 51 2075) and Greyhound (tel 212 1777) both operate from the Central Bus Station at 101-111 Franklin St. You'll also find Stateliner, Briscoes and other South Australian operators here. Briscoes have services to Alice Springs, Stateliner to other parts of South Australia and across the NSW border to Broken Hill. See the appropriate sections for details.

Rail There are two stations in Adelaide: the big one on North Terrace, now only for suburban trains, and the new interstate terminal at Keswick, just out of the centre.

Adelaide is connected by rail with Sydney, Melbourne, Perth, Broken Hill, Alice Springs and other centres. To Melbourne the daily overnight Overland has 1st class sleeping berths and 1st and economy-class seats. The trip takes about 13 hours and fares are $62 in 1st ($90 with sleeper) or $44 ($72 sleeper) in economy. There are some seat-only fares available a week in advance for $45 in 1st and $31 economy.

You can travel between Sydney and Adelaide either via Melbourne (daily) or via Broken Hill on the Indian-Pacific (four-times weekly). On the latter you connect with the Indian Pacific at Peterborough. Fares in 1st are $145 ($103 seat) via Melbourne, $180 ($159 seat) via Broken Hill. In economy it's $103 ($72 seat) via Melbourne, $149 ($106 seat) via Broken Hill. There's also a bus-train connection which is faster (and cheaper). A V-Line bus to Albury connects with the XPT train; travel time is about 20 hours, the fare $68.50 in economy, $75 in 1st.

Between Adelaide and Perth you can travel on the four-times-weekly Indian-Pacific or the three-times-weekly Trans-Australian. The latter originates at Port Pirie so in either case you have to change trains when travelling from Adelaide. Fares are $384 in 1st, $291 in economy, including sleeping berth and all meals. With only a weeks notice, the fares are $278 ($105 with no meals) in 1st and $212 ($80 with no meals) in economy. The Adelaide-Perth trip takes about 42 hours.

The Ghan between Adelaide and Alice Springs operates weekly and takes 24 hours. The fare is $236 in 1st, $171 in economy including sleeping berth and meals. An economy seat without meals is $118. You can also go by train to Broken Hill by taking the daily train to Peter-borough to connect with the four-times weekly Indian-Pacific. State rail services also operate to Port Pirie and Mt Gambier. Rail bookings in Adelaide are made by phoning 217 4455. It's wise to book ahead for interstate journeys, particularly on the Ghan which is very popular.

Hitching For Melbourne take the 161 bus from Pultenay St to Old Toll Gate and thumb from there. To Port Augusta and Perth take the 6 bus from King William St to Gepps Cross, walk or get a lift to Carvans Petrol Station and start from there.

Getting Around

Airport Transport Adelaide's modern international airport is conveniently located. There's an airport bus service (tel 381 5311) operating between hotels every half hour for $2.40 from 7 am to 10 pm. From the airport to central Victoria Square takes about 25 minutes.

You can get out to the airport entrance on a 27B or 27C public bus, otherwise count on about $7 for a taxi. Budget, Hertz, Avis and Thrifty have rent-a-car desks at the airport. There's also a reasonably-priced coffee bar/restaurant at the airport. In the city TAA (tel 217 3333) are at 144 North Terrace, Ansett (tel 212 1111) are at 150 North Terrace.

Bus, Train & Tram Adelaide has an integrated local transport system operated by the STA (State Transport Authority). For information you can ring 218 2345 until 10.30 pm daily. Adelaide is divided into three zones; travel within one zone costs 70c, two zones $1, or three zones $1.40. Tickets for zones one and two cover unlimited travel for up to two hours. You could, for example, come into Adelaide on the Glenelg tram, take a bus to the station and go out the other side by train, all on the same ticket. In fact, the ticket lasts from the start of the next hour so if you buy a ticket at 9.05 am your two hours isn't up until two hours from 10 am.

Between 9 am and 3 pm on weekdays the $1.40 fare drops down to $1; the $1 to 70c. In the city centre there are also a couple of free bus services: the Bee Line service basically runs down King William St from the Glenelg tram terminus at Victoria Square and round the corner to the railway station. It operates every five minutes from 8 am to 6 pm weekdays, to 9 pm on Fridays and 8 am to 12.15 pm on Saturdays.

Day Tripper tickets are available for unlimited use from 9 am daily. A single ticket covers two adults, and (unlimited?) children under 15, throughout the Adelaide metropolitan area for $4. The Transport Authority at 12A Grenfell St near King William St has tickets, timetables and maps; it opens 8.30 am to 5.30 pm weekdays, 8 to 11.30 am on Saturdays.

There are four buses a day leaving from the Ansett Building on North Terrace for the interstate train station for $2 – call the station on 217 4444 for times. For two or more people, a taxi is just as cheap.

Apart from buses and trains there's also a solitary tram service to Glenelg, which will whisk you out to the seaside suburb from Victoria Square for $1 (70c between 9 am and 3 pm). You can get a useful route guide and map from the STA. Buses are colour coded; silver for the plains, brown and cream for the hills and for express services, orange and white for the circle services. The free buses have fancier colours.

Tours Several companies offer sightseeing trips; check at the tourist office. Kay Hannaford offers Heritage Walks of 1½ hours leaving daily at 10 am from the SA Government Travel Centre at 18 King William St for $7.50.

Half-day tours around the city include the Festival Centre or go out to Glenelg and cost around $14. You can go out further, to Hahndorf in the Adelaide Hills, to Birdwood Mills and the Torrens Gorge, or to the Mt Lofty Ranges and the Cleland Reserve, also for around $14.

Day tours, such as those out to the Barossa Valley, to the valley and Kapunda, or to Goolwa and the Murray Mouth, cost around $24 to $32. Other tours include day excursions to Victor Harbor (transport only) for $11, flying day trips to Kangaroo Island for about $100 and in summer there are historic steam-locomotive rail tours organised by the Australian Railway Historical Society. Others like Intrepid Tours offer four-wheel drive trips through the Flinders Ranges for $20 a half-day and $40 for a full day with a maximum of eight people.

Car Rental The major firms – Avis, Hertz, Budget and Thrifty – are all represented in Adelaide. Action Rent-a-Car (tel 352 7044) offer small Suzukis for $19 and no mileage charge. They also have bigger cars and an eight-seater minibus is available for $50 per day. Cut Price Car Rentals (tel 211 7359) is on the corner of Morphett and Gouger Sts and has cars for $10 to $20 a day. Adelaide has a selection of the Rent-a-Wreck, Hire-a-Hack folk; find them in the yellow pages.

Motorcycle Rental The SA Motorcycle Centre (tel 51 2117) at 28 Compton St rent bikes from 80 cc up to 900 cc. Action Moped (tel 211 7060) at 269 Morphett St have mopeds for $25 a day or $5 an hour.

Bicycle Rental You can hire bikes from Elliotts Sports Shop at 200 Rundle St. Three-speed machines cost $5 for half a day, $10 a day or $25 a week. Out at Glenelg there's a bike hire place right next door to the information centre at the seashore end of Jetty Rd. They cost $2 an hour or there are cheaper daily rates and they have tandems as well.

Around Adelaide

Adelaide is fortunate to have so much so

accessible to the city; the Barossa is an easy day-trip, the wineries of the southern vales are a morning or afternoon visit and the Adelaide Hills are less than half an hour from the centre.

ADELAIDE HILLS
Adelaide is flanked by hills to the south and east. The highest point, Mt Lofty at 771 metres, is just a 30-minute drive from the city and offers spectacular views over Adelaide, particularly from Windy Point at night. The hills are scenic and varied, with tiny villages which look for all the world as though they have been transplanted straight from Europe. The Montacute Scenic Route is one of the best drives through the hills. Walking tracks, 1000 km of them in all, also criss-cross the hills.

Parks in the hills include the Cleland Conservation Park, just 19 km from the city on the slopes of Mt Lofty, with a wide variety of wildlife and open from 9 am to 5 pm daily. There are walking tracks, barbecues, waterfalls and a rugged gorge at the Morialta Park near Rostrevor. Other parks include the Parra Wirra Park to the north of the city and the Belair Recreation Park to the south.

Heading out of Adelade, on the Princes Highway in Glen Osmond you'll pass the Old Toll House at the foot of the hills. Tolls were collected here for just five years from 1841.

BIRDWOOD
Less than 50 km from Adelaide, Birdwood Hill Museum has the largest collection of old cars and motorcycles in Australia. The collection, which includes other pioneering exhibits, is housed in an 1852 flour mill and is open daily from 10 am to 5 pm. The town was once a gold-mining centre and has various other old buildings. You can get to Birdwood via Chain of Ponds and Gumeracha or via Lobethal. Gumeracha has a toy factory with a 20-metre high rocking horse – yes, another of those Australian 'big' attractions. Lobethal

has a fine little historical museum open on Tuesday and Sunday afternoons.

HAHNDORF (population 1300)
The oldest surviving German settlement in Australia, Hahndorf is 29 km southeast of Adelaide and is a popular day-trip. Settled in 1839 by Lutherans who left Prussia to escape religious persecution, the town took its name from the ship's captain Hahn; dorf means 'town'.

Various German festivals and celebrations are held in the town including the annual mid-January Scheutzenfest beer festival; and the German Arms Hotel at 50 Main St dates from 1834. The Hahndorf Academy, established in 1857, houses an art gallery and museum.

Fleurieu Peninsula

South of Adelaide is the Fleurieu Peninsula, so close that most places on it can be seen on easy day-trips from the city. The Gulf St Vincent has a series of fine beaches down to Cape Jervis, looking across to Kangaroo Island. The southern coast of the peninsula, from Cape Jervis to the mouth of the Murray, is pounded by the high seas of the Southern Ocean.

There are some good surfing beaches along this rugged coastline. Inland there's rolling countryside and the fine vineyards of the McLaren Vale area. The peninsula was named by Frenchman Nicholas Baudin after Napoleon's Minister for the Navy who financed Baudin's expedition to Australia. In the early days settlers on the peninsula ran a busy smuggling business but in 1837 the first whaling station was established at Encounter Bay. This grew to become the South Australian colony's first successful industry.

Places to Stay
The Fleurieu Peninsula is a popular

holiday area so there are plenty of places to stay whether you're looking for camp-sites, motels, hotels or guest-houses. There's a youth hostel in the Inman Valley, near Glacier Rock 20 km from Victor Harbor.

Getting There

You can get down to the peninsula by buses, all of which operate from the Central Bus Station on Franklin St. Premier Roadlines (tel 217 0777) have up to three services daily on the Adelaide-McLaren Vale-Willunga-Victor Harbor-Port Elliot route. It takes about two hours all the way and fares are McLaren Vale $2.60, Willunga $2.80, Victor Harbor and Port Elliot $6.20.

The Kangaroo Island Connection (tel 272 6680) run a twice-daily service to Cape Jervis via various towns on the peninsula. The fares are: Aldinga $2.40, Yankalilla $5, Cape Jervis $6.50; and to Goolwa with Johnsons (tel 339 2488) it's $5.45.

The railway line has now been closed to normal passenger services and at the time of writing was being refurbished. Due for completion sometime in '86, the line will re-open as a tourist run using steam trains.

GULF ST VINCENT BEACHES

There is a string of fine beaches south of Adelaide along the Gulf St Vincent coast of the peninsula. The beach stretch extends from Christie's Beach (a good beach below red sandstone cliffs) to Port Noarlunga, Seaford Beach and Moana Beach before you reach the best known beach on the peninsula – Maslins Beach, the southern end of which became the first legal nude bathing beach in Australia.

Further south, beyond Aldinga Beach and Sellicks Beach, the coastline is rockier but there are still good swimming beaches at Myponga, Normanville and a number of other places. The coast road eventually runs through the small town of

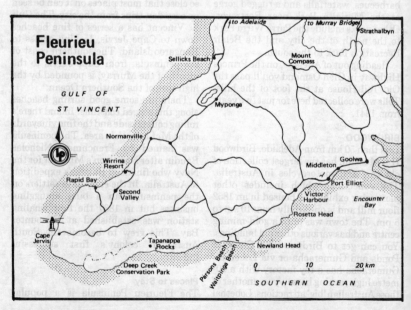

Delamere and ends at Cape Jervis at the tip of the peninsula. From here you can look across the narrow Backstairs Passage to Kangaroo Island, 13 km away. At one time ferries ran across the straits from Cape Jervis. Near Cape Jervis there's a 12-hectare fauna park. The cape, with its high cliffs and strong sea breezes, is a popular spot for hang-gliding and you can often see enthusiasts swooping above the coastline.

MORPHETT VALE

Adelaide has sprawled out so far that the small town of Morphett Vale has become an outer suburb of the city. Amongst the historic buildings in the town is St Mary's, the first Roman Catholic church in South Australia, built in 1846. On the Main South Rd, at the Noarlunga turn-off, the Morphett Vale Pioneer Village recreates an early South Australian settlement from around 1860. There are a number of historic buildings with period furnishings and equipment. The village is open from 10 am to 5 pm from Wednesday to Sunday and on public holidays.

SOUTHERN VALES

There is a string of wineries on the Fleurieu Peninsula; McLaren Vale is the centre of the wine-growing area but you'll also find winemakers at Reynella, Willunga and Langhorne Creek. The area is particularly well suited to red wines. There are around two dozen wineries in the McLaren Vale area alone and about 40 in the whole region. Many of them have tastings and also sell their wines; you can make a pleasant tastings crawl around the various wineries. The first winery in the area, in Reynella, was established in 1838 and some of the wineries date back to the last century and have fine old buildings. Most of them are open to the public Monday to Saturday; many of them on Sunday as well. A number have picnic or barbecue areas close to the cellar door sales.

The McLaren Vale Wine Bushing Festival takes place over a week in late

October to early November each year. It's a busy time of wine tastings and tours and the whole thing is topped by a grand Elizabethan Feast. At McLaren Flat, near McLaren Vale, there's the Manning Fauna & Flora Reserve.

WILLUNGA (population 500)

In the south of the Southern Vales winery area this small town has a long history and a collection of fine colonial-era buildings – several of them classified by the National Trust. Many of the old bluestone buildings and pug cottages have roofs made from locally-quarried slate. Some of the quarries still operate today. Buildings include the old Court House with a National Trust display and the fine old Bush Inn which now operates as a restaurant.

Willunga was once an important stopping point on the road from Adelaide to Victor Harbor. Today it's the centre for almond growing in Australia and the Almond Blossom Festival is held here each July. At the Mt Magnificent Conservation Park, 12 km east of Willunga, you can see grey kangaroos and take pleasant walks.

PORT ELLIOT (population 800)

On Horseshoe Bay, a smaller indent from the larger Encounter Bay, Port Elliot was originally established as the sea port for the Murray River trade and was the first town on Encounter Bay. At the time it was established in 1854, nearby Victor Harbor was still just a whaling station. Port Elliot proved less than ideal as a port, however, and in 1864 its functions were shifted to Victor Harbor where Granite Island provided a safer, more sheltered anchorage.

Today the town is a popular holiday resort with fine views along the coast to the mouth of the Murray and the Coorong. Horseshoe Bay has a sheltered, safe swimming beach with a good cliff-top walk above it. This stretch of coast is particularly popular with surfers and Boomer Beach, on the edge of town to the west, is one of the best surfing beaches. Middleton Beach, to the east of town towards Goolwa, is another beach that attracts the board riders.

VICTOR HARBOR (population 4500)

The main town on the peninsula, 84 km south of Adelaide, Victor Harbor looks out on to Encounter Bay where Flinders and Baudin made their historic meeting in 1802. Up on the headland known as the Bluff there's a memorial to the 'encounter' which took place on the bay below. It's a steep climb up to the Bluff from where there are fine views.

The port is protected from the high southern seas by Granite Island, a small island out in the bay which is connected to the mainland by a causeway. The old train connecting Granite Island has been stopped and replaced by a small ferry. The eight-minute ride costs $1.25 or you can go by one of the two 19th-century horse-drawn trams. On the island there's a chairlift up to the top from where there are fine views across the bay. You may see fairy penguins and seals on the shores of Granite Island.

Victor, as the town is often referred to, was established early in South Australia's history as a sealing and whaling centre. South of the town at Rosetta Bay, below the Bluff, is Whaler's Haven with many interesting reminders of those early whaling days. The first whaling station was established here in 1837 and another followed soon after on Granite Island but whaling ceased here in 1864, only 27 years later.

Other historic buildings in the town include St Augustine's Church of England from 1869, the Museum of Historical Art and the Cornhill Museum & Art Gallery.

There is also a number of interesting excursion points around the town. The Urimbirra fauna park, with a nocturnal house, is only five km out. You can make pleasant bush walks around the Hindmarsh Valley Falls. Spring Mount Conservation Park is 14 km to the north-west.

Also in this direction is the Myponga Conservation Park with many grey kangaroos, and Glacier Rock 19 km out. Along the coast from Victor Harbor towards Cape Jervis, Waitpinga Beach is another popular surfing beach and updraughts from the cliffs attract hanggliders; it's no good for swimming though.

The Victor Harbor Tourist Office is on Ocean St.

GOOLWA (population 1600)

On Lake Alexandrina near the mouth of the Murray, Goolwa initially rose to prominence with the growth of trade along the mighty Murray. The Murray mouth then silted up and large ships were unable to get up to Goolwa so a railway line, the first in South Australia, was built from Goolwa to nearby Port Elliot. In the 1880s a new railway line to Adelaide spelt the end for Goolwa as a port town.

Today Goolwa is a popular resort with a number of interesting old buildings including the National Trust museum which is in the first house built in the area. The house was built back in 1852. The old paddle-steamer *Captain Sturt* can be seen in the town and on the main street there's a horse-drawn railway carriage from the early days of the railway line. Goolwa is an access point to the Coorong Park. This long stretch of the beach to the actual mouth of the Murray can be driven along and there's a ferry crossing over to Hindmarsh Island. You can also take cruises on Lake Alexandrina on the *MV Aroona*.

Goolwa is the departure point for upriver cruises on the *Murray River Queen*. Milang, on Lake Alexandrina was a centre for the river trade even before Goolwa. In the early days of the rivershipping business, bullock wagons carried goods overland between here and Adelaide.

There's a Goolwa Tourist Office at 52 Hutchinson St.

STRATHALBYN (population 1750)
Situated on the Angas River well inland from the coast, this picturesque town was settled back in 1839 by Scottish immigrants. St Andrew's Church, the original 'kirk', is one of the best known country churches in Australia. It was built in 1848 and its tower overlooks the river. There's also an attractive Memorial Gardens on the riverbanks with a large contingent of resident waterbirds.

The town has many old buildings with a distinctly Scottish flavour to them: there's a National Trust pioneer museum, an old police station and court house, a historical folk museum, the Angas flour mill of 1852; in all, enough reminders of the region's early history to qualify Strathalbyn as a 'heritage town'.

The Barossa Valley

South Australia's most famous wine-producing valley vies with the Hunter Valley in NSW as the best-known in Australia. The gently sloping valley is about 40-km long and five to 11-km wide. The Barossa turns out a quarter of all the wine in Australia and since the valley is only about 50 km from Adelaide it's a very popular place to visit.

The Barossa still has some German flavour from its original settlement in 1842. Fleeing religious persecution in Prussia and Silesia, those first settlers weren't wine makers but fortunately someone soon came along and recognised the valley's potential. The name, curiously enough, is actually a mis-spelling of Barrosa in Spain, close to where the Spanish sherry comes from. Prior to WW I the Barossa probably sounded even more Germanic because during the war many German place names were patriotically Anglicised. When the jingoistic fervour died down some changed back.

There is a variety of places to stay in the Barossa and a leisurely tastings crawl around the various wineries is a popular activity for visitors. The valley is initially a little disappointing since it's rather wide and flat and from the central road doesn't really appear very valley-like at all. Furthermore, that main road through Lyndoch, Tanunda and Nuriootpa (the main valley towns) is rather busy and noisy; not at all like the peaceful valley you might expect. Get off the main road or take the scenic drive between Angaston and Tanunda and you'll begin to appreciate the Barossa.

Information
There's a tourist information centre in Coulthard House at 66 Murray St, Nuriootpa.

Wineries
The Barossa has something over 35 wineries around the valley and many of them are open to the public, offer guided tours or free wine tastings. Get a copy of the SAGTB's Barossa leaflet for full details of locations and opening hours.

Just some of the most interesting wineries include:

Chateau Yaldara (1) at Lyndoch. Established in 1947 in the ruins of a 19th-century winery and flour mill it has a notable art collection which can be seen on conducted tours.

Gramp's Orlando (2) at Rowland Flat, between Lyndoch and Tanunda, was established in 1847 and is one of the oldest wineries in the valley.

Krondorf (3) at Tanunda is currently one of the glamour wine makers with a high reputation for their wine.

Chateau Tanunda (4), also in Tanunda, is a magnificent old bluestone building built in 1889 but it it not open to the public at all.

Leo Buring Chateau Leonay (5) is also in Tanunda and is another winery fantasy with turrets and towers although it dates only from 1945.

Seppelts (6) in Seppeltsfield was founded

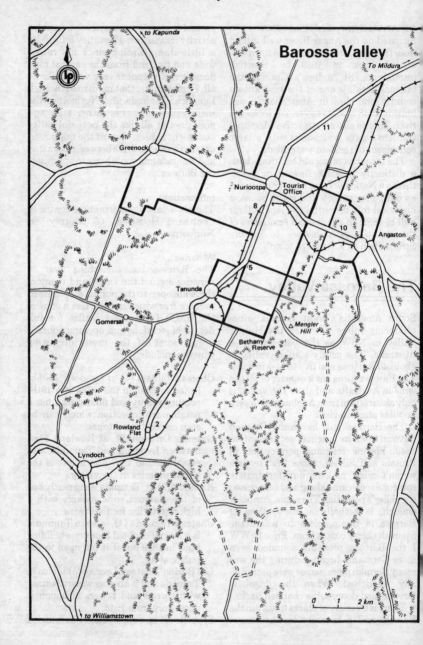

Barossa Valley

to Kapunda

To Mildura

Greenock

Nuriootpa

Tourist Office

11

6

8

7

10

Angaston

5

Tanunda

4

Mengler Hill

9

Gomersal

Bethany Reserve

3

1

2

Rowland Flat

Lyndoch

to Williamstown

0   1   2 km

Top: Adelaide's Festival Centre is well situated beside the Torrens River in the city centre (TW)
Left: The Rundle Mall is the main shopping street in Adelaide (SAGTC)
Right: The wine-producing Barossa Valley plays heavily on its German background (SAGTC)

Top: The sheer walls of Wilpena Pound show the beautiful colours and shadows typical of the Flinders Ranges (TW)
Left: Fording a river on an outback road in the Flinders Ranges (SAGTC)
Right: Seals on the beach at Kangaroo Island (SAGTC)

in 1852 and the old bluestone buildings are surrounded by gardens and date palms. The extensive complex includes a picnic area with gas barbecues.

Kaiser Stuhl (7) in Nuriootpa was established in 1931 and is the only wine-making co-operative in the valley. Its imposing building fronts on to the main road.

Penfolds (8), just down from Kaiser Stuhl, is one of the largest wineries in the valley; they can store 22.5 million litres of wine here!

Yalumba (9) in Angaston was founded way back in 1849 and the blue marble winery is surrounded by gardens and topped by a clock tower.

Seagrams (10), also in Angaston, is another old winery, originally established in 1859 and known until recently as Saltram.

Wolf Blass (11), out beyond Nuriootpa, was only founded in 1973 but by a combination of excellent wines and clever marketing they've quickly become one of the best known wine makers in Australia. There are plenty of other wineries around the valley and often the smaller, less well-known places can be the most interesting to visit.

Barossa Events

The Vintage Festival is the Barossa's big event, taking place over four days in March-April of odd-numbered years (1987, 1989). The colourful festival features processions, brass bands, tugs-of-war between the wineries, maypole dancing and, of course, a lot of wine tasting. It's not the only Barossa occasion though: Tanunda has a brass band competition on the first Saturday of each November and there are many other valley events.

Of course the main events in the Barossa move with the grape-growing seasons. It takes four to five years for grape vines to reach maturity after they are first planted in July-August. Their useful life is usually around 40 years. The vines are pruned back heavily during the winter months (July-August) and then grow and produce fruit over the summer. The busiest months in the valley are from March to early May when the grapes are harvested during the vintage season. The majority of the grapes are actually grown by small independent growers who sell them to the large wine-making firms.

After harvesting, the grapes are crushed and the fermentation process is started by the addition of yeast. Red wines get their red colouring not from the use of red grapes but from leaving the grape skins in with the juice during fermentation. With white wines the skins are separated and the juice fermented alone. Wines are usually aged in wood casks but white wines are not usually aged before they are bottled. Many of the wineries give free tours from which you can develop a better understanding of the wine-making process.

Places to Stay

Hotels & Motels Although there is no youth hostel in the Barossa there are quite a few fairly reasonably-priced hotels and a selection of campsites. Starting from the northern end in Nuriootpa, the *Vine Inn Hotel* (tel 62 2133) is right in the middle of town on Murray St. It's a big old place with comfortable rooms with wash-basins and tea/coffee-making facilities for $15/25. There is also a more modern motel section but it's rather expensive.

Also in Nuriootpa the *Angas Park Hotel* (tel 62 1050) at 22 Murray St is cheap at $16 per person for dinner bed & breakfast, or there's the *Karawatha Guest House* (tel 62 1746) on Greenock Rd with per person costs of $16 including breakfast. The *Sturt Highway Motel* (tel 62 1033) on Kalimna Rd is one of the cheaper motels in the valley at $25/32 for singles/doubles.

Angaston has the *Barossa Brauhaus* (tel 64 2014) at 41 Murray St, a fine-looking hotel with bed & breakfast rates of $16 per person. Just down the street at number 59 is the *Angaston Hotel* (tel 64 2428) at $15 per person, again bed & breakfast. Good for a splurge in Angaston is the National Trust's *Collingrove Homestead* (tel 64 2061), built in 1856. The two rooms are part of the old servants quarters and the rate of $38 for two people includes breakfast.

Tanunda has nothing particularly reasonably priced but in Lyndoch the *Lyndoch Hotel* (tel 24 4211) on Gilbert St is $12.50 per person for room-only. Five km north of Tanunda on Nuriap Rd, a family offers accommodation at $6 per person. They only have one room with a double and a single bed. Phone 62 2260 before 10 am or after 6 pm and get directions.

The tourist office has a list of 'alternative' accommodation in the valley, but most are a bit pricey ranging from $26 to $60 for two people.

Camping There are campsites in Lyndoch, Tanunda and Nuriootpa. They've all got on-site vans and the Lyndoch site also has cabins. The pleasant campground in Nuriootpa goes one better with possums who come down from the trees at night and monster you for their share of whatever's going down in the eats department.

Barossa Caravan Park (tel 24 4262), Barossa Valley Highway, Lyndoch, camping $5.50, on-site vans from $18, cabins $20.

Barossa Valley Tourist Park (tel 62 1404), Penrice Rd, Nuriootpa, camping $4.80 for two, on-site vans $16.50, cabins $20.

Langmeil Road Caravan Park (no phone), two km from PO, Tanunda,, camping $4.

Tanunda Caravan Park (tel 63 2784), Barossa Valley Highway, Tanunda, camping $5 for two, on-site vans $14.

Places to Eat

The valley is renowned for its solid, German-style eating places but most of them tend to be decidedly expensive. One definite exception is the *Heinemann Park Restaurant*, just on the Adelaide side of Tanunda, directly opposite the caravan park. It's simple and straightforward with good solid food at reasonable prices; most main courses around $9.

The *Zinfandel Tea Rooms* at 58 Murray St specialises in light lunches and continental cakes. At 51 Murray St in the town the *Tanunda Hotel* has a nice lounge with counter meals in the $6 to $8 bracket. The *Die Weinstube Restaurant*, south of Nuriootpa, is very pleasant with its outdoor eating area.

The valley is famed for its fine bakeries and one of the best is Linke's *Nuriootpa Bakery* at 40 Murray St, Nuriootpa.

Getting There & Around

There are several routes from Adelaide to the valley; the most direct one is via the Main North Rd through Elizabeth and Gawler. More picturesque routes go through the Torrens Gorge, Chain of Ponds and Williamstown or via Chain of Ponds and Birdwood.

It's $3 by Briscoes bus from Adelaide to the valley. You can book valley tours from the tourist office in Nuriootpa where you can also enquire about hiring bicycles; otherwise a car is nice to have in the valley, but don't plan on very much wine tasting if you're driving too.

LYNDOCH (population 550)

Coming up from Adelaide, Lyndoch (at the foot of the low Barossa Range) is the first valley town. The fine old Pewsey Vale Homestead is near Lyndoch.

TANUNDA (population 2600)

In the centre of the valley is Tanunda, the most Germanic of the valley towns. You can still see some early cottages around Goat Square or the Ziegenmarkt. At 47 Murray St there's the Barossa Valley Historical Museum with exhibits on the valley's early settlement; it's open Monday to Friday from 1 to 5 pm and on weekends from 2 to 5 pm. Storybook Cottage on Oak St is a creation for children. There are also a number of art and craft galleries around the town.

There are fine old churches in all the valley towns but Tanunda has some of the most interesting. The Tabor church dates from 1849 and is Lutheran; as is the 1868 St John's Church with its life-size wooden statues of Christ, the apostles Peter, Paul and John and of Moses.

The Tanunda Hotel was originally built in 1845 but was damaged by fire in 1895 and rebuilt 10 years later.

From Tanunda turn off the main road and take the scenic drive via Mengler Hill to Angaston. It runs through beautiful and peaceful country and the view over the valley from Mengler Hill is especially good.

NURIOOTPA (population 2850)

At the north end of the valley this is the commercial centre of the Barossa. Coulthard House was the home of a pioneer settler in the 1840s and is now used as the local tourist information centre. Nuriootpa also has several pleasant picnic grounds and a pheasant farm on Samuel Rd. The town was once a stopping place on the way to the copper mines at Burra.

ANGASTON (population 1750)

On the eastern side of the valley this town was named after George Fife Angas, one of the area's pioneers. Collingrove is a fine old homestead built by his son in 1853 and now owned by the National Trust; it's open Wednesday to Sunday from 10 am to 4.30 pm between 1 September and 31 May.

OTHER PLACES

Bethany, near Tanunda, was the first German settlement in the valley. Old cottages still stand around the Bethany reserve. Gomersal is near Tanunda and trained sheep dogs go through their paces twice daily here on Tuesday, Thursday and Saturday.

Springton, in the south-east of the valley, has the Herbig tree – an enormous hollow gum tree where a pioneer settler lived with his family from 1855 to 1860.

North of Adelaide

Two main routes run north of Adelaide:

the first is to Gawler where you can turn east to the Barossa Valley and the Riverland area, or continue north through Burra to Peterborough where you have the option of turning north-west to the Flinders Ranges or continuing on the Barrier Highway to the north-east for the long, dull run to Broken Hill in NSW; the second route from Adelaide heads off slightly north-west through Port Wakefield to Port Pirie and Port Augusta on the Spencer Gulf. You can then choose between the Flinders, the Eyre Peninsula or simply head west towards Western Australia.

This area to the north of Adelaide includes some of the most fertile and pleasant land in the state. Sunshine, rainfall and excellent soil combine to make this a prosperous agricultural region with excellent wine-making areas like the Clare Valley. Apart from the two main routes north there is a network of smaller roads which criss-cross this region.

ADELAIDE TO THE BAROSSA

On the way north to the Barossa or Clare Valleys you pass through Elizabeth (population 34,000), an industrial satellite city of Adelaide with major automotive manufacturing plants. Just after the turn-off from the Sturt Highway to the Barossa, Gawler (population 9500) is on the edge of the valley. Like Adelaide it was planned by Colonel Light and the old telegraph station, built in 1860, now houses a Folk Museum which is open Tuesdays to Thursdays from 2 to 4 pm. There is also a National Trust Telecom Telecommunications Museum in the same building; it's open the same hours plus on Sundays from 2 to 5 pm.

KAPUNDA (population 1350)

About 80 km north of Adelaide and a little north of the Barossa Valley, Kapunda is actually off the main roads north, but you can take a pleasant backroads route from the valley through Kapunda and join the

Barrier Highway a little further north. Copper was found here in 1842 and Kapunda became the first mining town in Australia, and for a while was the biggest country town in South Australia. At its peak it had a population of 10,000 with 22 hotels. The mines closed in 1888.

There's a lookout point in the town with views over the old open-cut mines and mine chimneys. Kapunda has a Historical Museum with old mining relics plus the old courthouse and jail tearooms – a good place for a country-style tea. It's a pleasant drive to Eudunda north-east of Kapunda.

BURRA (population 1200)
This really pretty little town was a copper-mining centre from 1847 to 1877. The district Burra Burra takes it name from the Hindi word for 'great great'. Pick up a guide-yourself leaflet from the tourist office by the centre of town (50c) and explore the town with its many old stone buildings and tiny Cornish cottages. A couple of old miners' dugouts by the riverbank have been preserved.

The town has a Folk Museum on Market Square in the tourist office building. The 33 cottages at Paxton Square were built for Cornish miners in the 1850s and are being restored by the National Trust. Other old buildings include Redruth Jail, the Bon Accord Mine Building and the courthouse and jail at Burra North. Burra Gorge is north of the town.

After Burra the country rapidly becomes drier and more barren. From the road you'll see galahs and possibly the odd emu. In the early morning or evening you may also see kangaroos, although driving along the road to Broken Hill during the '82 drought the number of dead roos was phenomenal – they were almost continuous all the way to the NSW border. Over one five km stretch I counted 47 recently killed. The unfortunate animals are attracted by the roadside vegetation due to water run-off from the road.

CLARE (population 2400)
This pleasant little town 135 km north of Adelaide is another important wine-producing centre although it is far less commercial than the Barossa. It was originally settled in 1842 and named after County Clare in Ireland. The first vines were planted here in 1848 by Jesuit priests and communion wines are still produced today. There are lots of wineries in the valley including the well-known Stanley Wine Company, dating from 1894.

The town has a number of interesting buildings including, in what seems to be a South Australian norm, a police station/courthouse, dating from 1850, which is preserved as a National Trust museum. The Wolta Wolta Homestead dates from 1864 while Christison Park has a fauna and flora reserve and picnic grounds. At the Pioneer Memorial Park there are walking trails and barbecue facilities.

You can visit the Barossa on your way north to the Clare Valley and in turn Clare can be visited en route to the Flinders Ranges. There's a daily bus to Riverton which connects with trains to Adelaide. The bus from Adelaide costs $8. There's a tourist office in the Town Hall at 229 Main St, Clare.

PORT PIRIE (population 14,700)
Just 84 km south of Port Augusta at the northern end of the Spencer Gulf, this is a major port and industrial centre with huge lead smelters that handle the output sent down by rail from Broken Hill. There are tours of the smelters on weekday afternoons. It's also an important port for shipping of agricultural produce.

Port Pirie has lots of interesting old buildings including some fine hotels down the main street of the town. On Ellen St the National Trust Museum includes the ornate old railway station and customs house. Near Port Pirie there's an interesting museum on Weerona Island, 13 km out, and the Telowie Gorge park is also within easy reach.

OTHER MID-NORTH TOWNS

Balaklava (population 1300) is a picturesque town on the northern edge of the Adelaide plains. There's a National Trust museum open on Sundays only and it's a short trip from here to Wakefield at the northern end of Gulf St Vincent. Jamestown (population 1400), north of the Clare Valley, is a country town with a Railway Station Museum open Sundays from 2 to 4 pm.

Peterborough (population 2600) is an important railway centre and also a place where the problems railway engineers in Australia have to cope with are clearly illustrated. The colonial bungling which led to Australia's mixed-up railway system managed to run three different railway gauges through Peterborough! Steamtown is a working railway museum and on holiday weekends narrow-gauge steam-train trips are made from Peterborough. The old town hall in Peterborough is now a museum and art gallery.

The area from Peterborough north to the Flinders saw a land boom in the 1870s as settlers established farming towns, encouraged by easy credit from the South Australian government. Sturdy farms and towns sprung up but the wet seasons that had encouraged hopes of wheat farming soon gave way to the normal dry conditions and as the land dried out the towns tumbled into ruins. Some of the most interesting reminders of those days can be seen in the southern Flinders.

Kangaroo Island
Population: 3000

The third biggest island in Australia (after Tasmania and Melville Island off Darwin in the Northern Territory), Kangaroo Island is a popular holiday resort from Adelaide. It's about 110 km from Adelaide to Kingscote, the main town on the island, but the north-east corner of Kangaroo Island is actually only 10 km off the southern tip of the Fleurieu Peninsula. Kangaroo Island is about 150 km long by 30 km wide but is sparsely populated. It offers superb scenery; pleasant, sheltered beaches along the north coast; a rough, rugged and wave-swept south coast plus lots of native

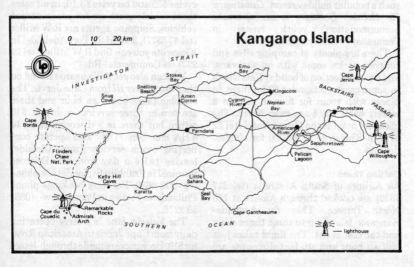

wildlife. There are no foxes, rabbits or other introduced wildlife that have upset the balance on the mainland. The island also has excellent fishing.

Like other islands off the south coast of Australia, Kangaroo Island had a rough-and-ready early history with sealers, whalers and escaped convicts all playing their often-ruthless part. Many of the names around the island have a distinctly French flavour to them since it was first charted by the French explorer Nicholas Baudin. He had just met Matthew Flinders who was in the process of circumnavigating Australia, at nearby Encounter Bay off Victor Harbor. Flinders had already named the island after the many kangaroos he saw there but Baudin went on to name many other prominent features on the island. Apart from beaches, bushwalks and wildlife, the island has also attracted more than its fair share of shipwrecks and there are a number of these which are of interest to skindivers.

Places to Stay

There is a wide variety of accommodation all over the island – hardly surprising for such a popular holiday resort. *Guestward Ho Holiday Cottages* is an 'alternate accommodation' youth hostel in Penneshaw; nightly cost is $5.

There are plenty of camping sites and caravan parks, some with on-site vans, and a wide selection of holiday flats which in some cases cost under $30 a night in places with room for four to six; on a weekly basis costs are even lower. The cheapest hotel is the *Ozone Hotel* (tel 22 011) in Kingscote at $17/30 for singles/doubles.

Getting There

Air Airlines of South Australia (tel 217 7332) are booked through Ansett at 150 North Terrace. They fly Adelaide-Kangaroo Island up to three times daily and the cost is $44. The flight takes just half an hour and student discounts are

available if you're under 26. Apex return fares of $68 are also available on certain 'off-peak' flights.

Commodore Airlines (tel 267 2400) fly three-times daily to Kingscote via Penneshaw with one-way fares of $44 and $34 respectively; return fares are double. Lloyd Aviation (tel 352 6944) have an apex return fare of $66 to Kingscote if you book seven days in advance. Albatross Airlines (tel (0848) 2 2296) also fly Adelaide-Kingscote twice daily for $60 return.

There's an airport bus running from the Kangaroo Island Airport to Kingscote for $2.50.

Ferry The *MV Troubridge* crosses to Kingscote from Port Adelaide anything from two to four-times weekly, depending on the season; the crossing takes 6½ hours. Once weekly it continues on to Port Lincoln on the Eyre Peninsula. There are some seasonal variations in summer, over school holidays and on public holidays. Fares to Kingscote from Port Adelaide are: adults $23, cars $57, motorcycles $19 and bicycles $2.10. From Port Lincoln the rates are: adults $33, cars $75, motorcycles $25 and bicycles $3.10; in all cases these vehicle costs are for accompanied vehicles. Shipping agents are R W Miller (tel 47 5577), 3 Todd St, Port Adelaide. In Kingscote you can find R W Miller (tel 22 273) on Commercial Rd.

You can also get to Kangaroo Island on the *Philanderer III* from Cape Jervis. The crossing takes about an hour and there are two or three services a day at $40 return but there is a discount given to YHA members. They also operate connecting coach services from Adelaide, leaving twice a day from the Briscoes terminal in Franklin St; for details phone (08) 272 6680. For ferry bookings phone Philanderer Ferries in Penneshaw – (085) 59 2276.

The *Valerie Jane* is a ferry operating daily from Cape Jervis to American River for $19. Bookings are made through Jetset tours in Adelaide (tel 212 3677) and Linnet's Island Club in American River (tel 33 053).

Getting Around

Kingscote Taxi and Tours Service provides a twice-daily service between American River and Kingscote for $6 and between Penneshaw and Kingscote for $5.

There are a variety of rental cars and motorcycles; the SAGTB has a car hire leaflet for the island. The 'big three' have agencies and there are a number of independent operators with typical charges being a Gemini for $44 with 250 free km per day plus 20c a km after that plus insurance of $8! Cheaper is Kangaroo Island Rental Cars (tel 22 390) in Kingscote with unlimited-km rates of $35 per day plus $5 insurance.

It's possible, but often difficult, to hitch around the island and it's especially hard in the off-season. Similarly, bicycling is hard work; the roads are mainly gravel and get very dusty plus the distances are surprisingly large. From Penneshaw to Cape Borda is 140 km. Bicycles can be hired at Kingscote Take-Away (tel 22585) in Kingscote, Linnet's Island Club (tel 33053) in American River, and the Sorrento Motel (tel 31028) in Penneshaw.

KINGSCOTE (population 1250)

The main town on Kangaroo Island, Kingscote is also the arrival point for the ferries and flights to the island. This was actually the first settlement in South Australia although it was soon superseded by Adelaide and other mainland centres. It was formally settled in 1836 and all but abandoned a few years later but there were other Europeans on the island many years earlier.

In Kingscote there is a rock-pool for swimming. Another good place to go for a swim is Brownlow Beach. The old cottage 'Hope', built in 1858, is a National Trust museum and the headstones in Kingscote's cemetery make interesting reading.

AMERICAN RIVER (population 120)

Between Kingscote and Penneshaw the small settlement of American River takes its name from the group of American sealers who built a boat here in 1803-4. The town is situated on a small peninsula and shelters an inner bay, named Pelican Lagoon by Flinders, which today is a bird sanctuary. American River is a popular tourist resort, good for sailing and fishing.

PENNESHAW

Looking across the narrow Backstairs Passage to the Fleurieu Peninsula, Penneshaw is a quiet little resort town with a pleasant beach at Hog's Bay and the tiny inlet of Christmas Cove is a boat harbour. You can sometimes see penguins on the rocks below the town. Frenchman's Rock is a monument housing a replica of the rock Baudin left here in 1803; the actual rock he marked to note his visit is now in the South Australian Art Gallery.

The Dudley Peninsula, the knob of land on the eastern end of the island on which Penneshaw is located, has several other points of interest: there's surf at Pennington Bay, the sheltered waters of Chapman River are very popular for canoeing, and the Cape Willoughby lighthouse was first operated in 1852 and is the oldest in South Australia (open from 1 to 3.30 pm Monday to Friday).

NORTH COAST

There is a series of fine sheltered beaches along the north coast of the island. Near Kingscote, Emu Bay has a beautiful, long sweep of sand. Other good beaches include Stokes Bay, Snelling Beach and the sheltered, sandy stretch of Snug Cove.

FLINDERS CHASE NATIONAL PARK

Occupying the whole western end of the island the Flinders Chase National Park is the largest national park in South Australia. The park has beautiful forests of eucalypts plus koalas, wild pigs and possums as well as kangaroos and emus which have become so accustomed to humans that they'll come up and brazenly badger you for food. The popular picnic and barbecue area at Rocky River homestead is actually fenced off to protect park visitors from these free-loaders.

On the north-west corner of the island Cape Borda has a lighthouse built in 1858 with guided tours Monday to Friday from 2 to 4 pm. The lighthouse is on a cliff 150 metres above the sea. There's an interesting little cemetery nearby at Harvey's Return. In the southern corner of the park Cape du Couedic (named by Nicholas Baudin, of course) is wild, remote and rugged. An extremely picturesque lighthouse built in 1906 tops the cape and you can follow the path from the car park down to Admiral's Arch – a natural archway pounded by towering seas. You can often see seals and penguins here.

At Kirkpatrick Point, only a couple of km east of Cape du Couedic, the Remarkable Rocks are a series of bizarre granite rocks on a huge dome stretching 75 metres down to the sea. You can camp at the Rocky River park headquarters, or elsewhere with a permit.

SOUTH COAST

The south coast of the island is rough and wave-swept in comparison to the north coast. At Hanson Bay, close to Cape du Couedic at the western end of the coast, there's a colony of fairy penguins. A little further east you come to Kelly Hill Caves, a series of limestone caves discovered in the 1880s when a horse, appropriately named Ned Kelly, fell through a hole in the ground. There are tours hourly to 3.30 pm daily.

Vivonne Bay has a long and beautiful sweep of beach and there is excellent fishing here but swimmers should exercise great care. The undertows are fierce and swimmers are recommended to stick close to the jetty or the river mouth. Seal Bay is another sweeping beach with plenty of resident seals. They're generally quite happy to have two-legged visitors

on the beach but a little caution is required – don't let them feel threatened by your presence. Nearby and close to the south coast road is 'little Sahara', a series of enormous white sand dunes, ideal for playing Lawrence of Arabia.

The South-East

The south-east of South Australia is the area through which most travellers between Melbourne and Adelaide pass. Travelling between the two cities you can either take the Western and Dukes Highways or the Princes Highway through the south-east region.

The Western/Dukes is the most direct route between the two cities (729 km) but the Dukes Highway stretch in South Australia is not terribly exciting – it just runs through a lot of flat, dull, agricultural land. South of this route there is some rather more interesting country and you can take slightly longer detours off the usual route but the Princes Highway, along the coast, is of greater interest. Along this road from Victoria you pass through Mt Gambier, with its impressive crater lakes, and then run along the extensive coastal lagoon system known as the Coorong.

Getting There

Air Ansett fly from Melbourne to Mt Gambier most days of the week and twice on some days. The flight takes just over an hour and costs $88. Airlines of South Australia have a similar schedule between Adelaide and Mt Gambier; again, it's about a 1-1/4 hour flight and the fare is $87.

Bus Mt Gambier Motor Service (tel (08) 217 0777) operates from the Central Bus Station in Adelaide to Mt Gambier six days a week. The trip takes about six hours and fares are Kingston $19, Robe or Millicent $22, Mt Gambier $24. Ansett

Pioneer operate from Melbourne to Mt Gambier daily. The trip takes about six to eight hours (varies from day to day) and the fare is $34.

Rail Phone 217 4455 for rail bookings in Adelaide. There are daily services from Adelaide to Mt Gambier, twice daily on some days. The trains follow the Melbourne line to just beyond Bordertown before turning south to Naracoorte and Mt Gambier. By day Adelaide-Mt Gambier is about eight hours but overnight services take about 11 hours. Fares from Adelaide are: Bordertown $18, Naracoorte $23, Mt Gambier $30.

MENINGIE (population 400)

On the southern edge of Lake Albert and at the north of the Coorong this small town is a popular gateway to the Coorong. A wide variety of watersports is available on Lake Albert and there are also good bushwalks in the area. The birdlife around Meningie is prolific and varied.

THE COORONG

The Coorong is a unique national park – a long, narrow strip curving along the coast for 145 km south of Adelaide. The northern end of the Coorong is marked by Lake Alexandrina where the Murray reaches the sea and the southern end is marked by the small town of Kingston SE. The Coorong consists of a long, narrow, shallow lagoon and a complex series of salt-pans, all separated from the sea by the huge sand dunes of the Younghusband Peninsula, more usually known as the Hummocks.

The Coorong is a superb natural bird sanctuary with a vast number of waterbirds. Cormorants, ibis, swans, terns, shags, ducks and other waterbirds can all be seen but it is the pelicans for which the Coorong is best known. The film *Storm Boy*, about a young boy's friendship with a pelican, was filmed on the Coorong. At Salt Creek you can take the nature trail turn-off from the Princes Highway and follow the old road which runs along the shore of the Coorong for some distance.

KINGSTON SE (population 1300)

At the southern end of the Coorong, Kingston is a popular beach resort and a good base for visits to the Coorong. The town was originally named Maria Creek after a ship which was wrecked at Cape Jaffa on the Coorong in 1840. Nobody lost their lives in the actual shipwreck but as the 27 crew and passengers made their way south towards Lake Albert, they were all massacred by Aboriginals. There's a memorial to the Maria in Kingston, but it's said that Policeman's Point was named after the point where white mans' retribution caught up with the Aboriginals.

Other attractions are the National Trust Pioneer Museum and the nearby Cape Jaffa lighthouse which is open from 2 to 5 pm daily. Kingston is a centre for rock lobster fishing but Kingston's best known lobster, and a major landmark in its own right, is hardly edible. Towering by the roadside is 'The Big Lobster' – a superb piece of Australian kitsch. The amazingly realistic lobster is made of fibreglass and steel and marks a tourist centre with restaurants, souvenirs and tourist information. You can, however, buy crayfish freshly cooked at the jetty.

The Jip Jip National Park is 45 km north-east of Kingston and features huge granite outcrops in the bush. From Kingston conventional vehicles can drive 16 km along the beach to 'The Granites' while with four-wheel drive you can continue right along the beach to the Murray River mouth.

ROBE (population 600)

A small port, steeped in history, Robe was one of South Australia's first settlements, dating from 1845. Early buildings include the 1863 Customs House which is now a National Trust museum. It's open Tuesdays and public holidays (daily in January) from 2 to 4 pm, admission is 50c.

There is also an old jail up on the cliffs and a small arts and crafts gallery.

The citizens of Robe made a colourful fortune in the late 1850s due to the Victorian gold rush. The Victorian government instituted a £10 head tax on Chinese goldminers in 1855 and 16,000 ingenious Chinese circumvented the tax by getting to Victoria via Robe in South Australia; 10,000 arriving in 1857 alone. The 'Chinamen's Wells' in the region are a reminder of that time. There are fine views along the coast from the Obelisk at Cape Dombey.

BEACHPORT (population 400)

South of Robe this quiet little seaside town is, like other places along the coast, a busy lobster and crayfishing centre. There's a small National Trust museum in the old wood and grain store plus a couple of other old buildings. There's good surfing near Beachport at the 'blowhole' and a nearby salt lake called the 'Pool of Siloam'.

MILLICENT (population 5250)

At Millicent the 'Alternative 1' route through Robe and Beachport rejoins the main road. The town has a central swimming lake and there's a National Trust museum and the Admella Gallery both on George St. A narrow gauge steam engine is on display nearby. There's also a Historical & Maritime Museum in the town.

The Canunda National Park, with its enormous sand dunes, is 13 km west of Millicent. Tantanoola, 21 km away, has the stuffed 'Tantanoola Tiger' on display at the Tantanoola Tiger Hotel. This beast, actually an Assyrian wolf, was shot in 1895 after a lot of local publicity. It was presumed to have escaped from a shipwreck but quite why a ship would have a wolf on board is not clear! Tantanoola also has limestone caves which are open 9 am to 5 pm daily.

There's a National Trust tourist office at 7 Mt Gambier Rd.

MT GAMBIER (population 20,000)

The major town and commercial centre of the south-east, Mt Gambier is 486 km from Adelaide. The town is built on the slopes of the volcano which gives it its name. The volcano has three craters, each with its own lake. The beautiful and spectacular Blue Lake is the best known although from about March to November the lake is more grey than blue. As nature would have it though, in November it changes back to blue again; just in time for the holiday season! The lake is 197 metres at its deepest and there's a five-km scenic drive around.

Mt Gambier also has many parks including the Cave Park with its deep 'cave', actually more of a steep-sided hole, which is right in the centre of the city. Mt Gambier is in a rich agricultural area but timber and limestone, cut in blocks for use as a building material, are the main products. The poet Adam Lindsay Gordon, who committed suicide in 1870, is also connected with Mt Gambier where he lived for some years.

Black's Museum, open daily, has displays of Aboriginal artefacts. On Sunday afternoons you can also visit the museum in the old courthouse. There are tours of the sawmills around Mt Gambier. Check with the Mt Gambier Tourist Information Centre on Casterton Rd for more details.

PORT MACDONNELL (population 700)

South of Mt Gambier this quiet little fishing port is a centre for rock lobster fishing. At one time it was a busy shipping port, hence the surprisingly big 1863 customs house, now used as a restaurant. Adam Lindsay Gordon's home, Dingley Dell, is now a museum.

There are some fine walks around Port MacDonnell including the path to the top of Mt Schank, an extinct volcano crater. On Wednesdays and Thursdays from 2 to 4 pm you can visit the Cape Northumberland Lighthouse on the superb coastline west of the port.

ALONG THE DUKES HIGHWAY

The Dukes Highway, the main Melbourne to Adelaide route, is not terribly exciting, particularly from the South Australian border through to Tailem Bend. Bordertown (population 2150), just across the border, is in a prosperous agricultural area. There's a good picnic area by the stream on the east side of town with a small wildlife sanctuary nearby.

Keith (population 1150) is another farming town and it also has a small museum and the Mt Rescue Conservation Park 16 km to the north. This area was once known as 90-mile desert. Tintinara (population 350) is the only other town of any size and also an access point to the Mt Rescue park. Coonalpyn (population 400) is a tiny township and jumping-off point for the Mt Boothby Conservation Park.

NARACOORTE (population 4750)

Settled in the 1840s, Naracoorte is one of the oldest towns in South Australia and one of the largest country towns in the south-east. The town has the Old Mill Museum, a National Trust museum and the Naracoorte Art Gallery. On Jenkins Terrace the Naracoorte Museum & Snake Pit (!) has gems, antiques and a reptile park. It's open daily from 10 am to 5 pm except Sundays when it's open 2 to 5 pm. Pioneer Park has restored locomotives and the town also has a swimming lake.

Naracoorte Caves are 11 km out of town – Fossil Cave has ice-age fossils and there are three others with stalactites and stalagmites; it's open daily. Bat Cave, with lots of bats that make a spectacular departure every evening, is 17 km out of town. At a similar distance from the town at Bool Lagoon Reserve you can see different types of waterbirds at different times of the year.

The Naracoorte Tourist Information Centre is at 128 Smith St.

COONAWARRA

A fine wine-producing area 10 km north of Penola, there are 10 wineries in the area. Wynn's Coonawarra Estate is the most well-known of the wineries here although it is not open to the public unlike some of the smaller wineries. Most of them are open Monday to Friday, some also open on Saturdays and Sundays. Penola (population 1200) is the main town in the area. Bushman's Inn in Penola North has displays of coins and Aboriginal artefacts.

Murray River

Australia's greatest river starts in the Snowy Mountains in the Australian Alps and for most of its length forms the boundary between NSW and Victoria. It's in South Australia that the Murray comes into its prime, though. First it flows west through the Riverland area, a region where the wonders of irrigation have turned an unproductive land into an important region of wineries and fruit growing. Although names like the Barossa and Hunter receive much more recognition, this region does actually produce 40% of Australia's wine. Then at Morgan the river turns sharply south and flows through the Lower Murray region to the sea. In all it is 650 km from the South Australia/NSW-Victoria border to the sea.

The Murray has lots of watersport possibilities, plenty of wildlife (particularly waterbirds) and, in the Riverlands section, a positive surfeit of wineries to visit. This, however, is also a river with a history for until the advent of the railways the Murray was the Mississippi of Australia with paddle-steamers carrying produce from the interior down to the coast. Many of the river towns still have a strong flavour of those riverboat days and if you've the cash and inclination you can still ride a paddle-steamer, forging its leisurely way on a cruise down the mighty Murray.

Life on the River

The Murray River region has plenty of conventional accommodation including a youth hostel by the Riverfront Caravan Park in Loxton, but to really get to grips with the Murray the ideal way is, of course, out on the river. You can do that by a number of methods. Simplest and cheapest are day trips such as those operated by the *MV Barrangul* from Renmark, the *MV Kookaburra* from Murray Bridge, the *MV Mary Ann* from Berri or the *MV Swamplander* which operates across Lake Bonney to Chambers Creek where there is abundant birdlife.

If you've got a family or a group of people a very pleasant way to explore the Murray is to rent a houseboat and set off along the river by yourself. These boats can be hired in Morgan, Waikerie, Loxton, Berri, Renmark and other river centres but they are very popular so it's wise to book well ahead. The SA travel centre offices can advise you about prices and make bookings. The cost depends on what you hire, where you hire it and, most importantly, when you hire it. Typical prices are around $300 a week for a four-berth houseboat, around $400 for larger eight or 10-berth boats; these costs can drop in low seasons.

Finally there are the riverboats such as the huge paddle-wheeler *Murray River Queen* which makes five-day trips from Goolwa to Swan Reach and back, or the *MV Aroona* with regular day-cruises to the Murray mouth and the Coorong, also from Goolwa.

You could take the *MV Murray Explorer* from Renmark up to the NSW-Victoria stretch of the Murray, then back down to Loxton and finally up to Renmark again but these trips are definitely not cheap!

Getting There

Air Murray Valley Airlines (tel 217 7711) can be found at TAA, 144 North Terrace, Adelaide. They fly to Renmark from Adelaide twice daily Monday to Friday; the fare is $62.

Bus Alternatively you can get there by bus. Stateliner (tel 212 1777) operates Adelaide-Blanche Town-Waikerie-Loxton with fares of $10 to Blanchetown, $13 to Waikerie and $16 to Loxton and Renmark. Briscoes and Stateliner are both at the Central Bus Station, Franklin St, Adelaide.

RENMARK (population 3500)

In the centre of the Riverland irrigation area 295 km from Adelaide, this was not only a starting point for the great irrigation projects that revolutionised the area, but also the first of the river towns. Irrigation was started by the Canadian Chaffey brothers in 1887 and you can see one of their original wood-burning irrigation pumps on Renmark Avenue. Olivewood, Charles Chaffey's home, built around 1890, is also on Renmark Avenue. It's open from 2.30 to 4 pm daily except Wednesday.

Today the area earns its living from vineyards, orchards and other fruit growing. In the town you can inspect the 1911 paddle-steamer *Industry* which is now a museum. There are several art galleries in the town centre while Goat Island in the river is a wildlife sanctuary with many koalas.

Around Renmark there is Bredl's Reptile Park & Zoo five km out of town with lots of snakes and crocodiles. And of course there are plenty of wineries in the area which provide free tastings.

There's a tourist office on Murray Avenue – phone 86 6703.

BERRI (population 3400)

At one time a refuelling stop for the wood-burning paddle-steamers, the town takes its name from the Aboriginal words 'berri berri' – 'big bend in the river'. It's the economic centre of the Riverland and there are a number of wineries in the area. Berri Estates Winery at Glossop, 13 km to the west, is the biggest winery in Australia, if not in the whole southern hemisphere.

Berri also has a large fruit juice factory

with tours four times a day over the weekends. Lovers of Australian kitsch should take a visit to the 'big orange'. It is four km out of Berri on the road to Renmark. This 16-metre diameter, fiberglass 'orange' has exhibits relating the economic story of the Riverland region. There's also a display of vintage cars and motorcycles in the adjacent Riverland Display Centre. It is open from 9 am to 5 pm daily.

In the town you can climb up to the lookout on Fiedler St for views over the town and river. There's a koala sanctuary near the Martins Bend recreation area on the river. Near Berri the small town of Monash has a huge children's playground with no less than 120 different children-amusers! The annual big event in Berri is the Berri Rodeo which takes place each Easter Monday. Punts still cross the river from the Berri Hotel on Riverside Avenue to Loxton.

There's a tourist office on Vaughan Terrace.

LOXTON (population 3100)

From Berri the Murray makes a large loop south of the Sturt Highway and Loxton is at the bottom of the loop. It's an additional 38 km to follow this loop off the main road. The town follows the usual Riverland activities of fruit-growing and wine-making and has expanded dramatically since WW II due to a land settlement scheme instituted for returned servicemen.

The town's major attraction is the Historical Village on the riverbank. This village includes a replica of the town's first house, a pine-and-pug hut built by William Charles Loxton in 1878. In all, over two dozen buildings re-create a working village of the Riverland district at the turn of the century. It's open daily from 10 am to 4 pm on weekdays, to 5 pm on weekends.

There's a tourist office – the Loxton Tourist & Travel Centre – in the Loxton Hotel on East Terrace.

BARMERA (population 2000)

On the shores of Lake Bonney, where English record-holder Donald Campbell made an attempt on the world water-speed record in 1964, Barmera was once on the overland stock route along which cattle were driven from NSW. The ruins of Napper's Old Accommodation House, built in 1850 at the mouth of Chambers Creek, is a reminder of that era as is the Overland Corner Hotel, on the Morgan road 19 km out of town. It is now preserved as a National Trust museum and is open Wednesday to Sunday from 10 am to 5 pm.

There's also a National Trust Art Gallery & Museum in the town. Lake Bonney, with sandy beaches, is popular for swimming and watersports. There's even a nude beach at Pelican Point.

There's a Barmera tourist office on Barwell Avenue.

WAIKERIE (population 1600)

The town takes its name from the Aboriginal word for 'anything that flies', after the teeming birdlife on the lagoons and river around Waikerie. Curiously, anything that flies also includes gliders, for Waikerie has the most active gliding centre in Australia. You can arrange to take a joy ride in a glider here, phone 41 2644.

Wine tasting, Pooginook Conservation Park (12 km north-east which has echidnas and hairy-nosed wombats), the Kangaroo Park, Holder Bend Reserve and the Waikerie Producers Co-op, which is the largest citrus packing-house in the Southern Hemisphere are other attractions in and around the town.

There is a tourist centre at 20 McCoy St.

MORGAN (population 400)

In its prime this was the busiest river port in Australia and the massive wharves, towering 12-metres high, may be quiet today but they're certainly still there. Morgan is off the Sturt Highway to the north and from here a pipeline pumps water to Whyalla on Spencer Gulf.

BLANCHE TOWN

The site of the first river lock on the Murray, built in 1922, Blanche Town also has the small Brookfield Conservation Park near town, specifically intended for the hairy-nosed wombat.

SWAN REACH (population 200)

This sleepy little old town has very picturesque river scenery and, hardly surprisingly, lots of swans. Just down-river the river makes a long, gentle curve lasting 11 km in all. The bend is appropriately known as Big Bend and there's a picnic reserve here and many white cockatoos. The *Murray River Queen* ends its up-river cruise at Swan Reach.

MANNUM (population 2000)

The *Mary Ann*, Australia's first river-boat, was built here and made the first paddle-steamer trip up the Murray from Mannum in 1853. The river is very wide here and there are many relics of the pioneering days on the river to be seen, including the 1898 paddle-wheeler *Marion*, now a floating museum, open daily 10 am to 4 pm.

You can also see a replica of Sturt's whaleboat and relics of the *Mary Ann*. The Halidon Rd Bird Sanctuary has pelicans, ducks, swans and other water-birds. The Cascade Waterfalls, 11 km from Mannum on Reedy Creek, are also worth visiting. Off Purnong Rd there's a lookout tower.

MURRAY BRIDGE (population 8700)

South Australia's largest river town is only 82 km from Adelaide. It's a popular area for fishing, swimming, water-skiing and barbecues and from here you can make day-cruises on the *MV Kookaburra*. There's a Folk Museum at Johnston Park and the Murray Bridge Folk Museum has 600 antique dolls and toys and a wide range of Australiana. In the Sturt Reserve by the river there's a 20c coin-in-the-slot bunyip!

Near Murray Bridge is Monarto – the town that never was. A grandiose plan was drawn up to build a second major city for South Australia by the end of this century. This site was chosen and land purchased in the early 1970s but nothing further happened and a few years ago the project was totally abandoned.

TAILEM BEND (population 1700)

At a sharp bend in the river, Tailem Bend is near the mouth of the Murray river. After Wellington the Murray opens into huge Lake Alexandrina – lots of water-birds but sometimes tricky boating. The river mouth is near Goolwa – see the Fleurieu Peninsula section. You can take a ferry across the river at Jervois from where it's 11 km to the interesting old town of Wellington.

Yorke Peninsula

An easy drive from Adelaide, the Yorke Peninsula is a popular holiday area with some pleasant beaches along both sides of the peninsula, plenty of opportunity for fishing and the Innes National Park on the tip of the peninsula. The Peninsula's economy was originally based on the copper mines of 'little Cornwall'. As the mining declined, agriculture took its place and much of the land is now devoted to growing barley and other grains.

Places to Stay

There are campsites, hotels, motels and a variety of holiday accommodation all over the peninsula. Port Vincent has an associate youth hostel.

Getting There

Air Commodore Airlines (tel 212 3355), at the TAA office on North Terrace, Adelaide

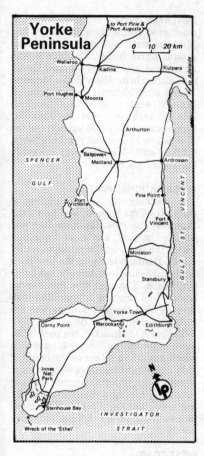

hours, depending on where you get off. There are two services daily Monday to Friday and one each on Saturday and Sunday.

Briscoes (tel 268 9444) have a couple of routes to the peninsula. Monday to Friday and on Sunday a bus runs from Adelaide to Ardrossan ($8.70), Port Vincent ($11.70), Stansbury ($11.90), Edithburgh ($12.50) and Yorketown ($12.50). The trip takes 2½ hours to Ardrossan and four hours to Yorketown. Their other service goes from Adelaide to Maitland ($8.80), Minlaton ($11.70) and Warooka ($12.50). It takes four hours to Warooka and runs daily except Saturday.

CORNWALL & COPPER MINES
In the early 1860s copper was discovered in the Moonta/Kadina/Wallaroo area of the Yorke Peninsula and within a few years a full-scale copper rush was on. The majority of the miners who worked these copper deposits were from Cornwall in England and the area still has a strong Cornish influence. There are many old cottages and churches which look for all the world as if they have been transplanted straight from Cornwall. The mining boom continued right through into this century, reaching its peak around the turn of the century, but in the early 1920s a slump in copper prices, rising labour costs and competition from mines abroad forced the closure of all the peninsula copper mines.

Over the long holiday weekend in May in odd-numbered years, a festival known as the Kernewek Lowender is held in 'little Cornwall'. It's a chance to try Cornish pasties or watch a wheelbarrow race. There are National Trust museums in each of the towns of the 'Cornish Triangle' and they're open on Wednesdays, Saturdays, Sundays, school holidays and certain other days during peak holiday seasons.

KADINA (population 2950)
The largest town on the peninsula,

have daily flights from Adelaide to Minlaton and on to Port Lincoln and return. Adelaide-Port Lincoln costs $47.

Bus There are a number of bus services between Adelaide and towns on the Yorke Peninsula. They all depart from the Central Bus Station, 111 Franklin St. Premier Roadlines (tel 217 0777) operates Adelaide-Kadina-Wallaroo-Moonta-Port Hughes-Moonta Bay. The fare is $8.20 and the journey takes from two to three

Kadina was once the centre of the copper-mining activities. The old Wallaroo mines are beside the town. The National Trust's Kadina Museum includes a number of buildings, one of which was the former home of the Matta Matta mine manager and was known as Matta House. There is also a blacksmith's workshop, a printing museum, displays of early agricultural equipment and the Matta Matta mine. Kadina has some fine old hotels with laceworked balconies and wide verandahs. There's a tourist office on Graves St.

WALLAROO (population 2000)

The second part of the Yorke Peninsula's 'Cornish triangle', this port town was a major centre during the copper boom. One of the great chimneys from the copper smelters, 'the big stack' built in 1861, still stands but today the port's main function is as an export point for agricultural products. Situated in the original town post office, the National Trust Maritime Museum has ship models and items from the town's early port history. There are other interesting old buildings in the town and good beaches.

MOONTA (population 1900)

A little south of Wallaroo the copper mine here was once said to be the richest mine in Australia. The town grew so fast that its school once had over a thousand students; the building now houses the largest country museum in the state. Other sights include numerous old Methodist churches (the town had 14 at one time), a National Trust restored Cornish miner's cottage, the Arts & Crafts Centre in the old railway station and ruins of the various mining works. Moonta Bay, the port for Moonta, is three km west of the town.

MAITLAND (population 1100)

In the centre of the peninsula this agricultural commercial centre also has a National Trust museum.

MINLATON (population 900)

Another agricultural commercial centre, Minlaton was the home town of pioneer aviator Harry Butler. His 1916 Bristol monoplane, nicknamed the 'Red Devil', is on display in the Harry Butler Museum. Nearby is the National Trust museum on Main St, while close to town there's an arts and crafts centre at the Gum Flat Homestead Gallery (two km out) and the Koolywurtie Museum with pioneer exhibits (11 km out). Minlaton was originally known as Gum Flat.

INNES NATIONAL PARK

The southern tip of the peninsula, marked by Cape Spencer, is all part of the Innes National Park. Stenhouse Bay, just outside the park, and Pondalowie Bay within the park, are the principal settlements. Pondalowie Bay is the base for a large crayfishing fleet and also has a fine surf beach. The park has fine coastal scenery and camping is permitted with permits from the park rangers who are stationed at Stenhouse Bay.

The main landmark in the park is the wreck of the barque *Ethel*, a 711-ton ship which was driven ashore on the beach in 1904. Despite an almost successful attempt to refloat her later that year, she has remained, rusting away, high and dry ever since. The ship's anchor is mounted in a memorial on the cliff-top above the beach.

WEST COAST

The west coast, looking out onto the Spencer Gulf, also has plenty of beaches but the road generally runs some way inland. The main port towns are Port Broughton and Wallaroo and Moonta Bay in the little Cornwall area.

EAST COAST

The east coast road from the top of Gulf St Vincent right down to Stenhouse Bay close to Cape Spencer closely follows the coast. There are many pleasant sandy beaches and secluded coves along the coastline. Port Clinton is the northern-most beach resort while a little south is Price, where salt is produced at salt-pans just outside town.

Ardrossan (population 1000) is 150 km from Adelaide and is the largest port on the east coast. There's the Ardrossan & District Historical Museum on Fifth St and ploughing enthusiasts will be delighted to hear that Ardrossan was the place where the 'stump-jump plough' was invented.

Continuing south the road runs through Pine Point, Black Point, Port Julia and Port Vincent in the next 50 km, each with a sandy beach. The road continues to hug the coast through Stansbury, Wool Bay, Port Giles and Coobowie before turning away from the coastline at Edithburgh.

Edithburgh has a rock swimming pool in a small cove and from the clifftops you can look across to the small islands of the Troubridge Shoals where there is good scuba diving. The town also has a small Maritime Museum and nearby Sultana Bay is a good spot for swimming. The southern part of the peninsula is sparsely populated but the road from Edithburgh to Stenhouse Bay is very scenic.

Eyre Peninsula

The wide Eyre Peninsula points south between Spencer Gulf and the Great Australian Bight. It's bordered on the north side by the Eyre Highway from Port Augusta to Ceduna. The coastal run along the peninsula is in two parts: first the Lincoln Highway south-west from Port Augusta to Port Lincoln and then the Flinders Highway north-west to Ceduna. It's 468 km from Port Augusta direct to Ceduna via the Eyre Highway while making the loop south totals 763 km.

This is a popular beach resort area with many fine beaches, sheltered bays and pleasant little port towns. Further along the Port Lincoln-Streaky Bay-Ceduna

stretch there are superb surf beaches and some of Australia's most spectacular coastal scenery. Off-shore further west is home to the great white shark. This is a favourite locale for making shark films – some of the scenes from *Jaws* were filmed here. The Eyre Peninsula also has a flourishing agricultural sector while the iron ore deposits at Iron Knob and Iron Baron are processed and shipped from the busy port of Whyalla.

The stretch of coast from Port Lincoln to Streaky Bay had one of the earliest European contacts. In 1627 the Dutch explorer Peter Nuyts sailed right along the north and west coasts of Australia in his ship the *Gulden Zeepard*. He continued along the south coast, crossed the Great Australian Bight but finally gave up at Streaky Bay and turned back to more hospitable climes. It was left to Abel Tasman, 15 years later, to complete the circumnavigation of the continent and it was not until over a century after that Cook 'discovered' the fertile east coast.

In 1802 Matthew Flinders charted the peninsula and named many of its prominent features during his epic circumnavigation of Australia. The peninsula takes its name from Edward John Eyre, the hardy explorer who made the first east-to-west crossing of the continent.

Places to Stay

There are plenty of places to stay on the Eyre Peninsula since many of the coastal towns are popular resorts – lots of camping grounds, holiday flats, hotels and motels.

Getting There

Air Airlines of South Australia (tel 217 7442) are at the Ansett terminal at 150 North Terrace, Adelaide. They fly to Port Lincoln ($66), Streaky Bay ($102) and Ceduna ($123) on the Eyre Peninsula. The Port Lincoln flights operate several times daily. There are also flights from Adelaide to Whyalla and other towns at the head of the gulf. Commodore Airlines fly between Minlaton on the Yorke Peninsula and Port Lincoln every day for $33.

Bus Greyhound and Ansett Pioneer's Adelaide-Perth services operate through Port Augusta ($17) and Ceduna ($36). It takes 9-1/2 hours from Adelaide to Ceduna. Stateliner (bookings and departures from the Greyhound terminal) operate to Streaky Bay ($23.50) and Ceduna.

Ferry The *MV Troubridge* sails once weekly from Adelaide via Kangaroo Island to Port Lincoln. It takes 6½ hours Adelaide-Kangaroo Island and another 9½ hours on to Port Lincoln. Fares are $45 from Adelaide, $33 from Kangaroo Island. Cars cost $75 from Kangaroo Island, motorcycles $25, bicycles $3.10.

Port Lincoln services stop between mid-December and early January when extra trips are made to Kangaroo Island from Adelaide. Agents for the ferry are R W Miller (tel 47 5577) at 3 Todd St, Port Adelaide. In Port Lincoln they are at Patrick Agencies (tel 82 1011), 33 Edinburgh St.

PORT AUGUSTA (population 15,300)
At the head of Spencer Gulf this busy port city is a crossroads for travellers. From here roads head west across the Nullarbor to Western Australia, north to Alice Springs and Darwin in the Northern Territory, south to Adelaide and east to Broken Hill and Sydney in New South Wales. It is also on the main railway line between the east and west coasts and serves as the terminus for the Ghan service to Alice Springs. Apart from its importance as a supply centre for goods going by rail or road into the outback it's also a major electricity generating centre, burning coal from the Leigh Creek open-cut mines. You can take a tour of the Thomas Playford Power Station or the Australian National Railways workshops,

the latter at 2 pm from Monday to Friday.

Other city attractions include the Curdnatta Art & Pottery Gallery in what was Port Augusta's first railway station. Old buildings include the Greenbush Gaol from 1869, the old town hall, the Grange from 1878 and Homestead Park pioneer museum which also includes a railway museum; it is on the corner of Elsie and Jaycee Sts.

WHYALLA (population 30,000)
The largest city in South Australia after Adelaide, Whyalla is a major steel-producing centre and also a busy deep-water port for shipping the steel and iron products. The town was originally known as Hummock Hill. Whyalla also had a major shipyard but it was closed down during the '70s. There are free tours of the steel works in Whyalla at 9.30 am on weekdays and 11 am on Saturdays; they start at the visitors' reception centre on Steelworks Rd. Ore comes to Whyalla from Iron Knob, Iron Monarch and Iron Baron and there are also tours of the Iron Knob mining operation at 10 am and 2 pm on weekdays and at 11 am on Saturdays. Iron Knob was the first iron ore deposit in Australia to be exploited. For safety reasons visitors on either of the Whyalla area tours must not wear sandals, thongs or other open shoes.

Apart from its industrial aspect, Whyalla also has fine beaches and a fauna and reptile park on the Lincoln Highway near the airport. On Ekblom St there are historical exhibits in the National Trust Mt Laura Homestead Museum which is only open on Sundays and public holidays from 2 to 4 pm. Studio 41, on the corner of Wood and Donaldson Terrace, includes an exhibition of local art. The Whyalla Tourist & Information Centre is at 3 Patterson St.

WHYALLA TO PORT LINCOLN
It's 280 km from Whyalla to Port Lincoln at the tip of the peninsula and there are

quite a few places of interest along the way. Cowell (population 600) is close to a very large jade deposit and the stone is cut and polished here. There's a jade workshop on West Terrace and the town also has a small National Trust museum in the old post office. Cowell has good beaches on Franklin Harbour, an expanse of water which is only open to the sea through a very narrow inlet. Cleve (population 800), 43 km inland from Cowell, has an interesting fauna park with a nocturnal house. Continuing 47 km further south, Arno Bay (population 400) is a popular little beach resort.

South again you reach Port Neill, another beach resort, and then Tumby Bay (population 900) which has a long, curving, white-sand beach and a number of interesting old buildings around the town. The Sir Joseph Banks group of islands are 15 km offshore from Tumby Bay and there are many attractive bays and reefs here plus a wide variety of sea birds which nest on the islands.

PORT LINCOLN (population 10,700)

At the southern end of the Eyre Peninsula, 662 km from Adelaide by road but only 250 km as the crow flies, Port Lincoln was named by Matthew Flinders in 1801. The first settlers arrived in 1839 and the town has grown to become the tuna fishing capital of Australia; the annual Tunarama Festival in January of each year signals the start of the tuna fishing season with boisterous merriment over the Australia Day weekend.

Port Lincoln is pleasantly situated on Boston Bay with a variety of opportunities for water sports. There are a number of historic buildings in the town including the Old Mill on Dorset Place which houses a small pioneer museum. The Lincoln Hotel dates from 1840 making it the oldest hotel on the peninsula. On the Flinders Highway, Mill Cottage is another museum and it's open from 2 to 5 pm daily. There are also a number of islands off Boston Bay.

Fourteen km offshore from the town is Dangerous Reef, the world's largest breeding area for the white pointer shark. Believe it or not a charter company runs trips out here for divers looking for that extra little bite. Even at $350 they're always fully booked, bringing in gamblers from the USA, Europe and Japan.

At one time Port Lincoln was considered as an alternative to Adelaide as the state capital. It still operates as an important deep-water port today. There is a tourist office (tel 82 3781) at the Town Hall on Tasman Terrace, the main street.

AROUND PORT LINCOLN

Cape Carnot, better known as Whalers' Way, is 32 km south of Port Lincoln and a permit to enter the conservation reserve must be obtained in Port Lincoln before you travel down there. A 15-km drive around the reserve takes you past stupendous cliffs, pounded by huge surf. It has some of the most impressive coastal scenery in Australia and at Sleaford Bay there is the remains of an old whaling station.

Also south of Port Lincoln is the Lincoln National Park, again with a magnificent coastline. You can visit offshore islands like Boston Island, Wedge Island or Thistle Island; the tourist office will help you find a boat to get out to them. Just north of Port Lincoln, Poonindie has an unusual old church.

PORT LINCOLN TO STREAKY BAY

Soon after leaving Port Lincoln the road passes by Coffin Bay, a sheltered stretch of water with some fine beaches. Coffin Bay itself is a tiny township and from here you can find spectacular coastal scenery at Point Avoid, Almonta Beach and Yangie Bay. There's a 25-km trail to Yangie Bay but you need four-wheel drive from there to Point Sir Isaac. You can see emus, Cape Barren geese and other wildlife at the Kellidie Bay Conservation Park. Elliston, further along the coast, is another beach resort and from here you can get out to a number of offshore islands. Flinders Island is 30 km off Elliston in the Bight, an $85 return flight from Cummins. Club 15 Holiday Homestead offers self-contained units from $20 per person. There are good swimming beaches around Waterloo Bay while Blackfellows has fine surf. Talia, further up the coast, has impressive granite rock faces and the limestone Talia Caves.

At Port Kenny on Venus Bay there are more beaches, and whales are often seen off the coast in October, when they come here to breed. Venus Bay has an active fleet of prawn trawlers. Shortly before Streaky Bay the turn-off to Point Labatt takes you to the conservation park where you can see the only permanent colony of sea lions on the Australian mainland. There's magnificent coastal scenery from here to Streaky Bay, 40 km north.

STREAKY BAY (population 1000)

This popular little resort town takes it name from the 'streaky' water, caused by seaweed in the bay. The town is surrounded by bays, caves and high cliffs. It was at Streaky Bay that the Dutch explorer Peter Nuyts gave up and turned back.

Curious granite outcrops known as *inselbergs* are found at numerous places around the Eyre Peninsula. You can see a particularly good group in the wheatfields close to the highway about 20 km southeast of Streaky Bay. They've been nicknamed 'Murphy's Haystacks'.

CEDUNA (population 2800)

Just past the junction of the Flinders and Eyre Highways, Ceduna marks the end of the Eyre Peninsula area and the start of the long, empty stretch of highway across the Nullarbor Plain into Western Australia. The town was founded in 1896 although a whaling station had existed on St Peter Island, off nearby Cape Thevenard, back in 1850.

There is an overseas telecommunications earth station 34 km north of Ceduna,

from where microwave communications are bounced off satellites. Tours are made every two hours from 10 am to 4 pm from Monday to Friday.

There are many beaches and sheltered coves around Ceduna while 13 km out of town you can see the old McKenzie Ruin at the earlier township site of Denial Bay. On the way from Streaky Bay you pass Smoky Bay, a small coastal fishing town. Near Point Sinclair, 95 km beyond Ceduna, is Cactus Beach with huge sand dunes and strong surf that draws enthusiasts to this remote surfing spot.

OTHER PLACES

Cummins (population 800), inland and north of Port Lincoln, is a small town with the Koppio Museum showing early agricultural equipment. Along the Eyre Highway the road passes through Kimba, Kyancutta and Wudinna, all important as agricultural centres but otherwise of little interest. Kimba (population 850) is on the very edge of the outback and you can visit Lake Gilles and the Gawler Ranges from here. Mt Wudinna, near Wudinna (population 600), is the second largest rock in Australia – nowhere near as well known as the largest! Tortoise Rock, also near Wudinna, looks much like a tortoise.

The Flinders Ranges

Rising from the northern end of Gulf St Vincent and running north for 800 km into the dry outback region, the Flinders Ranges is a desert mountain range offering some of the most spectacular scenery in Australia. It's a superb area for bushwalks, wildlife or simply taking in the ever-changing colours of the Australian outback. In the far north of the Flinders region the mountains are hemmed in by barren salt lakes.

The ranges, like so much of Australia, are geologically ancient but, worn though

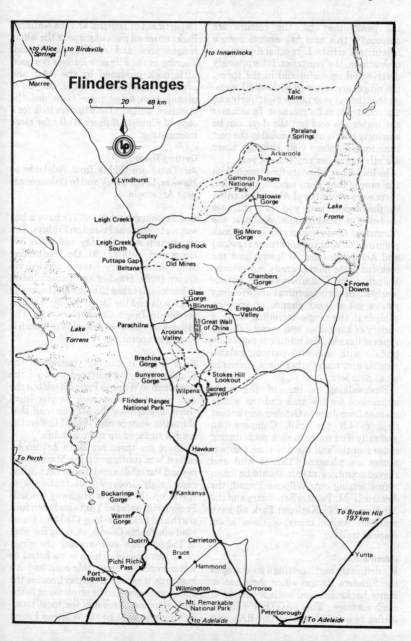

Flinders Ranges

0   20   40 km

to Alice Springs

to Birdsville

Marree

to Innamincka

Talc Mine

Lyndhurst

Paralana Springs

Arkaroola

Gammon Ranges National Park

Leigh Creek

Italowie Gorge

Copley

Lake Frome

Leigh Creek South

Big Moro Gorge

Puttapa Gap

Sliding Rock

Beltana

Old Mines

Chambers Gorge

Glass Gorge

Parachilna

Blinman

Eregunda Valley

Frome Downs

Lake Torrens

Aroona Valley

Great Wall of China

Brachina Gorge

Bunyeroo Gorge

Stokes Hill Lookout

Wilpena

Sacred Canyon

Flinders Ranges National Park

To Perth

Hawker

Buckaringa Gorge

Kankanya

Warren Gorge

To Broken Hill 197 km

Quorn

Carrieton

Bruce

Yunta

Pichi Richi Pass

Hammond

Port Augusta

Wilmington

Orroroo

Mt. Remarkable National Park

Peterborough

to Adelaide

to Adelaide

the peaks may be, the colours are amazing – this area has always been a favourite of artists. Like other dry regions of Australia, the vegetation is surprisingly diverse and colourful and in the spring the ranges are carpeted with wildflowers. At that time of year rain is most likely and the country is at its greenest. In summer the nights are cool but the days can be searingly hot. Winter is probably the best time for a Flinders visit although there are attractions for any time of year.

In 1802 when Flinders first touched on the ranges that were named after him, there were a number of Aboriginal tribes in the region and you can still see evidence of these people. Amongst the Aboriginal sites you can visit are the rock paintings at Yourambulla (near Hawker) and Arkaroola (near Wilpena) and the rock-cut patterns at Sacred Canyon (near Wilpena) and Chambers Gorge. Particularly in the early mornings and evenings you've got a good chance of spotting wildlife in the ranges including emus, a variety of kangaroos and many different types of lizards. The birdlife is especially prolific with colourful parrots, galahs, rosellas and many other birds – often in great numbers.

Bushwalking is one of the main attractions for the area and the winter months from June to October are the best time to hit the trail. Campers can generally find water in rock pools during those months and the day time temperatures are pleasant. This is wild and rugged country and care should be taken before setting out. Wilpena Pound, the Arkaroola-Mt Painter Sanctuary and the Mt Remarkable National Park all have excellent walks, many of them along marked trails.

Information

It's definitely worth getting a good map of the Flinders Ranges since there are so many backroads and such a variety of road surfaces. The SAGTB's Flinders leaflet is quite good and the RAA, SA Department of Tourism and the National Parks office all put out maps of the whole ranges area and of Wilpena Pound. *Touring in the Flinders Ranges* is a good little book produced by the RAA and available from their offices. If you're planning on doing more than just the standard walks in the Flinders look for a copy of *Flinders Ranges Walks* for more information.

Getting There

Air There are flights from Adelaide to Hawker, Leigh Creek and to Balcanoona, near Arkaroola.

Bus Stateliner (tel 217 0777) have a bus service to Wilpena Pound on Fridays. The return trip is on Sunday and takes 6½ hours and costs $27.50. On Wednesday and Saturday they have a service via Quorn ($20), Hawker and Parachilna to Arkaroola. It takes 12 hours all the way to Arkaroola and the fare is $41.50. The bus service to Leigh Creek costs $35. The railway service from Adelaide to Quorn is no longer operating.

Road If you're driving yourself to the Flinders it's good surfaced road all the way north to Wilpena Pound itself but the dirt road begins as soon as you leave there. If you take the Marree road that skirts the western edge of the Flinders the road is surfaced up to Parachilna.

There are three routes to Arkaroola: fastest is to continue up the Marree road beyond Parachilna and turn off at Copley, near Leigh Creek; an alternative is to travel up the Barrier Highway towards Broken Hill as far as Yunta and then turn north and follow the long (310 km) gravel road via Frome Downs, skirting the edge of Lake Frome and crossing the dingo proof fence twice. There is no petrol or water available along this road and it's best to do it earlier in the day because the sun in your eyes can be unpleasant in the late afternoon. Probably the most interesting route is to go via Wilpena Pound and take the road via Chambers Gorge, meeting the Frome Downs road south of Balcanoona. This road does tend to be difficult after rain, however.

Getting Around

You can make a loop that takes you around an interesting section of the southern part of the Flinders. From Port Augusta you go through the Pichi Richi Pass to Quorn and Hawker and on up to Wilpena Pound. From the Pound you continue north through the Flinders Ranges National Park to Blinman then down through the Parachilna Gorge to Parachilna, back on the plains and back south to Hawker – thus looping right round Wilpena Pound. From the Pound you can also make loops north into the Flinders Range National Park through Bunyeroo Gorge and the Aroona Valley.

Tours There are plenty of tours from Adelaide to the ranges and also tours out from Wilpena Pound and Arkaroola. Air tours made from the Pound include day trips to Arkaroola. Road tours go to the Aroona Valley, Blinman and Parachilna Gorge, Chambers Gorge or to Arkaroola.

MT REMARKABLE NATIONAL PARK

South-east of Port Augusta and in the southern stretch of the Flinders Ranges, the Mt Remarkable National Park is near Wilmington and Melrose. From Wilmington you can drive into the park and walk through narrow Alligator Gorge; in places the walls of this spectacularly beautiful gorge are only two metres apart. Hancock's Lookout, near Horrock's Pass just north of the park, offers excellent views of Spencer Gulf.

MELROSE

This tiny town is the oldest settlement in the Flinders Ranges. It's on the southern edge of the Mt Remarkable National Park, at the foot of Mt Remarkable itself. There's a walking trail to the top of the mountain. The old police station and

court house now houses a National Trust museum while the North Star Hotel of 1854 is the oldest hotel in the Flinders. The Mt Remarkable Hotel is only a few years younger and its exterior has scarcely changed over the past 125-plus years. There are a number of other interesting and picturesque old buildings in this enjoyable little town. Pleasant walks lead alongside the creek through the town and there's a good campsite on the riverbanks.

OTHER TOWNS

Other towns in the south of the Flinders include Carrieton (population 200) where a major rodeo is held each October. Bruce and Hammond, near Wilmington, were both railheads at one time but have now faded away to ghost towns. Orroroo (population 600) is an agricultural centre and nearby Black Rock Peak has good bushwalks and terrific views over the surrounding countryside. You can see Aboriginal rock carvings at Pekina Creek by the town and the ruins of the nearby Pekina Station Homestead are also worth visiting.

QUORN (population 1050)

The 'gateway to the Flinders' is about 330 km north of Adelaide and only 46 km from Port Augusta. This was once an important railway town after the completion of the Great Northern Railway in 1878 and the town still has a lot of the flavour of the old pioneering days. The railway line was closed down in 1957 but since 1974 parts of the line have been re-opened as a tourist attraction by railway enthusiasts. On winter weekends and public holidays a vintage steam engine makes a 25-km round-trip from Quorn to the scenic Pichi Richi Pass $8 for adults.

The town, picturesquely sited in a valley in the ranges, has a couple of art galleries and the small Flinders Museum in an old bakery and flour mill. From Quorn you can make four-wheel drive trips into the Flinders and visit the nearby Warren Gorge (which has good rock climbing) and the Buckaringa Gorge (good for picnics). Closer to the town you can follow walking trails to the top of Devil's Peak and Dutchman's Stern.

KANYAKA

North of Quorn, about half way to Hawker, are the ruins of the old Kanyaka settlement. Founded in 1851 it supported 70 families at its peak before being abandoned in the 1870s. Only the ruins of the solid, stone-built houses remain to remind of the high hopes that early settlers had for this harsh area.

If you're coming from the north don't be fooled by the signs for the Kanyaka settlement; all there is here is a solitary gravestone by the creek bed. The ruins, deserted except for roos and galahs, are further south. There are two groups of ruins, the second group being a couple of hundred metres away along the dirt road, a rise obscuring them from view. The first group also has an old graveyard and note the solid stone dunnies – they were clearly built to last. It's about one km along the creek to the cookhouse and shearing shed. The track continues around 1½ km to a picturesque permanent waterhole, overlooked by the Kanyaka Death Rock.

HAWKER (population 350)

In a sheep-raising area, the town of Hawker has a tiny museum of minerals in the Mobil station. There are a number of places of interest which can be conveniently visited from here, including the Kanyaka ruins to the south and Wilpena Pound, only a short drive north. Willow Waters is another old property abandoned in the 1890s when crops failed. There are Aboriginal rock paintings south of Hawker at Yourambulla Cave, a hollow in the rocks, high up on the side of Yourambulla Peak.

Places to Stay & Eat

The *Hawker Hotel* costs $16/22 for old-fashioned but quite OK small rooms. In the new motel part, rooms are $33/42 for

singles/doubles. The counter meals here are certainly filling. There's another motel and also a campsite in Hawker.

WILPENA POUND

The best-known feature of the ranges is the huge natural basin known as Wilpena Pound. This vast basin covers about 80 square km, ringed by a circle of cliffs and accessible only by the narrow opening at Sliding Rock, through which the Wilpena Creek sometimes flows. From outside the Pound the cliff face is almost sheer, soaring to 1000 metres, but inside the basin floor slopes gently away from the peaks. There are many excellent walks within the Pound including the climb to 1190-metre-high St Mary's Peak with superb views over the Pound. There are day-walks on marked trails including the climb up St Mary's Peak. Other popular walks are the one to Edeowie Gorge and Malloga Falls or to Mt John.

There is plenty of wildlife in the Pound, particularly birdlife which includes everything from rosellas, galahs and budgerigars to wedge-tailed eagles. You can make scenic flights over the Pound (booking at the Wilpena Pound Motel) or make excursions to other places of interest in the vicinity. Sacred Canyon, with rock-cut patterns, is off to the east. North of Wilpena Pound is the Flinders Ranges National Park where scenic attractions include the Bunyeroo and Brachina Gorges and the Aroona Valley.

Walks

You can make an excellent day-long walk from the campsite to St Mary's Peak and back. The walk can be made either as an up-and-down or a round-trip expedition. Up and back it's faster and more interesting to take the route outside the Pound and then up to the Tanderra Saddle since the scenery is much more spectacular. The final climb up to the saddle is fairly steep and the stretch to the top of the peak is a real scramble. From the saddle and the peak the views are superb. The

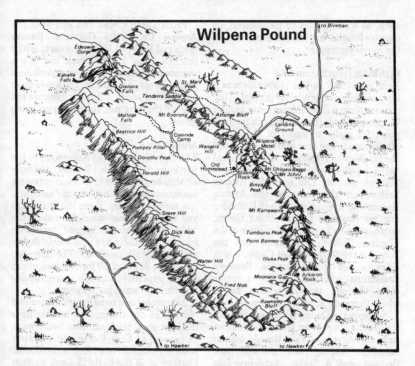

Wilpena Pound

to Blinman

Edeowie Gorge

Kanalla Falls

Glenora Falls

St. Mary Peak

Tanderra Saddle

Mt Boorong

Attunga Bluff

Landing Ground

Malloga Falls

Beatrice Hill

Cooinda Camp

Wilpena Motel

Pompey Pillar

Wangara Hill

Dorothy Peak

Old Homestead

Mt Ohlssen Bagge (Mt John)

Harold Hill

Sliding Rock

Binya Peak

Mt Karrawarra

Snave Hill

Dick Nob

Tumburru Peak

Point Bonney

Illuka Peak

Walter Hill

Moonarie Gap

Arkaroo Rock

Fred Nob

Rawnsley Bluff

to Hawker

to Hawker

white glimmer of Lake Torrens is visible off to the west and the long Aroona Valley stretches north of the Pound. Descending from the peak to the saddle you can then head back down on the same direct route or take the longer round-trip walk through the Pound via the homestead and Sliding Rock. This is the same track you take to get to Edeowie Gorge.

There is a series of bushwalks in the park, clearly marked by blue triangles along the tracks. Pick up a copy of the Wilpena leaflet issued by the National Parks & Wildlife Service, or the similar leaflet from the tourist office – either have maps which are quite OK for day walks on the marked trails. It is recommended that you do not walk solo and that you are adequately equipped – particularly with drinking water and sun protection in the summer. Most of the walks start from the campground and the walking times indicated are for a reasonably easy pace. The St Mary's Peak walk is probably the most interesting but there are plenty of others worth considering, varying from short walks suitable for those with small children to longer ones taking more than a day.

Places to Stay

Unless you've got a tent there is no cheap accommodation at the Pound. If you're equipped for camping there's a campsite at the Pound entrance with facilities including a well-stocked store. Cost for a site for two is $4.50. Otherwise the *Wilpena Pound Motel* has all mod-cons including a restaurant and swimming pool but you can count on $48 to $55 a night.

You can get pies and pasties in the

shop, as well as food to fix yourself, or counter lunches are available and there's the motel restaurant.

BLINMAN (population 100)

From the 1860s to the 1890s this was a busy copper town but today it's just a tiny country town on the circular route around Wilpena Pound. It's a useful jumping-off point for visits to many of the scenic attractions in the area and the delightful *Hotel North Blinman* has the real outback pub flavour – bed & breakfast is $17 per person. The beautiful Aroona Valley and the ruins of the Aroona Homestead are to the south of Blinman. Further south is the Brachina Gorge, another typically spectacular gorge of the Flinders. Between Blinman and the Pound is the Great Wall of China, a long ridge capped with ironstone. Between Parachilna and Blinman it's a scenic drive through the Parachilna Gorge where there are good picnic areas.

North on the Oodnadatta road, Beltana is almost a ghost town today but you can turn east here and visit the old copper mines at Sliding Rock. At one time Beltana was a major camel-breeding station and much of the town is now being restored. You can get a guide to the town from the old railway station which is now a museum. It's a long drive from anywhere to Chambers Gorge, well to the north-east towards Lake Frome. The deep gorge has rock carvings and from Mt Chambers you can see Lake Frome and the Flinders Ranges all the way from Mt Painter to Wilpena. There are camping facilities at Mt Chambers.

LEIGH CREEK (population 1000)

North again along the Oodnadatta road, Leigh Creek is the biggest town between Port Augusta and Alice Springs. The huge open-cut coal mine here supplies the Port Augusta power station. Tree planting has transformed this once barren town and you can do a drive-yourself tour of the works by following the green arrows.

From Leigh Creek you can visit the Aroona Dam; the Gammon Ranges National Park, 64 km to the east, is also reached from Leigh Creek but it's a remote and rugged area, for experienced bushwalkers only. In 1982 the whole town was shifted south a few km because the site of the original town is now being mined.

ARKAROOLA

The tiny settlement of Arkaroola, in the northern part of the Flinders, was only established in 1968. It's a privately operated wildlife sanctuary in rugged and spectacular country. From the settlement you can take a four-wheel drive along the 'ridge top' through rugged mountain country and there are also scenic flights and many walking tracks. The ridge-top tour costs $27 ($22.50 for children under two) – expensive but it's a spectacular trip through amazing scenery.

Arkaroola used to be a mining area and old tracks cut during the mining days lead to rock pools at the Barraranna Gorge and at Echo Camp and to waterholes at Arkaroola and Nooldoonooldoona. Further on is the Bolla Bollana Springs and some ruins of an old copper smelter.

Mt Painter is a well-known and very scenic landmark in the region while there are fine views from Freeling Heights across Yudnamutana Gorge or from Siller's Lookout from where you can see the salt flats of Lake Frome. This is the real, red outback country and Mt Painter is a spectacular example of that outback landscape. The Arkaroola area is of geological significance since Paralana Hot Springs is believed to be the site of the last volcanic activity to have taken place in Australia.

There are many interesting walks in the Arkaroola area but take water – and care. You get out of sight of civilisation surprisingly fast and you'll quickly realise what an inhospitable place the outback can be, particularly when it's hot. This is rough and rugged country.

Places to Stay & Eat

The resort campsite costs $2 ($3 more with power) for two and there is also a variety of other accommodation possible here. In the bunkhouse, bunk beds are $4 but these are intended mainly for groups. Same price, however, in the 'Shearers' Quarters'.

There are also a number of holiday-flat-style units at $25 with shared facilities. The motel units are $44 for a double in the *Greenwood Lodge* and $52 in the *Mawson Lodge*.

There's a small shop where you can buy basic supplies or in the restaurant main courses are $9 to $12.

Getting There

The Stateliner bus service from Adelaide cost $41.50 and comes up to Arkaroola on Saturdays and Wednesdays, returning on Sundays and Thursdays.

The Outback

North of the Eyre Peninsula and the Flinders area stretches the vast, empty area of South Australia's far north. It's sparsely populated and difficult to travel through yet has much of interest. Large parts of the far north are prohibited areas (either Aboriginal reserves or the Woomera military area) and without four-wheel drive or camels it's not possible to stray far from the main roads as there is virtually no surfaced road in the far north.

The main Stuart Highway stretches nearly 1100 km from Port Augusta to the Northern Territory border and is steadily being surfaced although in early '86 there was still about 300 km unmade. From the Territory border the road is surfaced all the way to Darwin. The alternative road to the Northern Territory, also not surfaced of course, runs from Port Augusta through the Flinders to Marree, Oodnadatta and eventually joins the Stuart Highway not far south of the Territory border. For most of the way it runs close to the old railway line route.

The two other routes of interest in the far north are the famous Birdsville Track and the Strzelecki Track. These routes are only possible in good conditions and with the right equipment. The South Australian outback includes much of the Simpson Desert and the harsh, rocky land of Sturt's Stony Desert.

There are also huge salt-lakes which every once in a long while fill with water. Lake Eyre, used by Donald Campbell for his attempt on the world's land-speed record in the '60s, filled up for a time in the '70s; it was only the second occasion since white men first reached this area. When the infrequent rains do reach this dry land the effect is amazing – flowers bloom and plants grow at a breakneck pace in order to complete their life cycle before the dry returns. There is even a species of frog that goes into a sort of suspended animation, remaining in the ground for years on end only to pop up with the first sign of rain. On a much more mundane level, roads can be washed out and the surface turned into a sticky glue. When this occurs vehicles on the road are often stuck for days, or even weeks, on end.

Places to Stay

Although Coober Pedy has a number of motels, in most other outback towns accommodation is rather limited. If you want to stay in a particular place it's wise to book ahead.

Getting There

Air There is a variety of flights to outback stations from Adelaide and Alice Springs. Opal Air (tel 217 7222) at the Ansett office at 150 North Terrace, Adelaide fly to Woomera for $118 and Coober Pedy for $180.

Bus Stateliner (tel 217 0777) at the Central Bus Station, 111 Franklin St,

Adelaide operate once or twice-daily to Woomera and Pimba ($30), Glendambo ($44), Andamooka ($50), Coober Pedy ($67) and Marla ($88). It takes 12 hours to Coober Pedy. There's a once-weekly service to Marree which takes 13 hours and costs $30. The Stateliner service continues through from Coober Pedy and Marla to Alice Springs ($95) daily – these are operated for Greyhound. Ansett Pioneer also operate on the Adelaide-Coober Pedy-Marla-Alice Springs run three times weekly with Briscoes. Fares are slightly cheaper than Greyhound/Stateliner.

Rail The new Ghan operates from Adelaide to Tarcoola, Marla and up to Alice Springs rather than along the old Marree-Oodnadatta route. Fares are $55 to Tarcoola and $85 to Marla.

COOBER PEDY (population 2100)

On the Stuart Highway 935 km north of Adelaide, Coober Pedy is one of the best known towns in the outback. The name is Aboriginal and means 'white fellow's hole in the ground', which aptly describes the place, as a large proportion of the population live in dugouts to shelter from daytime temperatures that can soar to over 50°C and winter nights which can get uncomfortably cold. Coober Pedy is in an extremely inhospitable area – even water has to be brought in to the town.

The town survives from opals which were first discovered here in 1911. Here, as in Andamooka, keen fossickers can have a go themselves after acquiring a prospecting permit from the Mines Department in Adelaide. There are literally hundreds of mines around Coober Pedy and there are tours, opal cutting demonstrations, and polished stones and jewellery on sale.

The Coober Pedy area was used for much of the filming of *Mad Max III*.

Places to Stay

The cheapest place is the *Umoona Opal*

Mine, owned and run by the local Aboriginal community. They provide underground camping ($5) and rooms ($10). Camping is no problem and although there are no youth hostels in the region, if you enquire at the bus station in Coober Pedy they'll put you on to places where hostellers get a special deal.

Getting There

Coober Pedy is about the only place with petrol between Glendambo (285 km south and 162 km beyond Pimba) and Kulgera, just across the Northern Territory border (478 km north).

Opals

Australia is the opal producing centre of the world and South Australia is where most of Australia's opals come from. Opals are hardened from silica suspended in water and the colour in an opal is produced by light being split and reflected by the silica molecules. Valuable opals are cut in three different fashions: solid opals can be cut out of the rough into *cabochons* – domed-top stones; *triplets* consist of a layer of opal sandwiched between an opaque backing layer and a transparent cap; and *doublets* are simply an opal layer with an opaque backing. In addition some opals from Queensland are found embedded in rock and these opals are sometimes polished while still incorporated in the surrounding rock.

An opal's value is determined by its colour and clarity – the brighter and clearer the colour the better. Brilliance of colour is more important than the colour itself. The type of opal is also a determinant of value – black and crystal opals are the most valuable, semi-black and semi-crystal are in the middle, milk opal at the bottom. The bigger the pattern the better, and visible flaws (like cracks) also have a bearing on the opal's value.

Shape is also important inasmuch as a high dome is better than a flat opal. Finally, given equality of other aspects, the size is important. As with any sort of gemstone don't expect to find great bargains unless you clearly know and understand what you are buying.

WOOMERA

During the '50s and '60s Woomera was used to launch experimental British rockets and conduct tests of an abortive European project to orbit a satellite. The projects were later abandoned and Woomera is once again just a large area of nothing much. What remains of the township of Woomera is six km off the Stuart Highway from the tiny settlement of Pimba.

ANDAMOOKA (population 400)

Off the Stuart Highway, north of Woomera and west of Lake Torrens, Andamooka is a rough-and-ready little town devoted to opal mining. Many of the residents live in dug-out homes to give some relief from the temperature extremes. It's about 100 km from Pimba to Andamooka and although the road is fair it very quickly becomes impassable after rain. Uranium has been discovered at Roxby Downs near Andamooka.

MARREE (population 400)

On the rugged alternate road north through Oodnadatta, Marree is a tiny township once used as a staging post for the Afghan-led camel trains of the last century. There are still a few old date palms standing as reminders of those days. Marree is also the southern end of the Birdsville track and just six km north of here is Frome Creek, a normally-dry creek bed that with rain can cut the track for weeks on end. Marree is likely to get even smaller in the future with the closing of the old railway line to Alice Springs.

BIRDSVILLE TRACK

Years ago cattle from the south-west of Queensland were driven down the Birdsville Track to Marree where they were loaded aboard the train – these days they're trucked out on the 'beef roads'.

It's 481 km between Marree and Birdsville, just across the Queensland border. Although in good conditions the track can even be managed by conventional vehicles, it's worth bearing in mind that it's a long way to push if you break down – and that traffic along the road isn't exactly heavy. There is, however, petrol usually available at Mungeranie, about 200 km north of Marree and 280 km south of Birdsville.

The track is more or less at the meeting point between the sand dunes of the Simpson Desert to the west and the desolate wastes of Sturt's Stony Desert to the east. There are ruins of a couple of old homesteads scattered along the track and artesian bores gush out boiling-hot salty water at many places. At Clifton Hill, about 150 km south of Birdsville, the track splits and one route or other may be better – seek local advice. The last travellers to die on the track took the wrong route, got lost, ran out of petrol and died before they were discovered.

STRZELECKI TRACK

The Strzelecki Track is even more rough and rugged than the Birdsville and at 494 km it's even longer. The track starts from Lyndhurst, about 80 km south of Marree, and runs to the tiny outpost of Innamincka. There's nothing by the way of supplies, petrol or help from one end to the other. Natural gas deposits have now been discovered near Moomba so there is likely to be much development here in the future. The new Moomba Strzelecki track is more well-kept but longer and less interesting than the old track which follows the Strzelecki Creek.

Innamincka is near Cooper's Creek, where the Burke and Wills expedition of 1860 came to its tragic conclusion. From Innamincka you can visit the Burke and Wills 'dig' tree, their graves and several memorials to them and to Sturt.

OODNADATTA (population 200)

A tiny town and, like Marree, likely to get even tinier with the old Ghan track's closure, Oodnadatta is at the point where the road and railway lines diverge. Oodnadatta was an important staging post during the construction of the overland telegraph line and later was the railhead for the line from Adelaide, from its original extension to Oodnadatta in 1884 until it finally reached Alice Springs in 1929.

THE GHAN
See the Northern Territory section for details of the famous train line from Adelaide to Alice Springs.

Tasmania

Area 68,000 square km
Population 450,000

Don't miss beautiful Hobart, the historic penal settlement of Port Arthur and the state's wild and rugged country where you'll find some of Australia's best bushwalks.

Tasmania was Australia's second settlement established fairly soon after Sydney was securely on its feet. It was first discovered by Dutch navigator Abel Tasman in 1642 and named Antony van Diemen's Land after the Governor of Batavia. It was then visited by the French Captain Marion du Fresne in 1772; accidentally by the first Englishman, Captain Tobias Furneaux, in 1772; and in later years by Captains James Cook and William Bligh – and all that time it was believed that Tasmania was part of the Australian mainland.

Contact with the Tasmanian coast became more frequent after the first fleet set up shop on the shores of Sydney Cove in 1770, as ships heading to the colony of New South Wales from the west had to sail around Tasmania. In 1789 Captain John Henry Cox, en route to China, recognised the commercial potential of the huge colonies of seals in the Tasmanian waters. The seal industry began in earnest and the skins and oils became Australia's first real exports.

Finally in 1798 Lieutenant Matthew Flinders, on the sloop *Norfolk*, circumnavigated Van Diemens Land proving the long-held theory that it was in fact an island, and named the strait after his ship's surgeon George Bass. Using Bass Strait the journey to Sydney from India or the Cape of Good Hope was shortened by a week.

Because of European rivalry over Tasmanian waters in the late 1700s, Governor King of New South Wales was prompted to establish a second settlement south of Sydney Cove before some other country decided to muscle in. After a cursory glance at Port Phillip Bay in Victoria (no good, was the report) they decided on the Derwent River estuary. Hobart Town was established in 1804 and quickly grew to be a rival city to Sydney, while other parts of the island colony were opened up for farming and mining.

Later, as the vast potential of the huge expanses of the land in NSW was utilised, Hobart began to slip behind but this had the beneficial effect of preserving the history of the island instead of sweeping it aside in the name of progress. In 1855 Van Diemens Land was officially renamed Tasmania. The following year the first election of a two-chamber parliament was held and transportation to Tasmania was abolished.

The convict days are especially evident in Tasmania as the worst of the cons were shipped here – it was dubbed 'that isthmus between earth and hell'. There are a number of interesting penal settlement ruins – Port Arthur being the best known – and many examples of convict-built bridges and buildings. Early mining also left its mark and Tasmania has a number of fascinating ghost towns, not to mention some more modern mining sites to visit.

For many visitors Tasmania's real fascination won't be charming old buildings or ruins but the wild natural scenery and the smaller, almost un-Australian scale of the island which brings it all within easy reach. There is spectacular coastline, rugged mountains, magnificent rivers, beautiful lakes and forests, excellent bushwalking trails and some of the best parks in Australia.

INFORMATION

The Tasmanian Government Tourist Bureau has a head office in Hobart and branch offices in Launceston, Devonport, Burnie and Queenstown. On the mainland they have branches in:

ACT
    5 Canberra Savings Centre, City Walk, Canberra 2600 (tel 47 0070)
NSW
    129 King St, Sydney 2000 (tel 233 2500)
Queensland
    217-219 Queen St, Brisbane 4000 (tel 221 7411)
South Australia
    32 King William St, Adelaide 5000 (tel 211 7411)
Victoria
    256 Collins St, Melbourne 3000 (tel 63 6351)
Western Australia
    55 William St, Perth 6000 (tel 321 2633)

There are also offices in Auckland and Christchurch, New Zealand. The offices have information on the usual tourist sights, accommodation, restaurants and travel. Every two months the bureau produces *Tasmanian Travelways*, a free comprehensive newspaper covering facilities, accommodation, public transport and current costs throughout the state.

The Wilderness Society, at 130 Davey St, Hobart (and in other Australian capital cities) can tell you just about anything you want to know about the natural Tasmania and has a wonderful selection of books, brochures and leaflets ideal for exploring the wild side of this beautiful island.

The Tasmanian Tourist Council has info at a variety of shops and restaurants plus at Golden Fleece petrol stations – look for a TAS sign. They produce an annual *Visitors' Guide to Tasmania*

($2.95) which is available from Tasbureau offices or newsagencies. It's an excellent publication with information on most places in Tasmania and good maps in the back. The council also produces a whole series of 'Let's Talk About' brochures, which provide more comprehensive local information on towns, areas around larger towns, wildlife, parks and so on.

The Royal Automobile Club of Tasmania produces a tourist map of the island for $2 (free to members and reciprocal members). They also put out an accommodation guide and have offices in most larger towns.

GEOGRAPHY

Tasmania is a varied and in places quite un-Australian island. It has a relatively dispersed population although despite its compact size there are still some areas that remain uninhabited. This is not, as in most other unpopulated Australian regions, due to a lack of water; Tasmania's south-west wilderness, for example, enjoys abundant rainfall. It was, however, distinct geographical features such as impenetrable rainforests and rugged mountains which governed the early regional development of the island and led to settlements being established in the fertile stretches inland and on the north and east coasts. Many parts of Tasmania that were originally too wild to attempt settlement are now protected from it.

So Tasmania's population is mainly in the east and along the north coast where the land is rolling and fertile. The coast and its bays are accessible and inviting and there are many beautiful coves and beaches. The Midlands region is almost a re-creation of the green England so beloved of early settlers and the highland lake country in the centre of the state, though less populated, is accessible and beautiful.

By contrast the south-west and the west coast are amazingly wild and virtually untouched. Strahan is the only

Top: Port Arthur was once the prison 'hell' of Tasmania; it's ruins make a peaceful scene (TGTB)
Left: Arthur's Circus is a small circle of quaint cottages in Hobart's historic Battery Point (TGTB)
Right: At Taroona, just outside Hobart, the old shot tower is a local landmark (TW)

Top: The bare hills around Queenstown are a stark reminder that pollution and wanton destruction of our environment are nothing new (TGTB)
Bottom: The 1824 Richmond Bridge is the oldest in Australia (TGTB)

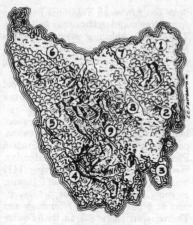

1 North East
2 East Coast
3 Tasman Peninsula
4 South & South West
5 West Coast
6 North West Coast
7 Tamar Valley
8 Midlands
9 Highland Lake Country

port of any size and its bay, difficult though it is to get in to, is the only safe harbour on the whole coast; the full length of the coast is often battered by raging seas. Inland, the forests and mountains of the south-west form one of the world's last great wilderness areas; this is also the region which has become a battlefield between conservationists and the 'profits today, to hell with tomorrow' developers intent on flooding more and more of the most beautiful rivers in their quest for hydro-electric power.

PLACES TO STAY

Hostels There are 19 youth hostels scattered around the island but in the peak holiday periods Tasmania is very popular with hostellers and it may be advisable to book ahead. You'll find the hostels at Bicheno, Bruny Island, Cygnet, Deloraine (summer only), Devonport, Hobart (Bellerive and Newtown),

Launceston, Lune River, New Norfolk, Oatlands, Port Arthur, Scamander, Sheffield, St Marys, Strahan, Swansea, Triabunna and Wynyard. There are other hostel-type places at Bronte Park and on King Island which also welcome YHA members and there's a special purpose-built family hostel at Coles Bay.

Guest Houses, Hotels, Motels & Holiday Flats There are places to stay all over the island with a whole range of prices depending on the amenities provided. Some lower priced guest houses and hotels have been mentioned under the relevant towns. *Tasmanian Travelways* has a good list of accommodation. Establishments have to be of a certain standard to be listed, so you'll probably find that there are a few places cheaper than the ones they list.

Camping *Tasmanian Travelways* and the automobile clubs' guides both list camping sites and caravan parks with on-site vans. *Tasmanian Travelways* has the more comprehensive listing. You'll find sites at most towns, in the national parks, at some beaches and at more out-of-the-way places – like Bruny and Maria Islands. Many caravan parks have on-site vans – including the sites at Hobart and Launceston. Camping charges in Tasmania are generally $3 to $6 per night for two people.

The Lands Department of Tasmania manages a number of areas of Crown land around the island where camping is permitted. Facilities are usually pretty basic or even non-existent but if you really want to get away from it all then you don't need a coin-operated laundry or even a toilet block! The Lands Dept produces a pamphlet *Camping on Crown Land* available from Tasbureau offices or the NPWS office in Sandy Bay.

GETTING THERE

Air There are only two ways to get to Tasmania and if you choose to fly then these days there are a number of options open to you. First of all, if you decide to fly into Hobart, you can choose between four airlines. With Ansett or TAA the fares from Melbourne are $136.30 one-way, $177.20 Apex return, $109 standby; and from Sydney it costs $219.40 one-way, $285 return.

East-West Airlines and Air New South Wales fly from Melbourne for $130; and from Sydney for $171. Air New South Wales also have a cheaper mid-week flight from Melbourne for $69; and a standby fare from Sydney for $147; and East-West operate to the Gold Coast from Hobart for $243.

Hobart is also an international port of entry. TAA and Air New Zealand operate flights between Hobart and Christchurch for as little as $336 for an off-peak-season Apex return. The regular one-way economy fare is $317.

You can also fly to other places in Tasmania from the mainland – fares for these flights are given under the Getting There sections of relevant towns and cities. TAA and Ansett both operate daily services from Sydney and Melbourne to Launceston. Ansett also fly to Devonport and Wynyard (Burnie). East-West Airlines fly from Sydney and Melbourne to Devonport and between Melbourne and Wynyard. Airlines of Tasmania fly from Melbourne to Launceston, Queenstown, Smithton, Strahan and Flinders Island. Promair flies from the Latrobe Valley in Victoria, to Launceston and from Melbourne (Essendon Airport) to Flinders Island. Air New South Wales fly from Sydney and Melbourne to Devonport. The Phillip Island Air Service runs flights between Phillip Island and Wynyard. And Kendell Airlines operates between Melbourne and King Island.

If you're under 25 you can join East-West's Club 25 (it's free) and get 20% off their fares to Hobart (from Sydney) or to Wynyard and Devonport (from Melbourne). This brings the ticket price almost down to standby level.

Ship You can reach Tasmania from the Australian mainland by sea as well as air. The regular shipping service between Melbourne and Devonport is particularly popular with people who want to bring their vehicles to Tasmania.

The relatively new, 'luxury' *Abel Tasman* makes three crossings a week each way between Melbourne and Devonport. The ship has a coffee shop, lounges, bar, a disco, restaurant, sauna, pool and gym. Departures from Station Pier, Melbourne are at 6 pm on Monday, Wednesday and Friday, arriving 14½ hours later at 8.30 am the following morning. The return trips depart Devonport at 6 pm on Sunday, Tuesday and Thursday, arriving at 8.30 am the following morning. There is a free bus service between the Melbourne city centre and the docks for departing and arriving services.

Fares vary between the holiday season (21 December to 24 January); the shoulder seasons (17 August to 20 December, 25 January to 23 May); and the bargain season (24 May to 16 August). The cheapest fares are for a four-berth cabin with private facilities. For bargain/shoulder/holiday season these cost $66/78/86 per person. After that there is a variety of different two, three and four-berth cabins ranging upwards in price to $143/165/180.

The cost for accompanied vehicles also varies with the seasons and with the size of the vehicle but rates start from around $76/85/95. You can take a motorcycle across for $18/20/26; bicycles cost $8/9/10.

One important point to consider if you plan to take the ferry in the holiday or even shoulder seasons is that it will be heavily booked and you must plan well ahead.

GETTING AROUND

Air Airlines of Tasmania and Kendell Airlines operate a fairly extensive network around Tasmania and also fly between

Tasmania and Melbourne's Essendon Airport. You can fly from Melbourne to Tasmania via Flinders Island at not a great amount more than a regular Melbourne-Tasmania flight. The price chart shows the main routes and costs around the island with the smaller airlines. Students aged 19 to 26 get a 25% discount with Airlines of Tasmania. More information is given in the relevant Getting There sections.

Bus All the main towns are connected by bus services. Tasmanian Redline Coaches are the main bus operator and Greyhound Eaglepasses are valid on their services. Ansett Pioneer also operate around the island via the main towns. They have offices in Hobart, Launceston and Devonport and their 15, 30 or 60-day Aussie-

passes can make travel quite inexpensive if you've only got a limited amount of time.

Tasmanian Redline also offers a Tassie Pass at $75 for 14 days or $60 for seven days. If, however, you intend to make the east coast trip between Hobart and Launceston this pass won't get you right along the coast as a number of the connecting services are run by private operators.

Redline have terminals in Hobart, Launceston, Devonport, Burnie, Smithton and Queenstown. Services operate between those towns via the Midland, Bass, Murchison and Lyell Highways. Redline's West Coast Service also operates from Hobart via Derwent Bridge and Queenstown to Strahan or north to Burnie. Some sample fares are: Hobart-Launceston

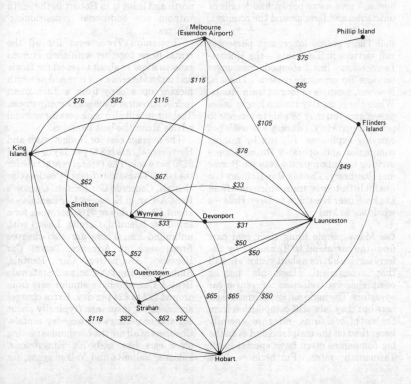

$11.40, Hobart-Devonport $19, Launceston-Burnie $10.60, Launceston-Devonport $7.60, Burnie-Queenstown $17.30, Queenstown-Hobart $20, Queenstown-Strahan $3.20, and Derwent Bridge-Hobart $13.60. So you could take your time to make a complete loop of the island for around the same cost as the seven-day Tassiepass.

You can make the east coast, Tasman Highway trip from Hobart to Launceston using a number of connections for $29.30. For more info on individual connections refer to East Coast Getting There section.

Coastliner Express operates between Hobart and Launceston and along the north coast to Smithton; and the Peninsula Coach Service runs between Hobart and Port Arthur (weekdays only). *Tasmanian Travelways*, the tourist bureau's give-away paper, has details of timetables and fares around the country.

Rail There are no longer any passenger rail services in Tasmania – the Hobart-Launceston line stopped passenger services 'for economic reasons'. There is, however, a couple of tourist train jaunts. While the Emu Bay run no longer takes passengers you may be able to arrange to get on it privately, but only when it's not carrying explosives. It's run by mining companies and operates through some exciting mountain passes between Burnie and Roseberry. The Ida Bay Railway is a quaint little tourist train which runs from Ida Bay, near Hastings, to Deep Hole – a whole seven km!

Car Many people bring their own cars from the mainland to Tasmania by the ferry service but for a short visit it's not all that economical. Tasmania has a comprehensive selection of rent-a-car operators. The main national firms are all here but they face stiff competition from the host of local firms – rates are generally lower than on the mainland and even the big companies often have special lower Tasmanian rates. Furthermore, the

compact size of the island also makes car rental cheaper and the rental firms are generally quite happy about one-way hire. You can pick up a car in Launceston, Devonport, Burnie or Wynyard in the north and leave it in Hobart in the south without any additional 'repositioning' charges.

Tasmanian Travelways list all the rental firms together with their current rates so if you're about to set off for Tassie and intend to rent a car it would be worth picking up a copy from a Tasmanian tourist bureau and making a comparison. Tasbureau will also book cars for you and advise about the best bargains.

The average cost for Budget, Avis and Hertz rental cars is $40 per day or around $230 per week. The typical rental rate for the larger Tasmanian firms – Costless Car Rentals, Concorde Car Rentals, Curnow's Rent-A-Car, or Economy Car Rentals – is about $26 per day or $160 per week for a small car (Gemini, Corolla, Laser) with unlimited km. There are also cheaper firms, such as Advance Travel Car Rentals, Alternative Car Rentals, Ambassador Rent-A-Car, and Statewide Rent-A-Car who have similar cars from around $22 to $24 per day. Extra charges are made for insurance (typically about $6) and sometimes for one-day rentals. Cheapest of all are the companies renting older cars like early-70s Kingswoods, Falcons, Valiants and Volkswagens, for

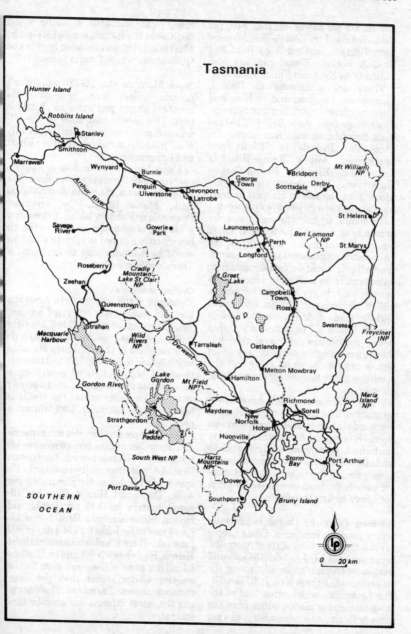

Tasmania

Hunter Island

Robbins Island

Stanley

Smithton

Marrawah

Wynyard

Burnie

Penguin
Ulverstone

Devonport
Latrobe

George
Town

Bridport

Scottsdale

Derby

*Mt William
NP*

Savage
River

Gowrie
Park

Launceston

Perth

Ben Lomond
NP

St Helens

St Marys

Roseberry

Zeehan

Cradle
Mountain-
Lake St Clair
NP

Great
Lake

Longford

Campbell
Town

Ross

Queenstown

Strahan

*Macquarie
Harbour*

Wild
Rivers
NP

Tarraleah

Oatlands

Swansea

*Freycinet
NP*

Gordon River

Lake
Gordon

Mt Field
NP

Derwent River

Hamilton

Melton Mowbray

Strathgordon

Lake
Pedder

Maydena

New
Norfolk

Hobart

Richmond

Sorell

Huonville

*Maria
Island
NP*

South West NP

Hartz
Mountains
NP

Storm
Bay

Port Arthur

Port Davie

Dover

Southport

Bruny Island

*SOUTHERN
OCEAN*

0   20 km

around $15 per day or less than $100 per week. You could try Rent-A-Bug, Mercury Auto Rentals, Lo-Cost Auto Rent and Rent A Rocket. Rental cars are also available on King and Flinders Islands.

There are companies in Hobart, Launceston, Longford and on King and Flinders Islands which hire campervans. Costs range from about $315 to $450 per week. Several companies rent motorcycles (Abel Car Rentals in Hobart and Launceston, Mike's Rent-a-Bike in Launceston, Kingston Rent-a-Car in Hobart and Launceston and Bargain Motor Bike Rentals in Hobart) at costs from about $20 a day or $140 per week.

Tasmania is just the right size for exploring on a small motorcycle. Or at least you'd think so – an entry in the Launceston youth hostel log book warned that 'all you would-be travelling bikers, unless you're on a 650cc or bigger, have pannier bags, heavy wet-weather gear, a pillion passenger to talk to, and you're slightly mad – don't consider riding around Tassie!' The note added that rental motorbikes are available but they're generally not worth it – you could rent a car for the same price and the condition of the bikes is not always good. Hmmm.

Not all Tasmanian roads have a good reputation. The highway from Hobart to Wynyard via Launceston, Devonport and Burnie is very good. Some other highways can be quite narrow and winding in places while the backroads vary from reasonable to very rough. Fortunately the distances are usually fairly short and the traffic is not heavy by any standards.

Hitching Travel by thumb is generally pretty good in Tasmania. Some people say it is the best in any state of Australia. It can get a bit hard on both the east and west coast though, especially during the off-season when there is very little traffic. The backroads, which often lead to the most interesting places, suffer from the same problem. And remember it can get mighty cold in Tassie in winter – you don't want to get stuck somewhere on the Murchison Highway between Burnie and Queenstown when it starts to snow!

Tours Many of the TGTB tours don't operate unless there are sufficient numbers or you pay extra to charter a taxi. This means that trips in the off-season tend to be non-existent, especially away from the major centres like Hobart and Launceston.

A number of small airline companies operate scenic flights to or over places like Cradle Mountain, the South West National Park, Maria Island, the Freycinet Peninsula or Flinders Island. Prices vary according to distances or time in the air but if you can afford to splurge a bit this would be a unique way to see some of Tassie's wilder parts.

Cycling Tasmania

Tasmania is the only state in Australia that can realistically be cycled around. Yes, I know lots of people ride bikes right round Australia, but lots of madmen do all sorts of crazy things! There are some long hills and some steep hills in Tasmania (more of both variety if you're on a bicycle) but the distances are relatively short and on many routes the traffic is light enough to make bike riding a pleasure.

Many people hire bicycles in Tasmania and a number of bike hire places are set up to cater for bicycle touring. Launceston Rent-A-Cycle has fully-equipped 10-speed touring bikes for about $42 per week; Devonport Hire A Bike has 10-speed tourers for $30 per week; and Hobart Mountain Bike Rentals has 12-speed mountain bikes for $14 a day or $60 per week. There are also bike renters in St Helens, Eaglehawk Neck and on Flinders Island but some of these are more for the one-day visitor rather than the long-distance tourer. *Tasmania Travelways* has the latest information on bike hire and rates.

If you want to bring your own bike with you then it's no problem on the *Abel Tasman* so long as you've booked far enough in advance to ensure you get aboard. By air, Ansett and TAA will carry one item of baggage free and that one item can be your bike. If you travel light enough it's even possible to make that your only item of baggage. Pack it well, if possible wrap it so that the baggage loaders aren't tempted to lift it by the wheel spokes or commit similar indignities upon it. It's probably easier to get your bike over to Tassie on the flights to Hobart or Launceston rather than the Wynyard or Devonport flights, because they use larger jet aircraft, not small F27s.

Gear Make sure your carrier rack is strong and that pannier bags are firmly attached. Try to balance the load about a third to the front, two-thirds to the rear. As many first-time bicycle tourers soon discover, it's very easy to carry far too much gear with you. Travel as light as possible; if it's not 100% necessary, leave it behind.

Getting Around Count on 10 to 14 days for a half-way round trip – Launceston-Hobart by east or west coast for example. For a full circuit of the island allow 14 to 28 days. Bikes can travel cheaply on the local bus services as freight and a short bus ride, even just 20 or 30 km, can make life a whole lot easier in some hilly sections. You're likely to suffer fewer headwinds if you travel around anti-clockwise. Many of the youth hotels are keen promoters of bicycle touring, the Launceston hostel in particular.

ACTIVITIES

Bushwalking Not unexpectedly, Tasmania, with its rugged, mountainous country, much of it still barely touched by man, is ideal for bushwalking. It has some of the finest bushwalking to be found in Australia and many walkers believe that the superb Cradle Mountain-Lake St Clair walk is the equal of any of the better-known walks in New Zealand.

Good information sources on bushwalking include the Federation of Tasmanian Bushwalking Clubs in Hobart and the National Parks & Wildlife Service (NPWS) also in Hobart. They can supply maps and guides to popular walks. Other sources are the book *100 Walks in Tasmania* and the excellent bush gear shops such as Paddy Pallin's in Hobart, or Allgoods in Launceston. The Tasmanian Wilderness Society at 130 Davey St, Hobart, dedicated to protecting Tasmania's superb wilderness areas, has books and pamphlets and people on hand who know what they're talking about. Summer is the best time for Tasmanian bushwalks although even then the mountain country can spring some nasty surprises on the unwary. Be prepared for sometimes viciously changeable weather.

Cradle Mountain-Lake St Clair, with its 80-km-long track, is one of the classic, long bushwalks in Australia (see the separate section on this walk). Frenchman's Cap National Park is for the experienced bushwalker only – there are shelter huts at Lake Vera and Lake Tahure. South-West National Park with Lake Pedder and the peaks of the Arthur Range is also mainly for the knowledgeable walker, although there are shorter, easier paths. The Hydro-Electric Commission (HEC) has several lodges. The South-West Track from Port Davey to Cockle Creek is a magnificent 10-day walk but again, only experienced walkers should tackle this one.

On the east coast the Freycinet National Park has good year-round coastal walks and a popular 27-km walking circuit. Ben Lomond National Park, south-east of Launceston, also has good walks and one shelter hut.

Water Sports There are good bayside beaches near Hobart including Bellerive, Long Beach, Kingston and Nutgrove. Good surf beaches are unpatrolled while

buses leave from Paddy Pallins Outdoor Shop, 124 St Johns St. The fare is $15 round-trip on a daily basis, less for longer-term tickets. From Jacob's Ladder to the ski village car park you can catch a shuttle bus.

Mt Mawson is in the Mt Field National Park 75 km west of Hobart. It's rather smaller and lower-key and the snow coverage is often not very good but the ski-touring can be exceptional.

Cross country skiing is popular on the western field at Cradle Mountain and at Mt Rufus in the Cradle Mountain-Lake St Clair National Park.

Tasmanian Aboriginals

The story of Australia's Aboriginals has not been a happy one since the European arrival, but nowhere has the story been more tragic than in Tasmania.

Tasmania's Aboriginals became separated from the Aboriginals of the mainland over 10,000 years ago when rising ocean levels caused by the close of the last ice age cut Tasmania off from the mainland. From that time their culture diverged from that of the mainland population. They lived by hunting, fishing and gathering, sheltered in bark or leaf lean-tos and, despite Tasmania's cold weather, they went naked apart from a coating of grease and charcoal. Their society was based on sharing and exchange – a concept the European invaders failed to come to grips with.

The Aboriginals were doomed as soon as the first Europeans settlers arrived in 1803, for Tasmania was fertile and easily divided and fenced to make farms. As the Aboriginals gradually lost their traditional hunting grounds they realised that the Europeans had come to steal their land, not share it, and they began to fight for what was theirs. By 1806 the killing on both sides was out of control. The Aboriginals speared stock and shepherds and in turn they were hunted and shot like animals. Europeans abducted Aboriginal children to use as forced labour; raped and tortured Aboriginal women; gave poisoned flour to friendly tribes and laid steel man-traps in the bush.

In 1828 martial law was proclaimed by Governor Arthur, giving soldiers the right to arrest or shoot on sight any Aboriginal found in the settled areas. The Aboriginal people fought

the west coast surf is ferocious and there are very few access points to the coast. Canoeing is a popular activity on several of the state's rivers.

The often-rugged Tasmanian coast also provides some fine skin-diving opportunities. Equipment can be rented in Hobart and Launceston and good diving can be found on the north-east, east and south-west coast.

Skiing

Tasmania has two ski resorts, Ben Lomond and Mt Mawson, which offer cheaper, although less-developed, ski facilities than the major resorts in Victoria and NSW. Despite its southerly latitude Tasmania's snowfalls tend to be fairly light.

Ben Lomond is 60 km from Launceston and every morning during the ski season Redline buses depart from the terminal at 112 George St, and Mountain Stage Line back with spears and fire and the settlers retaliated with the wholesale slaughter of men, women and children.

In 1830 the settlers launched a military operation known as *the Black Line* – a human chain, comprised of every able-bodied male in the colony. For three weeks they moved east and south across the settled areas in an attempt to corner the Aboriginals on the Tasman Peninsula. They only managed to capture an old man and a boy but succeeded in clearing the rest out of the settled districts.

Finally, between 1829 and 1834 George Augustus Robinson, the Conciliator, travelled the island collecting the survivors of this once-proud and peaceful race. The last 135 Aboriginals from the Tasmanian mainland were resettled on a reserve (prison) on Flinders Island – to be 'civilised' and Christianised. With nothing to do but exist, most of them died of despair, home-sickness, poor food and respiratory diseases. During those first 35 years of settlement 183 Europeans and nearly 4000 Aboriginals were killed.

The 47 survivors of the Flinders Island group were transferred to Oyster Cove in 1847. Of those all but Fanny Cochrane Smith, the daughter of an Aboriginal woman and a European sealer, were dead by 1876. The last full-blooded male died in Hobart in 1874 and Truganini, the last surviving full-blooded member of mainland Tasmania's Aboriginal population, died in 1876.

European sealers had been working in Bass Strait since 1798 and although they occasionally raided tribes along the coast for women, killing the men who tried to protect them, for the most part their contact with the indigenous people was based on trade. They exchanged flour, tobacco, tea and dogs for seal and kangaroo skins and women. Many of these sealers settled on the Bass Strait Islands with their Aboriginal women and the families they had started. By 1847 the new Aboriginal community, centred on the Furneaux Group of islands, had grown to about 50 people and had established a lifestyle based on both Aboriginal and European ways. It was this community which saved the Tasmanian Aboriginal society from total extinction, and it is their descendants who today wage a daily battle not only for their rights but for recognition of their very existence in a white society that is still taught that the last Tasmanian Aboriginal died in 1876.

Hobart
Population 180,000

Australia's second oldest capital city is also the smallest state capital and the most southerly; in winter the temperatures in Hobart often drop to near freezing and even in summer, sunny though it is, it rarely climbs above 25°C. Straddling the mouth of the Derwent River and backed by mountains which provide a fine view over the city, Hobart is an engaging, colourful little place which has managed to combine the progress and benefits of a modern city with the rich heritage of its colonial past. The time-worn buildings, busy harbour and easy-going atmosphere all make Hobart one of Australia's most enjoyable cities.

Hobart's life has centred on the magnificent Derwent estuary, one of the world's finest deepwater harbours, since the island's first little colony led by Lieutenant John Bowman set up camp at Risdon Cove in 1803. In February 1804 Lieut-Colonel David Collins, who was appointed governor of the new settlement in Van Diemens Land, sailed up the Derwent and decided a cove about 10 km below Risdon on the opposite shore was a better place to settle. Tasmania's future capital city began as a village of tents and wattle-and-daub huts with a population of 178 convicts, 25 marines, 15 women, 21 children, 13 free settlers and 10 civil officers. Hobart Town, as it was known until 1881, was proclaimed a city in 1842 and its development was based on trade and commerce. Early exports included corn and Merino wool. Many merchants made their fortunes from the whaling trade and ship building and one of Australia's great industrial empires, the IXL jam and fruit company, was founded here by Henry Jones.

Information
The Tasmanian Government Tourist

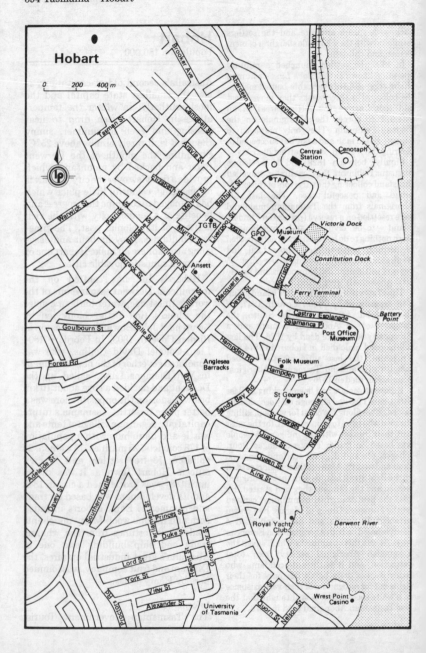

Hobart

0   200   400 m

Bureau (tel 34 6911) is at 80 Elizabeth St and is open Monday to Friday from 8.45 am to 5.30 pm, weekends and holidays from 9 to 11 am. The Royal Automobile Club of Tasmania (tel 34 6611) is on the corner of Murray and Patrick Sts. Colony 47 (tel 23 6159) at 47 Davey St is an info and referral centre and coffee shop.

The Tasmanian Youth Hostel Association office (tel 34 9617) is at 133A Elizabeth St and is open on Tuesdays and Thursdays between 12.30 and 5 pm and on Wednesday and Friday from 12 noon to 2 pm. The Wilderness Society is at 130 Davey St and the Wilderness Shop (34 9370) is at 155 Liverpool St. The Hobart Peace Centre is at 102 Bathurst St.

The National Parks & Wildlife Services (NPWS) has its head office at 16 Magnet Court, Sandy Bay (the shopping centre). They have lots of information on Tasmania's many parks and reserves and are an essential contact for would-be walkers.

Orientation

Hobart is an easy city to find your way around in. It's small enough to be manageable and very simply laid out. The central streets are in a straightforward grid pattern and Liverpool St is the main shopping street. Both TAA and Ansett have their city terminals along this street while the tourist office and the GPO are on Elizabeth St which runs across it.

Salamanca Place, the old warehouse area, is along the waterfront, while south of this is Battery Point, the delightful early colonial area of Hobart which has been maintained, basically, in its original form. Follow the river around from Battery Point and you'll come to Sandy Bay, site of the University of Tasmania and the Wrest Point Casino – Hobart's major landmark.

The north side of the centre is bounded by the Queen's Domain and the Royal Botanical Gardens, then the Derwent River. From here the Tasman Bridge crosses the river to the northern suburbs and the airport.

Walking Tour

One of the best ways of getting a feel for Hobart's interesting history is to take the Saturday morning walking tour organised by the National Trust and the TGTB. The 2½-hour tour starts at 9.30 am and costs $3 which includes morning tea. The walk centres around historic Battery Point, includes the small Maritime Museum and ends at the colonial warehouses at Salamanca Place. You can make a similar do-it-yourself tour with the aid of a leaflet from the TGTB.

Around Town

One of the things that sets Hobart apart from other Australian cities is its wealth of old buildings, built mostly from local sandstone or brick and remarkably well-preserved. More than 90 buildings in Hobart have National Trust classification and you'll find 60 of these, featuring some of Hobart's best Georgian architecture, in Macquarie and Davey Sts. Close to the centre St David's Park, with its lovely old trees and pioneer cemetery with graves dating from the earliest days of the colony, is a good place to pause and relax.

Built by convicts between 1835 and 1841 and originally used as a customs house, the old Parliament House is on Murray St, across from the park. The Theatre Royal at 29 Campbell St was built in 1837 and is the oldest theatre in Australia. The stage has played host to quite a few famous performers including Edmund Kean, Laurence Olivier, Vivien Leigh, Noel Coward and Dame Sybil Thorndyke. The theatre is being restored after being gutted by a fire in 1984.

The Cat & Fiddle Arcade in the centre of town is one of Hobart's most popular shopping areas and on Davey St you can see one of the only three royal tennis courts in the southern hemisphere. The other two are near the Lonely Planet office in Richmond, Victoria! You can look in at the courts on the walking tour.

Hobart's waterfront area, very close to the centre of the city, is still a colourful scene, although it's no longer the rough-house, brawling place it was in the early whaling days. Constitution Dock really comes alive at the finish of the annual New Year Sydney to Hobart Yacht Race and during the Royal Hobart Regatta in February. The regatta, first held in 1838, is the largest aquatic carnival in the southern hemisphere.

Salamanca Place

The row of Georgian sandstone warehouses on the harbour front at Salamanca Place is a prime example of Australian colonial architecture. Dating back to the whaling days of the 1830s they were the centre of Hobart Town's trade and commerce. These days they're occupied by galleries, restaurants, offices and shops selling everything from vegetables to antiques and arts and crafts of all kinds. A popular open-air market is held in Salamanca Place every Saturday morning during the summer – it's well worth dropping into; in winter it moves inside one of the old warehouses. From Salamanca Place you can climb up the precipitous Kelly's Steps, wedged between two warehouses, into Battery Point.

Battery Point

Behind the city docks and north of Sandy Bay is the historic centre of Hobart, the old port area known as Battery Point. It takes its name from the gun battery which stood on the promontory by the 1818 guardhouse, the oldest building in the area. In Hobart's early days this was a colourful maritime village of pubs, churches, conjoined houses and narrow, winding streets. It was home to master mariners, shipwrights, sailors, fishermen, coopers and merchants and the houses reflect their varying lifestyles. Battery Point has been lovingly preserved and is a real delight to wander around, highlighted by glimpses of the harbour between the many interesting buildings.

Places of special interest in Battery Point include Arthur's Circus – a small circle of quaint little cottages built around the former village green – the National Trust house 'Narryna', and old pubs like The Shipwright's Arms and The Lord Nelson.

Van Diemen's Land Folk Museum

Australia's oldest folk museum is housed in Narryna, a fine old Georgian home at 103 Hampden Rd, Battery Point. Built in 1836 it stands in beautiful grounds and the museum re-creates the early pioneering days in Tasmania. It's open Monday to Friday from 10 am to 5 pm and on weekends from 2 to 5 pm. Admission is $1.50. You can easily walk to it from the centre or take a Sandy Bay bus.

St George's Anglican Church & Maritime Museum

Only a short stroll from Narryna, the church is on Cromwell St, Battery Point. Construction started in 1836 but the tower was not completed until 1847. It was designed by two of the best-known Tasmanian colonial architects – James Blackburn and John Lee Archer (see Stanley).

Behind the church in historic Secheron House, is the fascinating Tasmanian Maritime Museum which has an extensive collection of photos, paintings, models and relics depicting Tasmania's (and particularly Hobart's) colourful shipping history. At only 50c admission, it's excellent value. Secheron House was built in 1831 and has been classified by the National Trust and the National Heritage Commission.

Anglesea Barracks

Built in 1811 this is the oldest military establishment in Australia which is still used by the army. During the week you can tour the grounds and inspect some of the restored buildings. The barracks are open from 9 am and 5 pm and there is no admission charge.

Museums

The excellent Tasmanian Museum & Art Gallery is itself a museum piece as it incorporates Hobart's oldest building, the Commissariat Store built in 1808. The museum features an Aboriginal display and exhibits on the state's colonial history; the Art Gallery has an excellent collection of colonial art. It's open daily and admission is free.

The Allport Museum & Library of Fine Arts has a collection of rare books on Australasia and the Pacific region. It's in the State Library in Murray St and is open weekdays from 9 am to 5 pm; admission is free.

The Post Office Museum at 19-21 Castray Esplanade has an interesting display on the development of the post and telegraphic services. It's open on weekdays from 9 am to 5 pm and Saturdays from 9 to 11 am; again, admission is free.

Others include the John Elliott Classics Museum at the University of Tasmania in Sandy Bay; Beatties Historic Photo Museum in Cat & Fiddle Arcade; and the Lady Franklin Museum in Lenah Valley, the first public museum in Australia.

Further Afield Hobart is dominated by the 1270-metre-high Mt Wellington, often dusted with snow in the winter. There are fine views over the city and the Derwent River from the summit and there are also many walking tracks in the area, but be warned – it can get very cold up there even in summer! The Old Signal Station on top of Mt Nelson, above Sandy Bay, also gives good views.

The city is on both sides of the Derwent, spanned by the Tasman Bridge, which collapsed disastrously in 1975 after being rammed by a runaway cargo ship. Government House and the Botanical Gardens are at the base of the bridge on the city side.

If you head west from the centre past Battery Point on the coast road, you soon come to the University of Tasmania and then the Wrest Point Casino at Sandy Bay. The hotel and casino, Australia's first (well, first legal one, anyway), quickly became a symbol of the city. Tasmania has very successfully capitalised on Australia's gambling mania!

Beyond Sandy Bay on the way to Taroona is the fascinating 'Tudor Court' in Lower Sandy Bay. John Palotta, a victim of poliomyelitis, spent most of his life creating a scale model of a Tudor village – his home town in Kent. It's in Sandy Bay Rd and open daily from 9 am to 5 pm. Take a Taroona bus from Franklin Square.

North of the city is Runnymede, a gracious, finely restored National Trust house with good views over the surrounding country. It was built in 1844 for Robert Pitcairn, the first lawyer to qualify in Tasmania and a leading advocate for the abolition of transportation. It's open daily, except Monday and during July, from 10 am to 12.30 pm and 1.30 to 4.30 pm. Admission is $1.50. It's at 61 Bay Rd, New Town.

Another popular short trip from the city is the guided tour of the Cadbury chocolate factory; it costs $10 including transport if you go on a TGTB tour. At Kangaroo Bluff there are the ruins of an old fort, built to repel a feared Russian invasion; similar forts can be seen in Sydney and Newcastle, NSW. Near here, Lauderdale, Seven Mile Beach and Cremorne are popular Hobart beaches and Clifton is the place to go for surf.

Places to Stay

Hostels Hobart has two *youth hostels*, one on either side of the Derwent River and both cost $5 a night. *Woodlands* (tel 28 6720), the larger of the two, is at 7 Woodlands Avenue, New Town, just three km from the city centre. It's a superb building and is one of New Town's original homes. The *Bellerive Hostel* (tel 44 2552), on the eastern shore of the Derwent at 52 King St, Bellerive, is an old stone schoolhouse built in 1859.

Guest-Houses There's not a lot available at a reasonable price in this category in Hobart. There are a few places to check out in the city, mostly at the south-west end, and a few at Sandy Bay, a short distance from the centre towards the university and the casino. Scan the *Hobart Mercury* for cheaper, longer-term accommodation.

Buckingham Accommodation (tel 23 1827), 51 Davey St, costs only $12 a single including a cooked breakfast, or $60 a week per person including dinner. Also in the city, *Narrara Guest House* (tel 34 3928) at 88 Goulburn St has singles for $12 a night and doubles from $18; breakfast and dinner are extra. By the week it's $50 full-board and it's a modern place with a pleasant atmosphere.

Other guest-houses tend to be more expensive. The *Astor Private Hotel* (tel 34 6384) at 157 Macquarie St has bed & breakfast singles/doubles for $22/35. It's an old-fashioned sort of place in the process of being restored – some rooms have showers, most don't. It does have the advantage of being very central.

At Sandy Bay *Number 27* is, as you might expect, at 27 Red Chapel Avenue (tel 25 2273). It costs $20/30 a single/double for bed & breakfast. It's a warm old-fashioned sort of place. *Adelphi Court* (tel 28 4829), 17 Stoke St, New Town, has bed & breakfast singles/doubles for $20/30. *Jutland House* (tel 28 4970), 53 Montagu St, Lenah Valley, has bed & breakfast singles for $17.

Hotels Hobart's hotels all tend to be a bit featureless and drab and mostly in the $20 bracket. For less than that per person you can get bed & breakfast singles/doubles at: the pleasant *Good Women Inn* (tel 34 4796), 186 Argyle St, for $14/24; the *Aberfeldy* (tel 23 7218), 124 Davey St, for $17/28; the *Customs House* (tel 34 6645) at 1 Murray St for $16/32; and the *Theatre Royal* (tel 34 6925) at 31 Campbell St for $17/27. The *Black Prince Hotel* (tel 34 3501) at 145 Elizabeth St

near the Mall is a good, clean place with rooms at $19/25 but breakfast is extra and the *Globe* (tel 23 5800) at 178 Davey St is $15/27 room-only.

Up a notch but still in the city there's bed & breakfast singles/doubles at: the *Telegraph Hotel* (tel 34 6254), 19 Morrison St, for $20/30; the *Brunswick Hotel* (tel 34 4981), 67 Liverpool St, for $20/32; and the *Brisbane Hotel* (tel 34 4920) at 3 Brisbane St for $22/34. *Hadleys Hotel* (tel 23 4355) at 34 Murray St costs $22/36 room-only. The *Racecourse Hotel*, 417 Main Rd, Glenorchy has bed & breakfast for $20/30 and *Claremont Hotel* (tel 49 1119), at 1 Main Rd Claremont, also has bed & breakfast for $18/28.

Motels & Holiday Flats The *Marina* (tel 28 4748) at 153 Risdon Rd, New Town, is about the cheapest motel around at $28/36 for singles/doubles. The *Lenton Lodge Motel* (tel 72 5044) at 238 Main Rd Derwent Park costs $39/44. *Motel Mayfair* (tel 34 1670) is very central at 17 Cavell St, West Hobart and costs $42/47. The *Argyle Motor Lodge* (tel 34 2488) at 2 Lewis St, North Hobart costs $49/53.

If none of these cheaper motels appeal you could always opt for the Wrest Point Casino where a single/double in the tower block will set you back $67/86 per night; or the charming *Lennah Motor Inn* where a double costs $105.

Hobart has a number of self-contained places where you are left to fend for yourself. In town the *Domain View Holiday Apartments* (tel 28 0690) at 352 Argyle St cost $28 for two and $5 for each extra person. There is a one-night surcharge. *Portland Lodge* (tel 25 3066) at 4 Portland Place, Sandy Bay, costs $25 a double. *Battery Point Holiday Flat* (tel 23 6592), 15 Secheron Rd, is $35 a double and $10 for each extra person.

Colleges During the December-February summer vacation and the the May and August holidays you can stay at the residential halls at the University of

Tasmania. *Christ College* (tel 23 5190) has a whole range of charges, depending on whether you are a student or not and what meals you want included. Room-only rates are $11 for students and $18.50 for others. *St John Fisher College* (tel 34 8955) is $15.50 per person and *Jane Franklin Hall* (tel 23 2000) costs $12 per person.

Camping The handiest camping ground is the *Sandy Bay Caravan Park* (tel 25 1264), less than four km from the centre at 1 Peel St, Sandy Bay. It's uphill from the casino intersection and a 54 or 55 bus will get you there. Camping costs $6 for two, on-site vans are $24 for two and $4 for each extra person. Other less convenient sites are located in the northern suburbs of Glenorchy and Berriedale.

Places to Eat

Hobart has a surprising variety of restaurants for a city of its size so to ease restaurant hunting you can divide it into three main food areas. In the city itself and in the Sandy Bay area you'll find a variety of places although you'll have to hunt around a bit. In Battery Point you'll find the smaller, more intimate places, most of the exotica and the prices to go with it. You can easily walk from the city to Battery Point and even Sandy Bay if you're feeling mildly energetic. Don't expect to find anything much apart from greasy spoon stuff or expensive meals on Saturday or Sunday afternoons.

Plain & Simple If it's plain, straightforward food you want then try the *Piccadilly* at 136 Collins St, a popular lunchtime snack place. The *Domino* at 55 Elizabeth St is another good place for an economically priced lunch, as is *Chequers* at 53A Murray St. The *Plaza Coffee Lounge* in the Elizabeth St mall has snacks and pancakes. There's also a whole selection of eateries across the river in Bellerive, near the youth hostel.

There's the usual selection of pizzerias

and Italian food specialists. *Etna Pizza House* is a good eat-there or take-away place at 201 Elizabeth St. You can get good-value food at the *Commonwealth Government Cafeteria* in the Commonwealth Centre at 188 Collins St.

For wholefood, try the *Pumpkin Eater* at 181 Liverpool St which has a restaurant and take-aways. The *Carlton Restaurant* at 50 Liverpool St (corner of Argyle St) is another no-nonsense sort of place and stays open until reasonably late in the evening. At Constitution Dock you can buy fresh fish from floating stalls.

Counter Meals There are lots of these and, of course, for down-to-earth value they are the places to head for. You can get a huge meal for around $5 at the *Queen's Head*, 400 Elizabeth St, North Hobart. Similar prices at the *Brunswick* at 67 Liverpool St (schnitzels, etc), the *Wheatsheaf Hotel* at 314 Macquarie St, and the *Telegraph Hotel* at 19 Morrison St. You can get a steak or similar meal for around $4.50 at the *Shamrock* on the corner of Liverpool and Harrington Sts. *Stoppy's Waterfront Inn* in Salamanca Place also has reasonably priced counter meals plus night-time entertainment from Thursday to Saturday.

More expensive but excellent food at the *Iron Duke Steak Bar* in the Duke of Wellington Hotel, 192 Macquarie St. The *Bavarian Tavern* at 281 Liverpool St has good solid food in sombre surroundings with stern waitresses and a rollicking band to complete the German feel!

Up a Notch *Barton Cottage*, a nice old house at 72 Hampden Rd, Battery Point, serves Devonshire teas for $4. *Mr Wooby's* is a trendy little place in Salamanca Place. Good atmosphere and good food with prices in the $1.50 range for snacks and $6 for main meals. It's licensed and stays open quite late.

For pasta lovers, *Romano's* at 112 Liverpool St is right in the city centre. It's fully licensed and open later than most

Hobart restaurants. *La Supremo* in Liverpool St has excellent homemade pasta; *Marti's Zucco*, 364 Elizabeth St is also good; and in Princes St, Sandy Bay you can get a great Italian meal for around $9 at the fully licensed *Tarantella*. *Don Camillo's*, in the Sandy Bay shopping centre, has a good reputation in Hobart; main courses are in the $8 to $10 bracket – good veal dishes and saltimbocca. There's a cheaper coffee bar section in the front, as well as the pricier, licensed restaurant behind.

Beards is in an old brick cottage in town, at 101 Harrington St, and has an interesting blackboard menu and open fires in winter. It's BYO and main dishes are around the $7.50 mark. *Tattersalls's Bistro & Bar* at 112 Murray St is another Hobart favourite (more about it under entertainment). It's a steak and seafood place and main courses are around $8. *Mom's* in Battery Point offers quite a few taste treats in the snack line, though it's not cheap.

Exotica Well, for Japanese food there's *Sakura*, next door to the Ball & Chain at 85 Salamanca Place (around $10 for a main course). *Taco Bill* at 41 Hampden Rd, Battery Point is Mexican of course. Back in town you can find Indian food at the *Kashmir*, 109 Elizabeth St; Malay food at the *Malayasian Tea House*, 466 Macquarie St; Afghani delights at *Shafi's*, 150 George St; and Indonesian meals at *Satay House* in the Kings Court Shopping Centre. The *Mandarin* at 177 Elizabeth St is a Chinese restaurant of the bare-tables and straightforward food variety. It's another place which is open every day of the week.

Top End Hobart has some very pleasant, if sometimes rather pricey, restaurants around Battery Point. *Mure's Fish House*, at 5 Knopwood St, won Bulletin Magazine's 1986 award for the best seafood restaurant in Australia. It has main courses for around $8 to $10 at lunchtime, $9 to $12 for dinner. *Dirty Dick's Steak House*, on the corner of Hampden Rd and Francis St, is quite a nice BYO place.

The *Ball & Chain* in the fine old warehouse of Salamanca Place is pseudocolonial style – the staff dress up. It's olde English food in olde worlde surroundings with distinctly modern prices! The *Red Fox* at 47 Hampden Rd, Battery Point, also specialises in traditional old English fare. They're open for lunch on weekdays and dinner every night. It'll cost you upwards of $12, depending on how many courses you have.

Entertainment

Check the *Hobart Mercury* for a guide to what's on and where. You tend to run into the 'no jeans, no running shoes' nonsense at quite a few of Hobart's entertainment spots, especially discos.

You can find rock bands of varying sorts at *Ye Old Red Lion* at 129 Macquarie St, *Hadley's* at 34 Murray St, the *Foreshore Tavern*, *Stoppy's Waterfront Inn* and the *Portlight Bar* in the Wrest Point Casino.

For jazz, head to the *Dog House* on the corner of Barrack and Goulburn Sts. They have something on every night except Sunday; no cover charge, no hassles and counter meals available. The *Ingmar Hotel* at 34 Patrick St also has jazz. *St Ives*, on Sandy Bay Rd, has jazz, folk and rock.

For folk, there's the *Bothy Folk Club* on Fridays and Saturdays in the Sir William Don Hotel, 304 Elizabeth St, North Hobart. *Tattersalls* at 112 Murray St has a wine-bar nightclub called *Pip's*. They have laid-back music, a solo guitarist till midnight Monday to Saturday and country rock on Sunday afternoons.

Getting There

Air You can fly to Hobart from Melbourne or Sydney as well as from other places in Tasmania. Hobart is even an international port of entry – there are two flights a week between Hobart and Christchurch in New Zealand. See the introductory

Getting There section for more details on flights from the mainland.

Airlines of Tasmania operate a number of services around the state. You can fly between Hobart and the following places: Launceston $50 (or $18 on the 'Dawn Buster Flight'); Devonport $64.50; Queenstown $62; Smithton $82; Strahan $62; Wynyard $64.50; Flinders Island $90; and King Island $118.

Bus See the various sections for more details on buses and schedules. The two main bus depots in Hobart are Tasmanian Redline Coaches (tel 34 4577) at 96 Harrington St and Cape Country Coaches (tel 34 9081) at Hobart Railway Station. Services in brief are:

Hobart-Port Arthur The Peninsula Coach Service operates services on weekdays but you have to stay overnight. Buses leave from the Tasmanian Redline depot in Hobart at 7.45 am and 3.45 pm and from Port Arthur at 7.45 and 11 am. It costs $8 a single, $14 return. Without your own transport, it is not possible to day-trip to Port Arthur except on tours. The TGTB coach tour, on Mondays, Wednesdays, Fridays and weekends costs $27.50.

Hobart-Launceston (Direct) Tasmanian Redline Coaches and Coastliner Express operate a total of about five services a day on weekdays and two on weekends. The Midlands Highway trip takes about 2½ to 3½ hours, and fares are $11.40 on Redline, $14.40 on Coastliner.

Hobart-Launceston (East Coast) Via the Tasman Highway it takes at least a couple of days because a number of different bus lines operate on the east coast and connections between the towns don't always coincide. See the East Coast & North-East section for details on fares between the Tasman Highway towns and check *Tasmanian Travelways* for the latest schedules. The total fare from Hobart to Launceston is $29.30.

Hobart-Queenstown Monday to Saturday

there are daily departures on Redline. The trip takes nearly seven hours and costs $20. If you're only going as far as Derwent Bridge it costs $13.60.

Hobart – North-West Coast Some of the services to Launceston continue through to the coast, or there are connections from Launceston. Typical fares from Hobart include Devonport $19 with Tasmanian Redline ($23.40 with Coastliner Express), Burnie $22 ($27.40), Smithton $33.40 with Coastliner.

Getting Around

Airport Hobart's airport is across the river some distance from the city centre. Tasmanian Redline Coaches run an airport bus service for $3. It departs from their depot at 96 Harrington St an hour before flight departures. Alternatively, a taxi costs about $15. In Hobart, TAA (tel 38 3333) are at 4 Liverpool St. Ansett and Airlines of Tasmania (tel 38 1111) are at 178 Liverpool St on the corner of Elizabeth St.

Buses Local buses are run by the Metropolitan Transport Trust (MTT) and depart from various central city streets. For only $2 you can get an unlimited-travel bus ticket for use between 9 am and 4.45 pm and after 6.30 pm on weekdays, all day on weekends. The tourist bureau has free timetables.

For the Bellerive Youth Hostel catch a bus from outside Fitzgerald's in Collins St to Bellerive via Bluff Stop 19. If there's no other bus to Bellerive take a Tranmere or Howrah bus, get off at Stop 19 and walk south along Scott St. For Woodlands Youth Hostel you can take a New Town bus from various places in the city including outside the Tasbureau office in Elizabeth St.

For Mt Wellington, the alternative to taking a tour is to catch a Fern Tree bus from Franklin Square, Macquarie St to the base of the mountain – after which it's a 12 to 13 km walk! You might be lucky enough to get a ride.

For getting out of town to hitch north, a Bridgewater bus could be your best bet, but they don't run very often so you may have to be content with a bus to somewhere like Glenorchy. In the south there are bus services to Huonville and Dover.

Ferry There's a ferry service across the river from Hobart to Bellerive for 90c, a pleasant way to get to the youth hostel but it operates only on weekday rush hours. There's even a bar on board! Departures from Hobart are from 6.35 to 8.20 am and 4.35 to 6.55 pm. From Bellerive there are services from 6.55 to 8.40 am and 4.50 to 6.10 pm.

Cars See the introductory Getting Around section for information on the many car rental firms in Hobart. *Tasmanian Travelways* gives you a comprehensive run-down on the latest hire rates. Rent-a-Rocket (tel 32 4512 or 34 4390) probably have the cheapest rental cars but they get mixed reports from users. Some complain about the mileage you get from them, breakdowns, large deposits and age restrictions. Other cheapie hire places include Rent-a-Bug (tel 34 9435), Bargain Car Rentals (tel 34 4122) and Mercury Auto Rentals (tel 72 1755).

Bicycles You can hire bikes in Hobart from the Sandy Bay Caravan Park. Straightforward pedal-brake bikes cost $8 a day, 10-speed bikes are $10, tandems $14, plus there's a security deposit. These bikes are really intended more for day use than bicycle touring, but longer-term rentals can be negotiated. If you want a bike on the weekend, it's necessary to book ahead. Hobart Mountain Bike Rentals (tel 34 3300) have 12-speed mountain bikes for $14 a day or $60 a week plus deposit.

Tours The TGTB operate a variety of day and half-day tours in and around Hobart. Typical half-day local tours include trips to Mt Wellington and Kingston, Richmond

and Risdon Cove, New Norfolk, Mt Nelson and the Cadbury factory at Glenorchy; fares are $10. There are day trips to Port Arthur ($27.50), Lake Pedder and Russell Falls ($23), Huon Valley and Hastings Caves ($20) and Maria Island; coach and cruise (27.50).

There are also boat trips on the Derwent River and around Hobart's harbour. It costs $9 for a two-hour afternoon or evening cruise with afternoon tea or supper included. On Friday and Saturday nights you can take a five-hour jazz-and-dinner cruise for $32.

Around Hobart

Roads fan out from Hobart in all directions and you can make a number of day-trips from the capital. Places of interest include Richmond on the way to Port Arthur and New Norfolk on the way up the Derwent Valley towards the west coast. There's also a few good beaches within easy driving distance of the city.

TAROONA (population 3300)
Continue on beyond Wrest Point and you'll soon see Taroona's famous shot tower. Completed in 1870, the top of the 66-metre tower gives a fine view over the Derwent River estuary. The small museum at the base was built in 1855 and the adjoining residence in 1835. The tower, museum, art gallery and beautiful grounds are open daily until dusk. Lead shot was once produced in high towers like this by dropping molten lead from the top. On the way down the globule of lead formed a perfect sphere and solidified when it hit water at the bottom.

KINGSTON (population 8560)
Eleven km south of Hobart, Kingston is the headquarters of the Commonwealth Antarctic Research Division. It's open for inspection from 9 am to 4 pm on weekdays. There are good beaches around

Kingston including Blackman's Bay, Tinderbox and Howdon and fine views across to Bruny Island from Piersons Point.

BRIDGEWATER (population 2800)

This market town 19 km north of Hobart is so-named because it marks the main north-south crossing of the Derwent River. The causeway here was built in the 1830s by 200 convicts undergoing secondary punishment in chain gangs. Despite the chains, they managed to move two million tonnes of stone and clay. The old watch house at Granton on the other side of the river, was built in 1838, also by convicts, to guard the causeway. It's now a petrol station.

PONTVILLE (population 910)

Further north on the Midlands Highway, the historic town of Pontville has a number of interesting buildings dating back to the 1830s. Pontville's quarries supplied much of the freestone used in Tasmania's early buildings and two of the quarries are still working today.

NEW NORFOLK (population 6250)

Set in the lush rolling countryside of the Derwent Valley, New Norfolk is one of the most historically interesting towns in Tasmania. First settled in 1803, it's the centre of hop growing in Australia and is dotted with old oast houses, the conical buildings used to store hops.

Originally called Elizabeth Town it was renamed after the arrival in 1807 of settlers from the abandoned Pacific Ocean colony on Norfolk Island. Early hop growing experiments proved successful and by the 1860s nearly all the farmers in the valley were in the same business. The hop field planted at Bushy Park in the Styx Valley in 1864 became the largest and most successful in the southern hemisphere. Although hop growing is no longer the domain of the small farmer the oast houses, colonial buildings and the tall poplars planted to protect the crops from winds give New Norfolk its special charm, particularly in autumn.

In 1864 the first rainbow and brown trout in the southern hemisphere were bred in the Salmon Ponds at Plenty, 11 km west of New Norfolk, making possible the stocking of streams and lakes of Australia and New Zealand. You can visit the ponds and museum and enjoy the restaurant's specialty – guess what! The Australian Newsprint Mills is the other major industry of the area and produces 40% of the country's newsprint. The mill (tel 61 2222) can be inspected.

The Oast House Museum is devoted to the history of the hop industry and also serves Devonshire teas. St Matthew's Church of England, built in 1823, is Tasmania's oldest existing church; and the Bush Inn is claimed to be the oldest continuously licensed hotel in Australia. The Old Colony Inn, a museum of colonial furnishings and artefacts, also serves lunches. A modern New Norfolk diversion is a ride through the Derwent River rapids on a whitewater jet boat. If it takes your fancy you can book at the Bush Inn.

New Norfolk is 38 km from Hobart and Redline Coaches heading west along the Lyell Highway pass through the town.

Places to Stay

The New Norfolk *Youth Hostel* (tel 61 2591) is in the historic 'Bridge Toll House' and costs $4 a night. There are camping sites at the *New Norfolk Camping Ground*. Bed & breakfast singles cost $12.50 at the *Fairhaven Lodge Guest House* (tel 61 1171); bed & breakfast singles/doubles at the *Norfolk Lodge* (tel 61 3291) are $15/25 and at the *Bush Inn* (tel 61 2011) are $17/30.

MT FIELD NATIONAL PARK

Spectacular mountain scenery, alpine moorland, dense rainforest, lakes, waterfalls and abundant wildlife – all just 73 km from Hobart. Mt Field is the state's oldest national park and features the magnificent 40-metre Russell Falls, fine bush walks, Lake Dobson and the Mt Mawson ski-fields.

Places to Stay

There's a caravan park and camping ground; the *Lake Dobson Cabins* (tel 88 1149) cost $2.50 per person and *Russell Falls Holiday Cottages* (tel 88 1198) cost $35 a double.

ROKEBY (population 3500)

Tasmania's first wheat crop and the first export apples were grown here, across the Derwent River from Hobart. Rokeby has a village green and a few historic buildings still remain including the old St Matthew's Church. There are good beaches south of Rokeby at South Arm and good surfing at Clifton Beach.

RICHMOND (population 400)

Nowhere else in Tasmania is the romance and nostalgic charm of the colonial days of Van Diemens Land more alive and intact than in the little town of Richmond. The famous and much-photographed Richmond Bridge, built by convicts when the town was founded in 1823, is the oldest road bridge in Australia. Straddling the Coal River, Richmond developed as an important granary town and crossing place for travellers heading to the east coast but with the completion of the Sorell Causeway in 1872 the town was bypassed by traffic travelling between Hobart and Port Arthur.

Richmond jail, which predates Port Arthur by five years, is the best-preserved convict jail in Australia. It's open daily and has records of the road-gang convicts who were confined here. Other places of interest include St John's Church, the oldest (1836) Roman Catholic church in Australia, St Luke's Church of England, the court house, the old post office, the Bridge Inn (now a transport museum), Saddler's Court (now a craft shop) and the Richmond Arms. Barne's Museum of Photographica is in the restored Buscombe's

General Store and Colman's Kitchen Teashop serves Devonshire teas in a building built in 1850.

Richmond is an easy day-trip from Hobart or a detour en route to Port Arthur. The TGTB operate coach tours to Richmond via Risdon Cove for $10.

Sorell, south of Richmond at the junction of the Tasman and Arthur Highways, is the centre of an important agricultural area. In the early 1800s it was the granary for Tasmania and New South Wales. The Carlton and Dodges Ferry area has many good beaches.

Places to Stay

If you want to stay overnight the *Richmond Caravan Park* has on-site vans for $22 a double and camping space and the *Morville Host Farm* (tel 62 4299) has bed & breakfast singles for $21.

South-East Coast

South of Hobart are the scenic fruit growing and timber areas of the Huon Peninsula, D'Entrecasteaux Channel and Esperance as well as beautiful Bruny Island and the Hartz Mountains National Park.

While timber from the Huon and Channel areas was used as sleepers for the Trans-Siberian Railway and piers for the Melbourne docks it was the fruit, especially apples, from the Huon Valley which really put Tasmania on the international export map. Around January and February there's work available picking apples and hops but there's plenty of competition for jobs.

Getting Around the South-East

The Channel Highway runs out of Hobart past the Taroona Shot Tower, through Kingston and right around the Huon Peninsula. The Huon Highway runs south from Huonville through Franklin, Geeveston and Dover to Southport, 103 km from Hobart. The TGTB operates coach tours to the Huon Valley and Hastings Caves on Thursdays and Sundays. The day-trip costs $20 and can be booked at the Tasbureau in Hobart.

KETTERING (population 300)

This small port on a sheltered bay 34 km south of Hobart is the terminal for the Bruny Island car ferry. There are seven services daily to Barnes Bay on North Bruny. Eight km north of Kettering is the town of Snug which has good swimming at Coningham Beach, a walking track to Snug Falls, and the Channel Historical Museum which tells you all about the pioneer days. In Gordon, 29 km south of Kettering, there's a monument to the French navigator Bruny D'Entrecasteaux. There are camping grounds at Snug and Gordon.

BRUNY ISLAND (population 300)

The sparsely populated island of North and South Bruny, joined by a narrow isthmus, was visited by Furneaux, Cook, Bligh and Cox but was named after Rear Admiral Bruny d'Entrecasteaux who explored the area in 1792. It's believed that William (Mutiny on the Bounty) Bligh planted Tasmania's first apple tree on the island during a visit in 1788.

The island's history is recorded in the Bligh Museum of Pacific Exploration at Adventure Bay. It's open daily and also has a collection of antique celestial and terrestrial globes. The lighthouse on South Bruny was built in 1836 and is the second-oldest in Australia. A walking trail encircles Mt Bruny on the southern peninsula; there's good surf at Cloudy Bay, superb coastal scenery and fine swimming beaches.

The daily car ferry from Kettering to Barnes Bay costs $6 on weekdays and $10 on weekends.

Places to Stay

House Sofia (tel (002) 60 6277) is a hostel at Dennes Point. It costs $11 per person

for a bed and three meals or $4 for just the bed. In Adventure Bay the *Captain James Cook Caravan Park* has on-site vans for $16 and *Quiet Corner Seaside Holiday Units* (tel 39 6350) cost $25 each and can take four people. A unit at the *Karana Holiday Farm* (tel 25 1383), Barnes Bay costs $30.

CYGNET (population 700)

Port Cygnet, on which this small town stands, was named by d'Entrecasteaux for the many swans (*cygne* in French) seen on the bay. There are some good beaches in the area plus a winery four km out of town and plenty of accommodation.

Places to Stay

Balfes Tea House (tel 95 1551), a hostel on Sandhills Rd about five km from town, costs $5 a night; great food too!

You can get bed & breakfast singles at: *Lynhurst Guest House* (tel 95 1317) for $15; *Lower Bagot Farm* (tel 95 1615) for $15; the *Commercial Hotel* (tel 95 1368) for $17; and the *Crooked Tree Point Tea House* (tel 95 1495) for $20.

HUONVILLE & SOUTH

Named after D'Entrecasteaux' second in command Huon D'Kermandec, this busy small town on the picturesque Huon River is a major apple growing centre. The valuable softwood Huon Pine was first discovered here, though the main stands are now found only around the Gordon River.

A little further south is Franklin (population 500), also an apple growing town, although timber milling is the main activity here. First settled in 1804, it's the oldest place in the Huon area. It has an interesting apple-industry museum and the Huon River at Franklin is one of Australia's leading rowing courses.

Geeveston, 31 km south of Huonville through Port Huon, is another timber town. An administrative centre for Esperance, Australia's most southerly municipality, it is also the gateway to the wild Hartz Mountains National Park.

HARTZ MOUNTAINS NATIONAL PARK

This wild and spectacular area of glacial lakes, snow-capped mountains and dense rainforest is only 84 km from Hobart. The Arve Loop Road, which runs north along the Arve River, is one of Australia's most dramatic rainforest drives. There's a superb view from Waratah Lookout (24 km from Geeveston) and the jagged peaks of of Mt Snowy, the Devils Backbone and Hartz Peak are really something to see. Rugged mountains give way to deep gorges and alpine moorlands and there are superb bushwalks in the park including a track to Mt Picton and the Arthur Range near Federation Peak.

DOVER (population 400)

This very attractive little fishing port, another 20 km south on the Huon Highway, has curious old houses, fine beaches, excellent bushwalks and three islands in the bay called Faith, Hope and Charity. The felling, processing and exporting of Huon pine was the major industry last century. Sleepers made here and in the nearby timber towns of Strathblane and Raminea were shipped to China, India and Germany while street paving and wharf piles went to England. Casey's Living Steam Museum has working steam-powered exhibits and is open daily except in July and there's also an apple industry museum.

Places to Stay

The *Dover Hotel* (tel 98 1210) has room-only singles for $13 and also serves good counter meals. *Anne's Old Rectory* (tel 98 1222) has bed & breakfast singles for $18.

The *Dover Beachside Caravan Park* (tel 98 1301) has camping sites and on-site vans cost $20 a double. *Huon Hideaway* (tel 97 6282) has holiday flats for $28 a double. If you're heading towards the South East Cape this is the last chance to stock up on provisions, although petrol is also available in Southport.

There's a camping ground at Southport which is 24 km beyond Dover. It's a pretty little town with a history going back to the whaling days. The Huon Highway ends here although secondary roads lead further south.

HASTINGS

Today, the three spectacular limestone caves is all that attracts visitors to the once-thriving logging and wharf town of Hastings. A spiral staircase takes you down into the well-lit depths and NPWS officers operate daily tours all year round. Hastings is about six km off the Huon Highway, north of Southport. There's a good walk through rainforest to Adamsons Falls and a thermal pool.

LUNE RIVER

A few km south-west of Hastings is Lune River, a haven for gem collectors and the site of Australia's most southerly post office. The quaint Ida Bay Railway, which once carried limestone, now carries passengers on a scenic trip from the township of Ida Bay to The Deep Hole, a beautiful beach on the bay opposite Southport.

The most southerly drive you can make in Australia is along the secondary road from Lune River to Cockle Creek and beautiful Recherche Bay. It is an area full of nature's beauty – spectacular mountain peaks, endless beaches and secluded coves, it's ideal for camping and bush-walking.

Places to Stay

The Lune River *Youth Hostel*, also known as The Doing Place, has been getting rave reviews. Warden Trevor Cook knows all there is to know about the area and also hires-out caving equipment. Bring plenty of food with you as the hostel only has basic supplies.

Tasman Peninsula

Tasman Peninsula

to Hobart
Arthur Hwy
Tasman Memorial
Cape Frederick Henderson
Dunalley
FORESTIER
PENINSULA
Norfolk Bay
Saltwater River
Tesselated Pavement
Eaglehawk Neck
Tasman Arch
Blow Hole
Nubeena
TASMAN PENINSULA
Cape Hauy
Port Arthur
Remarkable Caves
Munroe Bight
Maingon Bay
Cape Pillar
TASMAN SEA
0   5   10   15km

PORT ARTHUR

Port Arthur has been Tasmania's premier tourist attraction since it ceased operation as a penal settlement in 1877. Even in the 1920s there were many visitors fascinated by tales of desperate convicts here and attracted by the superb scenery of the Tasman Peninsula.

In 1830 Governor Arthur chose the peninsula as the place to confine those prisoners convicted of crimes in the colony. The feature of this 'natural penitentiary' was the unique garrison at Eaglehawk Neck, the narrow isthmus connecting the peninsula to the mainland. All but a few escape attempts were thwarted by a line of ferocious guard dogs chained up across the Neck and the rumour that the waters on either side were shark infested.

About 12,500 convicts served sentences here between 1830 and 1877. The township of Port Arthur became the centre of a network of penal stations on the peninsula and was itself much more than a prison town. It had many fine buildings and thriving industries including timber, ship building, coal mining and brick, nail and shoemaking. Australia's first railway ran the seven km between Norfolk Bay and Long Bay with power provided by convicts who pushed the carriages along the tracks. A semaphore telegraph system allowed instant communication between Port Arthur, the scattered penal out-stations and Hobart. Convict farms provided fresh vegetables; a boys prison was built at Point Puer to reform and educate juvenile convicts and a church – today one of the most readily recognised tourist sights in Australia – was erected.

The Isle of the Dead, in the middle of the bay, was the cemetery for 1769 convicts and 180 free settlers and officers. Convicts were buried six or seven to a grave with no headstones; their bodies wrapped in sail cloth and covered with quicklime.

In 1979 the NPWS launched the nine million dollar government-funded Port Arthur Conservation & Development Project. Many of the town's surviving buildings have been restored and work is still going on. You can explore the penitentiary, the model prison, the roundtower guard house, several cottages and the beautiful church. The Lunatic Asylum is now an excellent museum with early records, photographs of the convicts with details of their crimes, and displays of their tools, leg irons, and clothing. There's a model of Port Arthur as it was in 1860 and an audio visual history of the settlement. Entry is $3. Guided tours are available and a tourist launch makes trips to the Isle of the Dead and Point Puer.

You'll need at least two days to make the most of the Tasman Peninsula and its many bushwalks, superb stretches of beach and beautiful bays. Places of interest include the Tasmanian Devil Park and the Port Arthur Marine Park at Taranna; The Bush Mill on the Arthur Highway; and the Country Life Museum at Koonya. You can also visit the remains of the penal out-stations of Cascades (now Koonya), Saltwater River and Impression Bay (Premaydena) and the ruins of the Coal Mines Station, the most dreaded place of punishment. Near Eaglehawk Neck there are several incredible coastal formations – on Pirate's Bay there's the Tesselated Pavement and further round, the Tasman Sea thunders in through the Devil's Kitchen, the Blowhole and Tasman's Arch. South of Port Arthur is Remarkable Cave – which is just that. When the tide is out you can walk through this amazing sea cave.

Places to Stay
The Port Arthur *Youth Hostel* (tel 50 2311), in the town of Port Arthur has an excellent view of the settlement and costs $5 a night. Camping sites at the spacious *Garden Point Caravan Park*, two km before Port Arthur overlooking Stewarts Bay, cost $3 per person. The park has cooking shelters and a laundry. There's basic camping facilities at Lime Bay, Fortescue Bay and White Beach and bush camping is permitted along the walking trails.

Motels and hotels in Port Arthur tend to be uncomfortably expensive. The *Tanglewood Host Farm* (tel 50 2210) is a guest-house on Nubeena Rd, Port Arthur with bed & breakfast doubles for $34.

Getting There
The only way to day-trip to Port Arthur if you don't have your own transport is on a TGTB tour from Hobart for $27.50. The two bus services which operate between Hobart and the Tasman Peninsula require at least one night's stop-over.

The Peninsula Coach Service (tel 50 3186), operates Monday to Friday and costs $8 a single and $14 return. Buses leave Hobart at 7.45 am and 3.45 pm; and depart from Port Arthur at 7.45 and 11 am. Remarkable Tours Service (tel 50 3355) operate on Thursdays only.

You can hire bicycles from Eaglehawk Neck Peninsula Cycle Hire (tel 50 3186) for $8 a day or $30 a week.

East Coast & North-East

The eastern seaboard with its magnificent coastline, long sandy beaches, fine fishing and quiet backwater atmosphere is probably the least visited of the accessible regions of Tasmania.

Exploration and settlement of the area, which was found to be most suitable for grazing, proceeded rapidly after the establishment of Hobart in 1804. Offshore fishing, particularly whaling, also became important as did tin mining and timber, but bush rangers, poor communication and isolation all contributed to the difficulties faced by the early settlers. The vital coastal traffic of the 19th century provided their only link with the outside world.

Many of the convicts who served out their terms in the area stayed on to help the settlers lay the foundations of the fishing, wool, beef and grain industries which are still important today. The largest town on the coast is St Helens with a population of only 1000. Although it's quiet, a leisurely trip down the Tasman Highway is highly recommended.

Getting Around the East Coast
It's 358 km by the east coast route between Hobart and Launceston if you turn off the coast from St Marys to Fingal and Avoca. If you continue up to St Helens and Scottsdale it's 434 km and further still if you go north to Bridport and George Town or branch off to the Tasman Peninsula and Port Arthur in the south.

Travelling by bus along this route involves a number of changes and it takes a couple of easy-going days – longer if the weekend intervenes. Tasmanian Redline Coaches operate Launceston-Scottsdale-Herric and Launceston-Conara-St Marys but along the coast you have to use a number of private bus companies. Check *Tasmanian Travelways* for the latest timetables and fares.

Starting from Hobart there are about five companies operating overlapping services along this route. Fares are Hobart-Launceston $29.30; Hobart-Swansea $10.50; Hobart-Bicheno $13.50; Swansea-St Marys $5.80; Bicheno-Coles Bay $3.35; Bicheno-St Marys $3; St Marys-St Helens $2; St Helens-Winnaleah $3.50; and Winnaleah-Launceston $7.50. You'll probably have to sit down with the timetables and pen and paper to work out your schedule since the services and departures vary from day to day.

BUCKLAND (population 200)

This tiny township, 61 km from Hobart, was once a staging post for coaches. Ye Olde Buckland Inn, which welcomed coach drivers and travellers a century ago, still provides refreshments and counter lunches.

The old stone church of St John the Baptist, dating from 1846, has a stained-glass window with an interesting history. Originally part of the 14th century Battle Abbey built on the site of the Battle of Hastings in England, it was rescued from the abbey before Cromwell sacked it in the 17th century. The Marquis of Salisbury presented the window to Reverend Fox, the first rector of the Buckland Church.

ORFORD (population 350)

Surrounded by tall hills, Orford is a popular little seaside resort on the Prosser River. There's good fishing, swimming and charter boats available for fishing and trips to Maria Island. Sandstone quarried from the nearby cliffs was used in many of Melbourne's early buildings.

Places to Stay

There's a camping and caravan park by the bay. *Orford Holiday Flats* (tel 57 1153) cost $24 a double and $4 for each extra body, and *Sea Breeze Flats* (tel 57 1375) also cost $24 for two.

TRIABUNNA (population 924)

A little further north the larger town of Triabunna was a whaling station and garrison town when nearby Maria Island was a penal settlement. The tall timbers of the east coast are processed at a woodchip plant south of the town. Triabunna is still a busy fishing port and is also the jumping-off point for boat charters to the Maria Island National Park.

Places to Stay

The Triabunna *Youth Hostel* (tel 57 3439), is in Spencer St and costs $5 a night. The *Triabunna Caravan Park* (tel 57 3248) has camping sites and their on-site vans cost $19 a double.

MARIA ISLAND

Named by Dutch explorer Abel Tasman after the wife of Governor Van Diemen of the Dutch East India Company in Batavia, Maria Island is now a National Park & Wildlife Sanctuary. In 1825 it became the site for Tasmania's second penal settlement (the first was Sarah Island near Strahan) but was abandoned in 1832. The remains of the penal village at Darlington are remarkably well-preserved but the peace and beauty of the island today belies its convict past. In later years there was a successful but short-lived cement industry and efforts were made to establish a winery and grazing lands but both proved uneconomic.

The isolation which proved such a barrier to the many attempts to settle the island now helps preserve its natural and historical heritage. It's very quiet (the only car on the island is used by the park rangers) and has plenty of wildlife and magnificent scenery, particularly the cliffs on the north and east coasts. The open forests, scrublands, paddocks and fern gullies are now home to Cape Barren geese, emus, Forester kangaroos, wallabies and other native animals. It's a great, out-of-the-way place for anyone into swimming, skin diving, bushwalking or fishing.

Places to Stay

The NPWS has restored many of the old buildings at Darlington and the rooms in the penitentiary have been converted into bunkhouses for visitors. There are extensive camping grounds but no facilities and all supplies must be brought with you from the mainland.

Getting There

There is ferry transport to the island, on the *MV James McCabe*, from Louisville (a resort between Orford and Triabunna) across the Mercury Passage to Darlington. It departs daily at 10.30 am and the return fare is $8 for day visitors and $10 for campers.

SWANSEA (population 400)

On the shores of beautiful Great Oyster Bay, with superb views across to the Freycinet Peninsula, Swansea is a popular place for camping, boating, fishing and surfing. It's the administrative centre for Glamorgan, Australia's oldest rural municipality, and was first settled in the 1820s. The original council chambers are still in use and other interesting historic buildings include Morris' General Store and the 1860 Community Centre; the latter now houses a museum of local history and a superb full-sized billiard table.

The Swansea Bark Mill & East Coast Museum, which won the national Museum of the Year award in 1983, is worth a visit. Last century the mill processed black wattle bark, a basic ingredient in the tanning of heavy leathers which was then one of the main local industries. The adjoining museum features whaling implements, farming equipment and photographs.

Places to Stay

The Swansea *Youth Hostel* (tel 57 8367) is at 5 Franklin St close to the beach and costs $5 a night. The *Kenmore Caravan Park* and *Swansea Caravan Park* have camping areas, on-site vans for $25 a double and cabins for $27 a double. *Swansea Holiday Lodge* (tel 57 8110) in Franklin St has bed & breakfast doubles for $35.

COLES BAY & FREYCINET NATIONAL PARK

The tiny township of Coles Bay is sheltered by the spectacular 300-metre-high red granite mountains known as the Hazards. It serves as the gateway to the many good beaches, secluded coves, rocky cliffs and excellent bushwalks of the Freycinet National Park. The park incorporates Freycinet Peninsula and beautiful Schouten Island and is noted for its coastal heaths, orchids, wildflowers and wildlife, which includes black cockatoos, yellow wattlebirds, Bennetts wallabies and possoms. Moulting Lagoon is a breeding ground for black swans. There's a 27-km walking circuit of the park plus more shorter tracks; the walk to Wineglass Bay is worth the effort.

A charter boat (tel 57 0180) provides a regular service to Schouten Island where there are good campsites, plenty of walks and fine fishing.

Places to Stay

Sites at the *National Park Caravan Park* (tel 57 0107) should be booked at the ranger's office. If you're planning to camp in the National Park you should also inform the ranger. The *Iluka Holiday Centre* (tel 57 0115) costs $22 per cabin and *Pine Lodge Cabins* (tel 57 0113) cost $25 each. *The Chateau* (tel 57 0101) is a charming guest-house with bed & breakfast singles for $26.

BICHENO (population 400)

This old coal-mining port on a grassy cape overlooking The Gulch, a tiny picturesque harbour, was first used by sealers and whalers in the early 1800s. The lookouts on the hills over the town, were used to keep watch for passing whales. In the 1850s coal was hauled into the port by horse-drawn carts from the Denison River mines. Crayfishing, abalone and oysters are the main industries today.

The Bicheno Sea Life Centre on the foreshore features many species of marine life. At low tide you can walk out to see the fairy penguin colony on Diamond Island; and the 35 hectare East Coast Bird & Wildlife Park is just north of the town.

About 30 km north of Bicheno the Tasman Highway climbs up over the spectacular Elephant Pass. If you're thirsty when you get to the top try the *French Tea House* which serves coffee and pancakes and has a great view of the coast.

Places to Stay

The Bicheno *Youth Hostel* (tel 75 1293) is four km north of the town on the beach opposite Diamond Island. It costs $5 a night. *Bicheno Campervan Park* (tel 75 1280) has on-site vans for $18 a double, the *Treasure Island Caravan Park* has vans for $24 for two and both have camping sites.

ST MARYS (population 700)

This charming little town, in the shadow of the Mt Nicholas Range, is 10 km inland at the headwaters of the South Esk River (which meets the sea at Launceston).

Fifteen km north, through St Marys Pass and four km off the Tasman Highway, is the tiny coastal township of Falmouth which has some early convict-built buildings and good beaches.

At St Marys the Tasman Highway meets the Esk Main Rd which heads west through Fingal and Avoca to Conara Junction where it joins the Midlands Highway. Fingal, 21 km from St Marys, is the headquarters of Tasmania's coal industry and has a number of historic buildings. The Fingal Hotel, built in 1850 as the Talbot Arms, features a collection of over 280 different brands of Scotch whisky. Avoca serves the mining areas of Rossarden and Story's Creek in the foothills of Ben Lomond National Park. The historic home 'Bona Vista' can be inspected by contacting the caretaker.

North of St Marys the popular resort town of Scamander has excellent beaches and good fishing in the sea and river. The Scamander *Youth Hostel*, one km north of the bridge, costs $4 a night.

Places to Stay

The superbly situated St Marys *Youth Hostel* (tel 72 2341) on 'Seaview Farm' has magnificent views of the coast, ocean and mountains. It's on German Town Rd, eight km uphill on a dirt road from St Marys; you can get a taxi! It costs $4 a night. St Marys also has a hotel and camping area.

ST HELENS (population 1000)

The largest town on the east coast is a popular beach resort on George Bay. Once again, fishing, particularly for crayfish, is a major business – you'll find good fresh fish in the restaurants here. St Helens was first settled in 1830 and 40 years later became the outlet for the Lottah and Blue Tier tin-mining fields. The town has a museum and history room, good fishing (including offshore game-fishing on charter boats), and the bay, estuaries and lagoons are good for bird watching. It's also a good base for visiting the scenic beach at Binalong Bay, Sloop Reef and Stieglitz on the coast, St Helens and Humbug Points or the St Columba Falls.

Places to Stay

St Helens Caravan Park (tel 76 1290) has plenty of camping space as well as on-site vans for $22 for two. *Halcyon Grove*

Holiday Homes (tel 76 1424) cost $25 per unit and *Corraleau Holiday Units* (tel 76 1363) cost $24 a double. The *Hillcrest Caravan Inn* (tel 76 1298) at Stieglitz has on-site vans for $22 a double and *Ocean View Units* (tel 98 2468) at Binalong Bay cost $28 a double.

WELDBOROUGH

The eastern approach to the Weldborough Pass, with its mountain scenery and dense rainforests, is quite spectacular. Hundreds of Chinese migrated to Tasmania during the tin-mining boom last century and many made Weldborough their base, bringing with them some of their most valuable possessions including a Joss House which is now in the Queen Victoria Museum in Launceston.

GLADSTONE

About 25 km off the main Tasman Highway between St Helens and Scottsdale, the tiny town of Gladstone is one of the few tin-mining centres still operating in the north-east corner of Tasmania. At one time there were a number of mining communities in the area and a large Chinese population. Today, most of them are ghost towns. An unsurfaced road leads from Gladstone to the Eddystone Light, built in 1887. There are camping facilities at Eddystone Point, which is the most eastern point of the Tasmanian mainland, but campers need to take their own water supplies.

SCOTTSDALE (population 1800)

The major town in the north-east is a quiet place in a beautiful setting. It serves some of the richest agricultural and forestry country in the state. There's a good caravan park in the town with camping sites and two hotels. Bridport is a beach resort 21 km north of Scottsdale on Bass Strait. There's a fine old 1839 homestead there. You can also get to the pine forests en route to Branxholm and the beaches of Tomahawk.

BEN LOMOND NATIONAL PARK

This 16,457 hectare park 50 km south-east of Launceston includes the entire Ben Lomond Range, and its magnificent scenery, dense rainforests and alpine slopes make it an ideal place for skiing, walking, climbing and photography.

The highest point is Legges Tor (1573 metres) and at the southern end of the plateau is Stacks Bluff, which overlooks the Midlands and the Fingal Valley.

The park is reached by back roads via White Hills or Evandale and onto the Blessington Rd and the final climb up Jacob's Ladder is very narrow, steep and winding. The ski slopes here are considered better than those of Mt Field and are ideal for beginners and intermediate skiers. Access during the season is easy as the Mountain Stage Line runs daily bus services from Paddy Pallins Outdoor Shop, 124 St Johns St, Launceston. There are also shuttle buses from the Jacob's Ladder carpark to the ski village.

The Midlands

The tranquil rolling midlands of Tasmania have a definite English feel about them due to the diligent efforts of early settlers who planted English trees and hedgerows. It was the fertility and agricultural potential of the area along the cart track and stock route between the two major towns of Hobart and Launceston that promoted Tasmania's rapid settlement and early prosperity.

Coaching stations, garrison towns, stone villages and pastoral properties soon sprang up along the route as convict gangs constructed the main road between Tasmania's northern and southern settlements. Fine wool, beef cattle and timber milling put the Midlands, and therefore Tasmania's early economy, on the map and are still the main industries of the area.

The course of the Midland Highway

has changed slightly from its original route and many of the historic towns are now bypassed, but it is definitely worth making a few detours. Using this road it's just 199 km from Hobart to Launceston. Melton Mowbray (54 km from Hobart) is the junction for the alternative Lake Highway to Bothwell and Tasmania's highland lake country.

OATLANDS (population 2151)

Eighty-four km north of Hobart and one of four military posts along the historic main road, Oatlands has the largest collection of Georgian architectural styles in Australia. The oldest building is the convict-built court house (1829), and most of the houses, hotels, schools and churches were constructed in the boom days of the 1830s. Life then revolved around military operations and the local industries of milling and brewing. The town stands on the shores of Lake Dulverton which is a wildlife sanctuary and popular fishing area. St Peter's Pass, just north of the town, features hawthorn hedges cut in the shape of animals.

Places to Stay

The Oatlands *Youth Hostel* (Tel 54 1320) in Wellington St costs $4 a night. The *Oatlands Fishing Lodge* (tel 54 1444), at

92 High St, is a guest-house with bed & breakfast singles/doubles for $30/35. The more expensive *Amelia Cottage* (tel 54 1264) and *Waverley Cottage & Croft* (tel 54 1264) are host farms with bed & breakfast doubles for $45.

TUNBRIDGE

First settled in 1809 and formerly called 'Tunbridge Wells' this town became the central stopover for coaches between Hobart and Launceston. Historical buildings of interest include the Tunbridge Wells Inn and adjoining stables, the Victoria Inn with its sandstone coaching steps, The Blind Chapel and Rosemere, former home of the local blacksmith. A sandstone bridge built in 1848 by convicts spans the Blackman River on the northern side of the town. Tunbridge is in the centre of the state's superfine wool growing area and stages a huge annual district sheep sale during the third week of January.

ROSS (population 3000)

This charming ex-garrison town, 120 km from Hobart, was established in 1812 to protect travellers on the main north-south road and was also an important coach staging post and stock market. The convict-built Ross bridge is the third oldest bridge in Australia and historically the most important. It was designed by the famous architect John Lee Archer and convict sculptors Daniel Herbert and James Colbeck were responsible for the bridge's unique craftsmanship. Herbert, who was granted a pardon for his work on the 184 panels which decorate the arches, also carved the memorial which marks his grave in the old military burial ground – an interesting place to visit. Ross was also famous for two of Australia's earliest and most highly regarded educational establishments, Ellenthorpe Hall and Horton College.

The Four Corners, in the traditional heart of the town, represent Temptation (Man O' Ross Hotel), Salvation (Roman

Catholic Church), Recreation (Town Hall) and Damnation (old jail). Other interesting historic buildings include: the Scotch Thistle Inn, first licensed in 1830 as a coaching inn and now fully restored as a licensed restaurant; the Old Barracks, restored by the National Trust and now used as a wool and craft centre; the Uniting Church and St John's Church of England; and the Ross Memorial Library. The former rectory of St John's is now the Village Tea Rooms.

The Beaufort Deer Park, six km from Ross, has native wildlife as well as deer and is open daily except Tuesday and Wednesday. The town's major annual event is on the first Saturday in November when horse riders come from all over Australia and overseas to take part in the annual Ross Rodeo.

Places to Stay

The *Man O' Ross Hotel* has bed & breakfast singles for $15 and basic counter meals for around $5.50. There is also a caravan park and camping ground adjacent to the Ross bridge.

CAMPBELL TOWN (population 900)

Another former garrison post, Campbell Town is 12 km from Ross and 66 km south of Launceston. The most interesting examples of its early colonial architecture include the large brick and stone house known as The Grange, St Luke's Church of England, the Campbell Town Inn, Balmoral Cottage, the building known as the 'Fox Hunters Return' and the old brewery (now the Masonic Temple). In High St there is a memorial to Campbell Town-born Harold Gatty who in 1931, as navigator of the *Winnie Mae*, made the first round-the-world flight with American aviator Wylie Post.

There's a secondary road from Campbell Town through the excellent fishing and bushwalking area around Lake Leake (32 km), to Swansea on the east coast. From Conara Junction, 11 km north of Campbell Town, the Esk Main Road

heads east from the Midland Highway to St Mary's.

Places to Stay

The *Laird O' Lake Leake Hotel* (tel (003) 81 1329) has bed & breakfast singles for $20.

Launceston
Population 86,000

Launceston, the 'Garden City' of Tasmania, is renowned for its quiet charm, beautiful old homes and grand public buildings. Nestled in the wide, rich agricultural valleys formed by the Tamar and Esk river systems it has long been the geographic and commercial hub of northern and midland Tasmania. It is Australia's third oldest city and the state's second largest.

The discovery of the Tamar River estuary in 1798 by Bass and Flinders, who were actually trying to find out if Van Diemen's Land was joined to the rest of Australia, led to early settlement attempts in the area closer to the coast.

It wasn't until 1805 that the city of Launceston, on the upper reaches of the Tamar River at the confluence of the North and South Esk Rivers, was officially founded by Lieutenant-Colonel William Paterson. Originally called Patersonia, the city's first commandant later changed the name in honour of Governor King who was born in Launceston, a town settled 1000 years before on the Tamar River in Cornwall, England.

Like Hobart, its early history was one of rapid growth and many stately buildings were erected at the time to serve its developing commercial and social needs. Launceston's early settlers must also have been blessed with an appreciation of the area's natural beauty as the city is recognised for its long-established, well-maintained and very beautiful public and private gardens.

Launceston

Charles Bridge

Victoria Bridge

Royal Park

City Park

Cimitiere St

Cameron St

Paterson St

Brisbane St.

mall

York St.

Elizabeth St.

Princes Square

Frederick St.

Canning St.

Balfour St.

Frankland St.

Trewllyn Rd

Tamar Rd

Hillside Crescent

Margaret St.

Bathurst St.

Wellington St.

Charles St.

George St.

St John St.

High St.

Arthur St.

Abbot St.

Anne St.

Mary St.

Inman St.

Invermay Rd

0   200 m

1 Cataract Gorge
2 Gunpowder Mill
3 Penny Royal Mills
4 Museum & Art Gallery
5 Post Office
6 Tourist Bureau
7 Ansett
8 Tasmanian Design Centre
9 TAA
10 Tasmanian Redline Coaches
11 Youth Hostel
12 Tourist Information

Information

The Tasbureau office (tel 32 2488) is on the corner of St John and Paterson Sts.

It's open from 8.45 am to 5.30 pm on weekdays and 9 am to 1.30 pm on weekends and public holidays. The TAA office (tel 31 4411) and the Ansett office (tel 31 7711) are both on corners of George and Brisbane Sts. The post office is on the corner of Cameron and St John Sts and the Redline Coach terminal is on George St.

The central section of Brisbane St, between Charles and St John Sts, is a pedestrian mall and the town centres around the mall. The main attractions of Launceston are all within walking distance of the centre.

Cataract Gorge

The magnificent Cataract Gorge, where almost vertical cliffs line the banks of the South Esk River as it enters the Tamar, is Launceston's best-known attraction. The tranquil Cliff Grounds Reserve still exudes the wild beauty that so impressed the first European visitors to the gorge during the exploration of the Tamar River in 1804.

Development of the area was initiated in 1899 by a private organisation which constructed a walking trail along the north face of the gorge to the huge natural basin filled by the surging waters of the South Esk River. The Launceston City Council now administers the 158-hectare reserve which is rich in native flora and fauna.

Only 10 minutes walk from the centre of the city, the 1½-km path winds up the gorge to the Cliff Grounds and the First Basin recreation area on the other side of the river. A flock of magnificent peacocks lord it over the beautiful gardens and there's a swimming pool, kiosk and restaurant – a popular place for picnics and Devonshire teas. A visitor information centre in the old Bandstand features a changing display of historic and general info.

A chairlift links the two sections of the reserve and the breathtaking six-minute ride covers a distance of 457 metres across the river. The 308-metre central span is believed to be the longest single span of any chairlift in the world.

A good walking trail leads further up the gorge to the deserted ruins of the old Duck Reach turbine-driven power station which provided electricity for the city from 1895 to 1955. Launceston has the distinction of being the first city in the southern hemisphere to be lit by hydro-electric power.

Penny Royal World

The development of the Penny Royal entertainment and accommodation complex began with the relocation of an 1825 cornmill, moved stone by stone from Barton, about 60 km from Launceston. Penny Royal World now features working examples of the water and wind driven technology of the 19th century including a gunpowder mill, windmill, watermill and paddle steamer. The cornmill building includes the shops of the millwright, blacksmith and wheelwright as well as a gift shop and museum. The nearby watermill is now part of the luxury Penny Royal motel. Admission is $2 to each mill or $3 to both.

A farmhouse, jail, gunners' quarters, underground armoury magazine, a 10-gun sloop, a cutter, waterfalls and a restaurant are other attractions of the complex. A restored Edwardian tram takes visitors to the gunpowder mill at the old Cataract quarry where there's also a foundry for casting cannons and a model steam railway system. Penny Royal World is quite interesting but the $5 entry fee is a bit of a rip-off.

Parks & Gardens

Launceston's beautiful public squares, parks and private gardens have earned it the well-deserved reputation of being Tasmania's 'garden city'.

The 13-hectare City Park is an outstanding example of the landscape gardener's art and features an elegant fountain, Victorian bandstand, a charming zoo and a monkey park. The John Hart Conservatory within the grounds is noted for its amazing display of native and exotic hot-house blooms; and Albert Hall, built in 1891 for the Tasmanian International Exhibition, features a magnificent water organ.

Princes Square (between Charles and St John Sts) features a bronze fountain bought at the 1858 Paris Exhibition.

Other public gardens include Royal Park on the North Esk River by the junction of the Tamar River, the Trevallyn Dam recreation area, and Punchbowl Reserve with its wildlife sanctuary and magnificent rhododendron garden.

Buildings

The Queen Victoria Museum & Art Gallery in Royal Park was built late last century and still maintains the splendour of the period both inside and out. It has a unique collection of Tasmanian fauna, Aboriginal artefacts, penal settlement relics, colonial paintings and a planetarium. A major attraction of the museum is the splendid Chinese Joss House donated by the descendants of Chinese settlers who lived in north-eastern Tasmania. It came from Weldborough, a small town in the north-east of the state, where it was the southernmost working joss house in the world. The museum, in Wellington St, is open daily (afternoon-only on Sunday).

Macquarie House in the City Square was built in 1830 as a warehouse but was later used as a military barracks and office building. Following a massive restoration programme it now houses a section of the Queen Victoria Museum & Art Gallery and a restaurant. It is open daily but only afternoons on weekends.

The Old Umbrella Shop, built in the 1860s, is the last genuine period-shop in the state. Tasmanian blackwood lines the interior of this unique shop which has been classified by the National Trust. Three generations of the Shott family ran the business and a selection of their umbrellas is on display. The Trust uses the building, at 60 George St, as an information centre and gift store and it's open from 9 am to 5 pm on weekdays and 9 am to 12 noon on Saturdays.

Franklin House, one of Launceston's most attractive early homes, has been beautifully restored and furnished by the National Trust. An outstanding feature of the interior of this charming two-storey Georgian house is the woodwork, which is all New South Wales cedar. It was built in 1838 for Mr Britton James, a Launceston brewer and innkeeper, but in 1842 it became the W K Hawkes School for Boys. Franklin House is six km from the city centre on the main Hobart Rd (Midland Highway); open daily and entry is $2.

Other Attractions

The Design Centre of Tasmania has displays of design work by the state's top artists and craftspeople. The centre, on the Tamar St side of City Park, is open daily but closed Saturday afternoon and Sunday morning.

Ritchie's Flour Mill on Bridge Rd (near Penny Royal) has been transformed into an art gallery. Built in 1845, the four-level complex includes a quaint Georgian miller's cottage which is now a tearoom.

The Waverley Woollen Mills, established in 1874, is the oldest operating woollen mill in Australia. It is open daily till 4 pm and you can watch the process of turning greasy wool into finished items such as blankets and fashion garments. The mill is five km from the city centre on Waverley Rd.

The paddle-steamer *Lady Stelfox* can take you back in time on a leisurely 40-minute cruise up Cataract Gorge and around the harbour. The charming old vessel leaves Ritchie's landing stage (near the Penny Royal) on the hour daily between 10 am and 5 pm.

There are also Tamar River cruises that leave from Goondooloo berth near Royal Park daily at 1 pm. The modern cruiser takes three hours to get to Blackwall and back and costs $9 for adults and $4.50 for kids. You can book at the Tasbureau office.

There's a good view over the city from the Talbot Rd lookout (south-east of the centre), and from Freelands Lookout Reserve, off Bald Hill Rd.

Places to Stay

Hostels The Launceston *Youth Hostel* (tel 44 9779) is two km from the GPO at 36 Thistle St. Set in park-like grounds in the former woollen mills canteen, it has dorm beds and family rooms and costs $5 a night. There are 10-speed bicycles, wet-weather gear and walking boots for hire.

Unless you're into push bikes – in which case you'll get along famously with the infamous warden – be warned that this hostel has the reputation of being the least popular in Tassie.

Guest Houses The *Ashton Gate* (tel 31 6180), 32 High St, is good value at $14 per person. The hostess is charming and the breakfast is delicious. At the *Rubina Joy Private Hotel* (tel 46 9900), 375 Hobart Rd, bed & breakfast costs $14 a single. The *Windmill Hill Tourist Lodge* (tel 31 9337), at 22 High St, costs $17 for a single, $8 for each extra adult and breakfast is extra.

Hotels Launceston has quite a good selection of hotels for a town of its size. The *Crown Hotel* (tel 31 4137) at 152 Elizabeth St is comfortable and costs $15 per person including breakfast. The *Enfield* (tel 31 4040), 169 Charles St, is also $15 per person but for room-only. The *California* (31 4348), at 17 Lower Charles St, is very cheap at $8 a single, room-only – but it's what you'd expect for the price. Not far away at 43 Lower Charles St the *Riverview* (31 4857) has bed & breakfast singles for $14.

The following hotels all cost $16 for a bed & breakfast single: the *Richmond* (tel 31 3302) at 32 Wellington St, the *Star* (tel 31 9659) at 113 Charles St, the *TRC* (tel 31 3424) at 131 Paterson St, and the *Royal* (tel 31 2526) at 90 George St.

Lloyds Hotel (31 4966) at 23 George St costs $18 for a bed & breakfast single and the *St George* (tel 31 7277) at 119 St John St, is $20 a single and $15 for each extra adult for bed & breakfast.

Motels The *Mews Mini-Motel* (tel 31 2861) is at 89 Margaret St quite close to the centre, and you get an excellent breakfast included in the tariff. It's $22/33 for singles/doubles and $10 for each extra adult. The *Motel Maldon* (tel 31 3979) at 32 Brisbane St costs $28/36 a single/double for bed & breakfast.

Launceston also has some holiday flats and other self-contained accommodation

which may be worth checking. The *Frederick St Holiday Flat* (there's just one!) at 79 Frederick St (tel 31 8307) costs about $20 per night for two with a three-night minimum. A little way out of Mowbray, *Barton Lodge* (tel 26 2581) is at 11-13 Barton St and costs $26 for two, $5 for each extra person.

Camping The most convenient of the three caravan parks in Launceston is one of the *Treasure Island* chain but the management doesn't seem to be too enthusiastic about campers with their own tents. The park gets very crowded and at $5 for a tiny camping space it's expensive and claustrophobic. It is well-equipped though and has on-site vans for $18 a double. It's in Glen Dhu St, Glen Dhu but phone first (44 2600) before you lug your tent all the way there.

The other two caravan parks are both 12 km out of town but worth the trouble to get to. The camping sites are spacious and there's facilities for cooking, washing and relaxing. The *Legana Tourist & Caravan Park* (30 1714, after hours 30 1462) is on the West Tamar Highway near Westlands nursery; and the *Launceston Caravan Park* (93 6391) is on the Bass Highway near Hadspen.

Places to Eat Launceston has a few more eating places than it used to but if you arrive on a Saturday afternoon or Sunday don't expect too much in the appetising cheap snack department – all the interesting places close for the weekend. One exception is *Banjo's* – for hot bread, cakes and coffee – in Yorktown Square which is open weekdays from 7.30 am to 5.30 pm, Saturdays till 6 pm and even Sundays from 7.30 am to 2 pm. Yorktown Square also features the *Parthenon* for souvlaki, the *Pasta House* licensed restaurant and take-away, and *Sat's Coffee House*.

The *Cameo Coffee Lounge* in George St has tasty breakfasts and light lunches in the $3 to $6 range and is open Monday to Saturday from 8.30 am to 4.30 pm.

Bobbies in Quadrant Mall is another good low-priced place but it's not open Saturdays. For pretty good pizzas and other Italian food of the eat-here or take-away type you can try *Akka's* on Brisbane St opposite Kingsway, the *Pizza House* on George St and the *Capri Pizza Restaurant* at 76 St John St.

The *Canton*, 203 Charles St, does tasty sweet & sour numbers; for a cheap schnitzel or steak try the *Sorrento* also on Charles St; and the *Winton* on York St has steaks and other main courses for around $6 to $7.

Counter Meals Launceston's hotel bistro and counter meals are probably your best bet for a filling, reasonably-priced meal. The *Richmond Hotel* in Wellington St, the *Royal Oak* on the corner of Brisbane and Tamar Sts and the *TRC Hotel* in Paterson St have a good selection of counter lunches and evening meals in the $4 to $6 range. The *Batman Fawkner* in Cameron St has a lunchtime carvery where you can eat as much as you like for $8.50 and an a-la-carte menu at night.

More Expensive In the $8 to $12 bracket Launceston boasts quite a few good restaurants. *Romeo & Juliet* at 114 Elizabeth St has a great Italian menu; the *Akbar* at 63 Cimitiere St has an Asian menu – Indian, Indonesian, Chinese; *Pierre's* at 88 George St is worth trying; *Clayton's Coffee Shoppe* on Quadrant Mall has mouth-watering cheesecake and other taste treats as well as meals; *Shrimps* in George St is a good choice for seafood; and the *The Smiling Toad*, 91 George St, is good for vegetarian and game.

Dicky White's in the Launceston Hotel, 107 Brisbane St, has a satisfying and varied menu. The hotel lays claim to being the longest-running in the country. Dicky White was a convicted highwayman who reformed when he finished his time and became a colourful figure in early Launceston and founded the hotel.

On the corner of York and Kingsway Sts, the *Old Butter Factory* has a steakhouse-style menu where the emphasis is on do-it-yourself. You pick your hunk of steak from the display then grill it yourself and heap the salads on board from the selection on the table.

If you want to go up-market there is the *Owl's Nest* in the Penny Royal Watermill, *Rowel's* in George St, *Old Masters* at 58 Elizabeth St, and *Aces* at 136 Wellington St.

Entertainment Most of the hotels in Launceston have some sort of entertainment, either bands or disco. The *Hotel Tasmania* seems to provide music for all tastes. If you enter the hotel from Elizabeth St then *Rock Central* has a band or disco from Thursday to Saturday and if you take the Charles St entrance into *Nick's Bar* you'll find local rock, country or folk musicians. For jazz or rock try *Rosie's* on the corner of Elizabeth and George Sts, from Thursday to Saturday. If you're into folk music try and get out to the *Country Club Hotel* at Longford on the first Saturday night of each month.

In the disco department there's the terribly pretentious *Josephine's* in the Launceston Hotel, Brisbane St which is open Wednesday to Saturday. *Ragine's* is an expensive disco at the casino – and the drink prices are over-the-top all the time but admission is free from Sunday to Thursday. The *Old Tudor Inn* at Prospect, has a crowded disco from Thursday to Saturday and the *Butter Factory* has a disco from Tuesday to Saturday after 9 pm.

If you want to risk a few dollars or just observe how the rich people play then check out Tasmania's second casino, 10 km out of the city centre at Prospect. It doesn't have the Monte Carlo feel of Hobart's Wrest Point but it does provide an interesting diversion.

The *Launceston Federal Country Club Casino* is set on 85 hectares, has a golf course, lake, horse riding, tennis and squash courts, pool, sauna and spa – wonderful if you can afford to stay there. The casino, however, is free – to get in that is. The drinks are expensive but the gambling is not – as long as you don't get carried away!

Most Launceston venues are annoyingly fussy about suitable attire so if you didn't bring along your best clothes at least make sure you're neat or you could spend your evening just looking for a place that will let you in. If you're staying at the youth hostel, beware that you don't get locked out at night, whatever the warden might say about the door being open.

Getting There

Air Ansett and TAA both have a number of daily flights to Launceston from Sydney (1½ hours) and Melbourne (one hour), some flights from Sydney go direct. Fares from Melbourne are $117.20 one-way, $152.40 Apex return and $94 standby. From Sydney it costs $204.20 one-way, and $265.50 return. Airlines of Tasmania fly Melbourne (Essendon Airport) to Launceston for $105; and Promair have a service from the LaTrobe Valley in Victoria for $90 one-way.

You can fly TAA or Ansett between Hobart and Launceston for $69.40 but with Airlines of Tasmania it's just $50, or $18 if you take their 'Dawn Buster Service'. Airlines of Tasmania also have flights between Launceston and the following places: Devonport $30.50; Flinders Island $49; Wynyard $32.50; King Island $78; Queenstown $50; and Strahan $50.

Bus Tasmania Redline Coaches have a number of services to and from Launceston. To Hobart (three services daily) it costs $11.40; there are four daily buses to Devonport ($7.60) and Burnie ($10.60). There are also three services daily to George Town and buses run to Bell Bay, the north-east coast and St Marys. It costs $11 to St Helens and $29.30 to Hobart via the east coast. Coastliner

Express buses cost $19 to Smithton; Staffords Coaches (tel 24 3628) from Launceston airport cost $40 to Lake St Clair and $32 to Cradle Valley; and a Mountain Stage Line bus to Mienna and Great Lake costs $15.

Road Launceston is 199 km from Hobart by the direct route, 434 km by the east coast route. It's 89 km from Launceston to Devonport and another 54 km on to Burnie.

Getting Around

Airport Bus fare out to Launceston Airport on the Tasmanian Redline bus is $3; by taxi it's about $10.

Bus The MTT run the local buses and a $2 all-route all-day bus ticket is available from the tourist office, from Teague's at 102 Brisbane St and from the MTT office at 168 Wellington St. Most routes do not operate in the evening and Sunday services can be very sketchy if they operate at all. The Punch Bowl bus leaves from Brisbane St opposite Kingsway but there's no evening service and next to none on Sunday. A free bus map is available with a route map on the back.

If you're hitching to Devonport and the north-west catch a Prospect bus from outside the Launceston Bank for Savings on St John St. For Hobart and the east coast, catch a Franklin Village bus near the HEC on St John St. The Tasman Highway route to the east coast is longer and more scenic but also harder. For this route catch a Waverley bus from opposite Quadrant Mall on St John St. There is no bus service north of George Town on the Tasman Highway apart from the twice-daily service to Bridport. There's no traffic either, especially to Tomahawk.

Car & Bicycle See the Tasmania introductory Getting Around section for information on renting cars and bicycles. The major car rental firms have offices in Launceston or at Launceston Airport.

Tours Day and half-day tours operate around Launceston and the northern area. Scenic Air operate sightseeing flights from Launceston airport ranging in price from $33 to $170. Sights include the Tamar Valley, Cradle Mountain, Lake Pedder, South Coast, Gordon River, Maria Island or Flinders Island.

Around Launceston

Early in the 19th century Launceston was a gateway for the settlers and farmers who were opening up the north of Tasmania. They headed inland and along the north-west coast to exploit the region's fertile soils and grazing lands and south to develop one of the wealthiest farming areas in the state. The number of towns and fine early houses around Launceston is indicative of the prosperity the new colony quickly developed from this rich agricultural potential.

HADSPEN (population 950)
Tasmania's best-known historic home is the beautiful Entally House at Hadspen, built in 1819 by Thomas Haydock Reibey. As a historic showpiece it creates a vivid picture of what life must have been like for the well-to-do on an early farming property.

The Reibeys didn't always have it so good though; in 1790 Mary Haydock, the matriarch of this prosperous family, was convicted of horse stealing and transported to New South Wales. She was then 13-years-old. On the voyage out from England she met and later married Thomas Reibey, a sub-lieutenant in the service of the East India Company. The young couple prospered and Mary, being a very astute businesswoman, made quite a name for herself in the early days of the colony. It was Reibey family shipping enterprises that brought Mary's sons to Tasmania, where Thomas built Entally House on the 1050 hectare property and

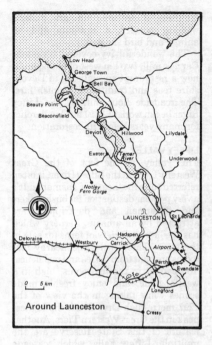

Around Launceston

his son Thomas became one of the state's first Premiers.

Entally House, 13 km from Launceston and just west of Hadspen, has been faithfully restored by the National Parks & Wildlife Service of Tasmania. The garden is beautiful, the house has antique furnishings and the outbuildings include stone stables, a coach house with vehicles and a bluestone chapel. Entry is $2 and it's well worth it.

In Hadspen itself you'll find the Red Feather Inn which was built in 1843 and served as the first coaching station on the road from Launceston. Tea-rooms and a craft shop now operate in an adjoining building and the village has a caravan park and camping ground.

Nearby Rutherglen Village, on the banks of the South Esk River, is primarily a convention and entertainment centre but as well as accommodation and leisure facilities it features an art gallery, working pottery, a museum and an animal and bird sanctuary.

The wonderful ivy-covered bluestone Carrick mill, two km west of Hadspen, is now a restaurant specialising in Devonshire teas and traditional English fare. The roadside flour mill by the Liffey River began work in 1810 but lay derelict for many years before its restoration.

LIFFEY VALLEY

This valley, at the foot of the Great Western Tiers on the Liffey River, is often referred to as the 'heart' of Tasmania. It's a very popular destination for bushwalkers and fishermen and daytrippers are attracted by an amazing fernery which has the largest variety of ferns for sale in the state. The fernery and nearby tea-rooms are built from ti-tree and melaleuca. You can sit in the tea-rooms, high in a wattle glade, and enjoy freshly made scones while taking in the view of the 1297-metre-high Drys Bluff, the highest peak in the Great Western Tiers. Another feature of this State Reserve are the multiple Liffey Falls which cascade through beautiful rainforest. Liffey is 34 km south of Carrick on a surfaced road.

EVANDALE

The town of Evandale, 19 km south of Launceston in the South Esk Valley, has been declared a historic town. A charming place, it remains unspoilt by progress; its buildings are in excellent condition and many of the shop fronts are original.

Clarendon, the National Trust's property near Nile, is one of the grandest Georgian mansions in Australia. Completed in 1838, the house and 22 hectares of superb parkland was given to the Trust in 1962 and parts of the building have been restored. Clarendon is eight km south of Evandale and entry is $2.

Places to Stay

There is accommodation at the *Prince of Wales Hotel* (tel 91 8381) in Nile St,

Evandale. It cost $13.50 a single for bed & breakfast.

PERTH (population 1230)

There are many historic buildings (surprise, surprise!) in this charming little town by the South Esk River, 19 km from Launceston. The site for the town was chosen by Governor Macquarie in 1821 and it eventually became an important coaching station on the Midlands Highway to Hobart. Noteworthy buildings in the town are the Eskleigh Home, the Methodist and Baptist churches and the Leather Bottle, Old Crown and Jolly Farmer inns.

LONGFORD (population 2030)

Longford, also a National Trust classified town, is set in the midst of a rich pastoral area watered by the South Esk and Lake Rivers. Its many colonial buildings, mostly built by convict labour, include Christ Church, Jessen Lodge, the Queen's Arms Hotel and Brickendon mansion. It's an easy day-trip from Launceston (only 27 km) but there's a caravan park with tent sites on the bank of the Lake River so you can take your time to explore the town's historic features.

The annual Tasmanian Folk Festival, which has an international reputation, is held in Longford on the Australia Day weekend in January. To cater for the more than 5000 people who attend each year the local council provides a 24 hectare camping area along the river.

The Longford Wildlife Park on Pateena Rd, about 14 km from the town, was created to provide a permanent conservation area for native Tasmanian flora and fauna. The 70-hectare bush and pasture park has kangaroos, wallabies, echidnas, Cape Barren Geese, wild ducks and native birds.

CRESSY

A little further south-west, in Cressy, you can visit historic Palmerston House. Cressy was once the richest wheat growing district in Tasmania but today earns its living from oats, barley, peas, beans and poppies – the latter for use in the production of drugs. The town, 36 km from Launceston, is also the jumping-off point for good trout fishing in nearby Brumby's Creek and the Macquarie, Lake and Liffey Rivers.

Places to Stay

At the *Ringwood Hotel* (tel 97 6161) bed & breakfast costs $15/25 a single/double.

The Tamar Valley

The beautiful Tamar River separates the East and West Tamar districts and links Launceston with its ocean port of Bell Bay. The Tamar runs 64 km from the confluence of the North and South Esk Rivers to Bass Strait and the estuary is Australia's longest navigable inland waterway for ships up to 4000 tonnes. The river is tidal to Launceston and wends its way through orchards, pastures, forests and the vineyards which are an important part of Tasmania's developing wine industry. The superb black swan is just one of the many species of wildlife that makes its home along the waterway and the river has become a popular recreation area.

The history of the valley dates from 1798 when Bass and Flinders discovered the estuary and named the stretch of water Port Dalrymple. Subsequent exploration of the river led to the discovery of Cataract Gorge and the founding of Outer Cove – now George Town. The valley's first five settlers arrived from Norfolk Island in 1805 bringing with them 612 Bengal cattle and 10 calves from India. The district developed slowly and was a port of call for the sailors and sealers from the Bass Strait islands and a sanctuary for some of the desperate characters who took to the bush during the convict days.

With the discovery of gold in the Cabbage Tree Hill (now Beaconsfield) area in the late 1870s the prosperity of the valley took a new turn. The region boomed and for a time Beaconsfield was the third largest town in Tasmania with being extracted before water seepage made conditions dangerous and the mines were forced to close.

Apart from its fascinating history the Tamar Valley has plenty more to offer the visitor in the way of scenery, beaches, fishing, swimming and boating. There are caravan parks as well as camping. There's also some reasonably priced hotels.

NOTLEY GORGE

Notley Fern Gorge is the only remnant of the dense rainforest that once blanketed the West Tamar. Originally saved from the settler's axe because of its inaccessibility, the 10-hectare reserve of ferns, trees and shrubs is also a wildlife sanctuary. Early last century the notorious bushranger Matthew Brady and his gang eluded capture for some time by hiding out in the Notley forests. The gorge is 23 km from Launceston off the West Tamar Highway via Legana.

EXETER

Near Exeter, base for the West Tamar farming and orcharding industries, are the river resorts of Paper Beach, Blackwell and Gravelly Beach.

Five km south of Exeter, Brady's Lookout is a high rocky outcrop used by the bushranger to check on troop movements and potential 'clients'. He was eventually captured in 1826 by a party led by John Batman (one of the founders of Melbourne) and was hanged in Hobart at the age of 27.

Places to Stay

There is accommodation at the *Exeter Hotel* (tel 94 4555) which has bed & breakfast singles for $15.

DEVIOT

The Tamar Valley Vineyards at Deviot (north of Exeter) are open to the public. Other vineyards and wineries are at Legana, Rosevears, Blackwall, Rowella, Glengarry and Lalla. The Tasmanian Rock Oyster Company also has its headquarters at Deviot and there's an unusual Proteas flower plantation.

BATMAN BRIDGE

Thirty km downstream from Launceston the Batman Bridge crosses the Tamar River. Dominated by a 100-metre-high, steel A-frame tower it was one of the world's first cable-stayed truss bridges.

The historic 'Auld Kirk' at Sidmouth is only minutes from the bridge. The church was built in 1846 by convicts and free labour.

BEACONSFIELD (population 900)

The once thriving gold-mining town of Beaconsfield is another attraction of the West Tamar district. The town is still dominated by the ruins of the three mine buildings, with their Romanesque arches, which were built at the pithead of the Tasmanian Gold Mine in 1904.

One of these buildings has been restored and houses the Grubb Shaft Museum with a fascinating display of local memorabilia including mining, orcharding and farming equipment. It's open Tuesday to Saturday from 10 am to 4 pm. You can also visit a restored miner's hut and the original Flowery Gully School.

There is a camping ground at Beauty Point, four km downstream from Beaconsfield. This picturesque little town was originally established to service the local gold-miners and is now the home of the Australian Maritime College.

At the mouth of the Tamar River the holiday and fishing resorts of Green's Beach and Kelso have good beaches and caravan and camping grounds.

LOW HEAD

There is also plenty to see in the East Tamar district on the other side of the river. The pilot station at Low Head on the north coast is one of the oldest in Australia. The original lighthouse overlooking the mouth of the Tamar was built in the 1830s and the present structure dates from 1888. The pilot station was restored by the Port of Launceston Authority and now houses a maritime museum. East Beach, on Bass Strait, is good for surfing and the quieter Lagoon Bay on the river is safe for swimming.

GEORGE TOWN (population 5600)

George Town, site of the original though accidental landing by Colonel Paterson in 1804 (his ship *HMS Buffalo* ran aground during a storm), was first settled in 1811 and is now a commercial and residential town for the Bell Bay industrial area. The old Watch House, built in 1843, has been restored as a folk museum and is open daily from 11 am to 3 pm.

The Grove, formerly the port officer's residence, has been classified by the National Trust and is open from 10 am to 5.30 pm. In this fine Georgian home on the corner of Elizabeth and Cimitiere Sts, the staff dress in period costumes; refreshments and lunches are available and handcrafts are on sale. Also of interest is the St Mary Magdalen Anglican Church in Anne St and the cemetery on the northern outskirts of town which has interesting headstones dating from 1833.

Places to Stay

There is a caravan and camping ground and the *George Town Hotel* (tel 82 1219) has bed & breakfast singles for $15.

BELL BAY

The Bell Bay area 'features' Tasmania's first thermal power plant, Comalco's aluminium smelter, TEMPCO's manganese steel furnaces, the Mobil Oil depot, freezer stores for meat and vegetables, and a little further south at Long Reach, the APPM and Forest Resources woodchip plants.

HILLWOOD

Keep heading south to the attractive rural area of Hillwood where you can pick your own strawberries and buy other berries and apples in season. Hillwood is also noted for its fishing and river views.

WINDERMERE

If you're into quaint old churches in picture-postcard settings then drop into Windermere where St Matthius Church sits above the river and lays claim to being the oldest church in Australia with a continuous history of regular usage since its foundation. It was built in 1842 by Dr Matthius Gaunt who, incidentally, won first prize at the Great London Exhibition of 1851 for his flour, produced in Windermere.

UNDERWOOD

In about 1940 the Alexander Patent Racquet Company planted more than 100,000 English ash trees near Underwood for the production of tennis racquets. Unfortunately – for them at least – the demand had diminished considerably before the trees had time to reach maturity. So now the magnificent stands of ash trees are now part of the 70 hectare Hollybank Reserve.

The Hollybank Apiary nearby is a commercial beekeeping enterprise where visitors can watch the bees going about their business in glass hives. Bee-type products like honey and honeymead are available for purchase.

LILYDALE

The small town of Lilydale, 27 km from Launceston, stands at the foot of 1187-metre Mt Arthur and is a convenient base for bushwalkers heading to the mountain and along a variety of other tracks and scenic trails in the area. Three km from the town the Lilydale Falls Reserve has two picturesque waterfalls and camping facilities.

North Central

Behind the northern coastal strip the Great Western Tiers rise up into Tasmania's central mountains and the Cradle Mountain National Park. There are some interesting and scenic spots in this area. The Bass Highway continues west from Launceston to Deloraine and the start of the north-west route.

WESTBURY (population 1200)

Westbury, 18 km west of Hadspen, is another classified historic town. The village green is believed to be the only such green in the southern hemisphere and is still used for fetes. Colonial furnishings are a feature of the White House built in the 1840s. Its outhouses display vintage vehicles, 'fashions of the day', and a collection of 19th century toys. St Andrew's Church features some superb examples of the work of Mrs Nellie Payne, one of Tasmania's most famous woodcarvers.

For accommodation try the *Westbury Hotel* (tel 931151) where bed & breakfast is $15/28 a single/double.

The beautiful St Mary's Church is the focal point of the little township of Hagley, five km from Westbury. The foundation stone was laid in 1861 by Sir Richard Dry, Australia's first knight who, in 1866, became Tasmania's first native-born Premier.

DELORAINE (population 1930)

This picturesque town, surrounded by lush countryside, has been the centre of an important agricultural district, noted for its oats since the 1840s. The Deloraine flour mills were established in 1859 and by 1870 there were 12,500 hectares under cultivation.

Many of the town's Georgian and Victorian buildings have been restored, some for commercial purposes and others as historic show pieces. The Bowerbank Mill Gallery, two km east of town, carries the National Trust's highest rating. Built in 1853, the old corn mill ceased production in 1929 and was re-opened in 1973 as an art and craft gallery.

Other places of interest include the Folk Museum and Cider Bar, the Deloraine Antiques and Old Sewing Box Museum, St Mark's Church of England, Bonney's Inn – which serves lunches and Devonshire teas – and a wildlife park. At Lemana Junction, seven km from the town on the Mole Creek Rd, there's a small smokehouse where eels, trout, abalone and scallops are smoked or processed.

There are also a number of waterfalls in the Deloraine area including Montana, Meander and Liffey Falls. (The latter is described in the Around Launceston section.)

Places to Stay

The Deloraine *Youth Hostel* (tel 62 2996) is in a spacious house at 8 Blake St. It offers a superb view of the Great Western Tiers and is open all day. There are bicycles for hire, snacks available and a bed costs $4.50. The hostel is closed during July, August and September. Deloraine also has a caravan park and camping area.

MOLE CREEK (population 300)

Limestone caverns, leatherwood honey and a wildlife park are the main attractions of the Mole Creek area west of Deloraine.

Marakoopa Cave, 11 km from the township of Mole Creek in the foothills of Western Bluff, consists of a large complex of caverns, two underground streams, gypsum formations and glow-worms. About 16 km from the town is King Solomon Cave, a more spacious, dry cavern with many passageways.

Mole Creek is a centre for the production of Tasmania's famous leatherwood honey which is produced by bees from the blossoms of the leatherwood tree.

Two km beyond Chudleigh, on the way to Mole Creek, is the Tasmanian Wildlife

Park with a noctarium for viewing nocturnal animals. There are a surprising number of animals found only in Tasmania and this park has one of the best collections anywhere.

PARRAMATTA CREEK

If you leave the main Bass Highway at Elizabeth Town (north of Deloraine) and head for Railton you'll find an extra-ordinary tea-house just off the road at Parramatta Creek. Built by a local guy who had 'money to spare', the Conservatory Teahouse looks like it's been transplanted from an English country estate. The high arched windows on all sides look out on the bushland, there are plants and classical music inside and nothing on the Devonshire tea and light lunch menu costs over $2.50.

SHEFFIELD (population 950)

Dominated by the impressive Mt Roland (1234 metres), the scenery around Sheffield in the Mersey Valley is absolutely superb. Set in the foothills of the Great Western Tiers, the town is surrounded by peaceful farmlands, virgin forests, quiet streams, rugged mountain gorges and rivers brimming with fish. Nearby Lake Barrington, formed by the Devil's Gate Dam which is part of the Mersey-Forth hydro-power scheme, is a major rowing venue and state recreation reserve. Apples are still an important crop in the Mersey Valley and mushrooms are also grown.

Places to Stay

Sheffield has a large comfortable *Youth Hostel* (91 1577) at 14 Main St which costs $4. There is also a caravan park and camping ground.

Devonport

Population: 23,000

The city of Devonport straddles the mouth of the Mersey River almost in the centre of Tasmania's north coast. Nestled behind the dramatic lighthouse-topped Mersey Bluff, it is the terminus for the vehicular ferry from Melbourne and a base for exploring the extraordinary north-west coast.

Bluff Lighthouse was built in 1889 to direct the colony's rapidly growing sea traffic and its light can be seen up to 27 km out to sea. A year later as the area became a vital port, the towns of Torquay and Formby joined to become Devonport.

Nearby Spreyton, where Tasmania's apple growing industry had its beginnings in 1898, is still one of the state's main orcharding districts. Devonport is the focal point for one of Australia's richest and most beautiful farming areas and has been exporting local products, including apples, vegetables, berries and fine wool, for nearly 100 years.

Devonport doesn't have a great deal of interest in its own right except for a couple of museums and the Aboriginal cultural centre but there's enough to occupy a bit of time either on arrival in Tasmania or prior to departure.

Information

If you're after info on bushwalking, canoeing, trout fishing, swimming, skiing, sailing, skin diving, mountaineering or cave exploring the place to go is the Devonport Showcase at 5 Best St. It has a complete range of tourist information, places of interest, activities, brochures, maps, accommodation and scenic routes in the Devonport area and across the north-west. There's also displays and workshop demonstrations of arts and crafts and a coffee shop. It's open every day from 9 am to 5.30 pm (tel 24 0520).

The Tasmanian Government Tourist Bureau (tel 24 1526) has its office at 18 Rooke St on the corner of King St and there is also an office at the ferry terminal in East Devonport. There's a Wilderness Info Centre in the Hub Arcade off Rooke St Mall. You'll find a laundrette at 157 Rooke St (the Victoria Parade end).

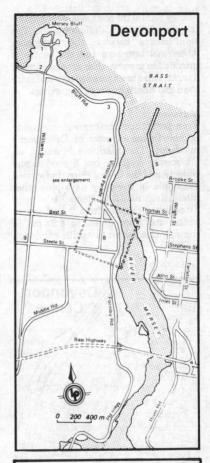

Devonport

1 Tiagarra
2 Bluff Caravan Park
3 Maritime Museum & Wheel House
4 Youth Hostel
5 Terminal Caravan Park
6 Ferry
7 Bass Strait Ferry Terminal
8 City Centre
9 To Don River Tramway

Tiagarra

The Tasmanian Aboriginal Cultural & Art Centre, known as Tiagarra, is on

Mersey Bluff at the north side of Devonport. It's open daily and admission is 80c. The word means 'keep' in the Tasmanian Aboriginal language and the centre is intended to preserve their art and culture. Tiagarra also has a rare collection of more than 250 Aboriginal rock engravings.

Museums

Transport of one form or another seems to be the theme of most of Devonport's museums. The Maritime Museum, on Gloucester Avenue, has a good model collection of the sailing ships that visited Tasmania in the early days plus other interesting nautical items. It's open Tuesday to Sunday from 2 to 4 pm in winter and from 10 am to 4.30 pm in summer (December to April); admission is 60c.

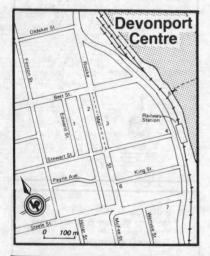

Devonport Centre

1 Tasmanian Redline Coaches
2 Ansett
3 TAA
4 Post Office
5 Ferry to East Devonport
6 Tourist Bureau
7 RAC

The Wheel House, on Victoria Parade, has a variety of early pedal-powered creations and its cycle collection is said to be the best in the southern hemisphere. It's open Tuesday to Sunday from 10 am to 4.30 pm and entry is $1.

Bramich's Early Motoring & Folk Museum takes you back to the nostalgic age of 'genteel motoring'. It's at 3 Don Rd and is open by appointment.

The Don River Railway, out of town on the Bass Highway to Ulverstone, has Tasmania's only full-sized passenger railway still in operation. Vintage steam locomotives haul carriages on a 30-minute trip along the banks of the picturesque Don River. During summer the train runs every day, except Saturday, between 10 am and 4 pm but in winter it only operates on Sundays and public holidays. At Don Village the Van Diemen Light Railway Society has a collection of restored locomotives, rolling stock and steam driven machines.

Other Attractions

The Devonport Gallery & Arts Centre at 43 Stewart St is open Tuesday to Friday from 10 am to 4.30 pm and Sundays from 2 to 4.30 pm. There's another art gallery at 46 Steele St.

Home Hill, once the home of Joseph Lyons and Dame Enid Lyons and built by them in 1916, is now owned by the City of Devonport and administered by the National Trust. Joseph Lyons was Premier of Tasmania from 1923 to 1928 before entering Federal Parliament in 1929 and serving as Prime Minister from 1932 to 1939. He is the only Tasmanian to have been Prime Minister and the only Australian to have been both the Premier of his state and leader of the Commonwealth. In 1943 Dame Enid Lyons became the first woman member of the House of Representatives and in 1949 was sworn-in as the first woman Federal Minister of the Crown. Home Hill, 77 Middle Rd, is only open to the public on the first Sunday of each month from 2 to 4 pm.

Places to Stay

Hostels The Devonport *Youth Hostel* (tel 24 7197) is in a wonderful old two-storey mansion at 26 Victoria Parade. It costs $5.50, is 50 metres from the Mersey River and 1½ km from the nearest surf beach. The hostel is closed during July and August.

Hotels & Guest Houses *Cara* (tel 24 4364) is a pleasant little guest-house at 22 Victoria Parade, before the youth hostel if you're coming from town. Singles/doubles are $12/20 with continental breakfast.

At *Limani Tourist Lodge* (tel 24 4928), 57 Percy St, it's $30 a double for bed & breakfast. At 44 MacFie St the *Trade-winds Private Hotel* (tel 24 1719) is $15 a single then $5 for each extra person, bed & breakfast. The *Tamahere* (tel 24 1898) at 34 Best St costs $14 single, $6 for each extra person, room only. At the *River View Lodge* (tel 24 7357) bed & breakfast costs $18/28 for singles/doubles.

Motels & Holiday Flats The *Sports Centre Lodge* (tel 24 4109) at 34 Forbes St costs $14 for one, $8 for each extra person. *Shoreline Holiday Units* (tel 27 8185) at 3 Rooke St costs $20 for two and only $1 for each extra person. *Edgewater Motor Inn* (tel 27 8441) is at 2 Thomas St, East Devonport, three km from the centre. Singles are $22 to $25, doubles $26 to $29.

Camping The *Mersey Bluff Caravan Park* (tel 24 2193) is out at the Bluff by Tiagarra and camping costs $3 for two. At the *Terminal Caravan Park* (tel 27 8794) in Terminal Park Rd, East Devonport, the cost is the same. The Terminal park also has on-site vans for $19 a double, $2.50 for each extra person.

Devonport Caravan Park (tel 27 8886) on Caroline St, East Devonport costs $3.50 for two to camp, $20 for an on-site van for two and $2 for each extra person. *Shoreline Caravan Park* (tel 27 8185) at 3 Brooke St, East Devonport also costs $3.50 for two to camp and has on-site vans at $20 for two and $1 for each extra person.

Places to Eat

Apart from counter meals in the pubs there's really just a few coffee lounges and take-aways. *Napoli* in the Mall is a café-style place which serves morning and afternoon teas and lunch dishes for around $5 but it closes at 4.30 pm. The *Coffee Shoppe*, in the Devonport Showcase, is open every day and even serves muffins and porridge for breakfast on Sundays.

The *Tamahere* at 34 Best St, the *Elimatta* at 12 Victoria Parade and the *Formby* at 82 Formby Rd all have counter meals for around $5.

Slightly up-market with meals in the $9 to $12 bracket, there's the *Mochador* at 12 Rooke St, the *Monterey Restaurant* at 117 Rooke St, the *Mandarin Inn* at 156 William St, the *Sunrise* at 140 Fenton St and the ever-present *Taco Bill* in Kempling St.

Entertainment

The *Tamahere* at 34 Best St has a disco from Thursday to Saturday from 8.30 pm. The usual Tasmanian no-denims rules apply. *Joo's Disco* at the Elimatta at 12 Victoria Parade runs on Wednesday, Friday and Saturday. *City Limits* is a nightclub on King St.

Getting There

Air Between Ansett, East-West Airlines and Air New South Wales there are about half a dozen flights a day between Melbourne and Devonport for $104.80 one-way. Ansett's Apex return fare from Melbourne is $138.80 and standby costs $84. From Sydney it costs $196 for one-way and $256.60 return with Ansett; or $160 one-way with East West or Air NSW.

Airlines of Tasmania operate between Devonport and the following places: Hobart $64.50; Launceston $30.50; Wynyard $32.50; and King Island $66.50.

Ferry See the introductory Tasmania Getting There section for full details on the ferry service between Melbourne and Devonport. From Devonport the ferry departs at 6 pm on Tuesdays, Thursdays and Sundays, arriving at Station Pier, Melbourne the following day at 8.30 am. If you have a car it must be there between 4 and 5 pm. If you're on foot embarkation is between 4.30 and 5.45 pm although the terminal is open earlier if you have nothing else to do.

Bus Tasmanian Redline Coaches have four services a day to Launceston and the fare is $7.60; the fare to Hobart is $19. There is no public transport to the caves around Mole Creek. Staffords Coaches (tel 24 3628) provide a charter service to Cradle Valley $20; Lake St Clair $35; Walls of Jerusalem $20; Frenchmans Cap and the walking tracks from the Franklin, Jane and Collingwood rivers for $40.

Getting Around

Morse's Motors run a local bus service but it's so limited you might as well forget it. The buses run from the corner of Rooke and Stewart Sts to East Devonport, North Devonport via Mersey Bluff and to West Devonport. Fortunately most places are within walking distance anyway; it's a pleasant stroll along the waterfront to most of Devonport's attractions.

There's a ferry across the Mersey (remember the song?) which operates Monday to Thursday from 7.15 am to 6.15 pm and on Fridays from 7.15 am to 10 pm. The one-way fare is 40 cents for adults, 25 cents for kids.

The major car rental firms all have offices in Devonport. You can hire bicycles from Hire-a-Bike (tel 24 3889) – 10-speeds are $8 a day or $30 per week, tandems are $16 a day or $50 per week, plus a $10 deposit.

AROUND DEVONPORT

From Braddon's Lookout, near Forth, seven km from Devonport, you have a fine view along the coast. The coastal resorts of Turners Beach and Leith are also west of the city. Turners Beach has two caravan parks and camping areas and there's good mullet and salmon fishing in the Forth River.

On the Rubicon River estuary just 19 km east of Devonport, is Port Sorell, a popular seaside resort with a wildlife reserve, picturesque Squeaking Point and the wide sands of Hawley Beach. Port Sorell is actually the oldest settlement on the north-west coast. In its early days it was visited by sealers and fishermen and before Devonport became more important as a port, it was doing a thriving trade in wattle bark. There's a caravan park and camping ground at Port Sorell and the *Moomba Holiday Park Cabins* (tel 28 6140), in Kermode St, cost $20 a double and $2 for each extra person.

Only a few km south of Devonport, at Latrobe, there is a scenic pathway and extensive picnic area which follows the winding Mersey River along Bell's Parade. In the 1870s, when Latrobe was the terminus for trains during the construction of the north-western railway, Bell's Parade was lined with warehouses handling goods from the railway and cargo from the small ketches and barges which came up the Mersey inlet. These days the town is famous for the annual Latrobe Wheel Race, held each Christmas, which is one of Australia's biggest cycling carnivals.

The North-West

Tasmania's magnificent north-west coast is a land as rich in history as it is diverse in scenery. Its story goes back 37,000 years to a time when marsupial rhinoceroses and giant kangaroos and wombats roamed the area. Aboriginal tribes once took shelter in the caves along the coast leaving a legacy of rock engravings and middens.

Europeans also quickly realised the

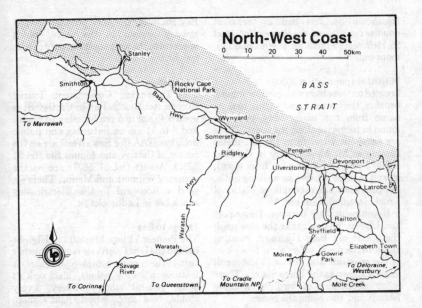

North-West Coast

potential of the region. As settlers moved further and further west building towns along the coast and inland on the many rivers, the area soon became a vital part of the young colony's developing economy. Goods exported in the early days included timber, limestone, wool, potatoes, chaff and thousands of tons of grey peas (the latter went to England for pigeon feed), and the many river and sea ports simply bristled with activity.

These days the north-west is a delightful melange of thriving towns and beach resorts served by deepwater harbours, with beautiful rivers, patchwork fields and pastoral plains rolling inland towards impressive mountain ranges.

ULVERSTONE (population 9500)

Ulverstone, at the mouth of the Leven River, is the business centre for a rich agricultural district that stretches almost 50 km from the coast south to the mountains. Ulverstone's major industry is International Canners, Australia's largest frozen vegetable processor. The fine beaches in the area make it a popular holiday resort and a good base for exploring the surrounding countryside.

You can make an interesting round trip (105 km) from Ulverstone out through Sprent, Castra and Nietta to Leven Canyon near Black Bluff (1339 metres) and back via Preston, Gunns Plains and North Motton. Leven Canyon is a spectacular gorge with a number of walking tracks, one of which leads to a lookout over the canyon – not for the faint-hearted! There's also a lower cliff walk to the Jean Brook waterfall. At Gunns Plains you can take a 30-minute tour of the limestone caves which are open daily between 10 am and 4 pm.

Places to Stay

Ulverstone has camping areas and the two caravan parks, one in Water St and the other in Queen St, have on-site vans for $18 a double.

The *Beachway Motel* (tel 25 2342) in

Heathcote St, has bed & breakfast doubles for $30, and the *Stones Hotel* (tel 25 1197 costs $12/22 for singles/doubles, room-only.

PENGUIN (population 2620)

Located on three bays with good swimming beaches, the township of Penguin took its name from the many fairy penguins found in rookeries along the coast. There are excellent views from the 471-metre summit of Mt Montgomery in the Dial Range State Forest (five km from town), as well as some interesting walking trails. Penguin also has a couple of National Trust classified churches.

If you're driving between Devonport and Ulverstone don't take the new road; the scenic old Bass Highway, running closer to the coast, offers some fine views of the coastline and across to the small islands known as the Three Sisters. There is an abundance of birdlife on these islands and also along the coast.

BURNIE (population 20,400)

Paper production is the main industry of Burnie, which makes the drive into Tasmania's third largest city a trifle unpleasant on a windy day. However, its setting on the shores of Emu Bay surrounded by green hills and backed by rich farming land, and its importance as an international deepwater port means it has a little more to offer than the average large industrial town.

Burnie was named after a director of the Van Diemen's Land Company, William Burnie, in 1828 and started life quietly until the discovery of tin at Waratah's Mt Bischoff. These days much of the output from several west coast mining centres is shipped out through Burnie as well as timber, dairy and paper products and vegetables. Port facilities have also improved considerably since the 1870s when visitors were brought close to shore in rowboats, then climbed into a basket and were hauled aloft by a crane.

Burnie is the headquarters of the Emu Bay Railway, the only privately owned railway system in the state, which operates to the west coast but only carries freight.

Information

The Tasmanian Government Tourist Bureau (tel 30 2224) at 48 Cattley St is open 8.45 am to 5 pm Monday to Friday and 9 to 11 am on Saturday and public holidays. TAA (for East-West) are on the corner of Cattley and Mount Sts (tel 31 6222). Ansett (tel 31 5677) are on the corner of Wilmott and Mount. There's a good noticeboard in the Electric Jug snack bar in Ladbrooke St.

Things to See

The Pioneer Village Museum in High St behind the Law Courts recreates Burnie's turn of the century commercial centre. It features a coffee palace, blacksmith's shop, general store, printery, livery stable, boot shop, wheelwright's shop, dental surgery and of course an inn. It's open Monday to Friday from 10 am to 5 pm and on weekends from 1.30 to 5 pm, admission is $1.50.

Burnie Park incorporates an animal sanctuary with wallabies, ducks, peacocks and Burnie's original 'settlers' – emus. It also features Burnie Inn, the town's oldest building, which was restored and moved to the park from its original site and is open during the summer.

Osbourne House, the Burnie Art Gallery and the Civic Centre, in Wilmot St are worth a visit.

Railway enthusiasts should visit the 'Loco Bar' in the Burnie Town House, in Wilson St, which features early Emu Bay Railway history.

It is possible to see cheese being made at the Lactos Pty Ltd factory and make a tour of the Associated Pulp & Paper Manufacturers Ltd factory.

There are waterfalls and viewpoints in the Burnie area including Roundhill Lookout and Fern Glade, three km from town and Guide Falls 16 km out.

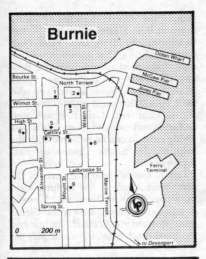

Burnie

1. Tourist Bureau
2. Webster Travel
3. Ansett
4. TAA (East West agents)
5. Tourist Bureau
6. Pioneer Village Museum
7. Circular Head Motor Services
8. Post Office
9. Tasmanian Redline Coaches

Places to Stay

There is no youth hostel in Burnie, the nearest one being 19 km away in Wynyard.

The *Bay View Hotel* (tel 31 2711), 15 Marine Terrace, has bed & breakfast for $15 per person, the *Club Hotel* (tel 31 2244) at 14 Mount St costs $13 for room-only and the *Regent* (tel 31 1933) at 26 North Terrace has singles for $15 and breakfast for an additional $3.

Three km west on the Bass Highway at Cooee there's a *Treasure Island* campsite where camping costs $5 for two. They have on-site vans for $22 a double, self-contained flats for $29 a double and both cost $3 for each extra adult.

Places to Eat

Burnie is short of places to eat – especially on Sundays when the town is very quiet. The *Rivoli* at 54 Cattley St (opposite Circular Head Motors) is open every day till quite late and does take-aways and sit-down grill meals for around $5 to $6. The *Regent Hotel*, 25 North Terrace, has counter meals and the *Beach Hotel* on the corner of North Terrace and Wilson St does counter lunches and teas from Monday to Saturday (noon to 1.30 pm and 6 to 8.30 pm).

Above Fitzgerald's there's *Napoli* with café-style meals for around $5 but it closes at 4.30 pm. The *Electric Jug* at 25 Ladbrooke St is a good snack bar; there's a Chinese restaurant at 28 Ladbrooke St and the *Steakhouse* at 104 Wilson St.

Entertainment

There's a disco from Thursday to Saturday at the *Top of the Town* at 195 Mount St, and the *Menai* on the corner of Menai and Edwards Sts has bands.

Getting There

Air Ansett and East-West Airlines fly to Wynyard, about 20 km from Burnie, several times a day from Melbourne. Some flights go via Burnie, some direct. The direct flight time is just over an hour by F27 and the cost is $104.80 one-way, $138.80 Apex return or $84 standby. From Sydney with Ansett it costs $196/257 one-way/return. Phillip Island Air Service have flights to Wynyard for $75.

Airlines of Tasmania operate between Wynyard and the following places: Hobart $64.50; Devonport $32.50; Launceston $61.50; and King Island $61.50.

Western Aviation (tel 42 3838) offer scenic flights over the rugged south-west, the Franklin River and Cradle Mountain.

Bus Tasmanian Redline Coaches operate services to Launceston for $10.60, to Hobart for $22 and Queenstown for $17.30. Their office is at 177 Wilson St. Circular Head Motor Services run out to Wynyard, Stanley and Smithton. There are infrequent services to Penguin,

Wynyard, Ulverstone and other places nearby plus more frequent services to Somerset.

Rail The Emu Bay railway service only takes passengers if it is not carrying explosives; it is also sometimes used for special holiday runs. It runs about twice a week, leaving around 12.30 pm on the way to Roseberry and returning about 4.30 pm, getting in to Burnie between 8 and 9 pm. There's no time to look around Roseberry (unless you want to stay for three or four days!) so it's really just a train enthusiast's trip. The trip back is mostly in the dark and the lights flicker too much for reading! Still, travellers have reported managing to ride part of the way in the driver's cab. Phone 31 2822 for information on the train; round-trip fare is about $10.

Getting Around

Local buses are run by MTT and, as in Launceston, you can get an unlimited-travel, all-day ticket. There are no bus services in the evenings or on weekends.

WYNYARD (population 4600)

Sheltered by the incredible Table Cape and unique Fossil Bluff, the township of Wynyard is built along the seafront and the banks of the Inglis river. Flying into Wynyard on one of the regular flights from the mainland is perhaps the best way to appreciate the incredible beauty of the patchwork farmlands that extend west along the coast from Table Cape to Stanley.

At Fossil Bluff, the oldest marsupial fossil found in Australia was unearthed and the soft sandstone of the area has many fossils of shells deposited when the level of Bass Strait was much higher. The Bluff is beyond the Wynyard Golf Course and the scenery alone is worth the seven-km trip. Table Cape has a lighthouse and spectacular, unforgettable views along the coast.

Attractions in the immediate area include the superb stretches of sandy beach at Boat Harbour Bay and Sisters Beach, nearby Detention Falls (just south of Myalla), the excellent walking area of the Rocky Cape National Park and the forests of Hellyer and other inland gorges. There is also splendid trout, fly and sea fishing in the Flowerdale, Inglis, Cam and Calder Rivers and estuaries and some of Tasmania's best diving grounds can be explored with the help of the Scuba Centre in East Wynyard.

One of the two major airports of the north-west is only a few minutes walk from the centre of Wynyard. Western Aviation (tel 42 3838) offer scenic flights from Wynyard over Cradle Mountain and the north-west coast for about $25 per person.

You can get tourist information from the Council Chambers in Saunders St, the Golden Fleece service stations on the Bass Highway in Wynyard and Somerset and the Seaway Motel at Boat Harbour Beach.

Places to Stay

The Wynyard *Youth Hostel* (tel 42 2013) at 36 Dodgin St is one block south of the main shopping centre and costs $5 a night. *Rod Walkers Leisure Ville* (tel 42 2291) has cabins for $25 a double and on-site vans for $22 a double – $3 for each extra person and there are a couple of hotels and a camping area.

AROUND WYNYARD
Boat Harbour Beach

Fourteen km west of Wynyard the sheltered township of Boat Harbour is noted for its white sand, rock and coral formations and crystal clear water.

Places to Stay & Eat There is a camping area and the caravan park (tel 45 1253) has on-site vans for $20 a double, cabins for $15 and flats for $22 a double.

Brownies is a restaurant and take-away specialising in seafood.

Sisters Beach

At nearby Sisters Beach, in a valley within the Rocky Cape National Park, you can enjoy a five-km expanse of glistening white sand, safe swimming and good fishing. There are more than 60 species of birds in the area and you may be lucky enough to see a rare sight – the eyrie of the sea eagle. Well-marked nature trails reveal an amazing variety of unique coastal flora. There's a 10-hectare Birdland Nature Park open Monday to Saturday from 10 am and Sundays from 2 pm.

The area of the Rocky Cape National Park was a favourite hunting ground of the Tasmanian Aborigines and evidence of their occupation has been found in a number of caves and middens.

Port Latta/Dip Falls

The largest bulk ore carriers to visit Tasmanian waters dock at the offshore loading facilities of this man-made port between Rocky Cape and Stanley. Port Latta is at the northern end of an 85-km pipeline that carries crushed iron ore in slurry form from the mines at Savage River to the enormous jetty and out to the waiting Japanese vessels. There are tours of the Port Latta plant every Friday at 2 pm. Children under 12 are not admitted and flat shoes and trousers must be worn.

The popular scenic and picnic area of Dip Falls, near Mawbanna, is reached via a turn-off from the Bass Highway at Black River. It's five km from Port Latta and an easy drive from Stanley or Smithton.

STANLEY (population 700)

Trading ships and whalers have been calling at this idyllic little town since the Van Diemen's Land Company established its headquarters here in 1826. Nestled at the foot of Circular Head – the extraordinary rock formation known commonly as The Nut – Stanley is the oldest town on the north-west coast and has changed little since its early days.

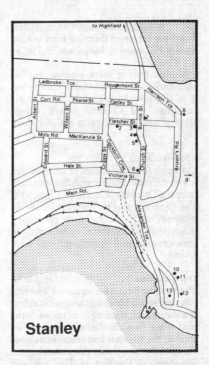

Stanley

1 The Rectory (1842)
2 St James Presbyterian Church (1855)
3 St Paul's Church of England (1880)
4 Stanley Discovery Centre
5 Plough Inn (1842)
6 Union Hotel (1849)
7 Commercial Hotel (1842)
8 Old Stanley Cemetery
9 To the Nut
10 Bay View Hotel (1849)
11 PM J A Lyon's birthplace
12 Poet's Cottage
13 Customs House
14 Old Wharf

The Van Diemen's Land Company, formed in London, was granted a charter in 1825 to settle and cultivate the Circular Head region to rear well-bred sheep with fine wool. The area boomed when large quantities of mutton, beef and potatoes were shipped to the Victorian gold-fields and its prosperity continued when settlers discovered the rich dairying land behind Sisters Hills and a 'Mountain of Tin' at Mt Bischoff.

Modern fishing boats, seeking crayfish and sharks, still operate from Stanley but it is the spectacular seascape, historic buildings and Cornish fishing village atmosphere that attracts visitors these days.

Information

Stanley has many places of interest and it's worth picking up a walking-tour map from the Discovery Centre on Church St. The Centre is also an amusing little folk museum with marine and pioneering relics, shell and mineral collections, old photographs and paintings by local artists.

Things to See

The striking basalt formation of The Nut can be seen for many km around Stanley. A walking trail starting from opposite the post office rises the 120 metres from sea level to the plateau and offers expansive views of the coastline. The charming old cemetery, at the foot of The Nut and overlooking the sea, has many interesting historical headstones, including those indicating the last resting place of the noted surveyor and explorer Henry Hellyer, and architect John Lee Archer. As cemeteries go, this wouldn't be a bad place to end up!

The Plough Inn, built in 1840, has been fully restored and is lived in by the present owners, who have furnished it with period furniture. It's in Church St, is open daily for inspection and features a cider bar and craft shop.

There's a particularly fine old bluestone building near the wharf which served as a grain store. Built in 1843, the stones were brought to Stanley as ballast in ships. Another seafront building – the VDL store – was designed by Tasmania's famous colonial architect John Lee Archer who was then a magistrate in

Stanley. His home, which is now a private residence, is known as Poet's Cottage.

The Union Hotel in Church St is now the only licensed hotel in Stanley. The original bluestone school is more than 100 years old and is owned by the National Trust. The Presbyterian Church, which is probably the first prefabricated building in Australia, was bought in England, transported and re-erected in Stanley in 1853 for the all-inclusive cost of £800. Lyons Cottage was the birthplace of former Australian Prime Minister Joseph Lyons; and Highfield, just out of the town centre, was the original headquarters of the Van Diemen's Land Company. Highfield was built in 1835 and is being restored by the National Parks & Wildlife Service.

Places to Stay

The *Union Hotel* (tel 58 1161) has bed & breakfast doubles for $26. At *Stanley Caravan Park* it costs $5 a double to camp, or $17.50 a double in an on-site van.

Places to Eat

The *Plough Inn* serves ploughman's lunches and Devonshire teas; the *Union Hotel* has counter lunches; and *Gull Cottage* overlooking Godfreys Beach also serves lunches and afternoon teas.

Warning: Don't arrive in Stanley on an empty stomach after dusk (especially in winter) or you may have to wait till breakfast to get a meal!

SMITHTON (population 3400)

The town of Smithton, which extends along the Duck River and onto the higher ground of Tier Hill, is the administrative centre of Circular Head and serves the agricultural and forestry areas of the far north-west.

Early settlers were quick to discover the value of the rich alluvial flats of the Duck River and the town soon overshadowed Stanley in economic importance. Smithton's economic growth began in the early 1900s with the building of the Duck River Butter Factory and several large sawmills and was assisted by the strength of its beef, dairy, vegetable and fishing industries. Although Stanley maintained its importance as the major port in the region, owing to the tidal limitations of Duck Bay the municipal government of Circular Head was transferred to Smithton in the 1920s.

These days the town is the centre of one of Tasmania's greatest forestry areas and has the largest hardwood sawmill in Australia. Dolomite, for agricultural use and some manufacture, is mined just one km from town. The district supplies more than 50% of the state's milk and dairy products; produces about 30,000 tonnes of vegetables a year (most of which are frozen at the General Jones plant); and the Duck River oyster beds have an annual yield of about 300,000 dozen. Fishing is also a multi-million dollar industry at Circular Head and there are processing plants at both Smithton and Stanley.

There's good fishing, swimming and boating in the river and Duck Bay, and Smithton is an excellent base for exploring the surrounding countryside.

Woolnorth, a 22,000-hectare property on the very north-western tip of Tasmania, is the only remaining holding of the Van Diemen's Land Company. Fully-escorted day coach tours of this historic property and magnificent coastline operate from Smithton or Burnie. For more info ring (004) 52 1252 or book through the Tourist Bureau.

Massive manferns, myrtles, fungi and lichen are features of the Milkshakes Forest Reserve, 45 km south of Smithton. A little further west of the reserve, set in beautiful virgin rainforest, is tranquil Lake Chisholm.

Places to Stay & Eat

Although the *Bridge Hotel* (tel 52 1398) is the only accommodation in Smithton, it is warm and friendly and has a relatively inexpensive bistro. There are adjoining motel units (at motel prices) but a bed & breakfast double in the hotel itself costs $28 a double with bathroom and TV; a single is $19; or a basic single (room-only) is $12.

Barb's Kitchen at 54 Emmett St has delicious cheap lunches (around $4.50) and great coffee.

Getting There

Air Airlines of Tasmania fly between Smithton and Melbourne ($82), Hobart ($82), Queenstown ($52) and Strahan ($52).

Bus With Coastliner Express it costs $33.40 to Hobart and $19 to Launceston.

MARRAWAH

Marrawah, the most western town in Tasmania, is at the end of the Bass Highway where the wild Southern Ocean occasionally throws up the remains of ships wrecked on the rugged coast. To the north much of the area along the Welcome and Montagu Rivers is swampy while to the south the rich dairying lands of Marrawah give way to plains of coastal heath which extend almost unbroken to the Pieman River.

This part of the coast was once a favourite home of the Tasmanian Aboriginals and particular areas have been proclaimed as reserves to protect the environment and remaining relics which include rock carvings, middens and hut depressions. The main Aboriginal sites are at Mt Cameron West, near Green Point, at West Point and Sundown Point.

Marrawah is a good base for trips into the Lands Department-designated Arthur Pieman protected area. The proposed region comprises the Crown Lands of the coastal area between Marrawah and the Pieman River, and the hinterland of plains, swamps, hills and mountain ranges inland to the Frankland, Leigh and Donaldson Rivers.

The whole area is ideal for fishing, camping and bushwalking or just for getting away from it all. Attractions include magnificent ocean beaches, the beautiful Arthur River (14 km south of Marrawah), waterfalls on the Nelson River, Rebecca Lagoon, Temma Harbour, the old mining town of Balfour, the Pieman River and the Norfolk Ranges.

Marrawah has a hotel which provides accommodation and meals and a general store for petrol and supplies. Camping is permitted in the Crown Land areas but except for a few selected sites where amenities are provided, camping conditions are basic.

Some roads are suitable only for four-wheel drive vehicles, others are off-limits to all vehicles and permits are needed in some areas. Before setting out it is best to contact the National Parks & Wildlife Service Ranger or the Crown Lands Warden in Smithton.

SOUTH TO QUEENSTOWN

From Somerset on the north coast (between Burnie and Wynyard), to the historic mining town of Queenstown, 170 km to the south, the Waratah/Murchison Highway passes through some pretty impressive scenery.

Hellyer Gorge is a serene myrtle forest reserve on the banks of the Hellyer River 40 km from the coast. Further south in this mountainous and heavily timbered region is the old mining town of Waratah. This sleepy little place (eight km from the main highway) had its beginnings in 1871 when James 'Philosopher' Smith discovered the richest tin-mine ever found in the world.

The Mt Bischoff mine was operated for 50 years yielding thousands of tonnes of tin and the entire top of the mountain being removed before it was finally closed.

The town has public caravan and camping facilities and there is also the *Waratah Hotel* where you can get a bed & breakfast.

Savage River (population 1400)

More than a century ago prospectors pushed their way through the bush and up the banks of the Savage River sluicing for gold. Iron ore was found at the time but it wasn't until the 1960s that an economical method of extracting the ore was devised. The township of Savage River was built to house the workers of this international mining project which involves Australian, American and Japanese companies. The ore is extracted and crushed, then mixed with water to form a slurry and pumped down an 85 km pipeline to Port Latta. There are tours of the mine at 9 am and 2 pm every Tuesday and Thursday.

Corrina (population 2)

This almost-ghost-town, 28 km south-west of Savage River, was once a thriving gold-mining settlement. These days it's the scenery and a popular cruise on the Pieman River that attracts the visitors. The launch *Arcadia II* makes a regular four-hour trip from Corrina to Pieman Heads through forests of eucalypts, ferns and Huon pine. Bookings should be made in advance at a Tasbureau office or the Savage River Motor Inn.

Roseberry (population 2700)

Mining began in Roseberry in 1900 with the completion of the Emu Bay Railway between Burnie and Zeehan but with the closure of the Zeehan lead smelters in 1913, operations here also shut down. The Electrolytic Zinc Company then bought the mine and with new mining processes it was re-opened in 1936 and has operated successfully ever since. There's a spectacular series of aerial buckets which transport ore down the mountainside from Williamsford, seven km away. Roseberry is 55 km from Queenstown in the Pieman River Valley at the base of Mt Murchison.

The *Roseberry* and *Kirkpatrick* hotels have accomodation and there's a caravan park.

The West Coast

Nature at its most awe-inspiring is the attraction of Tasmania's rugged and magnificent west coast. Formidable mountains, lonely valleys, unique buttongrass plains, deep ancient rivers, tranquil lakes, dense rainforests and a treacherous coastline – such is the compelling beauty of this incomparable area.

Were it not for its vast mineral and timber wealth, the region would probably still be uninhabited. In fact until the completion of the road from Hobart to Queenstown in 1932 the only way into the area was through the port of Strahan and even then the difficulty of access into Macquarie Harbour meant that only small boats could use it. The sparse population of the west coast today is a strong reminder of the pioneering spirit that tried to tame and exploit this inhospitable and often impenetrable land.

However, centuries before the white man arrived to extract the minerals and harvest the Huon pine, the west and south-west was home to Aboriginal tribes who lived in harmony with the harsh climate and rugged terrain. Australia's richest archaeological material has been found just above the Franklin River in an area abandoned by its original inhabitants some 20,000 years ago.

European settlement of the region has been turbulent, brutal, courageous, profitable and heartbreaking. The west coast has seen explorers, convicts, soldiers, loggers, prospectors, railway gangs, road builders, fishermen, settlers, outdoor adventurers, environmentalists and blockaders.

It has seen the flooding of Lake Pedder and the creation of a huge system of lakes on the upper reaches of the Pieman River to establish massive hydro-electric schemes and it is home to the Franklin River Australia's most controversial river

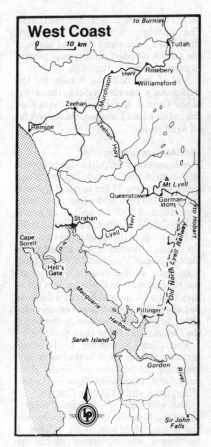

and scene of the greatest environmental debate in the nation's history.

The surviving mining towns such as Zeehan and Queenstown still thrive on their rich mineral resources and tourism is booming in the historic coastal town of Strahan where thousands of people come to experience the incredible natural beauty of the Gordon River.

While the environmentalists and big business continue to battle over the issues of wilderness versus electricity and world heritage area versus wood chip, nature herself has begun to reclaim what is hers. The rusting relics, disused railways, abandoned mines and deserted towns of the early west coast mining days remain as mere spectres in the bush.

And if just half the battles for the wilderness are as successful as the saving of the Gordon and Franklin rivers then the untamed wild west should survive for all to enjoy.

ZEEHAN (population 2000)

The discovery of rich silver-lead deposits in Zeehan in 1882 changed the face of this quiet little town 38 km north of Queenstown. By the turn of the century it had a population of 5000 (it peaked at nearly 10,000), its 26 hotels did a roaring trade and the stage of the Gaiety Theatre, then the largest in Australia, was graced by the likes of Nellie Melba and Caruso. More than eight million pounds worth of ore was produced at the Zeehan mines before they began to fail and the town declined just after 1908. Zeehan is now experiencing a revival however with the re-opening of the Renison Tin Mine at Renison Bell.

There are a number of buildings remaining from those early boom days including the once-famous Grand Hotel (now flats), the Gaiety Theatre, the post office, bank and St Luke's Church.

The excellent West Coast Pioneers' Memorial Museum is housed in what was the School of Mines, built in 1894. It features a working model of the Mt Bischoff Mill at Waratah, a mine diorama of underground workings, one of the best mineral collections in the world, and displays of Tasmanian birds, animals and Aboriginal artefacts. Outside there's an exhibit of steam locomotives and carriages used on the early west coast railways.

Rough roads leads to Trial Harbour, 23 km away on the coast, and Dundas, a mining town which has now all but disappeared. The road south-west from Zeehan has been upgraded for the 47 km to Strahan.

Places to Stay

The *Cecil Hotel* (tel 71 6221) in Main St has bed & breakfast doubles for $30 and the *Crocoite Caravan Park* in Hurst St has on-site vans for $18 a double.

QUEENSTOWN (population 4300)

The view during the final winding descent into Queenstown is dramatic, strangely beautiful and totally unforgettable. There is no escaping the fact that this is a mining town and that the destruction of the surrounding hills is a direct result of the region's major industry but it is nevertheless a stunning sight. Queenstown sits, almost defiantly, in a valley surrounded by deep eroded gullies and naked, multi-coloured hills.

It was the discovery of alluvial gold in the Queen River valley in 1881 that first brought prospectors to the area. Two years later mining began on the rich Mt Lyell deposits around an outcrop known as the Iron Blow. For nearly a decade miners toiled on the Mt Lyell ore, extracting a few ounces of gold a day and ignoring the millions of pounds of copper in it. Finally in 1891 the Mt Lyell Mining Company transported 100 tons of ore to Strahan for smelting and copper became the most profitable mineral on the west coast. American metallurgist Robert Sticht produced the first copper on-site at his smelter in 1896 and later became manager of the Mt Lyell Mining Company.

The first major link with the outside world was the company's Queenstown to Strahan railway built in 1899 to transport copper and passengers to the coast. It covered 35 km of spectacular terrain, required 48 bridges and some sections were so steep that the rack and pinion system had to be used to assist the two steam engines hauling the train.

The North Lyell Copper Company, which had set up in opposition to the Mt Lyell mine, built a second railway line from Linda via Crotty to Pillinger, also on Macquarie Harbour. However after the failure of the furnaces at Crotty the company merged with Mt Lyell and the tracks were pulled up.

At the turn of the century Queenstown, with a population of 5051, was the third largest town in Tasmania. It had 14 hotels, there were 28 mining companies working the Mt Lyell deposits, and 11 furnaces involved in the smelting process. The Mt Lyell Mining & Railway Company eventually acquired most of those mines or leases and since 1933 it has worked the area without a rival.

Within 20 years of the start of mining, the area around Queenstown, which had been thick rainforest, was denuded of vegetation. In that short space of time hundreds of timber cutters managed to cut down some three million tons of timber to feed the furnaces. By 1900 uncontrolled pollution from the copper smelters had killed all the vegetation that had not already been cut down. Because of the sulphur impregnated soils and dead stumps, bush fires raged through the hills every summer till there was no regrowth left at all and then the area's heavy rainfall (the highest in the state) completed the total destruction of the surrounding hills. With no growth to hold the original soil it was simply washed into the Queen River.

Information

The Tasmanian Government Tourist Bureau office (tel 71 1099) is at 39-41 Orr St. You can also get information from the local hotels and there's a guide map in Driffield St near Orr St.

Things to See

The Galley Museum, on the corner of Sticht and Driffield Sts, began life as the Imperial Hotel and was the first brick hotel in Queenstown. It has since served as a hospital (during the 1919 flu epidemic), a guest-house, and single men's quarters for the Mt Lyell Company. The museum features an excellent photographic history of Queenstown and the west coast as well

as mining equipment, personal effects and household goods from the early days. Have a chat with Eric Thomas who runs the place – he's a wonderful character who was born in Waratah and worked underground in the Mt Lyell mine for six years; admission is $1.50.

There are guided tours of the Mt Lyell Mine and the new Mining Museum on weekdays at 9.15 am and 4.30 pm, and weekends and public holidays at 9.15 am and 4 pm. The tours leave from Farmer's Store in Driffield St and cost $2.50 for adults and $1 for kids. Apart from the millions of tons of copper being mined, the present-day mining operations also produce significant quantities of gold, silver and pyrite.

The Miner's Siding in Driffield St is a public park area which features a restored ABT steam locomotive and a display detailing the history of the Queenstown to Strahan railway.

Even though the tracks have been torn up, if you have a trail-bike or four-wheel drive vehicle you can take a trip down part of the old Linda to Pillinger line, built by the North Lyell Company, to the magnificent railway bridge that crosses the fast-flowing King River.

The Western Arts & Crafts Centre in Orr St opposite the Tasbureau has local wood crafts, pottery, paintings and leatherwood honey. It's open daily.

Places to Stay

Hunter's Hotel in Orr St has bed & breakfast singles/doubles for $16/26 or room-only for $12/20. The *Pine Lodge* (tel 71 1852) is a small guest-house at 1 Gaffney St with bed & breakfast singles for $16 to $20 and doubles for $26 to $30. The more expensive rooms have attached shower and toilet.

The *Empire Hotel* (tel 71 1699) at 2 Orr St has a good coffee lounge and costs $20 a single and $5 for each extra adult – room-only. On Driffield St the *Commercial Hotel* (tel 71 1511) is $22/34 a single/double for bed & breakfast.

There are camping sites with modern facilities in the *Mountain View Caravan Park* in Grafton St. The park also has bunkhouse accommodation for $5 a person and on-site vans for $20 a double.

Places to Eat
Deidre's Coffee Shoppe in Orr St has delicious cakes and light snacks for about $3 and light lunches for around $5.

Getting There
Airlines of Tasmania fly to Queenstown from Melbourne ($115), Hobart ($62), Smithton ($52) and Launceston ($50).

By road Queenstown is 254 km north-west of Hobart and 175 km south-west of Burnie. Redline Coaches operate through Queenstown to Hobart ($20), Burnie ($17.30) and Strahan ($3.20) from Monday to Saturday. The Queenstown depot of Tasmanian Redline Coaches (tel 71 1011) is on Orr St.

Hitching into Queenstown along the Lyell Highway from Hobart is quite easy as there's a fair bit of traffic. The Waratah/Murchison Highway from the north coast may be a little harder though. Remember that it gets pretty cold here in winter and snowfalls along these two highways are not uncommon.

FRENCHMAN'S CAP
The reserve at Frenchman's Cap, south-east of Queenstown, is now part of the Wild Rivers National Park. The Lyell Highway passes close to the northern section of the pass and there are a number of walks in the immediate area. You can take a short trip from the highway to Donaghy's Hill for a view of the magnificent white quartzite dome of Frenchman's Cap and the Franklin River or spend a few days walking right into the Cap and Irenabyss over buttongrass fields and through rainforests.

STRAHAN (population 400)
Strahan today may be but a shadow of its former glory but the town and its harbour are rich in the history of its convict, logging and mining days.

Forty km from Queenstown on Macquarie Harbour, Strahan is the only town actually on the rugged and treacherous west coast. Rough seas, the lack of natural harbours and the high rainfall discouraged any early ideas of settling the region until Macquarie Harbour was discovered by explorers searching for the source of the Huon pine that frequently washed up on the southern beaches. The harbour's main disadvantage was its narrow entrance – the formidable sand-bar and rushing tides of Hell's Gates allowed access to only shallow-draught boats.

In 1821, in order to isolate the worst of the colony's convicts and use their muscle to harvest the huge stands of Huon pine, a penal settlement was established on Sarah Island. This barbaric institution in Macquarie Harbour became the most notorious place of punishment in Australia's history. The convicts worked up-river 12 hours a day, often in leg irons, felling the pines and rafting them back to the island's sawpits where they were used to build ships and furniture.

Punishment for the slightest infringements of settlement law was brutal and sadistic. A total of 33,723 lashes was inflicted on an average of 167 prisoners a year from 1822-26. The most dreaded punishment was confinement on tiny Grummet Island, where up to 40 convicts at a time were held in appalling conditions on what was little more than a windswept rock – for some, death was a welcome release. There were many escape attempts during the 12 year history of the prison but once off Sarah Island there was really nowhere to go. Of the 112 convicts who made a bid for freedom 15 were recaptured and executed for further crimes while at large, 68 perished in the bush and six were murdered and eaten by their desperate comrades. Sarah Island, which was abandoned in 1834 following the establish-ment of the 'escape proof' penal settlement at Port Arthur, is the setting for Marcus Clark's graphic novel of convict life *For the Term Of His Natural Life*.

As the port for Queenstown, Strahan reached its peak of prosperity with the west coast mining boom and the completion of the Mt Lyell Company's railway line in the 1890s. At the turn of the century it was a bustling centre with a population of more than 2000. Steamers operated regularly between Strahan and Hobart, Launceston and Melbourne carrying copper, gold, silver, lead, timber and passengers. The closure of many of the west coast mines and the opening of the Emu Bay railway from Zeehan to Burnie, led to the decline of Strahan as a port. These days it's a charming seaside village making a living from fishing and tourism.

The imposing post office and Union Steam Ship Company building, probably the finest buildings on the west coast, hint at the town's former importance and the lighthouse on Cape Sorell on the south head of the harbour is the third largest in Tasmania. There's an interesting little museum by the caravan park. Strahan's botanical gardens are worth visiting and its just a short walk to the delightful Hogarth Falls. Six km from the town is the impressive 40-km-long Ocean Beach where huge seas crash onto enormous sand dunes.

Strahan also has another unique, if rather odd, attraction: it is home to Tasmania's own self-styled eccentric aristocrat – Prince John, the Duke of Avram, who lives in historic Ormiston mansion, deals in his own currency and runs the 'Royal Bank of Avram'.

Places to Stay & Eat

There's an associate *Youth Hostel* (tel 71 7255), in Harvey St which costs $5 a night. There are camping grounds at Ocean Beach and Macquarie Beach and two caravan parks.

The owners of *Happy Hamer's Hotel* (71 7191), opposite the wharf, have every

reason to be happy – they charge $20 per person for breakfast and a bed in a shoebox! Their counter meals are quite good though.

Getting There

Airlines of Tasmania fly into Strahan from Hobart ($62), Launceston ($50) and Smithton ($52). The bus from Queenstown to Strahan costs $3.20.

Gordon River Cruises

The Gordon River rises in Lake Richmond, high in the King William Range, and crosses the unique buttongrass plains known as the Vale of Rasseleas before it turns westward. It then plunges through rugged mountains and sheer splits to the magnificent calm of its lower reaches, finally making its way to the ocean through Macquarie Harbour.

If you don't have time to explore the spectacular gorges, white water rapids, waterfalls, quiet reaches, rainforests and rugged mountains of the Franklin and Gordon Rivers from your own canoe or raft, then one of the excellent cruises that operate out of Strahan is the best way to appreciate the indescribable beauty of the Gordon River.

Three modern, comfortable launches make day or half-day trips up the Lower Gordon River, taking in Marble Cliffs, St John Falls and Warners Landing – site of the 11-week blockade to save the river. The boats return across Macquarie Harbour via Sarah Island and Hell's Gates.

The *Gordon Explorer* and *James Kelly II* half-day tours cost $18 for adults, $9 for kids and leave at 9 am and 1.30 pm. The Denison Star day tour (9am to 3.45) includes lunch and costs $20 for adults, $10 for kids.

SOUTH-WEST NATIONAL PARK

There are few places left in the world as isolated and untouched as Tasmania's south-west wilderness. The unique grandeur and extraordinary diversity of this ancient land is home to some of the

Earth's last tracts of virgin temperate rainforest. It is the habitat of the endemic Huon pine, which lives for more than 3000 years; and the swamp gum, the world's tallest hardwood and flowering plant. About 300 species of lichens, mosses and ferns (some rare and endangered), festoon the dense rainforest; superb glacial tarns decorate the jagged mountains and in summer the delicate alpine meadows are ablaze with wildflowers and flowering shrubs. And through it all, wild rivers race through rapids and deep gorges by caves, and countless waterfalls and cliffs.

Each year more and more people are venturing into the heart of this incredible part of Tasmania's World Heritage area, seeking the peace, isolation and challenge of a region as old as the last ice-age and unspoilt by human development.

The traditional walk in the South-West National Park is between Cox Bight or Port Davey and Cockle Creek near Recherche Bay and takes about 10 days but should only be tackled by experienced, well-prepared hikers. Light planes are used to airlift bushwalkers into the south-west (and for scenic flights) and there is vehicle access to Cockle Creek. There is also a variety of escorted wilderness treks that offer flying, hiking, rafting, canoeing, mountaineering, caving and camping. More information can be obtained from Tasbureau or the Wilderness Society.

At the edge of the wilderness lies Lake Pedder, once the crown jewel of the region, but now part of the Gordon River Power Development which generates more than 1400 million units of electricity a year. Lake Pedder was flooded in the early 1970s to help feed the giant underground power station at the Gordon Dam. Together with nearby Lake Gordon it covers over 500 square km and contains 27 times the volume of water in Sydney Harbour. It is the largest inland freshwater storage in Australia – man-made by the Hydro-Electric Commission.

The HEC township of Strathgordon is the base for visiting Lake Pedder and the Gordon Dam and power station. There is a walking track between Port Davey on the south-west coast and Scott's Peak Dam at the southern edge of Lake Pedder. You can also make day or overnight walks off the Scott's Peak road to Mt Eliza or Mt Anne.

Vehicle access to Strathgordon is along the 85-km Gordon Road from Maydena, reached via the Derwent Valley.

Places to Stay

Strathgordon has camping and caravan facilities and the Lake Pedder Motor Inn (tel 801166) has doubles for $24, room only.

Cradle Mountain-Lake St Clair

The best-known feature of Tasmania's superb central highland lake country is the 126,205 hectare Cradle Mountain-Lake St Clair National Park. It is one of the most glaciated areas in Australia and includes Tasmania's highest mountain, Mt Ossa (1617 metres). The rugged mountain peaks, tarns, lakes, streams, alpine moorlands, and the reserve's incredible variety of flora and fauna extend from the Great Western Tiers in the north to the Lyell Highway at Derwent Bridge in the south.

The spectacular 85-km overland trail between Cradle Mountain, which dominates the northern end of the park, and beautiful Lake St Clair, Australia's deepest natural freshwater lake, is not only one of the finest bushwalks in the country but is world famous. The walk takes five or six days at an easy pace but there is so much to see and do along the way that it's a great temptation to spend more time here. The only limitation is the amount of supplies that can be carried from the start of the trek.

Despite its magnificence and easy

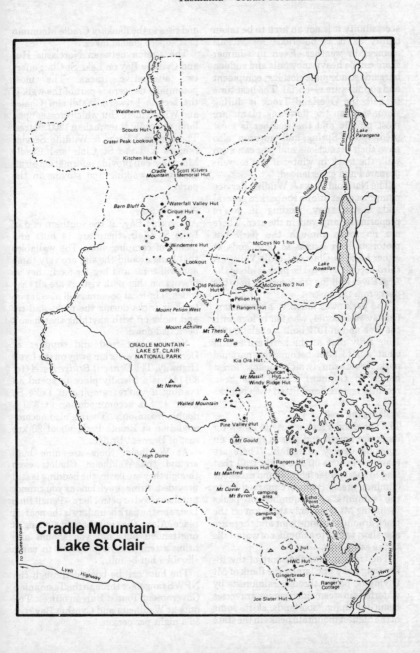

Cradle Mountain — Lake St Clair

Cell Mountain Road

Lake Parangana

Forest Road

Waldheim Chalet

Scouts Hut

Crater Peak Lookout

Kitchen Hut

Cradle Mountain

Scott Kilvers Memorial Hut

Barn Bluff

Waterfall Valley Hut

Cirque Hut

Mersey Road

Maggs Road

Arm Road

Patons Road

Windermere Hut

Lookout

McCoys No 1 hut

Innes Track

Lake Rowallan

camping area

Old Pelion Hut

McCoys No 2 hut

Pelion Hut

Rangers Hut

Mount Pelion West

Mount Achilles

Mt Thetis

Mt Ossa

CRADLE MOUNTAIN – LAKE ST. CLAIR NATIONAL PARK

Kia Ora Hut

Mt Nereus

Mt Massif

Duncan Hut

Windy Ridge Hut

Walled Mountain

Overland Track

Pine Valley Hut

Mt Gould

High Dome

Narcissus Hut

Rangers Hut

Mt Manfred

Mt Cuvier

Mt Byron

camping area

Echo Point Hut

camping area

Lake St Clair

hut

HWC Hut

Gingerbread Hut

Ranger's Cottage

Joe Slater Hut

to Queenstown

Lyell Highway

Lyell Hwy

to Hobart

accessibility it is not an area to be taken lightly as it is notorious for vicious changes in weather. Even in summer there can be heavy snowfalls and sudden blizzards so adequate clothing, equipment and supplies are essential. The best time to walk the Overland Track is during summer when the flowering plants are most prolific and the weather is *most* predictable. Spring and autumn also have their attractions and you can even walk the track in winter if you're well-prepared and experienced.

The National Parks & Wildlife Service pamphlet gives info on the park in general and is necessary reading if you're preparing for any walk in the area. There are no roads through the park but motorists have access to both ends at either Lake St Clair or Cradle Valley. A third access route to the park is along the Arm River walking track coming in to the park from the east.

The park owes much to an Austrian, Gustav Weindorfer, who fell in love with the area and in 1912 built a chalet out of King Billy pine at the northern end of what was to later become the national park. Waldheim (which means 'forest home' in German) Chalet has been recently restored and fitted with bunks.

Walking the Trail

The Overland Track is easy to follow for its entire length and passes through an amazing variety of terrain. There are many diversions off the main trail that lead to spectacular features and excellent climbing areas. Paths are marked up to the summits of a number of peaks including Mt Ossa, only three km off the track around the mid-point and there are also short tracks to a number of waterfalls in the same area.

The track follows the shore of the 18-km-long Lake St Clair by the flank of Mt Olympus, passes through rainforests by waterfalls in steep-sided gorges, traverses beautiful alpine moorlands, skirts some of the highest mountain peaks in the state

and rises to the flanks of Cradle Mountain past superb glacial lakes.

The stretch between Narcissus Hut and Cynthia Bay on Lake St Clair offers two alternative tracks. The most potentially dangerous part of the walk is the section between Waldheim Chalet and Windermere Hut which crosses open land, generally at more than 1200 metres. The National Parks & Wildlife Service rangers at Lake St Clair and Cradle Mountain can provide information on all aspects of walking and staying in the park.

Places to Stay

At Cynthia Bay, at the southern end of Lake St Clair, there are 14 huts and plenty of camping sites. The wallabies that hang around the site are very tame and will come and beg for food; they've discovered that park visitors are an easy touch. The local possums will also get up to their tricks during the night and try and make off with anything that hasn't been tied down.

You can get food and supplies at Derwent Bridge, six km away on the Lyell Highway. The *Derwent Bridge Hotel* (tel 891144) is a friendly place to spend an evening if you're camping at Lake St Clair. It has accommodation at $30 a double, room-only. There's also accommodation at Bronte Park, about 20 km east of Derwent Bridge.

At Waldheim there are nine huts around the Waldheim Chalet; even though they are basic, the bedding is still provided. Bring provisions as you cannot purchase food or petrol here – Pencil Pine Lodge on the park boundary is the nearest place. Along the trail there is a string of unattended huts but you should also bring a tent and be prepared to camp should a hut be full.

The huts can be booked through the NPWS rangers or through the Tasmanian Government Tourist Bureau offices. The huts at Waldheim and Cynthia Bay cost $6 a night per person.

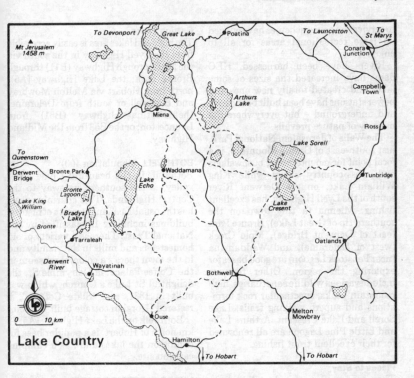

Lake Country

Getting There

Lake St Clair is six km from Derwent Bridge which is on the Lyell Highway 178 km from Hobart and 83 km from Queenstown. Cradle Valley is 95 km from Devonport via Sheffield and Gowrie Park. The final 30 km to Waldheim Chalet is over a narrow gravel road which ends at Dove Lake.

For Cynthia Bay any bus travelling between Hobart and Queenstown goes by Derwent Bridge. It costs $13.60 to travel to Cynthia Bay from Hobart and $6 from Queenstown.

Stafford Coaches (tel 004 24 3628) provide transport to Waldheim Chalet from Devonport ($20) and Launceston ($32), and to Lake St Clair for $35 from Devonport and $40 from Launceston.

Lake Country

The highland lake country of Tasmania's central plateau is a region of breathtaking scenery, fine trout fishing and ambitious hydro-electric schemes. There are steep mountains, hundreds upon hundreds of glacial lakes, crystal clear streams, waterfalls and an amazing variety of flora and fauna.

Until the development of the central highlands for hydro-electric power production, the region was the sole domain of hardy bushwalkers and adventurers and even now it remains one of the most sparsely populated of Tasmania's settled areas. However, the access roads that have been constructed to service the power schemes have opened up large recreational areas for all to enjoy.

Rivers have been harnessed, HEC dams have increased the sizes of some lakes and created totally new ones and power stations have been built both above and underground – but everywhere the majesty of nature prevails.

The Walls of Jerusalem National Park, just south-east of Cradle Mountain, is a focal point for mountaineers, bushwalkers and cross-country skiers while King William Lake, on the Derwent River south of the Lyell Highway, has excellent fishing. Mienna (a tiny town on the southern tip of Great Lake), Bronte Park (east of Derwent Bridge), Mole Creek (west of Deloraine), and Waddamana (near Penstock Lagoon) are good bases for exploring the region. Other features include various wildlife sanctuaries, high mountain peaks, spectacular rock formations and superb walking trails. Lake Sorell and Lake Crescent, Arthurs Lake and Little Pine Lagoon are all renowned for their excellent trout fishing.

Places to Stay

There are camping grounds at Tarraleah, Bronte Park, Arthur's Lake and Lake Sorell. At the *Bronte Park Highland Village* rooms in the hostel are $6 per person and in the chalet $12.

The *Great Lake Hotel* (tel 596179) at Hadden's Bay near Mienna costs $25 a single, room-only.

In Poatina the HEC's *Poatina Chalet* (tel 003 978245) has bed & breakfast singles/doubles for $21/32.

There's a caravan park in Tarraleah and the *Chalet* there, which has to be booked through Hobart (tel 002 305678), has bed & breakfast singles/doubles for $19/30.

There is dormitory-style accommodation in Waddamana through the Division of Recreation (tel 002 303745). The *Lachlan Hotel* (tel 87 1215) in Ouse has room-only singles/doubles for $15/24

Getting There

The highland lakes area is easily accessible from the Lyell Highway in the south via the Marlborough Highway (B11) through Bronte Park; the Lake Highway (A5), north from Hobart via Melton Mowbray and Bothwell or south from Deloraine; the Poatina Highway (B51) from Launceston; or the B53 from the Midland Highway.

BOTHWELL (population 400)

Bothwell, in the beautiful Clyde River valley, is the southern gateway to the Central Highlands. This charming town has the usual Tasmanian quota of historic buildings including 18 classified by the National Trust. There is a variety of old homesteads and mills in the vicinity and in the town there's a colonial museum in the 'Coffee Palace' in Dalrymple St, the delightful St Luke's Church, which was built in 1831, and 'Slate Cottage', a restored Georgian cottage built in 1835.

Bothwell, on the Lake Highway (A5) 72 km north of Hobart, is a popular base for fishing on the lakes and has a camping caravan site.

HYDRO-ELECTRIC POWER

Tasmania has the largest hydro-electric power system in Australia – it's larger than the far more well-known Snowy Mountain scheme in NSW and generates about 10% of Australia's total electricity output. Dam building for the hydro power stations is, however, a subject of considerable controversy due to the great potential these dams have to harm the environment. The flooding of Lake Pedder in the mid-70s raised the first public outcry against uncontrolled damming of Tasmania's magnificent rivers.

The first hydro-electric dam was constructed on Great Lake in 1911 and subsequently the Derwent, Mersey, Forth and Gordon Rivers were also dammed and work is proceeding on the Pieman River Scheme on the west coast. The dams, power stations, pipelines and canals of this enormous power network have involved amazing feats of engineering mostly in rugged country.

Visitors can inspect the power schemes and visit the Tungatinah, Tarraleah and Liapootah power stations along the extensive Derwent scheme between Hobart and Queenstown. The Derwent River rises in Lake St Clair and all but the final 44 km of its journey to the sea at Hobart is used to produce power. The northern schemes on the Mersey and Forth Rivers are smaller than the Derwent system but are much more spectacular as they lie in a short length of very steep river valley.

Although the conservationists won the battle over the proposed damming of the Franklin and Lower Gordon Rivers there are still on-going disputes over other projects; the majority of Tasmanians are opposed to the construction of these dams, so if you can, try to support the Tasmanian Wilderness Society in their brave fight against the powers of big business.

Bass Strait Islands

Tasmania has two islands which guard the eastern and western entrances to Bass Strait. Once the temporary and sometimes notorious home of sealers, sailors and prospectors and a refuge from the treacherous waters of the Strait, King and Flinders Islands are now retreats of unspoiled beauty, rich in bird and marine life. Though their early history of white contact is marred by bloody and tragic periods, it is the isolation and natural beauty of these islands which attracts visitors today. They're rough and rugged places; great if you really want to get away from it all and both of them have excellent fishing, bushwalking and scuba diving opportunities.

KING ISLAND

At the western end of Bass Strait this

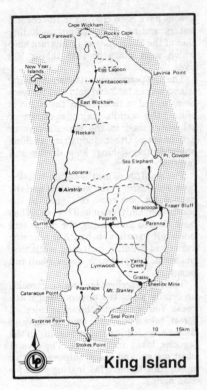

King Island

rugged island is 64 km across at its widest point and has over 145 km of unspoilt coastline with beautiful beaches and quiet lagoons.

Named after Governor King of New South Wales, the island was discovered in 1798 and in the early days of the century gained a worldwide reputation as a home and breeding ground for huge colonies of sea elephants and seals – which were then, of course, hunted almost to the point of extinction. The violent 'Straitsmen' – sealers and sailors with a reputation similar to the pirates of the Spanish Main – decimated vast populations of seals for their valuable skins and oil.

The stormy seas of Bass Strait claimed many ships over the years and at least 57 wrecks have been charted in the coastal waters around King Island, including that of the *Cataraque*, an immigrant ship which went down in 1845 taking 399 lives.

The first permanent settlement of King Island was in 1855 and gold and tin were being mined in 1905. Today the island is one of the world's major producers of scheelite, used in the manufacture of armaments. Other industries include abalone, cray-fishing, kelp drying and farming.

The main towns are the administration centre of Currie on the west coast and the deep-water port town of Grassy in the south-east. Only about half the island has been cleared for farming, the rest is still undisturbed native bush with an amazing variety of wildlife including wallabies, pheasant, rare platypus, ducks, quail and penguins.

There are excellent bushwalking tracks, especially along the unpopulated north coast. You can wander through a calcified forest, take a pony ride over rolling sand dunes or go fishing and swimming in the lagoons, lakes and beaches. The crystal clear waters and many shipwrecks also make King Island a fascinating place for skin diving.

Places to Stay

There is a *Youth Hostel* (tel 62 1294) in Clare Cottage on Charles St, Currie. Advance booking is essential and it costs $4 per night.

Naracoopa Lodge (tel 62 1124), a guest-house in Naracoopa on the east coast, costs $5 a night, room-only.

Also in Currie: *Daisy Flats* (tel 004 62 1563) on South Rd have bed & breakfast doubles for $30; the *Naracoopa Holiday Units* (tel 61 132 on Beach Rd cost $30 for two and $5 for each extra person; and the *Boomerang Motel* (tel 62 1288) costs $42 a double, room-only.

On-site vans in the *Bass Caravan Park* cost $20 a double and $3 for each extra person. The best way to see the island is to just take a tent and spend a week walking around the coast.

Getting There

You can fly to King Island from Melbourne with Kendell Airlines (tel (004) 62 1322) for $76 or $61 standby. Airlines of Tasmania service King Island from Hobart ($118), Devonport ($66.50), Launceston ($78) and Wynyard ($61.50).

Getting Around

You can rent cars from King Island Auto Rentals (tel 62 1272) in Currie from about $25 a day; from Bourke's Car Rentals (tel 62 1297) in Currie from $35 a day; or Avis (tel 62 1297) for $39 and up per day.

Some King Island roads are two-wheel ruts of deep sand and either four-wheel drive or lots of digging gear is recommended. The roads to Seal Rocks and Martha Lavinia Lake are bad.

FLINDERS ISLAND

Flinders is the largest of the Furneaux Group of islands which cover an area of 1968 square km off the north-east tip of Tasmania. The 50 islands in the group feature an incredible variety of scenery and wildlife.

The area was charted by the young navigator Matthew Flinders who first visited the islands as part of an expedition sent from Sydney in 1797 to rescue the survivor of the *Sydney Cove*, wrecked on tiny Preservation Island.

Like King Island, the Furneaux Group was used intermittently by sealers until the first permanent settlement in the 1830s. The early sealers were a notoriously cruel and rough lot, thinking nothing of leaving helpless seal pups to die having slaughtered the mothers. Nor were they able to resist the temptation of a little piracy from time to time, and apparently even lured ships on to the rocks by displaying false lights. It's likely that quite a few of the 120-odd ships wrecked around the Furneaux Group got there with a little outside help.

Map labels:
East Sister Is.
West Sister Island
North Point
Flinders Island
0 5 10km
Palana
Cape Frankland
Mt Killiecrankie
Killiecrankie
Mt Tanner
Leeka
Mt Boyes
Five Mile
FURNEAUX
Lughrata
Babel Is.
Settlement Point
Emita
Wybalenna Ruins
Memana
The Three Patriarchs
Blue Rocks
Blue Rocks Point
Mt Leventhorpe
Whitemark
Lackrana
GROUP
East Kangaroo Is.
Big Green Is.
Strzelecki Peaks
Loccota
Trousers Point
Lady Barron
Mount Chappell Is.
CHAPPELL ISLANDS
Great Dog Is.
Badger Is.
SOUND
Vansittart Island
Long Is.
FRANKLIN
Cape Barren Island
Mt Munro
Double Peak
Cape Sir John
CAPE BARREN ISLAND
Preservation Is.
ARMSTRONG CHANNEL
CLARKE ISLAND
BANKS
STRAIT

The most tragic saga in the history of Flinders Island was the part it played in the history of the white settler's treatment of the Tasmanian Aboriginals. In 1830 the first permanent settlement of Flinders Island was established with the last of mainland Tasmania's Aboriginals – those who had not been killed when martial law gave soldiers the right to arrest or shoot any Aboriginal found in settled areas. The 135 survivors transported to Flinders Island were to be Christianised and 'civilised' by the Europeans who had all but wiped out this entire race. They were settled at Wybalenna, an Aboriginal word

meaning 'black man's house', but this last-ditch attempt to save the original Tasmanians was doomed to failure. Many died of respiratory diseases, poor food, home sickness and despair. In 1847 the remaining 47 were taken on their last journey to Oyster Cove on the mainland; of these, all but one were dead by 1876.

It was not until 1888 that the island was finally and permanently settled though it remained sparsely populated till well after WW II when its agricultural potential was finally developed. It is the unspoilt scenery and unique wildlife of Flinders Island and others in the Furneaux Group that attracts visitors these days.

You can dive among the many shipwrecks dotted around the islands, a couple of which are clearly visible above water. The *City of Foochow* went down with a load of coal off the east coast in 1877 while the *Farsund* went aground near Vansittart in 1912. You can go walking in the Mt Strzeleki National Park and climb the 800-metre granite peak itself, fish or swim the many beautiful lagoons and secluded beaches, fossick for Killiecrankie 'diamonds' (actually white topaz) in Killiecrankie Bay, wander through wildlife sanctuaries or take a trip to Cape Barren Island to see the unique Cape Barren Geese. And if you're there in spring or summer you can see the amazing mutton birds – or *youla* as the Aboriginals called them. These migratory birds give Flinders its nickname – 'Island of the Moonbirds'.

The inscriptions in the cemetery at Wybalenna, (now known as Settlement Point), tell the tragic story of Tasmania's mainland Aboriginals who couldn't survive white domination long enough to die on their own land. The small settlement's church has been restored by the National Trust. There's a good museum at Emita, near Wybalenna, with items from the sealing and whaling days, the Aboriginal settlement and relics salvaged from shipwrecks.

Whitemark is the main town on the

island and is close to the airport but Lady Barron, in the south, has the deepwater port.

Places to Stay
There are a number of hotels and motels on Flinders Island. At Whitemark, *Bluff House* (tel 59 2084) costs $18.50 per person for bed & breakfast; the *Interstate* (tel 59 2144) is $13 per person for room-only.

The more luxurious *Furneaux* (tel 003 59 3521) at Lady Barron is also rather more expensive at $28/40 room-only for singles/doubles but this does include colour TV and other mod cons.

Greenglades Host Farm (tel 59 8506) in Emita costs $25 per person for full board. The *Flinders Island Cabin Park* (tel 59 2188) in Whitemark has self-contained cabins for $25 a double and $5 for each extra person. You can also find private accommodation on the island and there are many camping sites.

Getting There
Promair fly from Melbourne's Essendon Airport to Flinders Island on Tusedays and Thursdays for $75. You can book through any Tasbureau or Promair agent. Airlines of Tasmania operate services between Flinders Island and Melbourne ($85), Hobart ($90) and Launceston ($49).

Getting Around
Cars can be hired in Whitemark from Flinders Island Transport Services (tel 59

2060) for around $23 a day; Flinders Island Car Hire (tel 59 2188) for $30 a day; Bowman Flinders Island Hire (tel 59 2008) for $15 a day plus 20c a km.

You can hire bicycles from Mike's Rent-a-Bike (tel 59 2159) for $6 a day.

Mutton Birds
Each September the mutton birds (also known as stormy petrels or shearwaters) return to Flinders, King and other Bass Strait islands. They arrive from their northern summer haunts along the Japanese, Siberian and Alaskan coasts to clean out and repair their burrows from the previous year. They then head out to sea again before returning in November for the breeding season which lasts till April.

All the millions of eggs are laid in one three-day period and the parents then take turns, two weeks at a time, to incubate their charge. Once they have hatched their single chick, both parents feed the fluffy little fledgling until mid-April when all the adult birds depart, leaving the young to fend for themselves and hopefully follow their parents north. Unfortunately for the well-fed little mutton birds, they are tasty little creatures and once the adult birds leave the nests the 'birders' or mutton-bird hunters move in for their short season.

The Furneaux Group is also home to the Cape Barren goose. At one time it was feared that it would be hunted to extinction but the completely protected bird is no longer at risk.

Victoria

Area   228,000 square km
Population   4,100,000

Don't miss Melbourne (Australia's second largest city), the mountains of the Victorian Alps, the gold country and the interesting Murray River.

When the founding fathers up in Sydney decided it was time to get a foothold on some other part of the continent they had a go at establishing a settlement on Port Phillip Bay in 1803. Through a combination of bad luck and bad management they soon decided it was a lousy place to live and moved down to Tasmania. So it is not surprising that when Melbourne did become established, a long lasting rivalry with Sydney was to be the order of the day.

It was 1835 when the first permanent European settlement was made in Melbourne although whalers and sealers had used points along the Victorian coast as shelters or harbours for a number of years previously. The earliest settlers, John Batman and John Pascoe Fawkner, came to Melbourne in search of the land they were unable to obtain in Tasmania. Not until 1837, by which time several hundred settlers had moved in, was the town named Melbourne and given an official seal of approval.

The independent spirit naturally led to clashes with the staid powers of Sydney. The settlers were not interested in the convict system for example, and on a number of occasions turned convict ships away. Finally in 1851 the colony of Victoria was formed and separated from New South Wales. At about the same time, gold was discovered and the population doubled in little more than a year. As with a number of other Australian gold rushes, few people made fortunes but many stayed on to establish new settle-

ments and work the land. Some of the most interesting historical areas in Victoria are associated with these gold-rush days.

Melbourne, as Australia's second city, is naturally the state's prime attraction. Although it is not as intrinsically appealing as Sydney, it does lay claim to being the fashion, food and cultural centre of Australia and also the financial focus. Victoria is the most densely populated of the Australian states and also the most industrialised.

Of course Victoria is much more than its capital city. The Great Ocean Road runs south-west towards South Australia and has some of the most spectacular coastal scenery in Australia and evocative reminders of the whaling days in some of the small port towns that actually predate Melbourne. To the south-east of the capital is Phillip Island with its nightly penguin parade. Further south is Wilsons Promontory – the southernmost point on the Australian mainland and also one of the best-loved national parks with excellent scenery and bushwalks. Continuing east towards the NSW border there's more great coast in the Gippsland region.

Victoria's stretch of the Snowy Mountains includes some of the best skiing in Australia and it is much closer to Melbourne than NSW's fields are to Sydney. Skiing on weekends is easy for Melbournians while in summer the mountains are popular for camping, walking and a whole host of outdoor activities. Of course you don't have to go all the way to the Snowies to get into the hills; the ever-popular Dandenongs are less than an hour from the centre of Melbourne while the spectacular Grampians are another popular mountain area further to the west.

Finally there's the Murray River region in the north with historic river towns like Swan Hill and Echuca. Victoria also has its wine growing areas, particularly in the north on the slopes of the Great Dividing Range. And the gold country certainly shouldn't be forgotten; towns like Bendigo and Ballarat still have a strong flavour of those heady gold-rush days and lucky prospectors are still finding gold today.

INFORMATION

The Victorian Tourism Commission operates the following offices around Australia:

ACT
    Jolimont Centre, corner of Northbound Avenue & Rudd St, Canberra, 2601, (tel 47 6355)
NSW
    150 Pitt St, Sydney 2000, (tel 233 5499)
Queensland
    221 Queen St, Brisbane 4000, (tel 221 4300)
South Australia
    16 Grenfell St, Adelaide 5000, (tel 51 4129)
Tasmania
    Corner of Murray & Collins Sts, Hobart 7000, (tel 31 0499)
Western Australia
    16 St Georges Terrace, Perth 6000, (tel 325 1243)

GEOGRAPHY

Victoria's geography is probably more complex than any other Australian state as it includes both the final stretch of the Great Dividing Range and associated outcrops plus a swath of the flatter country to the west. The Great Dividing Range reaches its greatest altitude across the Victoria-NSW border and the Victorian alpine region is a popular area for skiing

in winter and bushwalking in the summer. The mountains run south-west from the NSW border, then bend around to run more directly west as the range crosses north of Melbourne and finally fades out before the South Australian border.

The Victorian coast is particularly varied. On the eastern side is the mountain-backed Gippsland region while to the west is the scenic Great Ocean Road and the spectacular coastline towards South Australia. The north-west of the state, beyond the Great Divide, is flat and often tedious plains; especially dull and dry in the extreme north-west of the state. For most of the length of the border between NSW and Victoria, the mighty Murray River forms the actual boundary.

CLIMATE

Victoria, and Melbourne in particular, has a single major drawback – the bloody climate. Statistically it's not that bad; the average temperature summer or winter is only a few degrees less than Sydney and it's certainly far less humid than Sydney or Brisbane. The annual rainfall is also less than either of those damp cities. The trouble with Melbourne's climate is that it's totally unpredictable; you can boil one day and shiver the next. What the hell am I talking about – it's the next minute, not the next day! In Melbourne if you don't like the weather, so they say, just wait a minute. It's not that Melbourne has four distinct seasons, it's just that they often all come on the same day. You simply can't trust the sun to shine in summer or, for that matter, the winter to be cold; it's totally fickle. The weather is basically somewhat cooler in Melbourne than elsewhere in continental Australia and you'll need at least an overcoat or warm jacket if you are here from April to September.

GETTING AROUND

V-Line has a fairly comprehensive rail network of InterUrban and InterCity services. The rail services are sup-

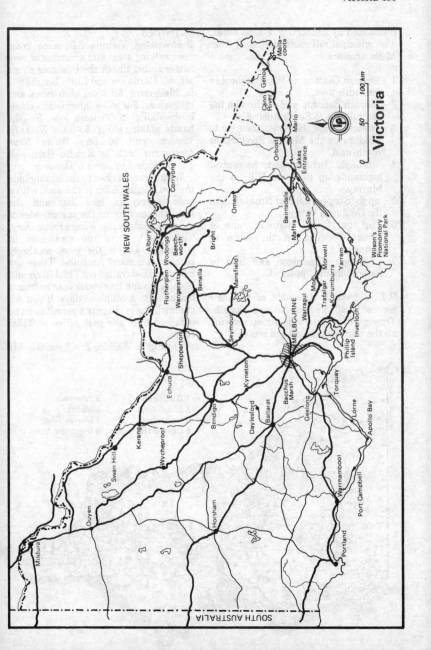

Victoria

0   50   100 km

NEW SOUTH WALES

SOUTH AUSTRALIA

plemented by connecting V-Line buses.
The principal rail routes radiating from
Melbourne are:

1 – through Geelong to Warrnambool in
the south-west.
2 – through Ballarat and on through the
central west to South Australia.
3 – also through Ballarat, then up to
Mildura on the Murray River in the
north-west.
4 – through Bendigo and the central
highlands up to Swan Hill on the
Murray.
5 – up to Shepparton and Numurkah in
the Goulburn Valley.
6 – up the Hume Highway route to
Albury/Wodonga on the route to
Sydney.
7 – through Traralgon and Sale to
Bairnsdale in Gippsland.

V-Line have a timetable of all their
services, available from station bookstalls.
Transport in Victoria is a map showing
all the country bus and rail routes.

ACTIVITIES

Bushwalking Victoria has some great
bushwalking areas and a number of very
active clubs. Check the bushgear shops
around Hardware and Little Bourke Sts
in Melbourne for local club news and
magazines. For more information about
bushwalking in Victoria look for the
handy walking guides *50 Bush Walks in
Victoria* and *50 Day Walks Near
Melbourne* both by Sandra Bardswell
and published by Anne O'Donovan.

Walking areas close to the city include
the You Yangs, 56 km to the west, with a
wide variety of bird life; and the
Dandenongs right on the eastern edge of
the metropolitan area. Wilsons Promontory,
'the Prom', is to the south-east in
Gippsland and is the most southerly
point of mainland Australia. There are
many marked trails from Tidal River and
from Telegraph Bay – walks can be from a
few hours to a couple of days. If you are
overnighting in the park a permit must be
obtained from the park office at Tidal
River.

The Alpine Walking Track starts at Mt

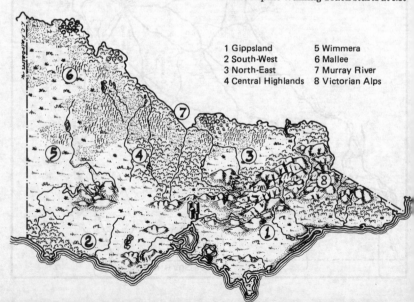

1 Gippsland   5 Wimmera
2 South-West   6 Mallee
3 North-East   7 Murray River
4 Central Highlands   8 Victorian Alps

Erica, 144 km east of Melbourne, and ends at Tom Groggin on the NSW border. This is a very long trail for the experienced walker. There are other popular marked trails in the Bright and Mt Buffalo areas of the Alps.

The Grampians are 256 km west where Victoria's only remaining red roos hang out. Mallacoota Inlet in east Gippsland is equally rugged inland but the coastal walks are easier.

Rock Climbing Again the Hardware St bushgear shops are good info sources. If you just want to scramble around in rather crowded conditions there is Hanging Rock (of Picnic fame) 72 km north-west. Sugarloaf and Jawbones are 112 km out in the Cathedral Range State Park, a popular weekend spot. The Grampians, 256 km from Melbourne, have a variety of climbs as does Mt Arapiles, 334 km (near Natimuk). At Mt Buffalo, 359 km north, the hardest climb is Buffalo Gorge.

Swimming & Surfing Although there is reasonably good swimming on the eastern side of Port Phillip Bay you have to get outside the bay to find surf. Some of the bay beaches close to the city are not too special but as you get further round the bay they get a lot better. Along the Mornington Peninsula you have the choice between sheltered bay beaches on one side and the open ocean beaches, only a short distance away on the other side of the peninsula.

Further out there are excellent beaches at Phillip Island and right along the Gippsland coast. Similarly, on the western side of the state the area from Point Lonsdale to Apollo Bay is particularly popular surfing ground.

Skin Diving Flinders, Portland, Kilcunda, Torquay, Anglesea, Lorne, Apollo Bay, Mallacoota, Portsea, Sorrento and Wilsons Prom are all popular diving areas. There are clubs and equipment renting organisations in Melbourne.

Boats & Sailing At Studley Park in the Melbourne suburb of Kew you can hire a whole selection of row boats, canoes and kayaks by the hour. Good fun although a fair few people seem to find themselves upside down in the muddy Yarra! Canoes can also be rented by Como Park, further down the Yarra towards the city. At Albert Park Lake you can hire row boats and sailing boats. There are many sailing clubs all around the bay in Melbourne and on Albert Park Lake. Elsewhere around the state there are many lakes popular for sailing.

Running & Cycling The four-km jogging track around the Domain park in central Melbourne is one of the most popular running circuits in Australia. Albert Park Lake is also busy. With it's relatively flat terrain Melbourne is very popular with bike riders – quite a few of us at Lonely Planet ride bicycles to work.

It's easy to hire bicycles along the popular Yarra-side bicycle track but not so easy to find them for longer-term hire in Melbourne. The state as a whole is pretty good for biking; it's relatively compact and has many good areas for two-wheeled travelling – such as along the Great Ocean Road.

Melbourne
Population: 2,900,000

Melbourne has always been the poor relation of Sydney; despite their fierce rivalry Melbourne has always come off second best. It goes right back to their founding; Sydney had nearly 50 years head start on its southern sister and even then the foundation of Melbourne was a rather haphazard affair. The first attempt at establishing a settlement on Port Phillip Bay in 1803 was an abject failure and the colonists soon transferred to the more inviting situation of Hobart. Not until 1835, following exploratory trips

Melbourne

0   500 m

1 Miami Hotel
2 Ansett
3 TAA
4 YWCA Hostel
5 Old Melbourne Gaol
6 Museum
7 Asian Food Plaza
8 Pellegrini's
9 GPO
10 Victoria Hotel
11 Town Hall
12 VGTB (Tourist Office)
13 City Square
14 Greyhound
15 Kingsgate Hotel
16 Spencer Hotel/Motel
17 Great Southern Hotel

from Tasmania, was Melbourne eventually founded by a group of Tasmanian entrepreneurs.

In 1851 the colony of Victoria became independent of NSW and at about the same time Melbourne actually became a rival for Sydney when it was the centre for Australia's biggest and most prolonged gold-rush. In just a few years Melbourne suddenly became a real place on the map and the city's solid, substantial appearance essentially dates from those heady days. For a time around a century ago Melbourne was actually the larger city but Sydney has gradually pulled back ahead and Melbourne now ranks number two to its more glamorous northern sister.

In population there's little between them; they're both large cities in the 2½ to three million bracket, yet somehow Sydney is far more the metropolis than Melbourne. It's brighter, more active and more hurried than its younger sister. Quite why is hard to pinpoint – Melbourne is certainly less attractively situated, on a flat coastal plain whereas Sydney rises, dips and curves around its beautiful harbour. Melbourne is certainly better planned – wide, sweeping boulevards against Sydney's narrow and often convoluted streets. Melbourne's much more solid, more permanent, more 'Victorian' in appearance. Even more dull?

Part of Melbourne's inferiority complex is due, no doubt, to the architectural kiss of death the city seems to suffer from. Spend as much as you want, plan as far ahead as you like, nothing seems to work in Melbourne. When every Australian city had to have a central pedestrian mall Melbourne had one too, except trams run through Melbourne's, people huddle to the sides and all in all it's a disaster. Melbourne's city square, the product of much planning and competition was an instant total flop. When Sydney built a performing arts centre they ended up with the opera house. When Melbourne did the same thing they ended up with something that worked very well but in appearance was so dull and innocuous you'd barely know it was there; even it's pointy spire is cunningly coloured to blend into a typical cloudy Melbourne sky with such precision as to be invisible. And Melbourne's biggest and most impressive bridge actually fell down during its construction.

Information

In Melbourne, the Victorian Government Travel Centre (tel 602 9444) is at 230 Collins St and is open 9 am to 5 pm on weekdays, 9 am to 12 noon on Saturday mornings. It's a place with a rather Victorian atmosphere too! The RACV (tel 607 2211) is at 123 Queen St and has a bookshop and information section on the 8th floor. The National Parks Service of Victoria, (tel 651 4011) with their head-office at 240 Victoria Parade, East Melbourne, has about 40 national, state and coastal parks. The National Trust puts out a useful walking-tours leaflet.

The Melbourne GPO is on the corner of Bourke St and Elizabeth St. There's an efficient poste restante here and also phones for interstate and international calls. Phone centres can also be found right behind the GPO on Little Bourke St, right across the road on Elizabeth St and up Bourke St just across Swanston St.

The YHA (tel 654-5422) has its helpful Melbourne office at 122 Flinders St. If you're after bushgear or information on bushwalking the centre for bushgear shops is around the junction of Hardware St and Little Bourke St, close to the GPO. The Environment Centre at 285 Little Lonsdale St has a wide variety of books, calenders, posters and magazines and is a good place for information about activities in the environment and conservation movements.

Melbourne has a lot of excellent bookshops including a big Angus & Robertson on Elizabeth St, several Collins Bookshops around the city, the agreeably chaotic McGills on Elizabeth St opposite the GPO (good for interstate and overseas newspapers) and several alternative bookshops. Best of these are Whole Earth at 83 Bourke St and Readings on Lygon St in Carlton. Readings also has an excellent window noticeboard where you'll find all sorts of offers to share accommodation or rides. It's actually mostly accommodation and some of the requirements are quite amazing - will that lesbian household really find the vegetarian, cat-loving, musician with leftist political leanings? The *Entertainment Guide* which comes free with *The Age* newspaper on Friday is the best source of info on what's happening around Melbourne for the following week.

Aboriginal Handcrafts is on the ninth floor of Century House at 125 Swanston St and is open weekdays from 10 am to 4.30 pm. There are a number of other Aboriginal craft shops and countless junk souvenir places. Melbourne also has a number of delightful Australiana shops selling amusing (and intentional) examples of Australian kitsch.

In the city there are a number of intimate and elegant little shopping arcades apart from the glossier modern affairs. The Royal Arcade off Bourke St Mall is noted for its figures of Gog and Magog which strike the hours.

Orientation

Melbourne's city centre, the 'Golden Mile', is deceptively simple. Wide boulevards run south-west to north-east and south-east to north-west but the south-west to north-east roads are interspersed with narrow streets from which a veritable maze of little alleys and lanes run off, giving the otherwise overpoweringiy orderly and planned centre a little human chaos. The main streets are Collins and Bourke Sts (south-west to north-east) crossed by Swanston and Elizabeth Sts (south-east to north-west). Swanston St is the real main artery of Melbourne as it crosses straight over the river on the southern side and runs right out of the city into Carlton on the north. Most traffic coming into the city from the south enters by Swanston St while most traffic from the north comes in on parallel Elizabeth St, since this is the direct route in from the airport or from Sydney.

The Yarra River forms a southern boundary to the city area, with railway lines running alongside it and Flinders St (the city centre street running closest to the riverbank). Right beside the river at the corner of Swanston and Flinders St is the ornate although rather elderly-looking Flinders St railway station. This is the main railway station for suburban railway services. The other Melbourne station, for country and interstate services, is the Spencer St station. The Spencer St end of town also has a number of old hotels and cheaper places to stay.

The Collins and Bourke St blocks between Swanston and Elizabeth Sts are Melbourne's shopping centre, the Bourke St block being a pedestrian mall. On the mall you'll find Myers (the biggest department store in Australia) and right next door on the Bourke and Elizabeth Sts corner is the GPO.

The Yarra River

Melbourne's prime natural feature, the 'muddy' Yarra, is about all the city has to offer as a competitor for Sydney's harbour and it's a loser from the start. There's no way a river, which is the butt of countless jokes about 'running upside down', can win against beautiful Port Jackson. This is all a little unfair because actually the Yarra is very pretty and hopefully, if plans currently held for it come to fruition, will be even more attractive in the future.

When the racing row boats are gliding down the river on a sunny day, or you're driving along Alexandra Avenue towards the city on a clear night the Yarra can really look quite magical. Best of all there's a bicycle track along the riverbank so you can bike it for miles along the riverside or ride to work without risking being wiped out by some nut in a Holden. The bike track has been gradually extended further upstream and hopefully will eventually start to move further downstream as well. On weekends you can hire bicycles from beside the Botanical Gardens and near Como Park.

There are also riverside barbecues beside the river and near Como Park in South Yarra you can also hire canoes and rowboats although further upstream, Studley Park in Kew is the most popular place for boating. Two-person canoes here cost $10 for the first hour, or $12 for three-person canoes. Subsequent hours are $5 and $6. They also hire kayaks and row boats.

A more leisurely way to boat down the river is on one of the pseudo-paddlewheeler tour boats which operate on the river from Princes Walk beside Princes Bridge (across from Flinders St Station). There are some really beautiful old bridges across the Yarra; and Alexandra Parade, the riverside boulevard on the south side, provides delightful views of Melbourne by day or night.

Polly Woodside

Close to Spencer St Bridge, immediately south of the city centre, is the *Polly Woodside*. Built in Belfast, Northern Ireland in 1885 she's an old iron-hulled sailing ship involved in freight carrying in the dying years of the sailing era. Recently restored it's hoped the Polly Woodside and the adjacent nautical museum will eventually form the centre for a major redevelopment project on this run-down riverside docks area. The ship and museum are open 10 am to 4 pm weekdays, 12 noon to 5 pm on Saturday and Sunday; admission is $4 for adults, or $10 for a family ticket. Across the river stands the recently completed World Trade Centre office block.

City Square

At the intersection of Collins and Swanston St is Melbourne's disastrous city square. Plans for a city square were discussed for years but despite all the advance planning and architectural competitions the city square still suffered from Melbourne's kiss of death. It's a nice enough square with lots of fountains and even a graffiti wall but for some reason it has simply never worked.

The only interest the city square has ever really had for the people of Melbourne was in the early days of the 'yellow peril'. This big chunk of modern sculpture was intended to give the square a central focus but, unfortunately, it was the sort of thing that makes the you-call-that-art brigade foam at the mouth. Doubly unfortunately Melbourne's city council at that time had absolutely nothing better to do than foam at the mouth and after endless arguments and veritable Zeppelins full of hot air the council got the sack and the yellow peril was spirited away to a new (and obscure) home in a riverside park down towards Spencer St. Now the square has no focus at all although it does have a rather good statue of Burke and Wills looking heroic and unlucky. This statue has had quite an interesting history moving from place to place all over the city.

On Around the City

Continuing up Collins St beside the City Square you come to the 'Paris End' where graceful trees shade the street and do give it something of a Parisian look although callous development has seen many of the fine old buildings that used to line the street replaced with more big, featureless office blocks. Up Collins St the other way you come to the Melbourne Stock Exchange at 351. You can visit the 3rd floor visitors' gallery from 9 am to 12 noon and 2 to 5 pm, Monday to Friday. Those interested in the forces of capitalism at work can also have a free tour of the exchange.

Bourke St has more shops but less style than Collins St but it too can boast a Melbourne fiasco: when, in the '70s, every Australian city had to have a pedestrian mall Melbourne got one too but the Bourke St Mall has been a non-starter from the very beginning. Melbourne has one big difference to any other Australian city – trams. It soon became very clear that there's no way a pedestrian mall can work if you've got 30-ton trams barrelling through the middle of it every few minutes. Or at least it soon became very clear to the likes of you and me; it's still not at all clear to the powers that be and several multi-million dollar re-arrangements of the potted plants and the benches still hasn't made it any clearer. In my opinion (and my opinion comes free) there are only two ways to make the Bourke St Mall work: the cheap way is to stop the trams running through the mall by putting the terminus at the Swanston St end of the mall; the expensive way is to stop the trams running through the mall by putting them in a tunnel underneath it.

Half a block up from Bourke St is something that's much more of a Melbourne success story – the Chinatown on Little Bourke St. This narrow lane was a thronging Chinese quarter even back in the gold-rush days and it's now a busy, crowded couple of blocks of often-excellent Chinese restaurants (though also often very expensive), Asian supermarkets and shops. The successful touch here was the addition of decorative street

lamps and Chinese tiled arches over the lane. Yes, I know they're artificial and garish but they look great. Another half block up to Lonsdale St brings you to the central city's Greek quarter.

City Buildings

Melbourne's an intriguing blend of the soaring new and the stately old. Carrying the 'new' banner are buildings like the Rialto on Collins St and Nauru House on Exhibition St. Nauru is a tiny Pacific island whose entire population could comfortably be housed in this big office block. It is an extremely wealthy island since it's basically solid phosphate, hence the building's nickname of 'birdshit house'. Only a sparrow hop away is the equally soaring Regent Hotel with its central atrium, starting on the 35th floor. A great place to stay if you can stretch to $100+ a night. The Rialto building, up the other end of the city, is the tallest office building in Australia. Beside it is the imaginative Rialto-Menzies Hotel which uses the facades of two old buildings and cleverly incorporates an old stone-paved alleyway which used to run between them.

On Spring St is a hotel of quite another era: the gracious old Windsor Hotel. Across the road from this is the imposing State Parliament House, a relic of Melbourne's gold-rush wealth. Other old buildings in the centre include the 1853 Treasury Building in the Treasury Gardens, the 1872 Old Royal Mint and the 1842 St James Cathedral, both beside Flagstaff Gardens. Victoriana enthusiasts may find some very small Melbourne buildings of interest – scattered around the city are a number of very fine cast-iron men's urinals (like French *pissoirs*). They mainly date from 1903 to WW I and one on the corner of Exhibition and Lonsdale St is classified by the National Trust. Other fine examples include one outside the North Melbourne Town Hall where there is also a very fine drinking fountain.

On the corner of Swanston and Flinders

Sts is the main railway station for local trains in Melbourne, the grand old Flinders St Station. 'Under the clocks' at the station entrance is a favourite Melbourne meeting place. Across the road from the station is one of Melbourne's best known pubs, Young & Jacksons. It's famed mainly for the painting of Chloe hanging in the public bar. Judged indecent at the Melbourne Exhibition of 1880 she's gone on to become a much-loved symbol of Melbourne. The pub, which supposedly gets through more Fosters than any other in Australia, has recently been carefully restored.

The Melbourne Club, pillar of the Melbourne establishment, is off Spring St up at the Treasury Gardens end of town. This end block of Bourke St is popular and has a number of excellent restaurants, bookshops and record shops. St Patrick's Cathedral, one of the city's most imposing churches, is also at this end of town.

Over the other side of the city the Victoria Market on the corner of Peel and Victoria Sts is the city's main produce centre, a colourful and popular scene Tuesdays to Saturdays when the stall operators shout, yell and generally go all out to move the goods. On Sundays the fruit and vegies give way to general goods – everything from cut price jeans to second-hand records.

Museum & Library
Extending for a block between Swanston St and Russell St beside La Trobe St is the inter-connected collection of the National Museum and the Science Museum, plus the State Library and La Trobe Library. The National Museum is entered from Russell St, the Science Museum from Swanston St, but you can actually get to either collection from either end. Exhibitions range from the first car and aircraft in Australia to the stuffed remains of Phar Lap, the legendary racehorse which nearly disrupted Australian-American relations when it

died a suspicious death in the US. The complex also includes a planetarium. The museum is open 10 am to 5 pm Monday to Saturday, 2 to 5 pm Sunday; admission is free.

Old Melbourne Gaol
A block further up Russell St is this gruesome old gaol and penal museum. It was built of bluestone in 1841 and was used right up to 1929; in all, over 100 prisoners were hanged here. It's a dark, dank, spooky place which often terrifies young children. The museum displays include death masks of noted bushrangers and convicts, Ned Kelly's armour, the very scaffold from which Ned took his fatal plunge and some fascinating records of early 'transported' convicts, indicating just what flimsy excuses could be used to pack people off to Australia's unwelcoming shores. It's an unpleasant reminder of the brutality of Australia's early convict days. It is open 10 am to 5 pm daily, admission is $2.50.

Melbourne Zoo
Just north of the city centre in Parkville is Melbourne's excellent zoo. There are numerous walk-through enclosures in this well-planned zoo. You walk through the aviary, around the monkey enclosures and even over the lions' park on a bridge. The zoo is open 9 am to 5 pm every day of the week and admission is $4.40. This is the oldest zoo in Australia and one of the oldest in the world. You can get to it on an 18, 19 or 20 tram from Elizabeth St. The zoo is beside Royal Park; a marker in the park indicates where the Burke and Wills expedition set off on its ill-fated journey in 1860.

Melbourne Cricket Ground
The MCG is one of Australia's biggest sporting stadiums and was the central stadium for the 1956 Melbourne Olympics. In Yarra Park, which stretches from the city and East Melbourne to Richmond, the huge stadium can accommodate over

100,000 spectators, and does so at least once a year. The big occasion is the annual football Grand Final in September. This is Australia's biggest sporting event and brings Melbourne, which engages in a winter of football mania each year, to a fever pitch.

Football as played in Melbourne is quite different to football i. other parts of the world, indeed even to raost other parts of Australia. It's Australian Rules football, somewhat akin to a cross between soccer and rugby but most closely related to Gaelic football. The teams play on an oval field with a 'double' goal – you score more points within the inner goalposts than the outer ones. Aussie rules football is principally a Melbourne activity, in Sydney they play rugby. The only other sporting event which generates the same sort of national interest in Australia is the Melbourne Cup horserace each November.

Cricket is, of course, the other major sport played in the MCG; intenational test and one-day matches as well as interstate Sheffield Shield and other local district games take place here over the summer months. You can tour the MCG museum on Wednesday mornings at 10 am.

Cultural Centre Complex

As you cross the river to the south of the city Swanston St becomes St Kilda Rd, a very fine boulevard which runs straight out of the city towards the war memorial, takes a kink around the shrine and then runs straight on to St Kilda. Beyond the memorial it's ad agency alley with many office blocks lining the road.

Right by the river is Melbourne's large arts centre. The National Gallery was the first part of the complex to be completed, back in 1968, and although it's a rather dull cubic building and the 'urinal' front window is something of a local joke, it houses a very fine collection of art. The gallery has local and overseas collections and many excellent temporary exhibits. The stained-glass ceiling in the Great Hall is a highpoint of the gallery. I particularly like the strange water fountains in the central courtyard. The gallery is open 10 am to 5 pm Tuesday to Sunday and the regular entry charge (higher for special exhibits) is $1 (students 50c).

Beside the gallery is the recently opened Concert Hall complex. It may look rather like a grounded prison ship from Star Wars but it houses an excellent concert hall, the state theatre, playhouse, studio and a performing arts museum, all topped by that tall pointy spire; well it does look nice at night. The construction of the centre certainly caused some problems while at the hole-in-the-ground stage. The more they dug the more it filled up with water and the more they pumped the water out the more the whole locality began to sink! Furthermore the water that drained in proved to be acidic and a low voltage has to be fed through the centre's foundations to prevent them rotting away! Tours of the centre are available for $1.50.

Parks & Gardens

Victoria has dubbed itself 'the garden state' and it's certainly true in Melbourne; the city has many swathes of green all around the central area. They're varied and delightful – formal central gardens like the Treasury and Flagstaff Gardens, wide empty parklands like the Royal Park, particularly fine botanic gardens and many others. In the summer months the FEIP (Free Entertainment in the Parks) programme puts on a wide variety of entertainment in city parks on weekday lunchtimes and on weekends.

Royal Botanic Gardens Certainly the finest gardens in Australia and arguably one of the finest in the world, this is one of my favourite spots in Melbourne. There's nothing more genteel to do in Melbourne than to have scones and cream by the lake on a Sunday afternoon – and Maureen and I do most Sundays we're in town! The

Royal Botanic Gardens Melbourne

beautifully laid out gardens are right beside the Yarra River; indeed the river once actually ran through the gardens and the lakes are the remains of curves of the river, cut off when the river was straightened out to lessen the annual flood damage when it used to wind back and forth across the flood plain at this point. The garden site was chosen in 1845 but the real development took place when Baron Sir Ferdinand von Mueller took charge in 1852.

There's a surprising amount of fauna as well as flora in the gardens. Apart from the ever-present water fowl and the frequent visits from cockatoos you may also see rabbits and possums if you're lucky. In all more than 50 varieties of birds can be seen in the gardens. In '82 a large contingent of fruit bats, usually found in the warmer climes of north Queensland, took residence for the summer. You can pick up guide-yourself leaflets at the park entrances; these are changed with the seasons and tell you what to look out for at the different times of year.

Kings Domain The gardens form a corner of the Kings Domain, a park which also contains the Shrine of Remembrance, Governor La Trobe's Cottage, the Sidney Myer Music Bowl and is flanked by the majestic St Kilda Road, the grand avenue which leads straight out from the heart of the city. The whole park is encircled by the 'tan track', a four-km running track which is probably Melbourne's favourite venue for joggers. It's another of my Melbourne regulars, I do a couple of laps every Sunday morning. The track has an amusing variety of exercise points – a mixture of the stations of the cross and miniature golf someone once said.

Beside St Kilda Rd stands the massive Shrine of Remembrance, a WW I war memorial which took so long to build that WW II was well underway when it eventually opened. The shrine is another example of the Melbourne architectural jinx – huge though it is and imposing though it was intended to be the shrine somehow manages to look completely anonymous; you can almost forget it was there. It's worth climbing up to the top walkway as there are fine views from there into the city along St Kilda Rd. From up there you can clearly see how St Kilda Rd runs so straight out of the city and on to St Kilda, but makes a distinct detour around the memorial. The shrine's big day of the year is Anzac Day. Back during the Vietnam era some commendably enterprising individuals managed to sneak up to the well-guarded shrine on the night before Anzac Day and paint 'PEACE' across the front in large letters. The shrine is open to visitors Monday to Saturday from 10 am to 5 pm, Sunday from 2 to 5 pm.

Across from the shrine is Governor La Trobe's Cottage, the original Victorian government house sent out from the mother country in prefabricated form in 1840. It was originally sited in Jolimont, near the MCG, and was moved here when the decision was made to preserve this interesting piece of Melbourne's early history. The simple little cottage is open daily and admission is $1.60 (students 80c). Beside the cottage is the Old Observatory and the National Herbarium, where amongst other things marijuana samples are tested to make sure they really are the dreaded weed. The imposing building overlooking the botanic gardens is Government House where Victoria's governor resides. It's a copy of one of Queen Victoria's palaces on England's Isle of Wight.

Up at the city end of the park is the Sidney Myer Music Bowl, a functional outdoor performance area in a natural bowl. It's used for all manner of concerts in the summer months but rock concerts here tend to become rather disreputable as young drunks create havoc with the flora and leave mountains of garbage – a real shame.

Treasury & Fitzroy Gardens These two popular formal parks lie immediately to the east of the city centre, overshadowed by the Hilton Hotel. The Fitzroy Gardens, with its stately avenues lined with English elms, is a popular spot for wedding photographs; on virtually every Saturday afternoon of the year there's a continuous procession of wedding cars pulling up here for the participants to be snapped. The pathways in the park are actually laid out in the form of a union jack! The gardens contain several points of interest including Captain Cook's cottage. It was uprooted from its native Yorkshire and reassembled in the park in 1934. Actually it's not certain that the good captain ever did live in this house but never mind, it looks very picturesque there. The house is furnished in period style and has an interesting Captain Cook exhibit. It's open 9 am to 5 pm daily and admission is 80c.

In the centre of the gardens, by the refreshment kiosk, is a small miniature Tudor village and a fairytale carved tree. Off in the north-west corner of the park is the people's pathway – a circular brick paved path made with individually engraved bricks. Anybody who dropped by here on 5 February 1978 got to produce their own little bit of art for posterity and it's quite intriguing to wander around.

Other Parks The central Flagstaff Gardens were the first public gardens in Melbourne. From a lookout point here, ships arriving at the city were sighted in the early colonial days. A plaque in the gardens describes how the site was used for this purpose. Closer to the seafront is Albert Park Lake, a shallow lake created from a swamp area. The lake is popular for boating and there's another popular jogging track around the perimeter. You can hire boats on the lake, the Jolly Roger Boathouse is at the city end of the lake

and rents rowboats for $7 an hour, sailing boats at $10 to $15 an hour. On Saturday the two sailing clubs here have races on the lake – I'm usually bringing up the rear in the Mirror class with *Tangkuban Prahu*.

On the north side of the city the Exhibition Gardens are the site of the Exhibition Buildings, a wonder of the southern hemisphere when they were built for the Great Exhibition of 1880. Later they served as the Victorian parliament building for 27 years while the Victorian parliament was used by the national legislature until Canberra's parliament building was finally completed. They're still a major exhibition centre today and a new extension is one of the few really successful uses of the 'mirror building' architectural craze which appears to have gripped Melbourne. There are some fine old fountains around the building, one of them well-reflected in the mirror building.

Trams

If Melbourne has a man made symbol then it's a moveable one – trams. Not those horrible, plastic-looking modern ones either; real Melbourne trams are green and yellow, ancient looking and half the weight of an ocean liner. Trams are the standard means of public transport and they work remarkably well. More than a few cities which once had trams probably wish they still did today. The old trams are gradually being replaced by new ones and some of the older trams have been turned into mobile works of art, painted from front to back by local artists. I like the one covered in sheep. If you like old trams then watch out for them on weekends when some delightful old vintage trams are rolled out on summer Sundays and used in place of the modern ones on the Hawthorn run from Princes Gate, and there's even a tram restaurant!

To get to grips with Melbourne and its trams try a ride on a number 8. It starts off along Swanston St in the city, rolls down St Kilda Rd beside the Kings Domain, turns round by the war memorial and on to Toorak Rd through South Yarra and Toorak. As you near Chapel St on Toorak Rd look for my 'it should be bombed' prize for ugly monstrosities: the ANZ Bank computer building on your left.

Another popular tram ride is number 15 which cruises right down St Kilda Rd to St Kilda. Trams are such a part of Melbourne life they've even been used for a play – act one of *Storming Mont Albert by Tram* took place from Mont Albert to the city, act two on the way back. The passengers were the audience, the actors got on and off along the way. It wasn't a bad play!

Melbourne trams should be treated with some caution by car drivers. You can only overtake a tram on the inside and must always stop behind one when it halts to drop or collect passengers. In the city centre there are a number of junctions where a peculiar path must be followed to make right hand turns, in order to accommodate the trams. Note that in rainy weather tram tracks are extremely slippery, motorcyclists should take special care. Cyclists must beware of tram tracks at all times, if you get a wheel into the track you're on your face immediately. I've done that twice in Melbourne, smashing a pair of glasses on one occasion.

Melbourne Suburbs

Melbourne's inner city suburbs have gone through the same 'trendification' process that has hit Sydney suburbs like Paddington and Balmain. Carlton is the most obvious example of this activity but Parkville, South Melbourne, Albert Park, Richmond and Hawthorn are other popular inner city suburbs with a strong Victorian flavour.

Carlton This is one of Melbourne's most interesting inner city suburbs – partly because here you'll find probably the most attractive collection of Victoriana, partly because the university is here and partly because Carlton is also the Italian quarter of Melbourne with the biggest collection of Italian restaurants in Australia. Lygon St is the backbone of Carlton and along here you'll find enough Italian restaurants, coffee houses, pizzerias and gelaterias to satisfy the most rabid pasta and cappuccino freak. The Lygon Street Festa is held annually in November and always gets a good turnout. Carlton is flanked by gracious Parkville and the seedy/trendy mixture of Fitzroy.

South Yarra & Toorak South of the Yarra River (as the name indicates) South Yarra is one of the more frenetic Melbourne suburbs, Toorak one of the most exclusive. The two roads to remember here are Toorak Rd and Chapel St. Toorak Rd is one of Australia's classiest shopping streets, frequented by those well-known Toorak matrons in their Porsches and Benzes. Apart from expensive shops and some of Australia's best (though also most expensive) restaurants, Toorak Rd also has a number of very reasonably priced places to eat. Toorak Rd forms the main artery through both South Yarra and Toorak.

Running across Toorak Rd is Chapel St in South Yarra; if the word for Toorak Rd is 'exclusive' then for Chapel St it's 'trendy'. The street is virtually wall-to-wall boutiques ranging from punk to Indian bangles and beads, op-shop to antique. Plus restaurants, the imaginative Jam Factory shopping centre and the delightful Prahran Market. The market is a great place for fruit and vegetables and you'll find me here early every Friday morning. Chapel St fades away into Prahran but take a right turn by the Prahran town hall and wander along Greville St, at one time Melbourne's freak street but it has now become a little ordinary and dull.

South Yarra also has one of Australia's finest colonial mansions, Como House, overlooking the Yarra River from Como Park. Built between 1840 and 1859 it's now authentically restored and furnished and is the headquarters of the National Trust. Aboriginal rites and feasts were still being held on the banks of the Yarra when the house was first built and an early occupant writes of seeing a cannibal feast from her bedroom window. Como is open 11 am to 3 pm Wednesday to Friday, 10 am to 5 pm on the weekends, admission is $3 (students $1.50) and you can get there on a number 8 tram from the city.

Richmond As Carlton is to Italy so is Richmond to Greece; this suburb just to the east of the city centre is the Greek centre for the third largest Greek city in the world. That's right, after Athens and Thessaloniki, Melbourne is the next largest city in terms of Greek population. Richmond is another centre for Victorian architecture, much of it restored or currently in the process of restoration. Richmond is, of course, the best place for a souvlaki in Melbourne! It's also where Lonely Planet has it's office; even though our post office box address is across the river in South Yarra.

St Kilda This seaside suburb is Melbourne's most cosmopolitan and most lively on weekends, particularly on Sundays. It's also the somewhat feeble excuse for a Melbourne sin centre; if you're after seedy nightlife you'll do better in Sydney's Kings Cross. St Kilda is definitely Melbourne's drug centre however, and is a sorrier scene for that. If you want a meal late at night or some activity on the weekends then St Kilda is the place to be. Fitzroy St with its many restaurants, snack bars and take-aways is the main street in St Kilda and also the red-light centre.

Sunday morning along the Esplanade in St Kilda features an interesting amateur art show while along Acland St gluttons will have their minds blown by the amazing selection of cakes in the coffee shop windows. St Kilda has lots of local Jewish and ethnic colour. The huge old Palais Theatres and the raucous Luna Park amusement centre, with roller-coasters and the like, can also be found here.

Williamstown At the mouth of the Yarra this is one of the oldest parts of Melbourne and has many interesting old buildings and lots of waterside activity. Williamstown remained relatively isolated from developments in the rest of Melbourne until the completion of the Westgate Bridge suddenly brought it to within a few minutes drive of the centre. *HMAS Castlemaine*, a WW II minesweeper is now preserved as a Maritime Museum and is open on weekends; admission is $1.60. Williamstown also has a Historical Museum on Electra St and the Railway Museum on Champion Rd, North Williamstown has a fine collection of old steam locomotives.

Other Suburbs South of the centre are other Victorian inner suburbs with many finely restored old homes, particularly in the bayside suburbs of South Melbourne, Middle Park and Albert Park. Emerald Hill in South Melbourne is a whole section of 1880s Melbourne, still in relatively authentic shape. Wealthier inner suburbs to the east, also popular shopping centres, include Armadale, Malvern, Hawthorn and Camberwell. Sandwiched between the city and Richmond is the compact area of East Melbourne, and like Parkville, it's one of the most concentrated areas of old Victorian buildings around the city with numerous excellent examples of early architecture.

Ripponlea is at 192 Hotham St, Elsternwick, close to St Kilda. It's another fine old mansion with elegant gardens inhabited by peacocks. Ripponlea is open 10 am to 5 pm daily and admission is $3.50 (students $1.50). In Eltham, the

mud-brick and alternative lifestylers suburb, Montsalvat on Hillcrest Avenue (26 km out) is an artists' colony open dawn to dusk daily.

Beaches
Melbourne hasn't got fine surf beaches like Sydney, at least not close to the city, but it's still not at all badly equipped for beaches and you can find surf further out on the Mornington Peninsula. Starting from the city end, Albert Park has a popular beach, a local meeting place, although the water here is probably not 100% healthy; the same applies to nearby St Kilda. Elwood, Brighton and Sandringham are not bad and Half Moon Bay is very good for a suburban beach. Beyond here you have to get right round to the Mornington Peninsula before you find the really excellent beaches.

Places to Stay
Melbourne has a fairly wide range of accommodation. It's not centred in any particular area although the old-fashioned hotels are found mainly in the city, particularly up around Spencer St railway station. The seaside suburb of St Kilda is probably the best general accommodation centre in Melbourne. There you'll find a wide variety of reasonably priced motels, private hotels, guest-houses and holiday flats. St Kilda also has an excellent selection of eating places ranging from cheap take-away places to some of Melbourne's finest restaurants. It's the most cosmopolitan area of Melbourne and a bit like a lower-key version of Sydney's Kings Cross.

For places to share, the university noticeboards, the board in the youth hostel office and the front window of Readings bookshop in Carlton are all worth checking. *The Age* classified columns on Wednesdays and Saturday are the place to look for longer-term accommodation. It is much easier to find places to rent in Melbourne than in Sydney. Note that most of the cheaper hotels, guest-houses and the like will also offer cheaper weekly rates. These are typically about four times the daily rates so it soon becomes better value to stay for a week.

Hostels There are actually two Melbourne *Youth Hostels* these days. Initially one was simply an overflow for the main hostel but demand is such that both are in full time operation. They're only about a minute's walk apart and only about three km from the city centre in North Melbourne, easily accessible by tram 54, 57, 59 or 68 from Elizabeth St. The 500 Abbotsford St hostel (tel 328 2880) has 42 beds while the 76 Chapman St hostel (tel 328 3595) has 100. The Chapman St hostel is a more modern building with 50 double rooms while the Abbotsford St one is normal dorm style. Both hostels have good noticeboards if you're looking for people to travel with, share lifts, airline tickets going cheap or just general information. Nightly charges are $7.50 at Abbotsford St and $8 at Chapman St. If you're coming in from the airport ask the driver to drop you near the YH (the buses go by Abbotsford St along Flemington Rd soon after leaving the Tullamarine Freeway) and he should be obliging. You can also arrange for the airport bus to pick you up from the hostel and save you the trek into town.

The Y The *YWCA Family Hostel* (tel 329 5188) is conveniently central at 489 Elizabeth St and very competitively priced. Singles/doubles are $23/34 and all rooms have shower and toilet, heating and cooling and tea-making facilities. Outside it's very much '70s bare concrete but inside it's functional and well-equipped. There's also a rather basic cafeteria here. The YWCA is almost directly across the road from the airport bus office.

Hotels Melbourne's cheap hotels tend to be concentrated at the Spencer St end of the city, around the railway station and also close to the Greyhound bus terminal. At 44 Spencer St the *Spencer Hotel/Motel* (tel 62 6991) has rooms at $18/28 in the older hotel section or motel-style rooms at $20/30 and $32/42. It's rather brighter inside than its somewhat gloomy exterior would indicate.

Close by at 131 King St the *Kingsgate Hotel* (tel 62 4171) used to be the old Peoples Palace. It's still very big (over 200 rooms) with prices including a light breakfast from $18 to $32 single, $28 to $42 double. The rooms vary widely – the most expensive have private facilities, air-con, fridges, and so on. In between there are rooms with attached shower and toilet, or just a wash-basin, or right at the bottom they're very bare and basic. The *Royal Arcade Hotel* (tel 63 8695) at 301 Little Collins St has cheap singles/doubles for $18/24.

Very centrally located at 215 Little Collins St, the *Victoria Hotel* (tel 63 0441) is a notch up-market from the cheapest city hotels. It's a big place with no less than 520 rooms. There are 135 basic rooms without private facilities which cost $26/33 for singles/doubles. The majority of the rooms have private facilities, colour TV and other mod-cons and are rather more expensive at around $43/53. The Victoria is one of the most conveniently located hotels in Melbourne, you could hardly ask to be more centrally located.

There are also numerous private hotels in and around the central city area. The *Great Southern* (tel 62 3989) is an old-fashioned place at 16 Spencer St, another reminder of the days of rail travel. With rooms at $14/20 its prices are pretty old-fashioned too. None of the rooms have attached bathrooms and most of them don't even boast a wash-basin. Other very basic city cheapies include *Purnall's* (tel 329 7635) at 445 Elizabeth St at $20/25 and the *Hotham* (tel 62 2681) at 2 Spencer St which is $15/25 but apart from the price has little to recommend it.

Suburban Accommodation – East & West Melbourne In the inner suburbs around the central city there are a number of places in the private hotel/guest-house/bed & breakfast categories. All these places will quote cheaper weekly rates. In West Melbourne the *Miami* (tel 329 8499) at 13 Hawke St has wash-basins with hot and cold water in all the rooms and breakfast is included in the $17/24 nightly tariff. Although it's very simple and straightforward the Miami is also very well-kept and it's an easy walk from here to the centre. It's a big, square block of a place with over 100 rooms.

Similarly convenient and well-kept, the *Magnolia Court* (tel 417 2782 or 419 4518) is in East Melbourne at 101 Powlett St which is also only one km from the centre. Rooms here are $30/36 room-only for singles/doubles. *Georgian Court* (tel 419 6353) at 21-25 George St, also in East Melbourne, has rooms from $8 a night, cheaper weekly rates and share cooking facilities. George St is a quiet, tree-lined street and the genteel looking Georgian Court is right across the road from the post office. Although East Melbourne is very close to the city centre it's generally a fairly quiet area.

Suburban Accommodation – South Yarra A little further out in South Yarra the *Westend* (tel 266 3135) is up at at 76 West Toorak Rd. There are tea-making facilities and rooms cost $16/26 including breakfast. The Westend is pleasantly situated looking across Toorak Rd to Fawkner Park. Right in the heart of the South Yarra shopping area, about midway between the South Yarra railway station and Chapel St, the *Toorak Private Hotel* (tel 241 8652) is at 189 Toorak Rd. It's a big, dark-green building and nightly costs are just $14/18 for singles/doubles; weekly rates are $50/66.

Suburban Accommodation – St Kilda It's very easy to get out to seaside St Kilda, just a straightforward tram ride (number

12 or 15) from Swanston St in the city, down the wide, tree-lined St Kilda Rd to Fitzroy St will get you there. Alternatively suburban train services run from Flinders St station to St Kilda where the line terminates right at the junction of Canterbury Rd and Fitzroy St.

Up at the top end of Fitzroy St there's a couple of possibilities. First of all at 151 Fitzroy St is the big, genteelly old-fashioned *Majestic Court Private Hotel* (tel 94 0561). Rooms here cost $15/20 for singles/doubles with private facilities. Next door at 149 is the *Regal Private Hotel* (tel 534 5603 or 4053) with bed & breakfast (a 'nice breakfast' they say) at $18 for singles, $27 for doubles. Rooms have hot and cold water but not private facilities. The restaurants and shops along Fitzroy St start just down from these two places.

Just around the bay from St Kilda is Elwood where the *Bayside* (tel 531 9238) is at 65 Ormond Esplanade, a rather busy road separated by a narrow park from the bay. All rooms have TVs, fridges and tea-making facilities, some have attached bathrooms. Nightly costs including an evening meal and breakfast are $20/30. Again, cheaper weekly rates are available.

Motels The *Spencer Hotel/Motel* and the *YWCA* both offer motel-style accommodation in the city centre and are reasonably priced. There's no real motel strip in Melbourne but you can find reasonably priced and fairly central motels in South Yarra and St Kilda in particular. The *Domain* (tel 266 3701) is at 52-54 Darling St in South Yarra and has rooms at $36/40. Rooms have all the usual motel mod-cons and it's conveniently close to the tram lines for the centre and to the Yarra River.

In St Kilda the *Carlisle Lodge* (tel 534 0416) at 32 Carlisle St is cheap at $28/30. It's a plain, slightly older motel but rooms have fridges and cooking facilities as well as air-con and the other usual motel facilities. Almost on the corner with

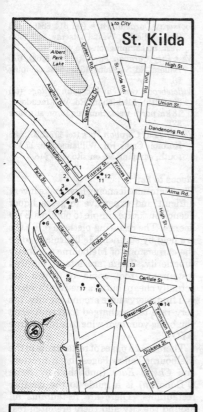

St. Kilda

1 Railway Station
2 Executive Motel
3 Tolarno's
4 Gatwick Private Hotel
5 Massoni's
6 Cleopatra's
7 Prince of Wales Hotel
8 Leo's Pizza Bar
9 Topolino's Bistro
10 R & M Books
11 Regal Private Hotel
12 Majestic Court Private Hotel
13 Carlisle Lodge
14 City Gate
15 Cosmos Books
16 Scherezade Restaurant
17 Luna Park
18 Palais Theatre

Fitzroy St, directly opposite the station, the *Executive* (tel 534 0303) is at 239 Canterbury Rd, St Kilda and has rooms at $30/35. It's a square, featureless block looking more like a block of flats than a motel, but conveniently close to all the noise and colour of Fitzroy St.

You'll also find some reasonably priced motels in less attractive suburbs on the main routes into and out of Melbourne. In Coburg the *Coburg Coach House* (tel 350 2844) is at 846 Sydney Rd (the road from Sydney) and has rooms at $29/35. In Footscray, on the route from Adelaide, there's the *Mid Gate Motor Lodge* (tel 689 2170) at 76 Droop St which has rooms for $28/32.

Holiday Flats There are a couple of places in St Kilda with motel-style rooms which also have cooking facilities. *Melbourne Gate* (tel 51 5870) is at 87 Alma Rd on the corner with Chapel St while *City Gate* (tel 534 2650) is at 6 Tennyson Rd. Melbourne Gate is a more modern building while City Gate is on a rather quieter street. Typical costs for singles are $22 for motel-style rooms with kitchenettes, $34 for one-bedroom flats. Equivalent weekly rates would be $70/95 while as a double a one-bedroom flat would cost $120 a week. They also have larger holiday flats with two and three bedrooms but the majority are just one-bedroom.

Colleges Melbourne has three universities: the long established Melbourne university and two newer 'bush universities' – La Trobe and Monash. Visitors would probably find the latter two too far away from the centre to be worth considering.

Melbourne University, by contrast, is very central, just to the north of the city centre. The following colleges have accommodation in the vacations, and the rates include breakfast:

Ridley College (tel 387 7555) with non-student rates from $11 a day room only

St Hilda's College (tel 347 1158) at \$21.50
Ormond College (tel 347 1319) from \$27
Trinity College (tel 347 1044) from \$25
St Mary's College (tel 347 4311) from \$21 per day including dinner as well as lunch on the weekends.

There are cheaper rates for students at all these colleges.

All these places are conveniently central, most of them in Parkville. There are some other Melbourne University colleges which only offer accommodation to convention groups. Generally the colleges above are available during the vacations although some close over Christmas. Only some require advance booking but almost all of them prefer it. International House is one of the best bets and also has accommodation year-round although your chances are best in the vacations.

Camping Melbourne is not too badly off for city campsites although none of them are too close to the centre. The Coburg East site (10 km north) and the Footscray site (eight km west) are probably the most convenient. The Footscray site only has on-site vans but the Coburg one is quite comprehensively equipped as well as being conveniently located. The following are some of Melbourne's closer campsites:

Half Moon Caravan Park (tel 314 5148), corner Geelong & Millers Rds, Brooklyn, 14 km out, camping \$7, on-site vans \$16.

Northside Caravan Park (tel 305 3614), corner Hume Highway & Coopers Rd, Campbellfield, 14 km north, camping \$8, on-site vans \$19.

Sylvan Caravan Park (tel 359 1592), 1780 Hume Highway, Campbellfield, 14 km north, camping \$8, on-site vans \$18.

Melbourne Caravan Park (tel 354 3533), 265 Elizabeth St, Coburg East, 10 km north, camping \$6, on-site vans \$17, flats \$22.

Crystal Brook Holiday Centre (tel 844 3637), corner Warrandyte & Andersons Creek Rd, Doncaster East, 21 km north-east, camping \$9, on-site vans \$22.

Footscray Caravan Park (tel 314 6646), 163 Somerville Rd, West Footscray, eight km west, no camping, on-site vans \$15.

West City Caravan Park (tel 363 3262), 610 Ballarat Rd, Sunshine, 13 km west, camping \$8.

Willowbrook Gardens Caravan Village (tel 333 1619), Mickleham Rd, Westmeadows, 18 km north-west, camping \$8, on-site vans \$21.

Hobsons Bay Caravan Park (tel 397 2395), 158 Kororoit Creek Rd, Williamstown, 17 km south, camping \$8, on-site vans \$18.

Places to Eat

The Victorian licencing laws make it very difficult and expensive to get a liquor licence but quite simple to obtain a BYO licence. The resulting plethora of BYO's are held by staunch Melbournians to be the cornerstone of Melbourne's culinary superiority. There are lots of licenced restaurants too, some of which are actually cheap, but it's the BYO's which you find everywhere around the city. It's very rare to be charged 'corkage' when you bring your own wine to a Melbourne BYO.

There are 28 pages of restaurants in the Melbourne Yellow Pages phone directory and *Cheap Eats* (published by Anne O'Donovan) is a guide to the cheaper restaurants. There are restaurants all around the city and there are often real national quarters – go to Lygon St, Carlton for Italian food; Swan St, Richmond for Greek food; Sydney Rd, Brunswick for Turkish; Little Bourke St in the city for Chinese.

City – Chinese While elsewhere around Melbourne food tends to be regional by area, in the city you'll find a bit of everything. The city is, however, the centre for Chinese food and you'll find a superb variety along Little Bourke St, the Chinatown of Melbourne. Most of the Little Bourke St Chinese restaurants tend to be more expensive, however. You have to dive off into the narrow lanes off Little Bourke, or abandon it altogether, to find the real bargains, like *Nam Loong* at 223 Russell St where even the blackboard menu is in Chinese. You almost feel like they're being condescending when they produce an English menu and you can certainly expect nothing but chopsticks. The prices are, however, something to smile about. Eat early though, Nam Loong closes at 9 pm. At 30 Crossley St the *Malaya* does filling Malaysian-Chinese food, especially the soups and noodle dishes.

Peony Gardens at 283 Little Lonsdale is more of a take-away place, less a restaurant. They say you'll find good Chinese food in restaurants patronised by the Chinese, so a restaurant patronised by Chinese students should be not only good but cheap too. At Peony Gardens most dishes are $3 or less and at that price you really can't complain about plastic plates and utensils or having to clear the table off after you've eaten. It's mainly a lunchtime place as it closes early in the evening.

On Little Bourke St there are some bargains to be found, however, like the pleasant Malaysian-Chinese *Golden Orchid* at 126. The big *Asian Food Plaza* on the corner of Little Bourke and Russell Sts has a menu featuring all manner of Chinese, Malaysian, Vietnamese, Korean and other Asian food. The kitchens around the dining area are all open so you can see what's going on and the prices are generally pretty reasonable. They do Hainan chicken rice, one of my favourite Chinese dishes, and on Sundays at lunch time they have *yum cha* where you choose small dishes of food off a trolley wheeled around the restaurant. Around the city you'll also find plenty of Japanese and Korean places.

City – Other Open from 7 am to midnight every day and 24 hours over the weekend the *Pancake Parlour* is the place to go for a meal from breakfast to a late night snack. It's at 25 Market Lane, is fairly fast-foodish in atmosphere and a bit expensive but very popular. There's another branch in Centrepoint on Bourke St. The *Pancake House* is next to the main Pancake Parlour and offers similar fare and an open-air courtyard in the back.

Further up Bourke St is another Melbourne institution – *Pelligrini's* at 66. It's a quick meal sort of place with the usual pasta dishes. If you want to take things a little easier then go round the corner to Crossley St where you can relax over the same food at slightly higher prices. *Campari Bistro* at 25 Hardware St, a hop, step and jump from the GPO, is a busy little Italian bistro which can get very crowded at lunchtime.

Carlton You can take a 1, 15, 21 or 22 tram from the centre but you can also walk to Lygon St, it's no distance at all from central Melbourne. This is not only the Italian centre of Melbourne it probably also qualifies as the restaurant centre of the city as there are literally dozens of places to eat scattered along Lygon St. Starting from the city end there's *Toto's Pizza House* at 101. They claim to be the first pizzeria in Australia and true or not they certainly make some of the best value pizzas in Melbourne – large pizzas are $6 to $8. Toto's is licensed but drinks are very reasonably priced – house wine is $2.50 a half litre or $4 a litre. As a final plus it's open past midnight every night of the week.

Head on up Lygon St after your pizza for an excellent coffee and cake at *Notturno* at 167. There are tables out on the pavement and it's open 24 hours. Or continue to 215 where *Il Gambero* is another long runner. They're a seafood specialist and also do pizza. The food can be variable but but it's open until after midnight and is reasonably priced. *Papa Gino's Pizzas*, a couple of doors up at 221, is another long-running pizza place with a good reputation. On the other side of the street is the equally long-running *Caffe Sport* at 262 Lygon St. It's one of those hidden places; you have to walk through the coffee bar and up the anonymous stairs at the back. And what do you find there? The Lygon St Italian standard menu – fairly good food at fairly reasonable prices.

Between Faraday and Elgin Sts there's a whole collection of places to eat but first turn off Lygon St to *Johnny's Green Room* at 194 Faraday St. This is another place that's open 24 hours a day, a place where you can get a cheap bowl of spaghetti and a cup of strong coffee (a game of pool too if you want) at any hour of the night. *Brunetti's Cakes Gelateria* has moved round the corner from Lygon St to Faraday St. They have good rolls, cakes and superb ice cream. Back on Lygon St there's *Tiamo's* at 303 – old-timers still refer to it as Tamani's. It's a straightforward pasta place and popular with students from Melbourne University, only a short stroll up Faraday St.

There's a popular theory that hidden somewhere in the middle of Lygon St there's an enormous Italian kitchen that turns out all the food for all the restaurants in Carlton – they're that much alike! There are, however, some different places such as *Shakahari* at 329 Lygon St. This is one of Melbourne's longest running and most popular vegetarian restaurants with a really interesting menu. Count on around $30 for a complete meal for two in this pleasantly relaxed restaurant. Almost next door is the famed *Jimmy Watson's Wine Bar* – see pub food.

The *Carlton Curry House* at 204 Rathdowne St does great Indian food at pleasantly low prices. Starters are just $1 to $2, main courses $5 to $6, you can stagger out replete for $20 for two. In fact this rates as my favourite new cheap restaurant in Melbourne for this edition. Reservations are advisable as it's a popular place. At 157 Elgin St *Bali House* is, despite the name, predominantly Malay and Chinese. Main courses are $5 to $8, the service is friendly, the decor basic.

Richmond Take a 70, 71 or 77 tram from Batman Avenue, by the river in the city, and get off on Swan St at the Church St junction in Richmond, the Greek centre of Melbourne. The hundred metres or so along Swan St away from the city past Church St is virtually wall-to-wall Greek restaurants, one of the simplest and best-known being the *Laikon* at 272. Inside, the Laikon is as plain as you could ask for, there's no menu so just go to the counter and order zatsiki and taramasalata (both dips), pitta bread to dip in it, and souvlaki (kebabs) which comes with salad. With a sticky sweet dessert and coffee you'll pay about $10 a head here and the food is as delicious and straightforward as you could ask for. While you're at the counter you better grab the wine bottle opener to uncork your wine too – the bottle shop on the corner of Swan and Church Sts sells retsina. The *Laikon* does good take-aways too.

The Laikon is just one of a number of Greek restaurants along here – *Elatos* at 213 Swan St and *Agapi* at 262 are also popular, straightforward and good value. Round the corner at 455 Church St *Ariston* also does excellent Greek food but in slightly swishier surroundings – tablecloths and the like!

Greek food isn't all you'll find in Richmond. Across the road from the Ariston is *Sweetman's* at 484 Church St. It's big and bright but also rather more expensive. There's also a variety of cuisines along Bridge Rd and Victoria St, parallel to Swan St. Victoria St has become Melbourne's 'Little Saigon' and there are numerous bargain priced Vietnamese restaurants along here. Try *Vao Doi* at 120 Victoria St where the food is very cheap and authentic. Main courses are $3 to $5, two people can eat well for less than $15. There are also Vietnamese restaurants along Bridge Rd, like the *Viet Huong* at 338 Bridge Rd opposite the Richmond Town Hall. They do specials for two people – five course for $20, six for $24. The glossy and popular

Que Huong at 176 Bridge Rd has main courses from $7 to $13; no skimping on the quantity here.

Or you could continue further along Swan St to the *Rumah Makan* which does really excellent Malay food – great curries and some unusual dishes. Richmond also has some Indian restaurants, some good pub food specialists and even Melbourne's only Argentinian steak house!

Sydney Rd Head directly north of the city centre along that majestic avenue Royal Parade and you suddenly find yourself in the narrow, congested shopping street of Sydney Rd, Brunswick. This is indeed the road to Sydney but it's also one of the worst bottlenecks in Melbourne, at least in the rush hours. In the evenings it's no problem at all and this is Melbourne's Turkish restaurant area. You can get there from the city centre on an 18, 19 or 20 tram.

If you've not tried Turkish food before it's very straightforward, honest fare, closely related to Greek or Lebanese food. Lots of interesting starters, main courses like kebabs, spiced lamb, various grilled meats, a wide variety of interesting desserts. Best of all it's generally very cheap and the Turkish restaurants along Sydney Rd often bake their own delicious bread (*pide*) on the premises – Turkish bread is superb.

Alasya at 555 Sydney Rd, it's so popular that it's engulfed the places next door and spawned an identical offshoot, *Alasya 2*, closer to the city at 163 Sydney Rd. Here, as at most of the other Turkish places, you can choose from the menu or opt for a fixed-price meal which gets you a dozen (yes!) starters, a mixture of main courses, a selection of desserts, heaps of freshly baked bread and coffee all for a fixed price. It's terrific value and you'd better bring a healthy appetite with you.

Quite a bit further up Sydney Rd, the *Golden Teras* (or Terrace) at 820 is a smaller place and equally popular. Just across the road the spacious *Sultan Ahmet* at 835 is more of the same with a fixed-price menu or you can choose items.

South Yarra Along Toorak Rd you'll find some of Melbourne's most expensive restaurants – places where a couple would have no trouble paying $70 to $100 for a meal. Fortunately there are some more relevant places in between – like *Pinocchio's* at 152 Toorak Rd. This is my favourite pizzeria on this side of town and it also has a blackboard menu of other standard Italian favourites. It's a pleasant and convenient place to eat and the pizzas are excellent; the take-away prices are lower.

Only a couple of doors away at 156 is *Tamani's*, Italian once again, a popular restaurant with good pasta dishes and salads. Just across the railway tracks at 164 *Alfio's* is almost too smoothly trendy-looking for its own good but the prices aren't bad, there's a nice sunny courtyard out back and their pasta is superb. Backtrack down Toorak Rd to number 74 where you'll find similar ambience and similar food at the *Barola Bistro* – a pleasant little espresso bar with a blackboard menu and snappy service.

South Yarra's not all Italian; there are also a number of the currently trendy deli-style places, in particular *The Deli* at 26 Toorak Rd. This large, airy place has good food, excellent salads and is fine for a late night coffee. Tables are also set out on the footpath. Upstairs at 177 Toorak Rd the *Mt Lebanon* has excellent Lebanese food (and a belly dancer) but it's more expensive than the regular string of Middle East eateries.

Deli food and open-air eating are also popular along Chapel St. Right turn from Toorak Rd and you'll almost immediately come to *Amigo's* at 596 Chapel St, a pleasant little Mexican restaurant which also does a steady take-away business. Across the road is *Spaghetti Graffiti* at

571, open around the clock. Continue along Chapel St to 517 where *The Tandoor* has probably the best Indian food in Melbourne; definitely not cheap though.

Right on down Chapel St almost to Commercial Rd and you'll find *Soda Sisters Drugstore* at 382. It's a facsimile of a '50s American soda fountain with ice cream sodas, sundaes, hamburgers and other representatives of American kulcha. A couple of doors down is the *Polonia*, where you get good, solid serves of home-cooked Polish food at very reasonable prices. The immensely popular Prahran market is back from the Chapel St-Commercial Rd junction – go here for some of the best fresh vegetables, fruit and fish in Melbourne.

Other Places – North of the City Brunswick St in Fitzroy has developed as a whole new restaurant area in the past few years. It's international – everything from Italian to Indian including Melbourne's only Afghani restaurant. The *Afghan Gallery Restaurant* is at 327 Brunswick St, certainly something a bit different although also a bit more expensive. The *Black Cat* at 252 is an ultra-with-it coffee bar, ideal for coffee and a cake at late hours. At 266 the *Thai Room* has superb Thai food and this is one place where when they say it's hot it really is *hot*!

Round the corner on Johnston St you'll find Melbourne's Spanish quarter with restaurants like the very Spanish *Costa Brava* at 36 – try their terrific paella for two or more. Turn the other way to Johnston St, Collingwood where at 32 *Jim's Greek Tavern* has typical Greek food but in a rather more 'restaurant-like' setting; the prices are still low.

Still in Fitzroy at 199 Gertrude St is *Macedonia*, a pleasantly basic and straightforward Yugoslav restaurant offering the Central European regulars including excellent schnitzels. For dessert you've got a choice of pancakes, pancakes or pancakes.

Other Places – South & East of the City Cross town to South Melbourne where you'll find several places worth considering along Clarendon St. The *Old Paper Shop Deli* at 266 is another place where you can eat outside, on the pavement breathing in the traffic fumes. The food is superb but it's wise to keep an eye on the prices – with care you can eat very reasonably but it's quite easy to keep making additions from the counter and end up with a surprising bill. A bit further along at 331 is the *Chinese Noodle Shop* – excellent authentic noodles dishes at reasonable prices in pleasant surroundings and fast, friendly service. Further again to *Taco Bill's* at 375 – strictly mass-market Mexican food but good value for all that. There's a whole string of Taco Bills around Melbourne, all very similar; check the addresses in the phone directory. To any Americans out there Taco Bill's is about a hundred times better than Taco Bells!

If you continue down Chapel St in South Yarra you'll come to Prahran where at 310 Chapel St the *Ankara Restaurant* does the Turkish regulars, just like Sydney Rd, with a good fixed-price complete meal. Or for Greek food there's *Lemnos Tavern* at 445 High St where you can fill yourself up just on the dips and bread. Main courses are $6 to $10. Also on High St at 408 *Arjuna* serves spicy Indonesian food at very reasonable prices.

Further east in Camberwell (or more correctly Hawthorn East) there are a number of good places along Camberwell Rd including the *Borobudur* at 159 with reasonably priced and reasonably good Indonesian food.

Head towards the sea where at Fitzroy St, St Kilda if you were going to have one super splash out meal in Melbourne then *Tolarno's* would be the place to do it. It's licensed and moderately expensive but the food and service are the equal of much more expensive places. Still on Fitzroy St but right at the other end of the price scale is *Cleopatra's* at the seaside end at number 1. It's Lebanese (or Egyptian?) and mainly take-aways but they produce some of the best quality Middle Eastern food in Melbourne and at very reasonable prices. Round the corner at 107 Acland St the *Danube* does good plain Central European food in large quantities; even their half serves fill you up!

Pub Food Melbourne has a good assortment of these, ranging from the humble corner place to some trendy, flashy establishments. The *Palace Hotel* at 893 Burke Rd, Camberwell isn't quite as good as it once was but it's still worth the trip out there; take a Camberwell tram from Swanston St which loops round through Prahran to run up Burke Rd, or take a train straight to Camberwell Station, right beside the Palace. Inside there's a long menu featuring all the pub food regulars from steak, fish or schnitzel to veal parmigana or chicken kiev and with a good salad table. It closes at 8.30 pm.

Since it's a wine bar rather than a pub it's probably not correct to put *Jimmy Watson's* in this section, but never mind. At 333 Lygon St this ever-popular place does excellent food as well as reasonably priced wine by the bottle. You'll find its courtyard is packed to capacity on any sunny Saturday morning.

You'll also find quite a few pub-food places around South Yarra and Prahran. The *Fawkner Club* (which isn't a club) is only a couple of blocks along Toorak Rd from St Kilda Rd. You can get there on any St Kilda Rd tram (walk up Toorak Rd) or the Toorak tram but then you have to walk back along Toorak Rd from where the tram joins it. The Fawkner Club's main attraction is the fine open-air courtyard out front – it's not been altered by a recent up-market trendification inside. There's the counter meal regulars plus a serve-yourself salad table.

On Chapel St at number 270, the *Court Jester* serves slightly up-market pub food. They have some slightly adventurous

dishes amongst the counter regulars and a good reputation for their food. Now U-turn and go right back along Chapel St through South Yarra, across the Yarra River into Richmond and on your right at 481 Church St (Chapel St changes names with the river) is the *Anchor & Hope*. *Molinas*, the restaurant part in front, is more expensive with starters at $5.50, interesting main courses at $9. The Bugatti Bar in back (with its amazing collection of car badges, number plates and assorted automotive memorabilia) has bistro food at $6 to $8. Come here only when you're hungry, the quantities are large.

The *London Tavern* at 238 Lennox St, Richmond is a pretty straightforward place but with a very good chef so the food is excellent (and reasonably priced) and with a bright and sunny courtyard, you can eat outside. Finally out at Williamstown the remarkable *Yacht Club Hotel* at 207 Nelson Place has what must be the cheapest pub food around. You can eat for $1.95 and all the pub regulars, with chips and a serve-yourself salad table, are only $2.95 or $3.50. Williamstown also has a *Taco Bill's* a couple of doors down and the *Ice Cream Shoppe* has a mind boggling selection of excellent ice cream.

ENTERTAINMENT

The best source of 'what's on' info in Melbourne is *The Age Entertainment Guide* which comes out every Friday. During the summer months watch out for the FEIP (Free Entertainment In the Park) programme with activities put on in city parks on weekday lunchtimes and on the weekends. There's also often something going on in the City Square.

Melbourne has a number of concert halls and other venues, none of them too good for big rock concerts. The old Festival Hall is big but barn like and the new riverside Entertainment Centre has unbelievably bad acoustics. The Arts Centre concert hall, also by the river, is the focus for opera and concert music.

There's also the Dallas Brooks Hall and the outdoors Sidney Myer Music Bowl.

Rock Music A lot of Melbourne's night time scene is tied up with rock pubs – some of the big crowded places can afford the top Australian bands and it's for this reason that Melbourne is very much Australia's rock music centre. It's on the sweaty grind around the Melbourne rock pubs that Australia's best bands really prove themselves. *The Age Entertainment Guide* and stations like EON-FM or 3XY will tell you who's on and where. Cover charges at the pubs vary widely – some nights it's free, generally it's from around $6, big names on weekend nights can cost $8 or more. Music generally starts around 9.30 pm. Those that follow are just a few of the places offering a variety of music.

Although it's not what it once was the small *Station Hotel* on Greville St, Prahran still attracts the crowds. It's one of the longest running of the rock pubs, a place with a bit of a Melbourne rock history. The Saturday arvo sessions are popular. At the opposite end of the scale are places like the *Bombay Rock* a monster place on Phoenix St, Brunswick. It's crowded, rough, expensive, impossible to get to the bar, the bands tend to start late and the bouncers are terrible but you do get the big name bands here – if you don't mind paying $10 or more for them. In St Kilda, *The Venue* is similar though not quite so bad. Also in the same vein is the *Prince of Wales Hotel* in Fitzroy St, St Kilda.

Between these extremes are places like the *Armadale Hotel* in Armadale, not a bad place with upstairs and downstairs rooms (harder rock upstairs?). The *London Tavern* in Caulfield caters mainly for students with middle-of-the-road to bland music. Ditto for the *Prospect Hill* in Kew which attracts fairly big bands, *The Central Club* in Richmond is another student type of pub which caters mainly for small bands.

In North Fitzroy the *Aberdeen Hotel* is a small, friendly sort of place catering mainly for fringe bands, something a bit different. *The Club* in Collingwood is similar, attracting interesting fringe bands. The big *Club Chevron* on St Kilda Rd, Prahran is free some nights and has quite a good atmosphere. Finally in the city there's *Billboard* on Russell St – basically for rich trendies who like looking at themselves not listening to the music.

Folk Music Yes there are also folk pubs. In *The Age Entertainment Guide* check the acoustic music listings as well as folk. One of the most popular is the *Dan O'Connell Hotel*, (the 'Dan') on the corner of Princes and Canning Sts in Carlton. For those interested in Irish music they claim 'we sell more Irish whiskey than Scotch' as proof of their Irish authenticity. On High St, Malvern the long running *Green Man Coffee Lounge* is still a popular folk venue. Others include the *Hatters Castle* in South Yarra; the *Troubador* on Brunswick St, Fitzroy; *Renown Hotel* in Fitzroy. The *Spaghetti Theatre* restaurant in Collins St in the city has live folk or acoustic music on most nights.

Jazz Just like there are pubs that specialise in rock or folk there are also pubs that specialise in jazz. Popular ones include the *Tankerville Arms* on Nicholson St in Fitzroy or the *Victoria Hotel* in Albert Park, the *Limerick Arms* in South Melbourne and the *Beaconsfield Hotel* in St Kilda are others. *I D's Nitespot* in Greville St, Prahran also has jazz in the evenings.

Discos For those who like their music canned rather than live Melbourne also has it's fair share of discos ranging from the absurdly expensive on down. The *Melbourne Underground* on King St, near Flinders St in the city, is a much flashier establishment than the rock pub havens and has a 24-hour liquor licence. There are a number of restaurants in this sprawling establishment. Others include *Inflation* on King St, *Sheiks* on Collins St, *Madison's* on Flinders Lane and *Fame* at 536 Swanston St, all in the city. In South Yarra there's *Chasers* at 386 Chapel St, or there's *Casablanca* in Fitzroy St, St Kilda.

Pubs & Wine Bars Apart from the music pubs there are quite a few other popular pubs and wine bars. Top of the wine bar list would have to be *Jimmy Watson's* on Lygon St, Carlton – very much a place to see and be seen, especially at around lunchtime Saturday. It has a delightful (when the sun is shining) open courtyard out back.

Some of the places listed in the pub food places (*the Fawkner* or the *Argo Inn* for example) are also good places to drop in. Other popular pubs include the *Anchor & Hope* on Church St, Richmond with its amazing car-badge decor; *Lord Jim's* (very much a place for pick-ups) at 36 St George's Rd, North Fitzroy or the *Council Club* in South Melbourne. The *Capitol Wine Bar* at the corner of Toorak Rd and Chapel St in South Yarra is also popular.

Theatre Restaurants No mention of Melbourne's eating/entertainment possibilities would be complete without a section on theatre restaurants. They've always been a popular idea but Melbourne's particular inspiration is combining eating out with fringe theatre. To a large extent the source of that inspiration is the amazing John Pinder.

John started out with a hole-in-the-wall place called the Flying Trapeze and then moved on to greater things with the *Last Laugh*. On the corner of Smith and Gertrude Sts in Collingwood it's an old cinema/dole-office done up in a dazzling mish-mash of styles from high kitsch up and down. In fact look up as you come in – to see the weird and wonderful collection

of airplanes hovering in the entrance hall. Everything from a cigar smoking Concorde to a flying vacuum cleaner. Inside there's room for 200 people to have a good time – you arrive, pay your money at the door (it's getting pretty expensive, you can pay $25 depending on the night and the show), buy drinks at the bar. There's a blackboard menu and food is reasonably good (for a theatre restaurant where food often takes second place to the show). Like other fringe places vegetarians are well catered for. You have time to get through the appetisers, soup and main course before part one of the show and dessert comes up before part two. The shows can be almost anything; one of the best would have to be the repeat visits by Circus Oz where you could consider the possibility of a tightrope walker landing in your lap half way through your meal.

Afterwards the patrons can take their turn to perform as the stage becomes a disco. Upstairs there's the Last Laugh's upstairs bar, *Le Joke*, where aspiring acts appear late at night. Good grief, Lonely Planet researcher Alan Samagalski has even played 'atomic folk music' there. The upstairs bar is $6 or $8 most nights although some nights are cheaper.

The Last Laugh has probably become a little too establishment these days but there are other places like the *Comedy Cafe* on Brunswick St in nearby Fitzroy where one show in 1982 consisted of taking the audience off in a bus to invade some of Melbourne's ritzier establishments while dressed in Groucho Marx masks. The Comedy Cafe also has it's late-night upstairs bar, the Banana Lounge where fringe comedy gets a go.

Cinema Melbourne's best alternative cinema centres include the long running *Valhalla* at 216 Victoria St, Richmond which shows a different film every night. In fact they show two films most nights and since they also have student discount it's great value. They produce a superb six-month film calendar detailing all their shows. Go to the Valhalla on Friday night for the midnight showing of *Blues Brothers* if you want to see Melbourne let its hair down.

The *Carlton Moviehouse* at 235 Faraday St has a similar programme. Various other cinemas around Melbourne specialise in non-mainstream films. They include the *Longford Cinema* at 55 Toorak Rd, South Yarra; the popular *Brighton Dendy*; the La Trobe *Agora* (same company as Valhalla) way out in Bundoora; the *Astor* on the corner of Chapel St and Dandenong Rd in East St Kilda and lastly, the *Union Theatre* at Melbourne Uni with two features for $3 which must be one of the cheapest around.

GETTING THERE

Air There are frequent connections between Melbourne and other state capitals – Melbourne-Sydney flights are hourly during the airport operating hours. East-West are cheaper than the big two but are very heavily booked. Melbourne to Sydney is $139 (standby $90) on East-West. Fares on Ansett or TAA include Sydney $148 (standby $114), Brisbane $224 ($180), Canberra $116 ($93), Adelaide $140 ($112), Perth $341 ($273). Connections to Alice Springs are made via Adelaide.

Melbourne is the main jumping-off point from the mainland to Tasmania. Hobart flights cost $136 (standby $109), Launceston $117 ($94), Burnie $102 ($82), Devonport $104 ($83). Burnie and Devonport routes are operated by East-West Airlines rather than TAA. The TAA office (tel 665 3333) is at 50 Franklin St while Ansett (tel 668 2222) is at 501 Swanston St. Both have smaller offices dotted around the city. East-West (tel 63 7713) are on the first floor at 230 Collins St.

Bus Ansett Pioneer and Greyhound both have frequent services to and from Melbourne. Adelaide connections are made daily; the trip takes about 11 hours

and costs $37. Services connect through to Perth via Adelaide and the fare is $122. Canberra takes about 10 hours for $29. Melbourne-Sydney services go direct (via Canberra), via Wagga Wagga or up the coast along the Princes Highway. The direct trip takes about 15 hours and costs $37.

There are also direct services between Melbourne and Brisbane, either via the Gold Coast or via Toowoomba. The trip takes 31 or 32 hours and costs $70. There are also a variety of other services from Melbourne – to Bega, Mildura, Mt Gambier or Deniliquin for example. Ansett Pioneer 9tel 668 3144) operate from the Ansett terminal on the corner of Swanston and Franklin Sts. Greyhound (tel 614-4240) are at 667 Bourke St, right up at the Spencer St end.

There are quite a few alternative bus companies operating through Melbourne. Across Australia Coachlines (tel 62 3848) are at 56 Spencer St and offer Sydney for $30 ($27 for students), Adelaide $30 ($27) and Perth $110 ($99). VIP Express (tel 62-7395) at 490 Flinders St have similar fares and also go to Brisbane ($60) and Cairns ($125). Deluxe Coachlines (tel 663 6144) at 440 Elizabeth St do all the above (at slightly higher prices) plus Canberra for $29 and Noosa for $72.

Rail There are three train services between Melbourne and Sydney: the Southern Aurora and the Spirit of Progress both operate overnight every day of the week; the Intercapital Daylight Express operates by day, Monday to Saturday. The trip takes 13 to 14 hours and costs $59 in economy, $83 in 1st. A sleeping berth is an extra $33 on top of the 1st class fare, there are no berths in economy. You can take a car on the Melbourne-Sydney services for $75. To get to Canberra by rail you take the Intercapital Daylight as far as Yass Junction from where a bus connects for the one-hour trip into Canberra – total fare $40 ($56 in 1st.)

To or from Adelaide the Overland

operates overnight every day of the week. The trip takes 13 hours and costs $44 in economy, $62 in 1st, again with a $33 supplement for a sleeper. The Intercapital Daylight to or from Sydney connects with the Overland. To get to Perth by rail from Melbourne you take the Overland and then the East-West Express to Port Pirie where you connect with the Trans-Australian or the Indian-Pacific. The Melbourne-Perth fare is $335 in economy, $479 in 1st, including sleeping berths and meals on the Port Pirie-Perth sector in economy or 1st.

There is also a rail service between Melbourne and Mildura, the Vinelander, which runs from Sunday to Friday, takes 10 hours overnight and costs $27.50 in economy, $37.50 in 1st, sleeping berths $17 extra on 1st.

If you're travelling to or from any of the major cities and can book at least seven days in advance, you can get a 30% discount with the 'Caper' fares (Customer Advance Purchase Excursion Rail – would you believe). Rail tickets for interstate services can be booked at the Spencer St railway station in Melbourne (tel 62 3115), from where the interstate services depart. There is also a Railways of Australia office in the Embank Arcade across the corner of Elizabeth and Collins Sts in Melbourne.

Vintage train enthusiasts should enquire about the Steamrail Victoria monthly excursions in old steam locomotives.

GETTING AROUND

Airport Transport Although Melbourne's Tullamarine airport is a fair way (about 20 km) out from the city it's quite easy to get to since the Tullamarine Freeway runs almost into the centre. Melbourne's old airport, Essendon, is on the way out to Tulla.

A taxi between the airport and city centre will cost about $15 to $17 but there are two privately operated bus services. The Skybus Express cost $5 and departs from the TAA and Ansett ends of the airport terminal, runs about every half hour through the day and the city terminus is at the airlines bus terminal in Franklin St.

The Skybus VIP service costs $6 and runs less frequently, particularly on weekends. It departs from outside the international part of the terminal, in the middle. At the city end the VIP bus drops you at the airline bus terminal and from there a minibus does a loop of the major hotels and Flinders St and Spencer St stations.

There is also a fairly frequent bus by Gull Airport Service between the airport and Geelong. It costs $12 one-way, $22 return; a same-day return is $18. The Geelong terminus is at 45 McKillop St. You can get timetables for these services from the information counter in the international section at the airport.

Tullamarine is a modern airport with a single terminal; TAA at one end, Ansett at the other, international in the middle. There's an information desk upstairs in the international departure area. It's the most spacious airport in Australia and doesn't suffer the night flight restrictions which apply to some other Australian airports. Tulla's snack bar and restaurant sections are the airport norm for quality and price but if you're stuck at the airport for any reason you can stroll over to the customs agents building, turn right out of the terminal and it's about a 200-metre walk, where there's a cheap snack bar. There's another in the small centre beyond the car park by the Travelodge Motel.

Public Transport Melbourne's public transport system, The Met, is based on buses, suburban railways and the famous trams. The trams are the real cornerstone of the system; in all there are about 750 of them and they operate as far as 20 km out from the centre. They're frequent and fun. Buses are the secondary form of public transport, supporting the trams where tram lines do not go, even replacing them at quiet weekend periods. There are also a whole host private bus services as well as the public ones. The train services provide a third link for Melbourne's outer suburbs. There is even an underground city loop which was completed in 1985. For information on Melbourne transport contact either the Victorian Government Travel Centre (tel 602 9444) at 230 Collins St or phone the Transport Information Centre (tel 602 9011) between 7.30 am and 10 pm Monday to Saturday or 9.15 am to 10 pm on Sunday.

You've got a choice in Melbourne of either paying a straight fare for distance or getting a day travelcard. On trams and buses the straight fare is 65c for a short journey. Melbourne is also divided into 10 transport 'neighbourhoods' – the largest being the Inner, which extends out from the city as far as the end of the tram network. The tickets vary depending on the number of neighbourhoods you wish to travel in, and for how long. There are two-hourly, daily, weekly and periodical tickets covering all neighbourhoods. The basic two-hour single-neighbourhood ticket is $1.10, while the daily ticket is $2.20. These tickets are good for travel on trains, trams or buses. There are other concession tickets available on trains and trams. Train travellers can get off-peak return tickets for use after 9.30 am; or off-peak travelcards which start at a railway station and allow only the one rail journey but also permit tram and bus travel within the central area. Or there are tram concession cards – the City Saver, nine rides in the city centre for $4. There are numerous other deals but we don't want to make this too complicated do we!

The Met Authority put out a leaflet, *Getting Around Melbourne on The Met*, which tries to explain the whole relatively complicated system of tickets and travelcards – pick one up at the tourist office, or the leaflet *How to Track it down by Tram on The Met* shows all the tram routes and indicates the things worth seeing on these

various routes. For travel further afield pick up a copy of the *Transport in Victoria* map which not only shows the complete V-Line suburban bus and train network but also details bus routes and operators throughout the state.

Car Rental All the big car rental firms operate in Melbourne. Avis, Budget, Hertz and Thrifty have desks at the airport and you'll also find Thrifty and Natcar in the city. The city offices tend to be at the north end of the city or in Carlton or North Melbourne.

Melbourne also has a number of rent-a-wreck style operators, renting older vehicles at lower rates. Their costs and conditions vary widely so it's worth making a few enquiries before going for one firm over another. Typical are Rentabomb (tel 429 4003) at 129 Bridge Rd, Richmond. They rent older Holdens at $14 to $18 a day plus $5 for insurance including unlimited km but you're limited to a 100-km radius from the centre. Equivalent weekly rates are $110 to $130. Rentawreck (tel 267 5999) are at 391 St Kilda Rd, directly across from the Australian Tourist Commission. They have a wide variety of older models with rates of $25 per day including insurance and unlimited km. Longer-term rates are $3 a day less. They also restrict you to the metropolitan area at these rates but you can go anywhere in Victoria for the same daily rate plus 10c a km in excess of 100 km a day.

The telephone yellow pages list lots of other firms (like Dam Cheap Hire, Discount Rent-a-Car, Rent an Oldie and so on) but some rates do not include any free km and you soon get up to the level of the unlimited-distance firms.

Bicycle Rental Melbourne's not a bad city for biking – there's that lengthy riverside bicycle track and other bicycle tracks and lanes around the city plus it's reasonably flat so you're not pushing and panting up hills too often. Look for a copy of *Weekend*

Bicycle Rides for a pleasant introduction to bike rides around Melbourne. There are quite a few rides you can make in the surrounding country by taking one train out of Melbourne then riding across to a different line to get the train back. An example is to take the train out to Gisborne and follow the fine ridgetop ride to Bacchus Marsh from where you can get another train back in to the city.

Unfortunately, if you don't already have a bike, Melbourne's not a great place to try and hire one – at least not if you want to do more than just dawdle along the pleasant cycle-path by the river, a popular pastime on weekends. There are hire places opposite the Botanic Gardens, beside Como Park in Burnley and at the Kevin Bartlett Reserve in Richmond. Hire-a-Bicycle (tel 288 5177), one of the riverside operators, also hires out bikes at other times. The rates are: $4 per hour and $2 each hour after that; $12 per day and $20 per week, all with a small deposit.

Tours Melbourne's latest tourist attraction is the *Spirit of Victoria*, a high-speed ferry which takes visitors on trips around Port Phillip Bay. It departs from Station Pier in Port Melbourne at 10 am and 2 pm on Fridays and Saturdays, going to Mornington, Sorrento and Portarlington and takes about 3½ hours for the round trip. On Sundays it departs at 11 am for a 6 hour trip to Queenscliff, Sorrento and Port Island. The fare is $24 and tickets are available on the boat. For info or reservations phone 62 6997.

The Age 'City Explorer' double-decker bus operates hourly from 10 am to 4 pm from Flinders St station and calls at six major attractions around town. Tickets cost $5 and you can get on or off when and where you like.

The usual variety of tours is available in and around Melbourne. Typical costs include half-day city tours from around $18, to the Dandenongs for a similar price, to Healesville for $20. Longer full-day tours to Ballarat, Phillip Island for the penguins, Bendigo, Echuca, the central gold-fields or into the snow country cost from around $27 to $33.

The old steam tug *Wattle* makes two-hour trips on weekends around the Port of Melbourne and Williamstown, leaving from 20 Victoria Dock at 10 am, 1 pm and 3.30 pm for $8.

Heritage Walks leave the Victour office in Collins St at 10 am on Mondays, Wednesdays and Fridays for 1½-hour tours of Collins St and South Melbourne for $10.

Around Melbourne

There are places of interest all around Melbourne and in all directions from the city – north and west into the gold country, south-east and south-west around Port Phillip and out to the Dandenongs.

THE DANDENONGS

Right on the eastern edge of Melbourne the Dandenongs are one of the most popular day trips from the city. They're cool due to the altitude and lushly green due to the heavy rainfall. The area is dotted with fine old houses, classy restaurants, beautiful gardens and some fine short bushwalks – quite apart from Melbourne's TV transmitter towers on 633-metre Mt Dandenong, the highest point in the Dandenongs. You can clearly see the Dandenongs from central Melbourne (on a smog-free day) and they're only about an hour's drive out.

The small Ferntree Gully National Park has pleasant strolls and lots of birdlife including, if you're very lucky, lyrebirds for which the Dandenongs are famous. The Sherbrooke Forest Park is similarly pleasant for walks and you'll see lots of rosellas here. The William Ricketts sanctuary on Olinda Rd, Mt Dandenong is named after its delightfully eccentric

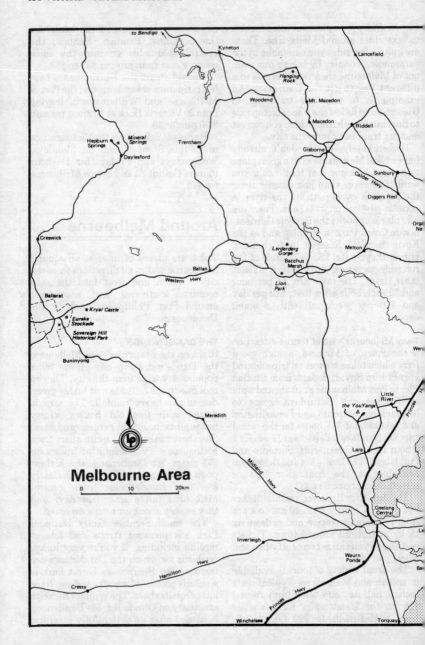

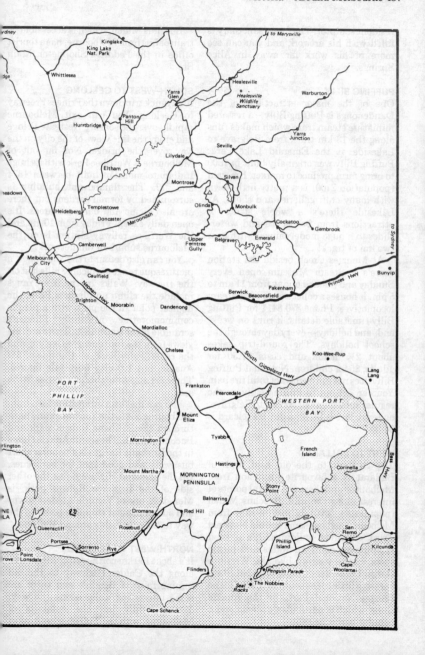

resident sculptor. The forest sanctuary is filled with his artwork and you can see more of his work far away in Alice Springs.

PUFFING BILLY

One of the major attractions of the Dandenongs is Puffing Billy – a restored miniature steam train which makes runs along the 13-km track from Belgrave to Lakeside at the Emerald Lake Park. Puffing Billy was originally built in 1900 to bring farm produce to market. Emerald (population 2100) is a pretty little town with many craft galleries and shops. At Lakeside there's a whole string of attractions from barbecues and water-slides to a huge model railway with over two km of track!

At Menzies Creek beside the station there's a Steam Museum open every Sunday and public holiday from 11 am to 5 pm. It houses a collection of early steam locomotives. Phone 870 8411 for Puffing Billy timetable details; it runs on weekends and holidays – every day through the school holidays. The round-trip takes about 2½ hours and costs $7.50 for adults, $5 for children. Note that Puffing Billy does not run on days of total fire ban. You can get out to Puffing Billy on the regular suburban rail service to Belgrave, one-way fare is $1.70, a day travelcard is $4.30.

WEST TO BALLARAT

The trip out to the old gold town of Ballarat is a favourite excursion from Melbourne and there are several points of interest along the way. Bacchus Marsh (population 5000) is just 49 km from Melbourne and has some fine old National Trust classified buildings. It's a good jumping-off point for walks and picnic spots in the vicinity like the Werribee Gorge, Lerderderg Gorge, Wombat State Forest, a little to the south in the Brisbane Ranges National Park, or the Anakie Gorge which is particularly scenic and a popular barbecue spot.

Bacchus Marsh, which is accessible by train or bus from Melbourne, has a tourist office in the Peddlers Shoppe on Main St.

SOUTH-WEST TO GEELONG

It's a quick trip down the Princes Freeway to Geelong. You can exit Melbourne rapidly over the soaring Westgate Bridge and enjoy the fine views of the city on the way over the bridge. Not far out of Melbourne is Werribee Park with its huge Italianate mansion built between 1874 and '77. The flamboyant building is surrounded by formal gardens but there are also picnic and barbecue areas. It's open daily except Friday from 10 am and the Werribee railway station is on the Melbourne suburban rail network.

You can also detour to the You Yangs, a picturesque range of volcanic hills just off the freeway. Walks in the You Yangs include the climb up Flinders Peak, the highest point in the park with a plaque commemorating Matthew Flinder's scramble to the top in 1802. There are fine views from the top, down to Geelong and the coast. Fairy Park, on the side of Mt Anakie, has 100 clay fairy tale figures. There are also a number of wineries in the area.

You can make an interesting loop from Melbourne out to the You Yangs and back through the Brisbane Ranges park and Bacchus Marsh. The scenic Anakie Gorge in the Brisbane Ranges is a popular short bushwalk and good spot for barbecues. On the Midland Highway, just the other side of the Brisbane Ranges park, is Meredith, one of Victoria's oldest towns and once a popular stopping point on the way to the gold-fields around Ballarat.

NORTH-WEST TO BENDIGO

It's about 150 km north-west of Melbourne along the Calder Highway to the old mining town of Bendigo and there are some interesting walks along the way. You've hardly left the outskirts of Melbourne, with the Tullamarine Airport control tower visible off to the east of the road, when you pass by the small Organ Pipes National Park on the right and Calder motor racing circuit on the left. A little further north is the turn-off to Sunbury, the site for a number of large Australian Woodstock-style rock festivals in the early '70s.

Gisborne (population 1700) is a pleasant little town, at one time a coaching stop on the route to the Bendigo and Castlemaine gold-fields. Soon after Gisborne you come to Macedon (population 1000) and the turn-off to Mt Macedon, a 1013-metre-high extinct volcano with fine views from the top. This area was devastated by the 1983 Ash Wednesday bushfires and the process of rebuilding is still continuing. Despite this, it is still a popular weekend day-out for Melbournians and there are a number of good walks in the country around here plus a few surviving elegant old houses with beautifully kept gardens.

Just north of Mt Macedon is Hanging Rock, a popular picnic spot which became famous from the book and later the film *Picnic at Hanging Rock*. At that mysterious picnic, three schoolgirls on a school trip to the rock disappeared without trace, only for one to equally mysteriously reappear a few days later. The rocks are great fun to clamber over and there are superb views from higher up. While it is highly unlikely that you'll find the missing girls, if you look carefully you may well see koalas lazing in the trees, high above the jumble of rocks.

Just south of the rocks, on the back road from Mt Macedon, there's a stretch of road where a stationary car will appear to roll uphill. This sort of optical illusion is not uncommon but I must admit that this particular piece of road is very convincing. Back on the Calder Highway, Woodend is another pleasant old town. This is the closest you can get to Hanging Rock by public transport; the train fare is $4.30.

The road continues through Kyneton (population 3800) with its fine bluestone buildings. The Historical Centre building was originally a two-storey bank, dating from 1855. Kyneton also has an eight-hectare botanic gardens. Although Kyneton did not directly participate in the Victorian gold-rush it prospered by supplying food and produce to the booming towns on the gold-fields. A further 11 km brings you to Malmsbury with a historic bluestone railway viaduct and a magnificent ruined grain mill, part of which has been converted into a delightful, if a little up-market, restaurant.

HEALESVILLE & THE HILLS

You don't have to travel far to the east of Melbourne before you start getting into the foothills of the Great Dividing Range. In winter you can find snow within a hundred km of the city centre. Healesville (population 4500) is on the outskirts of Melbourne, just where you start to climb up into the hills. There are some pleasant drives from Healesville, particularly the scenic route to Marysville, but the Sir Colin MacKenzie Wildlife Sanctuary is a prime attraction. This is one of the best places to see Australian wildlife in the whole country. Most of the enclosures are very natural, some of the birds seem to just pop in for the day. Some enclosures are only open for a few hours each day so you may want to plan your visit accordingly. The platypus, for example, is only on show in his glass-sided tank from 1.30 to 3.30 pm daily. The nocturnal house, where you can see many of the smaller bush dwellers which only come out at night, is open from 10.30 am to 4 pm while the reptile house is open to 4.30 pm. The whole park is open 9 am to 5 pm and admission is $4.70. There are barbecue and picnic facilities in the pleasantly wooded park. Healesville is on the regular Melbourne suburban transport network; trains operate to Lilydale from where connecting buses run to Healesville.

Beyond Healesville is Warburton

(population 2000), another pretty little hill town in the Great Dividing Range foothills. There are good views of the mountains from the Acheron Way near here and you'll sometimes get snow on Mt Donna Buang, seven km from town. Warburton, in the Upper Yarra Valley, is one of a number of picturesque spots along the upper reaches of the Yarra River. On the Melbourne side of Healesville there are a number of wineries from Yarra Glen along the Yarra Valley.

Marysville (population 600) is a delightful little place and a very popular weekend escape from Melbourne. The one-way bus fare there is $8.10. There are lots of bush tracks to walk, especially to Nicholl's Lookout, Keppel's Lookout, Mt Gordon and Steavenson Falls. Cumberland Scenic Reserve, with numerous walks and the Cumberland Falls, is 16 km east of Marysville. The cross-country skiing trails of Lake Mountain Reserve are only 10 km beyond Marysville.

LAKE EILDON

Continuing beyond the hill towns of Healesville and Marysville you come to Lake Eildon, a large lake created for hydro-power and irrigation purposes. It's a popular resort area with lots of boats and houseboats to hire. Trout breeding is carried out at Snob's Creek Fish Hatchery and there's a fauna sanctuary nearby. The Snob's Creek Falls drop 107 metres. On the shores of the lake the Fraser National Park has some good short walks including an excellent guide-yourself nature walk. On the south side of the lake is the old mining town of Jamieson. Alexandra (population 1800) and Eildon (population 800) are the main centres near the lake. One-way bus fare to the lake is $11.80, changing bus at Marysville.

The Goulburn Valley Highway starts from Eildon and runs to Seymour and Shepparton. North of Yarra Glen is Yea (population 1000), a good centre for the Kinglake National Park with waterfalls, fern gullies and other attractions including abundant wildlife. Gulf Station, a couple of km from Yarra Glen, is only open from time to time but it's an interesting collection of rough old timber buildings of a small rural settlement of the 1850s which has hardly been changed since that time.

Mornington Peninsula

The Mornington Peninsula is the spit of land down the east side of Port Phillip Bay, bordered on its eastern side by the waters of Westernport Bay. The peninsula really starts at Frankston, 40 km from the centre of Melbourne and from there it's almost a continuous beach strip, all the way to Portsea at the end (almost) of the peninsula, nearly 100 km from Melbourne. 'Almost' because the final tip of the peninsula, looking out across 'The Rip', the narrow entrance to Port Phillip Bay, is a restricted military base.

This is a very popular Melbourne resort area with many holiday homes; in summer the accommodation and campsites along the peninsula can be packed right out and traffic can be very heavy. In part this popularity is due to the peninsula's excellent beaches and the great variety they offer. On the north side of the peninsula you've got calm water on the bay beaches (the front beaches) looking out on to Port Phillip Bay, while on the south side there's crashing surf on the rugged and beautiful ocean beaches (the back beaches) which face Bass Strait.

Town development tends to be concentrated along the Port Phillip side; the Westernport Bay and Bass Strait coasts are much less developed and you'll find pleasant bushwalking trails along the Cape Schank Coastal Park, a narrow coastal strip right along the Bass Strait coast from Portsea to Cape Schank. Frankston is the start of the peninsula, linked by rail to Melbourne.

There's a Tourist Information Centre in Dromana on the coast road down the peninsula and the National Park Service's *Discovering the Peninsula* brochure tells you all you'll want to know about the peninsula's history, early architecture and walking tours.

Places to Stay & Eat

There is a string of campsites along the bay front but over the Christmas rush finding a place to set up tent can be very difficult. There are a number of hotels and motels along the peninsula but no travellers' bargains. Counter meals are available at the Sorrento hotels – the *Lady Nelson Bistro* in the Sorrento, the *Tavern Bar* in the Continental, the bistro in the *Koonya*. You can also get counter meals in the *Portsea Hotel* where there's a pleasant beer garden overlooking the beach. Excellent fish & chips at the *Hungry Eye* in Rye.

Getting There

There's a regular bus service from Frankston through to Portsea (ring 602 9444 for details) and Frankston is reached by rail from Melbourne.

During the summer months there's a ferry making the half-hour crossing from Sorrento and Portsea to Queenscliff on the other side of the heads; by road it's a couple of hundred km right round the bay. From 24 December to the end of January it operates 10 times daily, then to Easter five times daily, in November and December it operates three times daily on weekends and it also operates in the May and August school holidays. The adult return fare is $6 and for the first couple of morning departures there's a connecting bus into Geelong.

FRANKSTON TO BLAIRGOWRIE

Beyond Frankston you reach Mornington and Mt Martha, early settlements with some old buildings along the Mornington Esplanade and fine, secluded beaches in between. Dromana is the real start of the resort development and just inland from here a winding road leads up to Arthur's Seat lookout at 305 metres; you can also reach it by a scenic chairlift (weekends and holidays in summer only). On the slopes of Arthur's Seat, in McCrae, the McCrae Homestead is a National Trust property, dating from 1843 and open daily from 10 am to 5 pm from December to Easter and weekends the rest of the year. Coolart on Sandy Point Rd, Balnarring is another historic homestead on the peninsula. Coolart is also noted for the wide variety of birdlife which can be seen on the reserve. Balnarring is on the other side of the peninsula.

After McCrae there's Rosebud, Rye and Blairgowrie before you reach Sorrento. Rosebud has a Marine & Reptile Park and there's the Peninsula Gardens Tourist & Fauna Park (sounds like a great combination).

SORRENTO

Just as you enter Sorrento there's a small memorial and pioneer cemetery from the first Victorian settlement at pretty Sullivan Bay. The settlement party arrived here from England in October 1803, intending to forestall a feared French settlement on the bay. Less than a year later in May 1804 the project was abandoned and transferred to Hobart, Tasmania. The main reason for the settlement's short life was a lack of water; they had simply chosen the wrong place as there was an adequate supply further round the bay. The settlement's numbers included an 11-year-old boy, John Pascoe Fawkner, who 25 years later would be one of the founders of Melbourne. It also included William Buckley, a convict who escaped soon after the arrival in 1803 and lived with Aboriginals for the next 30 years as the 'wild white man'.

Sorrento has a rather damp and cold little aquarium and an interesting small historical museum in the old Mechanic's Institute building on the Old Melbourne Rd. From the 1870s paddle-steamers used to run between Melbourne and Sorrento. The largest, entering service in 1910, carried 2000 passengers. From 1890 through to 1921 there was a steam-powered tram operating from the Sorrento pier to the back beach. The magnificent hotels built of local limestone in this period still stand – the Sorrento (1871), Continental (1875) and Koonya (1878).

PORTSEA

Portsea, at the end of the Nepean Highway, offers another choice between front and back beaches. At the Portsea back beach there's the impressive natural rock formation known as London Bridge, plus a cliff face where hang-gliders make their leap into the void. There are fine views across Portsea and back to Melbourne from Mt Levy Lookout by the back beach.

At the entrance to the government zone at the end of the peninsula are two historic gun barrels which actually fired the first shots in WW I and WW II. In 1914 a German ship was on its way out from Melbourne to the heads when news of the declaration of war came through on the telegraph. A shot across its bows at Portsea resulted in its capture. The first shot in WW II turned out to be at an Australian ship!

Cheviot Beach, at the end of the peninsula, featured more recently in Australian history. In 1967, then Prime Minister Harold Holt went for a swim here and was never seen again. US presidents get shot by nuts, in Australia prime ministers presumably get eaten by sharks. Although the area is closed to the public tours are operated from the Sorrento Pier (tel 84 2000) – five times daily from 26 December to 1 February, four times daily on weekends from then to Easter.

THE OCEAN COAST

The southern (or eastern) coast of the peninsula faces Bass Strait and Western-port Bay. A connected series of walking

tracks is being developed all the way from London Bridge to Cape Schank and Bushrangers Bay. Some stretches of the Peninsula Coastal Walk are along the beach, some are actually cut by high tide, but in all the walk extends for over 30 km and takes over 12 hours to walk from end to end. The walks are best done in stages because the park is so narrow and is easily reached at various points.

Cape Schank itself is marked by the 1859 lighthouse and there are good walking possibilities around the cape. The rugged coast further east towards Flinders and West Head has natural features like the Blowhole. Towns like Flinders and Hastings on this coast are not quite as popular and crowded in the summer as the Port Phillip ones. Point Leo, near Shoreham, has a good surf beach. Off the coast in Westernport Bay is French Island which is virtually un-developed. A ferry operates between Stony Point and Cowes on Phillip Island.

Phillip Island

At the entrance to Westernport Bay, 128 km south-east of Melbourne, Phillip Island is a very popular holiday resort for the Melbourne area. There are plenty of beaches, both sheltered and with surf, and a fascinating collection of wildlife including the island's famous fairy penguin colony. The island is joined to the mainland by a bridge from San Remo to Newhaven.

Information & Orientation

There is an excellent information centre in Newhaven just after you cross the bridge to the island. Cowes is the main town on the island. It's on the north side of the island and has a pleasant, sheltered beach. The south side of the island has the surf beaches like Woolamai, Cat Bay and Summerland, which in the evenings

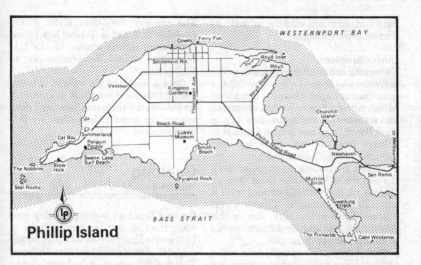

Phillip Island

is the site of the famous penguin parade. Rhyll is a small fishing village on the east of the island, while Ventnor is on the western coast.

Hotels, motels, camping grounds, restaurants, snack bars and other amenities can all be found in Cowes, which also has a Tourist Information Centre at 71 Thompson Avenue.

Penguins, Koalas & Seals

Every evening at Summerland Beach in the south-west of the island, the tiny fairy penguins which nest there, perform their 'parade', emerging from the sea and waddling resolutely up the beach to their nests – totally oblivious of the sightseers. The penguins are there year-round but they come in in far larger numbers in the summer when they are rearing their young. It's no easy life being the smallest type of penguin, after a few hours of shut-eye, it's down to the beach again at dawn to start another day's hard fishing.

The parade, which takes place like clockwork a few minutes after sunset each day, is a major tourist attraction so there will be big crowds here in summer. To protect the penguins you're strictly regimented – keep to the viewing ares, don't get in the penguins' way and no camera flashes. The admission charge is $4 but it's money well spent to see this unique sight.

Off Grand Point, the extreme south-west tip of the island, a group of rocks rise from the sea. They're known as The Nobbies and are inhabited by a resident colony of fur seals numbering about 5000. You can view them through coin-in-the-slot binoculars from the food kiosk in the carpark on the headland but unfortunately it shuts its doors early in the evening; too early if you want to come here just before continuing on to the penguin parade.

Koalas are the third wildlife attraction on the island. There are a number of koala sanctuaries around the island where you can see the lazy little creatures close up. Phillip Island also has mutton-bird rookeries, particularly in the sand dunes around Cape Woolamai. The birds arrive here in November each year from their migration flight from Japan and Alaska. You'll also find a wide variety of water-birds including pelicans, ibis and swans in the swampland at the Nits at Rhyll. Kingston Gardens Zoo has a variety of native Australian wildlife as well as domesticated animals.

Other Attractions

Swimming and surfing are popular island activities and there is also a now-defunct motor racing circuit where the Len Lukey Museum has a fine collection of veteran and vintage cars and racing cars. It's on Back Beach Road and is open Sundays to Fridays from 10 am to 5 pm and Saturdays from 12 noon to 5 pm.

There's a blowhole, spectacular when the seas are high, at Grant Point. Rugged Cape Woolamai with it's walking track is particularly impressive. There's a real contrast between the high seas on this side of the island and the sheltered waters of the northern (Cowes) side.

Churchill Island is a small island with a restored house and beautiful gardens. It's connected to Phillip Island by footbridge and the turn-off is well signposted about one km out of Newhaven. It's open on weekends from 10 am to 5 pm, and from 1 pm to 5 pm on Mondays, Wednesdays and Fridays.

Places to Stay & Eat

There are all sorts of guest-houses, motels, holiday flats and campsites in Cowes, Newhaven and San Remo. There's an alternate youth hostel at the *Anchor Belle Holiday Park* (tel (059) 52 2258) at 272 Church St and as there's only 10 beds, it's advisable to book; nightly cost is $6.50.

All the usual eating possibilities can be found in Cowes including counter meals at the *Isle of Wight Hotel* and some good fish & chip places.

Getting There

The usual route to Phillip Island by public transport is in three parts: first a train from Flinders St to Frankston, then a bus (once on Saturdays, twice daily the rest of the week) to Stony Point, followed by the twice-daily ferry service across to Cowes via Tankerton on French Island.

The one-way ferry fare is $5. Every weekday at 5 pm a V-Line bus leaves Dandenong railway station for the 1½-hour drive around Westernport Bay to Phillip Island.

Once a week there's a flight between Phillip Island and Smithton in Tasmania for $65. See the Tasmania 'Getting There' section for more information on this unusual route.

Geelong
Population 125,000

Geelong began as a sheep grazing area when the first settlers arrived there in 1836 and initially served as a port for the dispatch of wool and wheat from the area. This function was overshadowed during the gold-rush era when it became important as a landing place for immigrants and for the export of gold. Around 1900 Geelong started to become industrialised and that's very much what it is today – an industrial city near Melbourne.

Information

There's a tourist office (tel 97 220) at 83 Ryrie St. They are very helpful, have lots of information to hand and are very useful if you're going down along the coast to the Otways or other areas around Geelong.

Things to See

In general there are no real 'not to be missed' attractions in Geelong although the city has more than 100 National Trust classified buildings including some interesting pre-fabricated buildings brought

1 Kangaroo Hotel
2 Ferry Trip
3 Railway Station
4 Carlton Hotel
5 Art Gallery
6 Tourist Office
7 Post Office
8 Corio Hotel

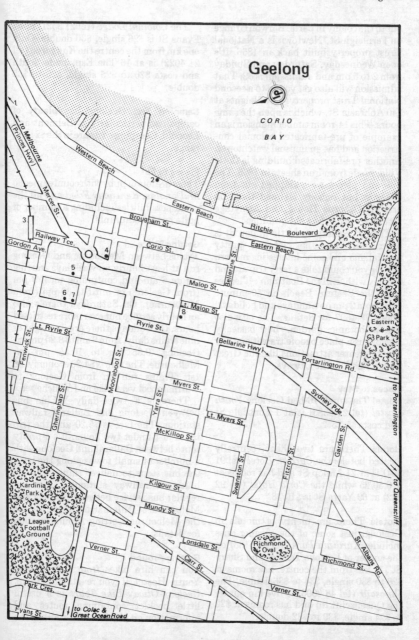

Geelong

CORIO BAY

out to the colony in parts. Barwon Grange on Fernleigh St, Newtown is a National Trust property built back in 1856. It's open Wednesday, Saturday and Sunday from 2 to 5 pm and admission is $2. That admission will also get you in to a second National Trust property: The Heights at 140 Aphrasia St, which is open the same hours. This 14-room timber mansion is an example of pre-fabricated colonial construction and has an unusual watchtower. Another pre-fabricated building is Corio Villa, made from iron sheets in 1856. The bits and pieces were shipped out from Glasgow but nobody claimed them on arrival! Osborne House and Armytage House are other fine old buildings.

The Art Gallery on Little Malop St is open daily and has lots of pretty Australiana and some interesting modern art. Or you could take a ferry trip around the bay with 'Bill the Boatman'. It leaves from the Eastern Beach on 50-minute trips from 2 pm on Sundays and holidays; phone 78 1697 for details. The city also has a botanic garden, but basically Geelong is a place people transit on their way to greater attractions like the Great Ocean Road or the Otways.

Places to Stay

Hostel The small 16-bed Geelong *Youth Hostel* (tel 21 6583) is at 1 Lonsdale St and costs $5.25.

Hotels There are two cheap, centrally located hotels: the *Carlton Hotel* (tel 91 954) is at 21 Malop St and has rooms at $16.50/25 while the *Corio Hotel* (tel 92 922) at 69 Yarra St is $10/18.

Motels There are plenty of motels in Geelong, just some of the cheaper ones include: *Kardinia Park* (tel 21 5188) on the corner of Latrobe Terrace and Sharp St 1½ km from the centre, has rooms at $28 to $30 single, $34 to $36 double. The *Dinosaur* (tel 48 2606) is five km out on the Queenscliff Rd and has rooms at $22 to $24 single, $30 to $32 double.

The *Colonial Lodge* (tel 21 3521) at 57 Fyans St is $26 single, $30 double. Only one km from the centre the *Kangaroo* (tel 21 4022) is at 16 The Esplanade South and costs $20 to $25 single, $26 to $32 double.

Camping Yes, Geelong has plenty of campsites, particularly at Belmont and Leopold. Camping costs are in the $2 to $7 range.

Places to Eat

There are lots of pubs with counter meals, *McDonalds*, *Kentucky Fried* and all the usual possibilities including a number of quite good restaurants.

Getting There

Trains between Melbourne and Geelong run at least hourly on weekdays starting before 6 am and continuing until 9 pm (from Geelong) or until 11.30 pm (from Melbourne). On Saturdays there's also an hourly service but over more restricted hours. On Sundays there are just eight or nine trains daily, from 8 am to 8.20 pm ex-Geelong, 9.35 am to 10.35 pm ex-Melbourne. The fare is $4.30 economy, $6 1st. Trains run on from Geelong to Warrnambool via Colac and Winchelsea.

There is a twice-daily V-Line bus between Geelong and Ballarat railway stations. The fare is $5.20 and the trip takes just under two hours. It's a pretty route between Ballarat and Geelong with a number of small towns along the way; the bus stops to deliver things to little bluestone railway stations. There's a regular bus service between Geelong and Melbourne's Tullamarine Airport – see the Melbourne Getting Around section for details.

Getting Around

You can hire bikes from the Geelong Youth Hostel if you're staying there. *Geelong-Otway Bike Tours* is a useful little booklet containing routes and information on possible bike-tours in the area. It's available free from the tourist office. Unfortunately there is no commercial bike hire facility in Geelong although you can hire bikes at the Barwon Valley Fun Park, near Barwon River, on weekends. Eagles bike shop at 64 Ryrie St in Geelong occasionally hire out bikes if they have any available.

Bellarine Peninsula

Beyond Geelong the Bellarine Peninsula is a twin to the Mornington Peninsula, forming the other side of the entrance to Port Phillip Bay. In summer a ferry crosses the heads between Portsea and Queenscliff and there's a connecting bus between Queenscliff and Geelong. Like the Mornington Peninsula this is a popular holiday resort and boating venue.

AROUND THE PENINSULA

Round the peninsula in Port Phillip Bay is Indented Head where Flinders landed in 1802, one of the first visits to the area by a European. In 1835 John Batman landed at this same point, on his way to buy up Melbourne.

At Portarlington (population 1900) there's a fine example of an early steam-powered flour mill. Built in 1856-57 the massive, solid building is open from 2 to 5 pm every Sunday. St Leonards (population 900) is a popular little resort just south of Indented Head.

QUEENSCLIFF (population 3400)

Fort Queenscliff was built in 1882 and houses the Australian Military College. It's open on weekends and public holidays. Queenscliff was originally established as a fishing port and fishing is still an important activity today.

Queenscliff has a fascinating little Historical Centre beside the post office on Hesse St. It's open daily from 2 to 4.30 pm and over the main school holiday seasons it's also open 10 am to 12 noon. You can get an interesting *Visitor's Guide to Queenscliff* here and explore the town with the walking-tour guide.

Along the front the Ozone and the Queenscliff are two hotels in the Victorian seaside 'grand' manner, very popular for leisurely weekend lunches. Queenscliff's Fort was built during the 1880s Russian scare. The 'Black Lighthouse', dating from 1862, is within the fort; tours take place on Sundays and public holidays at 2.15 pm and there's a fine ocean lookout below the fort.

Point Lonsdale and Queenscliff are practically joined. The lighthouse here guides ships through the narrow rip into the the bay and below the lighthouse is Buckley's cave. Here the 'wild white man', William Buckley, lived with the Aboriginals for 32 years after escaping from the settlement at Sorrento on the Mornington Peninsula. Actually this area is dotted with 'Buckley caves'!

Railway enthusiasts will enjoy the Bellarine Peninsula Railway which operates from the old Queenscliff station with a fine collection of old steam trains. On weekends, public and school holidays steam trains make the 16-km trip to Drysdale or shorter runs around Swan Bay.

OCEAN GROVE & BARWON HEADS

These resorts on the ocean side of the peninsula offer good skin diving on the rocky ledges of the Bluff at Ocean Grove and further out there are wrecks of ships which failed to make the tricky entrance to Port Phillip Bay. Some of the wrecks are accessible to divers. Barwon Heads has sheltered river beaches.

The Great Ocean Road

For over 300 km, from Torquay (a short distance south of Geelong) almost to Warrnambool where the road joins the Princes Highway, the Great Ocean Road provides some of the most spectacular coastal scenery in Australia. For most of the distance the road hugs the coastline, passing some excellent surfing beaches, fine skin-diving centres and even some hills from which hang-gliding enthusiasts launch themselves to catch the strong uplifts coming in from the sea in the evenings.

The coast is well equipped with campsites and other accommodation possibilities and if the seaside activities pall, you can always turn inland to the bushwalks, wildlife, scenery, waterfalls and lookouts of the Otway Ranges which back the coast. The Great Ocean Road was only completed in 1932 as a works project during the depression, and stretches of the country through which it runs are still relatively untouched.

Places to Stay

There are countless campsites and other holiday accommodation possibilities along the coastal stretch although they're often heavily booked during the peak summer season.

TORQUAY (population 2900)

This popular resort town marks the eastern end of the Great Ocean Road and is just 22 km south of Geelong. Some of the most popular surfing beaches are near here including Jan Juc and Bell's Beach. Bell's is the site for the Easter Australian surfing championship which each year attracts surfing enthusiasts from all over the world.

ANGLESEA (population 1500)

Another popular seaside resort, Anglesea is 44 km from Geelong and apart from beach activities it also offers the nearby Angahook Forest Park with many bushwalking trails, Iron Bark Grove, Treefern Grove, Melaleuca Swamp and the Currawong Falls. The golf course at Anglesea is well-known for the frequent visits by kangaroos which can be seen grazing the fairways. Another 10 km along the Great Ocean Road is Airey's Inlet, a pleasant smaller resort.

LORNE (population 900)

The small town of Lorne, 73 km from Geelong, was a popular seaside resort even before the Great Ocean Road was built. The mountains behind the town not only provide a spectacular backdrop but also give the town a mild, sheltered climate year round. Lorne has good beaches, surfing and bushwalks in the vicinity.

Climb up to Teddy's Lookout behind the town for the fine views along the coast. The beautiful Erskine Falls are also close behind Lorne; you can drive there or follow the walking trail beside the river, passing Splitter's Falls and Straw Falls on the way. There are numerous other

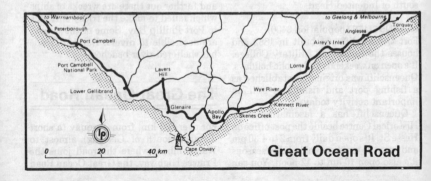

Great Ocean Road

short and long walks around Lorne. Pick up a copy of the useful little *Tourist Guide to Lorne* leaflet from the BP petrol station or the Ridgeway Supermarket.

When you tire of walking or the beach you can always poke around in the rock pools at low tide or catch a film at Lorne's little cinema. In the season there's music most nights at the Lorne hotels.

Places to Stay

Prices soar and the no-vacancy signs go out during the summer school holiday season when half of Melbourne seems to move down here. Even pitching a tent in one of the campsites could prove difficult at peak periods.

The *Lorne Hotel* (tel (052) 89 1409) on the Great Ocean Rd has rooms at $30 to $40, all with attached bathroom. Further along by the pier the *Pacific Hotel* (tel (052) 89 1609) has similar rooms at similar prices from $30 to $45. Motel and holiday flat prices are very variable with season. The *Chalet Lorne* (tel (052) 89 1241) at 4 Smith St is a guest-house with bed & breakfast from $18 to $22 per person.

The Lorne Foreshore Committee has four campsites at Lorne; the *Erskine River Section* is pleasantly sited by the river and right in the thick of things. The *Queens Park Section* is above it all, on the headland overlooking the pier. Site prices are in the $7 to $11 range and there are minimum booking requirements at peak periods.

Places to Eat

There's no chance of boredom when it comes to eating out in Lorne although at the fancier restaurants you should make sure you have a table booked during the season.

At the economical end of the scale there are counter meals at the *Lorne Hotel* and the *Pacific Hotel*; a collection of fast-food, pizza and take-away places; or great pita bread and other health-food at the *Beach Bite* on the beach by the swimming

pool. Plus there's a *Pancake Parlour* by the cinema with a pleasant open-air deck and the famous *Arab* which has been a Lorne institution since the mid-'50s.

Moving up the scale (and book a table in season) there's *Kosta's Tavern* which is much more international than it's Greek name would indicate; French-Mauritian food at *Au Dodo* while down at the pier, the *Pier* serves seafood (and vegetarian food and steaks) in a very Californian ambience. Just past the pier on the Apollo Bay side of town *Willo's Devonshire Teas* is famed for its scones.

APOLLO BAY & CAPE OTWAY

At Apollo Bay (population 1000), 118 km from Geelong, the road temporarily leaves the coast to climb up and over Cape Otway. The coast is particularly beautiful and rugged on this stretch and there have been many shipwrecks here. Cape Otway is covered in rainforest, much of it still relatively untouched, and although many of the roads through the cape are unsurfaced and very winding, they present no problems for the average car.

There are a number of scenic lookouts and nature reserves along here but Melba Gully is probably the best with the beautiful ferns for which the cape is noted. Just beyond this small park is Lavers Hill, a tiny township which once had a thriving timber business. Hopetoun Falls, Beachamps Falls and gemstones found at Moonlight Head are other Otway attractions. The 1848 convict-built Cape Otway Lighthouse is nearly 100 metres high and is open 10 am to 12 noon and 2 to 4 pm on Tuesdays and Thursdays. At Princetown the road rejoins the coast and runs right along it again, through the superbly spectacular Port Campbell National Park.

PORT CAMPBELL

If the Great Ocean Road offers some of the most dramatic coastal scenery in Australia, then the stretch through Port Campbell is

the most exciting part. The views along here are fantastic with beautiful scenes like the rock formations known as the Twelve Apostles where 12 huge stone pillars soar out of the pounding surf. Or there's London Bridge, a bridge-like promontory arching across a furious sea.

Loch Ard Gorge has a sadder tale to tell; in 1878 the iron-hulled clipper *Loch Ard* was driven onto the rocks offshore at this point. Of the 50 or so on board only two were to survive: an apprentice officer and an immigrant girl, both aged 18. They were swept into the narrow gorge now named after their ship. Although the papers of the time tried to inspire a romance between the two survivors, the girl, the sole survivor of a family of eight, soon headed back to Ireland's safer climes. This was the last immigrant sailing ship to founder en route to Australia.

A little further along the coast is Port Campbell itself, the main centre in the National Park and again sited on a spectacular gorge with some fine walks in the hills behind town. Soon after Port Campbell the Great Ocean Road leaves the coast at Peterborough to join the Princes Highway just before Warrnambool.

The South-West Coast

At Warrnambool the Great Ocean Road ends and you're on the final south-west coast stretch to South Australia on the Princes Highway. This stretch includes some of the earliest settlements in the state.

Getting There

V-Line operate Melbourne-Geelong-Colac-Warrnambool with connecting buses on to Port Fairy and Portland. Economy fares (1st class in brackets) are: Colac $10.10 ($14.10), Warrnambool $16.80

($23.50), Port Fairy $18 ($24.70), and Portland $22.80 ($29.50). There are buses and flights to Hamilton from Melbourne with connections to Portland, Warrnambool and Mt Gambier in South Australia.

WARRNAMBOOL (population 21,400)
Warrnambool is 264 km from Melbourne and has some good beaches. Gun emplacements intended to repel the Russian invasion which Australia feared in the 1880s can be seen near the lighthouse. This is now the site of the Warrnambool Maritime Village with a museum, restored sailing ships and port buildings of the era. It's open daily 9.30 am to 4.30 pm. Warrnambool also has a reptile park, a zoo and an antique vehicles museum, while 12 km west of the town is Tower Hill with its huge crater lake and a game reserve with many emus.

PORT FAIRY (population 2400)
This small fishing port was one of the first settlements in the state, dating back to 1835 although temporary visitors had stayed here right back in 1826. These first arrivals were whalers and sealers seeking shelter along the coast, but Port Fairy is still the home port for one of Victoria's largest fishing fleets.

The fishing boats are only one of the town's scenic attractions; the other is the many fine old buildings dating back to the town's early days. No less than 50 buildings in Port Fairy are classified by the National Trust and one of the finest is the bluestone home originally built for Captain Mills, a whaling boat skipper. Mott's Cottage, the early ANZ Bank, the old Caledonian Inn and Seacombe House are other interesting buildings. Built in 1844 the Caledonian is the oldest licensed pub in Victoria.

Port Fairy also has a historical centre on Bank St; the old fort and signal station at the mouth of the river; and Griffiths Island which is reached by a causeway from the town and has a lighthouse and a

mutton bird rookery. Port Fairy was originally known as Belfast and although the name was later changed there's still a Northern Irish flavour about the place and a Belfast Bakery on the main street.

Places to Stay
Port Fairy is 27 km west of Warrnambool and has several campsites and a number of motels. The *Youth Hostel* (tel (055) 68 1547) is at 8 Cox St and costs $6.75 (50c less off-season).

PORTLAND (population 9300)
Continuing west 72 km from Port Fairy you reach Portland, just 75 km from the South Australian border. This is the oldest settlement in Victoria. Established in 1834 it predates Port Fairy by one year. It's an indication of the piecemeal development of Victoria that the first 'official' visitor, Major Thomas Mitchell, turned up here on an overland expedition from Sydney in 1836 and was surprised to find it had been settled two years earlier. Whalers knew this stretch of coast long before the first permanent settlement and there were even earlier short-term visitors.

Portland has numerous classified buildings including the old Steam Packet Hotel, Mac's Hotel plus the Customs House and Court House on Cliff St. The lighthouse at the tip of Cape Nelson, south of Portland, is also classified by the National Trust.

From Cape Bridgewater you can make pleasant walks to Cape Duquesne and Discovery Bay. From Portland the Princes Highway turns inland through Heywood and Dartmoor before crossing the border to Mt Gambier in South Australia but there is also a smaller road which runs closer to the coast, fringed by the Discovery Bay Coastal Park. It actually meets the coast just before the border at the delightful little town (village even) of Nelson, a popular resort for Mt Gambier. This is also a good access point to the

Lower Glenelg National Park with it's deep gorges and brilliant wildflowers.

Western District

The south-west of the state, inland from the coast and stretching to the South Australian border, is particularly affluent sheep raising and pastoral country. Malcolm Fraser is just one of the wealthy Australian ex-prime ministers to come from the Western District. Early explorer Thomas Mitchell dubbed this fertile region 'Australia Felix'.

Getting There
Ansett-Pioneer buses operate from Melbourne to Hamilton ($19.20) and Mt Gambier ($34.00). You can also reach Hamilton by train and connecting bus via Ararat – $19.20 (1st class $24.60). Hamilton is quite a centre for local buses; you can travel from here to Mt Gambier, Portland, Horsham, Warrnambool or Ballarat.

Hamilton is also connected to Melbourne by air on the Melbourne-Hamilton-Mt Gambier-Adelaide route. The fare to Hamilton is $74.

MELBOURNE TO HAMILTON
You can reach Hamilton, the 'capital' of the Western District, via Ballarat along the Glenelg Highway or via Geelong along the Hamilton Highway. On the Glenelg Highway the small town of Lake Bolac (population 200) is beside a large freshwater lake, popular for watersports. Inverleigh (population 300) is an attractive little town along the Hamilton Highway.

The Princes Highway runs further south actually reaching the coast at Warrnambool. Winchelsea (population 900) is on the Princes Highway and has a museum in the 1842 Barwon Hotel and the National Trust operated Barwon Park Homestead, a fine old bluestone mansion which is open daily. The stone Barwon Bridge dates from 1867. You can reach the Grampians on a scenic route from Dunkeld on the Glenelg Highway.

COLAC (population 10,500)
On the eastern edge of the Western District there are many volcanic lakes in the vicinity of the town. Alvie and Red Rock Lookouts give good views over the area. Colac has a botanic garden on the shore of Lake Colac. Provan's Mechanical Museum has vintage cars and motorcycles. South of the town are the Otway Ranges and scenic routes run through the ranges to the Great Ocean Road.

CAMPERDOWN (population 3500)
There are many volcanic crater lakes around this pleasant town; you can see nearly 40 of them from the lookout on top of Mt Leura, itself an extinct volcano. Lake Gnotuk and Lake Bullen Merri, two crater lakes close to the town, are notable because although they are very close together their water levels are about 50 metres different! Also close to Camperdown is Victoria's largest lake: the salt Lake Corangamite. From Camperdown roads lead south through Cobden to Port Campbell and the Great Ocean Road.

There's a *Youth Hostel* (tel (055) 93 1864) at 15 Church St; nightly cost is $5.25.

HAMILTON (population 9700)
The major town of the area, Hamilton is particularly noted for its superb art gallery on Brown St; it's one of the best in any Australian country town. Lake Hamilton is right in the centre of town and there's a zoo in the botanic gardens.

Wannon Falls (15 km) and Nigretta Falls (seven km) are two local attractions. Mt Eccles National Park is 33 km out and has the crater lake Surprise. There are two other extinct volcanoes close to town. These reminders of volcanic origins are evident all through the south-west region. There are great views from the summit of Mt Napier.

Beyond Hamilton is Casterton (population 1900) with an historical museum in the old railway building and the very fine National Trust classified homestead Warrock, open daily. Coleraine (population 1200), another very early Victorian settlement, is between Hamilton and Casterton.

The South-West Regional Authority tourist office is on Lonsdale St.

Central West & the Wimmera

Several roads run west from the Victorian gold country to the South Australian border. The main road is the Western Highway which is also the busiest route between Melbourne and Adelaide. From Ballarat the road runs north of the Little Desert while to the north and south is the Wimmera – the seemingly endless Victorian wheatfields.

From Horsham the Wimmera Highway splits off the Western Highway and runs through this area which also extends north-east to Warracknabeal and Donald. In the south of the region is one of the area's major attractions, indeed one of the most spectacularly scenic areas of Victoria – the mountains of the Grampians.

Getting There
The Western Highway through the Central West is the main route between Melbourne and Adelaide and the Melbourne-Adelaide railway line takes the same route so there is no shortage of transport along this way. The nightly Overland runs right through to Adelaide while Monday to Saturday V-Line also have morning train as far as Serviceton and a nightly train as far as Dimboola. Fares from Melbourne include Ararat $13 economy ($19 1st), Horsham $20 ($29), Stawell $16 ($22), Dimboola $23, ($32), Nhill $23 ($32), Kaniva $24 ($34).

Ansett Pioneer and Greyhound use the same route with fares Ararat $24.10, Stawell $26.50, Horsham $32.50, Dimboola $32.50, Nhill $33.70, Kaniva $35. Buses head north from Horsham to Ouyen and Mildura or south to Hamilton in the Western District.

BALLARAT TO ARARAT
After leaving Ballarat by its long, tree-lined memorial drive you reach Beaufort (population 1200) about halfway to Ararat. For a brief period in its gold-rush heyday this small town had an enormous population chasing the elusive metal at Fiery Creek. Today it's a quiet farming centre with good bushwalking areas in the Mt Cole State Forest, 16 km to the north-west.

ARARAT (population 8300)
After a brief flirtation with gold in 1857, Ararat settled down as a farming centre. It has a folk museum with an Aboriginal collection, an art gallery and some fine old bluestone buildings.

Only 16 km north-west of Ararat on the Western Highway, Great Western is one of Australia's best-known champagne regions. Seppelt's Great Western vineyards were established in 1865. The unique Sisters Rocks are between here and Stawell. There are walks and barbecue sites in the Langi Ghiran State Forest, 14 km east. On the Melbourne side of Ararat there are some historic buildings in Buangor. Old gold towns in the area include Cathcart and Mafeking, which once had a population of 10,000.

STAWELL (population 6200)
A centre for visits to the Grampians and another early Victorian gold town, Big Hill was the site of the town's first gold discovery. Stawell's Mini-World is a local attraction with models of everything from the Eiffel Tower to a Dutch windmill. The attractive little town has a number of National Trust classified buildings, an illuminated fountain, an animated clock

in the town hall and a whole collection of war and other memorials.

Bunjil's Cave, with Aboriginal rock paintings, is 11 km south and other local attractions include Sisters Rock by the Western Highway to the south-east, Roses Gap Wildlife Reserve 17 km south, and the National Trust Tottington Woolshed, 55 km north-east.

There are a number of pubs in Stawell with good counter food – try the *Albion Hotel* on Gold Reef Mall in the centre.

THE GRAMPIANS

Named after the mountains of the same name in Scotland, the Grampians are the south-west tail end of the Great Dividing Range. The area is a state forest, not a national park, but it's renowned for fine bushwalks, superb mountain lookouts, excellent rock-climbing opportunities, prolific wildlife and, in the spring, countless wildflowers. The Grampians are at their best from August to November when the flowers put on their most colourful display. On a weekend in early spring there's a wildflower exhibition in the Halls Gap Hall. Mt Arapiles, 16 km west of Horsham near Natimuk, is a particular favourite of rock climbers. There are also many Aboriginal rock paintings in the Grampians.

There are many fine bushwalks around the Grampians, some of them short strolls you can make right from the middle of Halls Gap. Keep an eye out for koalas and kangaroos; you sometimes see koalas right in the middle of Halls Gap. The walk through the sheer-walled Grand Canyon is particularly impressive and there are some fine lookouts from the ridge that runs behind Halls Gap. Waterfalls, such as the spectacular McKenzie Falls, are another Grampians attraction. At Zumsteins, 22 km from Halls Gap, kangaroos gather in a paddock late every afternoon for the free feed they've grown to expect.

The Grampians lie immediately west of Ararat and south of the Western

The Grampians

Highway between Stawell and Horsham. The tiny town of Halls Gap (population 300) is the centre for the Grampians, indeed it's right in the middle of the region and has camping and motel facilities. Halls Gap is about 250 km from Melbourne.

Places to Stay & Eat

One km from the centre of Halls Gap on the corner of Buckler St and Grampians Rd the small *Youth Hostel* (tel (053) 56 4262) costs $5.25. There are a number of campsites, some of them right around the centre, and numerous motels.

There's a small café and take-away in the middle of Halls Gap but the Halls Gap restaurants are sometimes booked right out. It's a quick drive to Stawell where there are a number of pubs with counter meals.

HORSHAM (population 12,700)

A highway junction town and the main centre for the Wimmera, Horsham is also a good base for the Little Desert National Park and the Grampians. The town has an art gallery and 'Olde Horsham' with historic displays and a tea-room in an old tram. There are a number of picnic and recreation areas on the Wimmera River and the various lakes in the vicinity. North-east of Horsham towards St Arnaud on the Wimmera Highway is Murtoa (population 1000) in the heart of the wheatbelt and dominated by a gigantic wheat storage silo and a water tower for the railway.

LITTLE DESERT

Just south of the Western Highway and reached from Dimboola or Nhill, the Little Desert is noted for its brilliant display of wildflowers in the spring. The name is a bit of a misnomer because it isn't really a desert at all nor is it that little! Part of the 'desert' is a national park but it actually extends well beyond the park boundaries. If you really intend to explore the bushland of the park you'll need four-wheel drive. The desert is at its finest in the spring when it is carpeted with wildflowers. A little beyond Dimboola the Kiata Lowan Sanctuary is an easily accessible area in the north of the park with walks and a resident ranger. The Big Desert is further north of the Western Highway.

DIMBOOLA (population 1700)

The name of this quiet, typical Australian country town on the Wimmera River is a Sinhalese word meaning 'land of the figs'. The Pink Lake, just south of the highway, is a little beyond Dimboola. Beside the Wimmera River near here you can see Aboriginal canoe trees where canoes have been cut out in one piece from the bark. The Ebenezer Mission Station was established in Antwerp, north of Dimboola, to tend to local Aboriginals in 1859.

NHILL (population 2100)

Nhill is the mid-point between Melbourne and Adelaide and is another Wimmera wheat farming centre although it also acts as a centre for the Mallee region to

the north. The 1881 post office is classified by the National Trust and in the town centre is a memorial to the Clydesdale horses which were used extensively in the development of the Wimmera.

KANIVA (population 800)

Further west and just before the South Australian border, Kaniva is also on the edge of the Little Desert. There's an interesting three-km walking track, the Billy-Ho Bush Walk, about 10 km from the town with numbered examples of desert flora. Kaniva has a historical museum and Serviceton, almost on the South Australian border, has a National Trust classified railway station with basement dungeons.

NORTH TO THE MALLEE

You can make excursions from Nhill or from Dimboola to Lake Hindmarsh, about 40 km north. Jeparit (population 500) is north of Antwerp on the shores of the lake, the largest natural freshwater lake in the state. Jeparit has the Wimmera/Mallee Pioneer Museum, a collection of colonial buildings and old farming equipment. Australia's longest-serving prime minister, Sir Robert Menzies, was born here.

North again from Jeparit towards the Wyperfield park is Rainbow (population 700) with the National Trust classified Yuranga homestead and a tourist info centre on Federal St. It's open only on Sundays. North and west of the Mallee agricultural region is the dry Mallee bushland stretching for hundreds of square km.

HORSHAM TO EDENHOPE

From Horsham the Wimmera Highway runs slightly south-west through Edenhope to the South Australian border while the Western Highway goes slightly north-west, sandwiching the Little Desert between the two highways. Natimuk (population 500) has interesting old buildings and a museum in the old courthouse. There's plenty of birdlife on nearby Lake Natimuk. Just beyond Natimuk is Mitre Rock and soaring Mt Arapiles; fine views from the 213-metre summit of the monolith, 'Victoria's Ayers Rock', which is popular with rockclimbers although you can also drive all the way to the lookout on the summit.

There are a number of lakes around Edenhope (population 900) including Lake Wallace with its many water birds. The tiny town of Harrow, 32 km southeast, is a very early Victorian country settlement with old buildings including the 1851 Hermitage Hotel and an 1862 log jail.

WARRACKNABEAL (population 2700)

A major Wimmera wheat-growing town, there's a historical centre on Scott St and the town also has a number of interesting old buildings, some of them National Trust classified. The North-Western Agricultural Machinery Museum is just outside of town. North of Warracknabeal towards the Wyperfield National Park, Hopetoun (population 900) has the National Trust classified Hopetoun House, built for Edward Lascelles who was responsible for a lot of development in the Mallee area.

THE MALLEE

North of the Wimmera is the least populated part of Australia's most densely populated state. Forming a wedge between South Australia and NSW this area even includes the one genuinely empty part of Victoria. It also includes the dull, endless plains of the Mallee, a region which takes its name from the Mallee scrub which once covered the area. Although this area is so dry and there are still large tracts of sand plains and scrub, it's also a highly productive grain-producing area.

The Wyperfield National Park, entered from the small town of Albacutya, preserves a stretch of the Mallee in its original state. It's the largest national park in Victoria and has many emus and

kangaroos. Nhill and Ouyen are the main towns of the Mallee region. Ouyen (population 1600) is at the junction of the Sunraysia and Ouyen Highways, near the Hattah-Kulkyne National Park which is noted for its prolific birdlife. Note that the Mallee region becomes extremely hot in the summer and the flies can be a real pest.

Ballarat
Population: 62,600

Ballarat is the largest inland city in Victoria. It's 112 km from Melbourne on the main Western Highway to Adelaide. Ballarat was a major centre for Victoria's great gold-rush. When gold was discovered in 1851 Ballarat was just a small country town but two years later the population had already reached 40,000.

Today there are still many reminders of this gold-mining past although Ballarat doesn't have quite the historical flavour of Bendigo, the other large Victorian town from the gold era.

Information

The Gold Centre Regional Tourist Office (tel 32 2694) is just over the railway line on Lydiard St and is open Monday to Friday from 9 am to 5 pm and on weekends from 10 am to 3 pm. The people are very helpful and seem to be well stocked with lots of printed information. The RACV (tel 32 1946) have an office on Doveton St.

Around Town

Even before Ballarat's gold boom the town planners had the foresight to include a wide main street. With Ballarat's gold wealth to spend, Sturt St became a magnificent boulevard lined with the lavish buildings so typical of Australian gold towns. A wander along Sturt St takes you by verandahed Australian Victorian buildings bedecked with lacework plus a whole series of European styles from

Gothic to Renaissance. The tourist office puts out a walking-tours pamphlet for 30c.

Sovereign Hill

Ballarat's major tourist attraction is Sovereign Hill, a fascinating re-creation of a gold-mining township of the 1860s, complete with shops, a hotel and buildings along the main street including a post office, blacksmith's shop, printing shop, even a Chinese joss house. The site actually was mined back in the gold era so much of the equipment is original, as is the mineshaft. There's a variety of above-ground and underground mining works. It's open daily from 9.30 am to 5 pm and admission is $6.70 for adults – expensive but well worth it. This is one 'attraction' that is definitely worth seeing.

On the top of the hill overlooking the other buildings, the 'Government Camp' has been built. It's a reconstruction of part of the original 1857 Government Camp on the gold-fields with buildings such as the military barracks, court house and superintendent's office; and offers accommodation and houses the excellent Youth Hostel.

Gold Museum

Over the road from Sovereign Hill, this new museum, built on the mullock heap from an old mine, has imaginative displays and samples from all the old mining areas in the Ballarat region. There's also a large section devoted to the history of gold coins around the world. It's open 10 am to 5 pm daily except Friday when it's 12 am to 5 pm and is well worth the $1.20 admission.

Eureka Stockade

Australia never had a revolution which fired a national consciousness like America's did. The closest we ever came was the Eureka Stockade rebellion in 1854 when disgruntled miners refused to pay a government mining tax and mounted a futile opposition to the far superior

government forces. Second time around the redcoats won. Today there's a monument at the stockade site and a coin-in-the-slot diorama gives you the chance to see an action replay of the events and causes of this short lived 'revolt' against British rule. The park is on Stawell St South.

Eureka Exhibition

On Eureka St opposite the Eureka Memorial is this much-vaunted but disappointing museum. It's a series of walk-through, 'computer-controlled' scenes depicting various facets of the rebellion with taped commentary and slide-show. It's open daily from 9 am to 6 pm but is overpriced at $2.50 – the diorama across the road gives you much the same thing for 20c.

Botanical Gardens

In the city, Lake Wendouree is beside Ballarat's excellent 40-hectare Botanic Gardens. A paddle-steamer makes tours of the lake which was used as the rowing course in the 1956 Olympics. The cottage of poet Adam Lindsay Gordon stands in the gardens. On weekends and holidays there's a tourist tramway operating around the gardens. A little Ballarat joke is the Avenue of Past Prime Ministers, a pathway lined with busts of Australian PMs, there's a Fraser there but no Whitlam! Actually the whole garden is littered with statuary including the glasshouse-like 'Statue House'. There's also a Shell House in the garden.

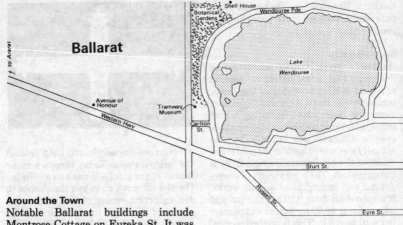

Ballarat

to Ararat

Botanical Gardens

Shell House

Wendouree Pde.

Lake Wendouree

Avenue of Honour

Tramway Museum

Western Hwy

Carlton St.

Sturt St.

Russell St.

Eyre St.

Around the Town

Notable Ballarat buildings include Montrose Cottage on Eureka St. It was the first stone cottage of the gold era in Ballarat and is furnished with relics of the time; it's only open during school holiday periods.

Ballarat has one of Australia's best art galleries outside of the capital cities in the Ballarat Fine Art Gallery at 40 Lydiard St North. It's particularly strong in its Australiana collection. The gallery is open varying hours Tuesday to Sunday and admission is $1 (students 50c). The gallery also has the original Eureka Flag, or at least what's left of it after souvenir hunters have chopped bits off over the last hundred years. When it was finally placed in the gallery it was, appropriately, unveiled by Gough Whitlam.

The Old Curiosity Shop at 7 Queen St South is a curious little house put together by a Cornish immigrant over a 40-year period from the 1850s. It's open daily and admission is $2. Golda's World of Dolls is at 148 Eureka St and has nearly 2000 dolls on display. It's open from 1 to 5 pm daily except Friday and admission is $1.50. For a view, you can climb Black Hill Lookout.

At the corner of York and Fussell Sts is the Wildlife and Reptile Park with a large collection of native animals including saltwater crocodiles; open from 9 am

daily, entry is a hefty $3.50 (students $2.50). The Silver Mine at 52 Victoria St is a replica silver mine selling new and used silverware – free admission.

Out of Town

Situated eight km on the Melbourne side of Ballarat, Kryall Castle is a modern bluestone 'medieval English castle'. Surprisingly it's a very popular attraction, no doubt helped along by the daily hangings (volunteers called for), 'whipping of wenches' and a weekly jousting tournament – kids love it. It's open 10 am to 5 pm daily and admission is $6 for adults.

Towards Adelaide, an Arch of Victory spans the road and for the following 22 km you pass through a continuous avenue of trees – one planted for every Ballarat resident who served in WW I. It's a surprising reminder of just how great the effect of that far away war was on Australia.

Places to Stay

Hostels There's an associate *Youth Hostel* (tel 31 1944) at the Government Camp at Sovereign Hill – a reconstruction

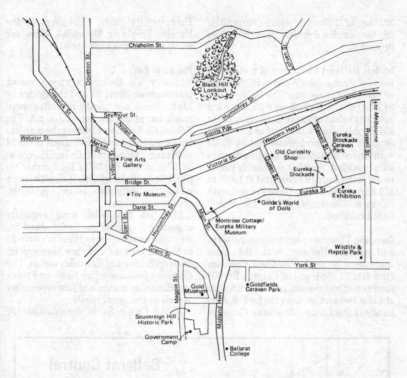

of the government administrative camp from the gold-fields in 1851. It has excellent facilities and costs $7.50 for YH members but $26/32 for others and it's wise to book in advance if at all possible. If you stay here you get a 10% discount on entry to Sovereign Hill. Entry to the hostel is from Magpie St, up behind the Sovereign Hill township.

During the summer months the College of Advanced Education students' residence on the campus at Mt Helen and Gilles Sts has beds at $6 a night for YH members. Phone the Campus Amenities Manager (tel 30 1800, ext 388 or 30 1768 after hours).

Hotels *The Provincial Hotel* (tel 32 1845) is at 121 Lydiard St, right across from the Ballarat railway station. Rooms are $16/ 28 including breakfast. Right outside the station is the rather dingy but cheap *Tawana Lodge* (tel 31 3461) at 128 Lydiard St at $12 per person, again including breakfast.

A short stroll down the street to 27 brings you to the *George Hotel* (tel 31 1031) with rooms at $18/31 for bed and breakfast. There's also four modern motel units. These places are all very central for the railway station (where buses also stop) and are about a 10-minute walk from the Mall.

Other hotels include the *Criterion Hotel* (tel 31 1451) at 18 Doveton St South with singles/doubles for $16/30 for bed & breakfast; *Craigs' Royal Hotel* (tel 31 1377) at 10 Lydiard St South, a rambling old place with rooms at $22/32 for bed & breakfast; and the *Western Hotel* (tel 32

2218) at 1221 Sturt St which charges $16/28 for singles/doubles also including breakfast.

Motels Ballarat has plenty of motels too, many of them on the Western Highway on either side of the centre. The *Ballarat* (tel 34 7234) on the Melbourne side, seven km east, has rooms at $21 to $27 single, $26 to $34 double. Just a bit further out is the *Brewery Tap Hotel-Motel* (tel 34 7201) with prices of $18/26 for singles/doubles with breakfast. Another reasonably priced motel is the *Eureka Lodge* (tel 31 1900) at 119 Stawell St South, three km out, with rooms at $26 single, $34 double with a light breakfast.

Camping There are plenty of campsites in and around Ballarat with the most convenient being the *Goldfield Caravan Park* (tel 32 7888) at 108 Clayton St, 200 metres north of Sovereign Hill, with sites at $7 for two and on-site vans for $18. Also handy is the *Eureka Stockade Caravan*

Park (tel 31 2281), right next to the Eureka Stockade Memorial. Sites are $7.50 and on-site vans are $13.

Places to Eat
Virtually all Ballarat's cheap eating places are on Sturt St and the Bridge St Mall. There are plenty of coffee-shop/snack-bar places but none stand out. The *Athens Cafe* on Sturt St near the mall has breakfast for $2 and other meals in the $4 to $6 range. Opposite is the *Log Tavern* at 23 with pizzas for $3 to $6. Further up Sturt St on the north side is *Health Hitch* where the emphasis is on vegetarian snacks and juices.

Most of the pubs serve typically uninspiring counter meals for about $6, although at the *George Hotel* it's only $3 to $5 for a big feed and they have special deals on Friday and Saturday nights. The *Criterion* features a live band on Friday and Saturday nights and jazz on Sunday as well as the usual meals.

At 10 Camp St is the *Number 10*

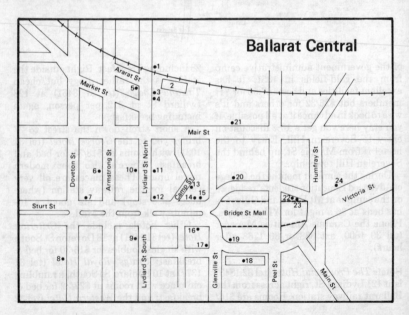

Ballarat Central

restaurant, a BYO place with a varied menu with main courses for $8 to $11. *Rudi's Bistro* on Sturt St has moderately-priced Italian dishes. For a splurge there's the very up-market *La Scala* at 120 Lydiard St, but here you're looking at $50 for two, plus drinks. It's in a restored bluestone warehouse with the *Winery* wine bar and has become Ballarat's trendy hangout. It's been extravagantly decorated to the point where it has become a tourist attraction in its own right. Similarly priced, but recommended is *Dyer's Steak Table*, a cosy, 120-year-old renovated horse stable on Little Bridge St.

If fast-food is what you're after, there's *McDonalds, Taco Bills* and *Pizza Hut*, all near the corner of Victoria and Humfray Sts. On Glenville St South is another of the *Pancake Kitchen* chain.

Getting There

Trains run regularly from Melbourne to Ballarat via Bacchus Marsh and there are also V-Line buses. The trip takes two

1	Tourist Office
2	Railway Station
3	Tawana Lodge
4	La Scala
5	Provincial Hotel
6	Cycle City
7	Health Hitch Cafe
8	Criterion Hotel
9	Craig's Royal Hotel
10	George Hotel
11	Fine Arts Gallery
12	Post Office
13	Number 10 Restaurant
14	Rudi's Bistro
15	Athens Cafe
16	Log Tavern
17	Pancake Kitchen
18	Supermarkets
19	Dyer's Steak House
20	Interstate Buses
21	Green Buslines
22	Taco Bill's
23	McDonalds
24	Pizza Hut

hours direct and the fare is $6.80 in economy, $9.50 in 1st.

Ansett Pioneer and Greyhound run through Ballarat on the Melbourne-Adelaide-Perth services but the buses go via Geelong so it's a rather roundabout route. The fare is $11 to Melbourne. There's no bus terminal in Ballarat but the Melbourne, Adelaide and Perth buses leave from just north of the Mall on Albert St.

Railway buses go to Warrnambool, Monday to Friday at 2.15 pm, $12.50; Hamilton, Monday to Saturday at 9.30 am, $12; Maryborough, weekdays at 7.15 am, $3.50; Donald, Monday to Thursday at 2.30 pm, $11.70; and Geelong, weekdays at 6.35 am and 3.15 pm, $5.20. Tickets are available at the railway station. Greens Buslines (tel 31 1488) on Mair St operate a weekday service to Bendigo at 2 pm for $14.70.

Getting Around

There's a tourist bus service, the Explorer Shuttlebus, which makes daily one-hour trips around the major sights with a running commentary on their history and the history of the town itself. The bus leaves from the tourist office although bookings can also be made at the railway station. Cost is $8 for adults, $6 for students.

Surprisingly, there is nowhere to hire bikes in Ballarat although you could try Cycle City at 35 Armstrong St.

There's a local bus service operated by Davis' Buses – check the timetable and route map at the railway station.

Gold Towns

Australia has had several gold-rushes but the Victorian rush was the biggest, the longest lasting and the one which has left the most visible reminders. In 1851 gold was first discovered in Clunes, which today is just a small town 40 km north of

Ballarat. Three months later 8000 people had poured into the region in search of the elusive metal and within a year the number had swollen to 30,000. Four years later Victoria had over 100,000 men working on the gold-fields. They had flocked there from all over the world but Melbourne had also been virtually denuded of workers as people rushed out in search of their fortune.

Although this was a classic gold-rush during it's early period with shanty towns, raucous bars, hard drinking and all the other popular features of gold-fever, that early phase didn't last long. Soon the easy surface gold was gone and the equally valuable subterranean deposits took large-scale equipment and major finance.

The mining companies were to bring unheard-of wealth to the region over the next 10 years. Money was spent lavishly on fine buildings and Bendigo in particular is still noted for its superb and grandiose Victorian architecture. It was in the 1880s that the gold towns reached their heights of splendour but although gold production was gradually to lose its importance after that time, the towns of the region now had a large and stable population and agriculture and other activities steadily supplanted gold as the economic mainstay of the area.

The major towns of the gold-rush era were Bendigo and Ballarat but even in the many smaller towns you'll still find some fine examples of the architecture which gold wealth brought to the region. The buildings here are solid and substantial – often quite unlike the impermanent look of so many Australian towns.

CRESWICK (population 2000)

Creswick is a pleasant small town 18 km from Ballarat, with many signs still visible of the diggings during the gold-rush days. At its peak, 60,000 people lived here. There's an interesting little Creswick Historical Museum, a graveyard with some early memorial stones from the gold

era as well as a Chinese section, an ornate town hall and many excellent bushwalks in the area.

CLUNES (population 700)

This town was the actual site for the first gold discovery in June 1851. Although other finds soon diverted interest from Clunes, there are still many fine buildings as reminders of the former wealth. The small hills around Clunes are extinct volcanoes.

DAYLESFORD (population 2900)

Picturesquely set around Wombat Hill Gardens and Lake Daylesford, the town boasts more of that sturdy gold-fields architecture. A few km north of the town is Hepburn Spa which has been noted for its medicinal waters since the last century; bottled mineral water is still big business here. The volcano crater of Mt Franklin is visible from the lookout point in the botanic gardens atop Wombat Hill.

CASTLEMAINE (population 7600)

A larger town, the centre of Castlemaine has been virtually unaltered since the 1860s. Castlemaine's rise to prosperity was rapid but the surface gold was just as quickly exhausted. Among the Victorian gems here is the fine market building which has been restored and now houses a museum with exhibits and an audio-visual display on the town and district and its gold-financed heyday. Castlemaine has numerous other fine examples of gold-field buildings including a couple of elegant hotels, a sandstone jail, an impressive town hall and a substantial old bank building.

Near Castlemaine it is possible to visit the Wattle Gully Gold Mine at Chewton. At Vaughan there's a mineral spring and an interesting Chinese cemetery. Guildford was a centre for the large Chinese population amongst the gold-miners.

MALDON (population 1000)

The current population is a scant

Top: A traditional green and cream Melbourne tram on the tree-shaded 'Paris end' of Collins St (TW)
Left: Melbourne skyscrapers reflected in the calm waters of the Yarra River (TW)
Right: The tall pointy spire tops the Melbourne Cultural Centre Complex (TW)

Top: A jumble of rocks rise from the surrounding countryside at Hanging Rock (TW)
Bottom: Near Port Campbell the Twelve Apostles are pounded by the seas of Bass Strait (TW)

reminder of the 20,000 who used to work the gold-fields near Maldon. The whole town is a well-preserved relic of the era with many fine buildings constructed from the local stone. The interesting buildings along the main street include Dabb's General Store with it's authentic shopfront and the restored hotel with the Eaglehawk Restaurant. There are some good bushwalks around the town and amateur gold hunters still scour the area with some success. On Phoenix St the Maldon Progress Association has tourist information.

MARYBOROUGH (population 7800)

Maryborough was already an established sheep-farming town when gold was discovered. It's still a busy town today and its Victorian buildings include a magnificent railway station. In fact a century ago Mark Twain described Maryborough as 'a railway station with town attached'. Bowenvale Timor, a short distance north of Maryborough, was a busy mining town at the height of the rush.

DUNOLLY (population 600)

This small town was once the heart of the gold-field area. More gold nuggets were unearthed in and around Dunolly than anywhere else in Australia. The largest gold nugget ever found, which was named the 'Welcome Stranger', was found here. It is not surprising that there are some interesting buildings along the main street. There is also the Goldfields Historical Museum, which opens up only on the weekends. It has display replicas of some of the more notable finds.

BUNNINYONG

Just south of Ballarat, this was the scene for one of the first gold finds in the state. The impressive, tree-lined main street boasts several fine Victorian buildings from the gold days including the old Crown Hotel, first licensed in 1842.

Bendigo
Population 63,000

This was once one of the richest gold-mining towns in Australia and although the gold days are now just history there's plenty of evidence of the wealth they once brought to this pleasant town.

The buildings around the town centre are very solid, substantial and imposing. Many of them were designed by William Charles Vahland, a German architect. Bendigo also makes the most of its gold-mining past with a number of tourist attractions worth investigating. Gold mining commenced here in 1851 and continued right up into the 1950s.

Information

There's a Regional Tourist Office (tel 47 7161) on the Calder Highway four km south of the centre. It's open 9 am to 5 pm Monday to Friday and 10 am to 3 pm weekends. The Bendigo Trust Tourist Office (tel 42 1205) is in the centre at Charing Cross, open 9 am to 5 pm but is closed for lunch between 12 noon and 1 pm. The RACV (tel 43 9622) has an office at 72 Pall Mall.

Pall Mall/McRae Streets

There are some fine old buildings along this street including the Shamrock Hotel, the third hotel of this name on the site, built in 1897. It's a very large, fully-restored and very fine example of the hotel architecture of the period. Its size gives some indication of how important and prosperous the town must have been in the gold-mining era but the interior is a bit disappointing – some nicely carved woodwork around the dining hall bar but nothing spectacular.

Other large buildings along these streets are the Bendigo Technical College, the elaborate post office, the fountain at Charing Cross, the war memorial and the town hall at the end of Bull St.

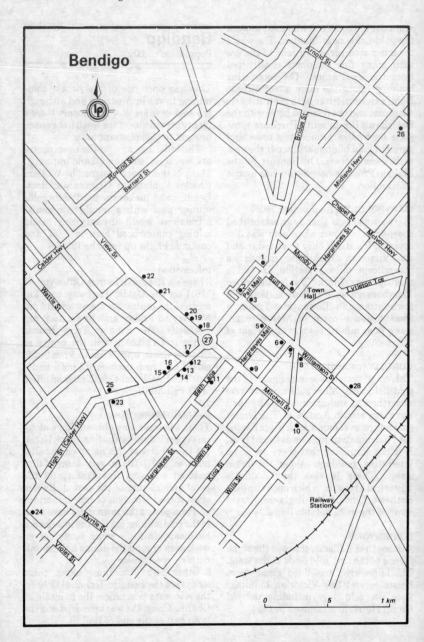

Bendigo

0   5   1 km

1	Conservatory
2	GPO
3	Shamrock Hotel
4	Metropolitan Hotel
5	Gillies Pie Shop
6	Limerick Castle Hotel
7	Chaplins Coffee Shop
8	Cumberland Hotel
9	Toi Shan Restaurant
10	Rechters Cafe
11	Green Olive Deli
12	City Family Hotel
13	Pears Restaurant
14	McDonalds
15	Rasoyer Indian Restaurant
16	Mexican Kitchen
17	New China Restaurant
18	Tourist Office
19	Dai Gun San
20	Militaria Museum
21	Art Gallery
22	Dudley House
23	Kentucky Fried
24	Central Deborah Mine-Talking Tram
25	Sacred Heart Cathedral
26	Tram Museum
27	Alexandra Fountain
28	Jolly Puddler Restaurant

Around Town

Rosalind Park is a pretty little place; in the middle is a lookout tower which was once the mineshaft head of the Garden Gully United Gold Mining Company – good views across the town from the top. The Bendigo Art Gallery on View St has an interesting collection with lots of Australian paintings – bush scenes, droving, mining. It's open Monday to Thursday from 10 am to 5 pm and Friday to Sunday from 2 to 5 pm; admission is $1.

Bendigo Tram

A vintage tram makes a regular tourist run from the Central Deborah Mine, through the centre of the city and out to the tramways museum and the joss house with a commentary along the way. On weekdays it departs from the Central Deborah Mine at 9.30 am and 2 pm, but you can catch it five minutes later than

that at the fountain. During weekends and school holidays it operates hourly from 9.30 am. For enquiries phone 43 8070; the fare is $3.

Central Deborah Mine

On Violet St this was one of the major gold-mining sites in Bendigo. It was the last mine to close on the gold-fields, operating for 103 years from 1851. Now restored and developed as a museum it's well worth a visit, particularly if you haven't been to Sovereign Hill in Ballarat. There are lots of interesting exhibits and many photographs taken from the mid-1800s onwards. It's open 9 am to 5 pm daily and admission is $2.50.

The Joss House

The Chinese joss house on Finn St is the only one remaining of the four which were known to exist in the area. Built of timber and hand-made bricks the building is painted red – the traditional Chinese colour denoting strength and good luck. It's a small place with a central temple, flanked by an ancestral temple and a caretaker's residence. Exhibits include embroidered and stone-rub banners, figures representing the 12 years of the Chinese solar cycle, commemorative tablets to the deceased, paintings and images of gods and Chinese lanterns. The only other joss houses known to remain in Victoria are two in Melbourne. The Bendigo Joss House is open 10 am to 5 pm daily and admission is $1.50

There's a Chinese section in the White Hills Cemetery on Killian St and also a prayer oven where paper money, and the other goodies which you can take with you, are burnt. Bendigo has an annual Chinese parade at Easter, featuring a 30-metre-long ceremonial dragon.

Dai Gum San

Dai Gum San is a small museum of life-size wax statues depicting scenes from Imperial China. The figures, made by a Chinese woman, originally formed part of a larger collection in Hong Kong until they were donated to the Bendigo Trust. The figures, some distinctly on the Chinese-gory side, include a beheading, a concubine with bound feet, removal of finger nails, tattooing, a fortune teller, Dr Sun Yat-Sen and many others. The museum is on View St, open daily from 10 am to 4 pm and admission is $1.75, ($1 for students).

Other Bendigo Attractions

Bendigo has a number of other 'attractions' of not such great interest. The massive Sacred Heart Cathedral is the only Gothic-style building still under construction in the southern hemisphere – it's taken a long time. Angels poke out of some of the nice wooden arches, there's a beautifully carved bishop's chair and some good stained-glass windows. Wesley Church on Forest St is also worth a glance. The Goldmines Hotel is OK but there are lots of OK hotels around.

Victoria Hill, the site of the richest mines, is now just some big holes plus a few rusting hulks of machinery. Classified by the National Trust, Dudley House is a fine old house with beautiful gardens. Fortuna Villa is a stately mansion with Italian fountain and lake, once owned by George Lansell, the 'Quartz King'. It's now the Army Survey Regiment Headquarters but is open to the public on Sunday afternoons. Note that admission is by pre-purchased tickets only, available from the Information Centre at the fountain for $2.

The Militaria Museum on View St has a collection of military paraphernalia. Entrance is $1 and it's open on Wednesdays from 12.45 to 4.30 pm and Saturdays from 10.30 am to 4.30 pm.

Places to Stay

Hostels With the closure of the youth hostel, Bendigo is no gold-mine when it comes to cheap accommodation. The only possibility is the College of Advanced Education which has cheap accom-

modation during the vacation periods. Phone the Residential Secretary on 40 3425 for details.

Hotels & Motels At 33 High St, close to Charing Cross, the *City Family Hotel/ Motel* (tel 43 4674) is $15 to $24 for singles and $25 to $34 for doubles. Close to the railway station at 150 Williamson St the *Brougham Arms Hotel* (tel 43 8144) is $22/30 for singles/doubles.

The *Limerick Castle Hotel* (tel 43 5075) at 257 Williamson St has single or doubles for $14 per person, breakfast is $4. The *Cumberland Hotel* (tel 43 4665) on the corner of Williamson St and Lyttleton Terrace charges $15 per person for bed and breakfast in its air-con rooms. It has a pleasant verandah upstairs to sit and have a beer or a meal.

Some other places to consider include the *Captain Cook Motel/Hotel* (tel 43 4168) at 358 Napier St at $26/32; or out on the Calder Highway, 7½ km south of the centre, the *Calder Motel* (tel 47 7411) has rooms at $23/28.

Camping There are lots of campsites in and around Bendigo, and up at Lake Eppalock. The closest to the centre is the *Central City Caravan Park* (tel 43 6937), three km south on the Calder Highway; sites are $6 for two, on-site vans are $18. Most other sites also permit camping and nightly costs are in the $4 to $8 range.

Places to Eat

Most of the city's 54 pubs do counter meals in the $4 to $7 range. One that stands out is the popular *Metropolitan Hotel*, on the corner of Bull and Hargreaves St – a recently renovated place but still with cheap meals in the bar. It also has a flash restaurant at around $40 for two.

For lunchtime snacks, there's *Gillies* on the corner of Williamson St and the Hargreaves St Mall – a Bendigo institution where you queue at the little window, order one of the five or so varieties of pie, then sit in the mall to eat it. Hopefully the mall's piped muzak won't give you indigestion.

There are many ordinary coffee shops dotted around. In Killian Walk in the mall is the *Golden Pine* milk-bar or there's *Chaplins* on Williamson St. Try *Rechters* for a step back to the '50s; good old-fashioned hamburgers and a collection of paraphernalia on the walls that has to be seen to be believed – everything from stuffed deers' heads to pool cues. It's on Mitchell St at the end of Myers St. The *Green Olive Deli* in Bath Lane has great salads, rolls and a variety of patés and cheeses.

Pears Restaurant at 57 High St is good value with main courses for $4 to $8 in a pleasant atmosphere. *Clog's Pizza* in Pall Mall have wholemeal pizza and other Italian food for $3 to $6.

For Chinese food, the *New China Restaurant* opposite the City Family Hotel offers a four-course lunch for $5.80, or the *Toi Shan* at 67 Mitchell St is a 10ther cheapie. *Coles* in the Mall have a restaurant upstairs. The *Rasoyee* is an Indian restaurant on High St with good food for $6 to $8.

For fast-food there's the usual bunch: *McDonalds*, *Kentucky Fried*, *Ollies* and the *Mexican Kitchen*, all on High St just south of Charing Cross.

The Jolly Puddler is an excellent restaurant at 101 Williamson St, but at about $25 a meal, it should be.

Getting There

Trains from Melbourne to Bendigo take about two hours and cost $10.70 in 2nd class, $15 in 1st. The first train departs from Spencer St station at 8.05 am and there are about half a dozen services a day on weekdays.

Ansett Pioneer and Greyhound buses operate through Bendigo on the route to Swan Hill and Mildura for $7.50. There is a minibus service between Bendigo and Ballarat; it departs from the Houlden Tours office at Charing Cross at 7.45 am

and arrives at Ballarat at 10.30 am. The cost is $14.70, tickets from the driver. The route between the two gold towns is through attractive rolling countryside, particularly at the Bendigo end, flattening out close to Ballarat.

Getting Around

Bendigo and it's surrounding area is well served by public bus. Check the route map at the bus stop on Mitchell St at the end of the Mall.

For bicycle hire the only real possibility is the Eaglehawk Leisure Centre (tel 46 9536). Other than that there's Daisy's Funbikes at the Ampol petrol station opposite the cathedral, who only hire out two-seater tricycles and other oddities, which are not well suited to going any distance.

Tours There are daily tours of Bendigo run by Bendigo Tours (tel 43 0659); the routes change daily so ring first. Barry Maggs runs Goldseeker Tours (tel 47 9559), taking people gold hunting with metal detectors.

AROUND BENDIGO
Close to Bendigo

Sandhurst Town at Myers Flats is a colonial era gold-town re-creation which includes a working 24-inch-gauge railway line. At Epsom you'll find Bendigo Pottery, the oldest pottery works in Australia. There are guided tours of the works and you can buy finished pieces here. Also at Epsom is the large under-cover market on Sundays. Hartland's Eucalyptus Oil Factory at Whipstick Forest was established in 1890 and the production process can still be inspected today.

Also in the area are the Mohair Farm and Woodstock Pottery on the Maryborough road, the Cherry Berry Farm Water Adventure Land and the Mandurang Orchid Nursery on Tannery Lane in Mandurang.

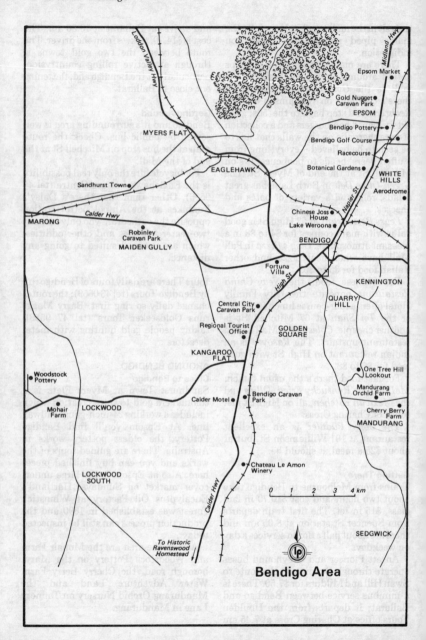

Bendigo Area

Epsom Market
Gold Nugget Caravan Park
EPSOM
Bendigo Pottery
Bendigo Golf Course
Racecourse
Botanical Gardens
WHITE HILLS
Aerodrome
Londan Valley Hwy
MYERS FLAT
Midland Hwy
EAGLEHAWK
Sandhurst Town
Calder Hwy
MARONG
Robinley Caravan Park
MAIDEN GULLY
Napier St
Chinese Joss House
Lake Weeroona
BENDIGO
Fortuna Villa
High St
KENNINGTON
QUARRY HILL
Central City Caravan Park
Regional Tourist Office
GOLDEN SQUARE
Woodstock Pottery
KANGAROO FLAT
One Tree Hill Lookout
Mohair Farm
LOCKWOOD
Calder Motel
Bendigo Caravan Park
Mandurang Orchid Farm
Cherry Berry Farm
MANDURANG
LOCKWOOD SOUTH
Chateau Le Amon Winery
0 1 2 3 4 km
Calder Hwy
To Historic Ravenswood Homestead
SEDGWICK

Further Afield

The large reservoir Lake Eppalock is about 30 km from Bendigo and provides the town's water supply. It's popular for all sorts of watersports – I learnt to sail there and set some sort of record for capsizing in the process. There are some fine lookouts in the vicinity of Heathcote (population 1200), a quiet little highway town.

Central Highlands & North Central Plains

The gold country of central Victoria, extending from Ballarat to Bendigo and beyond is part of the Central Highlands. Continuing north you drop down on to the north central plains, rich agricultural land which extends up to the Murray River. In the north-west of the state the country becomes steadily more sparsely populated in the dry Mallee region.

AVOCA (population 1000)

Already an established town when gold made its impact on the region, this is a good centre for bushwalking and relaxed wine tasting. The foothills of the Pyrenees Ranges around Avoca offer plenty of opportunity for the former; wineries scattered around the town are there for the latter. Avoca is at the junction of the Sunraysia and Pyrenees Highways.

AVOCA TO MILDURA

From Avoca the Sunraysia Highway runs north-west to Mildura, merging with the Calder Highway just before Ouyen. As the road descends from the Central Highlands in to the north central region and then the Mallee, the countryside becomes steadily drier and less populated.

Yet another old gold town, St Arnaud (population 2700) is in pleasant hill country and has many fine old lace-worked buildings and an excellent botanical gardens. Continuing up the highway Donald (population 1600) is a busy wheat-growing and sheep-raising centre with an agricultural museum. Birchip (population 900) is in one of the last areas of Victoria to be settled. See the Central West section for Ouyen.

BENDIGO TO MILDURA

The Calder Highway, like the Sunraysia, runs north-east from the Central Highlands right up to the Mallee. It runs more or less parallel to the Sunraysia, finally turning sharply east to meet it just before Ouyen. From Bendigo it's 45 km to Inglewood (population 1000) near where the 65-kg 'Welcome Stranger' gold nugget was unearthed. West of the town towards St Arnaud bushranger Captain Melville used to hide out in Melvilles Caves.

Wedderburn (population 900) is 74 km from Bendigo. It's another gold town and has a museum and general store set up just like it would have been at the beginning of this century. The town boasts a number of other early buildings and a boomerang factory. The road continues north through Charlton (population 1400) and Wycheproof (population 1000) on the edge of the Mallee. Wycheproof is 136 km from Bendigo and has another boomerang factory. It's also got 43-metre-high Mt Wycheproof, just 8805 metres lower than Mt Everest which probably makes it the lowest mountain in the world!

BENDIGO TO KERANG & ECHUCA

Two other highways also lead north from Bendigo. The Loddon Valley Highway follows the Loddon River to Kerang while the Midland and Northern Highway follows the Campaspe River to Echuca. Pyramid Hill (population 600) was named by the early explorer Mitchell after the strange pyramid-shaped, 187-metre-high hill by the town. The town has a historical museum while to the east near Terrick Terrick there's a picnic ground and walks by Mitiamo Rock. Rochester (population

2200) on the Northern Highway is a dairy-farming and market centre.

The Murray River

Although NSW and Victoria share the Murray from soon after its source all the

winding waterways. Many of the river towns have museums, old buildings from the riverboat era or well-preserved paddle-steamers to recall that colourful era.

Places to Stay
Apart from motels, hotels and campsites – of which there are plenty because the Murray is a popular holiday area – there is also an associate Youth Hostel in Echuca.

Getting There
Air East-West Airlines connect Albury/Wodonga with Melbourne ($75, standby $56) and Sydney ($105, standby $84).

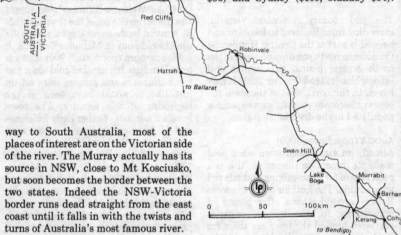

way to South Australia, most of the places of interest are on the Victorian side of the river. The Murray actually has its source in NSW, close to Mt Kosciusko, but soon becomes the border between the two states. Indeed the NSW-Victoria border runs dead straight from the east coast until it falls in with the twists and turns of Australia's most famous river.

The Murray is Australia's most important river for more than one reason. In terms of length it's the second longest in Australia and economically it is of great importance as irrigation schemes using Murray water have made huge areas of previously barren land agriculturally viable. It's also a river with a history; it was travelled along by some of Australia's earliest explorers and later became a great trade artery into the interior. Long before roads and railways crossed the land the Murray was an antipodean Mississippi with paddle-steamers cruising up and down its

Murray Valley Airlines have flights between Melbourne and Mildura.

Bus Ansett Pioneer connect Mildura with Sydney ($66), Melbourne ($29.30) and Adelaide ($32.50). The Melbourne-Mildura service operates through Swan Hill ($20) and Robinvale ($26) while there is also a Melbourne-Deniliquin service that goes through Echuca ($12). Greyhound have similar services and also connect Mildura with Broken Hill on their Melbourne-Broken Hill service.

Mildura-Broken Hill is $20. Albury/ Wodonga is on the regular Melbourne-Sydney Hume Highway route for both bus operators. Wodonga is $37 from Sydney, $24.10 from Melbourne.

Rail V-Line have services from Melbourne to Albury/Wodonga, Swan Hill and Mildura. Albury/Wodonga is on the regular Melbourne-Sydney route. The fare to Wodonga is $19.20 in economy, $26.90 in 1st. Swan Hill services operate via Bendigo but there is usually only one service daily all the way to Swan Hill. The fare is $19.50 economy, $27.30 1st. Mildura services are on the daily Vinelander via Ballarat. The trip takes about 10½ hours and the fares are $27.50 in economy, $37.50 in 1st.

CORRYONG (population 1400)
The Murray is still an alpine stream at this point. Corryong is the Victorian gateway to the NSW Snowy Mountains and also the last resting place of Jack Riley, The Man from Snowy River. His grave is in the town cemetery and there's also a 'Man from Snowy River' museum in the town.

TALLANGATTA (population 950)
With the construction of the Hume Weir

at Albury-Wodonga, Tallangatta was flooded by the rising waters of Lake Hume. The town was relocated on the shoreline of the new lake. Today it's popular as a watersports centre and as an access point to the alpine region.

WODONGA TO ECHUCA
See the Hume Highway section for details on Wodonga, the sister town to Albury on the NSW side of the Murray. By Wodonga the Murray has already become a large, steady river and the Hume Highway crosses the border over the Hume Weir. Further downstream at Yarrawonga another weir created Lake Mulwala back in 1939. The river is particularly pleasant along this stretch and Yarrawonga (population 3450) is a popular stopping point. Here and at Cobram (population 3800), a town noted for its fine peaches, there are many sandy beaches along the river. Downstream Barmah (population 600) is by a large loop in the river.

ECHUCA (population 8000)
In the riverboat days this was the busiest riverport in Australia. It's strategically situated where the Goulburn and Campaspe Rivers join the Murray. Those pioneering days are conjured up in the old Port of Echuca area and the restored paddle-steamers *Pevensey* and *Adelaide*. The Star Hotel and the Bridge Hotel also date back to the riverboat era.

Echuca has a Port of Echuca Museum, the Murray Museum and the Alambee Auto & Folk Museum. You can make short riverboat cruises on the modern paddle-steamer *Canberra* or for overnight trips there's the *Emmylou*; phone (054) 82 3801 for details.

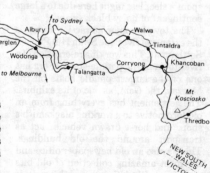

There's a Tourist Information Centre on Heygarth St in Echuca. The smaller NSW sister town of Moama is right across the river.

ECHUCA TO SWAN HILL

Cohuna (population 2200) is close to Gunbower Island, a long 'island' enclosed by the Murray and Gunbower Creek and with abundant animal and birdlife. Kow Swamp, to the south of Cohuna, is also a wildlife sanctuary.

Kerang (population 4000) is 30 km south of the Murray and between here and the river is a sprawling group of lakes and marshes particularly noted for their population of ibis. The lakes here are also popular for sailing. In the town itself there is plenty of birdlife in Korina Park while Strathclyde Cottage is a local arts and crafts centre.

North of the town, Murrabit is a small town on the Murray with a local market on the first Saturday of each month. From Kerang the Murray Valley Highway runs by the series of lakes all the way to Swan Hill. Just 16 km before Swan Hill is Lake Boga with its pleasant sandy beaches.

SWAN HILL (population 8400)

One of the most interesting and popular towns along the entire length of the Murray, Swan Hill was named by the early explorer Thomas Mitchell who spent a sleepless night here due to a large contingent of noisy black swans.

The town's major attraction today is the extensive riverside Swan Hill Pioneer Settlement. This working re-creation of a river town in the paddle-steamer era has one of the largest paddle boats on the Murray, the *Gem*, as one of its exhibits. The settlement has everything from an old locomotive to a working blacksmith's shop, and horse-drawn vehicles act as transport around the old buildings. There's also an old newspaper office and the most amazing collection of old bits and pieces. It's definitely worth a visit, is

open daily and the admission is $6.50. The paddle-steamer *Pyap* makes short trips from the pioneer settlement for $4.40.

Swan Hill also has a regional art gallery at Horseshoe Bend and a military museum. Continuing beyond Swan Hill it's worth a pause to visit the old Tyntynder Homestead, 17 km along the Murray Valley Highway. It's a beautifully restored old homestead from the earliest days of European settlement along the Murray. The homestead also has a small museum of pioneering and Aboriginal relics and many reminders of the hardships of early homestead life, like the wine cellar! Admission is $3.50.

Swan Hill is 340 km from Melbourne and has a Tourist Information Centre on Campbell St.

SWAN HILL TO MILDURA

From Swan Hill the Murray Valley Highway runs close to the river to near Robinvale, from where the most direct route to Mildura is to cross the river and continue on the Sturt Highway on the NSW side. The Murray Valley Highway takes a longer route around a great loop of the river, running beside and through the Hattah-Kulkyne National Park. This park is one of the few fragments of virgin Mallee scrub still remaining in the region. It's a valuable reminder that in this part of country the Murray is really running through a desert and only the great irrigation projects have made the desert bloom. North of the Murray is very empty country, stretching across the great expanse of outback NSW to Broken Hill.

On the river, though a little off the Murray Valley Highway, Robinvale (population 1750) is almost ringed in by a loop of the Murray. It's a centre for grape and citrus growing and has a busy wine industry with local wineries open for visits and tastings. Just downstream from the town is a weir and one of the largest windmills in Australia.

MILDURA (population 15,700)

On the banks of the Murray and nearly 550 km from Melbourne, this was the site for the first development of irrigation from the Murray. The Chaffey brothers came out to Australia to develop irrigation projects late last century. They were persuaded to come out here by Alfred Deakin, a great believer in the possibilities of irrigation and later to become prime minister. His vision proved to be correct and the extensive irrigated land here and down through South Australia all stems from the Chaffey brothers' early work.

W B Chaffey settled in Australia and later became the first mayor of Mildura; you can see his statue on Deakin Avenue. His original home, Rio Vista, is now a museum and part of the Mildura Arts Centre. Mildura also has an Aboriginal Arts Centre at 77 Orange Avenue while the Mildura Workingman's Club boasts one of the longest bars in the world – visitors can inspect the bar from 9.30 to 11 am. Amongst Mildura's other attractions one of the most interesting is the Orange World citrus plantation tour (one hour, $2). It's a fascinating introduction to how citrus fruit is produced.

Lest you forget that this is riverboat country you can take paddle-steamer trips from the Mildura Wharf. On weekday afternoons and Sundays the *PS Melbourne* does a two-hour round trip for $8. It's also wine country with a number of popular wineries around the town.

Leaving Mildura you don't have to travel very far before you realise just how desolate the country around here can be. Continuing west, now on the Sturt Highway, the road runs arrow-straight and deadly dull to South Australia, about 130 km away. Crossing into NSW you follow the Murray another 32 km to Wentworth, one of the oldest river towns, then strike off north for 266 km along the Silver City Highway to remote Broken Hill. A popular trip from Mildura is to Mungo Station to the strange formation called the Wall of China.

Mildura, which is noted for its exceptional amount of sunshine, has a Victorian Government Tourist Bureau on Deakin Avenue and a city Tourist Office at 41B Langtree Avenue.

Information

For fruit-picking work, write to or phone the Commonwealth Employment Service around the first week of February and the chances are good you will get a job as a grape picker or cart man. After a few days, you'll get used to the back-breaking 10 hour a day job. It usually starts around February and lasts for a month. It's hard work but if you've done it before, it can mean big bucks, like about $350 a week. Some farmers provide accommodation, but take a tent if you're not sure.

Goulburn Valley

The Goulburn Valley region runs in a wide band from Lake Eildon north-west across the Hume Highway and up to the NSW border. The Goulburn River joins the Murray upstream from Echuca. You'll also find Goulburn Valley centres in the Around Melbourne, Hume Highway and Murray River sections of this chapter but the stretch from Seymour on the Hume Highway up to the Murray River is covered below.

Getting There

Trains run between Melbourne and Shepparton and sometimes on to Numurkah. From Shepparton or Numurkah connecting buses operate to Cobram and across the Murray to Tocumwal, from where you can connect to Sydney. Fares from Melbourne are: Shepparton $11.70 ($16.40 1st), Numurkah $13.40 ($18.80) and Cobram $15.80 ($22.10).

Ansett Pioneer Melbourne-Brisbane bus services via Toowoomba operate up the Goulburn Valley with fares to

Shepparton of $10.40 and to Echuca $12.

NAGAMBIE (population 1100)

On the shores of Lake Nagambie which was created by the construction of the Goulburn Weir, Nagambie has some interesting old buildings, a historical society display and two of the best known wineries in Victoria are close by.

Chateau Tahbilk's winery is a beautiful old building with notable cellars while just a few km away the Mitchelton Winery is ultra-modern with a strange 'control tower' looming unexpectedly from the surrounding countryside. Mitchelton's winery is part of a whole complex including barbecue facilities and a swimming pool. Boat tours operate from Nagambie on the lake and up the river to the winery which is built on the river banks.

SHEPPARTON (population 28,000)

In a prosperous irrigated fruit and vegetable growing area, Shepparton and its adjoining centre of Mooroopna (population 2000) have a number of points of interest. Shepparton's modern Civic Centre has an art gallery and other facilities; there's an International Village, a Historical Museum open on Sunday afternoons, and a pottery a few km out of town. You can tour the Shepparton Preserving Company cannery (the largest in the southern hemisphere) at 10 am or 2 pm on weekdays.

From January to April is the fruit-picking season and it's a good time to pick up some casual work. Start looking in December as demand for jobs is high.

OTHER TOWNS

Rushworth (population 1000) is about 20 km west of the Goulburn Highway and was once a mining centre in the gold days. You can visit the local history museum on weekends or the Cheong Homestead a few km south of town at Whroo. Lake Waranga is popular for watersports.

North of Shepparton and not far from the Murray River, Numurkah (population 2700) is another irrigation-area town. has a Steam & Vintage Machinery Display. Kyabram (population 5400) is a little south of Echuca and has a fauna and waterfowl park at the southern end of the town. It's the centre for a prosperous fruit growing district.

Up the Hume

The Hume Highway is the direct route between Melbourne and Sydney. It's far from Australia's most exciting road; in fact it's downright dull in stretches, and the heavy (by Australian standards) traffic can make life a little tedious. En route to the NSW border you pass through the 'Kelly Country' area, around which Australia's most famous outlaw, Ned Kelly, had some of his most exciting brushes with the law. Not far to the east of the Hume are the Victorian Alps and in winter you'll catch glimpses of the snow-capped peaks from the highway.

Places to Stay

Although there are no youth hostels along the Hume there are plenty of other forms of accommodation. Beechworth, just off the Hume in a beautiful location in the alpine foothills, has an attractive hostel in a National Trust classified building.

Getting There

As the main artery between Australia's two biggest cities it's hardly surprising that there's plenty of transport possibilities along the Hume Highway.

You can fly to Albury-Wodonga with East-West from Melbourne ($75) or Sydney ($105) or take the buses or trains. Apart from the Melbourne-Sydney trains there are a variety of trains running just Melbourne-Albury or Sydney-Albury. From Melbourne fares (1st class in brackets) include Seymour $5.40 ($7.60),

Benalla $12.30 ($17.20), Wangaratta $14.60 ($20.40), Wodonga $19.20 ($26.90).

Ansett Pioneer and Greyhound run along the Hume of course. Fares include Benalla $22, Wangaratta $27.50 and Wodonga also $27.50. Bus services fan out from Wangaratta and Wodonga to Beechworth, Bright, Corryong and other towns in the foothills and to the snow resorts.

MELBOURNE TO BENALLA

The new Hume Freeway bypasses Kilmore and Broadford (population 1600) near Mt Disappointment and the Murchison Falls. Seymour (population 6500) is close to several interesting vineyards including the very old Chateau Tahbilk and very modern Mitchelton winery – see the Goulburn Valley section for more details. You can turn off the Hume here and take the alternate Newell Highway route to Sydney or Brisbane.

From Euroa (population 2700) you can take a scenic drive to Gooram Falls, near where Kelly performed one of his more amazing robberies at Faithfull Station; it's re-enacted every December.

BENALLA (population 8200)

The Kelly gang's exploits finally came to an end in a bloody shoot-out in nearby Glenrowan in 1880. Kelly was captured alive and eventually hanged in Melbourne. There's everything from a statue of Ned with his armoured helmet to a small museum of Kelly memorabilia but it's all terribly commercial. Benalla also has a Pioneer Museum with Kelly exhibits. There are picnic areas along the Broken River through town and an excellent art gallery by the waterside. Benalla is a good place from which to visit the various northern Victorian wineries or the mountains. The town is also a very popular gliding centre. The ruins of the Kelly family homestead can be seen just off the highway at Greta.

WANGARATTA (population 16,200)

'Wang', as it's known, is the turn-off point to Mt Buffalo and the north of the Victorian alps along the Ovens Highway. The town has some pleasant parks and bushranger Mad Dog Morgan is buried here. On the Boorhaman Rd, eight km from town, Bontharambo is a restored historic homestead. It's open on school and public holidays. There's lots of interest in the area around Wang including old gold towns, the alps and the Rutherglen wineries.

The North-East Victoria Regional Tourist Authority has an office at 29 Ryley St.

CHILTERN (population 870)

Only one km off the Hume Highway between Wang and Wodonga and close to Beechworth, this is another gold town with many reminders of its boom era. Author Henry Handel Richardson's home Lake View is preserved by the National Trust. In the old Grape Vine Hotel a courtyard is sheltered by the largest grape vine in Australia.

WODONGA (population 18,100)

The Victorian half of Albury-Wodonga is on the Murray River, the border between Victoria and NSW. Just south of the city off the Hume Highway on Coyles Rd there's the interesting Drage's biplane museum, open daily from 10 am to 5 pm.

Victorian Wineries

There's no Barossa or Hunter Valley in Victoria so the state's wine producing activities are less well known than those of NSW or South Australia but in actual fact some of Australia's best wines are made here. Grape growing and wine production started with the gold-rush of the 1850s and before the turn of the century Victorian wines had established a fine reputation in Europe. Then Phylloxera, a disease of grapevines, devastated the Victorian vineyards and changing tastes in alcohol completed the destruction. Only recently has the

Victorian wine industry started to recapture its former glory.

The oldest established wine-producing area is in the north-east, particularly around Rutherglen but also across to Glenrowan and beyond. Other fine wine-growing areas include the Goulburn Valley river flats south of Shepparton, Great Western between Stawell and Ararat on the Adelaide highway, around the Geelong area, and in the Yarra Valley near Melbourne. In the far north-west the irrigation areas along the Murray at Robinvale and Mildura also produce wine.

RUTHERGLEN (population 1400)
Close to the the Murray River, Rutherglen is the centre of Victoria's major wine-growing area. Amongst the wineries in the area is All Saints with a National Trust classified winery building. Just 11 km from Rutherglen, on the Murray, Wahgunyah was once a busy port for the Ovens Valley gold towns. Its customs house is a relic of that era.

YACKANDANDAH (population 500)
The pretty little 'strawberry capital' has been classified by the National Trust; not just the odd building but the entire town. Around here they have so many straw-berries they even make them into strawberry wine.

Yackandandah, only 25 km south of Wodonga and near Beechworth, was also a prosperous gold town and has many fine old buildings. The 1850 Bank of Victoria building is now a museum. Horse-drawn carriages are on display in the Millfield Carriage Museum and there are also a number of local craft centres. Near the town are picturesque little settlements and at Leneva you can ride the narrow-gauge railway at the Wombat Valley Tramway on the last Sunday of each month.

BEECHWORTH (population 3200)
This small town with its picturesque setting in rolling countryside and fine, National Trust classified buildings, is a pleasure to visit and explore for a few days. It's just 35 km from Wangaratta, and if you're travelling between Wang and Wodonga the detour through Beechworth makes a worthwhile alternative to the frenetic pace of the boring Hume Highway. Maureen and I once spent some time up here, exploring around Beechworth on bicycles – it's a great place.

In the 1850s Beechworth was the hub of the Ovens River gold-mining region and it became a very prosperous town. Signs of the gold wealth are still very much in evidence, reflected in the fact that some 30 buildings are classified by the National Trust.

Some of the more interesting buildings include Tanswell's Hotel with its magnificent old lacework, the post office with its clocktower, and the old jail which has a dank little cell where Ned Kelly once spent a night.

The old 1859 powder magazine is now a museum while the Robert O'Hara Burke Memorial Museum has relics from the gold-rush and a replica of the main street of a century ago, complete with 16 shop fronts. The hapless explorer Burke was a police officer in Beechworth during the early days of the gold-rush. There's a gemstone collection in the restored Bank of Victoria building.

Also of interest is the Harness & Carriage Museum behind Tanswell's Hotel, and the inevitable art and craft shops which always appear in towns of historic (and therefore tourist) interest.

Around Beechworth
There are a number of points of interest in the Beechworth area as well. On the outskirts of town on the road to Wodonga is the old cemetery with its Chinese section, a reminder of the Chinese presence on the gold-fields. Further out along the same road is the turn-off to Chiltern and to Woolshed Falls – a popular picnic area and the site of a major

alluvial gold-field which yielded over 85,000 kg of gold in 14 years. Further to the west is Eldorado where a gigantic gold dredge still floats on the lake where it was installed in 1936. At the time it was the largest dredge in the southern hemisphere.

Heading east from Beechworth along the Myrtleford road, you come to the Trout Farm at Hurdle Flat where fresh trout are for sale, and I mean *fresh*, or you can hire a fishing pole and catch your own. The small village of Stanley is 10 km out along this road and is the centre of a thriving little apple-growing industry.

Places to Stay & Eat

There's a good choice of accommodation here with the *Youth Hostel* in the National Trust classified old Star Hotel, the various other pubs and the caravan park.

Tanswell's Hotel does excellent counter meals and the bakery has a good selection of hot bread and cakes.

The Victorian Alps

As with the NSW Snowy Mountains, the Victorian Alps are popular in both summer and winter. They're best known for their winter skiing but in summer they offer excellent bushwalking. The mountains actually begin immediately to the east of Melbourne (the Dandenongs are a spur of the Great Dividing Range) and run north and north-east all the way to the NSW border. Only a few roads, none of them surfaced all the way, run right across the Great Dividing Range from north to south. In the north of the state the mountains slope down through delightful foothills into rolling country that includes some of Victoria's best grape-growing country.

Places to Stay

Apart from all the usual accommodation

possibilities there are also youth hostels at Beechworth, Mt Buller and Mt Baw Baw. In winter costs in the ski resorts tend to get pretty hair-raising and many skiing visitors prefer to stay in the towns lower down, often only a short drive from the snow.

Getting There

Buses and trains run from Melbourne to Albury-Wodonga – see the Hume Highway section for more details. You can also fly to Albury-Wodonga. Buses run from Wangaratta and Wodonga to many points in the northern part of the region. There are also buses from Melbourne to Mt Buller in the south while you can reach Omeo by bus from Bairnsdale in the Gippsland region.

MYRTLEFORD (population 2800)

Another Ovens Valley centre, Myrtleford is handy for old towns like Beechworth and Bright, the various wineries of the Rutherglen region and the popular Mt Buffalo National Park. In the town itself there's a historic park with a collection of antique steam engines.

MT BUFFALO

Mt Buffalo National Park is noted for its many pleasant streams and fine walks, apart from Mt Buffalo itself. The mountain was named back in 1824 by explorers Hume and Hovell on their trek from Sydney to Port Phillip Bay. The mountain is surrounded by huge granite tors – great blocks of granite broken off from the massif by the expansion and contraction of ice in winter and other weathering effects. There is abundant plant and animal life around the park as well as over 140 km of walking tracks. Walk leaflets are available for the Gorge Nature Walk and the Dicksons Falls Nature Walk. A road leads up almost to the summit of 1720-metre Mt Buffalo.

Places to Stay

You can stay in the park at the campsite

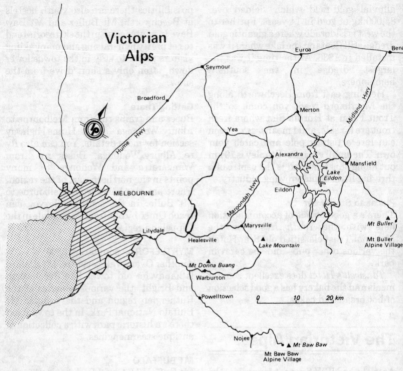

Victorian Alps

by Lake Catani (open only during the summer months) or at the Tatra Inn or The Chalet.

BRIGHT (population 1500)

Deep in the Ovens Valley, Bright today is a centre for the winter sports region, a summer bushwalking centre and in autumn it's renowned for its beautiful golden shades as the leaves change colour. In 1857 this was the centre for the notorious Buckland Valley riots when the diligent Chinese gold-miners were forced off their claims with much less than a fair go. Bright is an easy drive from the snowfields of Mt Hotham, Mt Buffalo and Falls Creek.

Bright has a museum in the railway station while around the town are a number of excellent walking trails. You'll also enjoy excellent views if driving from Bright along the Alpine Way. Places of interest in the vicinity include the Stony Creek Trout Farm, the Pioneer Park open-air museum and the pretty little town of Harrietville. A gold dredge continued operating in Harrietville right up to 1956 when it was sold and shipped off to Malaysia. The town is at the foot of 1979-metre Mt Feathertop and a regular bus runs to Mt Hotham. You continue through Harrietville to Mt Hotham and the Dargo High Plains, where in spring the wildflowers make for a colourful spectacle.

Mt Bogong, to the east of Bright, is the highest mountain in Victoria at 1985 metres.

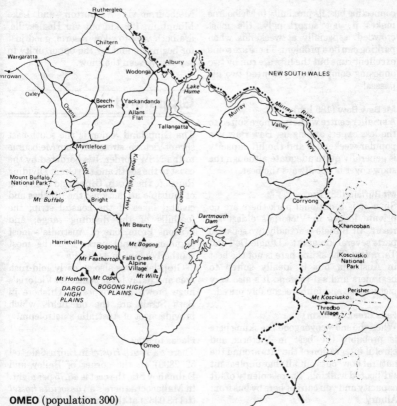

OMEO (population 300)

On the high plains on the southern side of the alpine region this small town is on the Omeo Highway, the southern access route to the snow country. In summer it's popular as a jumping-off point for the Bogong High Plains. The road from here to Corryong, near the NSW border, is scenic but rough. Omeo still has a handful of interesting old buildings despite two earthquakes and one disastrous bushfire since 1885. The town has also had its own little gold-rush.

MANSFIELD (population 1900)

Close to Lake Eildon and on the road up to Mt Buller there's a monument here recalling one of Ned Kelly's notorious clashes with the law. The graves of three police officers he shot at nearby Tolmie in 1878 are in the Mansfield cemetery.

SKIING

The Victorian resorts are closer to Melbourne than the Snowy resorts are to Sydney, so they're even more popular on weekends. See the NSW Snowy section for general information on skiing. The Victorian resorts are particularly good for ski-touring. Some of the main resorts, with distances from Melbourne are:

Mt Buller (241 km)

You can get there by rail to Mansfield and

connecting bus. Its proximity to Melbourne makes it, not surprisingly, the most crowded, especially at weekends when parking can be a problem. There are some excellent runs but the lifts are run by two opposing companies – you need two lift passes!

Mt Baw Baw (185 km)

A smaller centre with runs more suited to the less expert among us. Baw Baw is a popular weekender and the lift capacity is generally quite adequate although the snow cover is not always the best.

Mt Buffalo (332 km)

Since it is a national park there are no private lodges in Victoria's oldest ski resort. Mt Buffalo is actually two separate parts several km apart – Dingle Dell and Tatra Inn. The skiing here is not the best in Australia but is ideally suited to beginners and ski-tourers. It's also very picturesque and fairly reasonably priced.

Falls Creek (379 km)

When the snow cover good the skiing here is probably the best in Victoria and careful integration of the lifts around the natural bowl cuts out all that unpleasant ski-booted walking. There's plenty of lift capacity and you can get here by bus from Albury.

Mt Hotham (403 km)

A good-bad combination; Hotham is the furthest from Melbourne but enjoys the most consistent snow coverage. It has some of the best ski-touring areas but terrible inter-connection of the lifts necessitates lots of walking. The village is strung out along the road making a car a virtual necessity. There's very good cross-country skiing around Hotham, which can be reached from the north from Bright or from the south via Bairnsdale and Omeo.

Others

Mt Donna Buang, just 95 km from Melbourne via Warburton, and Lake Mountain, 109 km out via Healesville, are both very low-key resorts, good just for beginners and for the opportunity to say you've seen the snow.

Gippsland

The Gippsland region is the south-east slice of Victoria, stretching from Melbourne to the NSW border. It's bordered by the coast to the south and the Great Dividing Range to the north. Gippsland is an area of multiple attractions: the beaches and coastal lakes of the coastal strip; the foothills of the dividing range; and Wilsons Prom, one of Australia's most popular national parks and the most southerly point in Australia.

Gippsland was also an early gold-rush area and today is the centre for Victoria's huge brown coal deposits. Offshore in Bass Strait are the oil fields which provide most of Australia's petroleum.

Places to Stay

There's a *Youth Hostel* in Bairnsdale (tel 52 2896) on the corner of Bailey and Dalmahoy Sts, the cost is $5.75 per night. In Mallacoota there's an *associate hostel* (tel 58 0362) at the Shady Gully Caravan Park which charges $5.50 per night.

Getting There

V-Line operates a daily Melbourne-Traralgon-Sale-Bairnsdale service, sometimes by bus from Sale onwards. Fares from Melbourne are $9.60, $13.40, $16.80 respectively in economy; $13.40, $18.80, $23.50 in 1st.

By Greyhound bus, fares are Traralgon $18.10, Sale and Bairnsdale $21.70, Lakes Entrance and Orbost $24.10,

There's no public transport service all the way down to Wilsons Prom; about the closest you can get is Fish Creek; buses run there fairly regularly from Leongatha for $8.50.

DANDENONG TO SALE

Soon after leaving Dandenong the road divides; the Princes Highway continues east and the South Gippsland Highway heads off to the south-east to Phillip Island and Wilsons Prom. You can take the South Gippsland Highway and rejoin the Princes Highway at Sale. The Princes Highway runs at first through the Latrobe Valley, site of Victoria's huge coal deposits and the electricity generating stations.

Towns along the Princes Highway include Drouin (population 3500) with historical exhibits in the old police station. The Gippsland Regional Tourist Association has its headquarters at 231 Princes Highway, Drouin. A little further along you come to Warragul (population 7400), a dairy-farming centre. Trafalgar (population 1900) is another dairy centre before you reach the large town of Moe.

Moe (population 18,200) is a Latrobe Valley coal-mining centre and you can visit the Yallourn Power Station here. Old buildings have been collected here and reassembled in the Gippsland Folk Museum on the Princes Highway to re-create a 19th century community. From here there's a scenic road north to Walhalla, an historic old gold-mining town, and the road continues north across the Victorian alps. There are good views of the valley from Narracan and Coalville, small towns on a back road between Moe and Trafalgar.

Morwell (population 16,500) has huge coal deposits and electricity generating plants. In all, the Latrobe Valley generates more than 85% of Victoria's electricity. Traralgon (population 15,100) is, like Moe and Morwell, a major Latrobe Valley electricity centre.

WALHALLA (population 28)

This tiny ghost gold town is in the mountains 46 km north of Moe. At one time the richest gold-mine in Victoria was here; today the Long Tunnel Mine is open for visitors on weekends and holidays. There are a number of National Trust classified and other old buildings in the town so there's plenty of history but the spectacular drive up to the town is also attractive.

SALE (population 13,000)

At the junction of the Princes and Gippsland Highways, Sale is a supply centre for the Bass Strait oil fields. There's an Oil & Gas display centre on Princes Highway on the western side of town. The Port of Sale, also on this side of town, was a busy centre in the paddle-steamer days and you can still take cruises from Sale into the Gippsland Lakes. In the city centre Lake Guthridge has picnic and barbecue spots and the city also has some fine old buildings like the Criterion Hotel with its intricate lacework. On Princes Highway there is a Historical Museum.

There are many popular excursions and local attractions around Sale like Seaspray beach with good surfing south of the city. Lake Wellington is very popular for sailing and boating. Just beyond Sale at Stratford you can turn north on the unsurfaced road across the spectacular Dargo High Plains to Mt Hotham. There are also exciting roads into the mountains from Maffra (population 3800) and Heyfield (population 1700). The forest road to Licola and Jamieson, near Lake Eildon, is particularly spectacular.

Tourist information is available from the Oil & Gas centre.

THE GIPPSLAND LAKES

The long stretch of sand along 90 Mile Beach separates the sea from the extensive waterways of the Gippsland Lakes – an area offering lakes and sea, beaches and surf, fishing and boating.

Bairnsdale (population 9500), at the junction of the Princes and Omeo Highways, is a popular base both for the mountains to the north and the lakes immediately to the south. West of Bairnsdale is Lindenow and the small

Glenaladale National Park. The park has good bushwalking tracks and the Den of Nargun, an Aboriginal ceremonial ground in a gorge of the Mitchell River.

Paynesville (population 1600) is a resort on the lakes; you can cross to nearby Raymond Island by punt or to 90 Mile Beach by boat. Between Bairnsdale and Lakes Entrance you can turn off to Metung (population 350), a popular place to hire boats on Lake King. This interesting little fishing village has the small Angus McMillan cottage museum nearby at Chinaman's Creek. The Omeo Highway leads north from here onto the Bogong High Plains. Tourist info can be obtained from the Victorian Eastern Development Association at 63 Main St, Bairnsdale.

At the eastern end of the lakes is Lakes Entrance (population 3400) where there's a bridge across to 90 Mile Beach at Cunningham Arm. This is also a busy fishing port and lots of cruise boats operate on to the lakes. There's a Shell Museum on Marine Rd, an Antique Car Museum on the Princes Highway, and an Aboriginal Art Museum, also on the Princes Highway. You can visit the Buchan Caves from here.

TO THE NSW BORDER

From Orbost (population 2600) the Bonang Highway leads up through beautiful hill country into NSW. The route to Buchan and beyond is equally scenic so you can make a fine loop from Orbost around the Snowy River National Park by taking one road north and the other south. Most of this route is on unsurfaced road. There are a number of limestone caves around the tiny town of Buchan (population 220). Tours take place three times daily at the Royal and Fairy caves.

From Orbost you can also take the road down to the coast at Marlo and on to Cape Conran. Beyond Orbost is Cann River (population 350) and a series of coastal national parks stretching all the way to the NSW border. The Mallacoota National

Park around the Mallacoota inlet is the best known and most popular. Mallacoota (population 720) is the main centre for this area. There are some mud-brick flats (tel (051) 58 0329) for visitors to stay in. They've been built using recycled materials where possible and have been designed with the environment and ecology in mind.

SOUTH GIPPSLAND

Way back at Dandenong you can opt to take the route south into the south Gippsland area rather than continue east on the Princes Highway to Sale. This route takes you down to Phillip Island and Wilsons Promontory. On the way south to Wilsons Prom you pass Koo-wee-rup (population 1000) with the nearby Bayles Flora & Fauna Park. Wonthaggi (population 4800), close to the coast, was once a major coal-mining centre and from here there are good beaches at the small resort of Inverloch (population (1500), Tarwin Lower and Walkerville. Waratah Bay has good beaches from Walkerville right round to Sandy Point toward the Prom.

Near Korumburra (population 2800) is the Coal Creek Historical Park, a very popular re-creation of a coal-mining town of the 19th century. Coal was first discovered here in 1872 and the Coal Creek mine operated from the 1890s right up to 1958. A little to the south is Leongatha (population 3700) with some beautiful countryside around it. The turn-off to the Prom is at Meeniyan or at Foster (population 1000).

Welshpool (population 250) is a dairying town which is also involved in fishing at nearby Port Welshpool while the Bass Strait oil rigs are supplied from nearby Barry Beach. There's a Maritime Museum in Port Welshpool while the Agnes Falls, just north of the highway, are the highest in Victoria.

Further along the coast Port Albert (population 200) was the first port in the state and an entry point for Chinese

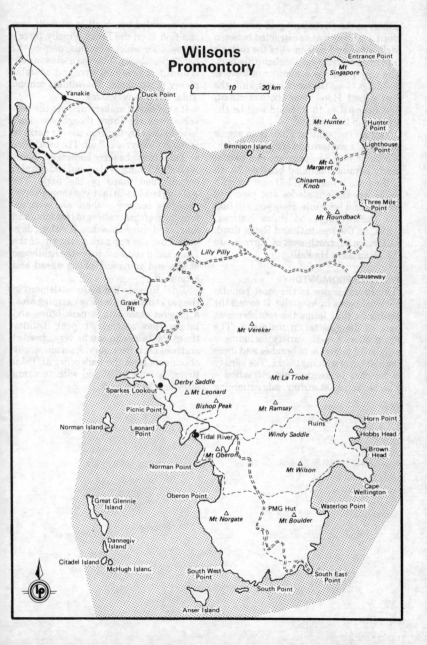

Wilsons Promontory

0   10   20 km

Yanakie

Duck Point

Entrance Point

Mt Singapore

Mt Hunter

Hunter Point

Bennison Island

Lighthouse Point

Mt Margaret

Chinaman Knob

Three Mile Point

Mt Roundback

Lilly Pilly

causeway

Gravel Pit

Mt Vereker

Sparkes Lookout

Derby Saddle

△ Mt Leonard

Bishop Peak

Mt La Trobe

Picnic Point

Leonard Point

Norman Island

Tidal River

Mt Oberon

Mt Ramsay

Ruins

Horn Point

Windy Saddle

Hobbs Head

Brown Head

Norman Point

Mt Wilson

Cape Wellington

Great Glennie Island

Oberon Point

Waterloo Point

PMG Hut

Mt Norgate

Mt Boulder

Dannegiv Island

Citadel Island

McHugh Island

South West Point

South Point

South East Point

Anser Island

miners in the Gippsland gold-rush days. Until a railway was constructed between Melbourne and Sale most of the region's trade was carried on through this port. The tiny town has a number of historic buildings along the main street while the Port Albert Hotel near the waterfront, first licensed in 1842, could well be the oldest pub in the state.

Yarram (population 2100) is an access point to the western end of 90 Mile Beach. Woodside and Seaspray are two particularly popular patrolled beaches. North of the town is beautiful hill country with dense woods, fern glades and plenty of rosellas and lyrebirds. Here you will find the Tarra Valley and Bulga National Parks, on the scenic Grand Ridge Road. At Hiawatha, north-west of Yarram, are the Minnie Ha Ha Falls.

WILSONS PROMONTORY

'The Prom' is one of the most popular national parks in Australia. It covers the peninsula that forms the southernmost part of the Australian mainland. The Prom offers superb variety including a wonderful selection of beaches and more than 80 km of walking tracks. The variety of beaches is another big attraction – whether you want surfing, safe swimming or a secluded beach all to yourself, you can find it on the Prom. Finally there's the wildlife which abounds, despite the park's popularity. There is a wide variety of birdlife, emus, kangaroos and, at night, plenty of wombats. The wildlife around Tidal River is very tame.

It's probably walkers who get the best value from the Prom though you don't have to get very far from the car parks to really get away from it all. The park office at Tidal River has free leaflets on 'Short Walks' and 'Long Walks' and you can also get detailed maps of the park. The walking tracks will take you through ever-changing scenery – there are swamps, forests, marshes, valleys of tree ferns and long, sand-duned beaches. It's a long day-walk from the car park to the tip of the Prom and if you want to see the lighthouse at the end you must phone ahead and arrange it.

Tidal River is the main settlement in the park with an extensive camping area, a general store and a park office and information centre. At peak holiday times the campsite can be very crowded and booking is necessary. A permit, easily obtainable from the park office at Tidal River, is required if you wish to camp elsewhere in the park.

Western Australia

Area 2,526,000 square km
Population 1,300,000

Don't miss beautiful Perth with its 'ideal' climate, the rugged gorge country of the Pilbara and the Kimberley to the north, and the interesting old gold-rush region around Kalgoorlie.

Western Australia is the largest, most lightly populated and most isolated state. Since the completion of surfacing of the Eyre Highway across the Nullarbor in 1976 it is now considerably more accessible from the east coast, and even if you travel the 4300 or so km between Darwin and Perth there is now only 100 km of dirt road in the Kimberley.

In the haphazard, fits-and-starts manner in which most of Australia was established, the first settlers arrived in Perth in 1829, three years after Britain had formally claimed it. They were there basically to beat any other Europeans to the area. Being so far from the main Australian development it is not surprising that growth was painfully slow. Not until the gold-rushes of the 1890s did WA really get off the ground. A larger and far more technologically advanced mineral rush forms the basis for the state's current prosperity.

The comparative newness of Perth accounts for its clean-cut look. It is a shiny, modern city, pleasantly sited on the Swan River with the port of Fremantle a few km downstream. Despite its late settlement WA has some of the oldest relics of European contact with Australia. A number of Dutch East Indiamen fell afoul of the WA coast while on their way to Batavia (Jakarta in Indonesia today) long before Captain Cook sailed up the east coast.

Away from the capital there are the gold-field ghost towns in the east of the state, the rugged coast and giant karri forests of the south plus the wine-producing Swan Valley area closer to the capital. Heading north there is the harshly beautiful Pilbara gorge country, site of the state's immense mineral wealth, plus the old pearling town of Broome, now enjoying a tourist boom all of its own. The wild Kimberley area forms the top corner of the state and is one of Australia's last frontiers.

INFORMATION

Western Australia is well represented in the eastern states with tourist offices in the major cities.

NSW
    92 Pitt St, Sydney 2000, (tel 233 4400)
Queensland
    307 Queen St, Brisbane 4000, (tel 229 5794)
South Australia
    108 King William St, Adelaide 5000, (tel 212 1344)
Victoria
    2 Royal Arcade, Bourke St, Melbourne 3000, (tel 63 3692)

GEOGRAPHY

Western Australia's geography is somewhat like a reverse of the eastern side of Australia – but with much less green and much more desert. The equivalent of the long fertile coastal strip on the east coast is the small south-west corner of the state. Here too a range of hills rises up behind the coast, but they're much smaller in scale than the Great Dividing Range on the east coast. Further north it's dry and

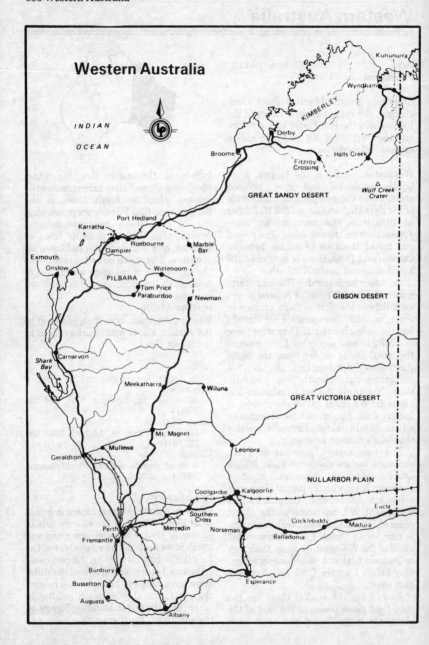

Western Australia

INDIAN OCEAN

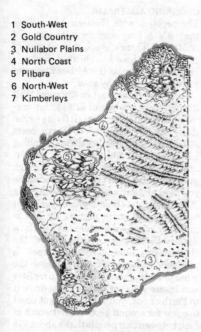

1 South-West
2 Gold Country
3 Nullabor Plains
4 North Coast
5 Pilbara
6 North-West
7 Kimberleys

the Great Sandy Desert in the north, and the Gibson and Great Victoria Deserts in between.

Wildflowers

Western Australia is famed for its wild-flowers and some people go all the way to WA just to see them. They spring into life in the late winter and early spring from August through October and can be seen all over the state. Even some of the driest deserts will put on a technicolour display with just a little rainfall as prompting.

The variety of flowers is enormous – the south-west alone has over 3000 different species, and because of WA's isolation from the rest of Australia many of the flowers to be seen here are unique to the state. They're known as everlastings because the flower petals stay attached even after the flower has died. The speed which the flowers appear is quite amazing – they seem to spring up almost overnight and transform vast areas within days. In some places the wildflowers form a virtual carpet of colour stretching as far as the eye can see with as many as one thousand million flowers per square km!

You don't even have to leave Perth to see WA's wildflowers; there's a section of Kings Park where they are cultivated. Elsewhere in the state you can find them almost everywhere but the jarrah forests in the south-west are particularly rich in wildflowers and WA's many coastal parks also put on brilliant displays. Near Perth the Yanchep National Park and the John Forrest National Park in the Darling Range are both excellent prospects.

GETTING AROUND

Air The state's internal air services are excellent, especially to the north-west. Ansett WA have a comprehensive network of flights connecting the northern towns with Perth with a frequency of flights which seems quite ridiculous when you look at the population up there. The reason why is quite simple: much of that

relatively barren and along the north-west coast the Great Sandy Desert runs right to the sea; this is a very inhospitable region.

There are, however, a couple of very interesting variations from the barren inland region of WA. The extreme north of the state is the Kimberley, a wild and rugged area with a convoluted coast and spectacular gorges inland. This area gets adequate annual rainfall – but all in one brief period each year. Taming the Kimberley has been a long-running dream which is still only partially fulfilled. Meanwhile it's a spectacular area well worth a visit.

Further south is the Pilbara, an area with more magnificent gorge country which is also the treasure house from which the state derives its vast mineral wealth. Away from the coast however, most of WA is simply a vast empty stretch of outback, the Nullarbor in the south,

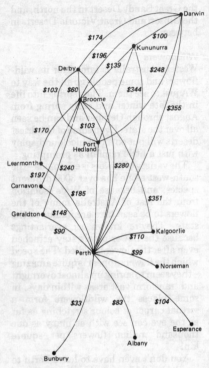

174
100
Darwin
Kununurra
196
139
248
Derby
103 60
344
Broome
355
170
103
Port
Hedland
Learmonth
240
280
197
Carnavon
185
Geraldton
148
351
90
Kalgoorlie
110
Perth
99
Norseman
33 83 104
Esperance
Albany
Bunbury

CROSSING AUSTRALIA

The problem with Western Australia is that it's a long way from the rest of Australia. There's absolutely no way of covering all those km cheaply. Sydney-Perth is 3284 km as the Airbus flies, and more like 4000 km by road.

But what is the least costly way? Well it's certainly not by rail at $442 for one-way economy ticket. Nor is it flying – even stand-by from Sydney to Perth costs $307. Hitching? Well possibly; thumbing a lift across the Nullarbor is not all that easy and you'll probably get through quite a few dollars of tacky fast food while you hang around roadhouses waiting for a lift, and waits of three or four days are not uncommon in some places. By bus is probably a good contender – say $130 for a Sydney-Perth ticket with one of the cheaper bus lines. Driving yourself is probably cheapest of all. Ignoring the other operating costs (you have to register and insure your car whether you drive it to Perth or not) you'll probably get coast to coast for around $300 to $350 worth of fuel; between four people that's about $75 to $90 a head.

ACTIVITIES

Bushwalking There are a number of bushwalking clubs in Perth. Popular areas include the Stirling Range National Park and Porongurup National Park, both near Albany. There are also a number of coastal parks in the south and south-west with good bushwalking tracks.

There are good walks in the hills around Perth at places like Piesse Brook, Mundaring Weir, the Serpentine, Kalamunda and Bickley. They're particularly pleasant during the August-September wildflower season. If you're a really enthusiastic walker there is 640 km of marked walking track all the way from Perth to Albany along old forest tracks.

Swimming & Surfing Perth sometimes claims, and with some justification, to have the best beaches and surf of any

northern population is involved in the mining and oil drilling projects and for the companies it's often easier to fly people back and forth from Perth rather than have them living up there. On some routes Skywest are in spirited competition with Ansett WA. The chart details the main WA routes and flight costs.

Bus & Rail Ansett Pioneer, Greyhound and Deluxe buses run from Perth up the coast (or through the interior to the Pilbara with Greyhound) to the Northern Territory. Other bus companies also connect Perth to the eastern states. Western Australia's internal rail network, on the other hand, is very small.

Australian city. Particularly popular surfing areas elsewhere in the state include Denmark (near Albany), Bunbury (south of Perth) and Geraldton (to the north).

Skin Diving Good diving can be found along a very large part of the WA coast from Esperance to Geraldton and then between Carnarvon and Exmouth. You can get to the islands and reefs off the coast with small boats. Good areas include Esperance, Bremer Bay, Albany, Denmark, Windy Harbour, Margaret River, Bunbury, Rottnest Island, Lancelin, Abrolhos Island (from Geraldton), Carnarvon and all around the North West Cape (Exmouth, Coral Bay).

Perth
Population: 980,000

On the banks of the Swan River, Perth is a clean, modern, attractive-looking city, claimed to be the sunniest state capital in Australia. It was founded in 1829 as the Swan River Settlement but it grew very slowly until the reluctant decision was taken to bring in convicts in 1850. Even then it still lagged behind the eastern cities until the discovery of gold in the 1880s sparked interest in the region.

A six-month-long sports festival is planned for the city in conjunction with the 1986-7 defence of Australia's recently acquired prize possession – the America's Cup yachting trophy. There will be football tournaments, horse-racing, a marathon run and other events. The actual cup races begin at the end of January '87.

Information
The Western Australian Government Travel Centre (tel 322 2999), also called Holiday WA, is at 772 Hay St, just down from Hay St Mall. The centre is open 8.30 am to 5 pm Monday to Friday, 9 to 11.45

am on Saturday. They can supply brochures and information and make bookings for tours and transport in WA. Useful brochures to pick up are the excellent series of town brochures, each with a good map; and the *In & Around Perth* brochure with a good colour map of the city centre and the metropolitan area plus lots of information. In the Hay St Mall is a Perth City tourist booth. There is a Travellers' Information Centre (tel 277 9199) in the domestic arrivals hall at the airport and it's open every day.

The Royal Automobile Club of WA (tel 325 0551) lives at 228 Adelaide Terrace. Their bookshop has an excellent travel section. Other good city bookshops are Angus & Robertsons at 196 Murray St and Down to Earth Books, downstairs at 874-876 Hay St. In Fremantle the Market St Book Arcade at 50 Market St is good.

The Youth Hostel Association has their office (not the hostel!) at 257 St Georges Terrace. The GPO is in Forrest Place. At the Perth Environmental Office on Hay St there's a noticeboard with info on cheap tickets, rides and accommodation.

Perth's daily newspapers are the *West Australian* and the *Daily News*. There are plenty of cinemas around the city but the Kimberley Cinema on Central Barrack St in the city is good for quality films, as is the New Oxford on the corner of Vincent and Oxford Sts. At 242 St Georges Terraces, right up at the King's Park end of town, Aboriginal Arts is a friendly place but its collection of Aboriginal arts and crafts for sale is not particularly good.

An interesting alternative to the usual hostel and hotel accommodation, although not necessarily in Perth, is offered by the Homestay of WA. They offer home and farm accommodation, will meet people at the Perth airport, guests can attend an Aussie barbecue (if they really want to) or have an evening meal with a family all for $18 per person for bed & breakfast. It may be more for long-term stays but you can contact them at Lot 40 Union Rd, Carmel 6076, or phone them on (09) 293 5347.

America's Cup The America's Cup races will be run out of Fremantle, the Perth port starting in late '86. Dates are:

1-15 October 1986
Defender & challenger eliminations begin
26 January 1987
Conclusion of eliminations
31 January 1987
America's Cup races begin

Orientation

The city centre is a fairly compact area situated at a sweep of the Swan River. Murray St and parallel Hay St are the main shopping streets, and the centre section of Hay St is a mall. On Thursday night the shops stay open late and the mall is at its busiest. Forrest Place, in front of the GPO, is also a small mall and a place for a quick rest in the centre of the city. The railway line forms a boundary to the central city area on the north side and immediately across the line in North Perth there's a restaurant enclave and a number of popular hostels and cheap accommodation centres. This section of town, over the bridge around William St where most of the activity is, is sometimes referred to as Northbridge.

The west end of the city slopes up hill to the pleasant Kings Park which overlooks the city and the Swan River. The Swan River serves as a spine from the city to Fremantle, the port of Perth, but it's suburbs all the way and also all the way out to Perth's superb Indian Ocean beaches.

Kings Park

The 400-hectare park overlooks the city and the river; there are superb views across Perth from the lookout tower. The park includes a 12-hectare botanical garden, a section of natural bushland and in the spring you can see a cultivated display of WA's famed wildflowers.

From the top of Kings Park the steep steps of Jacob's Ladder will take you down to Mounts Bay Rd by the river. In the park look for the huge karri trunk on display and the crosscut section of California redwood, showing just how old a tree can be and how short human history is in comparison.

Beside the park is the Legacy Lookout

1 Top Notch Hostel
2 Mamma Maria's
3 Entertainment Centre
4 Greyhound Bus Terminal
5 Plaka Shish Kebab
6 Sylvana Pastry
7 Northbridge Dining Bazaar
8 Francis St Youth Hostel
9 Brittania Hotel
10 Art Gallery
11 East Perth Railway Station
    (Country & Interstate)
12 Museum
13 Central Perth Railway Station
14 Barrack's Arch
15 Aboriginal Arts
16 Shafto Lane Tavern
17 'Down to Earth' Books
18 Citipak Food Centre
19 The Cloisters
20 Old Perth Boy's School
21 MPT Information
22 AMP Building
23 Travel Centre
24 Qantas
25 City Centre Market
26 GPO
27 Imperial Hotel
28 Miss Maud's
29 Angus & Robertson
30 Sunmarket Centre
31 Magic Apple
32 Grand Central
33 YMCA
34 Miss Maud's
35 Post & Telecom Museum
36 Town Hall
37 The Deanery
38 Court House
39 TAA
40 Airlines of WA
41 Government House
42 Ansett & Ansett Pioneer
43 Concert Hall
44 YHA Office
45 City Waters Lodge
46 RAC of WA
47 Downtowner Lodge
48 Jewell House, YMCA
49 Newcastle St Youth Hostel

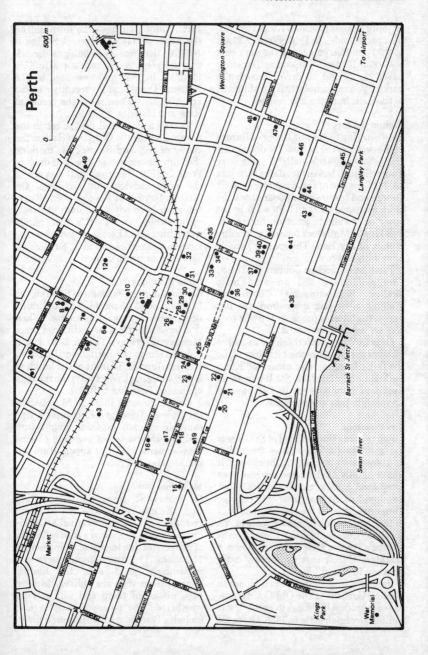

Perth

500 m

0

Market

Wellington Square

To Airport

Langley Park

Swan River

Kings Park

War Memorial

Barrack St Jetty

on top of Dumas House on Kings Park Rd. It's open Monday to Friday from 9.30 am to 4.30 pm. You can get to the park on a bus 106 or 107 from St Georges Terrace or buses 25, 27 and 28 drive through the park; or you can simply walk up Mount St to the park from the city centre.

Around the City

Between Hay St and St Georges Terrace in the centre is the narrow London Court; this photographer's delight looks very Tudor English but in fact dates from just 1937. At one end of this shopping court St George and his dragon appear above the clock each quarter of an hour while at the other ends knights joust on horseback. The Hay St Mall clock face is a miniature replica of Big Ben. The mall is usually alive with activity.

Perth has a modern Concert Hall on St Georges Terrace and an even more modern Entertainment Centre on Wellington St just down from the bus depot; the latter is probably the best rock concert venue in Australia.

Over in West Perth there are excellent views of the city from the 14th floor of the PWD Building at the corner of Kings Park Rd and Havelock St. It's open on weekdays from 9.30 am to 4.30 pm and Devonshire teas are available.

City Buildings

Down towards the park end of St Georges Terrace The Cloisters dates from 1858 and is noted for its beautiful brickwork. It was originally a school and has now been integrated into a modern office block development. At the corner of St Georges Terrace and Pier St the Deanery was built in 1850 and is one of the few houses in WA surviving from that period. Close by on St George's Terrace is Government House, a nostalgic Gothic-looking fantasy built between 1859 and 1864.

Behind the modern Council House in Stirling Gardens is the Old Courthouse, one of the oldest buildings in Perth. It was built in Georgian style in 1836. Other old

Perth buildings include the Town Hall on the corner of Hay and Barrack Sts (built 1867-70), the Treasury Building on Barrack St and St Georges Terrace opposite King St (built in 1854 and now used by the National Trust), and the recently restored His Majesty's Theatre on the corner of King and Hay Sts.

There's a memorial plaque set in the pavement near the Old Town Hall on the corner of Hay and Barrack Sts marking the announcement of the founding of Perth in 1829. The town hall was one of the early convict-built buildings. On Mounts Bay Rd at the foot of Mt Eliza, Governor Kennedy's Fountain utilises a spring which was Perth's first public water supply. There are tours of the modern Council House at 27 St Georges Terrace four times daily.

Other Buildings

You can tour the Parliament buildings at 11.15 am and 3.15 pm Monday to Friday when parliament is not in session. When it is in session there are still brief tours Monday to Friday. Take a 2, 3, 4 or 6 Subiaco bus to the Parliament House on Harvest Terrace. In front of the building is the old Barracks Archway, the remains of an 1860 Barracks building.

On the corner of Pier and Murray Sts, the Post & Telecom Museum is a fine example of early colonial architecture and its exhibits tell of communications developments in WA. It's open 10 am to 3 pm Monday to Friday.

Museums

On Francis St, across the railway lines from the city centre, the WA Museum includes a gallery of Aboriginal art, a 25-metre whale skeleton and a good collection of meteorites, the largest of which weighs 11 tonnes. The Australian outback is a particularly good area for finding meteorites as they are unlikely to have been disturbed there and will only be weathered. The museum complex also includes Perth's original prison, built in

1856 and used until 1888. Admission to the museum is free and it is open from 10.30 am to 5 pm from Monday to Thursday and from 1 to 5 pm on Friday, Saturday and Sunday.

The Small World Museum at 12 Parliament Place has the largest collection of miniatures in the country. The cars, kitchens, jigsaw puzzles and books are all one-twelfth scale. It's open on Monday to Thursday from 10 am to 5 pm and on weekends from 2 to 5 pm. To get there catch a Green Clipper bus.

The Collection Museum at 105 Swan St, Guildford displays antiques, furniture, musical instruments, cameras and tools from Georgian and Victorian England, Europe and Australia. It's open from 10 am to 4.30 pm daily except Monday and admission is $2.

Perth Zoo

Perth's popular zoo is across the river from the city at 20 Labouchere Rd, South Perth. It has an interesting collection including a nocturnal house which is open from 12 noon to 3 pm daily. The zoo itself is open from 10 am to 5 pm daily and admission is $3. You can reach the zoo by taking a bus 36 or 38 from St Georges Terrace or by taking the ferry across the river and then just strolling up the road from the Mends St jetty.

Art Galleries

On Jones St through to Roe St, behind the railway station, the Western Australian Art Gallery is housed in a modern building and has a very fine permanent exhibition covering European, Australian and Asian-Pacific art. Visiting exhibits are also shown here. The gallery is open from 10 am to 5 pm daily.

Other Parks

Between the city and the river the Alan Green Conservatory on the Esplanade houses a controlled-environment display which is open Monday to Saturday from 10 am to 5 pm and on Sunday from 2 to 6 pm. Also close to the city the Supreme Court Gardens are a popular place to eat your lunchtime sandwiches and in the summer there are often outdoor concerts in the Music Shell in the park.

Queens Gardens, at the eastern end of Hay St, is a pleasant little park with lakes; get there on a Red Clipper bus. Go up Williams St to Hyde Park in Highgate where the lake is a popular attraction for waterbirds. Lake Monger in Wembley is another hangout for local feathered friends, particularly Perth's famous black swans. Get there on a 90 or 91 bus from the Central Bus Station. The WA government is now planning a marine park in the waters off North Perth.

Beaches

Perth's claim to have the best beaches and surf of any Australian city really does have some justification. There are calm bay beaches on the Swan River at Crawley, Peppermint Grove and Como; or you can try a whole string of patrolled surf beaches on the Indian Ocean coast including Perth's very popular nude beach at Swanbourne. Some of the other surf beaches are Cottesloe, Port, City, Scarborough and Trigg Island and most of them can be reached by public transport. There's also Rottnest Island, just off the coast from Fremantle.

Old Mill

Just across the Narrows Bridge stands one of Perth's landmarks: the finely restored flour mill which was originally built in 1835. It's open Sunday, Monday, Wednesday and Thursday from 1 to 5 pm and on Saturday from 1 to 4 pm. On display inside the mill are relics from the pioneering era. You can get to the mill on a 34 bus from St Georges Terrace or you can walk there along the riverside from the Mends St jetty.

Perth Suburbs

There is a wide variety of old buildings, wildlife parks, pleasant picnic spots, tourist attractions and other places to visit around the city area. In particular Armadale to the south-east of the city, along the Swan River to the north-east and the places in the Darling Range (see Around Perth) are popular spots.

Armadale Pioneer Village is Armadale's major attraction. It's a working village of a century ago with shops, public buildings, gold-field operations and craftsmen working at now out-dated skills. It's open 10 am to 5 pm Monday to Friday, 1 to 9.30 pm on Saturday and 10 am to 6 pm on Sunday. You can get to Armadale by a 219 bus or a local train.

Just beyond Armadale is Elizabethan Village where, having left colonial WA behind, you move back to Shakespeare's England. It's open 10 am to 6 pm daily. At Kelsmcott, just before Armadale, the Museum of WA has its Historical Shanty Town which is open 10 am to 5 pm on weekends and is full of relics from the colonial era. Transport details are the same as for Armadale.

The Cohunu Wildlife Park has a miniature railway running through it for viewing the animals. It's open 10 am to 5 pm Wednesday to Sunday, daily during the school holidays. Boulder Rock is a pleasant picnic spot off the Brookton Highway near Armadale. Armadale is 27 km south-east of the city centre.

Up the Swan River There are a number of attractions in places up the Swan River from the centre of Perth, particularly in Guildford. Marylands Peninsula is enclosed by a loop of the Swan River and here you will find the beautifully restored old Tranby House of 1839. It's open daily, except Thursday, from 2 to 5 pm, and on Sunday from 11 am to 1 pm and 2 to 5 pm.

The Rail Transport Museum on Railway Parade, Bassendean has all sorts of railway memorabilia. It's open from 1 to 5 pm on Sundays and public holidays. The Hall Collection at 105 Swan St, Guildford is an enormous collection of Australiana and other items, housed in a building behind the 1840 Rose & Crown Hotel. It's open from 10 am to 4.30 pm daily except Monday; get there on a 306 bus.

Nearby on Meadow St, Mechanics Hall is now a small folk museum, open 2 to 4.30 pm from March to mid-December. Woodbridge is a restored and furnished colonial mansion overlooking the river. It's open Monday to Saturday from 1 to 4 pm and on Sunday from 11 am to 1 pm and 2 to 5 pm but closed all day on Wednesday. This is one of the few pioneer homes in Perth which you can visit; get there on a 306 bus. In West Swan the Caversham Wildlife Park has a collection of Australian animals and birds. It's open from 10 am to 5.30 pm daily except Friday.

The Swan Valley vineyards are dotted along the river from around Guildford right up to Upper Swan. Many of them are open for tastings except on Sundays. The river cuts a narrow gorge through the Darling Range at Walyunga National Park in Upper Swan, off the Great Northern Highway. There are walking tracks along the river and it's a popular picnic spot.

Other Suburbs In Subiaco there's a Museum of Childhood at 160 Hamersley Rd. Across the Canning River towards Jandakot Airport is the excellent Aviation Museum on Benningfield Rd, Bullcreek. It's open from 11 am to 4 pm on Tuesdays, Thursdays and weekends, admission is $2.

Just off the Canning Highway on the way to Fremantle is Wireless Hill Park & Telecommunications Museum in Melville. It has a variety of exhibits ranging from early pedal-operated radio equipment used in the outback to modern NASA communications equipment. It's open weekends from 2 to 5 pm.

The Claremont Museum is in the Freshwater Bay School, 66 Victoria Avenue, Claremont, and is open

Top: The Pinnacles Desert is a strange region north of Perth (WADT)
Left: An old minehead stands outlined against the sunset in Kalgoorlie (WADT)
Right: At the edge of the Nullarbor Plain the cliff face falls sheer into the surging waters of the Great
    Australian Bight (WADT)

Top: Wolf Creek Meteorite Crater in the north of WA is one of the largest in the world (WADT)
Left: Wave Rock, a unique natural rock formation near Hyden, WA (WADT)
Right: A few old pearling luggers can still be seen at Broome in the far north-west of WA
(TW)

Wednesday, Saturday and Sunday from 2 to 5 pm.

On the road to Armadale in Cannington is Woodloes, a restored colonial home of 1874. It's open Sundays from 2 to 4.30 pm. The small Liddelow Homestead in Kenwick is another restored homestead. It's open Thursday from 10 am to 2 pm and Sunday from 11 am to 3 pm. Yet another early home is the mud-brick and shingle Stirk's Cottage in Kalamunda. Built in 1881 it's open from March through to November on Sundays from 2 to 4.30 pm.

Out in Bibra Lake, south of the centre and accessible by MTT bus 600, is Adventureland – a large amusement park with rides, a zoo, the country's largest swimming pool and various other diversions. It's open daily in summer, and weekends-only in winter.

Places to Stay

Perth is really very well equipped for places to stay in almost any category you care to name. It's got no less than four youth hostels of various types (two official, two unofficial) plus guest-houses and lodges, some old-fashioned central city hostels, some reasonably central motel-type accommodation; in fact quite a variety and much of it conveniently central. If you have trouble finding a place try ringing the Westralian Accommodation Centre (tel 277 9199) who claim to find you just what you're after and at no cost to you. They also have a desk at the airport.

Hostels Perth is particularly well endowed in the hostel line and they're all reasonably central, particularly the two youth hostels. The main *YHA Hostel* (tel 325 5844) at 60-62 Newcastle St was at one time the busiest youth hostel in Australia. It still gets quite a throughput although other hostels have overtaken it. It's also a really international place since Perth is such an important arrival point for people coming from Europe and Asia.

The hostel is about a 15-minute walk (one km) from the city centre; just go straight up Barrack or William St, cross the railway line until you hit Newcastle St then turn right. The hostel has all the usual hostel facilities and is a great meeting place and info centre. Cost is $5.50. The office hours are 8 to 10 am and 5 to 10.30 pm.

The second *YHA Hostel* (tel 328 7794) at 46 Francis St serves to some extent as an overflow place but you can also go directly there if you wish. It's in an old house on the corner of William St and is a little closer to the city. It has small dorms with a capacity of 57 and has the same office hours and cost as the Newcastle St hostel.

A good alternative is the unofficial *Top Notch Hostel* (tel 328 6667) at 194 Aberdeen St, a 20-minute walk from the mall. Follow the same directions as for the Newcastle St youth hostel but turn left when you get to Aberdeen St. There's room for 50 people in five-bed dorms for $5 each or twin shares for $6 each. Weekly rates are six times the daily rates. The place has been recently repainted and there are all the usual facilities and a good kitchen.

Finally there's the long-running *Travel Mates* (tel 328 6685) at 496 Newcastle St; turn left at Newcastle St and it's then quite a distance. A 15 bus from Barrack St will help you if you don't want to walk from the centre. Dorm beds are $5 or by the week it's $33 and if you need linen there's a $3 charge. There's room for 30 and they can arrange rooms for couples. They've also got a late arrivals room where you can let yourself in, stretch your sleeping bag out and not disturb anybody should you arrive at some ungodly hour. There's a kitchen and laundry and the hostel is open all the time. The managers more or less let the place run itself. Motor vehicles are not popular at Travel Mates; it's intended for backpackers although motorcycles and bikes are OK.

YMCAs & Guest Houses Perth has two very central YMCAs, each taking both men and women. There are also a couple of modern 'lodges' a few km from the centre. The main *YMCA* building (tel 325 2744) is right in the centre at 119 Murray St. Much of the town thinks it's a real pit and though it's a bit grotty it's really not that bad. Residents include locals, pensioners and semi-permanents but a fair number of travellers pass through as well. Dorm beds are $6 per night or $30 per week. Rooms at the front are in better shape than the others and go for $9 or $50 per week for a single. Twin rooms are $8 per person in the front or $7 at the back; triples are cheaper still. Office hours are 8 am to midnight and the facilities are minimal.

The other *YMCA*, known as Jewel House (tel 325 6973), is only a couple of blocks further along Murray St at 180 Goderich St (as Murray St becomes after Victoria Square). This is an ex-nurses quarters building and offers 200 comfortable, clean, modern rooms. Singles are $16, doubles $20 and family rooms $40. Morning and evening meals are available and there are sandwiches at lunchtime. There are the usual lounges and a laundry. The office is open 24 hours and there's free baggage storage.

Centrally located and good value is the *Downtowner Lodge* (tel 325 6973) at 63 Hill St in a converted house opposite the Perth Mint. The 12 rooms are clean and pleasant and there are kitchen and laundry facilities you can use. It's a very quiet place with a TV room and car park. The rates are $10 for the first night, $9 for the second down to $7 for more than four nights, or $35 a week; doubles go for $70 to $80 per week.

The *Girls Friendly Society Lodge* (tel 325 4143) at 240 Adelaide Terrace takes women only at $16 per night and full board is available.

Hotels There are quite a number of old-fashioned hotels around the centre of Perth. Right across from the railway station there is a couple including the *Imperial Hotel* (tel 325 8877) at 413 Wellington St; a hotel of the 'old fashioned but majestic' school. The singles tend to be a bit minute but they've got wash-basins and you can make tea or coffee down at the end of the corridor. Nightly costs are $17/28 for singles/doubles. Breakfast in the Imperial's rather imperial-looking dining room will set you back from $3 for an equally old-fashioned (ie substantial) breakfast.

The *Grand Central* (tel 325 5638) at 379 Wellington St is rather more basic (no sinks in the room) but again quite OK. Rooms are $10/17 for singles/doubles and it's succinctly described by the manager as 'basic accommodation, mate'.

In the Mall is the *Savoy Hotel* (tel 325 9588) at 636 Hay St. It too is an older place that's had a face-lift or two and has a wide range of rooms. Singles are $20 to $27 depending on facilities, doubles $34 to $42 and all rates include a cooked breakfast.

Other cheaper hotels include the *George* (tel 321 9747) at the corner of George and Murray Sts and the *Bohemia* at 290 Murray St. Across the railway lines at 253 William St is the *Brittania* (tel 328 6121) with basic rooms for $10 per person. The better rooms are at the back on the verandah, the others are lit by skylight.

Motels & Units *City Waters Lodge* (tel 325 5020) at 118 Terrace Rd down by the river is conveniently central and good value. All the rooms have cooking facilities as well as the usual motel goodies – attached bathroom, colour TV and so on. There's also a laundrette in the block. Daily costs are $27/32 for singles/doubles and larger triples and family rooms are also available. Because they're so reasonably priced and so central they tend to be heavily booked so it's worth booking ahead with a one-night deposit.

The *Beatty Park Motel* (tel 328 1288) at 235 Vincent St, West Perth has singles/

doubles for $16/24 and family rooms with four beds for $38. The rooms have tea-making facilities and breakfast is available. To get there take a 250 or 260 bus from the city which goes by the rear of the motel on Carr St. A little further out is the *Ladybird Lodge* (tel 444 7359) at 193 Oxford St, Leederville. The prices and facilities are much the same as the Ladybird.

In East Perth the *Terminal Motor Lodge* (tel 325 3788) at 150 Bennett St has rooms at $18/27.

There is a couple of semi-reasonably priced places on Mounts Bay Rd at the bottom of Kings Park. The *Adelphi Centre* (tel 321 7966) at 130A Mounts Bay Rd costs $22 single, $27 double downstairs, $29/34 upstairs; extra beds cost $5. Like the City Waters Lodge the rooms are very well equipped and even have kitchen facilities although they are a step up in price. Here again it's wise to book ahead. Next door is the *Astoria* (tel 321 5231) which is marginally cheaper.

Across the bridge on the South Perth side, the *Canning Bridge Auto Lodge* (tel 364 2511) at 891 Canning Highway, Applecross costs $25 to $30 for doubles. The *Narrows Motel* (tel 367 7955) at 2 Preston St, Como costs $23/28 for singles/doubles.

Other reasonably central motels are: the *Lincoln Auto Lodge* (tel 328 3411) at 381 Beaufort St, Highgate; and the *Pacific Motel* (tel 328 5599) at 111 Harold St, also in Highgate and just a short walk from the Westrail East Perth terminal. The Pacific Motel has a pool and other mod-cons and costs $20/28 for singles/doubles.

In Scarborough the *Elsinore Holiday Flats* (tel 341 1824) at 49 Pearl Parade have one and two-bedroomed self-contained flats from $120 weekly. The tourist office has a list of other holiday flats in and around Perth.

Colleges There's college accommodation to try for during the vacations at the University of WA and at Murdoch University. University of WA colleges are St Columba's (tel 386 7177), Kingswood College (tel 386 8688), Currie Hall (tel 380 2772), St Thomas More College (tel 386 5080), St George's College (tel 386 1425), and St Catherine's (tel 386 5847) takes women. At Murdoch University (tel 332 2472) there are flats at Yarallda Court. One week is the minimum-stay period.

Camping Perth is not well endowed with campsites at a convenient distance from the centre although there are many about 20 km out. The list below covers the sites within a 20-km radius of the city centre. Central Caravan Park, Kenlorn Caravan Park and Como Beach Caravan Park are the most central; all within 10 km of the centre but the Como Beach site does not permit camping.

Forrestfield Caravan Park (tel 453 6378), 18 km east, Hawtin Rd, Forrestfield, camping $6 for two, on-site vans $16.

Perth Tourist Caravan Park (tel 453 6677), 15 km east, 319 Hale Rd, Forrestfield, camping $8 for two, on-site vans $13 for two.

Orange Grove Caravan Park (tel 453 6226), 19 km south-east Kelvin Rd, Orange Grove, camping $7 for two, on-site vans $18.

Guildford Caravan Park (tel 277 2828), 19 km north-east, 372 Swan Rd, Guildford, camping $5 for two, on-site vans $16.

Central Caravan Park (tel 277 5696), 7 km east, 34 Central Avenue, Redcliffe, camping $6 for two, on-site vans $70 per week.

Kenlorn Caravan Park (tel 458 2604), 9 km south-east, 229 Welshpool Rd, Queens Park, camping $8.50 for two, on-site vans $60 per week.

Como Beach Caravan Park (tel 367 1286), 6 km south, 4 Ednah St, Como, camping not permitted, on-site vans $70 to $130 per week.

Careniup Caravan Park (tel 447 6665), 14

Starhaven Caravan Park (tel 341 1770), 14 km north-west, 14-18 Pearl Parade, Scarborough, camping $7 for two, on-site vans $16.

Kingsway Caravan Park (tel 409 9267), 15 km north, Wanneroo Rd, Greenwood, camping $6 for two, on-site vans $18.

Caversham Caravan Park (tel 279 6700), 12 km north-east, Benara Rd, Caversham, camping $6 for two, on-site vans $45 per week.

Carine Gardens Caravan Park (tel 454 6829). Maida Vale Rd, Maida Vale, camping $6 for two, no on-site vans.

Springvale Caravan Park (tel 454 6829). Maida Vale Rd, Maida Vale, camping $6 for two, on-site vans $16.

Places to Eat

As with accommodation, Perth has a wide variety of places to eat. Look for the excellent food centres where you can find all sorts of different international cuisines all at very reasonable prices. Or head across the railway tracks from the centre to William St, the restaurant centre of Perth.

City There's a pretty good selection of places in the city centre, especially for lunches and light meals. *Bernadis* at 528 Hay St is a cut above the average lunch-coffee lounge. It has good sandwiches, quiches, salads, fruit salads and other hot items. It's a good place and is usually very busy. Further along Hay St at 570 is the very cheap but still good *Cini Coffee Lounge* with meat or steak & kidney pies for $1 or fish & chips, macaroni cheese and sandwiches all for under $3.

The *Granary* is downstairs on the west side of Barrack St south of Hay St. It offers a wide range of vegetarian dishes averaging about $3.60. It's a place popular with city office workers. At 138 Lower Barrack St is the very popular *Magic Apple*. It's a health-food place with all sorts of salads and smoothies but there have been some complaints about the scientologist leanings of the manager. Across the street at 129 the Hare Krishnas are setting up a restaurant. Back on Hay St, another cheap health-food place is *Tastes Galore*.

At the corner of Hay and Pier Sts, the *Singapore Restaurant* is the real thing – just like a corner in Singapore or Kuala Lumpur. It has cheap basic Chinese meals and soups. Down toward the other end of Hay St, near Kings Park, there's a whole string of places although many are a bit on the pricey side. *Fast Eddy's* on the corner of Milligan St is a big place where you sit up on stools and order one of the many types of burgers. There's other stuff too, like lasagna for $5 or less.

All over town you'll see small cafés which are good for an afternoon snack or light breakfast. They usually have things like desserts, toasted sandwiches and hot chocolate and a typical example is *Cherie Coffee Lounge* in the mall. For sandwiches there's the omnipresent *Miss Maud's* with shops at 113 Murray St by the YMCA and further along at 198 by the Angus & Robertson bookshop.

For a flashier lunchtime place with a Dutch flavour there's *Broodjeswinkel* beside the AMP building at the corner of William St and St Georges Terrace. Also by the YMCA at 117 Murray St is a pleasant and very reasonably-priced little Japanese restaurant called *Jun & Tommy's* where main courses are about $5 to $7.50. At 905 Hay St is *Pancho's*, one of many places in town offering Mexican food. Main courses are $5 to $8.

Near the Oxford Cinema, *Uncle Vinces* has great mussels in chilli sauce – a huge bowl between four will come to about $6 each, including a carafe of house red and spaghetti cabanara. They'll even give you a doggy bag to take the extra sauce home in. The *Pancake House* in Barrack St does a lunch special of spaghetti or fish with chips or salad, dessert and coffee for $2.50.

Lastly, *Cariban's* at 623 Wellington St has something for everyone – steaks, seafood, Italian and vegetarian dishes in the $5 to $7 range.

Counter Meals Perth has the usual selection of counter meals in the city centre area. At 196 Murray St counter meals in the basement *Albert Tavern* are around $5 – 'see through' barmaids too, something Perth seems to have an amazing enthusiasm for. There's also cheap counter meals (steak, salads & chips for $4) at the *Bohemia* at 290 Murray St. They run from 5.30 to 7 pm in the evenings. The *Railway Hotel* at 134 Barrack St has cheap meals from around $1.50 for a burger to more expensive meals around the $6.50 mark.

Sassella's Tavern, in the City Arcade off Hay St, does reasonably-priced bistro meals for about $5 and has entertainment too.

William St Area North of the city over the railway tracks, the area bounded by William St on the east and Lake St on the west is full of ethnic restaurants. Aberdeen St, Francis St and James St in particular have a plethora of eating places which include Chinese, Greek, Lebanese, Mexican, Indian, Italian, seafood places, Vietnamese, Dutch-Indonesian and even hamburger joints. They come in all price ranges too; from the very bottom to the very top; cheap cappuccino bars to posh seafood restaurants. There's quite a bit of nightlife in the area as well as adult movie and book parlours and strip bars.

Along William St itself, some places to try include *Kim Anh* at 178, a Vietnamese BYO place where two could have a good dinner for $20 to $25. Across the street at 175 *Café La Quan* is also Vietnamese but is cheaper. Nearby at 188 *Romanys* is one of the city's really long-running Italian places. It's moderately priced and popular.

Over on the other side again is *Sylvana Pastry* at 197 which is one of several

Lebanese coffee bars scattered about the city. They're comfortable and have an amazing selection of those sticky Middle Eastern pastries which usually look, and taste, delicious. There's a choice of Turkish delight, baklava, harisa, ladies fingers and palms, manoul dates, bookaj, bogasha, barazi, mamoul walnut, boorma cashews, kool shkodr, canary's nests and a few more unknowns! For a different type of snack, *Paradise Garage* at 234 William St has more than a rainbow of gelati flavours.

Further away from the town centre there's Mexican at *Los Gallos* at 276 William St. Most dishes are $7 to $8 with chile con carne $4.50 and all the other Mexican standards and some vegetarian dishes. *Agostino* is another Italian spot and the very good home-made dishes are all under $5. It's open from 11 am to 11 pm except Sunday when it's 11 am to 3 pm and it's closed on Tuesdays. They have eat-in or take-away.

Lorri's Place, at the corner of William and Newcastle Sts, has pizzas and burgers. Still further along there are more expensive places like *Domenic's* at 287 for Italian and the *Bohemia* at 311 for European although the latter has a $15 all-you-can-eat deal.

Off William St, *Mamma Maria's* at 105 Aberdeen St on the corner of Lake St has a pleasant ambience and reputation to match as one of Perth's best Italian eateries. Most main courses are up to $9 or more.

At 60 Lake St is *Young Joe's* with a restaurant on one side and a pizza bar on the other. It looks very plain but the prices are low and it has a BYO licence. *Adriano's* on the corner of Lake and James Sts is a small café open till at least 1 am on weeknights and 4 am on Saturday.

Over on James St, *Plaka Shish Kebab* is a large place with a huge green sign outside and posters of Greece on the inside with souvlaki, doner kebabs and the usual for $3 to $4.

Food Centres Easily some of the best meals I've had in Australia were in the Perth food centres – I'd actually look forward to getting hungry! Essentially the food centres are a group of kitchens where eaters share communal dining tables and chairs. Thus you can eat from one place, your partner can eat from another, have drinks from a third and dessert from a fourth. This terrific Singaporean idea has really taken hold in Perth and nightly crowds prove that it's a popular alternative to junk food.

A must is the *City Centre Market* in the Hay St Mall, downstairs near William St. Here there are stalls offering Chinese, Mexican, Indonesian, Indian and many other types of food. Excellent fresh food at the Singapore booth where a tasty meal of satay, bean sauce beef and rice costs $3. Try the pastry and coffee stall. The centre is open for lunch and dinner and is busy in the evenings when there's live entertainment.

There are several other centres in the city area but none match the City Centre. The *Citipak Food Market* at 895 Hay St is one of the oldest food fairs in town but surprisingly, it isn't very large. Beside the City Arcade between Hay and Murray Sts in the Carillon Centre there's another but it's a bit sterile. The *Sunmarket Centre* is also an older one and remains a little hard to find. It's down a lane off Murray St near the north-west corner of Barrack St. Here there are Chinese and Indian stalls as well as one or two Burmese ones. Meals are in the $3 to $4 range. Nearby, off Murray St, is the *Orient Food Feast* which also has several nationalities represented.

Bigger and busier is *Freddie's Food Factory*, north of the railway lines in the William St restaurant area. It's at 46 Lake St and is open from 5 to 11 pm most days except Friday and Saturdays when it doesn't close until 3 am. It's not open at all on Monday. There's a good variety of stalls here including one selling ice-creams for $3 to $6.

An older one in the same area is the *Northbridge Dining Bazaar* at 217 William St which also has a good selection to choose from but is a bit dead.

Entertainment

Perth has a busy selection of pubs, discos and night clubs to choose from in the evenings. In the centre *Sassella's Tavern*, upstairs in the City Arcade off the Hay St Mall, has music and no cover charge. There's a disco downstairs in the *Brass Rail Tavern* in the National Mutual Arcade, also off Hay St Mall. Further down at 395 Murray St, on the corner of Shafto Lane, the *Shafto Lane Tavern* is usually crowded and noisy later on with bands or a disco; also no cover charge.

Next door is *Pinocchio's* and across the road at 418 Murray St is *Beethoven's* – both with cover charges in the $5 to $10 bracket depending on who is on and what night it is. In the centre the *Melbourne Hotel* on the corner of Milligan and Hay Sts has a whole collection of bars – everything from a jungle bar to a piano bar. There's dancing and new music at *Jules* at 103 Murray St.

Popular clubs for interesting live music are the *Stoned Crow*, and the *Red Parrot* in Northbridge on the corner of Roe and Mulligan Sts. Also in this area is the dressier *Hannibal's* at 69 Lake St. There are several other nightspots in this part of town or there's the *Musos Club* at 418 Murray St where you can get in free and enjoy half-price drinks until 10 pm.

The *Silver Slipper* at the corner of James and Stirling Sts has rock music from 11 pm until late on weekends. For folk music you could try *Jenny's Place* in the back room at 24 Hedley St, Bentley on Sundays from 8 to 11.30 pm. Several pubs in and around town feature jazz on Saturday afternoons – check the listings in the daily papers.

At the corner of Murray and Milligan Sts, the *Skate Disco* has roller skating which can be good fun although a little hard on the knees.

Away from the centre there's the usual rock pub circuit with varying cover charges depending on the night of the week and who is playing. Popular venues include the *Leederville Stockade*, Vincent St, Leederville; the *Subiaco Hotel*, Hay & Rokeby Sts, Subiaco; *Hotel Cottesloe (The Cott)*, John St, Cottesloe; the *Boomerang Hotel*, 1120 Albany Highway, Bentley; the *Broadway Tavern*, Broadway Shopping Centre, Nedlands near the university.

Other places to try include the *Nedlands Park Hotel*, better known as *Steve's*, which is the uni pub, near the university. Out at Fremantle the *Newcastle Club Hotel* is popular.

On Fridays the *Daily News* has a fairly comprehensive Nightlife Guide.

Getting There

Air From the east coast there are TAA and Ansett flights from Sydney, Melbourne, Brisbane and Adelaide. Some Sydney and Melbourne flights go direct, some via Adelaide or in the case of Sydney, via Melbourne. Brisbane flights all go via one or more of the other centres. Fares (standby in brackets) to Perth are Adelaide $294 ($236), Melbourne $341 ($273), Sydney $383 ($307), Brisbane $406 ($325).

The two airlines have two flights a week between North Queensland and Perth via Alice Springs and vice versa. Fares are $282 from Alice Springs, $442 from Mt Isa, $394 from Townsville. Darwin-Perth flights go via Alice Springs or Port Hedland – TAA have just a handful of flights a week, Ansett WA flies Darwin-Perth along the coast routes daily. Darwin-Perth is $355. See the introductory Getting Around section for details of Ansett WA fares.

Bus Ansett Pioneer, Greyhound and Deluxe have daily bus services from Adelaide to Perth. Fares are $85 with Greyhound and Deluxe, $99 with Ansett Pioneer and the trip takes about 37 hours.

There are also a few other operators doing the trans-Nullarbor run which used to be cheaper but the added competition forced the big companies to drop their prices, so apart from Ansett Pioneer which offers more stopover options, the fares are virtually identical. Typical of the prices are Melbourne $110, Sydney $130 and Brisbane $160.

Ansett Pioneer (tel 325 8855) operate from the Ansett Terminal at 26 St Georges Terrace. Greyhound (tel 478 1122) operate from the Central Bus Station on Wellington St and Deluxe (tel 322 7877) are at the corner of Hay and William Sts. All three operate buses up the coast to Port Hedland, Broome and through the Kimberley to Darwin. See the relevant sections for details. Perth-Darwin is a 60-hour journey costing $190. Greyhound also operate to Port Hedland via the more direct inland route through Newman.

Westrail operate bus services to a number of Western Australian centres including Bunbury-Collie ($12), Hyden (Wave Rock) ($16, twice weekly), Esperance ($38, twice weekly), Geraldton ($30, almost daily) and Mullewa ($30, twice weekly).

Rail Along with the ghan to Alice Springs, the long Indian-Pacific run is one of Australia's great railway journeys; a 65-hour trip between the Pacific Ocean on one side of the continent and the Indian Ocean on the other. It's a trip to talk about but it's certainly not the cheapest way across Australia – in fact it's even cheaper to fly. Despite the fares the service still loses money but people who can find the cash certainly don't regret it. You see Australia at ground level and at the end of the journey you really appreciate the immensity of this country.

From its starting point in Sydney you cross New South Wales in the late afternoon and overnight, arriving in Broken Hill around breakfast time. Then it's on to Port Pirie in South Australia and across the Nullarbor. From Port Pirie to Kalgoorlie the endless crossing of the virtually uninhabited centre takes nearly 30 hours including the 'long straight' on the Nullarbor – at 478 km long this is the longest straight stretch of railway line in the world. Unlike the trans-Nullarbor road, which runs south of the Nullarbor along the coast of the Great Australian Bight, the railway line actually crosses the Nullarbor Plain. From Kalgoorlie it's a straightforward run into Perth.

To or from Perth fares are: Adelaide $384 1st, $291 economy or $105 in an economy seat with no meals; Melbourne $479 1st, $335 economy; Sydney $580 1st, $442 economy. 'Caper' fares offer good reductions if you book at least seven days in advance. Melbourne and Adelaide passengers connect with the Indian-Pacific at Port Pirie. Cars can be transported between Port Pirie and Perth for $210.

The full distance from Sydney to Perth is 3961 km. You can break your journey at any stop along the way and continue on later as long as you complete the one-way trip within two months; return tickets are valid for up to six months. Westbound departures are made on Sunday, Thursday and Saturday (arriving in Perth on Wednesday, Sunday and Tuesday). Heading east the train departs on Sunday, Monday and Thursday (arriving in Sydney on Wednesday, Thursday and Sunday).

In either 1st class or economy your fare includes a sleeping compartment; the main difference is that 1st class compartments are available as singles or twins, economy as twins only. First class twins have showers and toilets, 1st class singles have toilets only – with showers at the end of the carriage. In the economy seating compartments the showers and toilets are at the end of the carriage. Meals are included in the fare for 1st class and economy berth passengers (not for economy seat passengers) and 1st class passengers

also have use of a lounge compartment complete with piano!

Between Adelaide and Perth you can also travel on the three times weekly Trans-Australian. This service starts at Port Pirie so you have to take the connecting train to get to or from Adelaide. Fares are as for the Indian-Pacific; the Adelaide-Perth trip takes 42 hours.

The only rail services within WA are the Prospector to Kalgoorlie and the Australind to Bunbury – see the relevant sections for details. The trains from the east coast and the WA services all run to or from the terminal in East Perth as do the Westrail Buses. Ring 326 2811 for Westrail bookings or you can book through the WA Government Travel Centre in Hay St.

Hitching & Rides The hostel noticeboards are worth checking for lifts and share trips to points around the country. Also check the alternative lifestylers noticeboard at the Perth Environment Centre in Hay St.

If you're hitching out of Perth to the north or east take a train to Midland. For travel south take a train to Armadale. Some sexist noted in the youth hostel visitors book that you shouldn't try hitching across the Nullarbor 'unless you've got big tits and nice legs'. Trans-Nullarbor hitching is not that easy and the fierce competition between bus companies has made bus travel much more attractive.

Getting Around

Perth has a central public transport organisation, the Metropolitan Transport Trust, or MTT. There are MTT information offices at 125 St Georges Terrace and at the Perth Central Bus Station in Wellington St, both open 7 am to 6 pm Monday to Friday and 7.30 am to 3 pm on weekends. The MTT operate buses, trains and ferries. They can give you information and advice about getting around Perth and supply route maps and timetables. Phone 325 8511 for information.

Bus Around the central city there are four free City Clipper services which operate Monday to Friday. The Yellow Clipper and a shortened Red Clipper route also operate on Saturday mornings.

Red Clipper buses make a loop up and down St Georges Terrace-Adelaide Terrace and Wellington St.

Yellow Clipper buses operates around the very central area of the city.

Blue Clipper buses run between North-bridge and the Esplanade along Barrack and William Sts then down Beaufort St. It goes past the Central Bus Station, the WA Museum and very close to the youth hostel.

Green Clipper buses ply between the Central Bus Station and West Perth.

On regular buses a short ride of two sections costs 50c but anything longer is a zone ticket which allows you unlimited travel within the zone for two hours from the time of issue and can be used on MTT buses, trains and ferries. Costs are: one zone 80c, two zones $1, three zones $1.20 or you can get an all-day three zone ticket for $4.20. Zone two extends out as far as Fremantle, 20 km from the centre, so you have quite an area of action. You could, for example, use your two-hour ticket to go down to the jetty in Perth, take the ferry from the city to the zoo, then an hour or so later take the bus back, all for $1. The ticket also covers all suburban train services. See the Tours section for the MTT Sunday bus tours. A Multirider ticket gives you 10 journeys for the price of nine.

Some useful bus services include 106 or the longer 105 to Fremantle. The 103 also goes to Fremantle after first heading around Kings Park. Routes 3 and 6 operate to Subiaco and for the university take a 70 or 72.

The MTT *Guide to Perth* pamphlet lists bus routes to many local attractions like the beaches and the Darling Ranges. Pick one up at the tourist office or MTT office.

Rail Suburban trains all go from the City Station on Wellington St. Your rail ticket can also be used on MTT buses and ferries within the ticket's validity.

Ferries Ferries all depart from the Barrack St Jetty in Perth. There are services across the river from there to Mends St in South Perth every half hour at a cost of 50c. Take this ferry to get to the zoo.

See Rottnest Island for details on the ferries from Perth and Fremantle to Rottnest.

The MTT also runs a couple of river cruises. Between September and May the *MV Countess II* goes up river daily except Saturday on a three-hour cruise towards the Upper Swan River. Departures are at 2 pm from the Barrack St jetty and the price is $7.

The old-fashioned double-decker *SS Perth* cruises down river towards Fremantle between January and April. Departures at 2 pm Sundays are also from the Barrack St jetty. The price is $4 for the three-hour trip and a running commentary is given. There are also special school holiday trips and other more expensive river cruises – see the Tours section.

Car Rentals The major rental organisations – Hertz, Budget, Avis and Thrifty – are all represented in Perth plus there's a string of local organisations. You could try Bateman Car Rental (tel 322 2592) at 789 Wellington St with cars from as low as $6 per day and 10c per km or $65 a week with 350 km included. Econo-Car (tel 328 6888) at 133 Pier St has Mokes at $16 per day with 100 km free. Bigger cars and even eight-seater vans are available at higher but still reasonable rates. Rent-A-Cheapie (tel 325 9411) is another bargain dealer at 59 Jewell St, East Perth. Thrifty, with two locations including the airport, has small cars starting at $29. All the above companies charge insurance on top of the daily rates.

Bicycle Hire The youth hostel rents bicycles for $5 per day and there's a bicycle route around the river area.

Airport Transport Perth's airport is busy night and day, unlike so many Australian airports which shut down at night. It has to operate at night since Perth's isolation from the east coast plus its function as an international arrival point means planes arrive and depart at all hours.

A taxi to the airport is around $8 with a 60c surcharge at night. Alternatively the Skybus costs $3.50 and runs frequently from Monday to Friday between 8.30 am and 1.30 pm and then from 6.30 to 10.30 pm. On weekends and holidays it runs from 9.30 am to 12.30 pm and from 7.30 to 10.30 pm. For details of this confusing system and to arrange pick-ups call 328 9777. They'll usually pick up from the hostels.

Alternatively you can get into the city for just 80c on a 338 MTT bus to William St. They depart from the northern end of the terminal every 30 minutes from 5.30 am to 10.57 pm on weekdays and for nearly as long on Saturdays. Sunday services are less frequent.

The airport terminal handles domestic and international flights so there are money changing facilities here. Budget, Avis, Thrifty and Hertz have rent-a-car desks at the airport and there's also a desk for the Westralian Accommodation Centre who claim to be able to book accommodation at any price level for you and at no cost.

Tours There is a tremendous range of Perth and area tours; see the WAGTB on Hay St for information. City tours are about $10 or for a similar price you could go up to Swan Valley. Tours to places like

Yanchep, El Caballo Blanco and other attractions in the Perth vicinity range from $14 to $30 with the average being about $22. There are half and full-day trips and some night trips which include drinks and dining or dancing.

Others go out to the Darling Ranges, Wave Rock ($43), Yanchep Park and Caves ($13.50) and other natural sites. Still others feature man-made attractions and one company even offers four-wheel-drive trips for women only for some reason.

There are a variety of tours up the Swan River. A nearly three-hour Swan River Cruise costs $7 with the MTT or $9.50 on the Captain Cook Cruise. There are others, one with lunch and wine included. For $27 a vineyard tour takes you to wineries up the river – 'good value' wrote some travelling wine enthusiasts.

Another favourite of imbibers is the free tour of the Swan Brewery. The tour takes two hours (followed by a half-price beer tasting) and they take place at 10 am and 2.30 pm daily. It's necessary to book ahead; phone 350 0650 to make reservations. The brewery is at 25 Baile Rd, Canning Vale.

Fremantle
Population: 21,000

Fremantle ('Freo' to enthusiastic name shorteners) is the port for Perth at the mouth of the Swan River, 19 km south-west of the city centre. Over the years Perth has sprawled to engulf Fremantle which is now more a suburb of the city than a town in its own right, but it does have a wholly different atmosphere than gleaming, skyscrapered Perth.

It's a place with a very real feeling of history and a very pleasant atmosphere. It's hardly surprising that so many visitors to Perth decide that Fremantle is one of their favourite places.

Like Perth, Fremantle was founded in

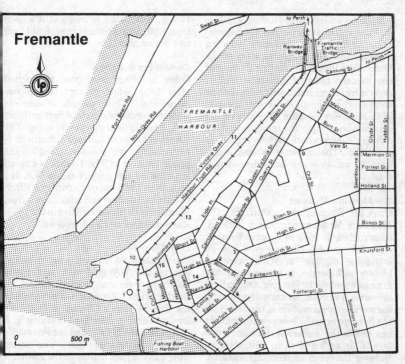

Fremantle

1 Round House
2 Town Hall
3 St John's Church
4 Maritime Museum
5 The Esplanade
6 Fremantle Market
7 Warder's Quarters
8 Gaol & Museum
9 WA Museum
10 Port Authority Building
11 Overseas Passenger Terminal
12 Post Office
13 Fremantle Station
14 Bannister Street Workshop
15 Old German Consulate

1829 but, also like Perth, the settlement made little progress until it was reluctantly decided to take in convicts. With this cheap and hard-worked labour, most of the town's earliest buildings, some of them amongst the oldest in WA, were constructed. As a harbour Fremantle was

an abysmal failure until the brilliant engineer C Y O'Connor (see the WA Goldfields section for more on his tragic story) built an artificial harbour in the 1890s. The town has numerous interesting old buildings and a couple of really excellent museums. The National Trust produces two walking-tour leaflets on Fremantle.

The 1987 America's Cup races will be run from Fremantle. The Australian defenders and several of the challengers, including the New York Yacht Club's boat, were already based in Fremantle and hard at work in 1985 preparing their 12-metre yachts.

Fremantle Museum & Arts Centre

Originally constructed by convict labourers as a lunatic asylum in the 1860s, the museum is on Finnerty St. It houses an intriguing collection including exhibits on Fremantle's early history, the colonisation of WA and the early whaling industry plus the intriguing story of the Dutch East Indiamen who first discovered the western coast of Australia and in several instances managed to wreck their ships on this inhospitable coast. It really is an excellent museum. The arts centre occupies one wing of the museum and it's a living centre where various crafts are practiced. The museum is open daily from 10 am to 5 pm and admission is free.

The Maritime Museum

On Cliff St near the waterfront, the Maritime Museum occupies a building constructed in 1852 as a commissariat. Recently opened, the museum has an intriguing display on WA's maritime history with particular emphasis on the famous wreck of the *Batavia*. One gallery is used as a working centre where you can see work on preservation of timbers from the *Batavia* actually being carried out. At one end of this gallery is the huge stone facade intended for an entrance to Batavia Castle in modern-day Jakarta, Indonesia. It was being carried by the *Batavia* as ballast when she went down. The museum is open from 1 to 5 pm from Friday to Sunday and admission is free. Like the Fremantle Museum, it's a 'not to be missed' attraction.

The Round House

On Arthur Head near the Maritime Museum, the Round House was built in 1831 and is the oldest public building in WA. It actually has 12 sides and was built as a local prison (in the days before convicts were brought into WA). Here the colony's first hangings took place and it was later used to hold Aboriginals before they were taken across to Rottnest. Since the building proved to be inconveniently sited smack between the jetty at Bather's Bay and High St, in 1837 a tunnel was cut through the hill underneath the Round

House. Admission is free and it's open from 1.30 to 4 pm on Saturdays and 11 am to 4 pm on Sundays.

Convict Era Buildings

Other buildings date from the period after 1850, when convict labour was introduced. They include Fremantle Gaol, the unlucky convicts' first building task. It's still used as a prison today. The entrance to the prison on Fairbairn St is particularly picturesque. Beside the prison gates at 16 The Terrace is a small museum on the convict era in WA. It's open from 1 to 4 pm on Saturdays, 10 am to 4 pm on Sundays and admission is free. Warders from the jail still live in the 1850s stone cottages on Henderson St.

Later Landmarks

Fremantle went through a boom period during the WA gold-rush and many buildings were constructed during, or shortly before, this period. They include the fine St John's Church of 1882, the former German consulate building at 5 Mouat St built in 1902, and the Fremantle Railway Station of 1907. The water trough in the park in front of the station is a memorial to two men who died of thirst on an outback expedition.

Around Town

Fremantle is well endowed with parks including the popular Esplanade Reserve beside the picturesque fishing boat harbour off Marine Terrace. St John's Reserve is beside the church of the same name. Fremantle has an excellent Art Gallery in Pioneer Reserve between Phillimore and Short Sts. It's open from Wednesday to Sunday from 12 noon to 5 pm.

The city is a popular centre for craft workers of all kinds and one of the best places to find them is at the imaginative Bannister St Workshops where a variety of craft workers can be seen in action and their work purchased. It's open 10 am to 4.30 pm weekdays, 10 am to 2 pm Saturdays and 1 to 5 pm Sundays.

There's a potters' workshop beside the Round House.

From the viewing platform on top of the Port Authority Building you can enjoy a panoramic view of Fremantle harbour. A statue of C Y O'Connor stands in front of the building. It's necessary to book ahead for a trip to the Port Authority Building as you need an escort and they're not always available if you just show up.

A prime attraction is the Fremantle Markets on South Terrace at the corner of Henderson St. Originally opened in 1892 the new market was re-opened in 1975 and attracts crowds looking for anything from craft work to vegetables, jewellery to antiques. There's a great tavern bar there and there are often buskers performing. It's open 9 am to 9 pm on Fridays and 9 am to 1 pm on Saturdays.

Places to Eat

There are plenty of places to drop in for a meal or a snack while exploring Fremantle, or you could sip a beer in one of the town's picturesque old pubs. There is a string of places to try along South Terrace – like the popular *Papa Luigis* for coffee and gelati at number 17. It's packed on Sunday afternoons. Next door is the *Mexican Cantina* and across the road is *Pizza Bella Roma*.

For something completely different you could try the barbecued haggis at the *Scottish Deli* in High St, or in the *Upmarkets Food Centre* opposite the market there's a stall where you can get cheap Brazilian and Argentinian food; eight dishes for $4, or 10 for $4.50 – excellent value.

Across from the Bannister St Workshops in the small shopping centre you could try a tasty panzerotto in *Vince's Panzerotto & Pizzas*. At 31 Market St, behind the GPO, the *Princess Coffee Lounge* is excellent value. Fish & chips on the Esplanade by the fishing boat harbour is something of a Fremantle tradition. There's good, cheap counter meals at the *Newcastle Club Tavern* on Market St.

Getting There

The passenger train service between Perth and Fremantle runs every half hour or so throughout the day. Buses 106 and 111 go from St Georges Terrace (north side) to Fremantle via the Canning Highway, or take the 105 which is a longer route but also goes south of the river. Buses 103 and 104 also depart from St Georges Terrace (south side) but go to Fremantle via the north side of the river.

Rottnest

Rotto, as it's known by the locals, is a sandy island about 19 km off the coast from Fremantle. It's 11 km long and five km wide and is very popular as a day's outing or longer-term escape for Perth residents, which is hardly surprising because it's quite a delightful place. The island was discovered by the Dutch explorer Vlaming in 1696. He named it 'Rats' Nest' because of the numerous king size rats he saw there. Actually they weren't rats at all but quokkas, miniature kangaroos which are even more prolific today.

What do you do on Rotto? Well, you bicycle around, laze in the sun on the many superb beaches (the Basin is the most popular, Parakeet Bay is the place for skinny-dipping), climb the low hills, go fishing or boating, ride a glass-bottom boat (Rotto has some of the southernmost coral in the world and also a number of shipwrecks can be seen), swim in the crystal clear water or you can even go quokka spotting (they're most active early in the morning).

The Rottnest settlement was originally established in 1838 as a prison for Aboriginals from the mainland – the early colonists had lots of trouble imposing their ideas of private ownership on the nomadic Aboriginals. The prison was abandoned in 1903 and the island soon

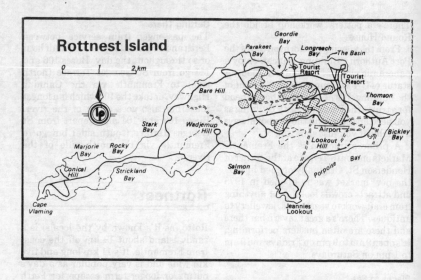

Rottnest Island

became a popular escape for Perth society. It's only in the last 20 years, however, that it has really developed as a day-trip city getaway. The original prison settlement is of great interest as the buildings here are the oldest in WA apart from a couple in Perth and Fremantle.

The '87 America's Cup races will be held in the waters close to Rottnest.

Information

The Rottnest Island Board has an information centre just to the left of the wharf as you arrive. Here and at the museum, you can get a number of useful publications about the island. Two of particular interest are the pamphlets on a walking tour of the old settlement buildings and a description of the various shipwrecks around the island. Rottnest is very popular in the summer when the ferries and the accommodation are both heavily booked – plan ahead.

Things to See & Do

There's an excellent little museum with exhibits about the island, its history, wildlife and shipwrecks. You can pick up

the walking-tour leaflet here and wander around the interesting old convict-built buildings including the octagonal 1864 'Quad' where the prison cells are now hotel rooms.

The island has a number of low-lying salt lakes and it's around them that you are most likely to spot quokkas although the bus tours have regular quokka feeding points where the small marsupials are programmed to appear on demand.

Some of Rottnest's shipwrecks are accessible to snorkellers but to get to most of them requires a boat. There are marker plaques around the island telling the sad tales of how and when the ships came to grief.

Places to Stay & Eat

Most visitors to Rotto day-trip but it's equally interesting to stay there and there is a wide variety of accommodation possibilities. You can camp for $5 for two in hire tents at *Tent-Land* (tel 292 5033) or there are safari cabins for $100 weekly. Book hired tents and cabin in advance but if you bring your own tent you can usually just turn up.

The *Hotel Rottnest* (tel 292 5011) is fairly expensive at $30 per person including breakfast. It was originally built in 1864 as the residence of the Governor of Western Australia. The *Rottnest Lodge Resort* (tel 292 5026) has units ranging from $30 to $90 per night for two people.

The island has a general store and a bakery which is famed for its fresh bread and pies. There's also a fast-food centre, the licenced *Rottnest Restaurant* for lunch and the *Hotel Rottnest*, affectionately known as the Quokka Arms.

Getting There

You can fly or take the ferry to Rotto. The *MV Temeraire II* plys between the Barrack St jetty and Thompson Bay on Rottnest once daily with a second service on Monday, Wednesday and Saturday. It also makes a stop at Fremantle. The fare is $20 return from Perth, $18 for a same-day return or $14 for students. Bicycles are an extra $3 return. If you board at Fremantle it's slightly cheaper. There's also the faster and more expensive *Seaflyte* motor launch.

You can also get across by air in just 11 minutes from Perth airport with Rottnest Airlines. The flight costs $19 return – where else can you make an overseas flight these days for under $10? It's even cheaper if there are two or more of you and there are slight reductions for students. The flights leave from the new Perth Flight Centre at the airport. There's a connecting bus between the Rottnest airport and the wharf area.

Getting Around

Bicycles are the time-honoured way of getting around Rottnest. The number of motor vehicles is strictly limited, which makes biking a real pleasure. Furthermore, the island is just big enough to make a day's biking fine exercise – not too far and not too short! You can bring your own bike over on the ferry or rent one of the 1200 available on the island. There are old

rattlers and better geared machines available for daily or weekly hire. As with rental bikes anywhere, choose carefully! If you really can't hack biking there's a two-hour bus tour round the island.

Around Perth

There is a great number of places of interest in day-trip distance from Perth. They include resorts and parks along the coast to the north and south of the capital and inland along the Avon River. The Darling Range runs parallel to the coast close to Perth and there are many places in the ranges for walks, picnics and barbecues. Many places can be reached on MTT city buses.

NORTH COAST

The coast north of Perth often has spectacular scenery with long sandy dunes. It quickly becomes the inhospitable land that deterred early visitors.

Yanchep

The Yanchep National Park is 51 km north of Perth – there's bush, caves (including the limestone Crystal and Yondemp Caves), Loch McNess, bushwalking trails and a wildlife sanctuary. Yanchep Sun City is a major marina and was the base for several unsuccessful Australian challengers for the America's Cup yacht races, which Australia finally won in 1983. Yanchep also has a seals-dolphins-sharks marine park.

Near Yanchep is Wanneroo (population 6700), an outer suburb of Perth and a popular wine-producing area. Wanneroo has a lion park and on weekends the Wanneroo Markets are a good outing from Perth. North of Yanchep is Guilderton, a popular holiday resort. Near here the *Vergulde Draek* (*Gilt Dragon*, a Dutch East Indiaman) went aground in 1656. The coast road ends at Lancelin, a small fishing port 130 km

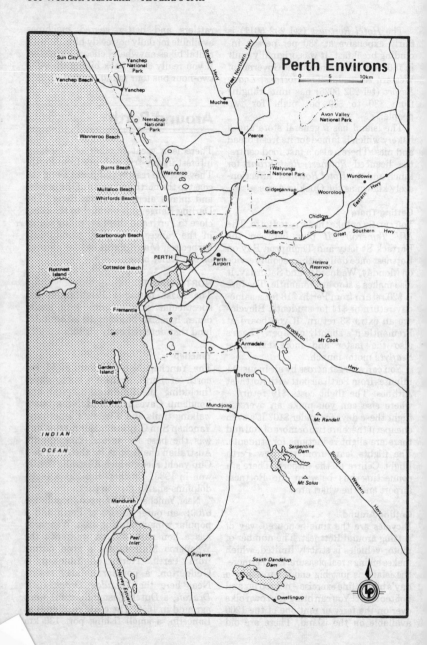

Perth Environs

0   5   10km

Sun City
Yanchep National Park
Yanchep Beach
Yanchep
Muchea
Brand Hwy
Great Northern Hwy
Neerabup National Park
Pearce
Avon Valley National Park
Wanneroo Beach
Burns Beach
Wanneroo
Walyunga National Park
Wundowie
Eastern Hwy
Mullaloo Beach
Whitfords Beach
Gidgegannup
Wooroloo
Scarborough Beach
Chidlow
Midland
Great Southern Hwy
Swan River
PERTH
Perth Airport
Helena Reservoir
Rottnest Island
Cottesloe Beach
Fremantle
Brookton
Mt Cook
Armadale
Hwy
Garden Island
Byford
Mundijong
Mt Randell
Rockingham
INDIAN OCEAN
Serpentine Dam
Mt Solus
South Western Hwy
Mandurah
Peel Inlet
South Dandelup Dam
Pinjarra
Harvey Estuary
Dwellingup

lp

north of Perth, but coastal tracks continue north and may be passable with four-wheel drive.

The Pinnacles

The small seaport of Cervantes (population 250), 257 km north of Perth by road, is the entry point for the unusual Pinnacles Desert. Here, in the coastal Nambung National Park, the flat sandy desert is punctured with peculiar limestone pillars, some only centimetres high, some towering up to five metres.

Check in Cervantes before attempting to drive into the park – four-wheel drive may be necessary. The Pinnacles are a very popular excursion from Perth – day tours from Perth cost around $38. It's possible to pick up the tour in Cervantes for $10 and save your car's suspension.

A coastal track, again four-wheel drive, runs north to Jurien (population 500), a crayfish fishing centre, and south to Lancelin. The coast has spectacular sand dunes along here.

Inland

The small town of New Norcia (population 130) has a curiously Spanish flavour; it was established as a Spanish Benedictine mission way back in 1846. Moora, further north, is a farming community. In the nearby Berkshire Valley an old cottage and flour mill have been restored and are now operated as a museum.

SOUTH COAST

The coast south of Perth is softer than the often-harsh landscape to the north. This is another very popular beach resort area for Perth and many people have holiday houses along the coast.

Rockingham (population 25,000)

Originally a port established in 1872, Rockingham was overtaken by Fremantle and is now a popular seaside resort just 45 km south of Perth. From here you can make trips to Penguin Island (yes, it does have penguins) and Garden Island, a naval base not open to the public. Boats run regularly to Penguin Island in the summer months or you can walk across at low tide.

From Rockingham you can also head inland to the Serpentine Dam and the Serpentine Falls National Park, with wildflowers and pleasant bushland. You can get to Rockingham on a 120 bus from Fremantle or a 116 from Perth.

Mandurah (population 11,000)

At the mouth of the huge estuary of the Serpentine River, Mandurah is yet another popular beach resort, 80 km south of Perth. Dolphins are often seen in the estuary. The town also has Hall's Cottage (open Sunday afternoon), built in the 1830s, and a geological museum. Prolific birdlife can be seen on the narrow coastal salt lakes Clifton and Preston, 20 km south. A 116 bus from Perth or a 117 from Fremantle will get you to Mandurah.

Inland

Head inland from the coast to Pinjarra (population 1300), a town with a number of old buildings picturesquely sited on the banks of the Murray River. Steam trains run from here on the Hotham Valley Railway to Dwellingup (population 450), another quiet little town with fine views over Peel Inlet behind Mandurah and out across the Indian Ocean. This is an area of jarrah forests, as is Boddington, further inland.

Avon Valley

The green and lush Avon Valley looks very English and was a delight to homesick early settlers. In the spring this area is particularly rich in wildflowers. The valley was first settled in 1830, only a year after Perth's foundation, so there are many early buildings to be seen.

Toodyay (population 600)

There are a great many old buildings in this historic town, many of them built by convicts. Even the local tourist centre is housed in one – Connor's Mill, dating from the 1850s. Close to town there's a winery which began operating in the 1870s while in the town itself there's a pleasant old country pub with a shady beer garden. Down river from Toodyay is the Avon Valley National Park.

Northam (population 6800)

The major town of the Avon Valley, Northam is a busy farming centre on the railway line to Kalgoorlie. At one time the line from Perth ended abruptly here and miners had to make the rest of the weary trek to the gold-fields by road. On the Avon River here, not only can can see the familiar black swans, but there's also white ones – a gift from Northam, England.

At Wooroloo, about midway between Northam and Midland, is El Cabello Blanco. This is a major Perth tourist attraction with performing Andalusian horses and plenty of other diversions to amuse the kids; admission is $7. Performances are at 2.15 pm from Tuesday to Sunday.

York (population 1100)

The oldest inland town in Western Australia, York was first settled in 1830. There are many old buildings right along the main street of town and a stroll down this street is a real step back in time. The excellent Residency Museum from the 1840s, the old town hall, Castle Hotel dating from the coaching days, Faversham House, the old railway station and Settlers' Hall are all of interest. Near York is the Balladong Farm Museum – a working farm of the pioneering era.

Beverley (population 750)

South of York, Beverley is noted for its fine aeronautical museum. Its exhibits include a locally-constructed biplane, built between 1928 and 1930. Further up river is Brookton (population 600) and Pigelly (population 1000) in an area well known for its wildflowers.

The Darling Range

The hills that run parallel to the coast, fencing Perth in against the coastline, are popular for picnics, barbecues and bush-walks. There are also some excellent viewpoints from where you can see over Perth down to the coast. Araleun with its waterfalls, the fire lookout at Mt Dale and Churchman's Brook are all off the Brookton Highway. Other places include the Zig Zag at Gooseberry Hill and Lake Leschenaultia.

The Cohunu Wildlife Park, where many of the animals can be fed by hand, is about a 35-minute drive from Perth. There are also plenty of waterbirds and a walk-in aviary. It's on Mill Rd, Gosnells. At Kalamunda you can get some fine views over Perth. Get there on buses 298, 300 or 302 via Maida Vale and Forrest-field; or 292, 299 or 305 via Wattle Grove and Lesmurdie. Taking one route out and the other back makes an interesting circular tour of the hill suburbs. There's a good walking track at Sullivan Rock, 69 km south-east on the Albany Highway.

Mundaring Weir

Only 40 km from Perth in the ranges, Mundaring (population 700), is the site of the Mundaring Weir – the dam built at the turn of the century to supply water to the gold-fields, over 500 km to the east. The reservoir has an attractive setting and it is a popular excursion and picnic spot from Perth. The C Y O'Connor Museum has models and exhibits about the water pipeline, an amazing engineering feat at the time. It's open Monday, Friday and Saturday from 2 to 4 pm, Wednesday from 10 am to 12 noon and Sunday from 1 to 4 pm.

Near Mundaring is the Old Mahogany Inn, originally built in 1837 as an outpost to protect travellers from unfriendly Aboriginals, it now houses a museum and tea-room. It's open from Wednesday to Sunday from 11 am to 6 pm. The John Forrest National Park in the Darling Range is also near Mundaring.

The Nullarbor

It's a little over 2700 km between Perth in Western Australia and Adelaide in South Australia, not much less than the distance from London to Moscow. Driving on the long, lonely Eyre Highway from one side of Australia to another is still quite an adventure as you cross the vast Nullarbor Plain – bad Latin for 'no trees', an accurate description of this flat, treeless wasteland.

The road across the Nullarbor takes it name from John Eyre, the explorer who made the first east-west crossing in 1841. It was a superhuman effort which took five months of nightmare hardship and resulted in the death of Eyre's companion John Baxter. In 1877 a telegraph line was laid across the Nullarbor, roughly delineating the route the first road would take. Later in the century gold-miners en route to the gold-fields of WA followed the same telegraph line route across the empty plains. In 1896 the first bicycle crossing was made and in 1912 the first car was driven across but in the next 12 years only three more cars managed to traverse the continent.

In 1941 the war inspired the building of a trans-continental highway, just as it had done for the Alice Springs-Darwin route. It was a rough-and-ready track when completed and in the '50s only a few vehicles a day would make the crossing. In the '60s the traffic flow increased to over 30 vehicles a day and in 1969 the WA government surfaced the road as far as the South Australian border. Finally in 1976 the final stretch from the South Australian border was surfaced and now the Nullarbor crossing is a much easier drive, but still a hell of a long one.

There are actually three routes across the Nullarbor. The new surfaced road runs close to the coastline on the South Australian side. The Nullarbor plains end dramatically on the coast of the Great Australian Bight, falling sheer into the roaring sea. It's easy to see why this was a seafarer's nightmare for a ship driven on to the coast would quickly be pounded to pieces against the cliffs and climbing them would be a near impossibility. On the South Australian side the old Eyre Highway is a little distance north of the coast while the third route, the Indian-Pacific Railway, is about 150 km north of the coast and actually on the Nullarbor Plain – unlike the road which only runs on the fringes of the great plain. For one 500-km-long stretch the railway runs dead straight – the longest piece of straight railway line in the world.

ALONG THE EYRE HIGHWAY

Ceduna is really the end of the line on the South Australian side of the Eyre Highway. You might travel this far west to see places in South Australia, but if you went any further west, it would only be for one reason – to leave South Australia and go to Western Australia. At Ceduna it's still 520 km to Eucla on the South Australia/Western Australia border and from there it's another 729 km to Norseman where the Eyre Highway ends. By anyone's standards, that's a long way.

Ceduna's name comes from an Aboriginal word meaning 'a place to sit down and rest' – perhaps it's quite aptly named. From Ceduna there are several places with petrol and other facilities along the road. Penong sees the end of all traces of cultivation and the start of the real treeless plain. You can make a short detour south of the town to see the Pink Lake, Point Sinclair and Cactus Beach – a little-known surf beach which is a 'must' for any serious surfer making the east-west journey. Nundroo is the real edge of the Nullarbor and Colona Homestead is the start of the last section of the highway to have been surfaced. The road passes through the Yalata Aboriginal Reserve and you'll often see Aboriginals by the side of the road seling boomerangs and other souvenirs.

For most of the way across, the highway

runs to the south of the Nullarbor Plain on the sloping stretch closer to the coast. From the tiny settlement of Nullarbor Station, where you can actually see the plain, to the WA border 184 km to the west, the new road has been built right along the coastline and offers superb views over the Great Australian Bight.

At the border there's a sign telling you to put your watch back 45 minutes. From here to Caiguna you're in an intermediate time zone, half-way between South Australian and Western Australian time. There's a Travellers' Village at the border with camping facilities, a motel, cabins and restaurant. Just across the border is Eucla with the picturesque ruins of an old telegraph station, first opened in 1877. The telegraph line now runs along the railway line, about 160 km to the north, and the station is gradually being engulfed by the sand dunes. The dunes are a spectacular sight as you leave Eucla and drop down into the Eucla Pass.

After Eucla the next sign of life is the tiny settlement of Mundrabilla with a bird sanctuary behind the motel. Next up is Madura, close to the hills of the Hampton Tablelands. At one time horses were bred here for the Indian army. You get good views over the plains as the road climbs up. Cocklebiddy has the stone ruins of an Aboriginal mission and the area has a number of interesting caves, for real caving enthusiasts. At Caiguna watches go back another 45 minutes to Western Australian time.

It's one of the loneliest stretches of the Nullarbor from here to Balladonia, including a straight stretch of road 144 km long! Shortly before Balladonia, three km north of the road, are a number of natural rock waterholes known as Afghan Rocks. They often hold water far into the summer. After Balladonia you may see the remains of old stone fences built to enclose stock. Clay saltpans are also visible in the area. Finally the mine shafts and mullock heaps around Norseman signal the end of the Eyre Highway and the decision point where you either turn north to the gold-fields of WA or south to the coastal area.

Crossing the Nullarbor

See the Perth 'Getting There' section for details of air, rail, hitching and bus information across the Nullarbor. Although the Nullarbor is no longer a torture trail where cars get shaken to bits by potholes and corrugations or where you're going to die of thirst waiting for another vehicle if you break down, it's still wise to avoid difficulties whenever possible.

The longest distance between petrol stops is about 200 km, so if you're foolish enough to run out of petrol mid-way, you'll have a nice long round-trip to get more. Getting help for a mechanical breakdown could be equally time consuming and very expensive, so make sure your vehicle is in good shape and that you've got plenty of petrol, good tyres and at least a basic kit of simple spare parts. Carry some drinking water just in case you do have to sit it out by the roadside on a hot summer day. Take it easy on the Nullarbor – plenty of people try to set speed records and plenty more have made a real mess of their cars when they run into big roos, particularly at night.

Gold Country

Fifty years after its establishment in 1829 the WA colony was still going nowhere rapidly so the government in Perth was delighted when gold was discovered at Southern Cross in 1887. That first strike petered out pretty quickly but more discoveries followed and WA went through a gold boom for the rest of the century. It was gold that put WA on the map and finally gave it the population to make it viable in its own right, rather than just a distant offshoot of the east coast colonies.

The gold boom was comparatively

short lived. The major strikes were made in 1892 in Coolgardie and nearby Kalgoorlie, but in the whole gold-fields area, Kalgoorlie is the only town of any considerable size left. Coolgardie's period of prosperity lasted only until 1905 and many other gold towns went from nothing to populations of as much as 10,000 then back to nothing in just 10 years.

Their rise to prosperity was meteoric, however, as the many magnificent public buildings in the old towns grandly tell. Life in the gold-fields in the early days was terribly hard. This area of WA is extremely dry – rainfall is erratic and never great. Even the little rain there is quickly disappears into the porous soil. Many early gold-seekers, propelled more by enthusiasm than common-sense, died of thirst while seeking the elusive metal, or later, of disease in the insanitary shanty towns. The completion of a 557-km-long water pipeline in 1903 solved that serious problem but couldn't ensure the gold supply. Today Kalgoorlie is the main centre for the area and some gold-mining still goes on there. Elsewhere there is a string of fascinating ghost and near-ghost towns plus the modern nickel mines that have recently revived some areas of the gold country.

WATER

Development of the Western Australian gold-fields faced an enormous problem right from the start: water, or rather the lack of it. Early miners faced terrible hardships due to this lack and more than a few died from thirst out in the bush or from the outbreaks of disease in the unhygienic shanty towns. It soon became clear to the government that gold was WA's most important industry and that development of the gold-fields was likely to come to a grinding halt without a reliable water supply. Stop-gap measures like huge condensation plants to produce distilled water from salt lakes or brackish bore water provided temporary relief and in 1898 the engineer C Y O'Connor proposed a stunning solution – he would build a reservoir near Perth and construct a pipeline 557 km to Kalgoorlie.

This was long before the current era of long

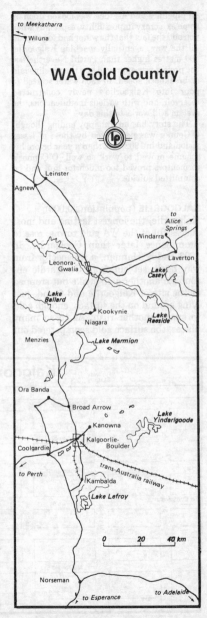

oil pipelines and his idea was looked upon by some as a crazy impossibility, especially when you add the fact that the water had to go uphill all the way, eventually reaching Kalgoorlie, 400 metres higher than Perth! Nevertheless, the project was approved and the pipeline laid at breakneck speed. In 1903 water started to pour into Kalgoorlie's newly constructed reservoir, and with various modifications, the system still works to this day.

The story has an unhappy ending though: O'Connor was persecuted by those of lesser vision and in 1902, less than a year before his scheme proved to work so well, O'Connor's tormentors proved too much for him and he committed suicide.

KALGOORLIE (population 20,000)

Kalgoorlie, the longest lasting and most successful of the WA gold towns, rose to prominence later than Coolgardie. In 1893 Paddy Hannan, a prospector from way back, set out from Coolgardie en-route to another gold strike but stopped at the site of Kalgoorlie and found, just lying around on the surface, enough gold to spark another rush. As in so many places, the surface gold soon petered out

but at Kalgoorlie the miners went deeper and more and more gold was found. It wasn't the storybook chunky nuggets of solid gold; Kalgoorlie's gold had to be extracted from the rocks by costly and complex processes of grinding, roasting and chemical action, but there was plenty of it.

Kalgoorlie quickly reached fabled heights of prosperity and the enormous and magnificent public buildings of the turn of the century speak clearly of just

1	Post Office
2	Palace Hotel
3	Exchange Hotel
4	Airlines of WA
5	RACWA
6	Golden Mile Museum
7	Hannan Tree
8	Surrey House
9	Victoria Tavern
10	Tourist Office
11	Kalgoorlie Hotel
12	Pizza Cantina
13	Geological Museum
14	Town Hall
15	Railway Hotel
16	Inland City Hotel

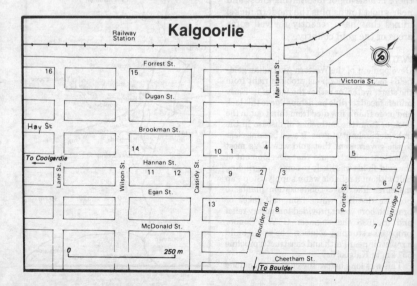

what a fabulously wealthy place this was. After WW I, however, increasing production costs combined with static gold values to push Kalgoorlie into a slow but steady decline. Today the famous 'golden mile' of Kalgoorlie's heyday is a shadow of it's once hectic self and the only major operation is the huge Mt Charlotte mine, close to Paddy Hannan's original find. The mining that is still carried on, Kalgoorlie's importance as an outback centre, the busy tourist trade plus the new nickel mines in the area combine to ensure the town's continued prosperity.

Information

There's an informative tourist bureau on Hannan St where you can get a good map of Kalgoorlie and buy the excellent and information-packed *Gold Rush Country* map. The office is open 8.30 am to 5 pm Monday to Friday and 9 to 11 am Saturdays. There's another tourist office on Burt St in Boulder. For an excellent book on the fascinating Kalgoorlie story read *The Glittering Years* by Arthur Bennet (St George Books, Perth, 1981). There's a daily paper in Kal (as it's known to it's friends), the *Kalgoorlie Miner*.

Kal can get very hot in December-January and overall the cool winter months are the best time to visit. From late-August through September, however, the town is packed out and accommodation of any type can be difficult to find. The RAC of WA (tel 21 1900) has an office on the corner of Porter and Hannan Sts.

Orientation

Although Kalgoorlie sprang up close to Paddy Hannan's original find, the mining emphasis soon shifted a few km away to the 'golden mile', a square mile which, area for area, was probably the wealthiest gold-mining area in the world. The satellite town of Boulder developed to service this town. There's a direct road between the two towns plus a longer route that runs by the airport.

Kalgoorlie itself is a grid of broad tree-lined streets. The main street, Hannan St, is flanked by imposing public buildings and is, of course, wide enough to turn a camel train in – a popular outback measuring stick! You'll find most of the hotels, restaurants and offices on or close to Hannan St.

Hainault Tourist Mine

Kalgoorlie's number one tourist attraction and it's 'not to be missed' feature is this mine, right in the golden mile near Boulder. Opened in 1898, the mine ceased operation in the 1960s. Today you can take the lift cage 60 metres down into the bowels of the earth and make an enthralling tour around the 'drives' and 'crosscuts' of the mine – guided by an ex-miner. There's also a tour of the surface workings and an audio-visual show on mining and Kalgoorlie itself. The underground tour costs $5.50, or $6.60 including a surface tour. You can wander around the surface workings yourself for free. Underground tours are made at 10.30 am, 1, 2.30 and 3.45 pm daily.

Near the mine the Lion's Lookout provides a good view over the golden mile, Boulder and Kalgoorlie. You can make an interesting loop around the golden mile by catching the 'Rattler', a tourist train complete with commentary which makes an hour-long trip around on Monday to Friday at 11 am and on Sunday at 1.30 and 3 pm. It leaves from Boulder railway station and you pass the old mining works and the huge mountains of 'slime', the cast-offs from the mining process.

Other Attractions

Just off the end of Hannan St you can climb the road (ignore the 'private' sign) to Mt Charlotte where the town's reservoir is situated. The view over the town is good but there's little to see of the reservoir which is covered over to limit evaporation. The School of Mines on the corner of Egan and Cassidy Sts has a geology display including replicas of big nuggets. It's

GOLDEN MILE MUSEUM
KALGOORLIE, W.A.

"BRITISH ARMS"   1899

usually open Monday to Friday from 2 to 4 pm but was closed at the time of writing due to vandalism.

Along Hannan St you'll find the imposing town hall and the even more imposing post office. In 1979 the largest chunk of debris from the fallen US Skylab space vehicle crashed to earth in WA and was put on display in the town hall. There's an art gallery upstairs while outside is a replica of a statue of Paddy Hannan himself, holding a water-bag drinking fountain. The original statue is on display inside the town hall, protected from the elements and the vandals.

A block back from Hannan St is Hay St and one of Kalgoorlie's most famous 'attractions', although it's quietly ignored in the tourist brochures. Kalgoorlie has a block-long strip of brothels where the red-lit ladies of the night beckon passing men to their true-blue Aussie galvanised-iron doorways. Nelson's eye has been turned to this activity for so long that it has become an accepted and historical part of the town. Usually Kalgoorlie's famous

(and illegal) two-up schools are also ignored but in late '82 a Perth gaming squad raid caused outrage amongst local citizens, including the mayor.

On Outridge Terrace the tiny British Arms Hotel (the narrowest hotel in Australia) now houses the interesting Golden Mile Museum with many relics from Kalgoorlie's pioneering days. It's open from 10.30 am to 4.30 pm daily, admission is $1. A little further along Outridge Terrace is Paddy Hannan's tree, marking the spot where the first gold strike was made. The Eastern Goldfields Historical Society also has a display at the June O'Brien Memorial Centre (open daily except Thursday). The Royal Flying Doctor Base can be visited Monday to Friday at 2.30 pm. Hammond Park is a small fauna reserve with a miniature German castle.

Boulder

There is another fine old town hall in Boulder which also has the Goldfields War Museum by the tourist bureau on Burt St. It's open 9 am to 1 pm and 1.30 to 4.30 pm daily. At the Golden Mile the rip-roaring hotels of the Boulder Block never closed and thirsty miners off the shifts poured into them night and day. There's nothing much to be seen there today.

Places to Stay

There is a string of pleasantly old-fashioned hotels right around the centre of Kalgoorlie. The *Exchange Hotel* (tel 21 2833) is the picture-postcard place right in the centre of town by the traffic lights on Hannan St. Rooms cost $20/34 for bed & breakfast. A few doors down at 9 Boulder Rd is *Surrey House* (tel 21 1340) where rooms cost $20/34, again, for bed & breakfast. It's a popular place in the budget category.

Other cheap hotels include the *Inland City* (tel 21 2401) at 93 Forrest St, the *Kalgoorlie* (tel 21 3046) at 319 Hannan St, the *Railway* (tel 21 3047) at the corner of Wilson and Forrest Sts and the *Criterion* (tel 21 2271) at 123 Hannan St. The very basic *Nullabor Guest House* (their spelling, not ours) (tel 21 2176) is at 300 Hannan St and has rooms for just $8/14 for singles/doubles.

Motels aren't cheap in Kalgoorlie but the *Auto* on Hannan St (tel 21 1433) has singles for $25, doubles for $27. There are a number of campsites in Kalgoorlie. If you're arriving late at night on the train or bus and are looking for a campsite, the closest is the *Golden Village Caravan Park* (tel 21 4162), on Hay St two km south-west of the railway station.

Places to Eat

There are plenty of counter-meal pubs and cafés in Kalgoorlie, particularly along Hannan St. The *Victoria Tavern* does good counter food at lunchtimes and in the evenings. The *Exchange Hotel*, on the corner of Hannan and Boulder Sts, has the Winter Lounge with main courses around $7. In the front bar there are also cheaper meals in the $3 to $5 range. The *Hotel York* also does counter meals in the Steak Bar where prices are around $7.

At 275 Hannan St is the *Kalgoorlie Cafe* with burgers, souvlaki and other similar fast foods while the *Pizza Cantina* at 211 does pretty good pizzas. Try the *Victoria Cafe* at 246 Hannan St for an early breakfast. In Boulder you can get counter meals at *Tattersalls*. Kalgoorlie also brews its own beer called 'Hannan's'.

Getting There

Air You can fly, rail or bus to Kalgoorlie. Ansett WA fly there two or three times daily from Perth. The flight takes just under an hour and costs $110. The Ansett WA office (tel 21 2277) is on Maritana St.

Bus Ansett Pioneer and Greyhound buses operate through Kalgoorlie on their Sydney ($144), Melbourne ($122) and Adelaide ($85) to Perth services. The fare to Perth is $35 but note that all the buses

pull into Kalgoorlie at an ungodly hour of the night when everything is closed up and finding a place to stay can be difficult. Unfortunately, most days of the week, the Prospector also arrives in Kalgoorlie at an uncomfortably late hour.

There's a three-times weekly bus service to Esperance – once via Kambalda and Norseman, twice via Coolgardie and Norseman, the trip takes 5½ hours and costs $27. To Perth by road from Kalgoorlie is 595 km.

Rail The daily Prospector railcar service from Perth costs $41.20 in 1st or $26.70 in economy. It's claimed to be one of the fastest railway services in Australia and takes about eight hours for the 600 km trip. It's modern, comfortable and provides good views of the generally monotonous scenery. The fare includes a meal en-route. From Perth you can book seats at the WAGTB office in Hay St or the Westrail Terminal (tel 326 2811). It's wise to book ahead as this service is fairly popular, particularly in the tourist season. The Indian-Pacific also goes through Kalgoorlie with fares to the eastern states of $105 to Adelaide, $149 to Melbourne and $211 to Sydney for economy class seats without meals. There are also economy and 1st class berths.

WESTERN AUSTRALIAN GOVERNMENT RAILWAYS

Getting Around

You can rent cars from Hertz, Budget, Avis or Letz (at the airport) and if you want to explore very far you'll either have to have wheels, hitch or take a tour since public transport is limited. A taxi to the airport would cost about $5. Make sure they use the meter around town! You can hire bicycles at Johnston Cycles (tel 21 1157) at 76 Boulder St for $1.50 an hour or $8 per day.

Between Kal and Boulder there's a regular bus service (timetable from the tourist office) costing 80c. You'll have to walk about two km from the Boulder junction to the Hainault Mine. Hitching shouldn't be too difficult. In the morning you can take the school bus to Coolgardie, which comes back in the afternoon.

Goldrush Tours are the main tour operators in Kalgoorlie. Book through the tourist office or direct from their office in Boulder St. They have town tours ($11, not including admission charges) and tours to Coolgardie ($14), Kambalda ($14), ghost towns ($20), a gold detector tour for avid fossickers ($13), and in August and September there are wildflower tours for $24.

Around the Gold Country

Kalgoorlie is the metropolis of the goldfields but there are many other towns of great interest although many of them are mere ghost towns today. Coolgardie, only 40 km from Kalgoorlie, is the best known while others vary from odd heaps of rubble to tiny outposts with superb town halls and equally magnificent hotels, kept alive today only by the tourist trade.

Before setting out to explore this area get a copy of the excellent and highly informative *Gold Rush Country* map. Remember that this is a remote, sparsely populated, rugged and very dry area – carry plenty of water and be prepared if you intend to wander off the beaten track. There is still quite a bit of local private

mining going on in the gold-fields – the lure continues!

COOLGARDIE (population 900)

A popular pause for people crossing the Nullarbor and also the turning-off point for Kalgoorlie, Coolgardie really is a ghost of its former self. You only have to glance at the huge town hall and post office building to appreciate the size that Coolgardie once was. Gold was discovered here in 1892 and by the turn of the century the population had boomed to 15,000. The gold then petered out and the town withered away just as quickly. There's plenty of interest to the visitor though.

For a start there are 150 informative historical markers scattered in and around the town. They tell what was once there or what the buildings were formerly used for. The Goldfields Museum is open 9.30 am to 4.30 pm every day of the week and has a fascinating display of gold-fields memorabilia. You can even find out about American President Herbert Hoover's days on the WA gold-fields. It's the largest museum in the gold-fields and worth the $2.50 admission, which includes a film, shown a few doors up the road at the Coolgardie Tourist Bureau. The railway station is also operated as a museum and here you can learn of the incredible story of the miner who was trapped 300 metres underground by floodwater in 1907, and his rescue by divers 10 days later!

Just out of town on the Perth side, the town cemetery includes many early graves including that of pioneer explorer Edward Giles. At Coolgardie's unhealthiest time it's said that 'one half of the population buried the other half'. Coolgardie's most amazing sight, however, is Prior's Museum. Right by the road a large empty lot is cluttered with every kind of antique junk you could imagine – from old mining equipment to half a dozen rusting old cars, it's all here. Open 24 hours a day, 365 days a year and admission is free!

Places to Stay & Eat

Coolgardie has a fine old *Youth Hostel* (tel 26 6051) at 56-60 Gnarlbine Rd. It costs $5 per night and has plenty of room. You can get bed & breakfast for $14 in the *Railway Lodge* (tel 26 6166) on Bayley St, or for $15 in the *Denver City Hotel* (tel 26 6031), also on Bayley St. The Denver City is one of Coolgardie's original hotels and it's a fine old building with long shady verandahs.

At the *Safari Village Holiday Centre* (tel 26 6037) at 2 Renou St bed & breakfast costs $21/34. There's also a campsite. The *Denver Hotel* does counter lunches and teas.

NORSEMAN (population 1900)

To most people Norseman is just a crossroad where you turn east for the trans-Nullarbor Eyre Highway journey, south to Esperance along the Leeuwin Way or north to Coolgardie and Perth. The town also has gold-mines still in operation today, many other old workings and a museum.

KAMBALDA (population 4500)

Kambalda died as a gold-mining town in 1906 but nickel was discovered here in 1966 and today this is the major mining centre in the gold-fields region. There are tours of the mining operation from Monday to Friday from the tourist office. The town is on the shores of salt Lake LeFroy and land-yachting is a popular activity.

NORTH OF KALGOORLIE

The road is surfaced from Kalgoorlie all the way to Leonora-Gwalia, 240 km north, and on from there to Laverton (130 km north-east) and Leinster (160 km north). Off the main road, however, traffic is virtually non-existent and rain can quickly cut the dirt roads.

Towns of interest include Kanowna, just 22 km from Kal along a dirt road. In 1905 this town had a population of 12,000, 16 hotels, many churches and an hourly train service to Kalgoorlie. Today, apart from the station and the odd pile of rubble, absolutely nothing remains!

Broad Arrow now has a population of 20, compared with 2400 at the turn of the century, but one of the town's original eight hotels operates in virtually unchanged condition. Ora Banda has gone from 2000 to less than 50. Menzies, 130 km north of Kal, has about 90 people today versus 5000 in 1900. Many early buildings remain including the railway station with its 120-metre-long platform and the town hall with its clockless clocktower. The ship bringing the clock from England sank en route.

With a population of 500, Leonora is still a reasonable sized little town. It serves as the railhead for the nickel from Windarra and Leinster. In adjoining Gwalia, the Sons of Gwalia Goldmine, closed in 1964, was the largest in WA outside Kalgoorlie. At one time the mine was managed by Herbert Hoover, later to become president of the USA. The Gwalia Historical Society is housed in the 1898 mine office; it's a fascinating local museum, open daily. Off the main road Koolkynie is an interesting little place with a population of just 10. In 1905 it was 1500. Nearby Niagara is a total ghost town.

From Leonora you can turn north-east to Laverton, where the surfaced road ends. The population here declined from 1000 in 1910 to 200 in 1970 when the Poseidon nickel discovery (beloved of stockmarket speculators in the late '60s and early '70s) revived mining operations in nearby Windarra. The town now has a population of 900. From here it is just 1710 km north-west to Alice Springs but you'll need four-wheel drive for the rough track, permission to enter the Aboriginal reserves along the way, enough fuel capacity for at least 650 km and don't even consider doing it from November to March when the route is closed for safety reasons due to the extreme heat.

North of Leonora the road is now

surfaced to Leinster, another modern nickel town. Nearby Agnew is another old gold town which has now all but completely disappeared. It's 170 km north to Wiluna from where it's another 170 km to Meekatharra on the surfaced Great Northern Highway which then continues on a further 860 km to Port Hedland. Arsenic was mined in Wiluna through the '30s when it had a population of 8000 and was a modern, prosperous town. The ore ran out in 1948 and the town went into a rapid decline. Today the small population consists mainly of Aboriginals.

The South & South-West

Many travellers on the road between the east and west coasts take the direct route through WA – across the Nullarbor then from Norseman north to Coolgardie and then directly west to Perth. It's certainly worth getting up into the gold-fields around Kalgoorlie and Coolgardie but turning south from Norseman to Esperance and then travelling along the Leeuwin Way, around the south-west corner of Australia, is an equally interesting trip. This is a very varied area with some real contrasts to the dry and barren country found in so many other parts of the state.

The southern stretch, 'The Great Southern', has some magnificent coastline pounded by huge seas but there is also beautiful country inland as well as Albany, the oldest settlement in Western Australia. Inland are the spectacular and rugged Stirling Range and Porongorups. The south-west corner is one of the greenest and most fertile areas of WA. Here you will find the great karri and jarrah forests, prosperous farming land and more of the state's beautiful wildflowers.

Places to Stay
The towns in the south-west and south coast regions are popular holiday resorts so there are plenty of hotels, motels, holiday flats and campsites. There is also a string of youth hostels right around the coastal region at Esperance, Albany, Denmark, Tingledale, Pemberton, Augusta, Bridgetown, Noggerup and Quindalup. Enough hostels, in fact, to make a really interesting hostelling circuit of the region possible.

Getting There
Air Skywest (tel TAA – 323 3333 in Perth) have a fairly comprehensive network of flights to towns in the south and south-west. They include Bunbury ($30), Albany ($87), Esperance ($129) and Norseman ($114).

Bus & Rail Westrail have a number of bus and rail services into the region including a three-times-weekly bus service from Kalgoorlie to Esperance. From Perth the Westrail Road Service bus to Esperance runs via Jerramangup on Mondays, via Lake Grace on Fridays. The trip takes about 11 hours and costs $38.20. A complete loop costs $93.10. There are also Westrail bus services to Albany ($25) and Hyden ($22.50), while to Bunbury there is a bus service ($11.70) and the 'Australind' train service ($9.30). Greyhound 'Eaglepass' holders can use Westrail bus services between Perth and Albany.

Esperance is 720 km from Perth via Lake Grace and 894 km via Albany. To do a complete road loop from Perth out to Kalgoorlie, down to Esperance and back around by the coast would involve something over 2000 km.

ESPERANCE (population 6400)
On the coast 200 km south of Norseman, Esperance has become a popular coastal resort for the region. Although the first settlers came to the area in 1863, it was during the gold-rush in the 1890s that the town really became established as a port.

When the gold-fever subsided Esperance went into a state of suspended animation until after WW II. In the 1950s it was discovered that adding missing trace elements to the soil around Esperance would restore it to fertility and since then the town has grown rapidly as an agricultural centre.

Esperance has some excellent beaches and the seas offshore are studded with the many islands of the Archipelago of the Recherche. The town's Municipal Museum has the usual pioneering exhibits but also has a major Skylab display. When the USA's Skylab crashed to earth in 1979, it made its fiery re-entry right over Esperance. The museum is on the corner of James and Dempster Sts and is open daily from 1.30 to 4.30 pm. George's Oceanarium has a marine life display and you can also see the town's original homestead on Dempster St, although it's not open to the public.

Only three km from the town the Pink Lake, with its prolific birdlife, really is pink; as much as half a million tonnes of salt are dredged from the lake annually. Twilight Bay and Picnic Cove are popular local swimming spots while you can look out over the bay and islands from nearby Observatory Point or from the Rotary Lookout on Wireless Hill. There are about 100 small islands in the Recherche Archipelago with colonies of seals, penguins and a wide variety of waterbirds. Woody Island is a wildlife sanctuary and there are regular trips to this and other islands in January and February.

Cape Le Grand National Park is a coastal park extending from about 20 to 60 km east of Esperance. The park has spectacular coastal scenery, some good beaches and excellent walking tracks. Frenchmans Peak, at the western end of the park, gives fine views. Further east is the coastal Cape Arid National Park, at the start of the Great Australian Bight and on the fringes of the Nullarbor.

Esperance has a Tourist Bureau on Dempster St, next to the museum.

Places to Stay

The *Youth Hostel* (tel 71 1040) is on Goldfields Rd, two km north of the town centre. It is a popular place which has room for 98 people and charges $5 a night.

Nobards Private Hotel (tel 71 2705) is not too central at 85 Pink Lake Rd but has single/double rooms for $13/22. The *Esperance Motor Hotel* (tel 71 1555) is well located in Andrew St and has singles/doubles for $14/28.

There are numerous camping grounds around Esperance, the most central being the *Esperance Bay Caravan Park* (tel 71 2237) on the corner of the Esplanade and Harbour Rd, down near the wharf. Camping sites are $5.50 for two and on-site vans are $15.

ESPERANCE TO ALBANY (476 km)

From Esperance the road runs inland, skirting the Fitzgerald River National Park before turning back to the coast at Albany. The tiny town of Ravensthorpe (population 300) was once the centre of the Phillips River gold-field and later copper mining also took place here. Of interest here is the historic homestead 'Cocanarup', built in 1868, with it's display of farm machinery. The fine beaches and bays around Hopetoun are immediately to the south. Access to the Fitzgerald River National Park can be made from here or from Jerramangup further west. Ongerup (population 200), a small wheatbelt town, has an annual wildflower show in mid-September with literally hundreds of species on show, collected from the region.

ALBANY (population 15,000)

The commercial centre of the southern region, the pretty town of Albany is the oldest settlement in the state, established in 1826, shortly before Perth. Its excellent harbour on King George Sound led to Albany becoming a thriving whaling port. Later, when steamships came into operation between the UK and Australia,

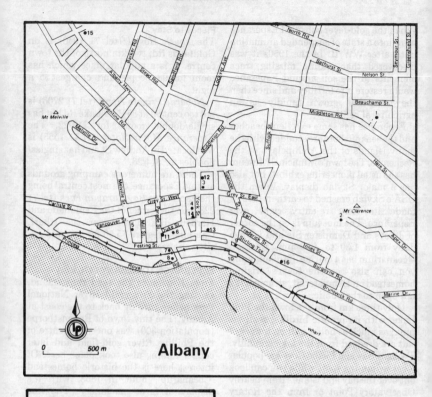

Albany

1 Strawberry Farm
2 Desert Mounted Corps Memorial
3 Post Office
4 Tourist Office
5 Post Office
6 Patrick Taylor Cottage
7 Old Gaol & Museum
8 Residency Museum
9 Old Post Office
10 Railway Station
11 Youth Hostel
12 Albany Hostel
13 London Hotel
14 Camberlea Guest House
15 Melville Caravan Park
16 Parkville Guest House

Albany was a coaling station for ships bound for the east coast.

With this long history, it's not surprising that Albany has some fine old colonial buildings and Stirling Terrace is particularly noted for its Victorian shopfronts. The Old Gaol & Museum dates from 1851 and is now a folk museum. There's also a full scale replica of the brig *Amity*, the ship which brought Albany's founding party to the area. Historical exhibits can also be seen at the Albany Residency Museum, originally built in the 1850s as the home of the Resident Magistrate.

Patrick Taylor Cottage dates from 1832 and has been restored and houses a collection of period costumes and furniture. On top of Mt Clarence is the Desert Mounted Corps Memorial, originally erected in Port Said as a memorial to the events of Gallipoli. When the Suez crisis in 1956 made colonial reminders less than popular in Egypt, it was brought here. The old farm at Strawberry Hill is the oldest in the state having been established in 1872 as the government farm for Albany.

There are fine views over the coast and inland from the Twin Peaks overlooking the town. Near Albany there are good beaches at Jimmy Newhill's Harbour, Emu Point, Frenchman's Bay and in town at the long sweep of sand at Middleton Beach. At Frenchman's Bay, 21 km from town, the Cheyne's Beach Whaling Station only ceased operations in 1978. Impressive rock formations and blowholes along the coast include The Gap and Natural Bridge, 16 km south, and the Blowhole and Gorge.

Tourist information is available from the Albany Travel Centre (tel 41 1088) at 171 York St.

Places to Stay

The Albany *Youth Hostel* (tel 41 3949) is only 400 metres from the town centre at 49 Duke St and costs $5 per night.

There are many hotels and guesthouses in and around town. Some of the more central ones include the *Albany Hotel* (tel 41 1031) on York St with bed & breakfast for $15 and the *London Hotel* (tel 41 1048) on Stirling Terrace has singles/doubles for $15/28 including breakfast. The *Parkville Colonial Guest House* (tel 41 3704) at 136 Brunswick St has 14 rooms and charges $12/24 for room-only singles/doubles. The *Camberlea Guest House* (tel 41 1669) at 158 York St has similar prices but includes a light breakfast.

The *Mt Melville Caravan Park* (tel 41 4616) is one km north of the centre at the corner of Lion and Wellington Sts. There are campsites for $4 and on-site vans cost $18.

MT BARKER (population 1500)

Directly north of Albany, Mt Barker is south of the Stirling Ranges and west of the Porongorups. The town is overlooked by the enormous TV tower on top of Mt Barker. The town has been settled since the 1830s and the old police station and jail of 1868 is preserved as a museum. Today the area is developing a reputation for wine producing.

Kendenup, 16 km north of Mt Barker, was the actual site of WA's first gold discovery, though considerably overshadowed by the later and much larger finds in the Kalgoorlie area. North of Mt Barker, Cranbrook (population 300) is an access point to the Stirling Range National Park. Mt Barker has a tourist office at 47 Lowood St, a couple of hotels and a caravan park.

THE STIRLING RANGE & PORONGORUPS

The beautiful Porongorup Range provides panoramic views, beautiful scenery and excellent bushwalks. Castle Rock (570 metres) and Nancy's Peak (652 metres) are easy climbs. The Devil's Slide (670 metres) is another popular Porongorup walk. In the Stirling Range Toolorunup (for views), Bluff Knoll (for the height – at 1037 metres it's the highest peak in the range) and Toll Peak (for the wildflowers) are popular half-day walks. The 96-km-long range is noted for its spectacular colour changes through blues, reds and purples. The mountains rise abruptly from the surrounding flat and sandy plains.

DENMARK (population 1000)

Situated 55 km west of Albany, Denmark has fine beaches (William Bay for swimming, Ocean Beach for surfing) and is a good base for trips into the karri forests. The town is picturesquely sited on the Denmark River and first became established supplying timber for goldfield developments. In the town, Winniston Park is a modern house packed with fine English antiques and is open daily. Copenhagen House, opposite the tourist office on Strickland St, shows local crafts. You can get fine views from Mt Shadforth Lookout.

Places to Stay

There is a *Youth Hostel* (tel 48 1267) at the Wilson Inlet Holiday Park, three km south of Denmark and during the summer months it is necessary to phone in advance.

NORNALUP-WALPOLE

The road continues close to the coast to Nornalup, a small town on the banks of the tranquil Frankland River. The heavily forested Walpole-Nornalup National Park stretches between Nornalup and Walpole and contains the 'Valley of the Giants', a stand of giant karri and tingle trees including one which soars to 46 metres high. Pleasant shady and ferny paths lead through the forest. The Frankland River is popular with canoeing enthusiasts. From Walpole the road turns away from the coast to Manjimup, 120 km north.

MANJIMUP (population 4100)

The commercial centre of the south-west region, this is a major agricultural centre, particularly for apple growing and wood-chipping. The town has a Timber Museum and you can make excursions to the Warren National Park, One Tree Bridge and the four superb karri trees at Four Aces, just along the riverbank, are believed to be over 300 years old. Nine km south of town, the Diamond Tree Lookout provides spectacular views of the surrounding countryside.

Manjimup has a tourist office on Giblett St. The *Manjimup Hotel* (tel 71 1322) has rooms for $22/29 singles/doubles and there are two caravan parks in town with campsites and on-site vans.

PEMBERTON (population 900)

Situated in the superb karri forests, the delightful little town of Pemberton has a very good local museum displaying old forestry equipment, an art gallery housed in a restored squatter's cottage and a trout hatchery which supplies fish for the state's dams and rivers. The Brockman Sawpit is a restoration showing timber cutting activities of the 1860s.

If you're feeling fit you can make the scary 60-metre climb to the top of the Gloucester Tree, the highest fire lookout tree in the world and the view makes the climb well worthwhile. It's just south of Pemberton on the Northcliffe road.

There's a tourist office on Brockman St in Pemberton. Apart from during the winter months, there's usually farm labouring work available in the Pemberton area.

Places to Stay

The *Youth Hostel* (tel 76 1153) is an easy 10 km hitch at Pimelea and has a beautiful location in the forest. In town the *Pemberton Hotel* (tel 76 1017) on Brockman St has bed & breakfast for $10 or the *Pemberton Caravan Park* (tel 76 1176) has on-site vans for $14 for two in addition to campsites.

NORTHCLIFFE (population 200)

Situated 32 km south of Pemberton, Northcliffe has a pioneer museum and the popular and picturesque Lane Poole Falls. Windy Harbour, on the coast south of Northcliffe, is something of a hippie hangout and, true to its name, is very windy. The cliffs around here are popular with rockclimbers and there's a great lighthouse at Point D'Entrecaustaux.

BRIDGETOWN (population 1500)

A quiet country town in an area of karri forests and farmland, Bridgetown has some old buildings including Blechynden House. Built of mud and clay by the area's first settler in 1862, it has been restored by the National Trust.

Places to Stay

Bridgetown has an associate *Youth Hostel* (tel (097) 61 1934) which is housed in a historic mud-brick hotel built in 1870. It's on the corner of Steere and Roe Sts and cost $4.50 a night.

NANNUP (population 550)

Continuing west from Bridgetown you reach Nannup with the largest jarrah sawmill in WA and the fine old Colonial House, dating from 1895. Boyup Brook (population 650) has a number of points of interest including a fauna reserve and a large butterfly and beetle collection. Interesting features of the river valley here are the 'blackboys' and large granite boulders. Nearby is Norlup Pool with glacial rock formations, and Wilga with an old timber mill and vintage engines.

AUGUSTA & MARGARET RIVER

A popular holiday resort, Augusta (population 450) is only a little north of Cape Leeuwin with it's lighthouse and waterwheel dating back to 1895. Between here and Margaret River (population 800) to the north there are a number of limestone caves – they include the Jewel Cave, Lake Cave and Mammoth Cave, where fossilised skeletons of Tasmanian tigers have been found. In all, 120 caves have been discovered between Cape Leeuwin and Cape Naturaliste but only these three, and Yallingup Cave near Busselton, are open to the public.

There are some fine beaches and good surfing spots between Augusta and the town of Margaret River, which is prettily situated on – you guessed it – the Margaret River. The Augusta-Margaret River Tourist Bureau is on the corner of the Bussell Highway and Wallcliffe Rd. The direct Augusta-Margaret River-Busselton road runs slightly inland but the old road running right along the coast is a good alternative. The coast here has real variety – cliff faces, long beaches pounded by rolling surf and calm sheltered bays.

Places to Stay

There's an associate *Youth Hostel* (tel 58 1545) on Molloy St, adjacent to the Blackwood River estuary and 500 metres north of the Augusta town centre. Apart from this and the on-site vans at the various caravan parks, there is very little in the way of cheap accommodation in the area. Some of the holiday flats have reasonable rates but mostly on a weekly basis.

BUSSELTON (population 6500)

On the shores of Geographe Bay you can see relics of the founding family of the 1830s in Prospect Villa, now a small museum in the centre of town. Like Bunbury further north, Busselton is a popular holiday resort. The town also has a cinema museum with a collection of early cinematic equipment, the National Trust Wonnerup House of 1859 and, until it was shortened by a cyclone in 1978, the longest timber jetty in Australia. Yallingup, to the south-west is a Mecca for surfing enthusiasts. Near there is Yallingup Cave and some fine coastal viewpoints such as Cape Naturaliste. Dunsborough (population 400) is a pleasant little town with fine beaches like Meelup, Eagle Bay and Bunker Bay, just to the west of Busselton. The Bannamah Wild Life Park is two km from the town.

Places to Stay

Busselton has a tourist bureau in the civic centre. There are many, many guest-houses, holiday flats and caravan parks along this stretch of coast. Guest-houses are typically $12 to $15 for bed & breakfast.

BUNBURY (population 22,000)

As well as being a port, industrial town and holiday resort, Bunbury is also where the blue manna crabs – a gourmet's delight – are found. The town's old buildings include King's Cottage, which now houses a museum. The Shell Museum on Mangles St has a collection of shells, minerals and Aboriginal artefacts. Two old steam trains, the *Leschenault Lady* and the *Koombana Queen*, make trips from the town. The tourist information centre is in the Old Government School Buildings on Arthur St.

AUSTRALIND (population 800)

Australind, yet another holiday resort, is a pleasant 11 km drive from Bunbury. The town takes it's name from an 1840s plan to make it a port for trade with India. The plan never worked but the strange name (Australia-India) remains. Australind has a tiny church just four by seven metres, said to be the smallest in Australia. There's also a motorcycle museum and a gemstone museum in the town as well as the Wellesley Wildlife Park nearby.

INLAND

Inland from the south-west coast, interesting centres include Harvey (population 2500) in a popular bushwalking area of rolling green hills to the north of Bunbury. There are dam systems and some beautiful waterfalls near here and the Yalgorup National Park is north of town. There's a tourist office on Young St.

Further south of Bunbury on the South Western Highway, Donnybrook (population 1200) is in the centre of an apple growing area. Collie (population 7700) is WA's only coal town and has a historical museum and a steam locomotive museum. There is some pleasant bushwalking country around the town and plenty of wild flowers in season.

Wheatlands

Stretching north from the Albany coastal region to north of the Great Eastern Highway (the Perth-Coolgardie road) is the WA wheatfields region. The area is noted for its unusual rock formations, best known of which is Wave Rock near Hyden, and for its many Aboriginal rock carvings.

CUNDERDIN & MECKERING

Meckering was badly damaged by an earthquake in 1968 and the Agricultural Museum in Cunderdin (population 700) has exhibits related to that quake. The museum is housed in an old pumping station used on the gold-fields water pipeline. Further east, Kellerberrin (population 1100) has a historical museum in the old courthouse of 1897 and is overlooked by a hill, named Killabin by Aboriginals.

MERREDIN (population 3500)

On the Perth-Kalgoorlie railway line and the Great Eastern Highway, Merredin has a National Trust restored homestead and the old railway station is also preserved as a museum.

Not far to the north of Merredin are some interesting rock formations around Koorda.

SOUTHERN CROSS (population 800)

Although the gold quickly gave out, Southern Cross was the first gold-rush town on the WA gold-fields. The big rush soon moved further east to Coolgardie and Kalgoorlie. Like the name of the town itself, Southern Cross's streets are also named after the stars and constellations. Situated 378 km east of Perth, this is really the end of the wheatlands area and the start of the desert, and when travelling by train the change is very noticeable. In the spring the sandy plains around Southern Cross are carpeted with wildflowers.

HYDEN & WAVE ROCK

Just three km from the tiny town of Hyden is the unusual rock formation known as Wave Rock. It's a real surfer's delight – the perfect wave, 15 metres high and frozen in solid rock. Wave Rock is 350 km from Perth and is one of WA's major tourist attractions. The curling rock is marked with different colour bands.

Other interesting rock formations in the area bear names like Hippo's Yawn and The Humps; Bates Caves have Aboriginal rock paintings and there's a wildlife sanctuary not far from Wave Rock itself.

OTHER TOWNS

There is a fine rock formation known as Kokerbin, an Aboriginal word for 'high place', near Bruce Rock. Corrigin (population 900) has a folk museum. Jilakin Rock is 18 km from Kulin (population 350) while further south-east, Lake Grace (population 600) is near the lake of the same name.

Narrogin (population 5000) is an agricultural centre, with the Courthouse Museum in the town and a couple of unusual rock formations near the town. Dumbleyung (population 300) also has a historical museum. Wagin (population 1500) has an art gallery and some fine old buildings plus there is good bushwalking around Mt Latham, six km to the west.

The Great Northern Highway

Although most people heading for the north-west and the Kimberley will travel up the coast, there is also the more direct route via the Great Northern Highway. The route takes a more or less straight line from Perth to Newman and then skirts around the eastern edge of the Pilbara to Port Hedland via Marble Bar. Total distance is 1670 km and the last 480 km from the mining town of Newman is not yet surfaced.

This is not exactly the most interesting road in Australia – in fact for most of the way it passes through country which is flat, dull and dreary in the extreme. Once you've passed through the old gold towns of the Murchison River gold-fields – Mt Magnet, Cue and Meekatharra – there's really nothing for another 400 km until you reach Newman.

Getting There

Greyhound have three buses a week up to Newman ($84) via Meekatharra ($28). The trip takes about 15 hours to Newman

and once a week it continues on to Port Hedland.

The Newman-Port Hedland sector costs $37. Skywest (booked through TAA) fly to Meekatharra from Perth on weekdays for $183 one-way.

MT MAGNET (population 600)

Mt Magnet is an old gold-mining town which is today a popular stopping point on the long drive north.

CUE (population 300)

Like Mt Magnet, this was once an important centre in the Murchison gold-fields.

There are still some interesting old buildings of solid stone in the town. Mining ghost towns in the area include Day Dawn and Big Bell.

MEEKATHARRA (population 1000)

Meekatharra is still a mining centre today. At one time it was a railhead for cattle brought down from the Northern Territory and the east Kimberley. There are various old gold towns in the area and from Meekatharra you can approach the WA gold-fields area around Kalgoorlie from the north. It's a bit over 700 km to Kalgoorlie, more than half of it on dirt roads.

Up the Coast

The road up the coast is now surfaced practically all the way to Darwin. There is only a 100 km stretch between Fitzroy Crossing and Halls Creek left and that's due for completion some time in 1986. It's still a hell of a long way but it's no longer a rough endurance test. There's a fair bit to see along the way so you can easily break the journey up over a few days even if you travel straight through. But don't underestimate it – Perth-Port Hedland is 1950 km by the coast and in summer they can be very hot km.

Getting There

Ansett WA fly from Perth to Geraldton ($90), Carnarvon ($148), and Learmonth (for Exmouth) ($185) plus other centres further up the west coast in the north-west Kimberley region.

Westrail have bus services to Geraldton ($30) daily except Saturday with several services on Friday. Greyhound have three buses a week up the coast to Port Hedland and beyond, Ansett Pioneer have four and Deluxe have three. From Perth fares are: Geraldton $52, Carnarvon $63, Minilya (turn-off for Exmouth) $80 and Nanutarra (turn-off for Wittenoom) also $80 with Greyhound. Ansett Pioneer fares are about the same.

PERTH TO GERALDTON (424 km)

From Perth you follow the Brand Highway past the turn-off to Jurien and the Pinnacles Desert, which is a major tourist attraction. It's a wide sandy plain studded with weird-looking limestone pillars of varying sizes, ranging from stony 'twigs' to columns over six feet tall. Eventually the main road comes back to the coast at Dongara (population 1100) – a pleasant little port with fine beaches and lots of rock lobsters! Russ Cottage, open Sundays and public holidays from 2 to 5 pm, is a local attraction. Nearby is the similar small port of Port Denison (population 500).

Further north, only about 20 km south of Geraldton, Greenough was once a busy little mining town but now it's just a quiet farming centre. The Pioneer Museum, which is open daily from 10 am to 4 pm, dates from 1860. A few km east is the railway station at Walkway. It's open Saturday, Sunday and Wednesday from 2 to 4 pm.

INLAND

The area inland from Dongara and Geraldton is noted for its spring wild-flowers. Mingenew (population 400), Morawa (population 800) and Mullewa (population 900) all have brilliant wild-flower displays in the spring. Tallering Peak and Gorges, 58 km north of Mullewa, are particularly splendid. Mingenew has a small museum while Carnamah (population 400) is near the Yarra Yarra Lake, noted for its birdlife. This area is also a gateway to the Murchison gold-fields and there are old gold-mining centres and ghost towns around Perenjori (population 300). Yalgoo is a tiny outback settlement, way out in the middle of nowhere, about halfway between Geraldton and Mt Magnet.

GERALDTON (population 21,000)

The major town in the mid-west region, Geraldton is situated on a spectacular stretch of coast. It's 427 km north of Perth and has a fine climate, particularly in the winter. Geraldton was probably one of the first European 'settlements' in Australia. In 1629 the Dutch East Indiaman *Batavia* was wrecked on the Abrolhos Islands, about 60 km off the coast. Before the survivors could be rescued from the inhospitable island a bloody mutiny took place and the Dutch commander hanged some of the mutineers and dumped two of them off on the mainland – never to be seen again. In the following century at least two more Dutch ships were wrecked here.

The Maritime Museum tells the story of the early wrecks and has assorted relics from the Dutch ships. The museum is open daily but for rather varied hours. Geraldton also has a Shell Museum at 240 Chapman St and a Gem & Mineral Museum on the corner of Mark and Pope Sts, both open daily. Geraldton's St Francis Xavier Cathedral is just one of a number of buildings in Geraldton and the West Australian mid-west designed by Monsignor John Hawes, a strange priest-cum-architect who later left WA in 1939 and spent the rest of his life (he died in 1956) a hermit on an island in the Carribean. You can look out over Geraldton from the Waverley Heights Lookout on Brede St; view the lobster boats at Fisherman's Wharf on the end of Marine Terrace or go to Point Moore Lighthouse, in operation since 1878.

There are flights to Geraldton from Perth, or buses from the East Perth bus terminal. The Geraldton Tourist Bureau (tel 21 3999) is on the corner of Chapman Rd and Durlacher St and is open Monday to Friday, 9 am to 5 pm, Saturday 9 am to 12 noon.

Places to Stay

The Geraldton *Youth Hostel* (tel (099) 21 2549) is at 80 Francis St and costs $5 per night. On Marine Terrace in the centre at number 184, the *Swansea Guest House* (tel 21 2205) charges $10 including a light breakfast. Close by is the *Shepheard's Hotel* (tel 21 3368) with bed & breakfast for $15. Further along at 311 Marine Terrace is *Palumbo's Lodge* (tel 21 4770) with bed & breakfast for $12.

Motels in Geraldton are not cheap. One of the cheapest is the *Auto* (tel 21 2455), on Brand Highway about three km south of the centre, where singles/doubles cost $26/37.

Dutch Shipwrecks

During the 17th century ships of the Dutch East India Company, sailing out to Batavia in Java from Europe, would head due east from the horn of Africa then beat up the Western Australian coast to Indonesia. It only took a small miscalculation for a ship to run aground on the coast and a few did just that, usually with disastrous results. The west coast of Australia is often decidedly inhospitable and the chances of rescue at that time were remote.

Four wrecks of Dutch East Indiamen have been located including the earliest, and in many ways the most interesting, the *Batavia*. In 1629, the *Batavia* went aground in the Abrolhos Islands near Geraldton and the survivors set up camp, sent off a rescue party to Batavia (now Jakarta) in the ship's boat and waited. It took three months before a rescue party arrived and in that time a mutiny took place and more than 120 of the survivors had been murdered. The two ringleaders of the mutiny were unceremoniously dumped on the coast.

In 1656 the *Vergulde Draeck* (Gilt Dragon) struck a reef about 100 km north of Perth and although a party made their way to Batavia, no trace, other than a few scattered coins, was found of the other survivors who straggled ashore. The *Zuytdorp* ran aground beneath the towering cliffs near the mouth of the Murchison River in 1712. Wine bottles and the remains of fires were later found on the cliff top but again no trace of survivors.

In 1727 the *Zeewyk* followed the ill-fated *Batavia* to destruction in the Abrolhos Islands. Again a small party of survivors made their way to Batavia but many of the remaining sailors died before rescue came. Many relics from these shipwrecks, particularly the *Batavia*, can be seen today in the museums in Fremantle and Geraldton.

GERALDTON TO CARNARVON (482 km)

Northampton (population 750) is the jumping-off point for the Hutt River Province where a local farmer decided that tourism must be an easier game than farming, appointed himself 'Prince Leonard of Hutt' and seceded from Australia. Today 60,000 people visit his 'independent principality' annually although it's actually nothing much more than a bare outback station. The turn-off is north of Northampton, towards Kalbarri.

The area inland from Northampton is noted for its wildflowers in the spring. The town was founded to exploit lead and copper discovered in 1848 and lead is still produced here. An early mine manager's house, Chiverton House, is now a fine Municipal Museum. The stone building was constructed between 1868 and 1875 using local materials. Horrocks Beach, 21 km away, is a popular holiday resort. The nearby Gwalia Church cemetery also tells its tales of the early days.

Lynton, near Port Gregory, has the ruins of a convict hiring station. Kalbarri (population 820) is a pleasant coastal holiday resort in the Kalbarri National Park. There are many spectacular gorges on the Murchison River in the park and from Kalbarri it's only 35 km to the Loop and Z-Bend, two particularly impressive gorges.

On north towards Carnarvon it's a long, dull, boring and often very hot run. At the Overlander Roadhouse, 290 km north of Geraldton, is the turn-off to Shark Bay, a popular fishing spot but with plenty of sharks. Hamelin Pool is a marine reserve and at Monkey Mia, 26 km from Denham, dolphins come right in to the beach; it's possible pat and play with them in the shallows with no danger from sharks. There's a caravan park here with campsites for $3 per person or on-site vans for $18.50 but the facilities are very basic.

Denham (population 400) is the most westerly town in Australia and was once a pearling port. Today prawns are the local money maker. In 1616 Dutch explorer Dirk Hartog landed on the island in Shark Bay which now bears his name.

CARNARVON (population 5100)

At the mouth of the Gascoyne River, Carnarvon is noted for its tropical fruit production, particularly bananas. Subsurface water, which flows even when the river is dry, is tapped to irrigate the riverside plantations. Solar salt is also produced near Carnarvon. On the nearby Brown's Range the 'big dish' is the huge 26.5-metre reflector of the Overseas Telecommunications Commission earthstation. This was once a NASA station and there's a museum beside the tourist office relating its role in NASA space shots. The main street of Carnarvon is 40 metres wide, a reminder of the days when camel trains used to pass through here.

Pelican Point, only five km from town, is a good swimming and picnic spot but you'll need four-wheel drive to get to Bush Bay (turn-off 20 km) or New Beach (40 km). Other attractions in the vicinity are the spectacular blowholes 70 km north; there's a fine beach about one km south of the blowhole. Cape Couvier, where salt is loaded for Japan, is 100 km

north. Rocky Pool is a superb swimming hole, 55 km inland along the Gascoyne River. Remote Gascoyne Junction is 164 km inland from Carnarvon in the gemstone-rich Kennedy Range.

The Carnarvon District Tourist Bureau is in the Civic Centre on Robinson St.

Places to Stay

The *Carnarvon Hotel-Motel* (tel 41 1181) on Olivia Terrace charges $12 per person. There are numerous caravan parks with the most central being the *Carnarvon Tourist Centre* (tel 41 1438) on Robinson St with campsites for $3 per person or on-site vans for $47 per week.

Getting There

You can fly here from Perth for $148 or from Geraldton for $100 with Ansett WA. Ansett Pioneer and Greyhound buses stop here on the Perth-Darwin run. From Perth the fare is $62, to Broome $85 and to Darwin $185.

EXMOUTH (population 2600)

The road to Exmouth forks off the main coast road and runs up to the US Navy Base at the top of the North-West Cape. Here a very hush-hush communications base is marked by 13 very-low-frequency transmitter station towers. Twelve of them are higher than the Eiffel Tower but they're there to support the 13th, which is 396 metres high, the tallest structure in the southern hemisphere. The base cost almost $100 million to build.

Otherwise Exmouth is chiefly noted for its excellent fishing although there are also some fine beaches on the Exmouth Gulf. This is also a productive prawning area.

Exmouth is a new town built to service the navy base and to reach you have to travel along a long dirt road, but I've got a soft spot for the town as it was the first place I set foot in Australia. A few years back I hitched a ride from Bali on a yacht and ended up here.

CARNARVON TO PORT HEDLAND
(855 km)

After the Exmouth turn-off the road runs inland from the coast for some distance before rejoining it almost at Dampier. Onslow (population 600), on the coast, is some distance off the road. This was an early pearling port but now exists mainly to service the oil fields on Barrow Island. The town was actually shifted to its present location from its original site when cyclones seemed to arrive simply too often. The climate is OK in the April to September period but in the wet this is still 'cyclone city'.

Karratha (population 8400) is a dormitory town for the area, Dampier being the main working centre. On King Bay, Dampier (population 2500) faces the islands of the Dampier Archipelago. They were named after the English pirate-explorer William Dampier who visited the area in 1699 and immortalised himself as not only one of Australia's first knockers but also its first whinging pom – he thought it was a pretty miserable place. Dampier is the port for the Mt Tom Price and Paraburdoo iron ore deposits. The huge port facilities can handle ships up to 230,000 tons and there are also ore treatment works. Solar salt is also loaded for export. Permits are needed to inspect the port facilities. Off shore on the north-west shelf huge natural-gas fields are in the process of being developed.

Roebourne, only 32 km east, is the oldest active town of the north-west. It had an early history of gold and copper mining and there are still some fine old buildings to be seen. The town was once connected to Cossack, 13 km away on the coast, by a tramway. Cossack was also once a bustling town when in the late 1800s it became a district port. Its boom was short lived and from the early 1900s to the present it was nearly a ghost town – 'nearly' only because there have always been one or two residents in town. Today there are plans for restoration as the fairly remote Pilbara region becomes more

intriguing to visitors, much the way the Broome area has. There are excellent beaches in the area and the cooler, drier months are best for a visit.

In Cossack itself, the typically solid government buildings have been restored and the old general store has been renovated. Others are being worked on but bringing the place back to life will take some years. In 1984 Cyclone Chloe added to the damage that time had caused. There's a museum and the old graveyard to visit but as yet there is no hotel or even a campground. In the meantime, the modern port here is Wickham (population 2400) on Cape Lambert with its three-km-long jetty. In the summer months it's wise to keep well clear of the sea, inviting it may look but the water is full of nasties and swimming can be dangerous. Ask the locals as to which places are OK.

Port Hedland
Population: 11,500

Once Western Australia's fastest growing city, this is the port from where the Pilbara's iron ore production is shipped off to Japan – to return a few months later as shiny new Toyotas. The town is built on an island, connected to the mainland by causeways. The main highway into Port Hedland enters over a causeway three km long. The port handles the largest annual tonnage of any Australian port. Like other towns along the coast it's also a centre for salt production, huge 'dunes' of salt can be seen six km from the town.

Port Hedland had an early history with grazing in the area from 1864, then a fleet of 150 pearling luggers in the 1870s before the Marble Bar gold-rush put the town even more firmly on the map. By 1946 the population had dwindled away to a a mere 150. The port is on a mangrove-fringed inlet – there's good fishing, crabs, oysters and lots of bird-life to be seen. As

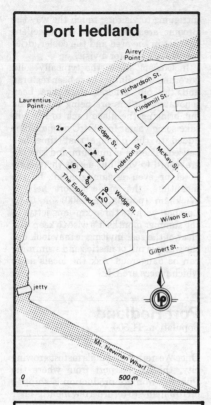

Port Hedland

Airey Point

Richardson St.

Laurentius Point

Kingsmill St.

2●

Edgar St.

●3
●4 ●5

Anderson St.

McKay St.

●6 ●7 ●8

The Esplanade

●9
●10

Wedge St.

Wilson St.

Gilbert St.

jetty

Mt. Newman Wharf

0   500 m

1 Hostel
2 Greyhound Buses
3 TAA
4 Picture Gardens
5 Tourist Office
6 Pier Hotel
7 Post Office
8 Airlines of WA & Ansett Pioneer
9 Bruno's Pizza
10 Esplanade Hotel

Port Hedland has grown, satellite towns have sprung up, both to handle the mining output of the area and also to accommodate the area's work-force.

You can visit the wharf area to see the huge ore carriers loaded without any prior arrangement. There's a tour of the Mt Newman Mining Company's operations at Nelson's Point every weekday at 2 pm. The bus leaves from the main gate at Wilson St. Next to the gate is a limestone ridge with Aboriginal carvings – if the site is locked you can borrow the key from the tourist office. The Drysdales Seashells International collection (plus gemstones and other items) is also worth inspecting.

Don't swim in the sea here – there's everything from sea snakes and stonefish to blue-ringed octopus and sharks. There's an Olympic swimming pool by the Civic Centre and Pretty Pool is a safe tidal pool. October to March is the cyclone season in Port Hedland. The Aboriginal Progress Association sells Aboriginal artefacts opposite the tourist office. The Tourist Information Centre (tel 091 73 1650) is at 13 Wedge St and is open Monday to Friday from 9 am to 5 pm, Saturday from 9 am to 12 noon. TAA, Ansett WA, Greyhound and the post office are all on Wedge St.

Places to Stay Geoff Schafer runs the hostel at 3A Kingsmill St. It's a bit rough and ready but friendly and costs $6 a night. At 20 Richardson St is the *Backpackers Hostel* (tel 73 2198). It's open from 6 am to 11 pm, has kitchen and laundry facilities and charges $5 but you need your own sleeping bag or linen.

The *Pier Hotel* (tel 73 1488) on the Esplanade has expensive motel rooms for $28/38 for singles/doubles. Just down at the corner with Anderson St, the *Esplanade Hotel* (tel 73 1798) is $28/34 – also expensive, like everything in Port Hedland. There are a couple of motels in town but they're prices are totally over the top.

You can camp in South Hedland by the airport or more conveniently in Port Hedland at the *Cooke Point Caravan Park* (tel 73 1271), three km from the centre on the waterfront. Camping there costs $3 per person but there are no on-site vans, as there are at the other two sites.

Places to Eat

The *Pier* and the *Esplanade* hotels do counter meals and bar snacks at lunchtime. There are also a number of coffee bars and other places where you can get a pie or pastie.

The *Hedland Hotel* does excellent value counter meals and the air conditioning in here is really popular in the summer. Counter meals in the evening are available only on Friday and Saturday nights until 8 pm. There are plenty of supermarkets if you want to put your own food together.

Getting There

Air You can fly to Port Hedland from Darwin ($248) five times a week or Perth ($190) up to five times daily with Ansett WA, which also flies to other north-west towns, or TAA. Phone numbers are Ansett WA 73 1777 and TAA 73 2222.

Bus Ansett Pioneer, Greyhound and Deluxe have services from Perth to Port Hedland. Some of the Greyhound services take the inland route via Newman and Marble Bar rather than going up the coast.

North of Port Hedland there are two Ansett Pioneer, two Greyhound and three Deluxe services through to Broome ($37), Derby ($56) and Darwin ($140) each week.

Travel time for the 1728 km trip from Perth to Port Hedland is about 24 hours; Port Hedland to Darwin is about 2600 km and takes 34 hours.

Getting Around

Buses arrive right in the centre of Port Hedland on Wedge St. The airport is about 10 km out – the only way to get there is by taxi for $15. There's a reasonably regular bus service between Port Hedland and South Hedland – it takes 40 minutes to an hour and costs $1.20. You can hire cars at the airport from Hertz, Budget or Avis.

The Pilbara

The Pilbara is the iron ore producing area which accounts for much of WA's prosperity – from some of the hottest country on earth. Gigantic machines are used to tear the dusty red ranges apart. It's isolated, harsh and fabulously wealthy. The Pilbara towns are almost all company towns – they're either mining centres where the ore is wrenched from the earth or ports from where it's shipped abroad. Exceptions are the beautiful gorges of Wittenoom and earlier historic mining centres like Marble Bar.

Places to Stay

There are campsites and motels in the various Pilbara towns.

Getting There

Greyhound have three buses a week from Perth to Newman – 15 hours, $84. One of them continues through to Port Hedland. Services are the same in the opposite direction – Port Hedland-Newman takes eight hours and costs $37.

There is no bus service to Wittenoom although it is sometimes possible to get on a tour bus from Port Hedland, otherwise you really need your own transport. Most of the roads in the Pilbara are dirt. The Great Northern Highway is surfaced as far as Newman but the rest of the way north through Marble Bar is all dirt. A new surfaced highway is being built from Hedland to Wittenoom, but until that's finished, it's 295 km of dirt. From Wittenoom to Newman via Roy Hill is 268 km and to Roebourne via Millstream it's 289 km. From Nanutarra on the North-West Coastal Highway to Wittenoom is 377 km.

INLAND TO WITTENOOM

A little beyond Roebourne a road turns inland to Wittenoom. It's 264 km from the turn-off and there are a number of interesting spots along the way. The road passes through the Chichester Range National Park where Python Pool is a pleasant swimming hole and picnic spot. The small Millstream National Park is a little distance off the road – a pleasant oasis with pools, trees, ferns and lilies. Water from the natural spring here is piped to Dampier, Karratha, Wickham and Cape Lambert.

WITTENOOM (population 250)

Wittenoom is the Pilbara's tourist centre. It had an earlier history as an asbestos mining town but mining finally halted in 1966 and it is the magnificent gorges of the Hamersley Range which now draws people to the town. Wittenoom is at the northern end of the Hamersley Range National Park and the most famous gorge, Wittenoom Gorge, is immediately

south of the town. A surfaced road runs the 13 km to this gorge, passing old asbestos mines and a number of smaller gorges and pretty pools.

Like other gorges in central Australia, those of the Hamersley Range are spectacular both in their sheer rocky faces and their varied colours. In the early spring the park is often carpeted in colourful wildflowers. Travel down the Newman road 24 km and there's a turn-off to the Yampire Gorge where blue veins of asbestos can be seen in the rock. Fig Tree Well, in the gorge, was once used by Afghan camel drivers as a watering point. The road continues through Yampire Gorge to Dales Gorge but only the first couple of km of its 45 km length can be reached. On this same route you can get to Circular Pool and a nearby lookout,

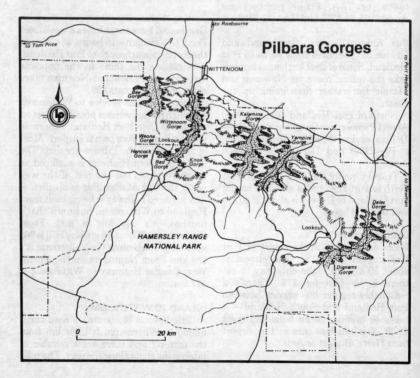

Pilbara Gorges

and by a footpath to the bottom of the Fortescue Falls.

The Joffre Falls road will take you to Oxer's Lookout at the junction of the Red, Weano and Hancock Gorges. Following the main road to Tom Price you pass through the small Rio Tinto Gorge, 43 km from Wittenoom, and just beyond this point, the Hamersley Range is only four km from the road. Mt Meharry (1245 metres), the highest mountain in Western Australia, is in the south-east of the Hamersley Range National Park.

If you're setting off on foot to do some exploring, be sure you can find your way back as the bush looks all the same and there are no people and no water. Notify somebody that you're going. For the more energetic there's a walk starting at the Asbestos Mine about 13 km from Wittenoom on the surfaced road. Walk up Wittenoom Gorge, then up Red Gorge (some swimming may be required!) until you come out at the pool below Oscar's Lookout. Then proceed up Hancocks Gorge, cross the road and follow the footpath into Weano Gorge, which can be followed back to the junction pool – it involves two quite scary climbs, so be warned! The circuit is a good day's walk – get detailed directions from the Wittenoom Tourist Bureau on Second Avenue. Weano Gorge, the most spectacular one, can be easily approached from near Oscar's Lookout and can be followed down almost to the junction pool with no difficulty.

NEWMAN (population 5500)

At Newman, a town which only came into existence in the 1970s, Mt Whaleback is being systematically taken apart and railed down to the coast. It's a solid mountain of iron ore and every day up to 120,000 tonnes of ore are produced, a task which requires moving nearly 300,000 tonnes of material. After crushing, the ore is loaded into 144-car, two-km-long trains which are sent down the 426 km railway line, Australia's longest private railway,

to Port Hedland from where it is shipped overseas. Guided tours of the operations are available from the Mt Newman Company office several times daily in winter and once a day at 1 pm in the summer. The town of Newman is a modern, green company town built solely to service the mine.

TOM PRICE & PARABURDOO

Similar mining activities are also carried on in these two towns. The ore is railed to the coast at Dampier. Check with the Hamersley Iron office about inspecting the mine works.

GOLDSWORTHY & SHAY GAP

Goldsworthy was the first Pilbara iron town and, like Newman, its production is shipped to Port Hedland and loaded on to bulk carriers at Finucane Island. At one time Mt Goldsworthy was 132 metres high but it's now a big hole in the ground. Since mining operations shifted 70 km east to Shay Gap, the mine at Goldsworthy is starting to fill with water and there's only a few workers living here now maintaining the electricity generators which run the massive shovels and provide town power at Shay Gap (population 1000). Both these towns were badly hit by Cyclone Enid in 1980.

MARBLE BAR (population 350)

Reputed to be the hottest place in Australia, Marble Bar had a period in the 1920s when for 160 consecutive days the temperature topped 37°C (100°F)! On one occasion in 1905 the mercury soared to 49.1°C. From October to March, days over 40°C are common – it's uncomfortable. The town is 193 km south-east of Port Hedland and takes its name from a bar of red jasper across the Coongan River, five km from the town. The town came into existence when gold was found here in 1891. At its peak the population was 5000 and other minerals as well as gold are still mined here today. In the town the old Government Buildings of

1895 are still in use. In late winter, as the spring flowers begin to bloom, Marble Bar is actually quite a pretty place.

The yearly race meeting attracts a large, noisy crowd from all over the Pilbara and is quite a spectacle.

Broome
Population: 3700

Broome is a delightful old pearling port. It's a small dusty place characterised by its Chinatown, looking for all the world like a set from a western movie – wooden side-walks and all. Although still isolated, Broome has recently been 'discovered' – the surfacing of the generally dull 624 km from Port Hedland across the fringes of the Great Sandy Desert has sparked a mini-tourist boom and perhaps surprisingly, it's become something of a travellers' centre.

Broome's colourful early history was based on pearling, established here in the 1880s. At its peak in the early 1900s Broome had 400 pearling luggers worked by 3000 men and it supplied 80% of the world's mother-of-pearl. Today only a dozen or so pearlers still operate. Pearl diving was a very unsafe occupation, as Broome's Japanese cemetery attests. The divers were from various Asian countries and consequently the town has a distinct oriental feel. In August the Shinju Matsuri or 'Festival of the Pearl' remembers those early pearling days.

Information

The shiny new Broome tourist office (tel 92 1176) is right across the road from the old crashed Garuda DC-3, not far from Chinatown. It's open from Monday to Friday from 9 am to 5 pm and on Saturday from 9 am to 12 noon.

Chinatown

Chinatown refers to the old part of town although there is really only one block or so that is both Chinese and historic. The plain and simple wooden buildings that line Carnarvon St house Chinese merchants as well as restaurants and shops. The bars on the windows aren't there due to outlaw gangs on horseback but rather to minimise cyclone damage.

Sun Pictures, the old open-air cinema dating from 1916 is near Short St and is once again showing movies. The Roebuck Bay Hotel still rocks along despite its sparkling new motel section. A noisy night at the Roebuck is like one of those cartoons where the walls of the bar continuously quake in and out and bodies come flying through the swing doors with reasonable regularity. Great fun, just stand clear of the occasional fights!

Note the Carnarvon St street sign which is written in English, Chinese, Arabic, Japanese and Malay. Over on Dampier Terrace near Short St by the dock area is a model of a Chinese temple encased in a big glass box. Most of the restaurants are in this part of town as is one of the campgrounds.

New Town

The centre of Broome's new development

1	Broome Caravan Park
2	Tourist Bureau
3	DC-3 Museum
4	Sun Pictures
5	Bakery
6	Streeter's Jetty (luggers)
7	Roebuck Bay Hotel
8	Pearl & shell shops
9	Pearl Lugger
10	Ali Baba Kasbah Restaurant
11	Aboriginal Gallery
12	Wing's Restaurant
13	Mango Jack's
14	Post Office
15	Airlines of WA
16	Library & Civic Centre
17	Wackett Aircraft
18	Mangrove Motel
19	Continental Hotel
20	Tropicana Motel
21	Bay Bistro Restaurant
22	Museum
23	Pioneer Cemetery
24	Coolarabooloo Hostel

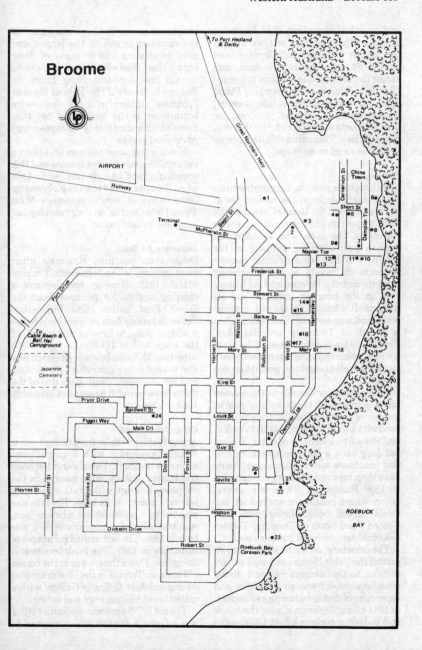

Broome

AIRPORT

Runway

Terminal

Port Drive

To Cable Beach &
Bali Hai
Campground

Japanese
Cemetery

Pryor Drive

Bardwell St

Piggot Way

Male Crt

Haynes St

Hunter St

Pembroke Rd

Dora St

Forrest St

Dickson Drive

To Port Hedland
& Derby

Great Northern Hwy

Carnarvon St

China
Town

Short St

Dampier Tce

Bagot St

McPherson St

Napier Tce

Frederick St

Stewart St

Barker St

Herbert St

Walcott St

Robinson St

Mary St

Weld St

Mary St

King St

Louis St

Guy St

Saville St

Hopton St

Robert St

Roebuck Bay
Caravan Park

Dampier Tce

ROEBUCK
BAY

• 1

• 3

• 2

9 •

6 •

4 • • 5

• 7   • 8

12 •
• 13

11 • • 10

14 •
• 15

• 16

• 17

• 18

19 •

20 •

21 •
• 22

• 23

and growth is away from old Chinatown in the southern portion of town around the corner of Dampier Terrace and Saville St. The museum is here, and across the street is the modern but semi-Chinese looking Seaview Shopping Plaza. The Tropicana Motel is also nearby. Across Dampier Terrace you can see beached boats at low tide and further out, Roebuck Bay. There are a couple of places to eat here and some shops.

Pearling

You'll often see pearling luggers drawn up by Streeter's Jetty in the mangroves at the end of Short St. Beside Carnarvon St there's a preserved lugger on display with statues of the men who founded the modern pearl farming industry in the region. The Broome Historical Society Museum on Saville St has interesting exhibits on both Broome and its history and on the pearling industry and its dangers. It's housed in the old customs house and is open from 10 am to 2 pm but is closed on Thursday and Saturday. Even these hours aren't fixed as the place is run by volunteers and often there aren't enough people around to warrant keeping it open.

Along Dampier Terrace in Chinatown are a number of shops selling pearls, mother-of-pearl and shells. They're quite good with some interesting stuff to look at and some fine jewellery. Mother-of-pearl has long been a Broome speciality and this continues today. Buccaneer Pearls has a shop here and a factory you can visit at 1690 Hunter St. There are several others where pearls are worked on and shells carved before being sold. The Golden Pearl Shop on Dampier Terrace has some second-hand books as well.

The cemetery, on the outskirts of town just off the Cable Beach road, also vividly testifies to the dangers of pearl diving when equipment was so primitive and knowledge of diving techniques so limited. In 1914 alone, 33 divers died of the bends and in 1908 a cyclone killed 150 seamen caught out at sea. The Japanese section of the cemetery is one of the largest and most interesting and so many of those buried there died very young. You can be certain few Japanese hung round in Broome to die of old age. Behind the neat Japanese section with its impressive tombstones is the interesting but run-down section containing European and Aboriginal graves.

Rivalries between pearlers of different nationalities was always intense and this sometimes took an ugly turn, as in 1937 when Europeans fled town as Koepangers (from what is now Indonesian West Timor) went on the rampage seeking out Japanese in particular.

Japanese Air Raid

Other than pearling, Broome's other great memory is the Japanese air-raid of March 1942. Broome had become a clearing station for refugees from the Dutch East Indies (now Indonesia). Seven Japanese Zero fighters had trailed a refugee plane to Broome and surprised the town with a 16-minute raid which wiped out 15 flying boats in Roebuck Bay and several other aircraft at the airstrip and left 70 people dead. Remains of the flying boats can still be seen out in muddy Roebuck Bay.

Other Attractions

Across Napier Terrace from Chinatown is Wing's Restaurant with a magnificent boab tree beside it. There's another boab tree behind, outside what used to be the old police lock-up, with a rather sad little tale on a plaque at its base. The tree was planted by a police officer when his son, who was killed in France in WW I, was born in 1898. The father died in Broome of sunstroke in 1920. The boab tree is still doing fine. Down the road near the corner of Dampier Terrace is the Goolarabooloo Aboriginal Arts & Crafts Gallery with a collection of boomerangs and gourds.

The old DC-3 opposite the tourist office was a Garuda aircraft which crashed in

Broome while on a charter operation. It was patched together and used as a unique tourist office for some years and is now a rather poor excuse for an aviation museum. Admission is $1 and it's only open from 9.30 am to 12 noon. On Weld St by the library and civic centre, there's a Wackett aircraft on display which used to belong to Horrie Miller, founder of Macrobertson Miller Airlines, now Ansett WA. He's buried in Broome cemetery.

There's an old pioneer cemetery by the old jetty site at the end of Robinson St. Nearby there's a park and small beach, which doesn't have a lot of sand but people do swim here. Out in Roebuck Bay at low tide the remains of several of the flying boats sunk by the Japanese can be seen. In the bay at the entrance to Dampier Creek, there's a landmark called Buccaneer Rock, dedicated to Captain William Dampier and his ship, the *Roebuck*. He is said to have careened his ship off it in 1699. You can see it from behind the Mangrove Hotel.

The old 1888 court house was once used to house the transmitting equipment for the old cable station here. There's also a small museum at the police station.

Ask at the tourist office about the 'Golden Staircase to the Moon', a phenomenon that occurs just a few times a year when the low tide and moon are just right. It's the effect of the moon shining on the rippling mud-flats.

Out of Town

Six km from town is Cable Beach, the most popular swimming beach. The telegraph cable used to cross to Java in Indonesia from here. The northern side of the beach is now a popular nude bathing beach. The beach here is a classic – white sand and turquoise waters as far as the eye can see. Wheeled windsurfers are available here for some sand sailing.

Just before reaching the beach, off Cable Beach road, is the British-owned Pearl Coast Wildlife Park, a new zoo which houses native birds and animals

and imported species that now breed in the wild. It's very large and animals lovers shouldn't mind the enclosures too much – they're spacious and look pleasant enough. Especially good is the bird collection with parrots, cockatoos and finches. All the well-known Australian animals are present including a couple of wary dingoes. It's open daily, except Thursday, from 10 am to 12 noon and from 2 to 5 pm, admission is $3. Next door is the crocodile farm with crocs brought in from the Fitzroy River.

There are other good beaches along Roebuck Bay to Gantheaume Point, seven km south of Broome. The cliffs there have been eroded into curious shapes and at low tide you may be able to find the 130-million-year-old dinosaur tracks although they haven't been spotted since the 1930s. There are casts of the tracks on the cliff tops, which is probably all you'll see.

At the end of Port Drive at Entrance Point, eight km from town, is the port which is deep enough for ocean-going vessels. If you ride out here, the small beach may be welcome for a cooling swim. Broome can have enormous tides – up to 11 metres in the spring.

There are several good fishing, swimming and camping spots outside Broome including among others Crab Creek, Willies Creek, Barred Creek, Quondon Beach and Manali.

Places to Stay

Not since the halcyon days of the pearling has Broome had an abundance of lodging options. Even now, despite its increased popularity as a tourist destination, the situation is not great and for a cheap bed you really need to bring a tent. Even for the less budget-minded, the choices are limited and overpriced at about $50 a night.

Although there is no youth hostel, one possible alternative worth checking is the *Goolarabooloo Hostel* (tel 92 1747) on Dora St at the end of Louis St. It's in an

Aboriginal compound area and though catering mainly to Aboriginals, it will take visitors. There are only a few rooms and they go for $10 including food, or $50 by the week. Meals are taken in the dining room in a separate building. The woman who runs it is friendly and helpful and hopes, if money is forthcoming, to open up a new hostel designed mainly for young travellers. Goolarabooloo is reached by continuing up the dirt road at the end of Louis St and it's on the left about 100 metres along. It's an idea to call ahead as the rooms are often occupied.

For a hotel, the legendary *Roebuck Bay Hotel* (tel 92 1221) at the corner of Carnarvon St and Napier Terrace in Chinatown is the cheapest but is still not cheap. Adequate rooms, without TV, in the old section are $35 single. In the new motel section rates are $42/52 for singles/doubles.

The *Continental Hotel* (tel 92 1002) is a modern place on Weld St at the corner of Louis St which charges $50 for a single, $58 double. The *Mangrove Motel* (tel 92 1303), between the Continental and Chinatown down near the water, is similarly priced at $48/60. From November to the end of March the *Tropicana Motel* (tel 92 1204) at the corner of Saville and Robinson Sts offers singles/doubles for $15/25 to 'Aussiepass' and 'Eagle Pass' holders. There are also a couple of pricey holiday resorts.

Fortunately there are three camping grounds although in the peak season they get very busy. Just on the edge of town is the *Broome Caravan Park* (tel 92 1776) along the Great Northern Highway past the tourist office. Campsites are $3.50 per person per night, on-site tents are $5 per person or $25 per week and on-site vans are $37/47 for single/double. There are also chalets for rent from $35 for two in the low season.

Also very central is the *Roebuck Bay Caravan Park* (tel 92 1366) on the waterfront at the south end of town at the end of Robinson St, two km from the tourist office. Camping is $4 per person or $20 per week. Caravan sites are $8 per person and there are extra charges for electricity.

Definitely the nicest place to camp is at the *Bali Hai Caravan Park* (tel 92 1375) out at Cable Beach. Campsites are $4 per person and there are no on-site vans. There are four-bed chalets available for $75 per night. It's strongly recommended that your tent is insect proof as the midges can be bad at times.

Since there's often such a shortage of space, a blind eye is turned to people camping in unofficial places. There are a host of quiet little turn-offs to the sand dunes along the road before Cable Beach, or just ask at the tourist office. They have a list of people who will let you camp in their backyards and use their facilities and they may also be able to suggest some other accommodation possibilities. If you're really stuck arriving late at night, the area of grass on the foreshore by the Cable Beach car park can be surprisingly comfortable.

Places to Eat

Finding a place to stay in Broome may be a real hassle but eating out is no sweat at all. *Kool Spot* is a sure sign of Broome's trendification – their food (breakfast and lunchtime only) would have been pretty odd in Broome not so long ago. Rolls, sandwiches, various fancy foods, exotic cakes, fruit juice and smoothies. It's very nice but not cheap.

Also seemingly out of place is the *Ali Baba Kasbah Restaurant*, at the corner of Napier and Dampier Terraces, with Lebanese and Italian foods. Pizza, shish kebab, felafels and tabouli, but also wiener schnitzel for $5.50. It's open in the evening and there are a few outdoor tables. It's a good place to sit with a cappuccino and watch the police paddy-wagon cruising in front of the bar, stopping occasionally to toss someone in the back.

Mango Jacks on Hamersley St and

Chipmonks on Short St dispense the usual fast food. Next door to Mango Jacks is a pizza place open from 5 pm with pizzas for about $6.

The *Roebuck Hotel* has several possibilities. The dining room meals are expensive, even breakfast is $4.50 to $6 and other meals are $6 to $8. In the quiet, spiffy new bar by the office, specials can be had for $4.50. Around the back entrance off Dampier Terrace in the old saloon bar, both beer and meals are cheaper. After 5 pm when everyone knocks off work, this place has an atmosphere conducive to heavy drinking.

Over in the newer part of town, both the *Continental Hotel* and the town's most expensive motel, the *Tropicana*, offer traditional counter meals from $5.50 in the Tropicana with a $9 carvery buffet on Sunday evening. Top choice out here however is the *Bay Bistro* at 384 Dampier Terrace across from the shopping centre. It's a very pleasant place overlooking the bay with a few tables outside on the lawn. Fish & chips at $3.30 through to all kinds of seafood for $6 to $9 and they also have take-aways.

Another place for a good meal is *Chin's* on Hamersley St off Napier Terrace near Mango Jacks, a friendly place serving Chinese food and a few Indonesian dishes, mostly in the $6 to $8 range. The cheapest thing on the menu, nasi goreng at $5.60, is excellent and the serving large. *Wing's* on Napier Terrace is more expensive and not as good. Other places come and go - a wander around Chinatown might turn up something new.

There's a bakery at the corner of Carnarvon and Short Sts. It's very good but tends to run out early. It's open from 7.30 am and also sells sandwiches, rolls and good breakfast treats.

Out at Cable Beach there's a take-away shop selling sandwiches, burgers and some basic foodstuffs such as bread, drinks and canned food.

Getting There

Air Ansett WA fly to Broome regularly on their Perth to Darwin route. From Perth the fare is $242, from Darwin $196. The Ansett WA office (tel 92 1101) is on the corner of Barker and Weld Sts.

Bus Greyhound buses leave from the tourist office both north and southbound on Wednesdays, Fridays and Sundays. Deluxe also leaves from the tourist office on Tuesday, Friday and Sunday northbound and on Monday, Wednesday and Friday heading south. Ansett Pioneer buses leave from the Tropicana Motel on Tuesdays and Fridays in both directions. Note that some arrivals and departures are either very late or very early. Fares include Port Hedland $37, Carnarvon $85, Perth $113, Fitzroy Crossing $39 and Darwin $105. The tourist office acts as agent for all bus lines and Ansett WA.

Getting Around

Airport Transport There are taxis and private cars to take you from the airport to your hotel and they ask about $4 - real highway robbery! If you're staying anywhere near Chinatown it's close enough to walk.

Around Town There is no public transport around Broome but you can hire bikes at a couple of places. Kabuki (tel 92 1487), beside the Roebuck Hotel, has top quality bikes for $10 a day or $8 for old rattlers. You can also hire them from the shop known just as 384 on Dampier Terrace which also has antiques and runs a book exchange. Their rates are $5 for a normal bike or $12 for a tandem, both for 24 hours. It's an easy area to ride around; it's flat and no problem riding out to Cable Beach (eight km) although you need to stay on the roads to prevent thorn punctures and if it's very windy the ride can be a real slog. Despite this, bikes are easily the best way to see the area.

Hertz, Budget and Letz have rent-a-car desks at the airport. You can hire

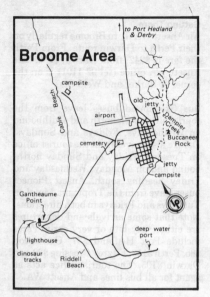

Broome Area

to Port Hedland & Derby

campsite

Cable Beach

old jetty

airport

Dampier Creek

cemetery

Buccaneer Rock

jetty

campsite

Gantheaume Point

deep water port

lighthouse

dinosaur tracks

Riddell Beach

Mokes for $18 per day plus 16c a km from Outback Car Hires on Hunter St (tel 92 1369) or Ricci's Moke Hire (tel 92 1557) which has similar prices.

Tours Happy Wheels offers day trips to sites out of town such as Lake Eyda – ask the tourist office for details. The Roebuck Hotel has a 15-seat bus it uses for tours to points of interest in and around town.

Camel Safaris leaving from Cable Beach and exploring the coastal area to the north can be booked at the Bali Hai take-away shop at the beach. One-day trips are $25 or five-day coastal caravans are $100 including food.

CAPE LEVEQUE ROAD
It's about 200 km from the turn-off nine km out of Broome to the Cape Leveque Lighthouse. About half-way is a diversion to the Beagle Bay Aboriginal Community with their beautiful church in the middle of a green. Inside is an altar stunningly decorated with mother-of-pearl. Just

before Cape Leveque is Lombadina Aboriginal Community with a church built from mangrove wood.

Cape Leveque itself has a lighthouse and two wonderful beaches. Beyond it is One Arm Point – yet another Aboriginal community. Take note that the communities won't want you to stay on their land, but if you want to see their church or buy something from the shop they will be helpful.

BROOME TO DERBY
There's a free campsite beside the Fitzroy River, 155 km along the Great Northern Highway from Broome. Just over the all-weather bridge is the Willara Bridge Roadhouse and shortly after that is the turn-off to Derby, 43 km to the north. The main road continues into the heart of the Kimberley and on to Darwin.

The Kimberley

The rough and rugged Kimberley at the northern end of WA is one of Australia's last frontiers. Despite enormous advances in the last decade this is still a little-travelled and very remote area of great rivers and magnificent scenery. The Kimberley suffers from climatic extremes – heavy rains in the wet followed by searing heat in the dry – but the irrigation projects have made great changes to the region.

Nevertheless rivers and creeks can rise rapidly following a heavy rainfall and become impassable torrents within 15 minutes. Unless it's a very brief storm, it's quite likely that they will remain impassable for three to four days. The Fitzroy River can become so swollen at times that after two or three days rain it grows from it's normal 100-metre width to a spectacular 11 km! River and creek crossings on the Great Northern Highway on both sides of Halls Creek become impassable every wet season. The completion of the surfaced road some time in 1986 will not necessarily solve this problem as several notorious crossings will still only be fords and not all-weather bridges.

The best time to visit is April to September. By October it's already getting hot – 35°C, and later in the year daily temperatures of over 40°C are common. On the other hand, from May to July, nights can be piercingly cold, especially in Halls Creek.

Kimberley attractions include the spectacular gorges on the Fitzroy River and the huge Wolf Creek meteorite crater.

DERBY (population 3000)

Only 216 km from Broome (and what's more 216 surfaced km), Derby is a major centre for the Kimberley – an administrative centre, a shipping port for the cattle production of the region and a jumping-off point for the spectacular gorges in the region. The road beyond Derby continues through to Fitzroy Crossing, another 259 km, before it reverts to dirt for 100 km of the 291 km to Halls Creek. The rest of the way to Darwin, over a thousand km, is all surfaced. Derby is on King Sound, north of the mouth of the Fitzroy River, the mighty river that drains the West Kimberley region. From Derby you can make trips right up into the north of the region as the roads have been much improved of late.

In the town itself there's a museum in the Derby Cultural Centre while seven km south the Prison Tree is a huge boab tree with a hollow trunk 14 metres around. It is said to have been used as a temporary lock-up years ago.

From Derby there are flights over King Sound to Koolan and Cockatoo Islands, both owned by Dampier Mining Company. You can't go there unless invited by a resident, but scenic flights are available to the adjoining islands of the Buccaneer Archipelago.

Places to Stay

The *Derby Caravan Park* (tel 91 1022) has camping sites for $7 for two and on-site vans for $30 per night with a maximum stay of three days. Otherwise there's the central *Spinifex Hotel* (tel 91 1233) right at the centre on Clarendon St with singles for $37 or doubles for $45. Also in the centre is the *YWCA* (tel 91 1522) on Loch St with rooms at $12/24 for singles/doubles. The *Boab Inn* (tel 91 1044) is more expensive at $45/53.

Getting There

By air it's $60 from Broome, $264 from Perth.

Ansett Pioneer, Greyhound and Deluxe buses run through Derby. Fares include Broome $14, Darwin $85, Port Hedland $50 and Perth $129.

THE GORGES

The roads into the Kimberley from Derby have been much improved recently. You can make an interesting loop from Derby to visit the spectacular gorge country – or you can pick them up between Fitzroy Crossing and Derby. The Windjana Gorge National Park on the Lennard River and Tunnel Creek National Park on Tunnel Creek are only about 100 km from Derby. It only adds about 40 km to the trip to Fitzroy Crossing, although the road is mostly dirt, if you want to visit these gorges.

The walls at the Windjana Gorge soar 90 metres above the Lennard River which rushes through here in the wet but in the dry it becomes just a series of pools. Three km from the river are the ruins of Lillimooloora, an early police station. Tunnel Creek is a 750-metre-long tunnel, cut by the creek right through a spur of the Oscar Range. The tunnel is generally from three to 15 metres wide and you can walk right through it. You'll need a good light and don't attempt it during the wet when the creek may suddenly flash-flood. Half-way through, a collapse has produced a shaft right to the top of the range. Flying

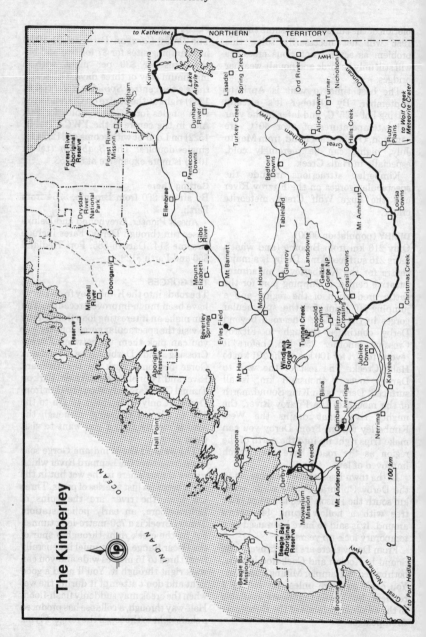

The Kimberley

100 km

INDIAN OCEAN

foxes (bats) also inhabit the tunnel for part of the year.

Windjana Gorge, Tunnel Creek and Lillimooloora were the scene of the adventures of an Aboriginal tracker called 'Pigeon'. Starting in November 1894, Pigeon unexpectedly shot two policemen colleagues and then led a band of dissident Aborigines, constantly and skillfully avoiding all official search parties. In the meantime he killed another four men, until in early 1897 he was trapped and killed in Tunnel Creek. He and his small band had hidden out in many of the inaccessible gullies of the adjoining Napier Range. Disappearing into the night or evading capture by fleetness of foot, he had evaded his hunters for 2¼ years.

If you haven't got your own transport, Kimberley Safaris in Derby (tel 91 1084), do a day trip ($60) and also two, four, six and 14-day safaris at prices from $170 to $880 per person.

GIBB RIVER ROAD

This is the 'back road' from Derby to Wyndham. It's more direct by several hundred km than the Fitzroy Crossing-Halls Creek route but it's almost all dirt. You can reach many of the Kimberley gorges from this road without four-wheel drive. Fuel is available at Mt Barnett station, near Manning Gorge.

There's quite a competition as to which is the best gorge along the road, but the first one – the Lennard River Gorge – usually wins. Though you'll need four-wheel drive to drive all the way in, you can walk the last five km as an alternative. Ask the Derby tourist office for details of the gorges as they are not too well signposted. Most have rock paintings in them. The Barnett River Gorge is also four-wheel drive territory.

Moll Gorge is hard to get to on a very sandy road through Mt House station. In fact this station doesn't recommend the road at all. At sunset along the road the many magnificent ranges change from brown to orange to crimson to mauve as the sun slowly sinks. After Gibb River Station the road deteriorates as far as the huge Pentecost River, which is negotiable only by four-wheel drive vehicles for much of the year. Before setting out on this road, check with the Derby tourist bureau and the police as to its condition because at times it is officially closed. Don't even think about hitching – there's just no traffic.

FITZROY CROSSING (population 430)

A tiny settlement where the road crosses the Fitzroy River, this is another jumping-off point for the gorges and waterholes of the area. The Geikie Gorge is just 19 km from the town. The gorge, on the Fitzroy River, flows through a small national park, only eight km by three km. During the wet season the river rises nearly 17 metres, and the campsite by the river is seven metres below the waterline! In the dry the river completely stops flowing although a series of waterholes remains. The ranges which the gorge cuts through are actually a fossilised coral reef some 350 million years old.

The vegetation around the beautiful gorge is dense and there is also much wildlife to be seen including the harmless Johnston crocodile. Sawfish and stingrays, usually only found in or close to the sea, can also be seen in the river. A variety of kangaroos and wallabies also live around the gorge which is a sanctuary area. Visitors are not permitted to go anywhere except along the prescribed part of the west bank. There is an excellent walk along that bank and you can also swim, with the crocodiles, in the gorge. Twice a day there's a national park boat trip lasting two hours and covering 16 km of the gorge, it costs $4. The campsite at the gorge costs $3 per night per vehicle. The campsite and the gorge trips are usually in operation only during the April to November dry season.

Ask at Brooking Springs station for directions to the very pleasant and peaceful Brooking Gorge. Also ask for permission to go through their land. Note that some cattle stations lately have been sealing off gorges on their land due to thoughtless littering by visitors.

The campsite in Fitzroy Crossing itself is right next to the pub and consequently, is pretty noisy. Camp sites are $3 and cabins are $20 per night.

HALLS CREEK (population 1000)

In the centre of the Kimberley and on the edge of the Great Sandy Desert, this was the site of a gold-rush back in 1885, the first in WA. The gold soon petered out and today the town is a cattle centre, 14 km from the original site where some crumbling remains can still be seen. Halls Creek Old Town is a fascinating place for poking around creeks and gullies in a four-wheel drive searching for that elusive gold nugget. If you're really interested in doing a bit of fossicking, it's best to go with a local. 'Old town' is in fact the general term for the hilly area behind Halls Creek and gold might be found anywhere here. For swimming there's Caroline Pool, Sawpit Gorge and Palm Springs.

Six km north of Halls Creek there's another natural China Wall, Australia seems to have a few of them! The major attraction in the area is the 135 km trip to the 835-metre-wide and 50-metre-deep Wolf Creek Meteorite Crater, the second largest in the world. The road to the crater is fairly good and you can camp and get supplies at the Carranya Station homestead nearby. Halls Creek is nearly 3000 km from Perth.

There's an Aboriginal art shop in the town where you can often see carvers at work making some very high quality artefacts. You can also take scenic flights for $25 over Bungle Bungle, an unearthly moonscape best seen from the air.

The caravan park in Halls Creek charges $5 for sites and has air-con on-site vans for $25. The *Kimberley Hotel* is not cheap at $28/41 for singles/doubles.

The road to Wyndham and Kununurra, 360 km away, passes through the Carboyd Ranges – catch them at their best at sunset. You can swim in the river at the Durham River bridge.

WYNDHAM (population 1500)

Wyndham, a sprawling town, is suffering from Kununurra's boom in popularity but it's Five Rivers Lookout on top of Mt Bastion is a must. From the top you can see the King, Pentecost, Durack, Forest and Ord Rivers. It's particularly good at sunrise or sunset. During the dry season saltwater crocodiles (man-eaters) congregate near the jetty and during the day one or two might be seen at the end of the outlet drain behind the meatworks. Be wary – crocs take foolish swimmers at the rate of about two per year, despite the signs warning swimmers of the dangers.

The Moochylabra Dam is a popular fishing and picnic spot about 25 km away. Near the town there's a rather desolate and decrepit little cemetery where Afghan camel drivers were buried in the last century.

Places to Stay

The *Three Mile Caravan Park* (tel 61 1064) charges $6 for campsites. The *Wyndham Community Club* has air-con rooms with facilities for $23. There are also some cheaper but more basic rooms available by the *Hungry Croc Restaurant*.

KUNUNURRA (population 2100)

Founded in the 1960s, Kununurra is in the centre of the Ord River irrigation scheme and is experiencing a rise in popularity. There are good views of the irrigated fields from Kelly's Knob Lookout. During the wet season, distant thunderstorms can be spectacular when viewed from here although caution is also needed as the Knob itself is frequently struck by lightning.

Lake Kununurra, a man-made lake beside the town, has plentiful birdlife and several swimming spots. There's good fishing below the Lower Dam and also on the Ord River at Ivanhoe Crossing. If you're swimming here, be careful – there's a saying that the Ord takes a life a year, and it usually seems to be at Ivanhoe Crossing.

There's a Visitor's Centre (tel 68 1177) on Coolibah Drive with information on the town and the Kimberley. Zebra stones with red stripes or dots on a white base, a local oddity, are sold as souvenirs or incorporated into jewellery. Scenic flights are available for $70 per person for trips over the Bungle Bungle, the Argyle Diamond Project and the irrigation area.

Places to Stay & Eat

There are four caravan Parks, two of them by Lake Kununurra. The *Kimberley Guest House* (tel 68 1411) at 111 Nutwood Crescent has rooms at $29/39. The *Country Club Hotel* (tel 68 1024) on Coolibah Drive has a good Chinese restaurant as well as air-con rooms for $32. *Gullivers Tavern*, noted for its Gulliver prints, is a very popular drinking place which gets very crowded. Go early if you want to have a meal here.

LAKE ARGYLE

Created by the Ord River Dam, Lake Argyle is the second biggest storage reservoir in Australia, holding 12 times as much water as Sydney Harbour! Prior to its construction, there was too much water in the wet season and not enough in the dry and so by providing a regular water supply, it has made agriculture on a massive scale possible in the area.

At the lake there's a pioneer museum in the old Argyle Homestead which was moved here when its original site was flooded. The *Argyle Tourist Village* has expensive rooms and a campsite and from here there are boat rides out on to the huge lake each morning and afternoon. All around the lake there is now green farmland with rice a principal crop.

Just off the Lake Argyle Highway are some Aboriginal rock paintings. One of the best tours out of Kununurra is a 28-km canoe trip down the Ord River through part of the gorge. Cost is $30 and a car picks you up and takes you back to the tourist village but there has to be a minimum of two canoes.

South of Kununurra is a huge diamond mine with a visitors' centre at the site. The Bungle Bungle Mountains, 200 km south of Kununurra, remain a difficult-to-reach, rugged wonderland. Colourful sandstone foundations, chasms, peaks and domes highlight the ancient area where pioneers set up a short-lived cattle station in the early 1900s.

From Kununurra it's a picturesque 108-km drive to the Grotto, a pleasant waterhole. There's another prison boab tree in the area and an Afghan cemetery, a memorial of the old camel caravans.

Getting There

Ansett WA connect Kununurra with Darwin ($104) and other Western Australian towns like Broome ($139), Port Hedland ($205) and Perth ($344). They also operate a bus service which connects Wyndham and Kununurra for $14.

Ansett Pioneer, Greyhound and Deluxe all come through Kununurra on their way to or from Darwin. The fare from Kununurra to Darwin is $57 and the trip takes nine hours. To Perth it's $179 and 42 hours. Deluxe Coachlines also serves the town from Perth and Darwin. Getting off the main roads in this area usually necessitates four-wheel drive. These and regular cars can be rented in Kununurra.

Index

Temperature

To convert °C to °F multipy by 1.8 and add 32

To convert °F to °C subtract 32 and multipy by · 55

Length, Distance & Area

	multipy by
inches to centimetres	2.54
centimetres to inches	0.39
feet to metres	0.30
metres to feet	3.28
yards to metres	0.91
metres to yards	1.09
miles to kilometres	1.61
kilometres to miles	0.62
acres to hectares	0.40
hectares to acres	2.47

Weight

	multipy by
ounces to grams	28.35
grams to ounces	0.035
pounds to kilograms	0.45
kilograms to pounds	2.21
British tons to kilograms	1016
US tons to kilograms	907

A British ton is 2240 lbs, a US ton is 2000 lbs

Volume

	multipy by
Imperial gallons to litres	4.55
litres to imperial gallons	0.22
US gallons to litres	3.79
litres to US gallons	0.26

5 imperial gallons equals 6 US gallons
a litre is slightly more than a US quart, slightly less
than a British one

Lonely Planet

Lonely Planet published its first book in 1973. Tony and Maureen Wheeler had made a lengthy overland trip from England to Australia and, in response to numerous 'how do you do it?' questions, Tony wrote and they published *Across Asia on the Cheap*. It became an instant local best-seller and inspired thoughts of a second travel guide. A year and a half in South-East Asia resulted in their second book, *South-East Asia on a Shoestring*, which they put together in a backstreet Chinese hotel in Singapore in 1975. The 'yellow book', as it quickly became known, soon became *the* guide to the region and has gone through five editions, always with its familiar yellow cover.

Soon other writers started to come to them with ideas for similar books – books that went off the beaten track and took an adventurous approach to travel, books that 'assumed you knew how to get your luggage off the carousel,' as one reviewer described them. Lonely Planet grew from a kitchen table operation to a spare room and then to its own office. It also started to develop an international reputation as the Lonely Planet logo began to appear in more and more countries. In 1982 *India – a travel survival kit* won the Thomas Cook award for the best guidebook of the year.

These days there are over 60 Lonely Planet titles. Nearly 30 people work at our office in Melbourne, Australia and another half dozen at our US office in Oakland, California.

At first Lonely Planet specialised exclusively in the Asia region but these days we are also developing major ranges of guidebooks to the Pacific region, to South America and to Africa. The list of walking guides is growing and Lonely Planet is producing a unique series of phrasebooks to 'unusual' languages. The emphasis continues to be on travel for travellers and Tony and Maureen still manage to fit in a number of trips each year and play a very active part in the writing and updating of Lonely Planet's guides.

Keeping guidebooks up to date is a constant battle which requires an ear to the ground and lots of walking, but technology also plays its part. All Lonely Planet guidebooks are now stored and updated on computer, and some authors even take lap-top computers into the field. Lonely Planet is also using computers to draw maps and eventually many of the maps will be stored on disk.

The people at Lonely Planet strongly feel that travellers can make a positive contribution to the countries they visit both by better appreciation of cultures and by the money they spend. In addition the company tries to make a direct contribution to the countries and regions it covers. Since 1986 a percentage of the income from each book has gone to aid groups and associations. This has included donations to famine relief in Africa, to aid projects in India, to agricultural projects in Nicaragua and other Central American countries and to Greenpeace's efforts to halt French nuclear testing in the Pacific. In 1988 over $40,000 was donated by Lonely Planet to these projects.

Lonely Planet Distributors

Australia & Papua New Guinea Lonely Planet Publications, PO Box 88, South Yarra, Victoria 3141.
Canada Raincoast Books, 112 East 3rd Avenue, Vancouver, British Columbia V5T 1C8.
Denmark, Finland & Norway Scanvik Books aps, Store Kongensgade 59 A, DK-1264 Copenhagen K.
Hong Kong The Book Society, GPO Box 7804.
India & Nepal UBS Distributors, 5 Ansari Rd, New Delhi – 110002
Israel Geographical Tours Ltd, 8 Tverya St, Tel Aviv 63144.
Japan Intercontinental Marketing Corp, IPO Box 5056, Tokyo 100-31.
Netherlands Nilsson & Lamm bv, Postbus 195, Pampuslaan 212, 1380 AD Weesp.
New Zealand Transworld Publishers, PO Box 83-094, Edmonton PO, Auckland.
Singapore & Malaysia MPH Distributors, 601 Sims Drive, #03-21, Singapore 1438.
Spain Altair, Balmes 69, 08007 Barcelona.
Sweden Esselte Kartcentrum AB, Vasagatan 16, S-111 20 Stockholm.
Thailand Chalermnit, 108 Sukhumvit 53, Bangkok 10110.
UK Roger Lascelles, 47 York Rd, Brentford, Middlesex, TW8 0QP
USA Lonely Planet Publications, PO Box 2001A, Berkeley, CA 94702.
West Germany Buchvertrieb Gerda Schettler, Postfach 64, D3415 Hattorf a H.
All Other Countries refer to Australia address.

Guides to The Pacific

Australia - a travel survival kit
Australia's Central lands home to more ... this guide
gives you the complete lowdown on Down Under - from how
to get around the coast, from cosmopolitan cities to
country towns.

Bushwalking in Australia
Australia offers opportunities for walking in many different
climates and terrains, from the tropical north to the snowy
peaks of the ranges to the mountains of the south-east.
Two experienced and enthusiastic walkers give details of the
best walks in every state plus notes on many more.

Tramping in New Zealand
Call it tramping, hiking, walking, bushwalking, or
trekking - the walking in some parts has no way to compare
here with New Zealand's natural beauty. This guide
gives detailed descriptions for 70 walks of various length
and difficulty.

Fiji - a travel survival kit
This is a comprehensive guide to the whole archipelago.
On a rundown of these beautiful islands ... comfortable
resorts, from catamaran cruises to interisland flights,
whatever you prefer, this book will help you enjoy the
islands' seas.

Solomon Islands - a travel survival kit
The Solomon Islands archipelago has been kept secret. If
you want to discover remote tropical islands, simple
unspoiled cultures and traditional Melanesian villages,
this book will show you how.

Guides to The Pacific

Australia – a travel survival kit
Australia is Lonely Planet's home territory so this guide gives you the complete low-down on Down Under, from the red centre to the coast, from cosmopolitan cities to country towns.

Bushwalking in Australia
Australia offers opportunities for walking in many different climates and terrains – from the tropical north, to the rocky gorges of the centre, to the mountains of the south-east. Two experienced and respected walkers give details of the best walks in every state, plus notes on many more.

Tramping in New Zealand
Call it tramping, hiking, walking, bushwalking, or trekking – travelling on your feet is the best way to come to grips with New Zealand's natural beauty. This guide gives detailed descriptions for 20 walks of various length and difficulty.

Fiji – a travel survival kit
This is a comprehensive guide to the Fijian archipelago. On a number of these beautiful islands accommodation ranges from camping grounds to international hotels – whichever you prefer this book will help you to enjoy the South Seas.

Solomon Islands – a travel survival kit
The Solomon Islands are the Pacific's best kept secret. If you want to discover remote tropical islands, jungle-covered volcanoes and traditional Melanesian villages, this book will show you how.

Tahiti & French Polynesia – a travel survival kit
The image of palm-fringed beaches and friendly people continues to lure travellers to Polynesia. This book gives you all the facts on paradise, and will be useful whether you plan a package holiday, or to travel the islands independently.

Rarotonga & the Cook Is – a travel survival kit
Rarotonga has history, beauty and magic to rival Hawaii, Tahiti or Bora Bora. Unlike those better known islands, however, the world has virtually passed it by. The Cook Islands range from mountainous islands to remote and untouched coral atolls.

Micronesia – a travel survival kit
Amongst these 2100 islands are beaches, lagoons and reefs that will dazzle the most jaded traveller. This guide is packed with all you need to know about island hopping across the north Pacific.

Papua New Guinea – a travel survival kit
Papua New Guinea is truly 'the last unknown' – the last inhabited place on earth to be explored by Europeans. This guide has the latest information for travellers who want to find just how rewarding a trip to this remote and amazing country can be.

Bushwalking in Papua New Guinea
Papua New Guinea offers exciting challenges for bushwalkers. This book describes 11 walks of various length and difficulty, through one of the world's most beautiful, rugged and exotic countries. Specific and practical information is provided.

Also Available:
Papua New Guinea phrasebook

Lonely Planet Guidebooks

Lonely Planet guidebooks cover virtually every accessible part of Asia as well as Australia, the Pacific, Central and South America, Africa, the Middle East and parts of North America. There are four main series: 'travel survival kits', covering a single country for a range of budgets; 'shoestring' guides with compact information for low-budget travel in a major region; trekking guides; and 'phrasebooks'.

Australia & the Pacific
Australia
Bushwalking in Australia
Papua New Guinea
Bushwalking in Papua New Guinea
Papua New Guinea phrasebook
New Zealand
Tramping in New Zealand
Rarotonga & the Cook Islands
Solomon Islands
Tahiti & French Polynesia
Fiji
Micronesia

South-East Asia
South-East Asia on a shoestring
Malaysia, Singapore & Brunei
Indonesia
Bali & Lombok
Indonesia phrasebook
Burma
Burmese phrasebook
Thailand
Thai phrasebook
Philippines
Pilipino phrasebook

North-East Asia
North-East Asia on a shoestring
China
China phrasebook
Tibet
Tibet phrasebook
Japan
Korea
Korean phrasebook
Hong Kong, Macau & Canton
Taiwan

West Asia
West Asia on a shoestring
Turkey

Mail Order

Lonely Planet guidebooks are distributed worldwide and are sold by good bookshops everywhere. They are also available by mail order from Lonely Planet, so if you have difficulty finding a title please write to us. US and Canadian residents should write to Embarcadero West, 112 Linden St, Oakland CA 94607, USA and residents of other countries to PO Box 88, South Yarra, Victoria 3141, Australia.

Indian Subcontinent
India
Hindi/Urdu phrasebook
Kashmir, Ladakh & Zanskar
Trekking in the Indian Himalaya
Pakistan
Kathmandu & the Kingdom of Nepal
Trekking in the Nepal Himalaya
Nepal phrasebook
Sri Lanka
Sri Lanka phrasebook
Bangladesh

Africa
Africa on a shoestring
East Africa
Swahili phrasebook
West Africa

Middle East
Egypt & the Sudan
Jordan & Syria
Yemen

North America
Canada
Alaska

Mexico
Mexico
Baja California

South America
South America on a shoestring
Ecuador & the Galapagos Islands
Colombia
Chile & Easter Island
Bolivia
Peru

Lonely Planet Update

We collect an enormous amount of information here at Lonely Planet. Apart from our research there's a steady stream of travellers' letters full of the latest news. For over 5 years much of this information went into a quarterly newsletter (and helped to update the guidebooks). The new paperback *Update* includes this up-to-date news and aims to supplement the information available in our guidebooks. There will be four editions a year (Feb, May, Aug and Nov) available either by subscription or through bookshops. Subscribe now and you'll save nearly 25% off the retail price.

Each edition has extracts from the most interesting letters we have received, covering such diverse topics as:
- how to take a boat trip on the Yalu River
- living in a typical Thai village
- getting a Nepalese trekking permit

Subscription Details

All subscriptions cover four editions and include postage. Prices quoted are subject to change.

USA & Canada – One year's subscription is US$12; a single copy is US$3.95. Please send your order to Lonely Planet's California office.

Other Countries – One year's subscription is Australian $15; a single copy is A$4.95. Please pay in Australian $, or the US$ or £ Sterling equivalent. Please send your order form to Lonely Planet's Australian office.

Order Form

Please send me

☐ One year's subscription – starting next edition.   ☐ One copy of the next edition.

Name (please print) ....

Address (please print) ....

....

....

Tick One

☐ Payment enclosed (payable to Lonely Planet Publications)

Charge my   ☐ Visa   ☐ Bankcard   ☐ MasterCard   for the amount of $ ....

Card No .... Expiry Date ....

Cardholder's Name (print) ....

Signature .... Date..

US & Canadian residents
 Lonely Planet, Embarcadero West, 112 Linden St,
 Oakland, CA 94607, USA
Other countries
 Lonely Planet, PO Box 88, South Yarra, Victoria 3141, Australia